0003. Sidewall, Japan, 1990–95

0004. Sidewall, Tile, 1958, Barbara White

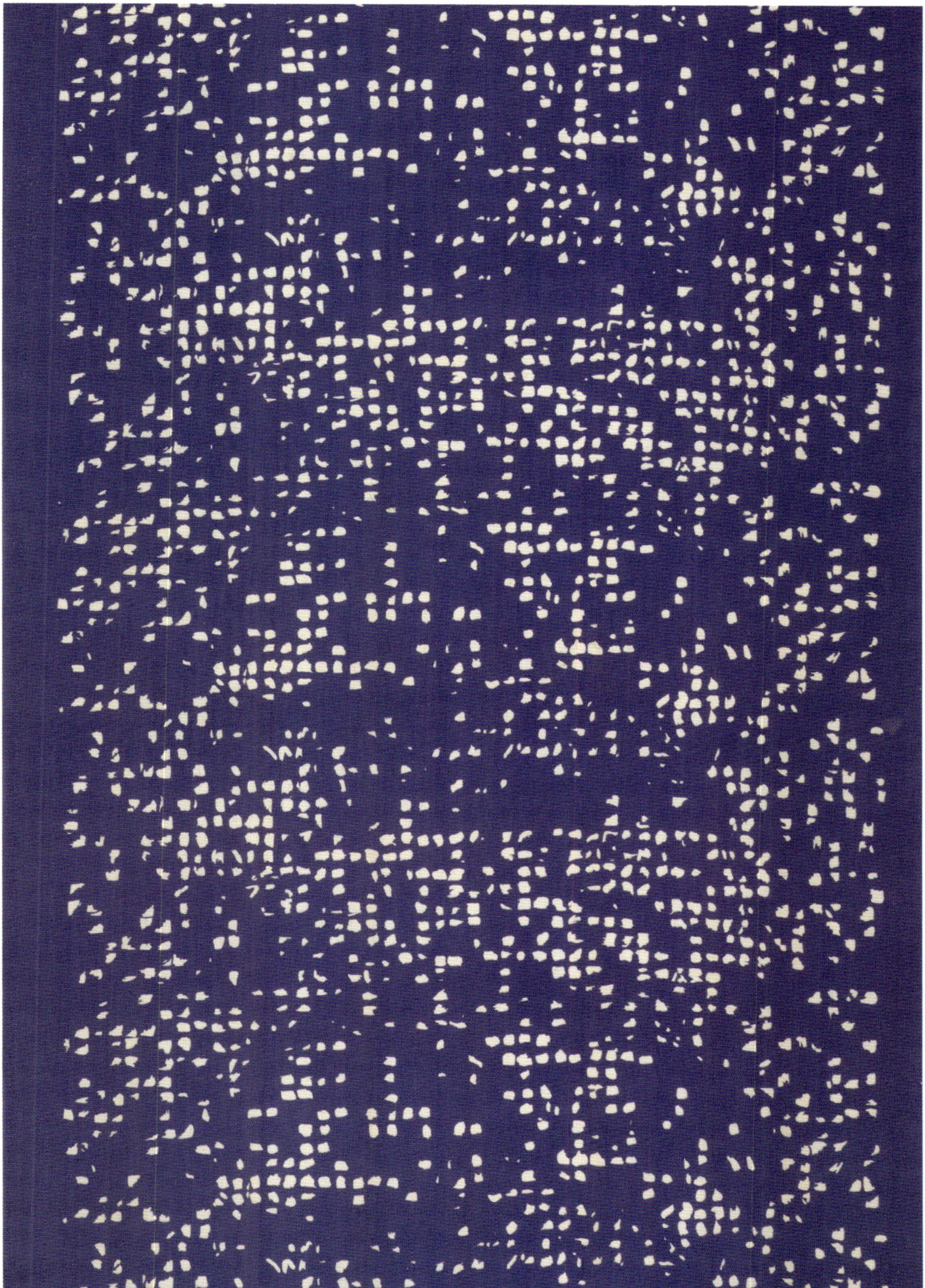

0005. Textile, Van Dyke Squares, ca. 1953, Philip Johnson

0006. Drawing, Textile Design: Optical Black and White, 1930s, Donald Deskey

0007. Poster, Ontwerpen van Tanaka, Ikko, 1965, Pieter Brattinga

0008. Zebra cup and saucer, Sweden, 1955, Eugen Trost

0009. Footed bowl, Austria, ca. 1914, Michael Powolny

0010. Hand-woven sample, USA, ca. 1945, Anni Albers
0011. Sidewall, Mauer, 1959, Le Corbusier

0012. Sidewall, Japan, 1990–95
0013. Textile, Campagna, 1948, Angelo Testa

0014. Red White vase, Netherlands, 1998, Hella Jongerius

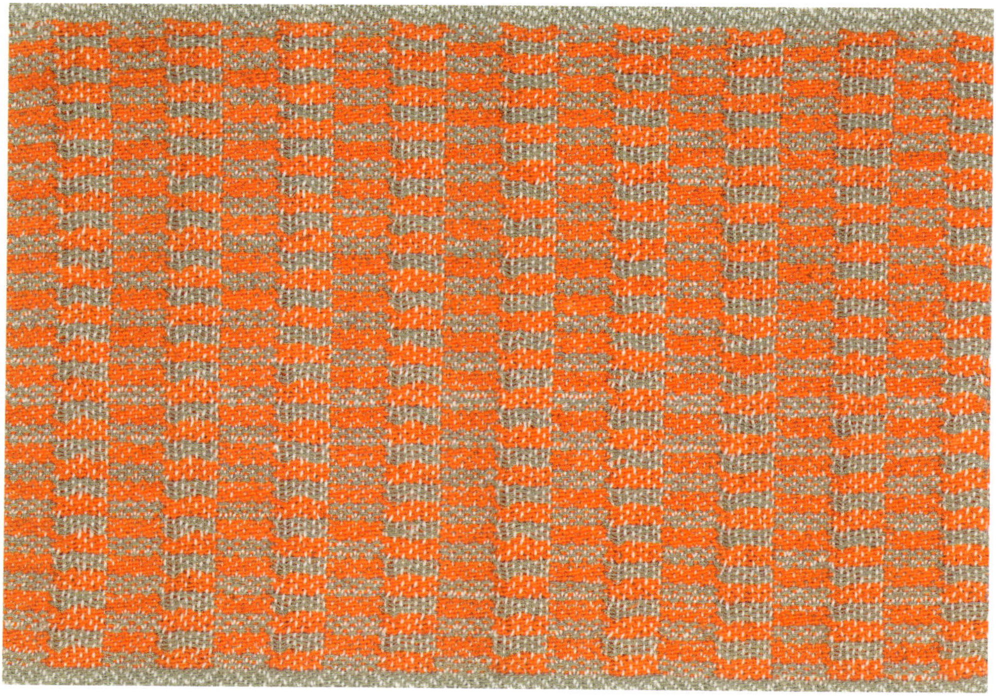

0015. Hand-woven sample, USA, ca. 1948, Anni Albers

0016. Sidewall, Zeppelin, 1998, Elizabeth Dow

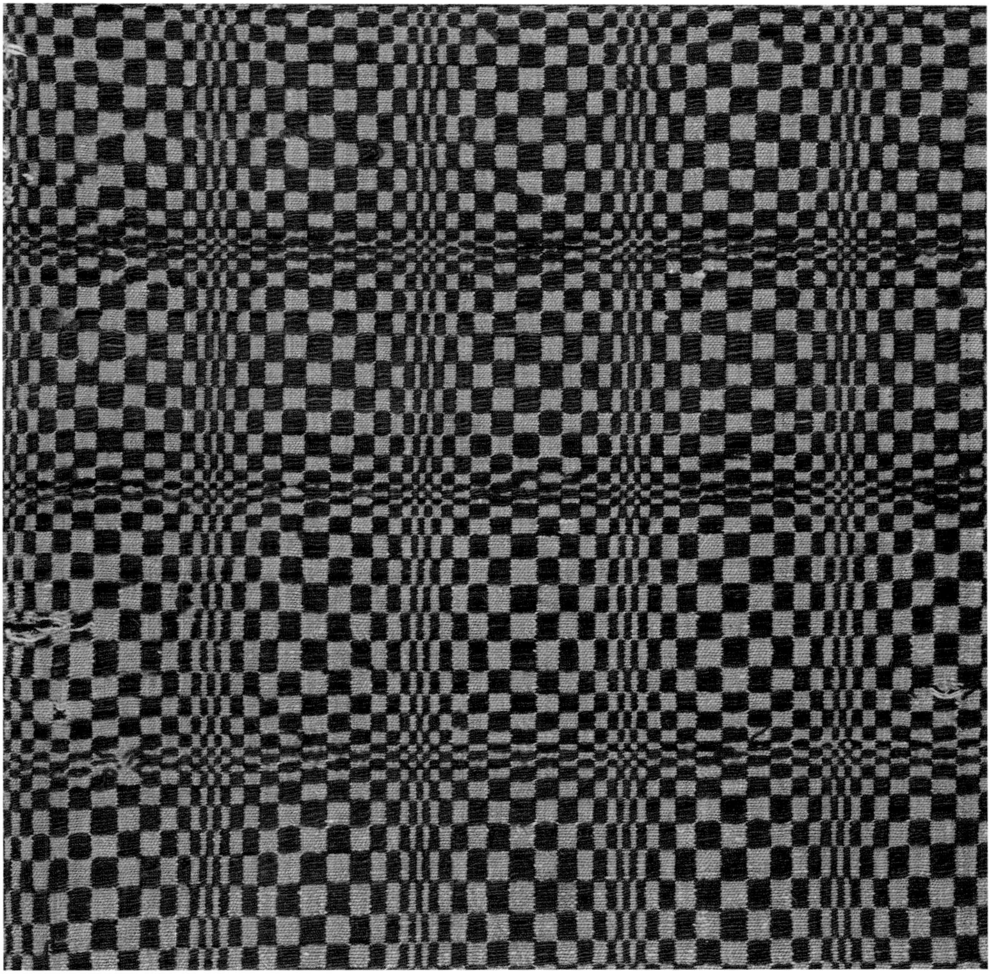

0017. Coverlet fragment, USA, ca. 1850

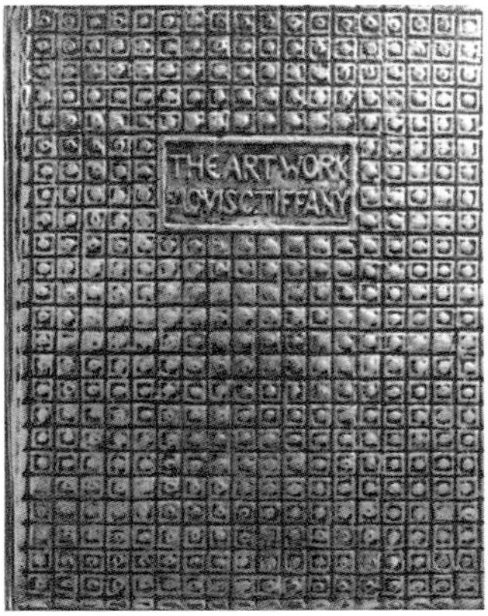

0018. Textile, Central Asia, 19th century
0019. Book cover, *The Artwork of Louis C. Tiffany*, 1914, Louis C. Tiffany

MAKING DESIGN

COOPER
HEWITT

Smithsonian Design Museum

COOPER HEWITT, SMITHSONIAN DESIGN MUSEUM

COLLECTION

Making Design Web-Based Edition
A searchable digital version for *Making Design* is under development. Readers of the print version and visitors to Cooper Hewitt can find the most current version at: cooperhewitt.org/publications/making-design

Published by
Cooper Hewitt, Smithsonian Design Museum
2 East 91st Street
New York, NY 10128, USA
cooperhewitt.org

This publication is made possible in part by
Furthermore: a program of the J.M. Kaplan Fund

Furthermore:
a program of the J.M. Kaplan Fund

Distributed Worldwide by ARTBOOK | D.A.P.
155 Sixth Avenue, 2nd floor
New York, NY 10013, USA
artbook.com

Library of Congress Control Number: 2014947908

ISBN 978-0-910503-74-7
ISBN 978-1-9423-0302-2/Limited Edition

Cooper Hewitt, Smithsonian Design Museum
Pamela Horn
Head of Cross-Platform Publishing

Matthew Kennedy
Image Rights & Publishing Associate

Design: Irma Boom
Font: Neuzeit S by C.W. Pischiner

2014 2015 2016 2017 / 10 9 8 7 6 5 4 3 2 1

Printed in China

Contents

Foreword

With this remarkable volume we celebrate Cooper Hewitt, Smithsonian Design Museum and its extraordinary collection of historic and contemporary design. Timed to mark the occasion of our reopening following a major renovation project, *Making Design* is one of the many ways we are making our collection widely accessible to readers and visitors, both near and far. Cooper Hewitt's renovation gave us the opportunity not only to re-envision how our galleries, garden, and public spaces would look and be used, but to completely rethink the role of museums and how visitors experience them.

At the new Cooper Hewitt, visitors are participants rather than observers, actively engaging with design and its creative process on myriad levels. All of us now have the world's knowledge at our fingertips thanks to smartphones, computers, and the Web. We've made innovation and groundbreaking technology key elements of our new visitor experience, enabling everyone to mine the riches of Cooper Hewitt's collection in ingenious, imaginative ways.

We chose Irma Boom, the brilliant, award-winning Dutch graphic designer, to be the creative force behind this book, and she has delivered something truly spectacular. After hearing about our mission to reveal more of our collection and actively engage our audiences, with process as a focus, Boom created the concept for the book. She turned the traditional role of designer on its head and became the "author." Cooper Hewitt supplied the content, and Boom created the visual narrative on the following pages. After looking at more than 37,000 images of our collection, Boom was inspired and exhilarated to dive in. Our only stipulation was that she include fifty-four essays about specific objects, a process glossary, and 450 works the curators provided. The organization, or narrative, of this book is purely visual and as you page through it, you'll see sequences of more than 1,200 images that are provocative, lyrical, funny, unexpected, ravishing, somber, and exquisite. The pairings emphasize looking at objects as well as making connections between them, highlighting their details, textures and patterns, forms, shapes, and colors. I know that in addition to being a beautiful window into Cooper Hewitt's collection, this book will be an invaluable resource for designers and design aficionados around the world for years to come.

Finding engaging, innovative ways to bridge the physical with the digital has been a focus for our galleries and website. We have created experiences that amplify your connection to our collection—and to design as a whole. With *Making Design,* our goal was to publish the ultimate book-as-object, in format and function, but it was also our aim to offer an exciting digital version of the book to reflect our digital prowess in the Cooper Hewitt galleries. Owning this print edition automatically offers each reader the keys to a new way of seeing Cooper Hewitt's holdings. Boom's design concept introduces readers to this user-centric approach and then puts it wholly in your hands to make connections with our more than 210,000 objects and the world beyond.

This project is the culmination of the dedication, support, and hard work of many people. Beginning, of course, with the core collection Sarah and Eleanor Hewitt assembled in 1897, we are indebted to all the donors over the decades who have so generously contributed to the collection either through gifts of objects or funding.
We appreciate the funding provided by the museum's Andrew W. Mellon Foundation Publications Fund and are grateful to Furthermore: a program of the J. M. Kaplan Fund for its support. I also thank everyone at Cooper Hewitt who contributed to *Making Design*.

I look forward to sharing Cooper Hewitt and its collections with you as, together, we experience the power of design to impact our lives.

Caroline Baumann
Director
Cooper Hewitt, Smithsonian Design Museum

0020. Textile, South China Sea, 1972, Jack Lenor Larsen

0021. Katagami, Water Pattern (detail), Japan, late 19th–early 20th century

0022. Print, Trial Proof for a Printed Textile (detail), ca. 1759–1815, Oberkampf & Cie. Workshop

0023. Scenic, Les Vues d'Italie, ca. 1830, Dufour et Leroy

0024. Drawing, Villa Albani, Italy: Design for a Fountain with Pegasus, ca. 1750, Carlo Marchionni

0025. Cooper Union

0026. Class of Women's Art School, ca. 1900

Introduction

The history of a museum's collection is primarily a story of its founders, donors, directors, and curators, and, with its richness and diversity, Cooper Hewitt's collection is no exception. From the very beginning, it was conceived as "a practical working laboratory," a "visual library" where students and designers could go to be inspired by actual objects. There were few restrictions: objects could be touched, moved, sketched, photographed, and measured. Even by today's standards, this vision of Sarah and Eleanor Hewitt for a museum in 1897 seems radical. Cooper Hewitt's 2014 complete renovation was the opportune moment to redefine its goals and ambitions for a twenty-first-century museum. Without doubt, the digital era is helping the reimagined Cooper Hewitt succeed even more in realizing the Hewitt sisters' original, user-focused ambition of participation and outreach, of creating a museum and collection "for anyone who wanted to use it as a place to work and learn." [1]

Originally located in Cooper Union for the Advancement of Science and Art, Cooper Hewitt's core collection was formed between the late nineteenth and early twentieth centuries by Sarah and Eleanor Hewitt, granddaughters of the industrialist and inventor Peter Cooper, who established Cooper Union in New York in 1859. They shared their grandfather's "love of beautiful and exquisite workmanship" [2] and wanted to fulfill his vision for a teaching museum within the school.
In 1897, the Cooper Union Museum for the Arts of Decoration was officially inaugurated. The sisters wanted to elevate the "appalling . . . state of decorative design" and production in America. [3] They strove to emulate the collections of the South Kensington Museum (Victoria and Albert Museum) in London and the Musée des Arts Décoratifs in Paris, where they sought inspiration and advice. Most of the objects they acquired were made prior to 1830: for them, France during the late seventeenth to early nineteenth centuries was, even more than Italy, the apogee of design.

From the time they were children, the Hewitt sisters made annual trips to Europe. In their efforts to collect and make available the best in design, they purchased works of technical and artistic merit from dealers and at auctions, both in the United States and abroad. Entire collections, as well as individual objects, came flowing in from their trips to France and their visits to dealers who offered access to major sources. Their collecting ambitions were augmented with bequests and generous gifts from great French design houses, manufacturers, and dealers they befriended, as well as from prominent New Yorkers in their parents' large social circle, such as J. P. Morgan and George A. Hearn. The foundation of this original collection provided logic and structure to all subsequent collecting. [https://collection.cooperhewitt.org]

The collection was transferred to the Smithsonian Institution in 1967. In 1976, what is now Cooper Hewitt, Smithsonian Design Museum, opened as Cooper-Hewitt, The Smithsonian Institution's National Museum of Design, in its current location, Andrew Carnegie's magnificent 1902 residence. Four curatorial departments were established: Decorative Arts, Drawings and Prints, Textiles, and Wallcoverings. Today, Cooper Hewitt possesses one of the most diverse and comprehensive collections of design works in existence, and is the only museum in the United States devoted exclusively to historic and contemporary design. The collection comprises more than 210,000 objects, spanning thirty centuries up through the present day, with the oldest work, an Egyptian faience cup, dating from 1330 to 1100 BC. Expanding and strengthening the collection remains vital to the museum's identity and mission, while its fundamental nature and emphases remain firmly rooted in the mission formed by the Hewitt sisters. The current collecting focus has shifted to the contemporary, to bolstering the American holdings, including works by National Design Award winners, and acquiring major historical pieces not yet represented.

Continuing the collection's original legacy as a teaching museum, Cooper Hewitt has become a center for scholarly and applied research, providing professional development and museum training to graduate students. In 1982, a collaborative effort between the museum and Parsons The New School for Design (previously Parsons) established a master's program in the History of Decorative Arts and Design. Not only are graduates of that program having an impact on this burgeoning field in the United States, but most of the museum's collections, exhibitions, publications, and research activities benefit directly from the students' scholarship. In fall 2014, the program was renamed History of Design and Cultural Studies.

A sampling from the vast, eccentric holdings of this extraordinary collection give this handbook its visually rich and unique character. Some of the works are vernacular and lowly; others are acclaimed masterpieces of their day—but the thrust has always been on history, innovation, process, technique, use, and social context more than on masterpieces. Collectively, the objects are a tribute to the remarkable plurality of design processes and manufacturing techniques. This attempt to present the concepts of design and the design process, including prototypes as well as technological innovations, differentiates Cooper Hewitt's acquisitions from design collections within art museums.

Making Design's layout reinforces another distinguishing characteristic of Cooper Hewitt: the novel ways it integrates its collections. The ability to draw on historic examples from various cultures, to access forgotten techniques and ideas and juxtapose them with contemporary works, creates provocative dialogues and amplifies the historic continuum. This range is an asset few museums have or utilize and provides a continuing source of inspiration to contemporary viewers and designers. Furthermore, because design can describe most everything humans have ever created, the curators are increasingly mining the larger Smithsonian's encyclopedic collections, archives, scientific research institutes, and extensive expertise for additional exhibition and collection-enriching opportunities. And, with the new Smithsonian-wide digitization initiative to open access to its collections as never before, possibilities for both the public and scholars to engage with the collections are now within fingertips' reach.

Department of Product Design and Decorative Arts

The Department of Product Design and Decorative Arts's approximately 38,000 three-dimensional objects form an important, comprehensive resource for decorative arts and design. International in scope, although predominantly from Europe and the United States, the collection contains an exceptionally diverse assortment of objects, from decorated Greek amphora, Roman glass, and Chinese ceramics to birdcages to mass-produced electronic products, reflecting a vast range of historical styles and design movements.

Objects are distinguished by their design, technological innovations, and use of materials. Works include prototypes and examples of early production models as well as iconic expressions of their medium or era. Categories of objects within the product design collection include a comprehensive ceramics collection, most notably European porcelain and earthenware, furniture, metalwork, lighting, glass, jewelry, models, architectural elements, and industrial design. Recent acquisitions have highlighted contemporary works in these categories, including objects such as Michael Eden's 3D-printed Tall Green Bloom urn.

Department of Drawings, Prints, and Graphic Design

The Department of Drawings, Prints, and Graphic Design, located in the Drue Heinz Study Center for Drawings and Prints, houses nearly 137,000 works of art and design on paper, mainly European and American, dating from the later fourteenth century to the present. The collections are encyclopedic and include both design drawings as well as fine arts. While the majority of objects pertain to eighteenth- and early nineteenth-century designs for architecture, decorative arts, and ornament, over 12,400 of which came from the Giovanni Piancastelli collection, and 13,788 from the Léon Decloux collection, the holdings also comprise discreet groupings of old master sixteenth- and seventeenth-century prints; Italian and French sixteenth- to nineteenth-century figure drawings; seventeenth- to twenty-first-century American and European graphic design; Japanese prints; American twentieth-century prints; American nineteenth-century landscapes, figure drawings, oil sketches, and important contemporary architectural drawings. Most notable among the fine arts holdings are highly important works by Frederic Edwin Church, Winslow Homer, and Thomas Moran, which are housed in the Henry Luce Study Room for American Art.

Department of Textiles

The Department of Textiles is home to an outstanding and diverse collection of over 26,000 objects, from humble, handmade domestic items to unique masterworks of textile art. The holdings span twenty-four centuries and five continents, ranging from a rare Han Dynasty (206 BC to AD 220) bonnet and mitts to the Greenleaf collection of fine lace to a twenty-first-century embroidered surgical implant. It represents a wide range of textile techniques: weaving, embroidery, knitting, **crochet**, braiding, knotting, lace, printing, and various forms of resist dyeing. Organized by technique and structure, the collection is notable for its embrace of process, including tools such as printing blocks and bobbin-lace pillows; dyers' record books and weavers' thesis books; embroidered, knitted, and lace samplers, unfinished work, manufacturer's samples, mass-produced yardage, finished garments and costume accessories, and home furnishings. The overall strength of the collection is in sixteenth-, seventeenth-, and eighteenth-century Western European textiles.

Department of Wallcoverings

Cooper Hewitt maintains the preeminent collection of wallcoverings in the United States. International in scope, it includes almost ten thousand examples from the seventeenth century through the present. The range allows the museum to document the history and development of wallpaper, with major strengths in artist-, architect-, and designer-designed wallcoverings; late eighteenth- to early nineteenth-century French wallpapers; twentieth-century American papers, especially from 1890 to 1910 and the 1950s; prominent pieces of mid- to late nineteenth-century English production; seventeenth-century gilded leather to current mass-produced vinyl-coated papers; and childrens' wallpapers.

In addition to actual wallcoverings, the holdings include printing tools, and approximately three hundred sample books that date from the late nineteenth and twentieth centuries. There is also a collection of one hundred nineteenth-century bandboxes covered in wallpaper; these document the styles and printing techniques of early American wallpaper.

Smithsonian Design Library and Archives
What could essentially be considered a fifth curatorial department is Smithsonian Design Library, a branch of the Smithsonian Libraries. A trove of over ninety thoudsand volumes, including ten thousand rare treasures pertaining to ornament, architecture, and decorative arts, it is an unparalleled resource in the United States for books, trade catalogs, serials, pictures, and archival material covering design and decorative arts from the Renaissance to the present. The library also oversees picture files and design archives that include the Caldwell Lighting Company, the M. Thérèse Bonney photography collection of art deco–era design, and the papers of such industrial/graphic designers as Donald Deskey, Henry Dreyfuss, George Nathan Horwitt, Gilbert Rohde, Tommi Parzinger, and Ladislav Sutnar. The library's holdings add a rich and important dimension to exhibitions.

Digital and Emerging Media
The computer is the most significant development to have impacted collecting since the twentieth century and offers the newest chapter in Cooper Hewitt's history. In addition to facilitating online public access to the collection, the digital frontier has spawned a brand-new collecting area as vital as the other arts of manufacture. Traditionally, the idea of design in a museum was made possible primarily through displayed objects. With digital works and an even broader definition of design today, many things can no longer be acquired, or collected—the physical possession of some objects is not possible. How does one, for example, build a collection of intangible designs and processes and virtual systems that aren't objects? As a design museum, how do we represent this loss of "thingness," this new and vastly expanding expression of our culture? To forge this new territory, in 2013, Cooper Hewitt took the bold step of adding digital code to the collection, acquiring the iPad application called Planetary.

Making Design
Pedagogy and the design process were central to the Hewitt sisters' philosophy and continue to inform how the museum acquires, displays, and interprets works. The pages of *Making Design*, sequenced by graphic designer Irma

Boom, is the ultimate example of how the museum is encouraging visitors to our galleries and website to "play with" our collection. It reflects our current approach to collecting, which increasingly includes supporting sketches, drawings, occasional prototypes, and videos that document the design process. Design is an agent of change and designers look at how solutions fit into human life. This user-centered approach is reinforced throughout these pages, with process-driven narratives that discuss individual objects through a design lens. The focus is on people, purpose, and making, emphasizing the communal nature of design. The people we celebrate are makers, users, designers, manufacturers, clients, commissioners, and the public. Purpose encompasses the myriad ways that design objects are useful. In our focus on making, we showcase materials and techniques as well as preparatory processes like research, drawing, and prototyping. The museum's primary goal is to inspire people to see how design can impact their lives.

As we move forward, collecting stories need to be told through new means—through narrative, display of fragments, and ingenious storytelling. Our curators, in collaboration with Cooper Hewitt's Education and Digital and Emerging Media Departments, have begun working in an interdisciplinary capacity to curate beyond the walls of the galleries. Digital interactives in the museum's galleries and further investigated on our site provide new venues for discussion and exploration around our collection. We are also creating a new terminology with which to delve deeper and search across our holdings. Our goal is to provide many more points of entry to serve greater numbers of communities who might benefit and enjoy Cooper Hewitt's collections.

As the nation's design museum, Cooper Hewitt's ambition is to be *the* design resource, giving all visitors, physical and virtual, the opportunity to access the museum like a glorious design library awaiting further exploration, leveraging all its assets—collections, exhibitions, educational programs, archives, publications, website, and Smithsonian Design Library. Offering content across both physical and digital platforms, our collections are becoming visible and readily accessible throughout the world in ways beyond the Hewitt sisters' greatest expectations. This digital resource, coupled with access to actual objects, will enhance design education, integrate our content with social networks, reach the global design community, and increase our scholarly impact. When he first conceived of the Smithsonian, James Smithson dreamed of "an establishment for the increase and diffusion of knowledge." This physical and virtual expansion of Cooper Hewitt rises to a level he never could have imagined.

Cara McCarty
Director of Curatorial
Cooper Hewitt, Smithsonian Design Museum

1 Russell Lynes, *More Than Meets the Eye: The History and Collections of Cooper-Hewitt Museum* (Washington, DC: Smithsonian Institution, 1981), 23.
2 Eleanor G. Hewitt, *The Making of a Modern Museum* (New York: The Wednesday Afternoon Club, 1919), 9.
3 Lynes, *More Than Meets the Eye*, 20.

About the Essays

The authors of the fifty-four essays in this volume comprise the curatorial staff of Cooper Hewitt, Smithsonian Design Museum, three librarians at Smithsonian Libraries, and two external contributors.

These case studies, indicated below by object image number, explore some of the collection's highlights while representing a range of time periods, cultures, and processes. The design lenses of user, purpose, and making are emphasized throughout to underscore the theme of "making design." Many of the essays include new research and contain bolded process terms that appear in the illustrated process glossary (see pages 833–45).

Essay Contributors

EB Elizabeth Broman, Reference Librarian, Smithsonian Libraries
0715

SB Susan Brown, Associate Curator of Textiles
0309, **0513**, **0893**, **1102**

SDC Sarah D. Coffin, Curator and Head of Product Design & Decorative Arts
0458, **0505**, **0518**, **0567**, **0579**, **0596**, **0685**, **0770**, **0824**, **0871**, **0879**, **1115**

JCB Jennifer Cohlman Bracchi, Reference Librarian, Smithsonian Libraries
0709, **0907**

LC Lucy Commoner, Head of Conservation
0052

CC Caitlin Condell, Curatorial Assistant of Drawings, Prints & Graphic Design
0027, **0296**, **0351**

GSD Gail S. Davidson, Curator and Head of Drawings, Prints & Graphic Design
0380, **0805**, **0839**, **0859**, **0865**, **0937**, **1007**, **1119**

GH Gregory Herringshaw Assistant Curator of Wallcoverings
0096, **0542**, **0591**, **0761**, **0976**, **1079**, **1084**, **1098**

SEL Sarah E. Lawrence, Dean of Design History, School of Art and Design History and Theory, Parsons The New School for Design
0601

EL Ellen Lupton, Senior Curator of Contemporary Design
1048

CM Cara McCarty, Director of Curatorial

MM Matilda McQuaid, Deputy Director of Curatorial & Head of Textiles
0121, **0173**, **0990**, **1051**

MMW Mary McWilliams, Norma Jean Calderwood Curator of Islamic and Later Indian Art, Harvard Art Museum
1044

KR Kimberly Randall, Collections Manager of Textiles
0902

CT Cynthia Trope, Associate Curator of Product Design & Decorative Arts
0377, **0381**, **0583**, **0632**, **0639**, **0723**, **0871**

SVD Stephen H. Van Dyk, Head of Art Libraries, Smithsonian Libraries
0858, **0982**

SELECTION

Katagami, Arrow Design Imitating Warp Ikat (Kasuri), late 19th–early 20th century
Japan
Cut mulberry paper treated with persimmon tannin and silk thread
Gift of Helen Snyder, 1976-103-289

The word **katagami**, the Japanese term for the paper stencil used to print patterns on fabric, translates literally as "pattern paper." Featuring designs and motifs drawn from nature, traditional folklore, and literature, katagami are crafted as tools to be used in the resist-dyeing process that is used to produce printed textiles in Japan. The patterns that are carved into katagami are not conceived of with the intention of being seen in isolation, as a single sheet, but as a seamless series of repeats in a larger textile. Yet the delicately rendered, rhythmic motifs of these stencils have often given them a second life, as collectibles and as inspiring objects of beauty. This remarkable Arrow Design Imitating Warp Ikat, which probably dates to the Meiji period (1868–1912), is one such example.

The tradition of using paper stencils to **resist dye** for printing dates back as early as the eighth century, around the beginning of the Heian period, and the use of paper stencils in the resist-dye process emerged during the Kamakura period (1185–1333).[1] Yet it was in the mid- to late Edo period (1603–1868) that dyeing with katagami became a flourishing method, one that continued through the Meiji period. While the resist-dye process can be used to produce textiles for many purposes, katagami have primarily been used to dye fabrics for kimonos.

Katagami are carved by craftsmen who train as apprentices for many years, often learning to specialize in a single method of cutting. The trade demands intense mental and physical concentration and dexterity. Stencil carvers typically focus on a single carving technique, by either pulling the blade toward or away from the body. Others specialize in designs composed of minute perforations. At the height of the stencil carvings' popularity, and even among some carvers today, an entire career might be built around a specialty of *shima-bori*, or stripe cutting, a technique that would have been essential to creating this remarkable design of arrows running in opposite directions.

Stencil carvers rely on the production of properly prepared mulberry paper. The paper is then treated with persimmon tannin and aged. The juice and the paper become one, turning a deep copper brown. The persimmon tannin makes the paper waterproof. By the time the paper is ready to be carved, it is durable enough to remain intact once it is soaked in preparation for each use, and flexible enough to retain its original dimensions without warping during the dyeing process. The stencils are crafted to be resilient to the rigorous process of printing, for a stencil is typically used hundreds of times before being retired. The carving process for a single design might take days or weeks, but several copies of the same design are carved at once by binding several layers of paper together.

The pattern design for any given sheet of katagami is dictated in part by the need to make the stencil hold together. Silk thread was commonly used as reinforcement between the sheets of paper, enabling delicate designs that maximized the relationship between positive and negative space that is at the heart of any sheet of katagami. Because Japanese garments were traditionally made without a shoulder seam, a pattern such as Arrow Design Imitating Warp Ikat, in which half the design points up and half points down, allows for a fluid repeat of the pattern on the front and back of

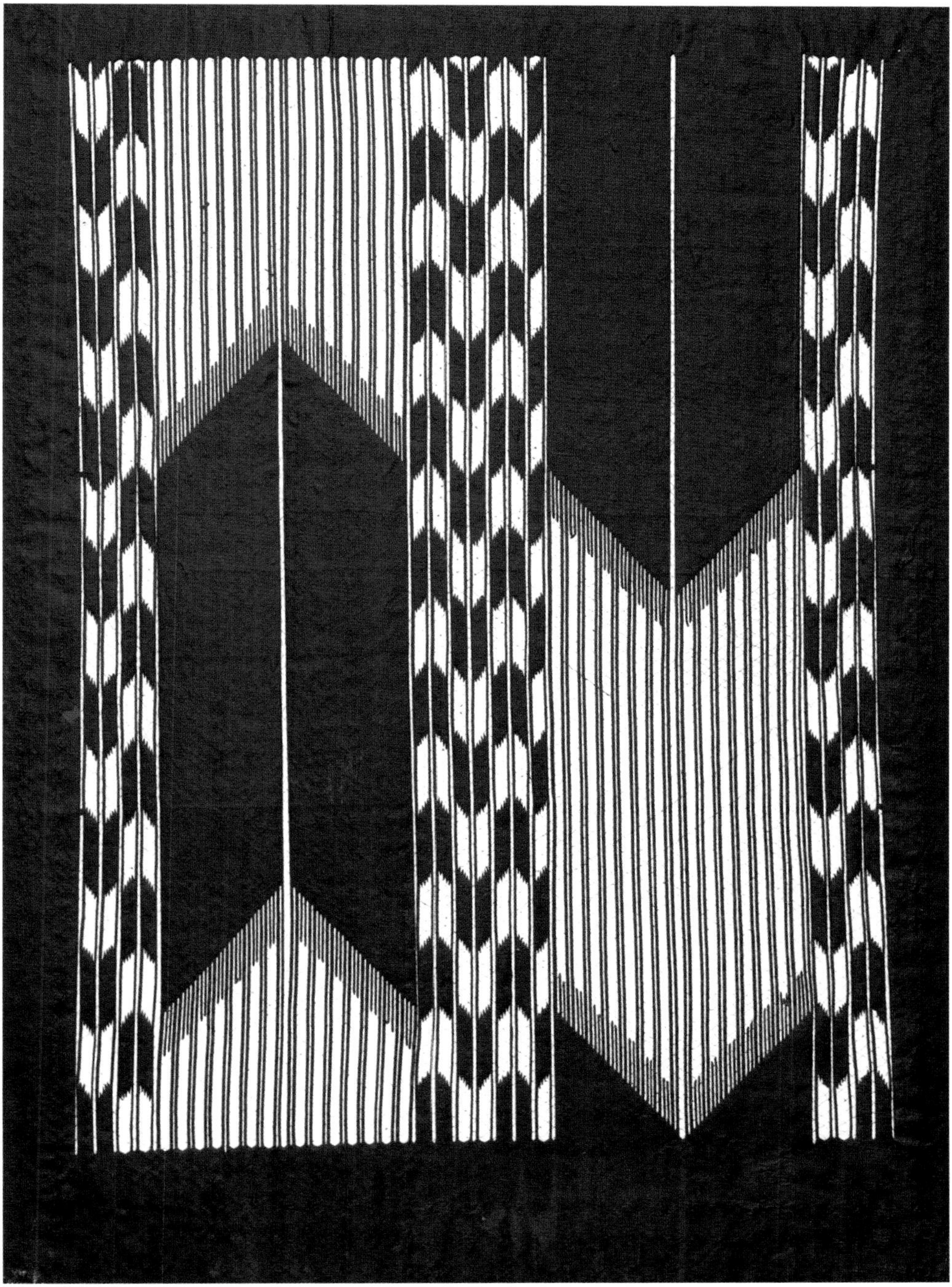

0027. Katagami, Arrow Design Imitating Warp Ikat (Kasuri), late 19th–early 20th century

the garment. Many designs also contain visual elements that hold special meaning in Japan. Arrow Design Imitating Warp Ikat not only makes use of the incalculable precision of a shima-bori carver and the rhythmic balance of positive and negative space, but also employs the meaningful motif of arrows, which are considered a protective talisman.

Although katagami were rarely collected as art objects in Japan, Western artists, designers, decorative arts schools, and museums began collecting the stencils as early as the 1860s. Designers as influential and diverse as Koloman Moser, Josef Hoffman, Eugène Grasset, René Lalique, Henry van de Velde, and Lockwood de Forest all used katagami as source material for their decorative work.[2] **CC**

1 Iwao Nagasaki, "The History of Printed Pattern Dyeing and Paper Stencils in Japan," in *Katagami Style*, Akiko Mabuchi, Yoko Takagi, and Iwao Nagasaki (Tokyo: Nihon keizai shinbunsha, 2012), 6–9.

2 Thomas S. Michie, "Western Collecting of Japanese Stencils and Their Impact in America," in *Carved Paper: the Art of the Japanese Stencil*, ed. Susanna Kuo, Richard L. Wilson, and Thomas S. Michie (Santa Barbara, CA: Santa Barbara Museum of Art, 1998), 160–61; Akiko Mabuchi, Yoko Takagi, and Iwao Nagasaki, *Katagami Style* (Tokyo: Nihon keizai shinbunsha, 2012).

0028. Purse, USA, early 19th century

0029. Textile, England for African market, early 20th century

0030. Purse, USA, ca. 1880

0031. Grasscloth, Japan, 1954

0032. Sidewall, Checks and Balances, 1998, Elizabeth Dow

0033. Sidewall, Edo, 1967, William Justema
0034. Sidewall, Frames, 2004, Craig Wood and Chris Taylor

0035. Textile, Staccato, 1951, Angelo Testa

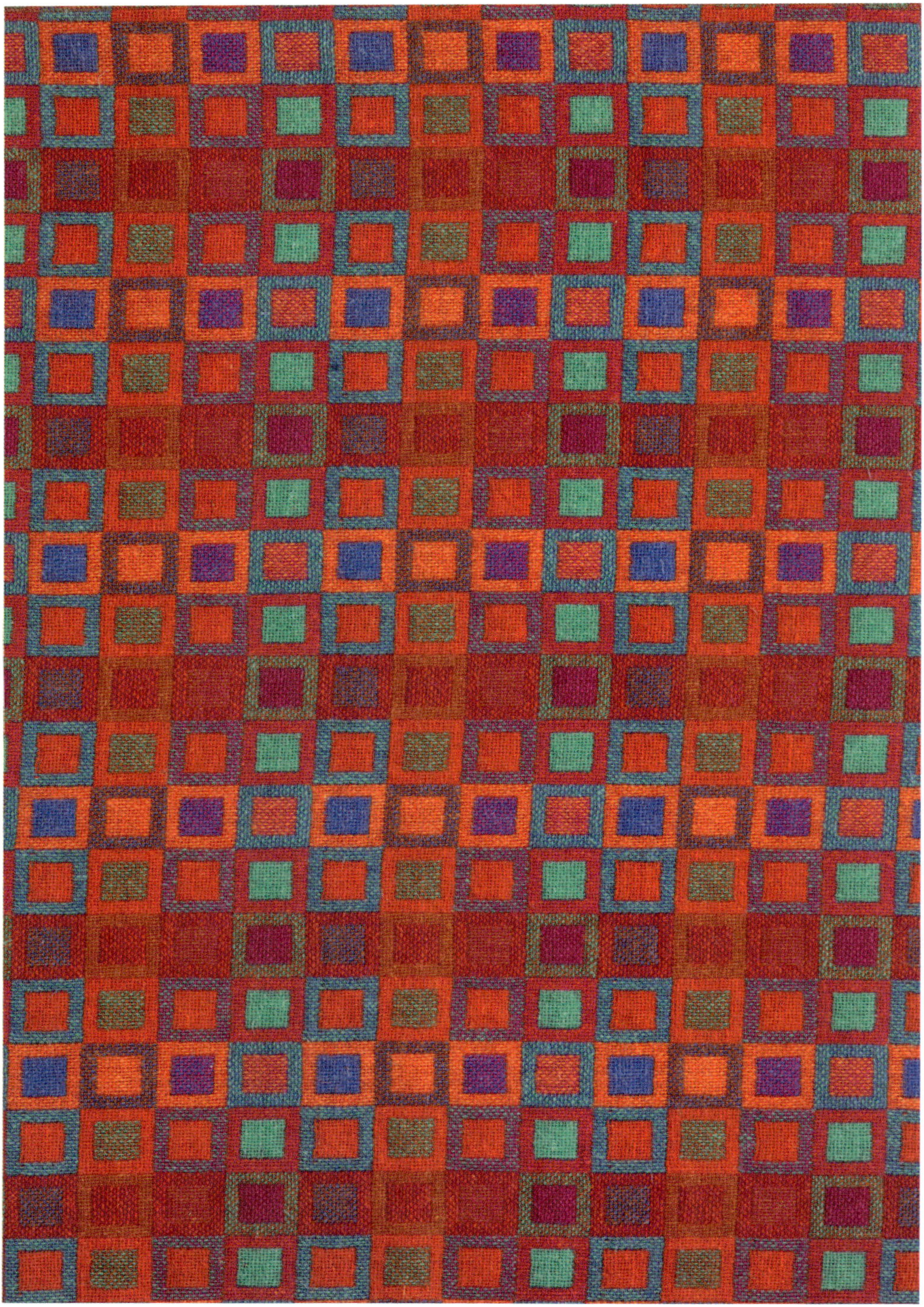

0036. Sample, Matrix, 1973, Jack Lenor Larsen

0037. Mural miniature, Quadrati, 1971, James Seeman Studios Inc.

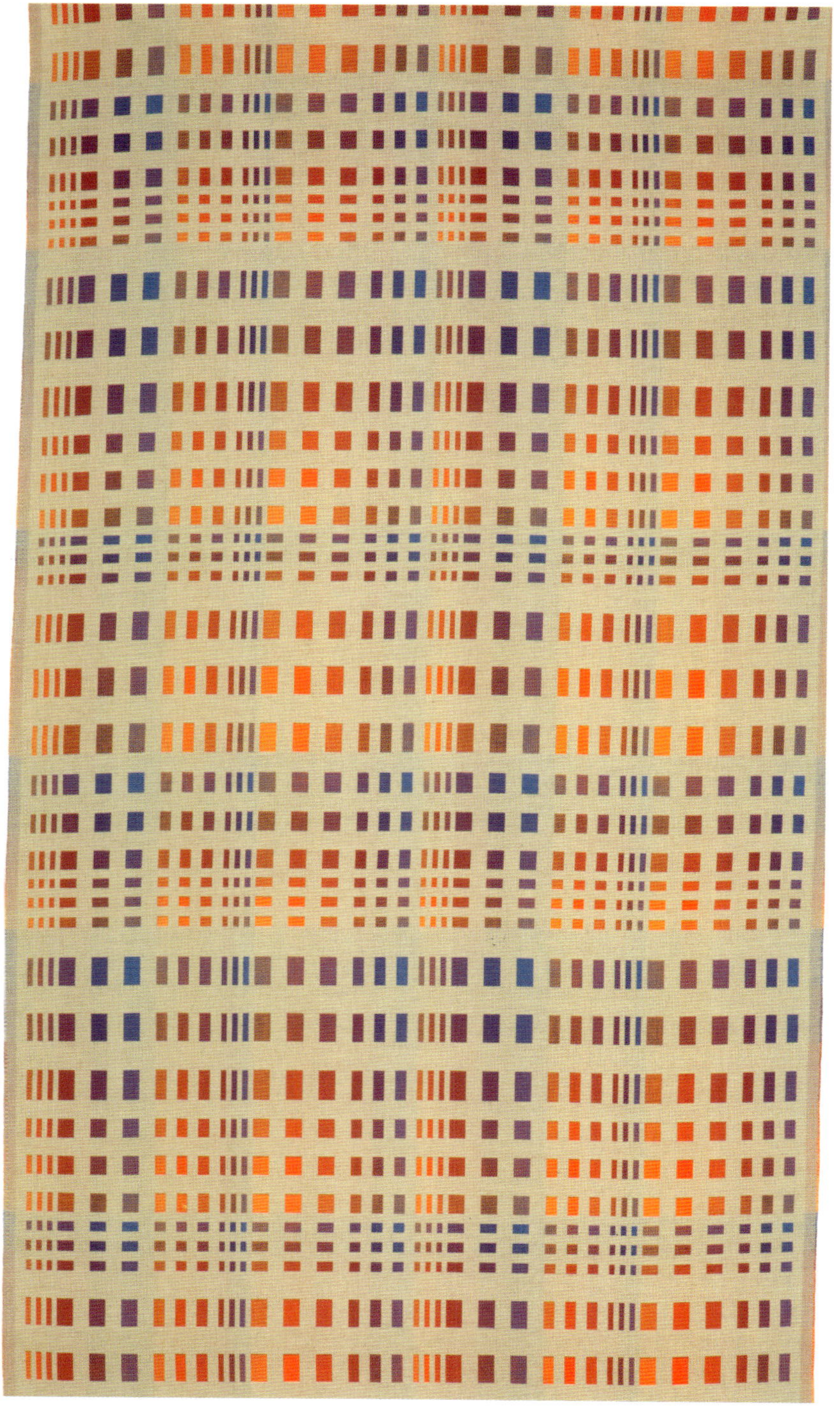

0038. Textile, Landis II, 1973, Richard Landis

0039. Textile, Suora, 1980, Markku Piri

0040. Textile, Mexican Plaid, ca. 1938, Dorothy Wright Liebes

0041. Book, France, 1822–30, Jacquemart & Benard

0042. The Weighing of the Heart brooch in art form holder, England, ca. 1998, Kevin Coates

0043. Hand-woven sample (detail), USA, 1948, Anni Albers

0044. Textile, USA, 1930–31, Donald Deskey

0045. Sample (detail), USA, 1949, Anni Albers

0046. Darning sampler, Germany, 1841, S. Hille

0047. Sewing sampler, Germany, late 19th century
0048. Darning sampler, Netherlands, 1711

0049. Darning sampler, Netherlands or Denmark, early 19th century

0050. Darning sampler, England, 1800, Hannah Walne

0051. Darning sampler, Netherlands, 1767

Darning sampler, Netherlands, 1735
Silk embroidery (pattern darning and eyelet stitches) on plain-weave linen foundation
Bequest of Gertrude M. Oppenheimer, 1981-28-234

The earliest European samplers date from the sixteenth century and functioned as portable and treasured repositories of stitch techniques, much like an artist's model book of stock figures and motifs. By the seventeenth century, samplers were exercises for young girls to practice needlework skills they were expected to master. Creating a sampler taught more than hand techniques; the concentration and focus on detail required discipline and patience. Needlework skills were generally viewed as a sign of culture, moral upbringing, and preparedness for marriage and family. Samplers remained an important aspect of a young woman's education well into the second half of the nineteenth century.

In samplers that were used to teach mending or darning, the maker learned the skills necessary for repairing and reweaving worn textiles and clothing, a requirement for running a thrifty and exemplary household.

As noted in this epigraph by the English poet John Taylor (1578–1653) from a popular seventeenth-century pattern book, mending was an essential craft for repairing household textiles.

> A Needle (though it be but small and slender)
> Yet it is both maker and mender:
> A graue Reformer of old Rents decayd,
> Stops holes and seames and desperate cuts displayed.
>
> —John Taylor, "The Prayse of the Needle"[1]

Mending worn or damaged textiles is as ancient as the art of **weaving** and was made possible by the invention of sewing needles. Examples of mending as early as the third millennium BC are found on woven linen Egyptian burial sheets from the Middle Kingdom that were excavated from royal Egyptian burial sites. In the Cooper Hewitt collection, a Tiraz textile fragment from the tenth to eleventh century AD has two areas of original mending, executed in the same fine **Z-spun** cotton as the **warp** and **weft** of the original textile (**0053**).

Mending samplers developed in the early eighteenth century in Northern Europe and spread to other countries later in the century.[2] This Netherlandish piece (**0052**) is part of a group of nearly forty mending samplers, many from the same donor, in the museum's larger collection of more than one thousand samplers. Dating from the eighteenth and nineteenth centuries, the majority of the museum's darning and mending samplers are executed with silk thread on a linen or cotton foundation (**0054**, **0055**). Although the production of mending samplers was codified through teaching traditions, samplers were nonetheless personal creations and often express a unique aesthetic in the maker's choice of color and layout. To the modern eye, the seemingly random placement of motif and color contributes to an accidental and charming beauty.

The darned mends of the samplers are created by cutting out a square hole in the foundation fabric to mimic an area of damage, then reproducing the original woven structure of the fabric through needle weaving. Often the vertical and horizontal elements of the mend, replicating the warp and weft of a woven pattern, are worked

0052. Darning sampler, Netherlands, 1735

in different colors of silk thread. Although the majority of household textiles repaired during this period were white cotton or linen, with the mends invisibly integrated into the surrounding material, the bright, contrasting colors in the samplers allowed the needle-woven structure to be clearly assessed by student and teacher. The use of silk for these exercises may be due to the fiber's strength and ability to withstand the needle weaving process without fraying.

The tightly executed darning seen in mending samplers was also made possible by the general availability of fine steel needles, which did not become plentiful in Europe until the seventeenth century.[3]

This skillfully executed mending sampler (**0052**) includes eighteen darned holes filled with a variety of simple needle-woven structures, including **plain weave**, **twill**, diamond twill, and **herringbone**. The silk darning thread is secured beyond the upper and lower cut edges of the hole and worked into the foundation fabric to secure the vertical warp elements for needle weaving. The horizontal weft elements are similarly needle woven into the foundation fabric and interlaced over and under the previously laid warp threads to create the desired structure. In the center of the sampler is a large patch of the foundation fabric that was cut out, embroidered in an eyelet stitch with the maker's initials, the date (1735), and a crown motif, and then darned back into place, the repair highlighted by a different color thread at each of the four sides. This insertion technique was used in the lower-right corner of the sampler, while the other three corners of the sampler were cut away and filled with needle weaving, with **selvedges** that were overcast on the two outside edges.

As design artifacts, mending samplers contain information about attitudes and practices in the eighteenth and nineteenth centuries: the value attributed to domestic textiles, the skills and responsibilities of young women, and the acceptance—or even appreciation—of the inherent imperfections in a mended textile. In a broader sense, mending is a sustainable approach to preservation and can be considered to be one of the precursors to the modern field of textile conservation. Today, needlework techniques are part of the vocabulary of treatments in use by textile conservators to preserve and restore valuable textiles so that they may continue to be studied and enjoyed. **LC**

1 John Taylor, "The Prayse of the Needle," in *The Needle's Excellency* (London: James Boler, 1631).
2 *Embroidered Samplers in the Collection of the Cooper-Hewitt Museum* (Washington, DC: The Smithsonian Institution, 1984), 9.
3 Sylvia Groves, *The History of Needlework Tools and Accessories* (Middlesex, England: Hamlyn, 1966), 17–23.

0054. Mending sampler, Germany, 1869
0055. Darning sampler, Netherlands, 1814

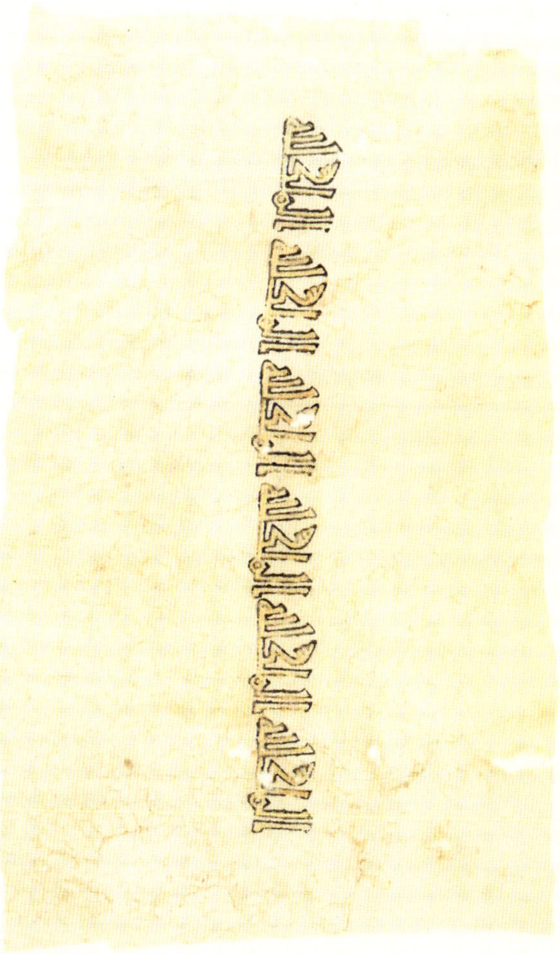

0053. Fragment of a garment, Iran or Iraq, 10–11th century

0058. Drawing, Design for a Jacquard Woven Textile (detail), ca. 1927, Adelgunde (Gunta) Stölzl

0057. Tea towels, Index Collection, 2012, Raw Color

0056. Sampler, Spain, 1753, Marie Claerejo

0063. Huipil (uncut), Guatemala, early 20th century

0061. Sampler, Mexico, 19th century
0062. Sampler, Mexico, 20th century

0059. Sidewall, Pindespil, 1970
0060. Sampler, Germany or Denmark, 1739

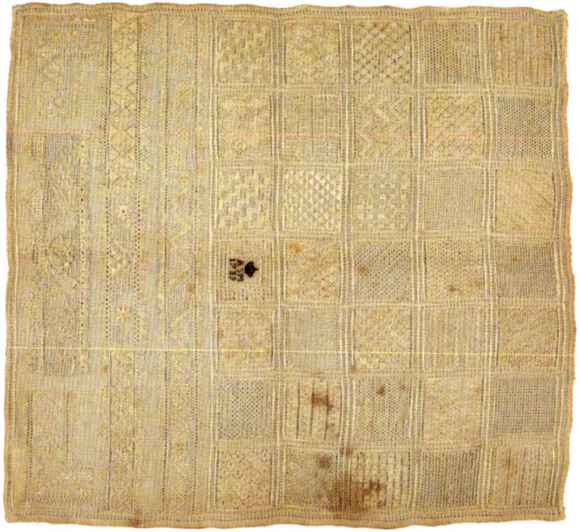

0064. Coif, England, late 16th–early 17th century

0065. Purse, Germany, 1815–40

0066. Sampler, Italy, 19th century

0067. Sampler, Mexico, 19th century

0068. Sampler, Austria or Germany, 19th century

0069. Poster, Zürcher Theater Spektakel, 1996, Benker & Steiner Werbeagentur AG

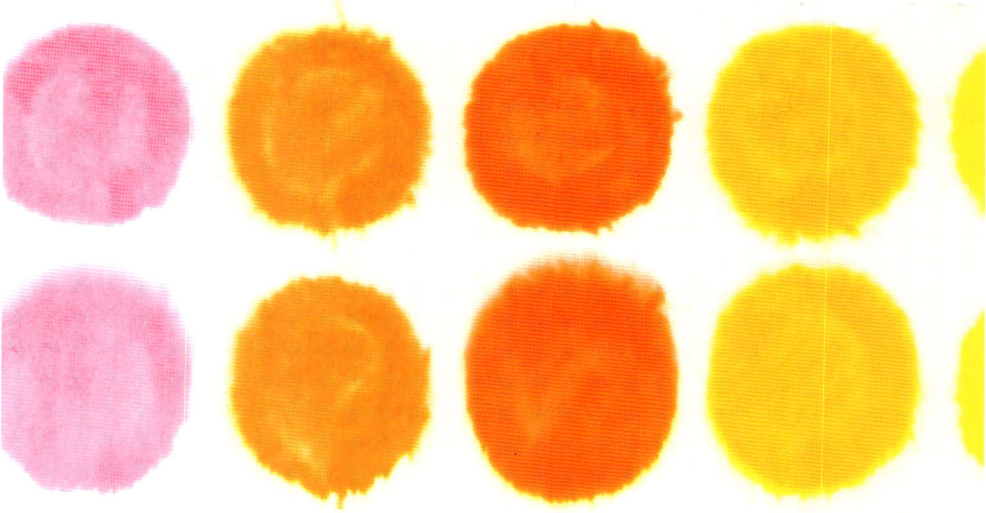

0070. Sidewall, Star Dots, 1969–70, Barbara White

0071. Textile, Discus, ca. 1955, Arundell Clarke Ltd.

0072. Purkersdorf Sanatorium side chair, Austria, 1904–06, Josef Hoffmann

0073. Textile, Golf Magic, ca. 1953, Brian Connelly

0074. Textile, Kivet, 1956, Maija Isola

0075. Border, France, 1800–20

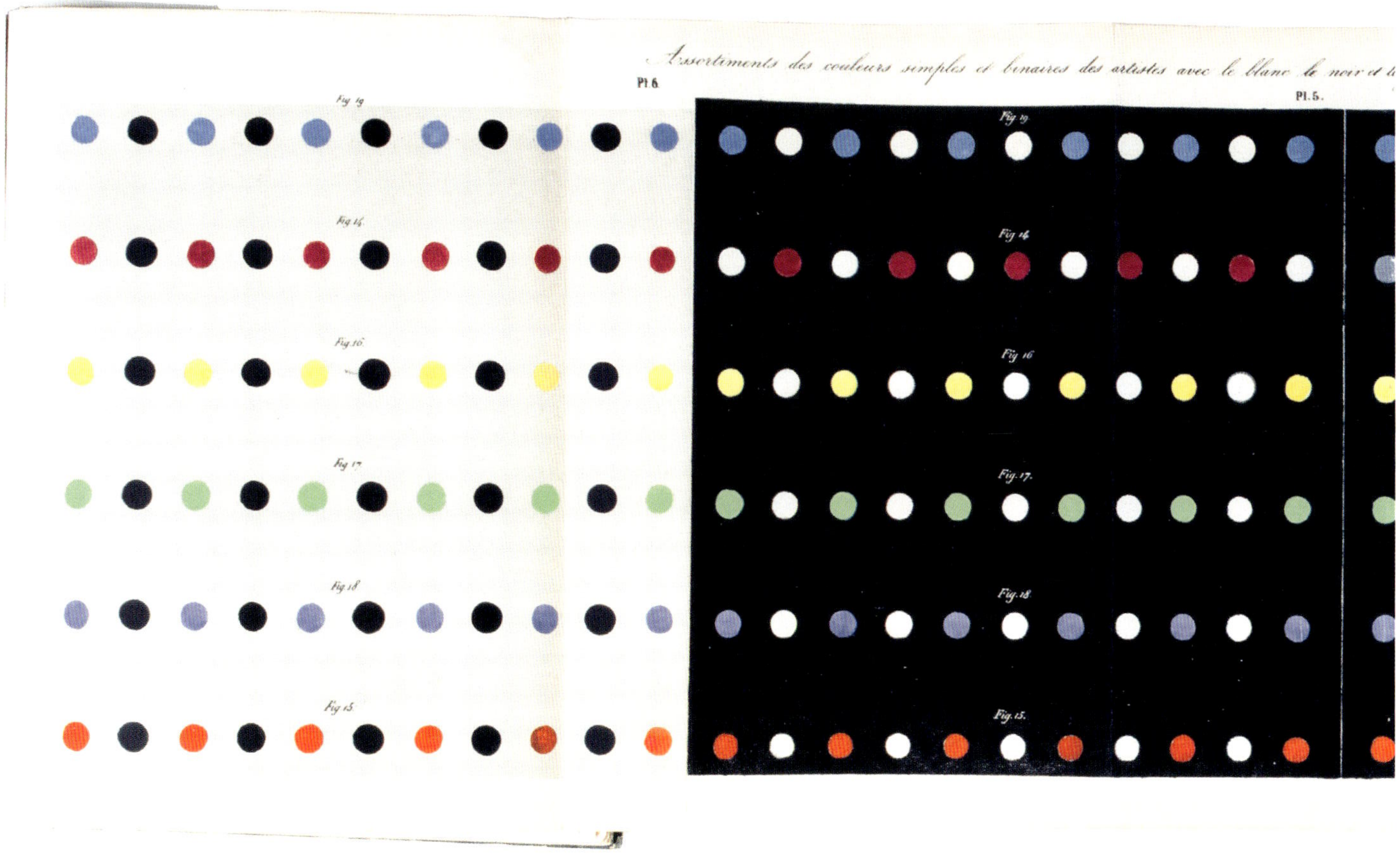

0076. Foldout (detail), *De la loi du contraste simultané des couleurs*, 1839, Michel Eugène Chevreul

0077. Textile, Repeat Dot Print, 2002, Hella Jongerius

0078. Sidewall, 1950, J. Line & Sons

0079. Hanging, Rush Hour 2/ Shanghai (detail), 2012, Grethe Sørenson

0081. Tile (detail), USA, 1877–83, J. & J. G. Low Art Tile Works

0080. Stencil, Katagami, Pine Needle Clusters (detail),, 1877–83

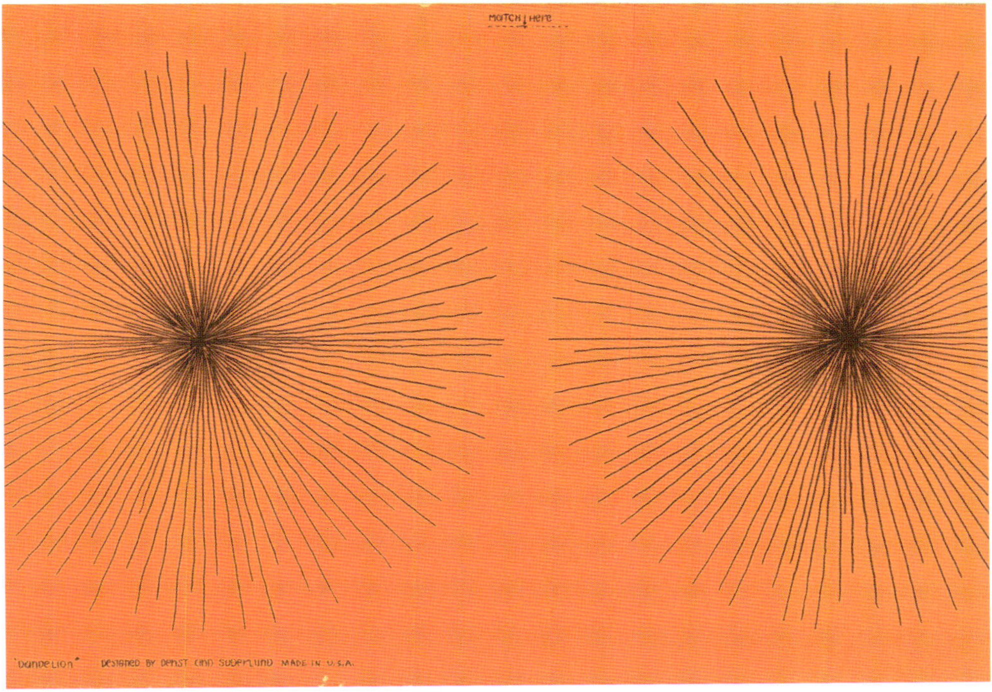

0082. Sidewall, Dandelion, 1952–53, Denst and Soderlund

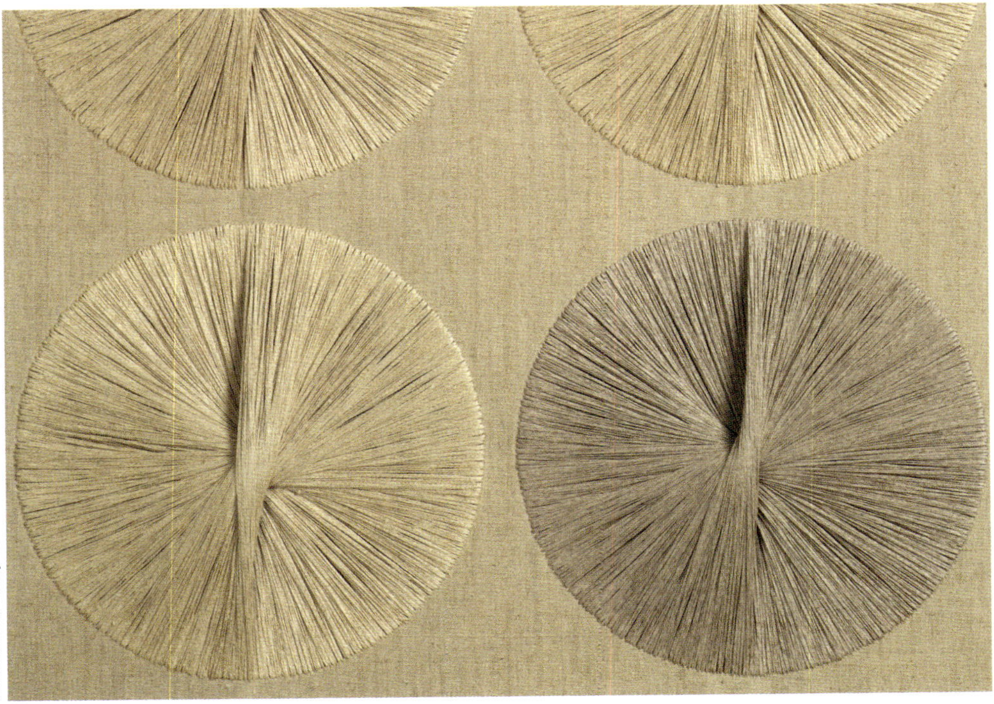

0083. Panel, Study for Ford Foundation wall panels (detail), 1967, Sheila Hicks

0084. Sidewall, Pause, 2004, 2x4

0085. Drawing, Textile Design: Abstract Snow Flake (detail), 1950–70, Tommi Parzinger

0086. Textile, Abacus, 1946, Paul Rand

0087. Textile, Armour, ca. 1955, Joseph Provato

0088. Sidewall, Paris, France, ca. 1872

0089. Frieze, USA, 1905–20

0090. Frieze, 1905–20, Carey Bros. W.P. Mfg. Co.

0091. Sidewall, Efeu/Ivy, 2006, Thomas Demand
0092. Sidewall, sample, USA, 1906–80

0093. Sidewall, France, 1850–60, Desfossé et Karth

0094. Sidewall, possibly England, 1770–80

0095. Sidewall, Fernery, 1967–69, Woodson Wallpapers, Inc.

Sidewall and frieze, 1905–15
M. H. Birge & Sons Company (American, 1834–1959)
Buffalo, New York, USA
Machine printed on paper
Gift of Philadelphia Museum of Art, 1971-58-8-a,b

Wallpapers were rarely designed to be used alone, and fashions in wall treatments changed frequently. In the eighteenth century, wallpapers were paired with one or more borders, hung over a wood wainscot or wallpaper dado. In the late nineteenth century the fashion was for tripartite wall divisions including a dado, sidewall paper, and wide frieze. Moving into the Mission style in the early twentieth century, wall treatments began to get simpler, consisting of a frieze and sidewall. It remained popular to paper ceilings, referred to as the fifth wall, from about 1850 into the 1950s.

This turf design is a matching set of sidewall and frieze. The sidewall contains an allover pattern of green turf, which continues up into the landscape frieze. As the grass reaches the frieze it is shown going to seed, then opens up to reveal a vast landscape with trees and iris blooms. Beginning around 1900, although papers were available separately, it was common to purchase matching sets containing a sidewall, frieze, and ceiling paper to create a continuity throughout the room, simplifying the selection process. The sidewall was frequently the darkest in color, the ceiling the lightest shade, and the frieze somewhere in between. This wallpaper was made during the period when wide landscape friezes were at their height of popularity. There were still many decorating conventions, including the appropriateness of certain papers to certain rooms. Landscape friezes were usually recommended for dining rooms, halls, and libraries. A repeating pattern of turf is unusual, and most likely would be used in a more casual setting. The popularity of landscape friezes began with Walter Crane's May Tree frieze in 1896. By 1902 there were numerous wide block-printed landscape friezes, printed across the full width of the paper, between eighteen and twenty inches. By 1904 they appeared in less expensive **machine-printed** versions with shorter repeats necessitated by the smaller surface of the printing roller. The use of wide friezes remained in vogue until around 1913, when the format changed to two repeats across the width of the paper, or about nine inches, and the landscape scenes were often interrupted or enclosed by architectural elements.

In the simplified Mission interiors, wide landscape friezes visually expanded the room. The frieze became the dominant element, while the other papers were secondary. These wide friezes were hung just below the crown or picture molding, with a sidewall paper running down to the baseboard.

A narrow wood molding normally separated the two papers. When not part of a matched set, the coordinating sidewall would be a solid or a tone-on-tone pattern in the dominant color of the frieze. It was common to hang the frieze at eye level in a dining room, with a sidewall rising up to meet it; their intersection would be covered with a plate rail molding. The ceiling paper could then be brought down to the top of the frieze.

M. H. Birge & Sons Company was the oldest wallpaper company in America when it was sold to a Canadian concern in 1959. Birge produced a wide range of patterns available to consumers in all price ranges. **GH**

0096. Sidewall and frieze, USA, 1905–15, M. H. Birge & Sons Co.

0097. Dish, England, 1749–60, Longton Hall

0098. Border, Germany, 1905–15

0099. Border, Germany, 1905–15

0100. Textile, Austria or Germany, early 20th century

0101. Sidewall, 1830–31, Zuber & Cie
0102. Sidewall, England, 1765

0103. Sidewall, England, ca. 1848, A. W. N. Pugin

0104. Border, France, 1840–45

0107. Textile, Fibra, 1953, Eszter Haraszty

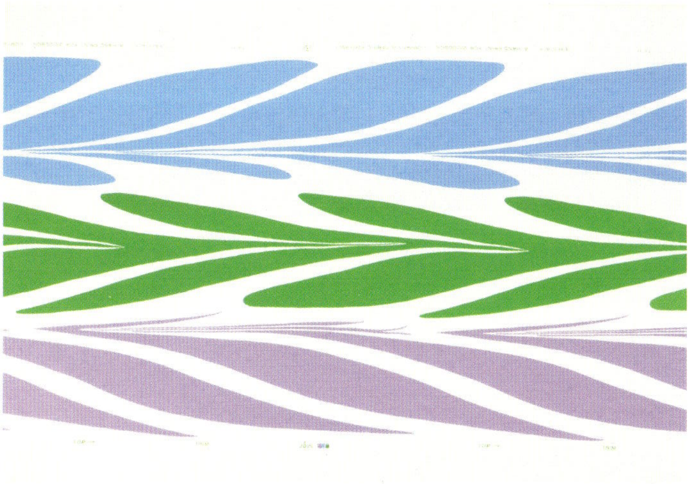

0105. Sidewall, Leafstalk, 1967–69, Woodson Wallpapers, Inc.
0106. Textile, Vågorna, 1949, Stig Lindberg

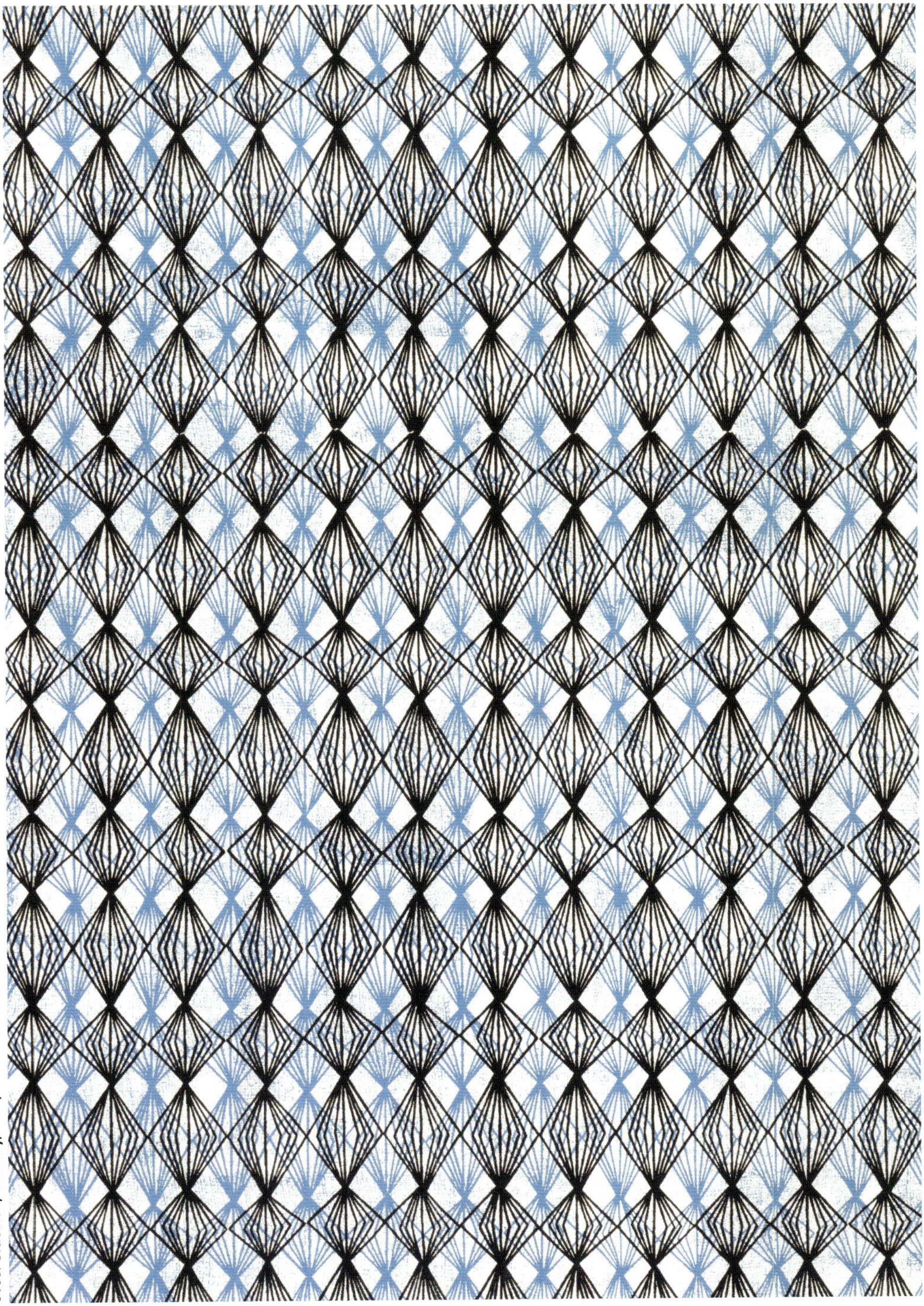

0108. Sidewall, Overlay, 1953, Gene McDonald

0109. Textile, USA, ca. 1950, Marianne Strengell

0110. Textile, Filo, 1942, Angelo Testa

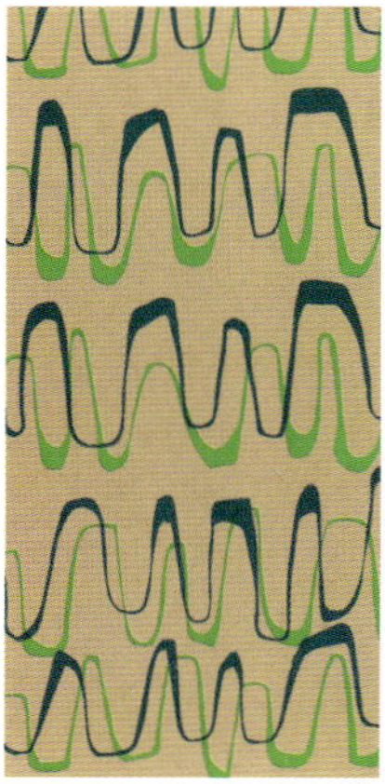

0111. Sidewall, 1080 Cadires, 2010, Javier Mariscal
0112. Sidewall, Sound Waves, 1948, Multiplex Display Fixture Co.

0113. Drawing, Textile Design: The Dance, 1950s, Angelo Testa

0114. Sample, Lines, 1952, Alexander Hayden Girard

0115. Sample, Pepitas, 1952, Alexander Hayden Girard

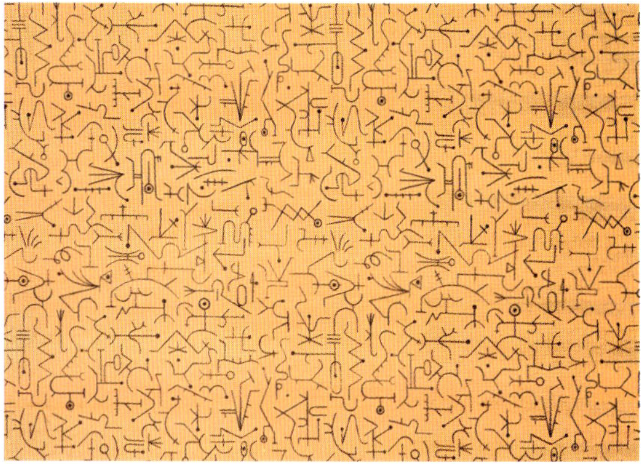

0117. Sidewall, 1953–54, Arthur Sanderson & Sons, Ltd.
0118. Textile, Incantation, 1947, Alvin Lustig

0116. Sidewall, 1954–55, Lucienne Day

0120. Textile, Stilts, 1951, Angelo Testa

0119. Sidewall, Listen and Record, 2009, Ilias Fotopoulos

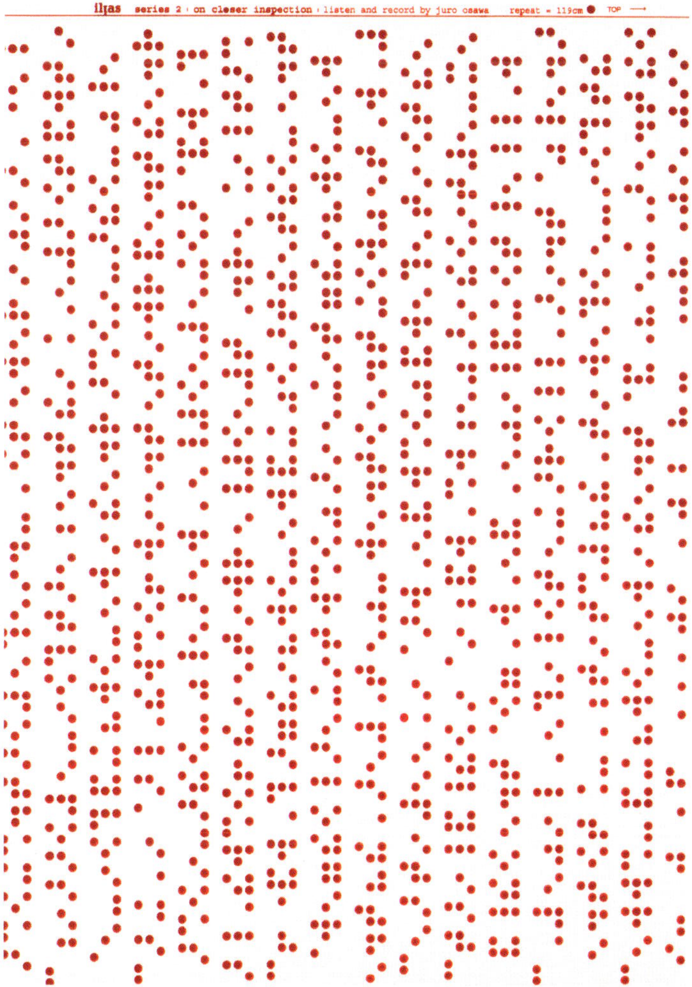

Textile, Eclat, 1975
Designed by Anni Albers (American, b. Germany, 1899–1994)
Manufactured by Knoll International (USA)
Screenprinted cotton
Museum purchase through gift of the Josef and Anni Albers Foundation and from General Acquisitions Endowment Fund, 2011-41-1

In 1970, artist and weaver Anni Albers abandoned **weaving** altogether to pursue a life devoted to printmaking. In an interview with Maximilian Schell in 1989, she said: "I could not stand the idea anymore of all the yarns and looms. It took too long and it always produced just one piece . . . I just outgrew it in some way."[1] She was seventy-one years old, and almost fifty of those years had been spent creating some of the most important textiles of the twentieth century.

She learned weaving at the Bauhaus school in Weimar, where she was admitted in 1922. Although she would have preferred studying other areas in the visual arts, the weaving workshop was the only one open to women. She experimented with different materials and techniques at the Bauhaus, working directly on the loom in order to retain the spontaneity that results from the immediacy between hand, loom, and material. Albers infrequently relied on drawn sketches for guidance, as "a design on paper . . . cannot take into account the fine surprises of a material and make imaginative use of them."[2] This led to an approach that was one of her greatest achievements at the Bauhaus and that would guide Albers throughout her artistic career.

She began experimenting with printmaking in the early 1960s, when she accompanied her husband, artist Josef Albers, to the Tamarind Lithograph Workshop in Los Angeles. "June Wayne, head of the workshop, asked me to try **lithography** myself. I found that in this medium the image of threads could project a freedom I never suspected . . . . Once having discovered this new freedom I was never able to let go."[3] This experimentation with lithography in the mid-1960s contributed to a new textile-making direction for Albers, represented by Eclat, a vibrant **screenprinted** textile for drapery and upholstery. Launched by Knoll under Barbara Rhodes, head of textiles at Knoll between 1973 and 1978, this textile was the first time that Albers translated her graphic art into fabric design for Knoll.[4]

Eclat was a variant of a drawing made around 1970 (**0123**) and two similar prints, PO I (**0122**) and PO II, made in 1973. The prints used a combination of **offset lithography** and **screenprinting**. Albers created a geometric arrangement of trapezoids in orange on gray (PO I) and in gray on gray (PO II), which had the illusion of oscillating between one continuous pattern and multiple pattern modules. Eclat has the same three-dimensional effect and animated surface created by the persimmon trapezoids (it was first available in twelve colorways) on an off-white background.

This was not the first textile that Albers designed for Knoll. She had begun her association with the furniture and textile company in 1957, when she was a consultant on a line of new textiles, including a series of casement fabrics. These were typical of Albers's work during her years as a student and teacher at the Bauhaus (1922–32), and later in the United States, where she and Josef emigrated in 1933 to teach at Black Mountain College (1933–49). The design of these casement fabrics recalls her functional approach to textiles and her curiosity about and experimentation with new fibers and techniques.

0121. Textile, Eclat, 1975, Anni Albers

Albers ended her business relationship with Knoll in 1979, although her fabrics have been reintroduced a number of times over the years. A version of Eclat was reintroduced by the company in 1997 as a cotton and mohair velvet upholstery fabric. In 2007 Knoll produced Eclat in a woven upholstery fabric for the Archival Collection "effectively recognizing it as an iconic Knoll design."[5] **MM**

1 Pandora Tabatabai Asbaghi, "Anni Albers 1899–1994," in *Anni Albers, eds. Nicholas Fox Weber and Pandora Tabatabai Asbaghi* (New York: Guggenheim Museum, 1999), 177.

2 Anni Albers, "Constructing Textiles," in *Anni Albers: On Designing* (New Haven, CT: Pellango Press, 1959), 13.

3 Gene Baro, "A Conversation between Gene Baro and Anni Albers," in *Anni Albers* (New York: Brooklyn Museum, 1977), 7.

4 Angela Völker, "Knoll without the Knolls: Change and Transformation 1963–78," in *Knoll Textiles 1945–2010,* ed. Earl Martin (New York: Published for Bard Graduate Center by Yale University Press, 2011), 262.

5 Ann Marguerite Tartsinis, "Designer Biographies" in *Knoll Textiles 1945–2010,* ed. Earl Martin (New York: Published for Bard Graduate Center by Yale University Press, 2011), 310.

0122. Screenprint, PO I, 1973, Anni Albers, The Josef and Anni Albers Foundation

0123. Drawing from a Notebook, ca. 1970, Anni Albers, The Josef and Anni Albers Foundation

0124. Sample, Celtic Fret, 1969, Ted Hallman

0125. Sidewall, Japan, 1935–39

0126. Poster, HorseProjectSpace Presents: Ritual Tendencies, 2007, Michiel Schuurman

0127. Textile, Unikko, 1965, Maija Isola
0128. Sidewall, Poppies, ca. 1968, Ben Morris

0129. Sidewall, Muguet, 1967–69, Woodson Wallpapers, Inc.
0130. Sidewall, Pasture Flowers, 1960–66, Phoebe Hyde

0131. Sidewall, Ramona, 1965–68, Don Elmer
0132. Textile, Collage, 1967, Wolf Bauer

0133. Sidewall, Orleans, ca. 1968, Eaglesham Accessories
0134. Sidewall, Poppies, 1912, Paul Poiret
0135. Sidewall, France, 1920, René Crevel for Nancy McClelland, Inc.

0137. Drawing, Textile Design: Butterfly Motif, France, 19th century

0136. Textile, Punchinello, 1960, Contessa Friedlinde di Colbertaldo Dinzl

0138. Sampler, Mexico, early 19th century

0139. Wrapping cloth (bojaggi), Korea, ca. 1900

0140. Textile, Bows, ca. 1960, Josef Frank

0141. Sample, Rain, 1954, Alexander Hayden Girard

0142. Textile, Pythagoras, 1953, Sven Markelius
0143. Book illustration (detail), *Tapis et tissus*, ca. 1929, Sonia Delaunay

0144. Textile, Pythagoras, 1953, Sven Markelius
0145. Drawing, Textile Design: Alternating Triangular Forms, 1930–31, Donald Deskey

0146. Book illustration, *Relais*, 1930, Édouard Benedictus
0147. Sidewall, Brighton, 1960–70, Joe Martin

0148. Textile, Zebra, 1971, Sven Fristedt

0149. Textile, Enku, 1965, Hans Krondahl

0150. Purse (detail), USA, 18th century

0151. Drawing, Textile Design: Colorways for Montezuma (detail), 1910–12, Josef Hoffmann
0152. Panel (detail), USA, 1952, Mariska Karasz (top)
0153. Sidewall, Sahara, 1928, Edward Bawden (bottom)

0154. Textile, Motus, 1970, Gaetano Pesce
0155. Sample, Ribbons, 1957, Alexander Hayden Girard

0156. Sidewall, Crazy Key, 1967, William Justema

0157. Spun chair, Italy, 2010, Thomas Heatherwick

0158. Sidewall, Compendium, 1968, Rosemary Newson

0159. Sidewall, Stitched Vertical, 2008, David Rockwell
0160. Sidewall, Citadel, 1959–60, Jack Lenor Larsen

0161. Sidewall, Yvonne Coordinate, 1950–56, Elsbeth Kupferoth
0162. Sidewall, Early Eighties, 1992, Matteo Thun

0163. Sample book, Bauhaus, 1929–30, Rasch & Company

0164. Sample book, Bauhaus, 1929–30, Rasch & Company

0165. Installation, Dutch Clouds (detail), 2011, Karel Martens

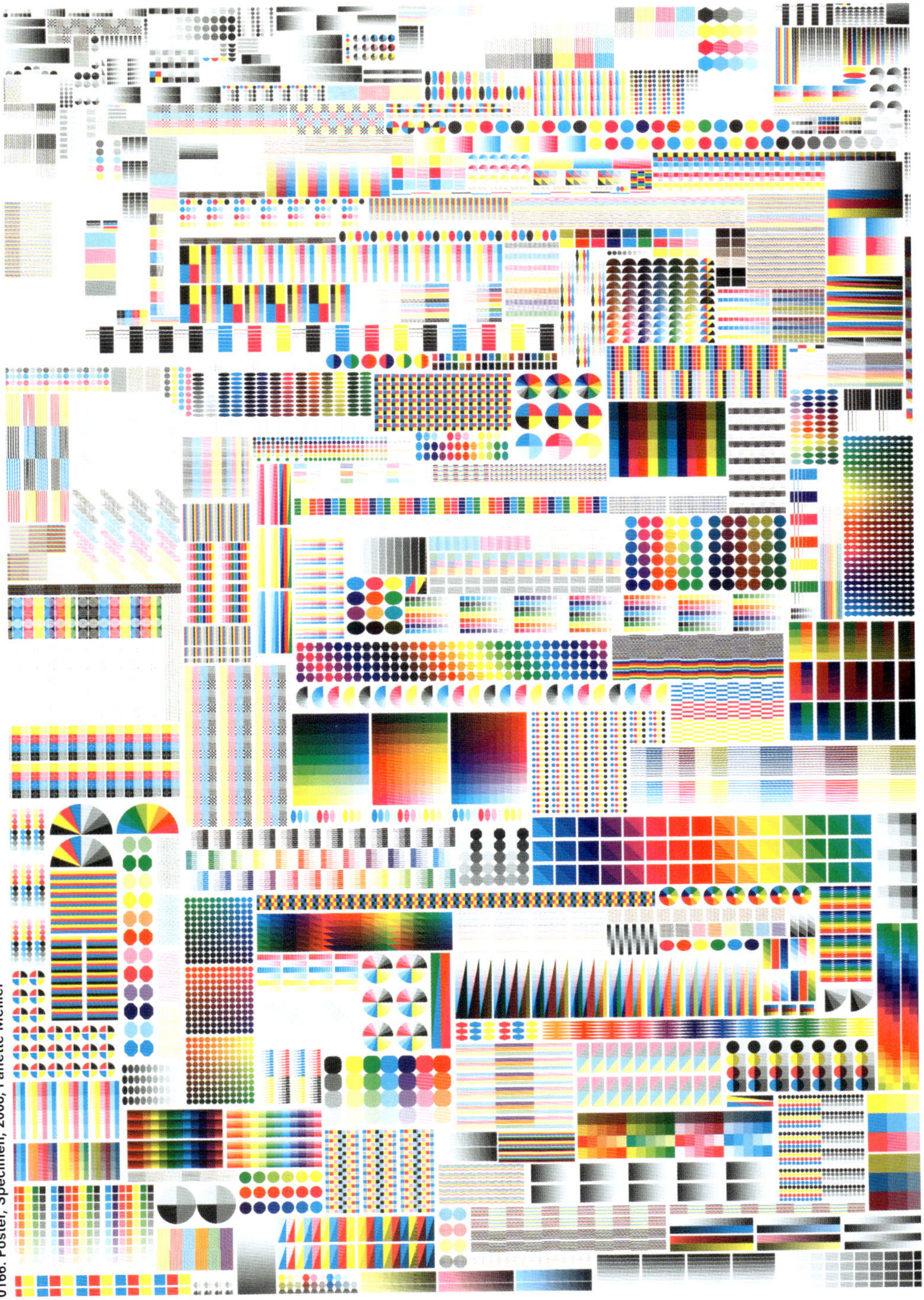

0166. Poster, Specimen, 2008, Fanette Mellier

0167. Blanket, Index Collection, 2012, Raw Color

0168. Hand-woven sample, USA, before 1953, Anni Albers

0169. Textile, Squares, 1950–55, Arundell Clarke Ltd.

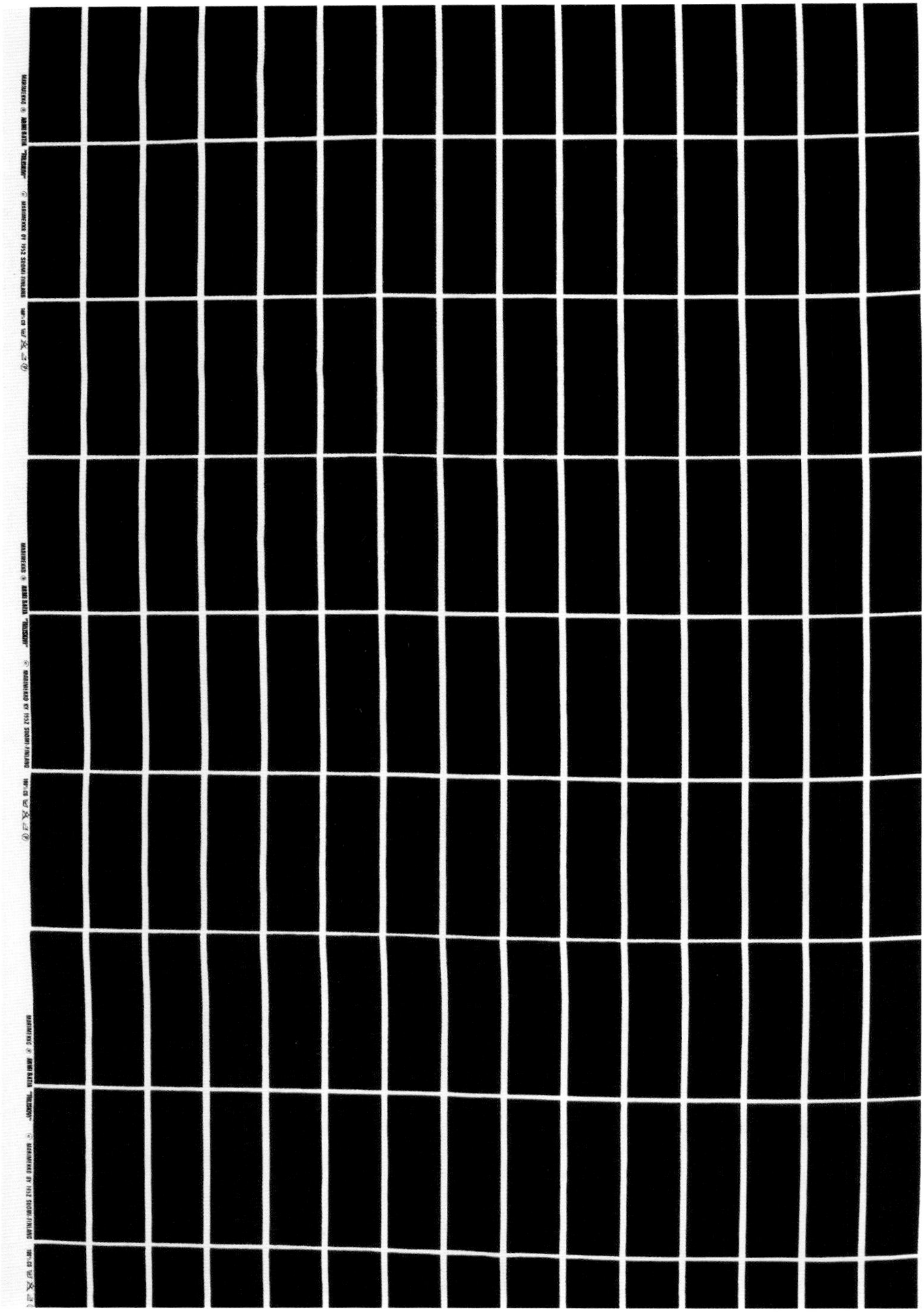

0170. Textile, Tiliskivi, 1952, Armi Ratia

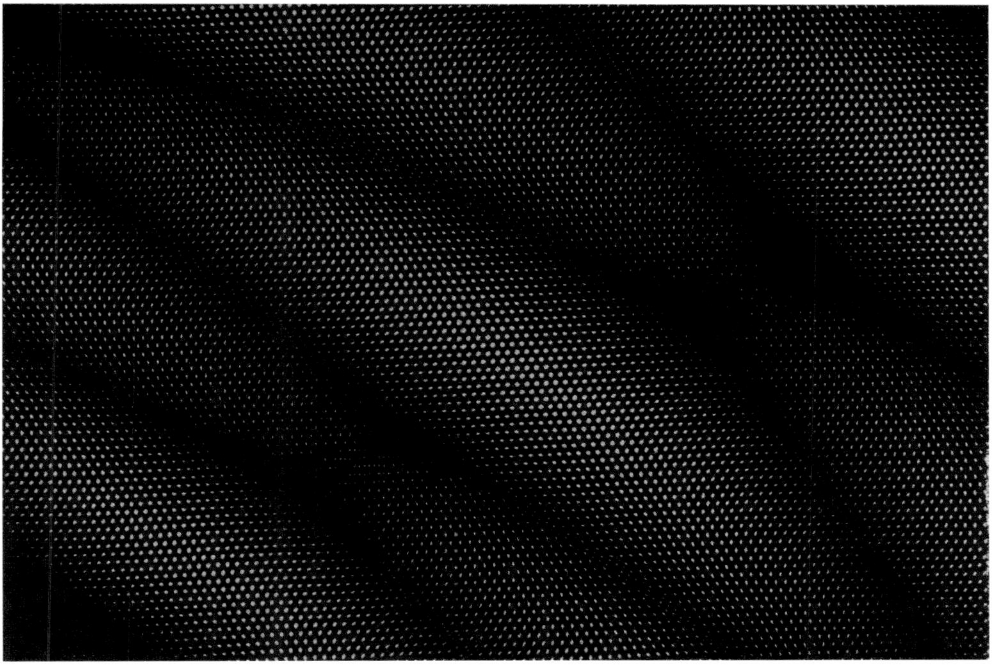

0171. Textile, Interferens, 2007, Grethe Sørensen

0172. Textile, Ghana, 20th century

Textile, Regenbogen (Rainbow), 1919
Designed by Dagobert Peche (Austrian, 1887–1923)
Printed by Clavel & Lindenmeyer, Wasservogel (Basel, Switzerland)
Block printed on silk
Gift of Frances Cogan, 1988-40-1

When the Austrian designer Dagobert Peche died on April 16, 1923, Josef Hoffmann, one of the founders of the Wiener Werkstätte, proclaimed: "Not even every hundred years, at most perhaps every three hundred years, does a country see the birth of such a genius. Dagobert Peche was the greatest ornamental genius Austria has produced since the Baroque. . . . All of Germany has arrived at a new stylistic epoch thanks to Peche's patterns." [1]

Peche designed over 110 different fabric patterns for the Wiener Werkstätte from 1911, when he started his collaboration with the textile department, until his death twelve years later. [2] His preeminence as a designer included other textile-related areas such as lace, embroidery, and beading, and extended to designs for interiors, glass, furniture, ceramics, and wallpaper. By 1915, when he officially became a member of the Werkstätte, he was already the chief designer for its wallpapers.

The Wiener Werkstätte was the idea of designers Josef Hoffmann and Koloman Moser and their friend, the industrialist, Fritz Wärndorfer, who in 1903 wanted to establish an alliance of artists and craftsmen based on the ideas of the Englishmen John Ruskin and William Morris. Officially registered as the Wiener Werkstätte-Produktiv-Gemeinschaft von Kunsthandwerkern in Wien (Viennese Workshops Craft Workers Association), its aim was to elevate applied arts to the fine arts and to promote its members' financial interests through schooling and training in the applied arts, and through the establishment of workshops (metalwork, ceramics, textiles, glass, graphic arts, fashion, jewelry, architecture, interior design, and furniture) to create objects for sale.

In the early years of the Wiener Werkstätte there was a strict adherence to more geometric patterns and forms with Hoffman and Moser as examples, but by 1915 Peche had changed the course of the workshop to embrace both naturalistic and fantastical ornamentation. For Peche, utilitarian objects became a surface for decoration.

Regenbogen (Wiener Werkstätte no. 653) was introduced in 1919 and was available in a variety of colorways—blues, purples, reds, grays—and almost limitless shading combinations within each color. Unlike the stark graphic quality of his posters, Peche's textiles have a more subtle and refined color sense. The ombré effect in Regenbogen, for example, where shades of color melt into one another, resulted from a type of **block printing**. Ink colors were spread in shaded bands by a brush or roller and then picked up with blocks by the printer, who transferred them to the cloth. It was almost impossible to detect the seams of the block or any printing flaws when using this technique. [3]

Block printing was the preferred printing technique in the textile department. Like other hand-crafted objects offered by the workshop, these textiles were quite expensive to produce, especially when using more complicated techniques as with Regenbogen. Only the wealthier clientele could afford most of the Wiener Werkstätte designs.

One of these individuals was Wolko Gartenberg, who commissioned Peche in 1921 to design an apartment interior—workroom and living and dining rooms (**0174**, **0175**). Peche used *Regenbogen* for virtually every surface that could be covered with a

0173. Textile, Regenbogen, 1919, Dagobert Peche

fabric—walls, chairs, cushions, and lampshades. Even the exquisite graining of the furniture, also designed by Peche, had a similar striped sensibility to Regenbogen. Peche's passion for ornamentation and pattern resulted in a spectacular living environment in which every solid structure—from the furniture to the walls—transformed into pulsating stripes.

Peche designed variations of the Regenbogen pattern often with bold floral motifs on top of the ombré striped patterns as if to underscore that the stripe itself was a plain ground to receive another layer of ornamentation. The textile was also used in the context of fashion and applied to textile corsages, handbags, and garments.

Peche was extraordinarily prolific during his years at the Wiener Werkstätte, a testament to his total commitment to the applied arts as conceived by the organization. In Peche's compilation of writings, titled "The Burning Bush" (1922), he laid out his thoughts about aesthetics, the relationship between art and technology, and the future of the Wiener Werkstätte. He wrote with a clear understanding about the need to expand the commercial ventures of the Wiener Werkstätte. At the same time, he maintained his prescient vision of the Wiener Werkstätte as a "culture emporium of the twentieth century. . . . It is the department store in the best sense of the word. . . . It is the fine-art department store, the emporium of humanity."[4] **MM**

1 Berta Zuckerkandl, "Errinnerung an Dagobert Peche," *Neues Wiener Journal* (April 19, 1923), quoted in Anne-Katrin Rossberg, "Who is Peche?," in *Dagobert Peche and the Wiener Werkstätte*, ed. Peter Noever (New Haven: Yale University Press, 2002), 30.

2 This amounted to about ten percent of the printed and woven designs over the course of the Wiener Werkstätte (1903–32), with approximately one hundred artists responsible for designing over 1,800 patterns.

3 Anne-Rose Bringel, conservator at Museum of Printed Textiles, Mulhouse, France, e-mail message to author, August 5, 2013.

4 Dagobert Peche, "The Burning Bush," 1922, quoted in *Dagobert Peche and the Wiener Werkstätte*, ed. Peter Noever, trans. Russell Stockman (New York: Neue Galerie, 2002), 187.

0174. Photograph, Wolko Gartenberg apartment: Corner seating in the living room, 1921, MAK – Austrian Museum of Applied Arts / Contemporary Art

0175. Photograph, Wolko Gartenberg apartment: Living room, 1921, MAK – Austrian Museum of Applied Arts / Contemporary Art

0176. Textile, Auden, 2009, Rodarte

0177. Sidewall, t.e.124, 2012, Irma Boom

0178. Sample, USA, 1959, Jack Lenor Larsen

0179. Textile, Sherman, 2013, Irma Boom

0182. Sidewall, Cord #1, 2003, Petra Blaisse
0183. Sidewall, Thorny Stripe, 1993, Christine Tarkowski

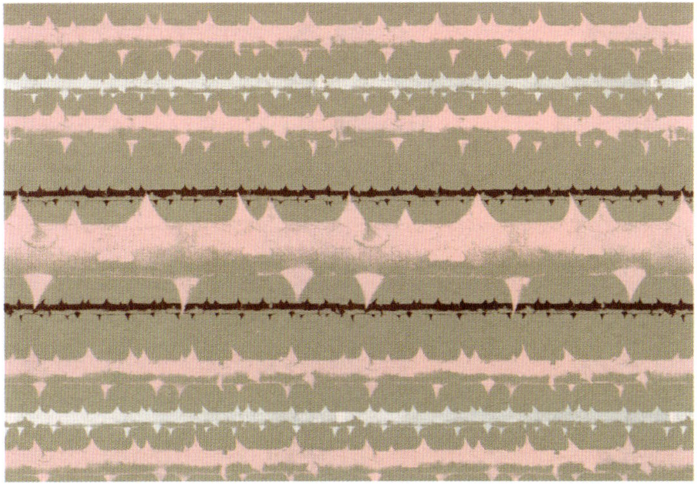

0180. Sidewall, 1950–56, Elsbeth Kupferoth
0181. Ornament, pilaster, Palm, 1947–51, Denys Fitzpatrick

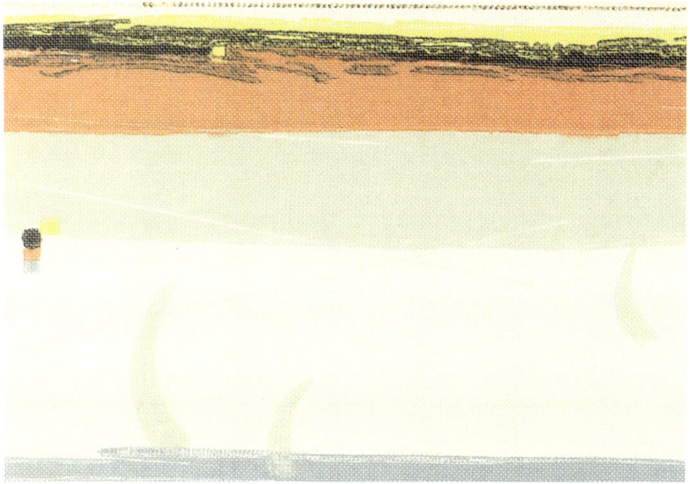

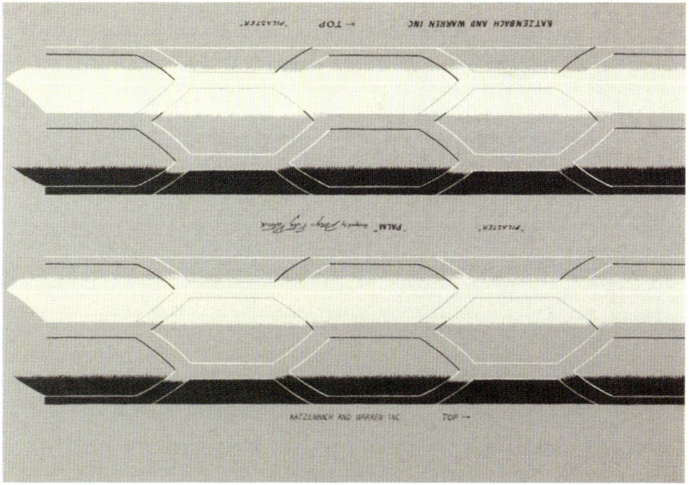

0184. Egyptian Story bangle bracelet, Germany, 2012, Stefan Hemmerle

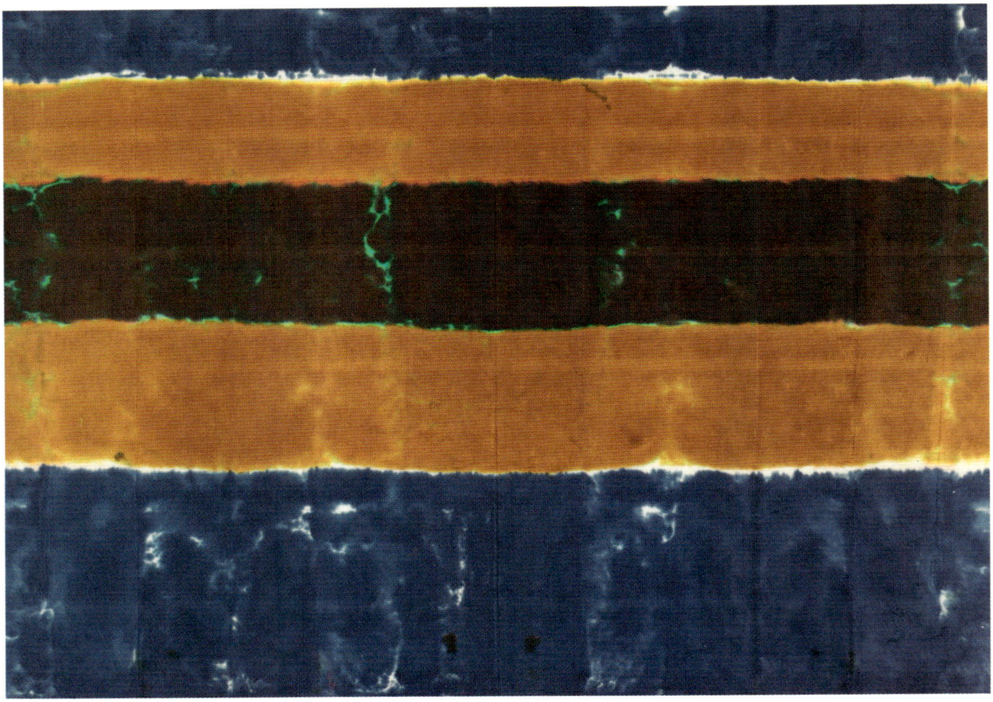

0185. Sidewall, Folded Stripe, 1965–69, Barbara White

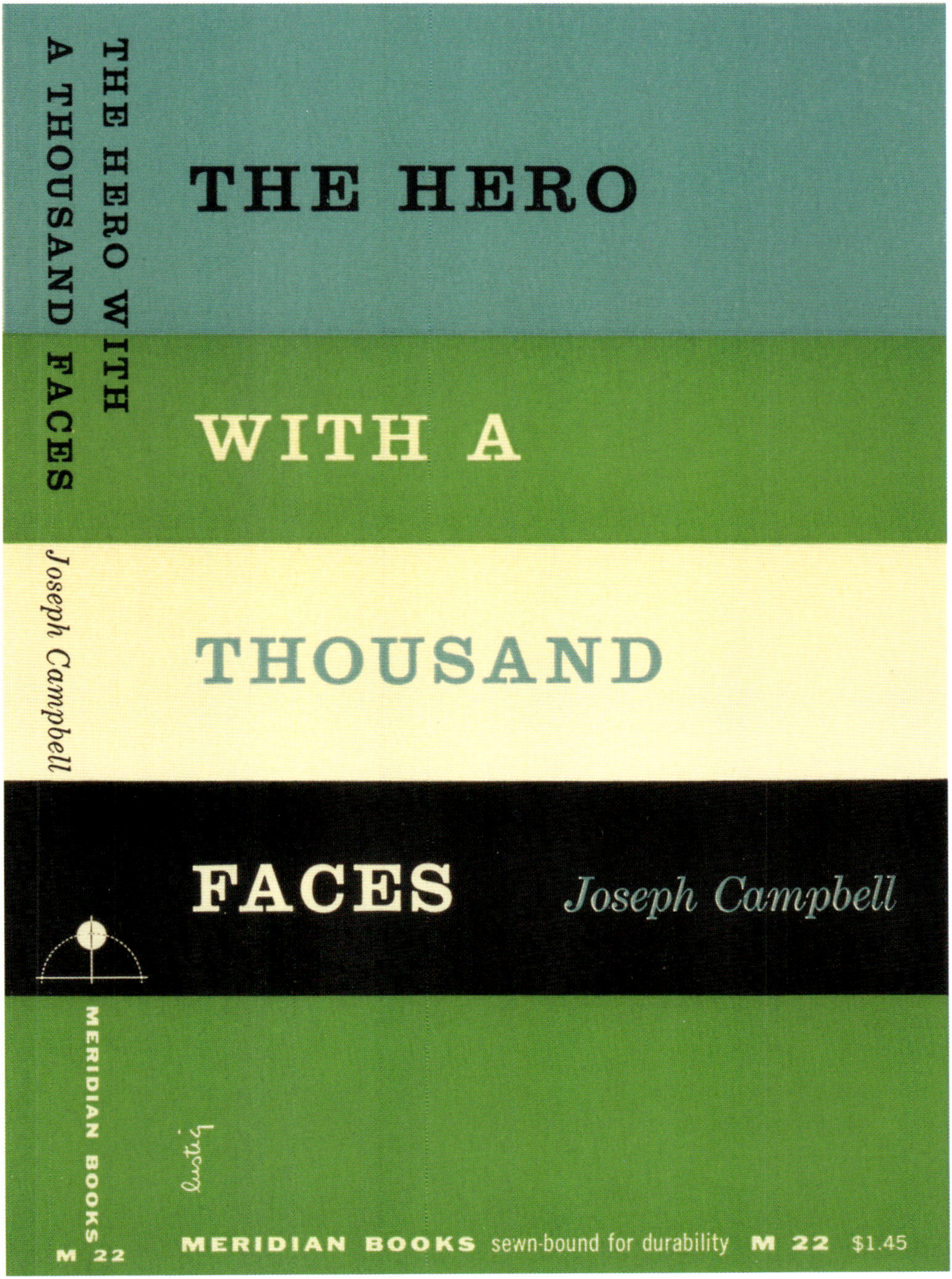

0186. Book cover, *The Hero with a Thousand Faces* by Joseph Campbell, 1955, Alvin Lustig

0187. Sidewall, Baroque Stripe, 1959–60, Jack Lenor Larsen
0188. Sidewall, der Spitz, 1921–22, Dagobert Peche

0189. Textile (detail), England, ca. 1795
0190. Sidewall, France, 1901–06, Zuber & Cie

0191. Textile, France, 1710–15
0192. Textile, France or Italy, 1700–05

0193. Sidewall, Acanthus, ca. 1925, William Morris
0194. Sidewall, Tulip, 1893–95, Charles Francis Annesley Voysey

0195. Textile, France or Italy, ca. 1700

0196. Textile, England, ca. 1740
0197. Sidewall, USA, 1828–50

0198. Textile, Compton, 1896, John Henry Dearle

0199. Textile, France, ca. 1785, Oberkampf & Cie.
0200. Textile, Juin, 1930, Paul Poiret

0201A. Sidewall, Meadow, 1967, William Justema

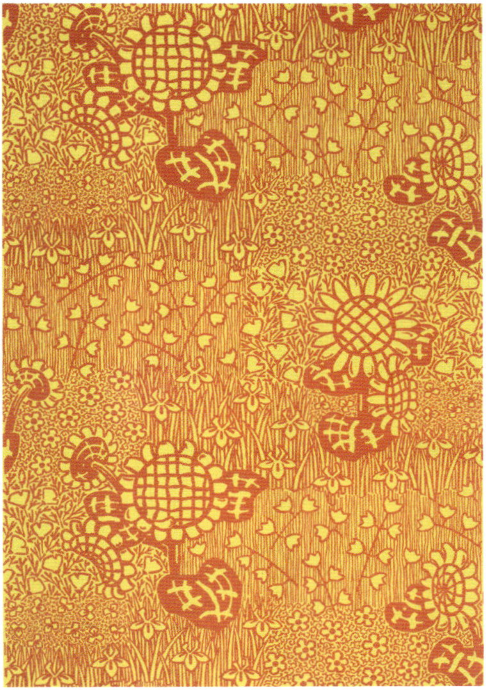

0201B. Sidewall, Meadow, 1967, William Justema

0202. Bed cover (suzani) (detail), Turkey, 19th century

0203. Textile, France, ca. 1792, Oberkampf & Cie.

0204. Sidewall, Tree of Wisdom, 1952, Kakegawa Grasscloth Manufacturing Co. and Orientex, Ltd.

0205. Sidewall, Love in Bloom, 1968, The Jack Denst Designs, Inc.

0206. Sidewall, England or USA, 1880–1900
0207. Textile, Primavera, 1959, Don Wight

0208. Sidewall, USA, 1938–40
0209. Sidewall, France, ca. 1920, René Crevel

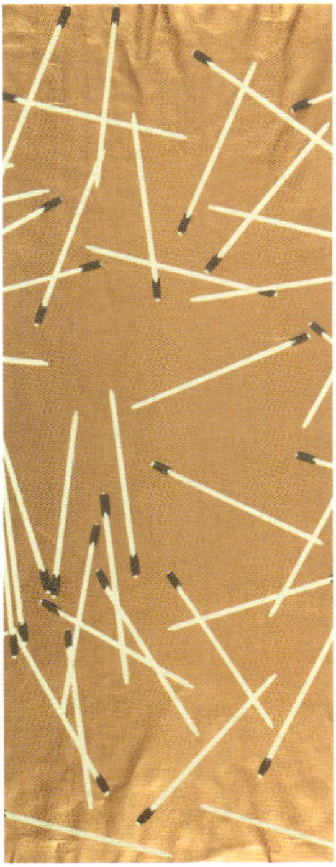

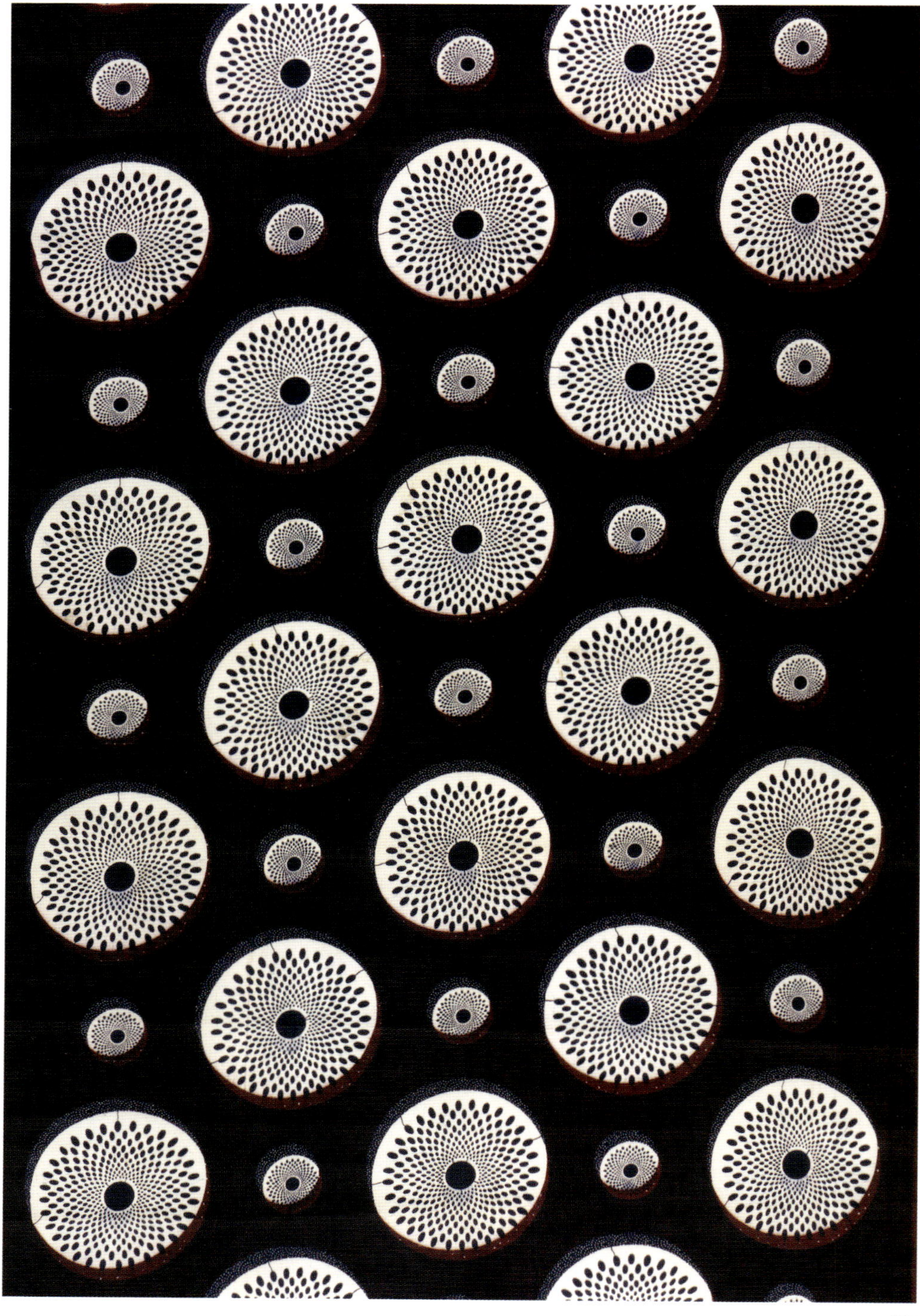

0210. Textile, England or Netherlands for African market, 1960s

0211. Textile, Fan, 1985, Theo Maas

0212. Textile, Netherlands, 2012, Nico Verbart

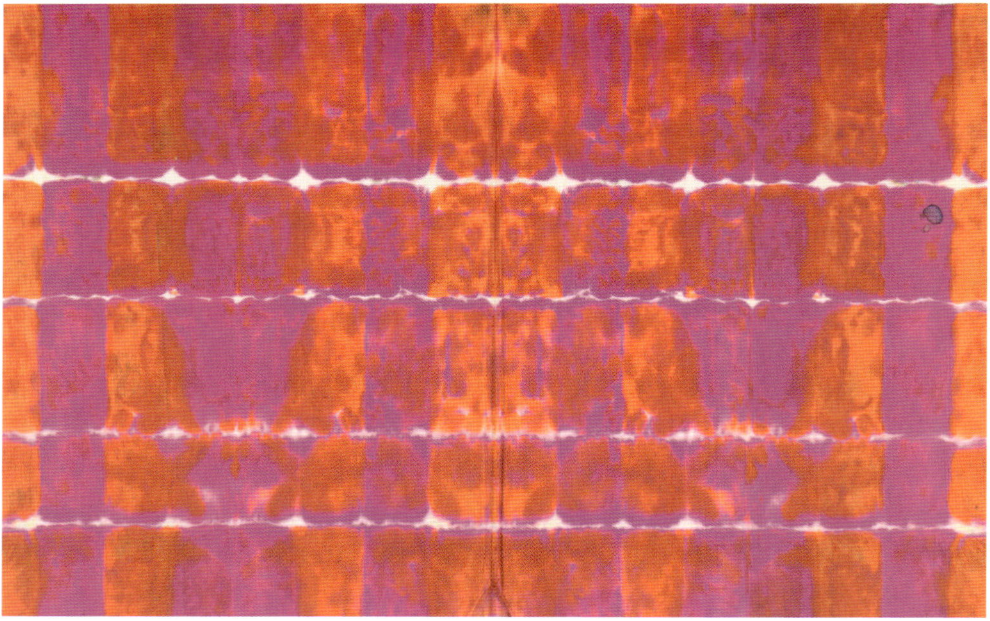

0213. Sidewall, Folded Stripe, 1965-69, Barbara White

0214. Textile, Melooni, 1963, Maija Isola
0215. Textile, Kyoto, 1965, Hans Krondahl

0216. Sidewall, Tie Dye, 1958, Barbara White

0217. Sidewall, Asters, 1959–65, Barbara White

0218. Sidewall, Roses, 1959–65, Barbara White

0219. Tea ceremony rug (mosen), China for Japanese market, late 19th century
0220. Textile, Felsenhuhn, 1910–12, Wilhelm Martens

0221. Sidewall, Homestead, 1962–69, William Justema
0222. Sidewall, France, 1810–20

0223. Textile, Santana, 1984, Johan Sleegers

0224. Poster, Knoll International, 1967, Massimo Vignelli

0225. Textile, Istuva Harka, 1967, Maija Isola

0226. Print, Invitation for Alvin Lustig: An Exhibition of His Work, Frank Perls Gallery, USA, 1949–50, Alvin Lustig

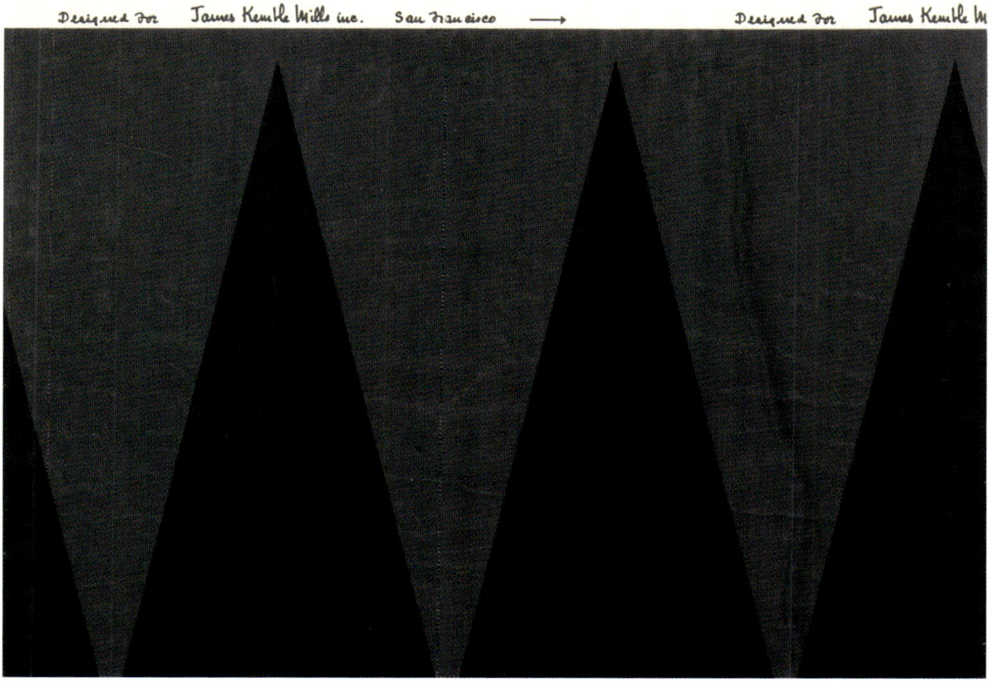

0227. Sidewall, Pennants, 1953, James Kemble Mills, Inc.

0228. Poster, Nippon Good Design Show, 1963, Taï Tsuge
0229. Sidewall, To the Point, ca. 1970, Perceptive Concepts, Inc.

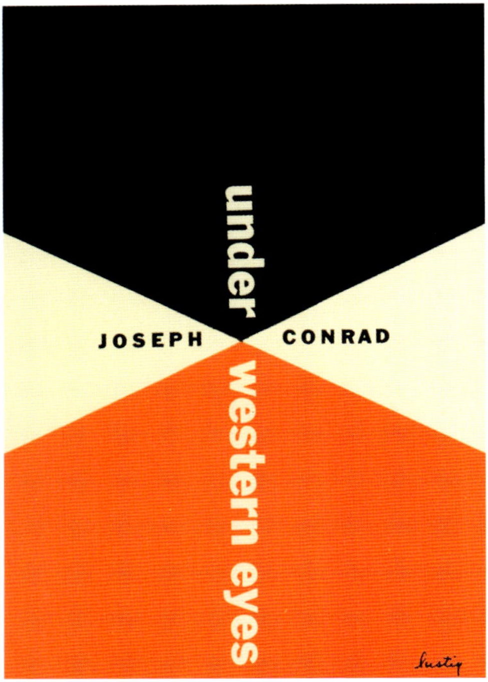

0230. Book cover, *Under Western Eyes* by Joseph Conrad, 1951, Alvin Lustig
0231. Book cover, *Selected Poems* by Ezra Pound, 1948, Alvin Lustig

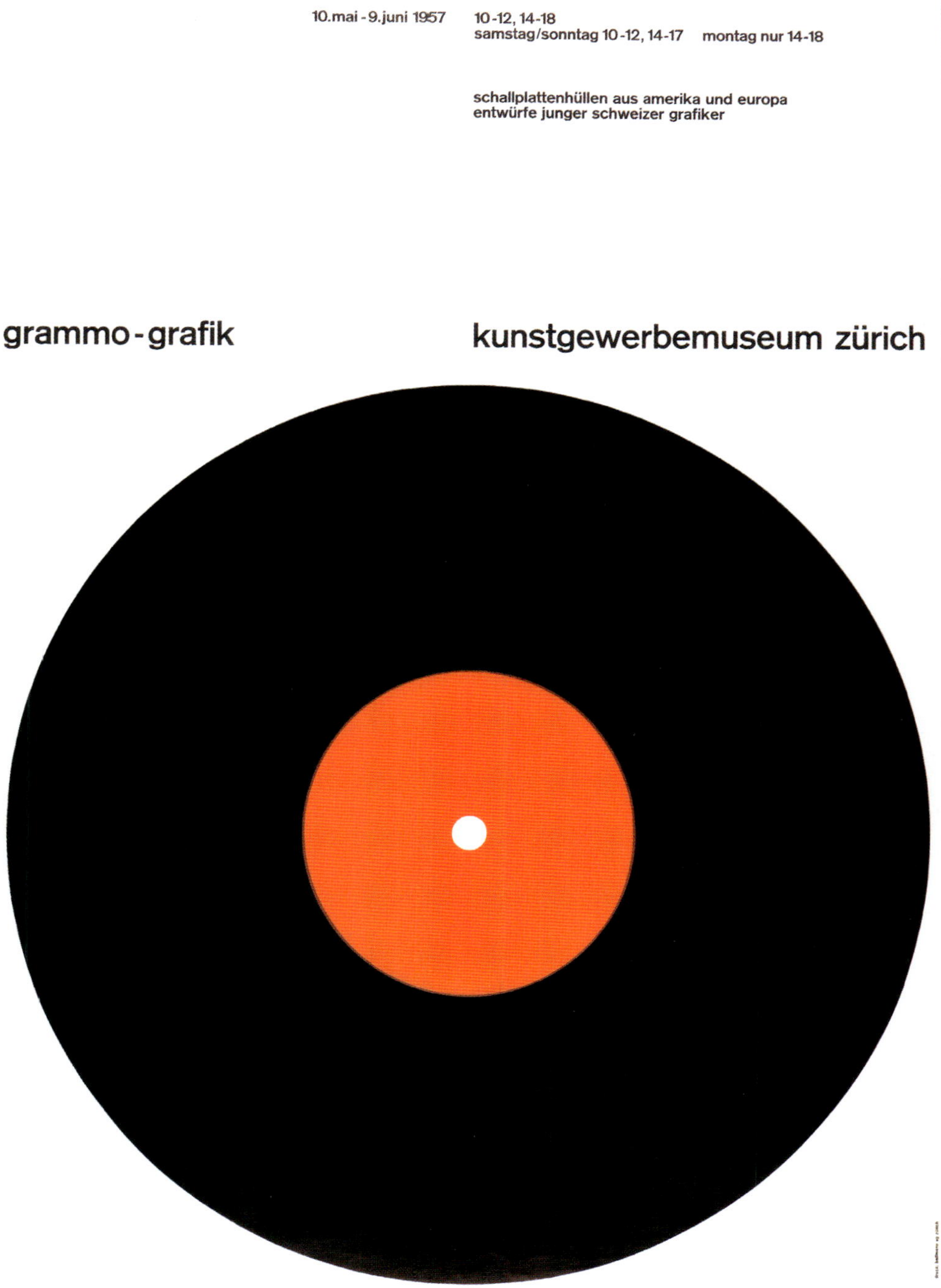

0232. Poster, Exhibition Grammo-Grafik, Kunstgewerbemuseum Zürich, Switzerland, 1957, Gottlieb Soland

0233. Poster, Alberto Flammer / Flavio Paolucci, Museo Cantonale d'Arte, Italy, 1988, Bruno Monguzzi

0234. Book illustration (detail), Aviation exposition, 1909 in *Décors éphémères*, 1948, Albert Chevojon

0235. Bulb lamp, Germany, 1966, Ingo Maurer

0236. Printed packaging, 100 Watt Soft White Bulbs, ca. 1968, Paul Rand

0237. Poster, Nouveaux Espaces, Pesce. Quasar, 1970, Jean Widmer

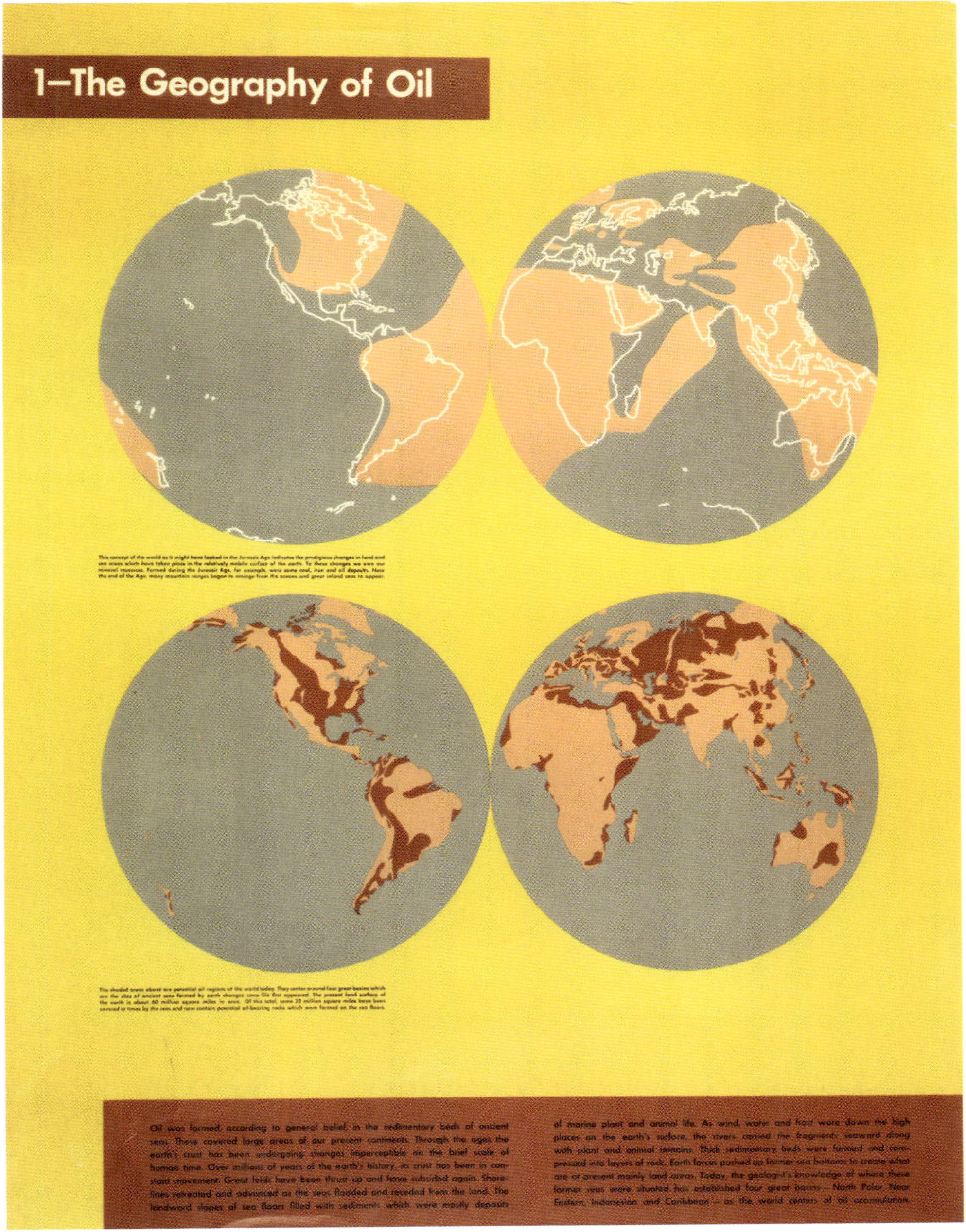

0238. Poster, The Geography of Oil, 1943, Ladislav Sutnar

0239. Poster, Yale University School of Art Graduate Program: 1991–1992, 1991, Paul Rand

0240. Book illustration, *Catalog Design*, 1944, Ladislav Sutnar

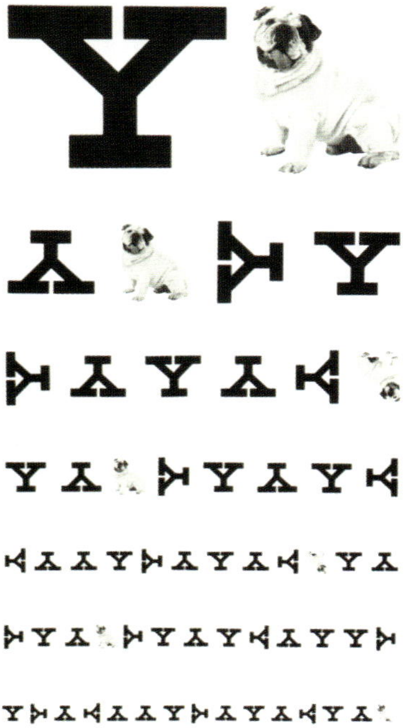

0241. Poster, Yale University School of Art, 1988, Paul Rand
0242. Envelope, *Industrial Design* magazine, 1953, Alvin Lustig

0243. Poster, Seduction, for the Yale School of Architecture Symposium, 2006–07, Marian Bantjes
0244. Poster, PhotoGraphie Zeit: Raum M. Mathys, 1973, Wolfgang Weingart

0245. Drawing, Design for Numerals for a Thermostat, ca. 1950, Henry Dreyfuss

0246. Poster, LIGHT/YEARS, 1999, Michael Bierut

0247. Book cover, *Catalog Design*, 1944, Knud Lönberg-Holm and Ladislav Sutnar

0248. Print, Citibank Golden Passbook Deposit Slip, ca. 1975, Dan Friedman
0249. Poster, Herman Miller Inc., Textiles & Objects, 1961, John Neuhart and Alexander Hayden Girard

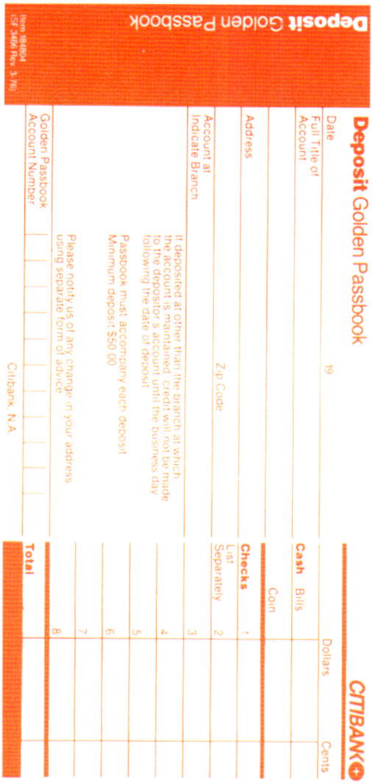

0250. Printed packaging, 60 Watt Extra Life* Bulbs, 1960s, Paul Rand
0251. Booklet, 2 pittori, 3 scultori, XXVII Biennale, Venice, 1954, Alvin Lustig

0252. Poster, Jazz Willisau: Charles Gayle Solo, 2009, Niklaus Troxler

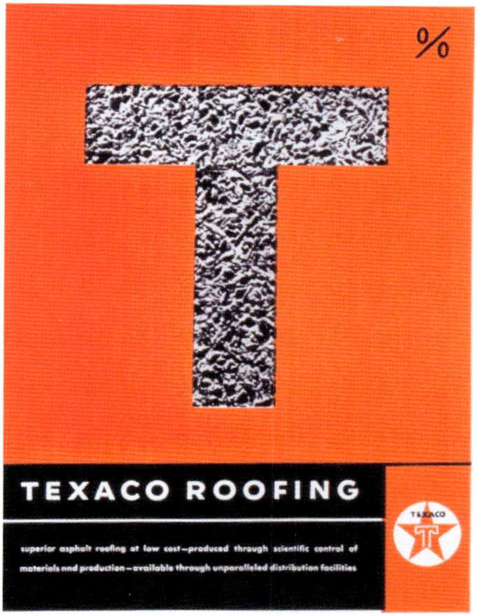

0253. Poster, Fucking A, The Public Theater, 2003, Paula Scher
0254. Book illustration (detail), *Catalog Design*, 1944, Knud Lönberg-Holm and Ladislav Sutnar

0255. Sample, Alphabet, 1960, Alexander Hayden Girard
0256. Drawing, Design for Public Theater Flyer, 1994, Paula Scher

0257. Alphabet border, 1993, William Wegman

0258. 'Ultima II' LOVE ring, USA, ca. 1972, after Robert Indiana

0259. Poster, Shakespeare in the Park 2007: Romeo and Juliet/ A Midsummer Night's Dream, The Public Theater (detail), 2007, Paula Scher

0260. Book illustration, *Alphabete*, ca. 1870, Friedrich Christmann and Hermann Junker

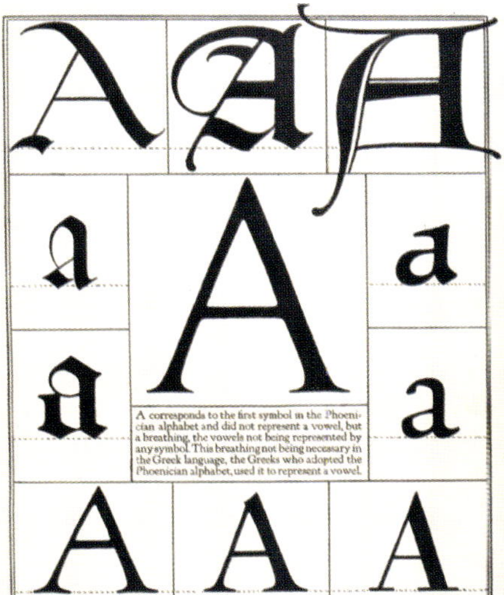

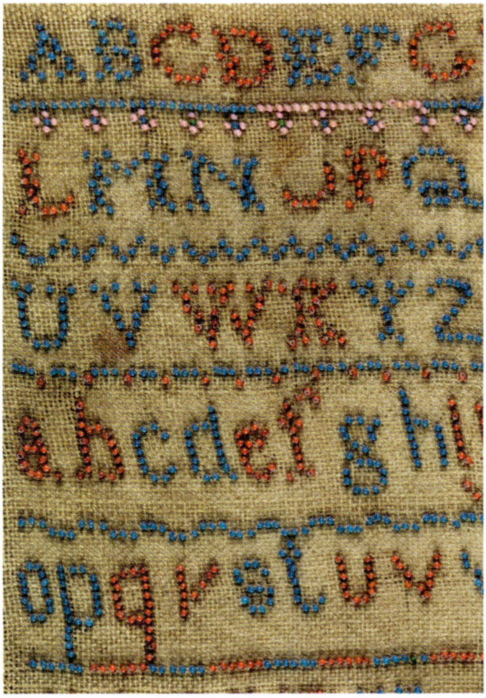

0261. Book illustration, *The Alphabet: Fifteen Interpretative Designs Drawn and Arranged with Explanatory Text and Illustrations*, 1922, Frederic W. Goudy
0262. Sampler (detail), England, 19th century, Jane Hall

0263. Print, Invitation for Knoll, ca. 1945, Herbert Matter
0264. Print, Tom E. Lewis, 1940, Alvin Lustig

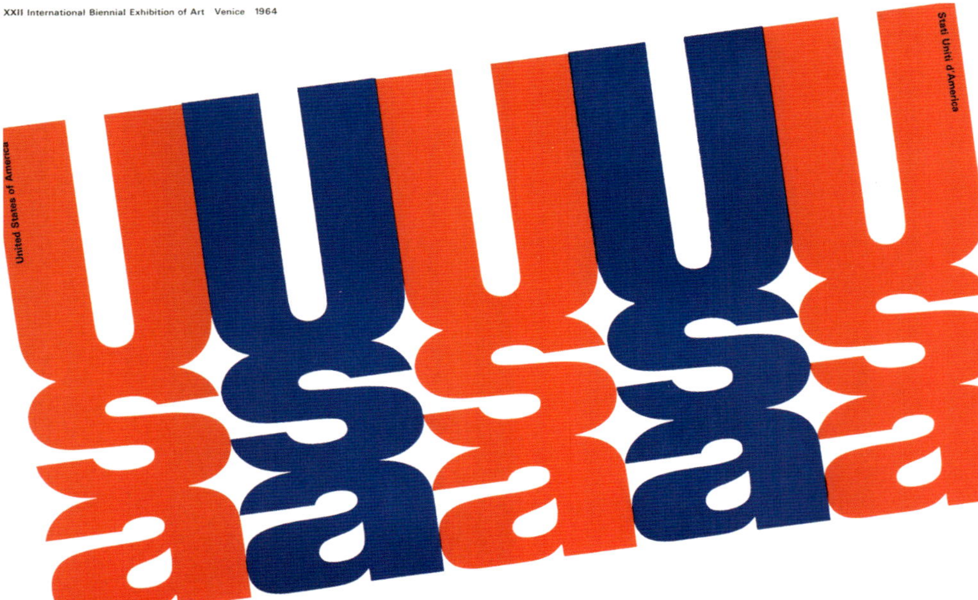

0265. Book cover, USA, for XXXII International Biennial Exposition of Art, Venice, 1964, Elaine Lustig Cohen

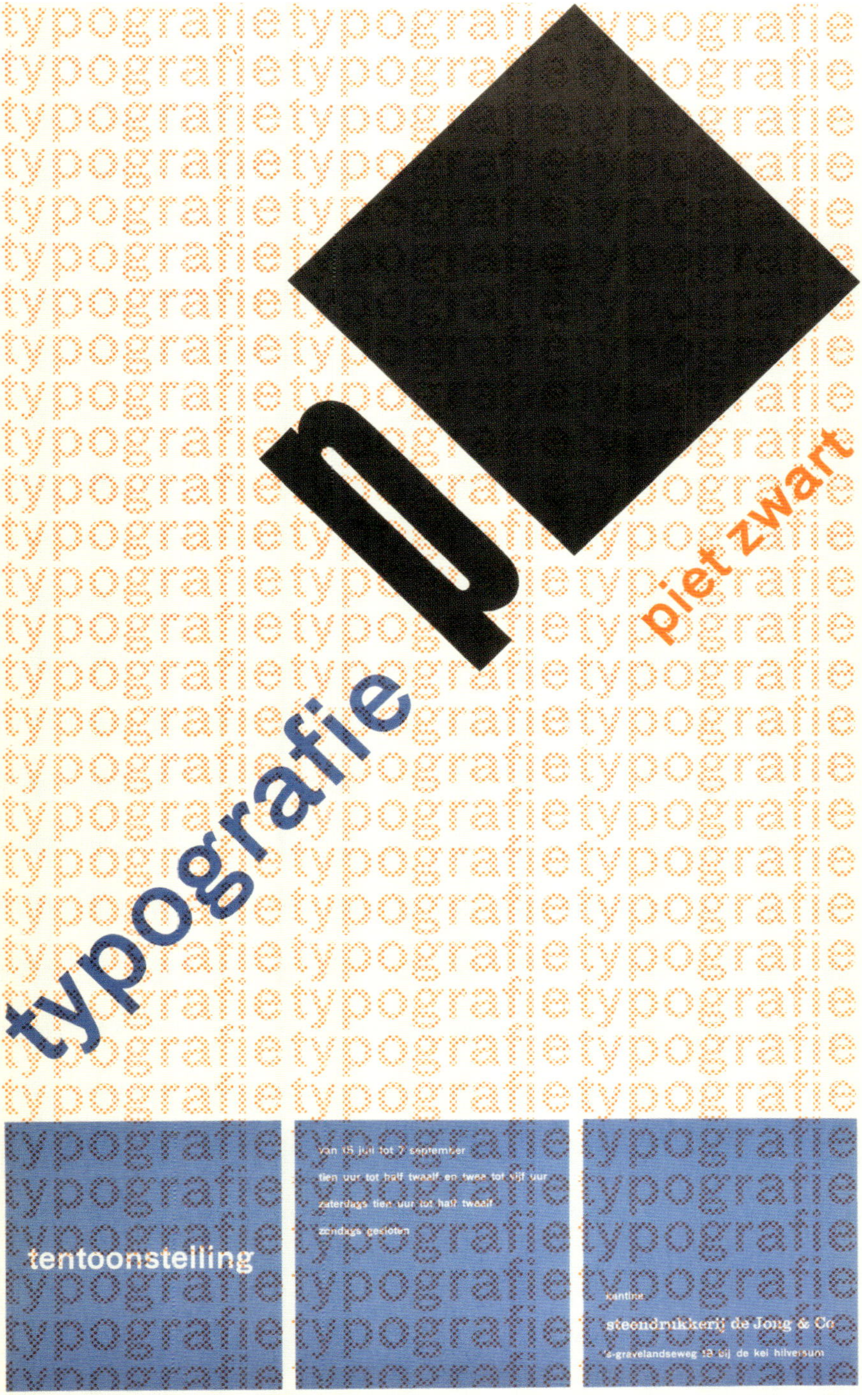

0266. Poster, Typografie Piet Zwart, 1960, Pieter Brattinga

0267. Poster, Max Bill: Werbegrafik und Buchgestaltung 1930–55, 1998, Robert & Durrer

0268. Poster, Alles Falsch: Imitationen, Nachahmung und Modell: von der Lust am Falschen, Museum für Gestaltung, Switzerland, ca. 1989, Michael Schirner

0269. Poster, Jazz Willisau: McCoy Tyner Sextet, 1980, Niklaus Troxler

0271. Print, Andrew Good, 1939, Alvin Lustig
0272. Poster, IBM Rebus, ca. 1992, Paul Rand

0270. Poster, Exposicion Litografias, Galeria de Arte de la Universidad Nacional, 1939, Francisco Dosamantes

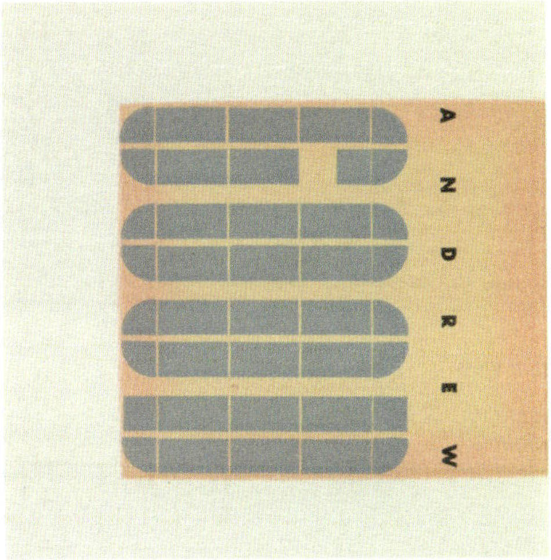

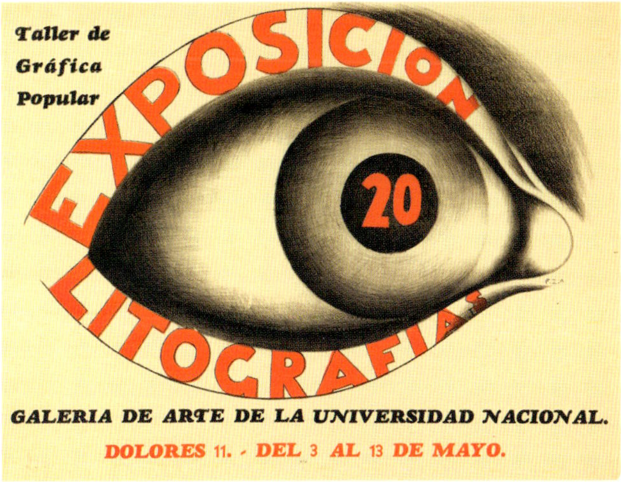

0273. Sidewall, Space Stations and Rockets, ca. 1950

0274. Sidewall, Constellation, 1938, Marion Dorn Kauffer

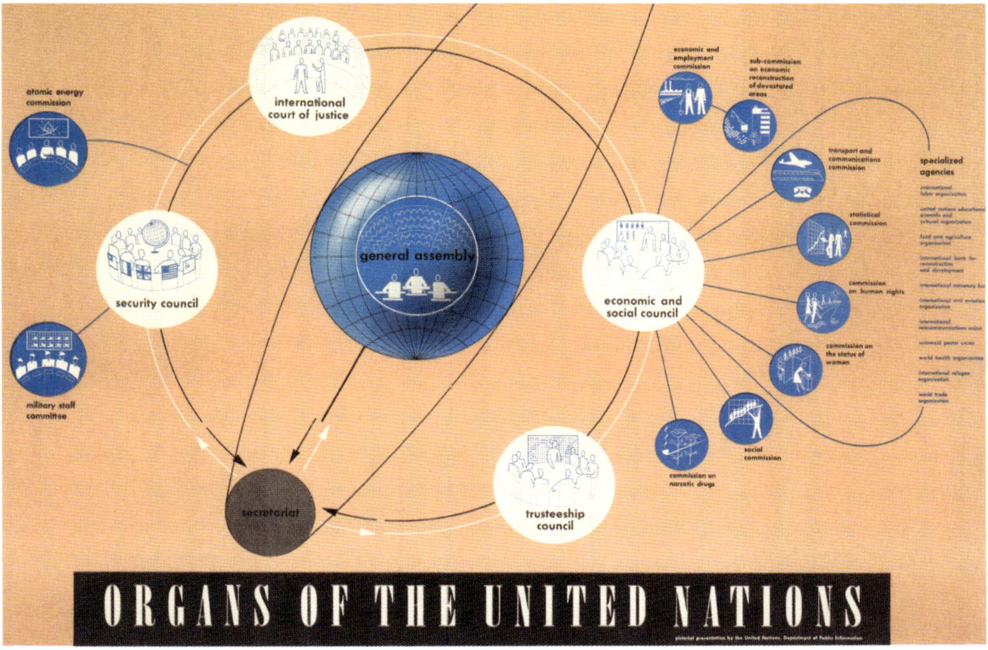

0275. Poster, Organs of the United Nations, 1946, Ladislav Sutnar

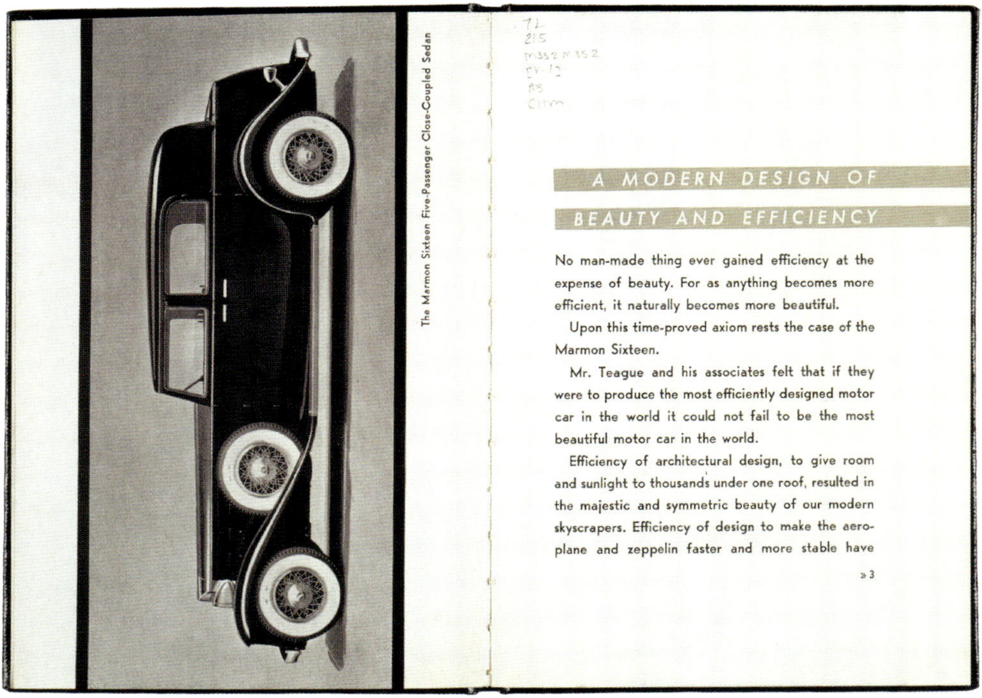

The Marmon Sixteen Five-Passenger Close-Coupled Sedan

A MODERN DESIGN OF

BEAUTY AND EFFICIENCY

No man-made thing ever gained efficiency at the expense of beauty. For as anything becomes more efficient, it naturally becomes more beautiful.

Upon this time-proved axiom rests the case of the Marmon Sixteen.

Mr. Teague and his associates felt that if they were to produce the most efficiently designed motor car in the world it could not fail to be the most beautiful motor car in the world.

Efficiency of architectural design, to give room and sunlight to thousands under one roof, resulted in the majestic and symmetric beauty of our modern skyscrapers. Efficiency of design to make the aeroplane and zeppelin faster and more stable have

» 3

0276. Book Illustration, *The Marmon Sixteen*, 1930, Walter Dorwin Teague

0277. Book cover, *Des Canons, des munitions?*, 1930, Le Corbusier

0280. Drawing, Textile Design: Plane Motif, 1950–70, Tommi Parzinger

0278. Poster, Vorm en Luchtfoto, 1960, Pieter Brattinga
0279. Business card, K2 Snowboards, 1994, Robynne Raye

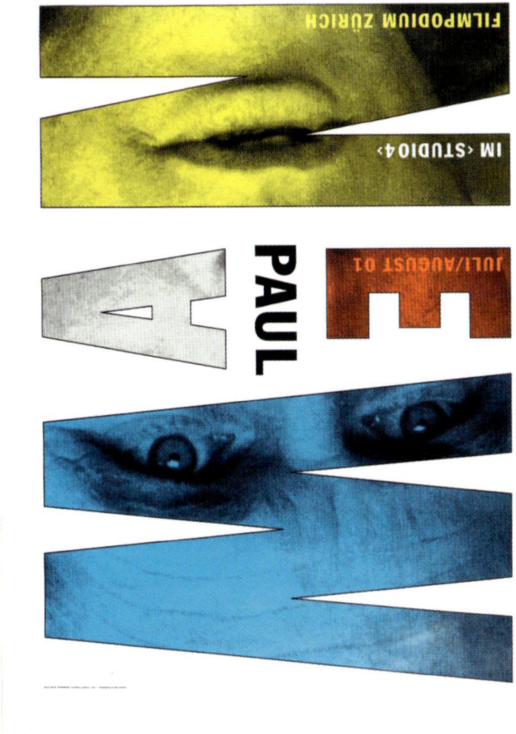

0282. Poster, Paul Newman, Filmpodium Zurich, 2001, Ralph Schraivogel

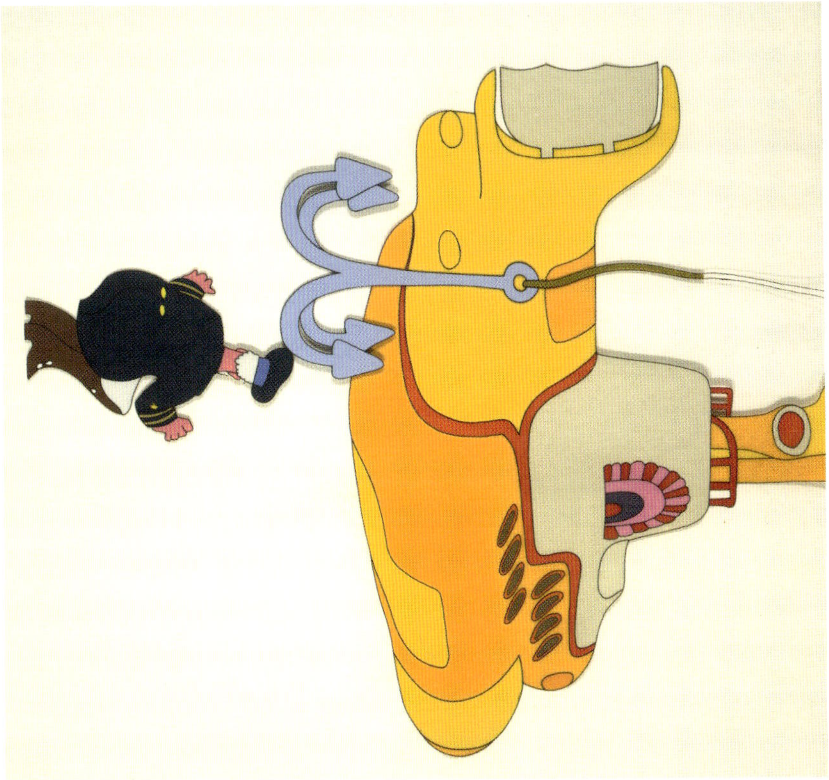

0281. Drawing, Yellow Submarine Film Celluloid, 1967–68, Heinz Edelmann for United Artists, made by King Features Production, for Apple Films

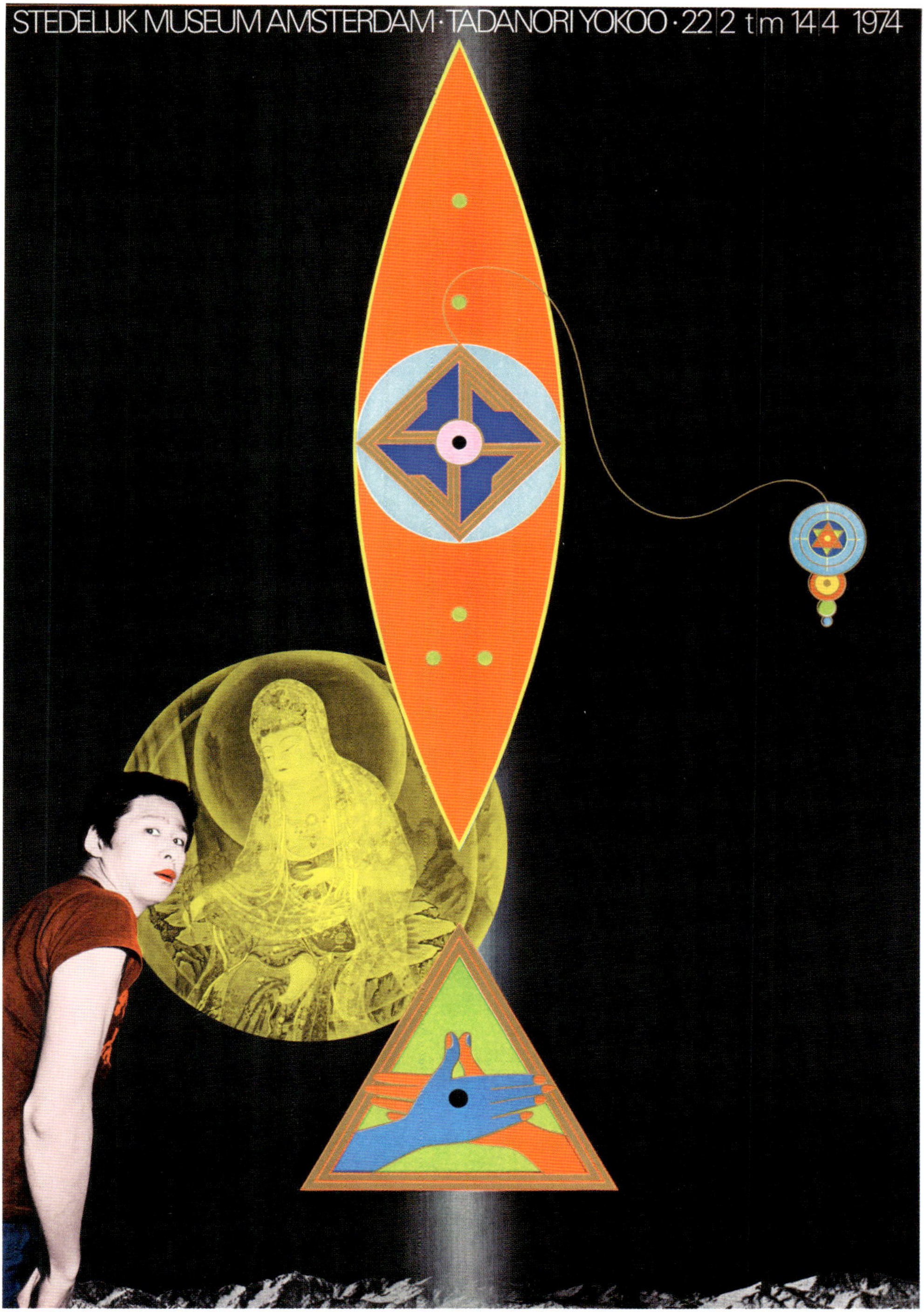

0283. Poster, Tadanori Yokoo, Stedelijk Museum, Netherlands, 1974, Tadanori Yokoo

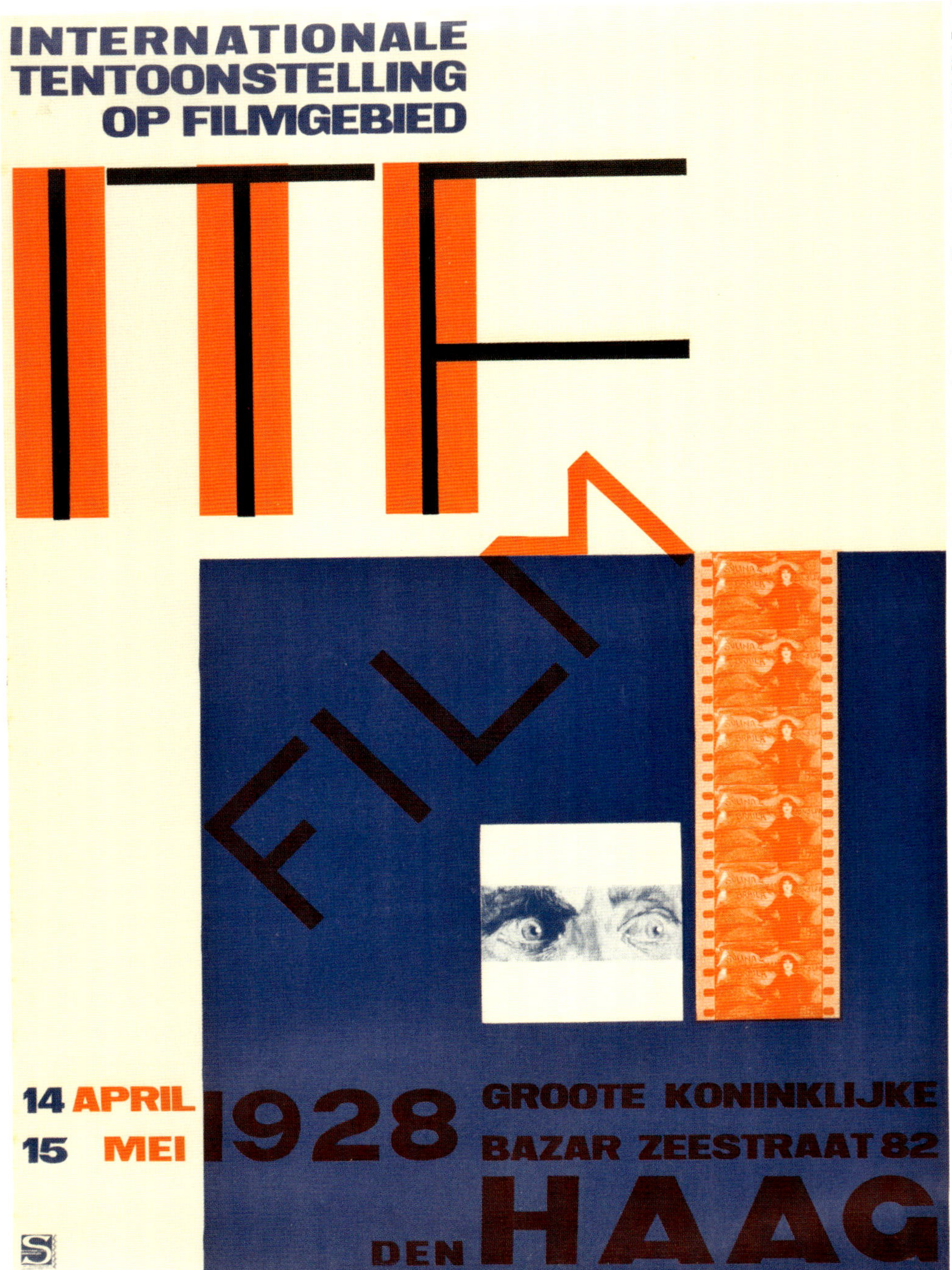

0284. Poster, ITF Internationale tentoonstelling op filmgebied, 1928, Piet Zwart

0285. Poster, Oskar Schlemmer, Les Noces, Igor Stravinsky, 1988, Bruno Monguzzi

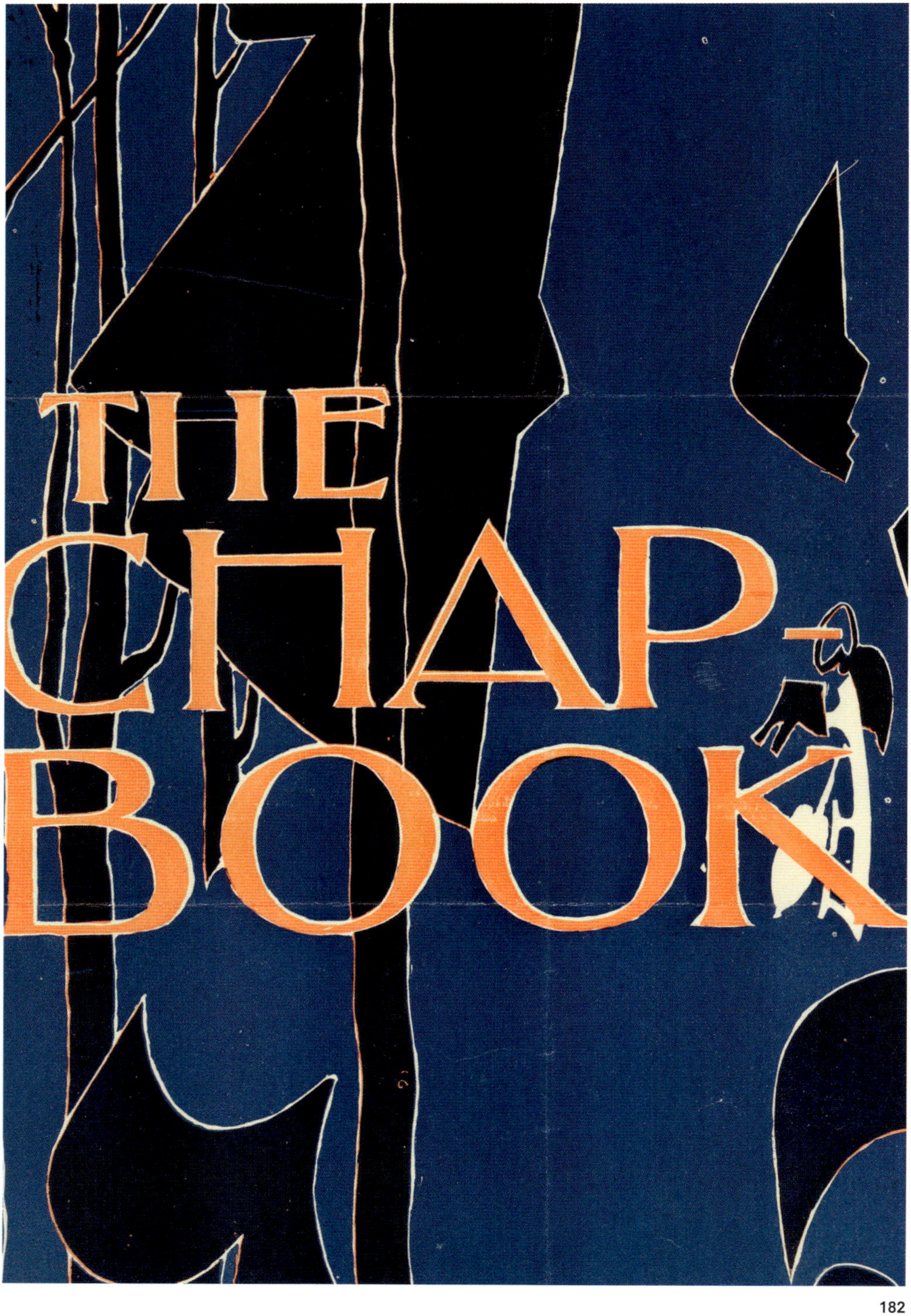

0286. Poster, The Chap-Book (Blue Lady) (detail), 1894, William Henry Bradley

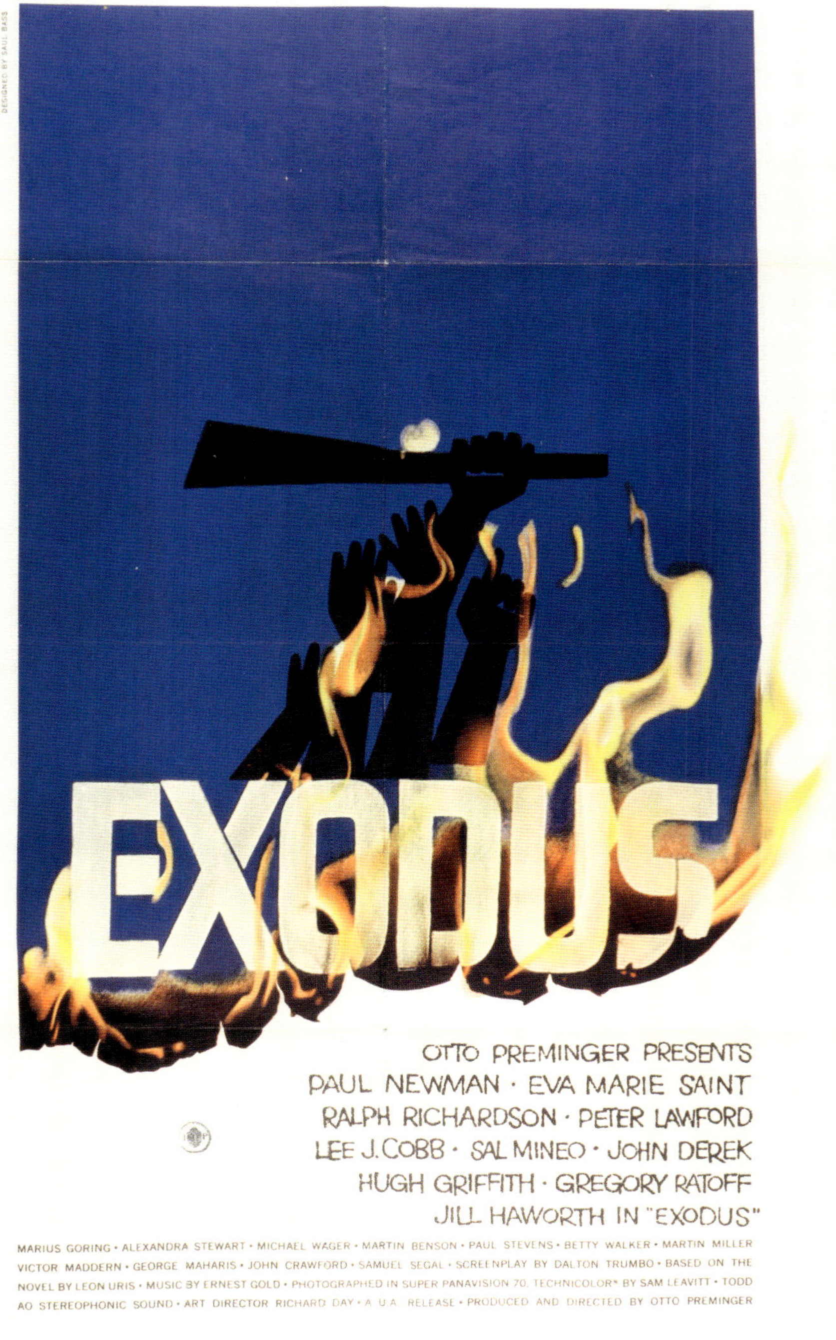

0287. Poster, *Exodus*, 1960, Saul Bass

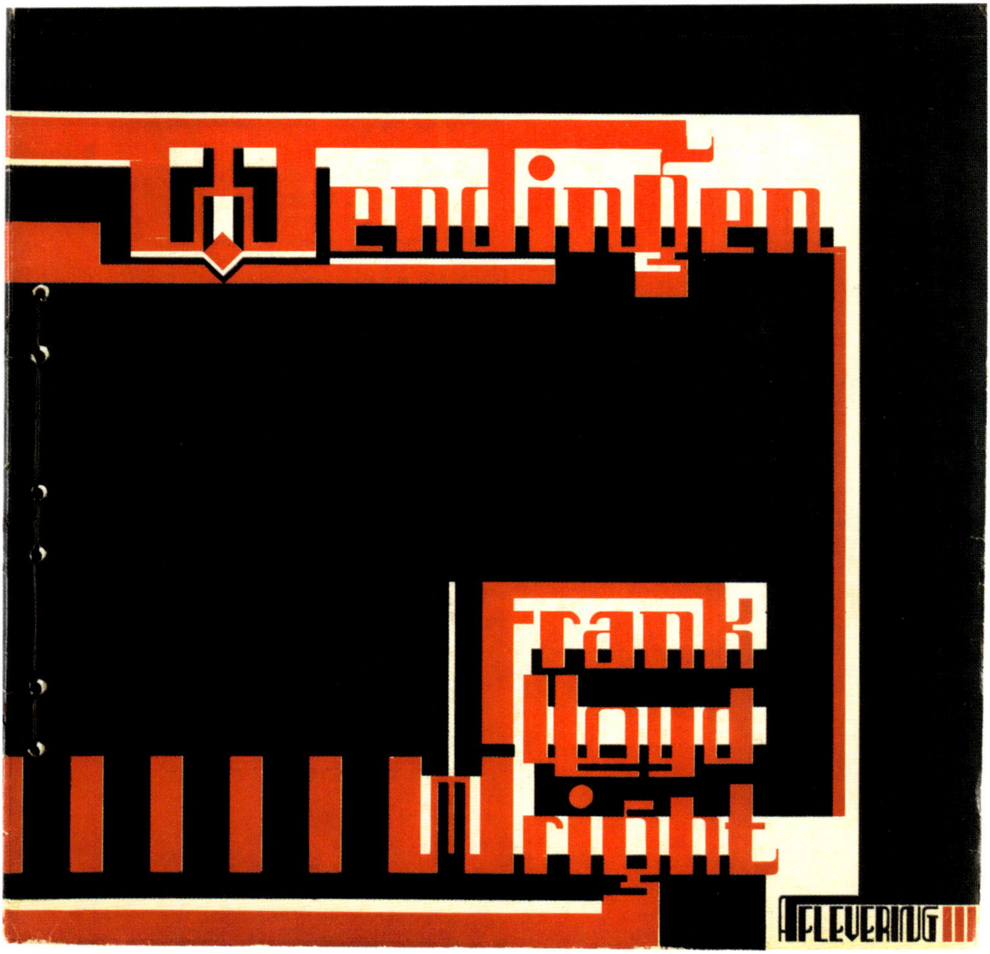

0288. Magazine cover, *Wendingen: Frank Lloyd Wright*, 1925, Hendrik Wijdeveld

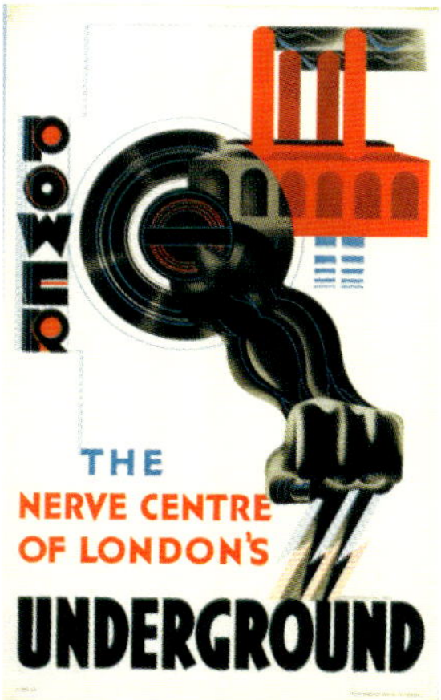

0289. Poster, Power—The Nerve Center of London's Underground, 1930, Edward McKnight Kauffer

0290. Trade catalog front and back cover, *Livery MDCCCXCIX*, ca. 1899, Will Bradley

0291. Printed blotter, Lijstwerk: de grootste en de kleinste partij direct uit voorraad, maart 1935, 1935, Piet Zwart

0292. Textile, Nuno me Gara (detail), 1981, Junichi Arai

0293. Poster, Vivo in Typo, 2008, Philippe Apeloig

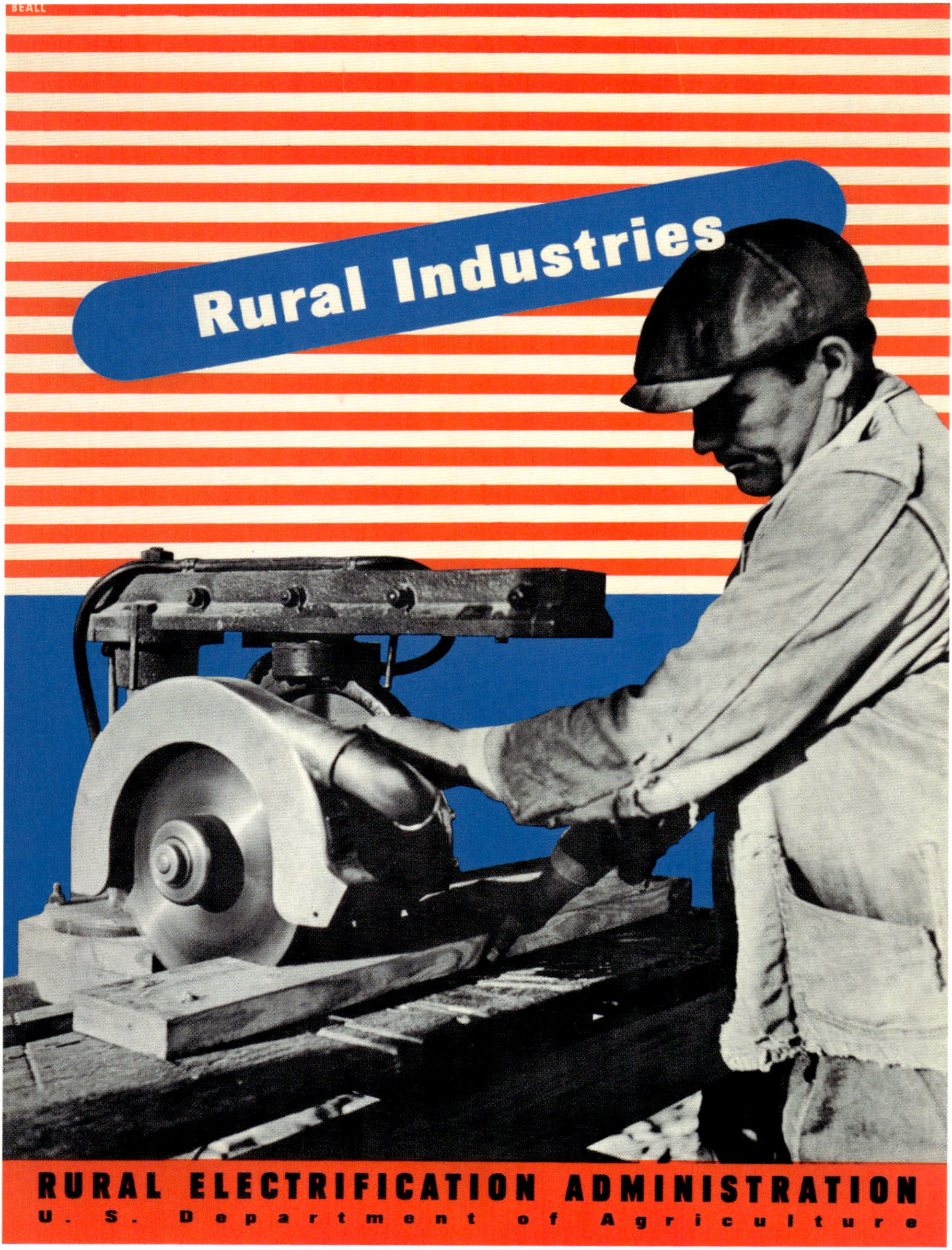

0294. Poster, Rural Industries, 1947, Lester Beall

0295. Poster, Semana de Cine Cubano en Boliva, 1985, Nestor

Poster, Symphony of a Big City, 1928
Georgii Augustovich Stenberg (Russian, 1900–1933)
Vladimir Augustovich Stenberg (Russian, 1899–1982)
Color lithograph on off-white wove paper
Museum purchase from Drawings and Prints Council and General Acquisitions Endowment Funds, 2008-1-1

Set against the image of a single skyscraper, a lone figure takes in his surroundings. With a megaphone for an ear, a camera for an eye, and a watch keeping time in place of his neck, the man has physically transformed to absorb and record the bustling energy of a booming metropolis. This poster, designed by the Stenberg brothers in 1928 for the film *Berlin: Symphony of a Big City,* is a striking example of the aesthetic shift that took place in the 1920s and early 1930s in the graphic arts. No longer reliant on realism in illustration, designers throughout Europe embraced the experiments of the avant-garde, maximizing the technological advancements in printing and photography, and exploiting collage to create an innovative graphic style.

Brothers Vladimir Augustovich Stenberg (1899–1982) and Georgii Augustovich Stenberg (1900–1933) were Constructivist sculptors in the post-revolutionary Moscow avant-garde. They applied their vision to theater design, ceramics, fashion, and architecture, but their greatest and lasting contribution to this revolutionary aesthetic was one that married the political potential of graphic design with the potent new medium of cinema—the film poster. During a time when illiteracy was commonplace across Russia, cinema was a unique and popular agitational tool. Cinema posters were plastered throughout the streets, with each film's narrative conveyed in bold images. But the Stenbergs' posters stand apart for their adoption of cinematic vocabulary—montage, close-ups, distortion—to create playful abstracted works. Their posters captured not only a film's narrative elements, but also the spirit of cinematic experience.

Photomontage—the process of creating a collage from photographic elements —had become popular in Russia by the early 1920s, but the technology was not yet available to reproduce these black-and-white images in the quantities required for mass-advertising. The Stenbergs invented a projection device that could enlarge, reduce, distort, and manipulate images. "All kinds of techniques were possible," Vladimir Stenberg later noted. "But rather than being scared of them, we motivated ourselves to integrate these new technologies for our own benefits." [1]

Their use of projection allowed them to incorporate a variety of elements into an unusual but unified representation that seamlessly blended abstracted designs with those sourced from photographic material. By drawing images that recalled the appearance of photographs, they were able to control the quality, tone, and gradation of their images into a cohesive aesthetic. The projection device also enabled them to engage the physical elements of cinema in their design process. To create a poster, they would lay frames from the spool of film directly onto the projector to insert an image from the movie, such as an actor's face. By projecting the film frames in a similar manner to how they were intended to be shown, the brothers translated the audience's experience of projected film into drawing, then mass-produced it through lithography.

Foreign films that were seen as promoting social content were shown widely in Russian cities. Originally released in 1927, *Berlin, Symphony for a Big City* was directed by the German filmmaker Walter Ruttmann. It was among the first feature-

0296. Poster, Symphony of a Big City, 1928, Georgii Augustovich Stenberg and Vladimir Augustovich Stenberg

length films whose primary subject was not a person, but a place. The film narrative relies on the rhythm and structure of following the life of Berlin's streets for a single day. The Stenbergs often worked under crushing deadlines. It was not unusual for them to see a movie one afternoon and have to finish the poster that day. For Symphony for a Big City, they crafted a composition that ingeniously captured the speed and movement of the life of a city. The part-man, part-machine figure at the heart of the poster replicates not a character in the film, but a photomontage by the Bauhaus-trained photographer Umbo (Otto Umbehr), who had worked with Ruttmann as a camera assistant on Berlin, Symphony for a Big City, and produced the original photomontage several years earlier for the cover of Austrian journalist Egon Erwin Kisch's book *Der Rasende Reporter*. How the Stenbergs became familiar with Umbo's photomontage, which features Kisch's head, remains a mystery. But by using selected elements of the photomontage, they transformed a representation of an individual into an evocative depiction of the overwhelming demands of a modern metropolis. Intriguingly, the skyscraper that stands in for Berlin in the poster bears no resemblance to the buildings in the film, nor to any Moscow building. For the Stenbergs, who had never seen a skyscraper, the simple grid-like structure that forms the background of the poster was an image of futuristic urban fantasy.

The Stenbergs were well aware of the challenges of producing a poster that would be noticed. Unlike their contemporaries, who used black type on white backgrounds, they frequently chose a black background with sans-serif lettering in vivid colors. Against the dark, bold red, yellow, and white, and the black-and-white gradient, the poster for *Berlin: Symphony for a Big City* is cinematic in its own right. **CC**

1 Quoted in Christopher Mount, *Stenberg Brothers: Constructing a Revolution in Soviet Design* (New York: Museum of Modern Art, 1997), 16.

0297. Print, Wandbehang die Reifezeit, 1901, Koloman Moser

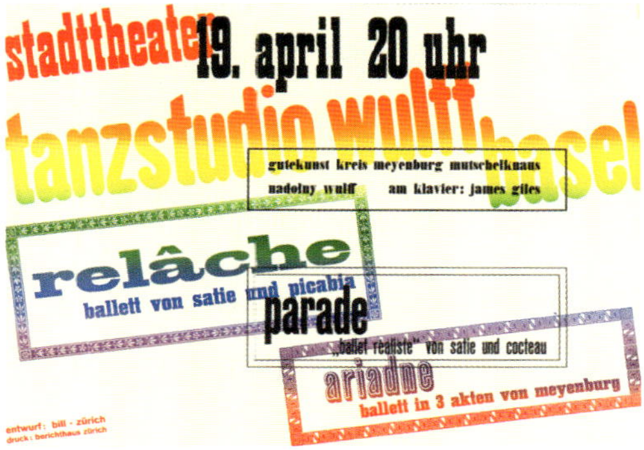

0298. Poster, Schule für Gestaltung Bern, 1998, Ralph Schraivogel
0299. Poster, Tanzstudio Wulff, Basel, 1931, Max Bill
0300. Poster, Bicycle, Public, 2012, Paula Scher

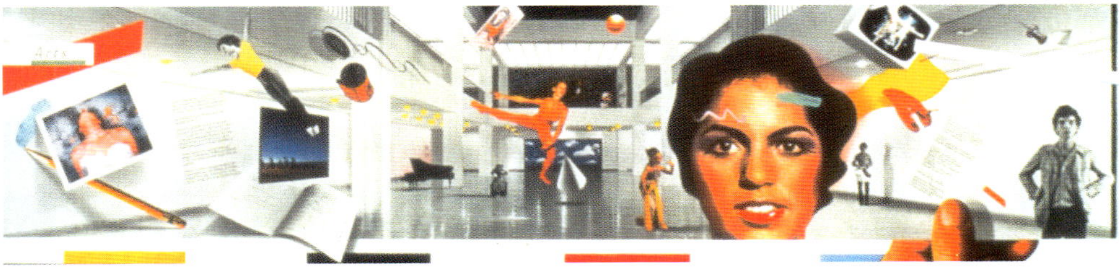

0301. Poster, California Institute of the Arts, 1978, April Greiman and Jayme Odgers

0302. Poster, Spitzen der Wiener Werkstätte, ca. 1919, Dagobert Peche

0303. Poster, Engelberg, Trübsee, Switzerland, 1936, Herbert Matter

0304. Textile, Futsu Crisscross, 2009, Reiko Sudo

0305. Sidewall, Hexagon, 2004, Marcel Wanders

0306. Album, Woven Paper Designs, 1902–4, Margarete Riessen

0307. Kimono (detail), Japan, 1926–45

0308. Poster, Dylan, 1966, Milton Glaser

Textile, Binary Traces: Kay, 2005
Lia Cook (American, b. 1952)
Berkeley, California, USA
Jacquard woven cotton double cloth
Museum purchase from General Acquisitions Endowment Fund, 2007-33-1

Binary Traces: Kay explores the complex interrelationship among memory, visual stimulation, and tactile experience. The tapestry is as monumental as the portrait is intimate—the face is nearly six feet high. From a distance it looks like a pixelated, over-enlarged photograph, but drawing closer, its textile qualities are revealed. It is about as heavy as a good sturdy blanket, and falls in soft waves at the hem; the cotton yarns are thick, and the rough texture of the weave is apparent. Lia Cook took the image from a well-handled family snapshot, with a physical life of its own having perhaps been piled in a box or pasted in an album. For those who knew Kay, the snapshot no doubt evoked a specific memory, while for the viewer of the tapestry the sense of memory is implicit and abstract.

Lia Cook was among the first artists to use **digital jacquard** technology in her studio practice and for over thirty years has been a pioneer in exploring the artistic possibilities of the technology. In the 1970s she began investigating the representation of cloth in cloth, fascinated by the illusion of drapery and the rendering of surface. In the 1980s and 1990s she began using photographs, in particular self-portraits and photographs of children. She often selects a close detail of snapshots, discolored slides, or video stills to intensify an intimate moment or fleeting emotion. The photographs are **digitized**, then JacqCAD software translates each pixel of the image into code for a digital jacquard head on the hand loom in her studio. Binary Traces: Kay is woven in **double cloth**, each pixel expressing the crossing of either a black or a white **warp** and **weft**. Cook uses pure black and pure white threads in her image, but through complex weave structures creates the illusion of a gradation of grays. The textile is woven by hand, the **shuttle** passed rhythmically back and forth by the artist; the hand is critical to this seemingly technology-driven work. Cook favors neither hand nor machine, but rather that place where they meet. Cook's mastery of the technology allows her to develop micro-structures to represent each nuance of shading in the faces. The structural language of weaving leaves a binary trace in the mazelike surface of the fabric.

Throughout her career she has been intrigued by the process of constructing imagery in textiles. The compelling place is where image and structure become one —"the image as physical object."[1] She has said, "I wanted to look deeper into understanding what a human being experiences when visually engaged in an object that has evidence of the hand."[2] The woven image carries with it many of the sensual experiences we associate with cloth. Using brain imaging technologies to measure response to large-scale photographic and woven images, Cook and her scientific partners were able to map the response to each and establish that the woven images provoked reactions of a different type and intensity, activating emotional and tactile centers in the brain. These explorations support what Cook has intuited for years —that we respond differently to textiles, even if we only touch with our eyes. **SB**

1 Lia Cook, "Weaving and Innovation: Digital Fibers Converse with Neural Networks," Ruth Davis Design Gallery, School of Human Ecology, University of Wisconsin-Madison, accessed November 25, 2013, at www.designgallery.wisc.edu/exhibits/Lia%20Cook/.

2 "UNC Asheville Center for Craft, Creativity & Design to Host Exhibition: 'Bridge 11: Lia Cook,'" last modified July 6, 2012, accessed November 25, 2013, www.unca.edu/news-events/news/2012/7/center-craft-creativity-design-lia-cook-bridge-11.

0309. Hanging, Binary Traces: Kay, 2005, Lia Cook

0310. Poster, Chambers Brothers Band, Neon Rose #12, 1967, Victor Moscoso

0311. Poster, Hoffnung und Widerstand, Museum für Gestaltung, Zürich, Switzerland, ca. 1998, Cornel Windlin

0312. Square (detail), Egypt, 5th–7th century

0313. Print, Self-Portrait, Rembrandt with Plumed Hat and Lowered Sabre (detail), 1634, Rembrandt Harmensz. van Rijn

0314. Sidewall, Bullies, 1992, Virgil Marti

0315. Sidewall, Bachelor's Wall Paper, 1969, Charles Dana Gibson

0316. Fashion plate, Modes de Paris, 1829

0317. Book illustration, *L'art de la coëffure des dames françoises*, 1768, Sieur Legros de Rumigny

0318. Sidewall, Beauty, 1972, Werner Berges

0319. Book illustration, *Les choses de Paul Poiret*, 1911, Paul Poiret and Georges Lepape

0320. Print, Portrait of Albrecht of Brandenburg (detail), 1524, Albrecht Dürer

0321. Poster, De Man achter de Vormgeving van de P.T.T. (detail), 1960, Pieter Brattinga

0322. Embroidered picture (detail), England, ca. 1840

0323. Sidewall, France, 1918–23, Émile-Jacques Ruhlmann

0324. Textile, Crossing Colors, 2013, Sheila Hicks

0325. Textile, Gazebo, 1960s, Win Anderson

0326. Fungo table lamp, Italy, 1956, Massimo Vignelli

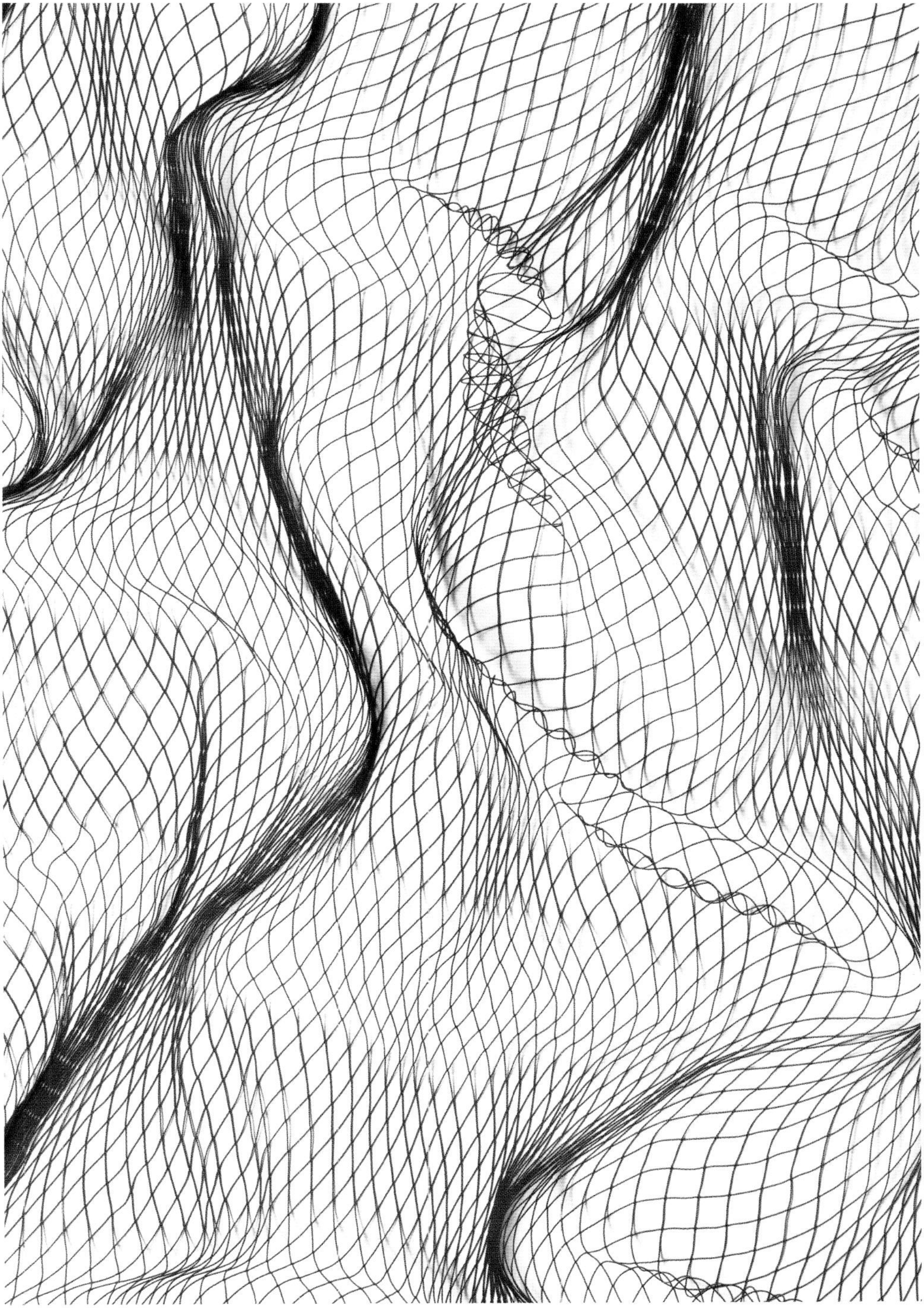

0327. Encircling fishing net, designed 1996, manufactured 2003, Toray Industries, Inc.

0328. Vase, Model 3461, Italy, ca. 1934, Carlo Scarpa

0329. Textile, Sticks, 1957, Joseph Provato

0330. Sidewall, Razzmatazz, 1967, William Justema
0331. Textile, Obelisk, 1958, Jack Lenor Larsen

0332. Sidewall, Japan, 1954

0333. Sidewall, Chopped Herringbone, 1971, Alan Buchsbaum

0334. Poster, Architektur und Kinder, 1995, Peter Frey

0335. Sidewall, Testura Grafica, 1971–72, Getulio Alviani

0336. Tile, Spain, 17th century

0337. Sidewall, France, ca. 1800
0338. Coverlet fragment, USA, early 19th century
0339. Magazine title page (detail), *The Repository of Arts,* 1810, Rudolph Ackermann

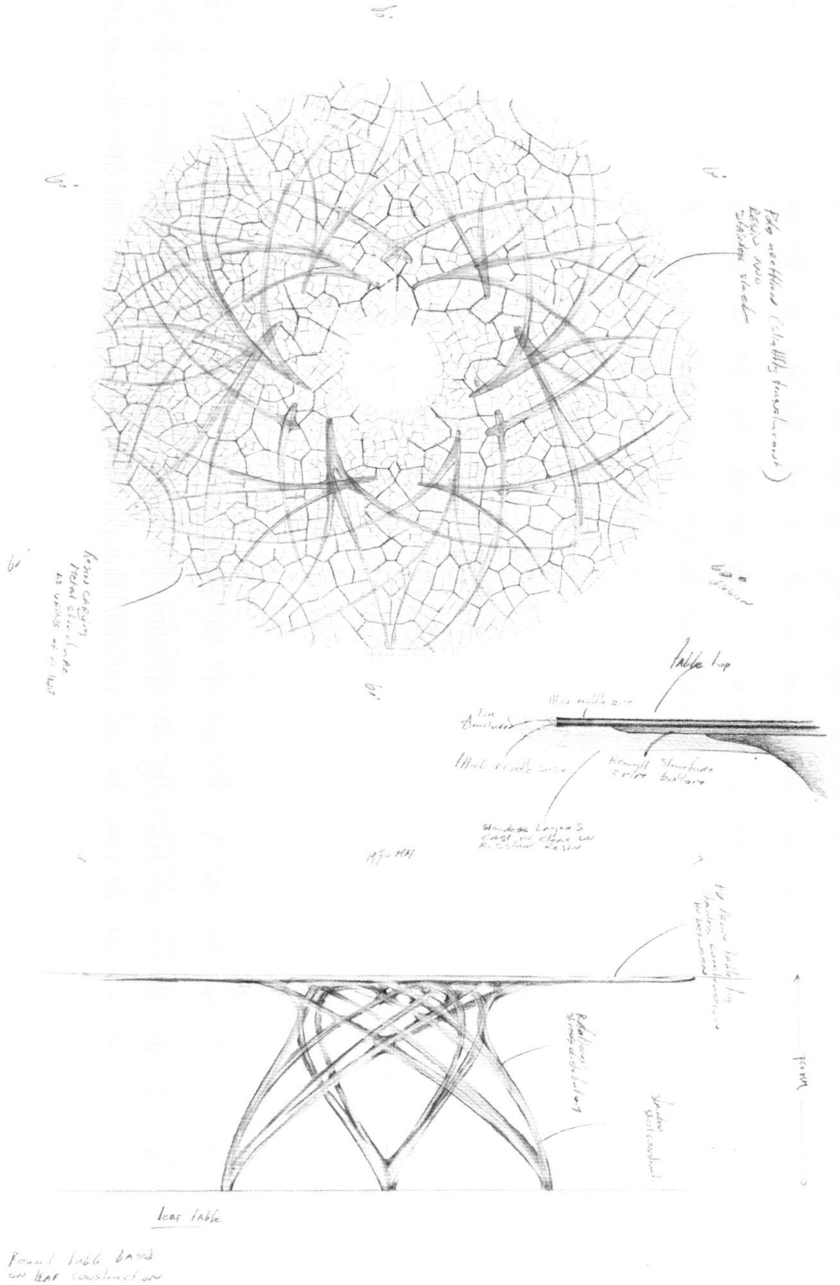

0340. Drawing, Leaf Table, 2010, Joris Laarman

0341. Plate, China (for export), ca. 1830
0342. Plate, France, 1760–80

0343. Kremlin Service dessert plate, Russia, ca. 1830, Fedor Grigorievich Solntsev
0344. Platter, England, 1888–98, William Frend De Morgan

0345. Plate, The Reign of Workers and Peasants Will Be Without End, USSR, 1920, Sergei Vasilievich Chekhonin
0346. Plate, Germany, ca. 1901, Peter Behrens

0347. Poster, el atomo para la paz, General Dynamics, 1955, Erik Nitsche

0348. Buffaloware sample plate, USA, 1950s, Oneida

0349. Sample plate, France, 1887, A. Lacroix & Cie

0350. Textile, Spectrum, 1950–55, Rolf Middelboe

Print, Interlace Pattern with White Medallion, from Knots
Albrecht Dürer (German, 1471–1528)
Woodcut on off-white laid paper
Museum purchase through gift of Eleanor and Sarah Hewitt, 1944-37-1-b

For centuries, this intricately wrought interlace design—one of six similar motifs produced by Albrecht Dürer—has entranced and perplexed those who have encountered it. The intended purpose of the Knots, as Dürer referred to the series, as well as the precise date of their execution, remains unknown. Some scholars have postulated that the designs are patterns for embroidery or textiles. Others have suggested that they were ornamental designs for ceramics, or as labyrinthine didactic tools for training draftsmen.[1] What is certain is that the story of the Knots traverses culture and time, touching on the relationship of master and student, and the reuse and reinvention of a series of graceful, rational motifs.

Born in Nuremberg on the cusp of the German Renaissance, Dürer was a virtuosic artist and intellectual, renowned for his painting and draftsmanship as well as for his theoretical writings on proportion and geometry. One of his greatest legacies was his visionary contributions to the medium of printmaking. A master of both **engraving** and the **woodcut**, Dürer brought an unprecedented tonal and descriptive range to his prints, endearing his audience to printmaking and revolutionizing the potential of the medium.

The decorative tradition of geometric interlace patterns predates Dürer by centuries, and was employed in Roman, medieval, and Islamic ornament. This remarkably complex woodcut, however, has its direct origins in the work of Dürer's Italian contemporary, Leonardo da Vinci (1452–1519). All six interlace patterns, in fact, are copies of designs by Leonardo, for whom interlace motifs may have served as an informal, lyrical coat of arms. Vinci, his birthplace, translates as "to entwine," and his notes reveal a preoccupation with the word *gruppi*, the Lombard term for "knots." Interlace designs appear in many of Leonardo's drawings and paintings, often as ornamental motifs worked into the hair or clothing of his subjects. The designs are also found in the decorative interlaced branches in the magnificent fresco ceiling for the Salle delle Asse at the Sforza Castle in Milan.

To compose his circular knot designs, Leonardo would have constructed a grid of dots, weaving his drawn lines around them. But Dürer would likely have come to know the six designs through a series of unattributed engravings after Leonardo's drawings during his transformative trip to Venice in 1494–95. The six Knots are a rare example of Dürer directly copying another artist's work.

The woodcuts appear to replicate not only the interlace configuration, but also the precise measurements of the designs, which suggests that Dürer traced the engravings.

Sometime after his return to Germany, it is presumed, Dürer carefully copied the designs onto blocks of wood, which were then cut by a craftsman so expert as to be able to carve out the delicate web of knots without breaking the wood between the carved lines. Black ink would have been spread across the surface of the woodblocks, catching only the astonishingly minute recesses between the maze of lines, before the blocks were pressed against the paper to produce the prints. The Knots put Dürer in the position of both student and master. On the one hand, the project offered Dürer the opportunity to study and replicate the remarkable work of Leonardo. But the decision to reproduce Leonardo's designs in woodcut allowed Dürer to

0351. Print, Interlace Pattern with White Medallion, before 1521, Albrecht Dürer

showcase his consummate dexterity in a medium that did not ordinarily lend itself to exquisite, intricately entwined lines.

Beyond enabling Dürer to demonstrate virtuosity in the woodcut, the intended use of the six prints remains an enigma. His only recorded mention of the prints, in his diary, describes his sale of a set to a glassmaker in the Netherlands.[2] Though we may never fully recover their original purpose, the beauty and complexity of the Knots continue to endure. **CC**

1 Carmen Bambach Cappel, "Leonardo, Tagliente, and Dürer: 'La scienza del far di groppi,'" *Achademia Leonardi Vinci: Journal of Leonardo Studies & Bibliography of Vinciana* 4 (1991): 72–98; Eileen Costello, "Knot(s) Made by Human Hands: Copying, Invention, and Intellect in the Work of Leonardo da Vinci and Albrecht Dürer," *Athanor* XXIII (2005): 25–33; Anada Coomaraswamy, "The Iconography of Dürer's 'Knots' and Leonardo's 'Concatenation,'" *Art Quarterly* 7 (Spring 1944): 109–28; Arthur M. Hind "Two Unpublished Plates of the Series of Six 'Knots' Engraved after Designs by Leonardo da Vinci," *Burlington Magazine* 12 (October 1907/March 1908): 41–42.

2 Albrecht Dürer, quoted in Costello, "Knot(s) Made by Human Hands," 28.

0352. Cut paper, Noah's Ark, 1982, Ernst Oppliger
0353. Hanging, Four Seasons, 1964, Luba Krejci

0354. Drawing, Perspective Design for a Painted Dome and Cupola of a Church, 1700–25, after Andrea Pozzo
0355. Skirt, China, 1950–60

0356. Tsuba (sword guard), Japan, 1830–43
0357. Lock, Spain, late 16th–early 17th century

0358. Sample plate, France, ca. 1875

0359. Poster, Sutnar: Visual Design in Action, The American Institute of Graphic Arts, 1961, Ladislav Sutnar

0360. Plate, France, ca. 1870, Léon Parvillée
0361. Volvelle, *Astronomicum Caesareum*, 1540, facsimile 1967, Peter Apian

0362. Plate, USA, ca. 1905
0363. Argenta ware plate, Sweden, ca. 1940, Wilhelm Kåge

0364. Plate, England, 1753–58, Chelsea Porcelain Manufactory
0365. Ianvarivs (January) plate, France, 1565–75, Martial Courteys

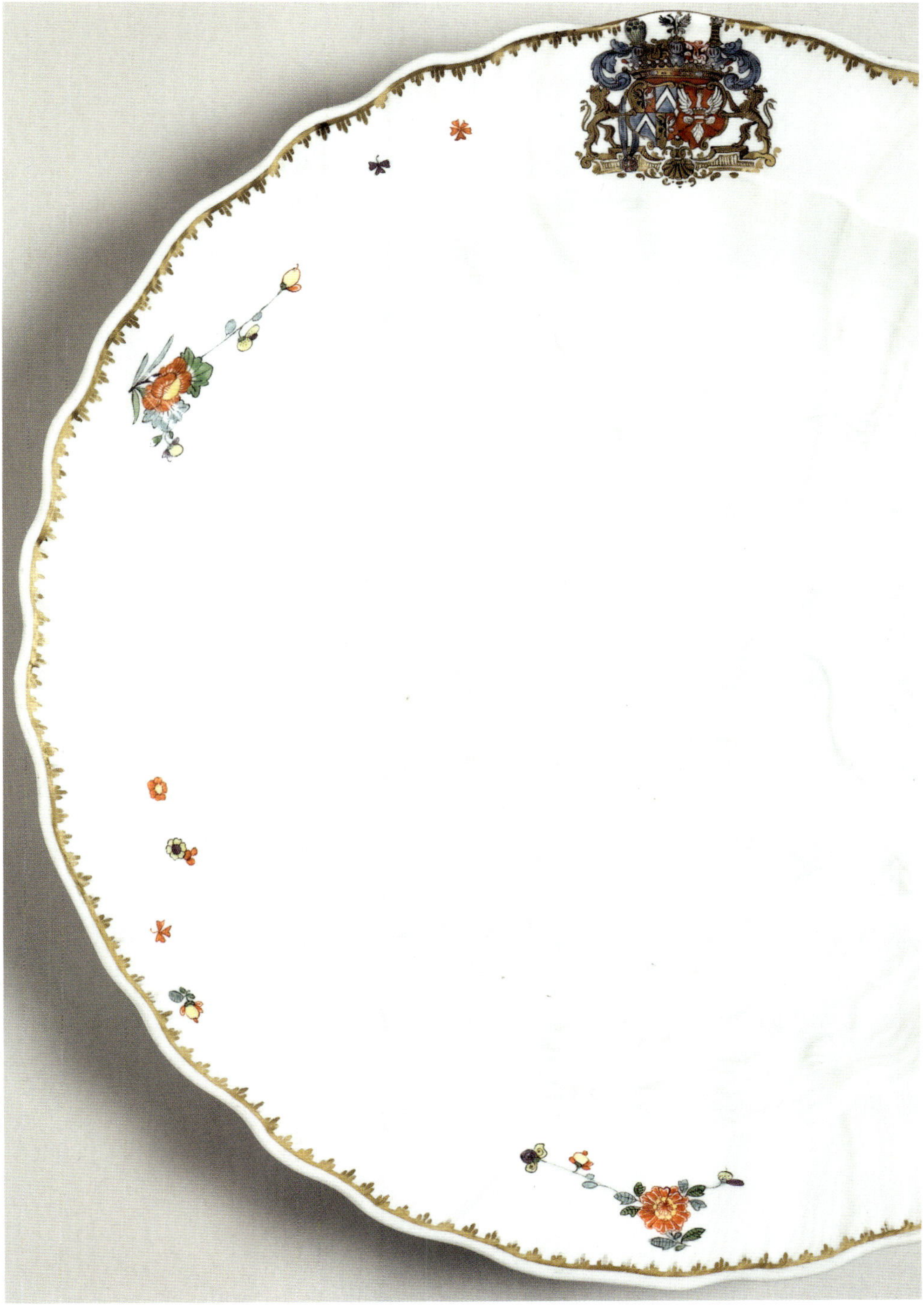

0366. Swan Service charger (detail), Germany, 1737–41, Johann Joachim Kändler

0367. Five buttons from a set of ten, France, 1775–80

0368. Fountain, France, early 18th century

0369. Cooling pail, France, ca. 1740

0370. Nest Learning thermostat, USA, 2011, Tony Fadell and Matt Rogers
0371. Big Ben Chime Alarm clock, USA, ca. 1944, Henry Dreyfuss

0372. Box and lid with portrait miniature, France, ca. 1770
0373. Box and lid with portrait miniature of a gentleman, England, 1793, Villers

0374. Vase, Austria, ca. 1925, Moser Glass Factory
0375. Box, probably Italy, early–mid-18th century

0376. Button, West Indies, late 18th century, attributed to Agostino Brunias

Vase, Paris, France, ca. 1925
Jean Dunand (French, 1877–1942)
Raised brass, hand-painted lacquer, nickel (rim)
Gift of Linda Lichtenberg Kaplan, 2004-21-1

This vase is an outstanding example of the work of the early twentieth-century master metalworker, lacquerer, and innovator Jean Dunand. Born in Switzerland and educated there and in Paris, Dunand started as a sculptor, learning to work in a variety of materials including wood, stone, ivory, and metal. He turned to the decorative arts after 1902. Although his early designs were naturalistic, by the 1910s he embraced the strong geometric forms and designs that would become characteristic of the art deco style. While Dunand worked with the sculptor Jean Dampt in Paris, he periodically returned to Switzerland, where he studied the art of hammering metal with a coppersmith named Danhauer. In 1905 Dunand presented his first group of metal vases and objects, each formed and hammered from a single piece of metal in a technique called dinanderie. This term derived from Dinant, the name of a Flemish town known as a center of brassware production since the Middle Ages. Dunand would start with a circular sheet of metal such as brass, copper, pewter, steel, lead, or silver, hammering it first with a wooden mallet, then with a steel hammer. This laborious process required a thorough knowledge of the various metals and their physical characteristics and properties. Dunand began the hammering or **chasing** process in the center of a seamless metal sheet and ended at the edges, avoiding hitting the same point twice. Doing this changed the metal's structure and hardened it. Dunand had to repeatedly heat the material to make it pliable again, sometimes requiring as many as thirty to forty reheatings to produce a vase or other form.
Fascinated by **lacquerwork** early in his career, Dunand may have also been influenced by the Swiss enamelwork he saw in his youth. He also admired Japanese lacquerware, and in 1912 had the opportunity to learn the craft from a Japanese master, Seizo Sugawara, who was then living and working in Paris and sought Dunand's advice about metalwork. In exchange, Dunand asked Sugawara to teach him traditional Japanese lacquer production and processes. Lacquer's resilient luster requires patience, since multiple thin coats of lacquer are slowly built up in layers to achieve a final surface. Dunand not only learned the craft, but over decades refined it and experimented with colors, surface treatments, and design. Rather than slavishly imitating a Japanese aesthetic and motifs, he adapted the material to the bold forms and geometric treatments of contemporary art, as seen in the Cooper Hewitt's vase of about 1925. This vase is a fusion of an understanding of the art of metalwork and the power of lacquerwork, combining the texture of the hammer marks with an informed understanding of lacquer techniques to produce a cohesive design. **CT**

References
Brunhammer, Yvonne. "Introduction." In *Jean Dunand, Jean Goulden*, 30–46. Paris: Galerie du Luxembourg, 1973.
Delorenzo, Anthony. *Jean Dunand*. New York: E.P. Dutton, 1985.

0377. Vase, France, ca. 1925, Jean Dunand

0378. Drawing, Design for Woven Silk and Embroidery: Woman Swallowed by Fish and Head of Christ Surrounded by Seraphim (detail), Italy, late 14th century

0379. Drawing, Ceiling Design: Iris and the Rainbow, 1810–25, Felice Giani

Drawing, Design for Acratherm Gauge, 1943
Designed by Henry Dreyfuss (American, 1904–72),
for Minneapolis Honeywell Regulator Company (Minneapolis, Minnesota, USA)
Rendered by Roland Stickney (American, 1892–1975)
Brush and gouache on illustration board
Gift of Honeywell, Inc., 1997-10-6

T-86 Round thermostat, 1953
Designed by Henry Dreyfuss (American, 1904–72)
Manufactured by Honeywell, Inc. (Minneapolis, Minnesota, USA)
Metal and molded plastic
Gift of Honeywell Inc., 1994-37-1

With its compact body and elegant gold casing, the Honeywell Round thermostat was designed to blend with any interior, from traditional to contemporary. It has been the most enduring design object created by the pioneering industrial designer Henry Dreyfuss. The story behind the development of the T-86 device reveals Dreyfuss's concern with creating products that put the user first. The thermostat project also illuminates the collaborative design process between a consultant industrial design firm and an American corporation in post–World War II America. As home to the Henry Dreyfuss archive, Cooper Hewitt, Smithsonian Design Museum holds twenty gouache and graphite drawings (out of many hundreds originally created) related to the ubiquitous round thermostat.

The genesis of the T-86 dates back to the late 1930s, when the Minneapolis-Honeywell Regulator Company first hired Dreyfuss to design housings for gas valves as well as their heating control device, then known as the Chronotherm. One of the early 1938 drawings (**0382**), by Dreyfuss's master **renderer**, Roland Stickney, shows the implement as a rectangle with one rounded corner, like a slick, miniature, streamlined radio. By around 1940 Dreyfuss convinced Honeywell president Harold W. Sweatt that a round thermostat form was more practical than the traditional rectangle, which frequently was attached crookedly to the wall.

The development of the Honeywell Round seems to have begun in earnest in 1942: Dreyfuss filed a design patent on June 19, 1942, and the company's in-house design engineer Carl Kronmiller filed a patent on the inner mechanics December 4, 1942.[1] The round device, in its first iteration revealed in Stickney's **gouache** drawing, had a metal or plastic casing with a dial in the middle to control the temperature and a curving thermometer above it. Through the early 1940s, Dreyfuss's team worked on a traditional rectangular device as well as a round thermostat, because the in-house engineers could not get the curved thermostat to function consistently. Between 1943 and 1948, as documented in the Cooper Hewitt drawings, the Round sported a clear plastic window over the thermometer, a removable plastic ring so it could be painted the color of the walls, and an electric clock. By 1949, Dreyfuss had separated the recording temperature scale from the setting dial, which now appeared on the bottom of the device, making the thermostat easier to use, but it took until 1953 for Kronmiller to work out the internal components. While Kronmiller always claimed to have created the Round, it was Dreyfuss, whose portrait had appeared on the May 1, 1951, cover of *Forbes* magazine, who became the public presence behind the design, as shown in the 1953 ad for the introduction of the device, published in the *Saturday Evening Post* and *Life* magazines (**0383**).

In looking at the final version of the T-86 introduced in 1953, its most distinctive

0380. Drawing, Design for Acratherm Gauge, 1943, Henry Dreyfuss, rendered by Roland Stickney

0381. T-86 Round thermostat, 1953, Henry Dreyfuss

feature is its bold hemispherical form of smooth metal and **molded** plastic. This simple shape, with its three visible elements—body, dial, and graphics—in a unified form, helps make the device easy to understand, almost intuitive for the user. Clearly printed numerals and calibrations in two-degree increments are laid out in a curved line under the transparent setting dial, with the temperature range of 66–74°F centered at the top of the curve, subtly suggesting a mid-range comfort zone. A red arrow indicates the current temperature, while a black arrow, fixed to the large dial with its easily gripped serrated edge, can be rotated to the desired temperature.[2] The Round thermostat has become a classic not only for its function, but for its visual and tactile qualities as well. **GSD, CT**

1 Russell Flinchum, *Henry Dreyfuss, Industrial Designer: The Man in the Brown Suit* (New York: Cooper-Hewitt, National Design Museum, Smithsonian Institution & Rizzoli, 1997), 143–46.

2 William Lidwell and Gerry Manacsa, *Deconstructing Product Design: Exploring the Form, Function, Usability, Sustainability, and Commercial Success of 100 Amazing Products* (Beverly, MA: Rockport Publishers, Inc., 2009), 162–63.

0382. Drawing, Design for a Chronotherm, 1938, Henry Dreyfuss, rendered by Roland Stickney

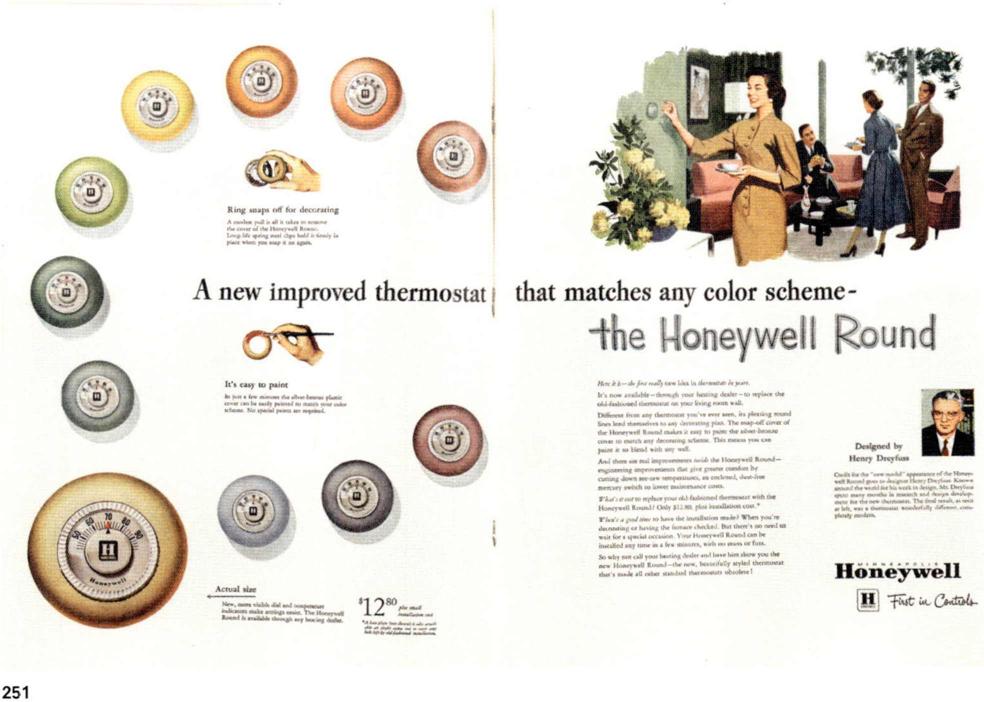

0383. Print, Honeywell Advertisement in *Life* magazine, 1953

0384. Beadwork picture (detail), France, early 19th century

0385. Drawing, Textile Design: No. 8359, 1918, Robert M. Davidson

0386. Drawing (detail), Textile Design: No. 8672, 1924, M. K. Ayling

0387. Drawing, Textile Design: Floral Motif, France, 19th century
0388. Textile, Austria, 1920–30, Josef Frank

0389. Drawing, Textile Design: Floral Motif, France, 19th century
0390. Sidewall, Field Flowers, 1952, Winifred Mury

0391. Sidewall, France, 1840–70

0392. Sidewall, Paris, France, 1788, Jean-Baptiste Réveillon

0393. Ornament—panel, France, 1856–57, Jules Desfossé
0394. Scenic panel, Le Jardin d'Armide, 1854, Edouard Muller

0395. Sidewall, France, ca. 1875
0396. Sidewall, Le Printemps, ca. 1785, Jean-Baptiste Réveillon

0397. Drawing, Hôtel de Salm, France: Panel of Arabesques, 1785, Jean-Guillaume Moitte
0398. Ornament, Decor Pastoral, 1851–64, Jules Desfossé

0399. Drawing, Design for a Bowl with Enamel Cover, 1950–70, Tommi Parzinger

0400. Sidewall, France, ca. 1800

0401. Sidewall fragment, France, 1855–70

0402. Sidewall, Daphnis, ca. 1921, Dagobert Peche

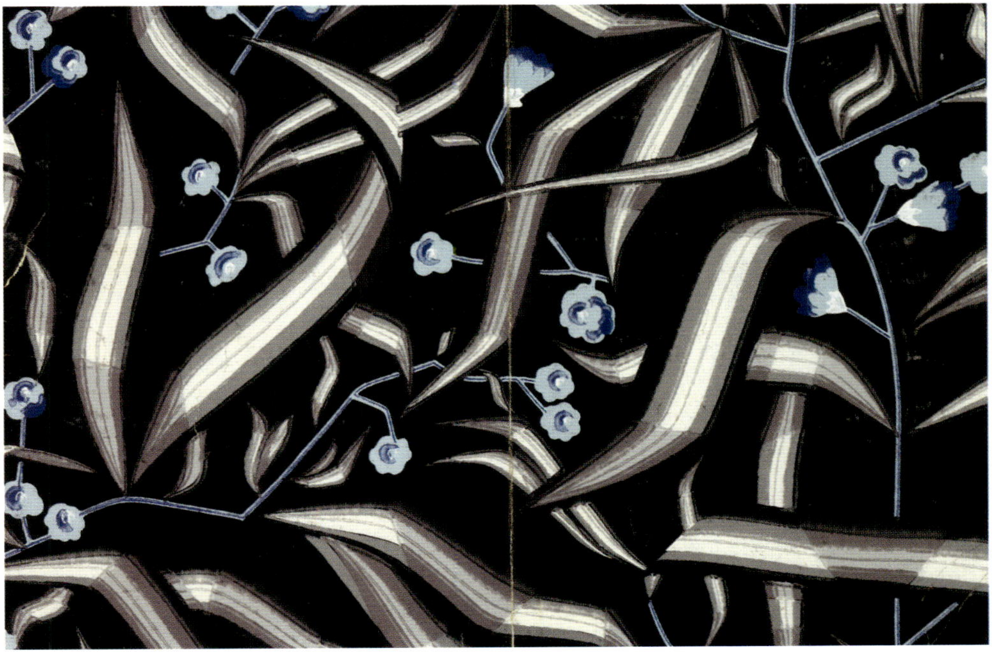

0403. Sidewall, Daphnis, ca. 1921, Dagobert Peche

0404. Pair of doors with handles, France, 1925–26, Seraphin Soudbinine and Jean Dunand

0405. Book illustration, *Magic in the Night: Official Souvenir, Golden Gate International Exposition* (detail), 1939, Gabriel Moulin

0406. Window shade, New York Crystal Palace, USA, 1853

0407. Oil sketch, Niagara from Goat Island, Winter, 1856, Frederic Edwin Church

0408. Drawing, Fisherman in Quebec, 1895, Winslow Homer

0409. Frieze (detail), USA, ca. 1900, Hobbs, Benton & Heath

0410. Indian Encampment vase, USA, 1909, Edward Timothy Hurley

0411. Drawing, Floral Design for a Printed Project, France, 1820–40

0412. Collar, China, 19th century

0413. Drawing, Brighton Pavilion, England: Design for the West Wall of the Music Room, ca. 1817, Frederick Crace

0414. Poster, Aeron Chair, 2012, Kam Tang

0415. Book illustration, *The Practical Ostrich Feather Dyer*, 1888, Alexander Paul

0416. Scarf, USA,1975, Alan Grinberg

0417. Drawing, Textile Design: Purpurnelke: Red with Teal and Brown, 1924, Felice Rix-Ueno

0418. Paper construction, *[2,3]*, 2010, Tauba Auerbach

0419. Pair of gates from the Chanin Building, USA, 1928, René Paul Chambellan

0420. Brooch, England or France, 1750–1800

0421. Fan, USA, ca. 1905

0425. Fan, possibly France, 1830–50
0426. Fan, France, 1885–90, Alouise van de Voorde

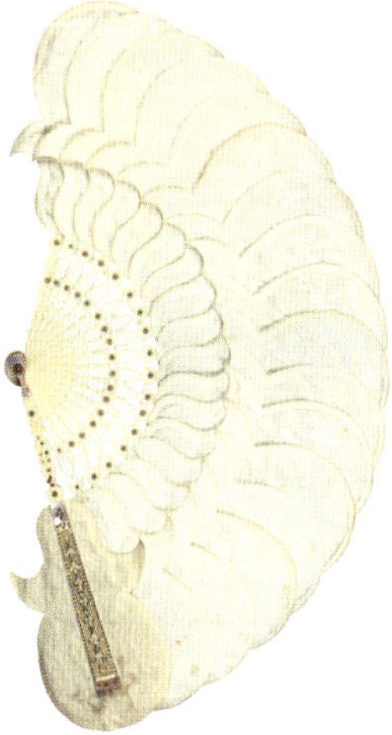

0423. Folding fan, England or France, 1800–10
0424. Folding fan, USA, 1890–1910

0422. Brisé fan, China, 1710–20

0427. Drawing, Floral Design, France, late 19th century

0428. Fan, Austria or Germany, early 20th century

0429. Peacock vase, USA, ca. 1901, Louis Comfort Tiffany

0430. Vase, USA, 1883–88, New England Glass Company

0431. Drawing, Designs for Colored Glass Vases, Czechoslovakia, ca. 1850

0432. Vase, France, late 19th–early 20th century, Émile Gallé
0433. Decanter and stopper, Model 5929S, USA, Wayne Husted, 1959

0434. Bud vase, France, ca. 1900, Émile Gallé

0435. Solifleur, Clutha series vase, Great Britain, ca. 1890, Christopher Dresser

0436. Vase, USA, ca. 1900, Louis Comfort Tiffany

0437. Scent bottle, England, ca. 1750

0438. Vase, Netherlands, 1875–1900

0439. Vase, probably for S. A. Weller Theater, Ohio, ca. 1902, Jacques Sicard

0440. Jeux de Fonds—Astronomie vase, France, 1951, Rabaey

0441. Lotus-shaped cup, Egypt, ca. 1100 BC

0442. Vase, Switzerland, 18th century

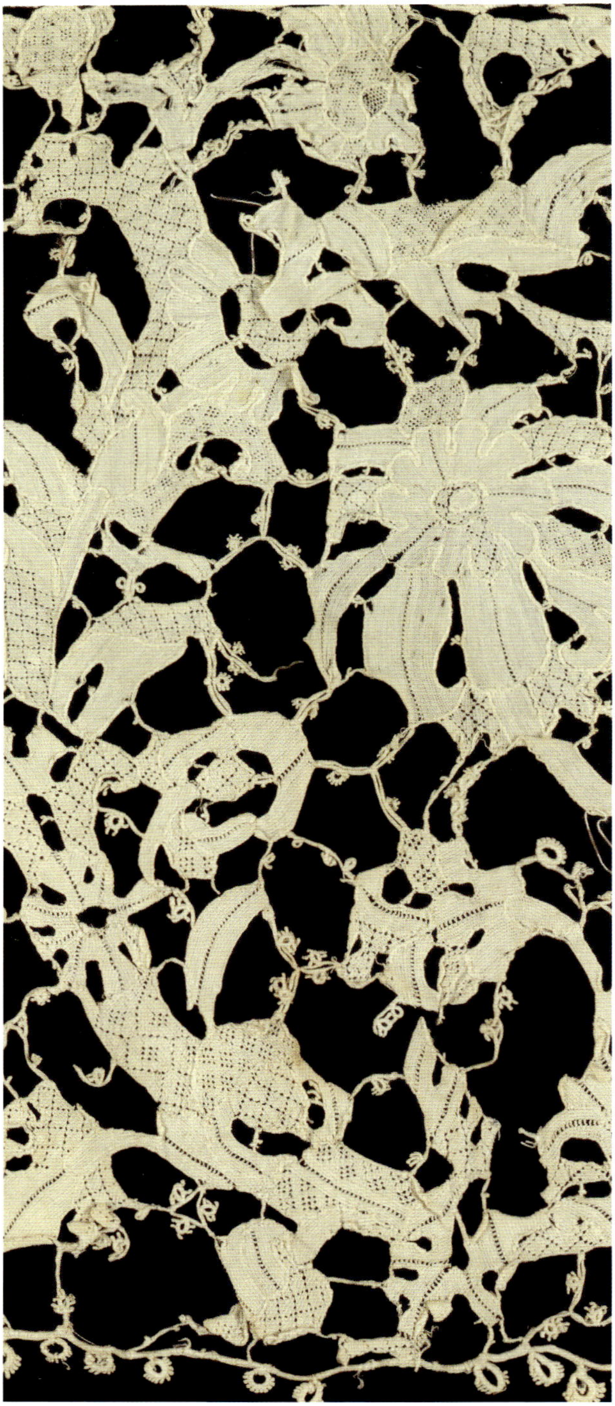

0443. Border, England, 1800–20
0444. Cravat end (detail), Italy, mid–late 16th century

0445. Ewer, Shape No. 469, USA, 1894, Pitts Harrison Burt and Matthew Andrew Daly

0447. Water pitcher, Austria, 1913–14, Karl Massanetz

0446. Drawing, Design for a Crystal Urn with Silver Mounts, ca. 1827–35, Joseph Anton Seethaler II

0448. Tall Green Bloom urn, England, 2012, Michael Eden

0449 Pitcher, Bohemia, ca. 1905, Johann Lötz Witwe

0451. Purse, USA, 1830–60

0450. Flask, Netherlands, mid-18th century

0452. Ewer, possibly Ireland, ca. 1810

0453. Flagon, USA, 1860-80, Peter L. Krider

0454. Standing cup and cover, Germany, ca. 1650, Georg Kraudi

0455. Ewer, Iran, 17th–18th century

0456. Drawing, Design for Majolica Pitcher, Italian, 18th century

0457. Vintage jug, England, 1854–55, Joseph Angell III

Pomander, Dijon, France, 1682–83
Probably made by Antoine Morelot (maker's mark "M") [1]
Pomander: cast, chased, engraved, and raised silver, gilt silver
Case: sharkskin over wood, silver
Bequest of Joan W. Leidesdorf, 1997-62-23

The word *pomander* comes from the Latin *pomum ambrae*, and more directly from old French *pome d'ambre* (apple of amber). While mention of perfume balls exists earlier in France, they were termed "pomander" by 1411 when the Duc de Beri (Berry) received "a beautiful pomander with musk, opening in the middle into two sections and closing with hinges hanging on a little chain." [2] Various forms of pomander exist, but many are apple- or pear-shaped and open into sections, much like a cut piece of the fruit for which they were named. They held concentrated fragrant herbs and spice mixtures, sometimes rolled into balls and sometimes in powders in the pomander, some of which were to perfume or sanitize the air and others had medicinal or flavoring values if applied or ingested.

Pear-form pomanders of this large size, with drop-down segments, were popular in the seventeenth century and often held powdered essences rather than solid waxy balls. Accessories for the wealthy, they were usually made of silver, gilt silver, or even gold, and worn almost as a piece of jewelry, hung on cords, necklaces, or on chains, from either the neck or waist, ready to work in the hand, or to raise to the nose. Sometimes the scented mixtures were put into openwork bracelets or necklaces. Early examples were New Year's gifts for the wealthy: in 1520 the Duke of Buckingham ordered a gold pomander to be made with the king and queen's badges for a New Year's gift for the queen, with a chain of gold to hang the pomander from her waist chain. [3]

As demand grew in the seventeenth century for simple pomanders holding just one paste for the less wealthy, the presence of eight gilded sections in this large pear-form pomander with its elaborate applied ornament shows, that in addition to the complexity of the decoration and size of the pomander, the number of compartments and the expense of their contents were also a social status commentary. That this was a prized treasure is confirmed by the protective sharkskin-covered wood carrying case, a newly fashionable use for this textured fish-leather.

It has eight numbered compartments: I Musque (musk); II Jeseme (a variant of jasmine); III Jonquille (jonquil); IV Tubereuse (tuberose); V Binjouin (probably for benzoin resin from the styrax tree and used in perfumes); VI Pastille (pastille, probably for throat lozenges); VII Ambre (probably ambergris, an aromatic waxy gray perfume ingredient from sperm whales); VIII empty (cover with name missing). The overwhelming concentration of scents rather than spice mixtures also implies that this was a purely luxury item, as none of the known compartments features concentrates for food preparation.

While pomanders exist from the Low Countries and England, both the word's origin and this example are French. Dijon had been a major cultural center under the Dukes of Burgundy, who were great patrons of the arts—especially sculpture and architecture, but also music—from the early eleventh until the late fifteenth century. But between the death of the last duke, Charles the Bold, in 1477 until 1682, when Louis XIV upgraded the status of Burgundy, the town continued with its artistic traditions but was not as powerful. The pomander, created in 1682, reflects the strong cultural heritage of Dijon and possibly the renewed political power of the region. Some of the

0458. Pomander and case, France, 1682–83

segments of the finely modeled body of the pomander have figures, modeled and cast as tiny sculptures, of cupids dancing and playing as if to music. These figures, as well as those from the scene of Hercules with the Nemean lion, were almost certainly based on engravings used by the designers and craftsmen who for centuries had produced silver and furniture in Dijon's Burgundian court. The choice of scenes references the amorous connections of perfumes along with the power of Hercules's feats, suggesting, like the high level of materials and contents, that the pomander may have been a love token for the wife of a politically and socially powerful person.

An example of the elite status of those who used this luxury item can be seen in an Anglo-Netherlandish school painting of about 1570–75 depicting Frances Sidney, Countess of Sussex, in a lavish fur-trimmed mantle with gem-encrusted animal-head chain with a pomander **(0459)**. **SDC**

1 There were five makers using an M mark in Dijon at this date, the others being Jean Malpoy, Clément Ménestrier, Louis Michel, and Denis Mauny: Thierry de Lachaise of Sotheby's Paris, who has helpfully provided this information, feels it to be more probably Antoine Morelot. He also provided the reference to these makers' marks in Arnaud de Chassey & Elizabeth Réveillon, *Les Orfèvres de Bourgogne*, 239. I am grateful to Kevin Tierney and Thierry de Lachaise for their contributions to this attribution.

2 G. Bernard Hughes, "Pomanders and Vinaigrettes," *Country Life* (December 30, 1949).

3 David Charles Douglas, *English Historical Documents*, vol. 1, V states "a pomander of gold to be made with the Kynge and quenes badgeys for a new yers gyfte for the quene and a chain of gold to hang the powmander at her gyrdyll," quoted in Diana Scarisbrick, *Tudor and Jacobean Jewellery* (London: Tate Publishing, 1995), 99.

0459. Painting, Frances Sidney Countess of Sussex, ca. 1570–75, Sidney Sussex College, Cambridge

0461. Drawing, Design for a Boat-Shaped Vessel, Possibly for a Festival Float, 1524–46, Giulio Romano

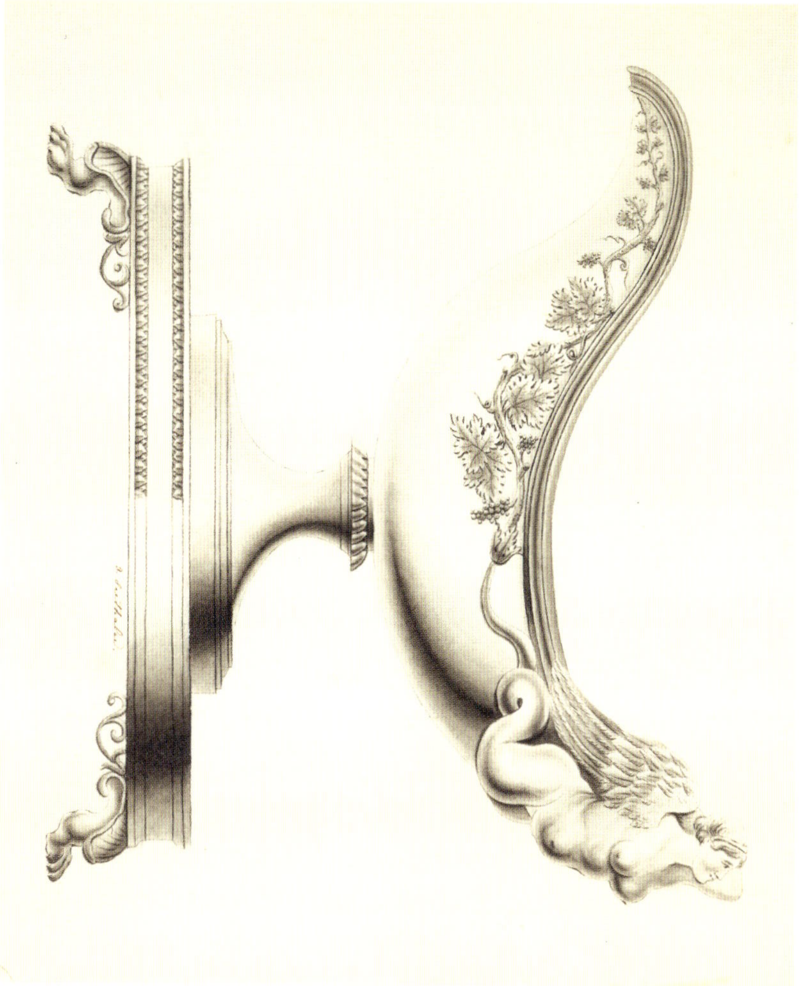

0460. Drawing, Design for a Sauce Boat, 1827–35, Joseph Anton Seethaler II

0462. Cake basket, England, 1758, Thomas Heming

0463. Cream pitcher, France, 19th century
0464. Ewer, Netherlands, 1686–1701, Adriaen Kocx for Grieksche A [de] (the Greek A factory)

0465. American Modern pitcher, USA, 1937, Russel Wright

0466. Jug, England, 1880–82, Christopher Dresser

0467. Teapot and lid, Czechoslovakia, ca. 1932, Ladislav Sutnar

0468. Teapot and lid, Germany, ca. 1770, Berlin Porcelain Factory

0469. Chocolate pot and lid, Germany, mid-18th century, Meissen Porcelain Factory
0470. Chocolate pot and lid, Germany, ca. 1735

0471. Chrysanthemum teapot, USA, 1891–1902, Tiffany and Co.
0472. Teapot, USA, ca. 1845, Samuel Kirk

0473. Book illustration (detail), Artistic Workers in Silver & Gold Plate, 1884, Reed & Barton,
0474. Teapot and lid, Austria, ca. 1925, Franz von Zülow

No. 1235. 2 No. 120 Bottles, $9.50. (ENDLESS)

0475. Book illustration (detail), Artistic Workers in Silver & Gold Plate, 1884, Reed & Barton,

0476. Kayserzinn tureen, Germany, 1902–04, Hugo Leven

0477. Bowl, Roman Syria, 1st century

0478. Kilta sugar bowl and lid, Finland, 1952, Kaj Franck

0479. Fruit basket and cover, Northern Ireland, 1890–1910, Belleek

0480. Mamluk cap, Egypt, late 13th or early 14th century

0481. Jazz punch bowl, USA, 1931, Viktor Schreckengost

0482. Cap, England, 17th century

0483. Cache-pot, France, ca. 1765

0484. Skygarden hanging lamp, Netherlands, 2011, Marcel Wanders

0485. Kylix, Greece, 6th century BC, attributed to the Heidelberg Painter

0486. Skyphos (drinking cup), Etruria (present-day Italy), 6th century BC

0487. Ecuelle and cover, Germany, 1872–88, Charles Thieme Saxonian Porcelain Company

0488. Scholten family tureen, lid, and stand, China for the Dutch market, ca. 1775–95

0489. Pot and lid, USA, 1930–40, Russel Wright

0490. Madame de Pompadour (née Poisson) covered tureen and stand, France, 1990, Cindy Sherman

0491. Monte Santo bowl, Italy, 1924–25, Gio Ponti

0492. Bowl, USA, ca. 1900, Louis Comfort Tiffany

0493. Sidewall, USA, 1936–56

0494. Rock crystal style flower bowl, Austria, 1923–24, Marianne Rath

0495. Bowl, Austria, 1917, Josef Hoffmann

0496. Sidewall, Batterie de Cuisine, 1965–68, Piazza Prints, Inc.

0497. Toddy lifters (syphons), Ireland or England, 18th–19th century
0498. Cup and saucer, Czechoslovakia, 1932, Ladislav Sutnar

0499. Decanters and stoppers, Ireland, ca. 1800
0500. Footed vase, Austria, 1910–14, Josef Hoffmann

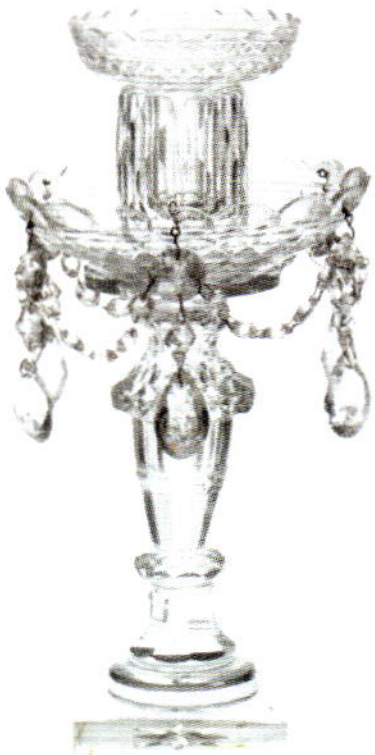

0501. Decanter and stopper, Ireland, 1st half 19th century
0502. Four Continents goblet, Bohemia, 1750–70
0503. Candlestick and drip pan, England, 1760–90
0504. Pinch drinking glass, USA, 1950, Russel Wright

Ambassador vase, 1924–25
Oswald Haerdtl (Austrian, 1899–1959)
Manufactured by J. and L. Lobmeyr,
Karlsbader Kristallglasfabriken A. G. (Vienna, Austria, founded 1823)
Mold blown glass (muslin)
Museum purchase through gift of Georgiana L. McClellan, 1958-98-42

This vase is a virtuosic performance in glass. An interpretation of a sixteenth-century Venetian vase, it epitomizes the technical achievements of the Lobmeyr glass firm and the geometric and smooth-surfaced designs of Oswald Haerdtl. More symbolic than useful, it celebrates the art of glassblowing.

Ludwig Lobmeyr, son of the founder of the firm, first used the plain, very thin glass called muslin glass in his 1856 beer tumbler both as a technical feat but also to contrast with the elaborate decoration of much glass of the era. However, in 1917, under the direction of his son-in-law and successor Stefan Rath, Lobmeyr further advanced the fineness of muslin glass, creating an ultra-thin muslin glass with a barely perceptible resilience and strength for Josef Hoffmann's Patrician pattern. This pattern, of which a number of different sizes of stemmed glass are in the museum's collection, uses the shape of the human lip to give sensuous curves to the glass. Both the cup and stem are barely felt by the lips and hand as the liquid slides into the mouth.

Some of Hoffmann's glasses and rum flagons had iridescent hues, more subtle than Louis Comfort Tiffany's, a Lobmeyr technique started much earlier, since Lobmeyr was exhibiting iridescent glass at least by the Philadelphia Centennial Exhibition (1876), where Tiffany might have seen it. However it is in his use of clear glass in the Patrician pattern that Hoffmann shows a stronger modernist aesthetic that paves the way for Haerdtl's colorless triumph of bold geometries whose almost only visible part is the outline.

The story of the user of this vase, along with a group of more functional table articles like wine and water goblets, plates and bowls, and bonbonnières (candy dishes) in various sizes, is one of the development of the International Style of the 1920s. This design and a number of others by Haerdtl were part of Lobmeyr's display at the Paris 1925 Exposition internationale des arts décoratifs et industriels modernes. It was there that Mrs. Agnes Carpenter, a wealthy woman who lived on Fifth Avenue in New York, saw them. She ordered a large array of objects, and Lobmeyr sent design drawings for her approval, with even the names of the objects in English **(0506)**. These drawings survive in the Drawings and Prints department, a rare example of Lobmeyr drawings outside the firm or the Museum of Applied Arts (MAK) in Vienna. Various entries in Lobmeyr's account books confirm several orders from her in 1927 and 1928. Through her viewing of European design in world's fairs, Agnes Carpenter helped bring the latest fashions to New York, although the necessary skills to make this glass remained in Austria. Carpenter's collection came to Cooper Hewitt after her death in 1958. It was not until 2009, when Cooper Hewitt acquired a large collection of Lobmeyr glass directly from the Rath family descendant owners, that another Lobmeyr collection entered the museum, this time with some examples designed by an American—Ted Muehling. **SDC**

0505. Ambassador vase, Austria, 1925-27, Oswald Haerdtl

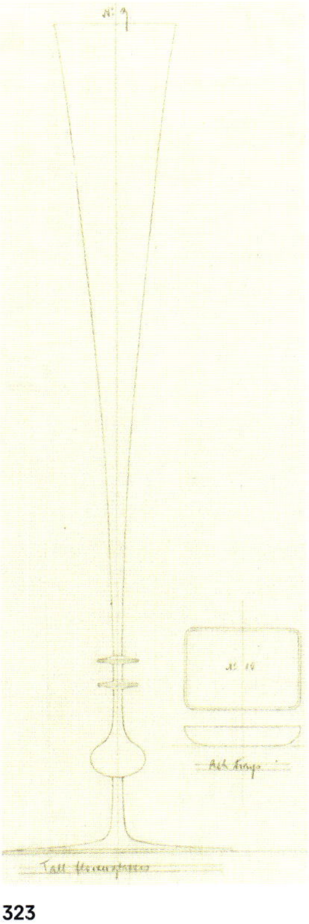

0506. Drawing (detail), Design for Tall Flower Glasses, Ashtrays, Table Ornament, ca. 1926, Flower Glasses designed by Oswald Haerdtl, Ashtrays designed by Stefan Rath

0507. Sculptural vessel, Netherlands, 1985, Toots Zynsky

0508. Drawing, Concept Design for Air Jordan XIII Sneaker, 1996, Tinker Hatfield

0509. Handkerchief vase, Italy, 1955, Fulvio Bianconi

0510. Savoy vase, Finland, ca. 1936–37, Alvar Aalto

0511. Collage, The Gates, Project for Central Park, USA, 2003, Christo

0512. Drawing, Design for a Verrière (Monteith) for Sèvres Porcelain Manufactory, France, 1765–75, Jacques-François Micaud

Woman's ceremonial skirt, early 20th century
Kuba Kingdom, Democratic Republic of the Congo
Woven and embroidered raffia palm fiber
Museum purchase through gift of Dr. and Mrs. Lewis Balamuth, Mr. and Mrs. DeWitt Clinton Cohen, Gertrude Crownfeld, Valerie Dreyfus, Norvin Hewitt Green, Rodman A. Heeren, Eleanor and Sarah Hewitt, Florence N. Levy, Mrs. Paul C. Pennoyer, Mrs. Bernard Reis, Mrs. William Jay Schieffelin, and Mr. and Mrs. Stephen B. Stanton, 1990-133-3

The visual arts of the Kuba Kingdom, an area delineated by the Kasai, Sankuru, and Lulua Rivers in the heart of what is today the Democratic Republic of the Congo, have long been admired for their vitality and complexity, especially in the handling of abstract geometric surface design, inspiring artists and designers from Henri Matisse to Sonia Delaunay to Josef Hoffmann.[1] Perhaps the most dynamic examples are raffia skirts worn by both men and women. The center panels of the long skirts are like extended canvases for dynamic abstract compositions, and their borders often draw the eye with the movement of massed pompoms or coiled edgings, as on this one. Worn wrapped several times around the body and secured with a belt, the upper edge flips back and creates a second zone of activation, along with a majestic girth. This skirt is part of a costume that could also include bangles, bells, cowrie shells, and whisks. It is easy to imagine how the bounce and sway of this ruffle-edged skirt enhance the visual and auditory spectacle during the dances that are part of almost every ceremony.

No single person designs, makes, wears, or owns the raffia skirts that feature so prominently in Kuba social life. Every adult is expected to contribute to the fabrication of textiles, and most do so daily, if only for short periods. Some may spend more time than others, each according to his skills and talents, and older people who are no longer able to hunt or work the fields may spend a much larger proportion of their time making textiles.[2] Each garment represents the rich complexity of community relationships and the interdependency of men and women.

Raffia is woven exclusively by men. Young leaflets of the raffia palm (*Raphia textilis*) are chosen, and the tender membranes are stripped from the underside of the leaf with the edge of a knife. The strips are tied in bundles to dry in the sun, then split lengthwise with the fingers into individual fibers. The fibers are not twisted or spun to form longer yarns therefore, the finished size of a woven piece is limited to about twenty-six to twenty-eight inches square. These woven units, called *mbala*, were formerly used as currency and as tribute to the paramount ruler, or *nyim*. Textiles are still seen as tangible wealth, and communities work together to accumulate them.

Once the weaving is complete, the stitching and decoration of men's or women's skirts is divided strictly between the genders. The female head of the clan, who directs the production of the women's skirts, first procures the mbalas from a male relative. These coarse squares are made soft and flexible by wetting and pounding in a mortar or wooden trough, then stitched together to form a long skirt. Both men and women use a broad repertoire of decorative techniques, including tie-dye, **appliqué**, patchwork, and **embroidery**, but only women use **cut-work** and cut-pile embroidery, the two dominant techniques in this skirt. Vertical stripes are created by removing the warps and wefts in certain areas, then stitching across the openings in zigzag stitches. These decorative elements can also camouflage the seams, giving the illusion of an uninterrupted field. A series of interlocking diamonds is outlined in dark brown embroidery, and the intersections are filled with tiny red embroidered

0513. Kuba woman's ceremonial skirt, Democratic Republic of the Congo, early 20th century

eyelets. The separate border is of dark brown cut-pile embroidery in an interlace motif. Each tuft of **pile** is a short length of raffia inserted with a needle under the warps of the foundation, and the two ends are cut short. Brushing the exposed ends with the edge of a knife further splits the raffia ends and gives a rich, velvety texture. The undulating coil edging of this piece is created by wrapping and binding a thick rope of raffia to the edge of the skirt with buttonhole stitches; the tension introduced causes it to flip back and forth like an unruly cable.

In addition to celebratory events, raffia textiles also serve important funerary functions for both the living and the dead. The deceased are buried wearing layers of raffia textiles, according to the person's wealth and status in life. Even today, when most men have adopted Western-style clothing and many women wear blouses and wrappers of imported cotton, it is believed that traditional dress is required for burial in order to be recognized and accepted by the ancestors on the other side. Decisions about which specific pieces to include in the interment are made collectively by all of the clan members who jointly own them, and a suitably abundant, skillfully made, and aesthetically pleasing display is of great importance to the family's prestige. Although a clan's supply of textiles can be greatly diminished by a funeral, the period of confinement and mourning is often when a family creates new textiles.[3] **SB**

1 Vanessa Drake Moraga, *Weaving Abstraction: Kuba Textiles and the Woven Art of Central Africa* (Washington, DC: Textile Museum, 2011), 110.

2 Patricia Darish, "Dressing for the Next Life: Raffia Textile Production and Use among the Kuba of Zaire," in *Cloth and Human Experience*, eds. Annette B. Weiner and Jane Schneider (Washington, DC: Smithsonian Institution Press, 1989), 124.

3 Ibid., 134.

0514. Kuba loom, Democratic Republic of the Congo, early 20th century

0515. Book illustration, *Insectes*, 1927, Eugène Alain Séguy

0516. Dragonfly and Cattail Pond Lily lamp, Models 1462 (shade) and 225 (base), USA, 1900–10, Louis Comfort Tiffany

Araiso U brooch
Paris (form), Wajima, Ishikawa Japan (lacquer), 2007
Made by Van Cleef & Arpels
Lacquered by Junichi Hakose (Japanese, b. 1955)
Raised white gold, gold beads, eggshell lacquer on mother-of-pearl support on white gold, round cut diamonds
Gift of Van Cleef and Arpels, 2011-42-1

The brooch was created by Van Cleef & Arpels in Paris. Made of gold, the brooch had mother-of-pearl cut and set into it as a ground for lacquering. The then-partial brooch was sent to Junichi Hakose to create the lacquer (*urushi*) in Japan. Born in 1955 in Wajima, Ishikawa, Japan, a center for enamel making, Hakose began collaborating with Van Cleef & Arpels in 2002. His technical skills make him sought after for lacquer boxes and other wares in addition to his collaboration with the firm. He often works in *Wajima-nuri* lacquer and *maki-e*.

Wajima-nuri requires more than twenty steps and over one hundred processes to complete a single piece and is the specialty of Hakose's birthplace. Maki-e is a process, requiring great levels of both painting and craftsmanship skills, in which, in this case, the maker drops hot, molten 99.9% gold and silver in the finest amounts from a special brush directly onto the surface of the lacquer. The brooch's surface is built up slowly with these layers, with drying between and at the end, totaling eight weeks. At the end of the lacquering process, the surface has a texture depicting waves, which are symbolic in Japan of strength, power, clarity, depth, and unity. Water can be calm as well as aggressive, and, although pure and serene, it is also, imperceptible at times. Here the water is made to sparkle, not only in the lacquer but with the addition of tiny diamonds set into the lacquered waves, and with a central body set by the Van Cleef & Arpels jeweler with nine diamonds.

This butterfly and another one with different lacquer that were given to Cooper Hewitt by Van Cleef & Arpels are part of a collection created by the firm of twenty-five different designs, with only twenty pieces made available for each design. The use of traditional jewelry and lacquer techniques from both Asian and Western cultures represents the global fusion of design that the museum seeks to represent. **SDC**

0517. Hanakarakusa W brooch, France and Japan, 2007, Van Cleef & Arpels

0518. Araiso U brooch, France and Japan, 2007, Van Cleef & Arpels

0519. J.B. Schmetterling (Butterfly) hanging lamp, Germany, 2011, Ingo Maurer

0520. Textile, Farfalle, 1963, Harvey Smith and Clayton Ryder

0521. Sidewall, The Peacock, ca. 1890

0523. Sidewall, The Cedar Tree, 1910, Louis Stahl

0522. Drawing, Textile Design: Bird Motif (detail), France, 19th century

0524. Figurine, Rooster, England, ca. 1760, possibly Derby Porcelain Factory

0525. Sidewall, Sommerfeld, 1917–28, Felice Rix-Ueno

0526. Drawing, Cartoon for Wallpaper and Textile: Peacock, 1960, Harvey Smith

Le Nébuleux, étalant ses parures. Pl. 16.

0527. Book illustration, Le Nébuleux, étalant ses parures, 1806, François Le Vaillant and Jacques Barraband

0528. Sidewall, Tumtin, ca. 1967, Philip Graf Wallpapers, Inc.

0529. Drawing, Textile Design: Birds (detail), France, 19th century

0530. Rank badge (buzi) (detail), China, Ming dynasty, 1368–1644

0531. Sidewall, Celui qui aime ecrit sur les murs, 1924, Jean Lurçat

0532. Textile, Japan, 1936

0533. Poster, Levi's 501, The Button Fly, 2010, Sagmeister Inc.

0534. Book illustration, 1832, Edward Lear

0535. Sidewall, Cat and Canary, 1958, John Rombola

0536. Drawing, Dog Wallpaper, ca. 1956, Saul Steinberg

0537. Compact disc, Imaginary Day by Pat Methany, 1997, Stefan Sagmeister

0538. Sidewall, Alice in Wonderland, 1968, John Rombola

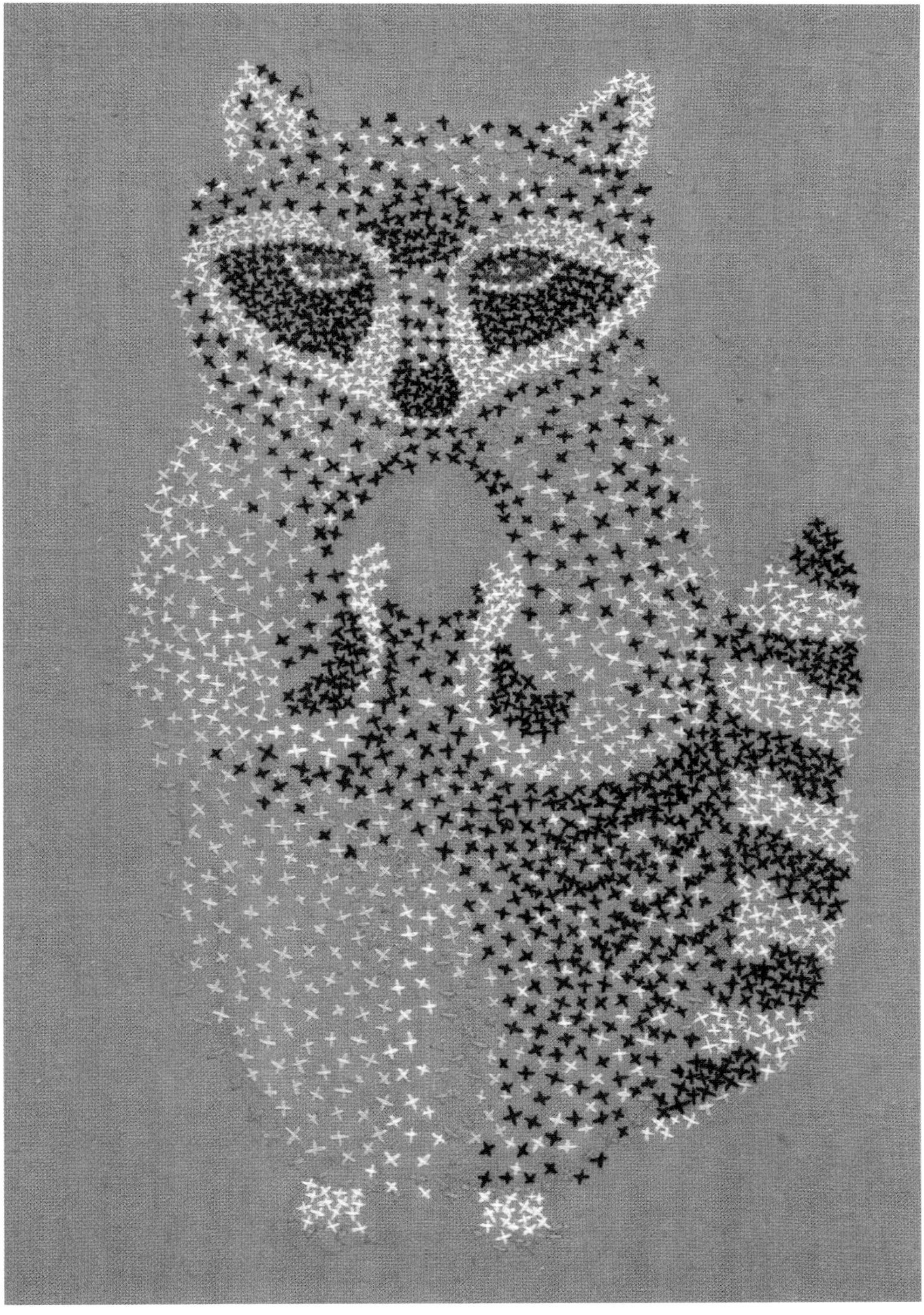

0539. Embroidered picture, USA, 1965

0540. Sidewall, Cow, 1971, Andy Warhol

0541. Scenic panel, L'Orage, France, 1861, Eugene Ehrmann, after a painting by Robert Eberle

Sidewall, Zodiac, 1942
Marion Dorn (American, active in England, 1896–1964)
Made by Bassett & Vollum, Inc. (Galena, Illinois, USA)
Screenprinted on paper
Gift of Anonymous Donor, 1967-49-1-a

Marion Dorn's Zodiac is an early **screenprinted** wallpaper with a large-scale design featuring the twelve signs of the zodiac, with six printed in brilliant colors and six overprinted in white outline against a deep green, almost black ground. The design, in the bold coloring and strong lines characteristic of Dorn's work, is printed in seven colors, applied one at a time with one screen for each color. Each sign is rendered in a simplistic manner and printed in a solid block of color, with only the most essential elements delineated. While many of her designs are abstract and geometric, she was inspired by nature and frequently incorporated shells, birds, and foliage.

Dorn was born and educated in the United States but traveled to Britain in the early 1920s to pursue her textile career. She started out designing printed textiles and batiks and later also designed rugs. Many of her designs were printed in limited editions and sold at upscale retailers. She founded her own studio, Marion Dorn Ltd., in London in 1934; by that time she had begun screenprinting some of her textiles. Her first screenprinted wallpaper, Constellation, was produced for Coles in 1938. She reluctantly returned to the States in 1940, when the American Embassy felt England was about to be invaded by German forces. She set up a studio in New York and began receiving commissions for wallpaper designs, initially from Bassett & Vollum and later Katzenbach & Warren.

Screenprinting was the major advancement in wallpaper production in the twentieth century. While the silkscreen technique was patented in England in 1907, its further development occurred mainly in the United States. Machine printing produced a greater quantity of wallpaper faster at a lower cost than screenprinting, but it was far less flexible. Printing machines were expensive, and it was necessary to print rolls by the thousands to be economical, which necessitated the designs be very mainstream. Screenprinting has a low startup cost with no minimum print requirements, so studios can print in small batches, which allows them to create more unusual and artistic designs for niche markets. The appearance of a screenprinted wallpaper is noticeably different from that of a machine-printed one in that the pigments are very dense and opaque. Machines require a thin, watery pigment that dries quickly as each of the colors is printed in quick succession in the paper's one pass through the printing machine.

The earliest wallpapers screenprinted for commercial production were introduced in 1938, and a number of these papers were included in a 1939 wallpaper exhibition at the Cooper Union Museum. However, the majority of screenprinted wallpapers were introduced after the war, as there was a moratorium on new wallpaper designs from about mid-1942 until November 1, 1945. While individual patterns were released at the end of 1945 it took fourteen months for the studios to produce and deliver their new collections to the public. After the war, screenprinting quickly established itself as a viable part of the industry. **GH**

0542. Sidewall, Zodiac, 1942, Marion Dorn

0543. Sidewall, Animal Kingdom, 1950, Edgar Miller

0544. Drawing, Still Life with Fish and Parrot (detail), 1740, Jean-Baptiste Oudry

0545. Scenic wallpaper, Sea Beauties, 1920–40, The P. Company

0546. Textile, L'Eau, ca. 1924, Yvonne Clarinval

0547. Frog paperweight, France, ca. 1910–20, François-Émile Décorchemont

0548. Ornament (detail), France, 1850–60

0549. Sidewall and frieze, France, 1928–29, J. Grantil Company

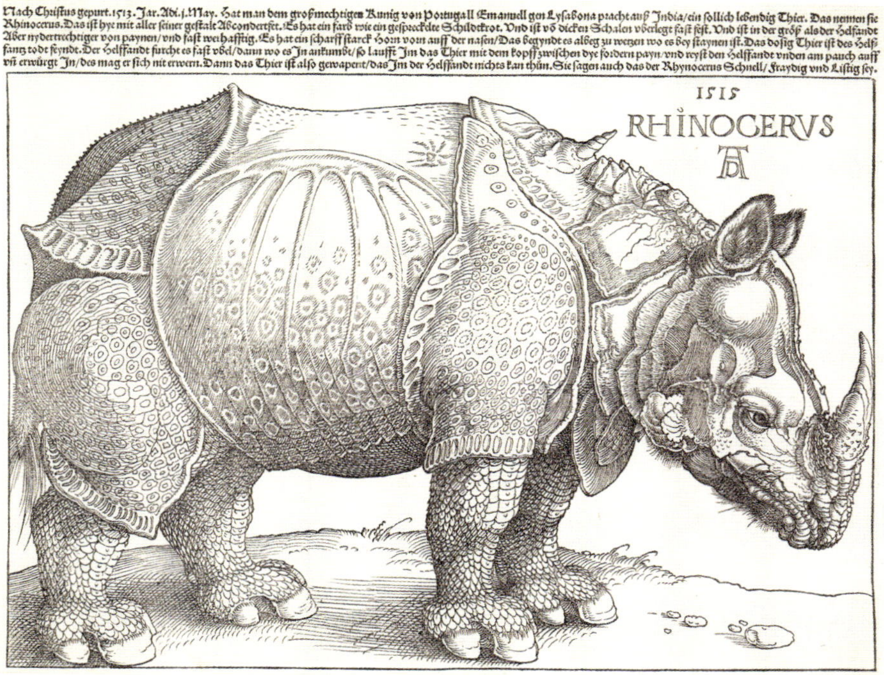

0550. Print, The Rhinoceros, 1515, Albrecht Dürer

0551. Inkwell, Germany, ca. 1735

0552. Print, Lion and Hare Composed of Ornamental Leaf-Work, 1698, Wolfgang Hieronymus Von Bömmel

0553. The "Hunting" Frieze, 1905, Cecil Aldin

0554. Frieze, Winnie the Pooh, after 1926

0555. Matchsafe, USA, 1905–15, Theodore B. Starr

0556. Allegorical Figure of America from the Four Continents, Germany, late 18th–early 19th century, Meissen Porcelain Manufactory

0557. Frieze, Kindergarten Cut-Outs, 1907, The Schmitz-Horning Co.

0558. Frieze, Jungle Cut-Outs, 1907–10, The Schmitz-Horning Co.

0559. Book illustration, *Mapje en Papje in het Hazenbosch*, ca. 1900–20, Marie Hildebrandt and Sibylle von Olfers

0560. Book illustration, *Studies in Design*, 1876, Christopher Dresser

0561. Paper construction, *The Model Menagerie*, ca. 1895, Ernest Nister

0562. Mantle, Peru (detail), 16th–17th century

0563. Book illustration, *Insectes*, 1927, Eugène Alain Séguy

0564. Drawing,Textile Design: Insect Motif (detail), France, 19th century

0565. Book illustration, *Locupletissimi rerum naturalium thesauri accurata description*, 1734–65, Albertus Seba

0566. Elefantenruesseltisch (Elephant trunk table), Austria, ca. 1910, Adolf Loos

Vase, ca. 1905–14
Louis Comfort Tiffany (American, 1848–1933) for Tiffany Studios
Manufactured at Tiffany Furnaces (Corona, New York, USA)
Glazed molded earthenware
Gift of Marcia and William Goodman, 1984-84-32

While Louis Comfort Tiffany's name is recognizable to many for his artistic productions in glass, his studios also produced artistic pottery. While very distinctive, and once seen, identifiably different from other American art pottery of its era, Tiffany's pottery was nonetheless far from the only force in this realm. Rookwood, Newcomb, and Grueby, to name just a few of the American art pottery companies, all produced works of both creative design and artistic decoration and glazes. French art pottery shown at the world's fairs was a huge influence on most of the biggest names in the United States—and on Tiffany. Tiffany returned from the 1900 Exposition Universelle in Paris brimming with ideas of what he would like to create. The matte glaze on this fern vase is one of the French influences, in contrast to a previous insistence on high-shine glazes. According to Keramik Studio:

> Mr. Louis Tiffany is busy experimenting with pottery, which no doubt means that he will finally produce something as artistic as his Favrile glass. In an interview with the manager, our representative was told that as yet, Mr. Tiffany is in the experimental stage, but that he was so charmed with the work of artist potters at the Paris exposition, that he came home with the determination to try it, and that he would probably produce something in the lustre bodies. [1]

Before he actually sold his own wares, Tiffany arranged an exhibition of French art pottery in 1901.[2] He wanted to create his own aesthetic through employing a variety of skilled craftsmen to work in his vision. However, the other firms, notably Rookwood, encouraged the individuality of the creators of the glazes and decoration, allowing signatures, so that many names are known.[3] Despite Tiffany's general ban on signing, excellent scholarship has identified a variety of people who worked for him at his glass studios, most notably Clara Driscoll, who was responsible for some key designs.[4] More recently, documents from his ceramics studio[5] have led to further discoveries and pursuit of identities for some of the staff there, including a few other women.[6] However, just as working molten glass was perceived to be a man's job, so throwing pottery for the kiln, with glazes and other surface treatments, was considered as a potential area for women to create. In the case of Tiffany it was also the area to which so much of the firm's creative energy turned. This did not mean that Tiffany was firing his own pots—he may not have known how—but he did know the effect he wanted to achieve, and hired people capable of creating it or who knew where to look for sources.

After Loius Tiffany took the company over from his father, Charles Tiffany, it became typical for the roles of individual subcontractors not to be identified. This meant, for instance, that the name or mark of Albert Coles, who supplied some of Tiffany & Co.'s silver patterns, was removed. Likewise, the LCT signature did not mean Louis Comfort Tiffany had participated in the making. The initials served much the way the Tiffany & Co. mark did for his father's firm. In this case, hand-etched initials rather than the stamped company mark further identified the producer in a way that suggested completely handcrafted work with Louis Comfort Tiffany himself the design director. Advertisements repeatedly implied production by phrases like,

0567. Vase, USA, ca. 1905–14, Louis Comfort Tiffany

"a unique art product" and "made under the supervision of Mr. Louis C. Tiffany" and the name "Favrile," based on the Latin *fabrilis*, meaning related to a craftsman.[7] This impression of complete handwork is not exactly accurate. Despite the considerable amount of handwork required to finish this vase **(0567)**, it was actually cast in molds. This vase had seven hand-carved molds. The complications of putting them together and finishing the details piece off by hand made it an expensive production, but the molds allowed for limited editions to be made.[8] In some cases, because either a few were made and/or its complex structure made it vulnerable to cracking, a fern vase this size is very rare.

The fern vase, with its furled ferns, represents Tiffany's continued commitment to naturalism. Other more upright vases show the ferns starting to unfurl.[9] The collaboration needed to make this vase included the artistic vision probably provided by Tiffany as the artistic design director, aided significantly by his manager; those who molded, threw, and articulated the various parts of the vase; and the glazers. The whole is Tiffany's, as is evident from the fact that the ceramics created in his studio, many of which had iridescent glazes like his glass, reflect his interest in iridescence or shapes that push the limits of the material in his own way. While his ceramics were never as commercially successful as his glass, they had a distinctive look that cannot be confused with any other factory. As beautiful as many pieces of some of the other factories are, their identification is more associated with their decorators, whose work might look like that of someone else, somewhere else, rather than conforming to a design aesthetic promoted by a particular firm. This latter principle is one that has governed many firms. It is only when they pass through more than one design director that one sees an individual style come through. Tiffany envisioned and saw to fruition technical skills not achieved before and too costly to maintain without the aesthetic environment needed to maintain them.

This vase is part of a large collection of American art pottery given by Marcia and William Goodman to the Museum in 1984.[10] It includes other Tiffany ceramics and examples by Rookwood, Newcomb, and Grueby, among others. **SDC**

1 "New York and Syracuse," *Keramic Studio* 2 (December 1900): 161, quoted in Martin Eidelberg, *Tiffany Favrile Pottery and the Quest of Beauty* (New York: Lillian Nassau, 2010), 12.

2 Anna B. Leonard, the New York–based china painter, listed Dalypayrat, Hoentschel, and Chaplet among others. See Eidelberg, *Tiffany Favrile Pottery*, 13.

3 All of the thirty-two pieces of Rookwood pottery in Cooper Hewitt's Goodman collection, from which this piece also comes, have known decorators or signatures.

4 Martin Eidelberg, Nina Gray, and Margaret Hofer, *A New Light on Tiffany: Clara Driscoll and the Tiffany Girls* (New York: Giles, 2007).

5 Martin Eidelberg and Nancy A. McClelland, *Behind the Scenes of Tiffany Glassmaking: The Nash Notebooks* (New York: St. Martin's Press in association with Christie's Fine Arts Auctioneers, 2001); Marilynn A. Johnson, ed., *Louis Comfort Tiffany: Artist for the Ages* (London: Scala, 2005).

6 Eidelberg, *Tiffany Favrile Pottery*, 15–17.

7 Ibid., 68.

8 Ibid., 64.

9 Johnson, *Louis Comfort Tiffany*, 135.

10 Selections were exhibited in 1987 when a catalog was produced. *American Art Pottery* (New York: Cooper-Hewitt Museum, 1987), 100–1.

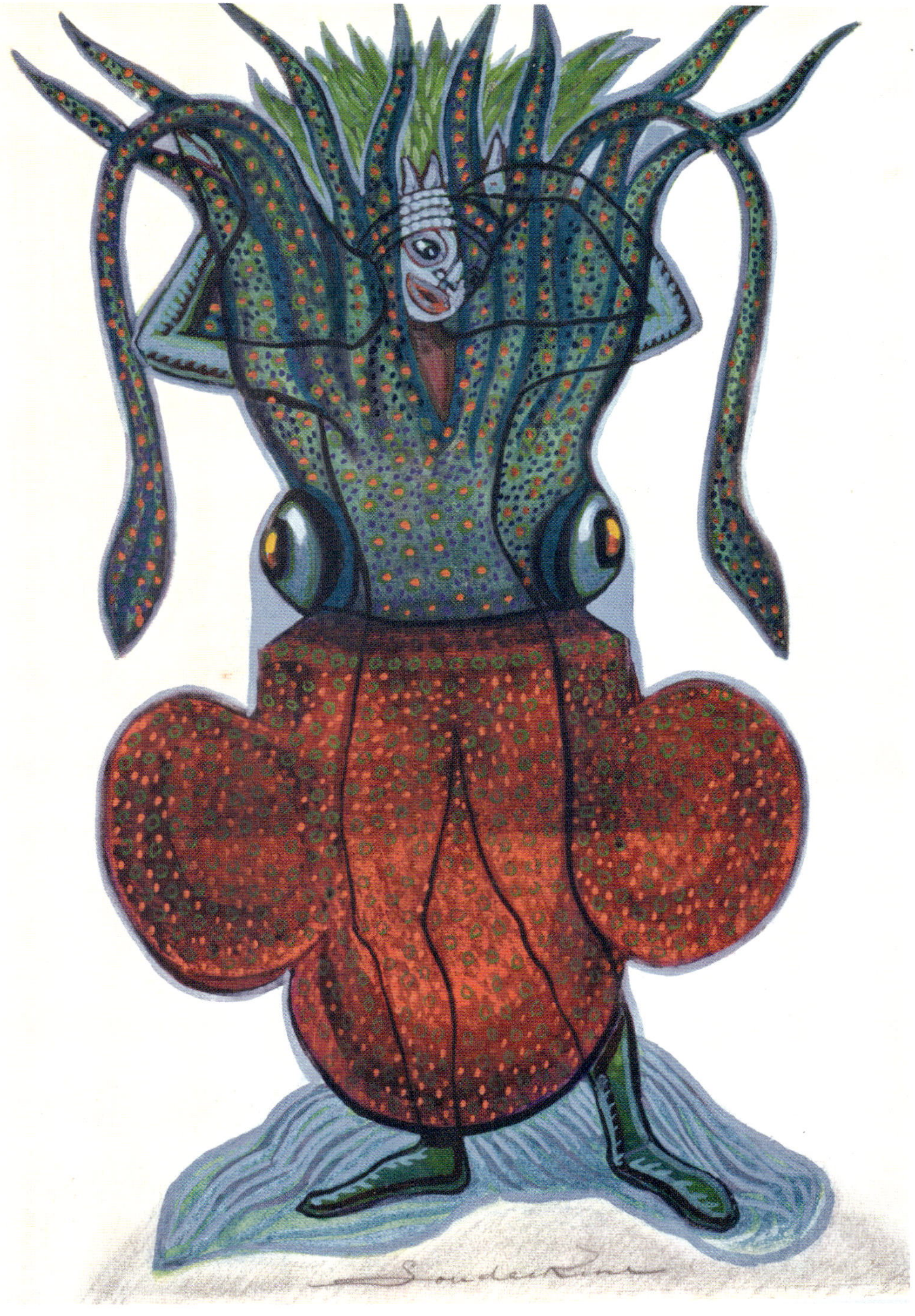

0568. Drawing, Squid Costume Design for the Opera *Sadko* by Rimsky-Korsakov, ca. 1929; Serge Soudeikine

0569. Man's hat (ashetu), Cameroon, after 1957

0570. Cap, Spain, late 18th century

0571. Bowl, USA, ca. 1893–1909, George E. Ohr

0572. Man's cap, England, late 16th century

0573. Man's hat, France, 18th century
0574. Man's hat, France, ca. 1730

0575. Kuba men's hat (laket), Democratic Republic of the Congo, 19th century
0576. Kuba Men's hat (laket), Democratic Republic of the Congo, 19th century

0577. Hat, France, 18th century

0578. Bonbonnière, England, ca. 1755

Melos necklace, ca. 1873
Made by Fortunato Pio Castellani & Sons (Rome and Naples, Italy)
Enameled, granulated, and rolled gold
Museum purchase through gift of Anonymous Donor, Annie Schermerhorn Kane, and various donors, 1969-40-17

The name Castellani is the most recognized of the Italian jewelers who worked "after the antique," meaning based on ancient jewelry. The firm produced both reproductions and pieces inspired by antiquity, mostly based on then-recent archaeological finds in what is now Italy, Greece, and southern Russia. They acquired and repaired all or most of the ancient pieces that served as their models or inspiration, giving them close access to study ancient techniques and design motifs.
Antiquity has been a design source, recurring in waves, throughout history. After the Renaissance, the renewal of interest in the era started with the rediscoveries and subsequent excavations of Herculaneum and Pompeii, beginning in 1738 and 1748, respectively. The neoclassical movement expanded in the early nineteenth century with additional excavations in Greece and other sites. But it was not until the 1830s and 1840s—when archaeological digs provided new discoveries, especially of Etruscan gold jewelry found in tombs, that archaeological jewelry design reached new heights of fashion. Publications of finds and exhibitions broadened the audience for the jewelry. German, English, Italian, and French texts from the eighteenth and early nineteenth centuries contained motifs from these ancient designs, giving new impetus and source material for designers.
Fortunato Pio Castellani, founder of the Castellani firm, was a Roman goldsmith, jeweler, and antiques dealer who opened his first jewelry shop in Rome in 1814–15, after he received his master's patent and at the end of Napoleon's occupation.
He experimented with different jewelry techniques, including tinting gold to imitate the deep yellow color of gold found in archaeological digs. Alessandro Castellani (1822–83), his eldest son and chief designer of the firm, made a special study of the ancient technique of **granulation**, meticulous work involving the application of a myriad of tiny little balls of gold to give texture and pattern to carefully shaped gold forms. While other members of the firm, most notably Alessandro's brother Augusto (1829–1914), were probably as involved in its production, Alessandro's interest in it guided the firm in the perfection of the granulation technique. Whether Alessandro reinvented the technique or learned it from information passed down from antiquity through peasant craftsmen remains unknown, but the firm attained a mastery of the technique, a contribution that inspired many others goldsmiths and jewelers, including Carlo Giuliano and Giacinto Melillo, both of whom worked for Alessandro in Castellani's Naples workshop before branching out on their own.
The Castellanis had the close support and some design input—including sketches—from archaeologist and later Duke of Sermoneta Michel Angelo Caetani (1804–82), as they turned to ancient-inspired pieces. Before selling desirable ancient pieces, they often made copies. The original necklace on which this superb example **(0579)** is based, dates to about 330 to 300 BC and was said to come from the Greek island of Melos. Alessandro supervised its repair (which analysis has revealed included the replacement of several missing elements) and initiated the making of copies.
He also designed variants. While faithful to the ancient techniques of granulation and **enameling**, this necklace features longer chains than the original to hold the pendants, and incorporates the adorsed "C's" (*text continued on page 388*)

0579. Melos necklace, Italy, ca. 1873, Fortunato Pio Castellani & Sons

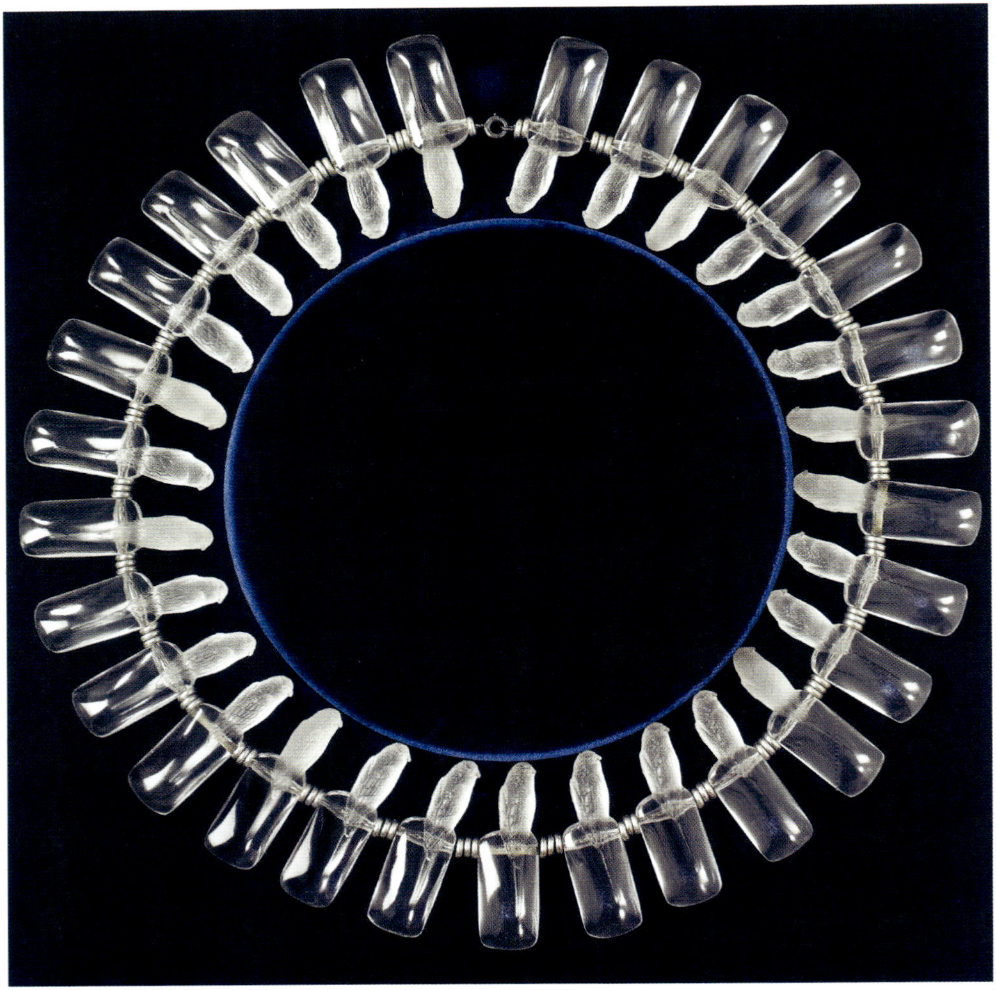

0580. Necklace, France, ca. 1930, René Lalique

0581. Necklace, Norway, 1983, Tone Vigeland

mark of the Castellani firm on the terminals of the clasp. The longer chains made the necklace somewhat easier to wear, thereby making it both an original and a reproduction.[1]

Castellani sold the ancient necklace as part of a collection to the British Museum in 1872. An exhibition there to garner support for the collection acquisition inspired demand for such copies or adaptations that continued after its sale. In fact, the young Guiliano, while in the Castellani shop in Naples, signed an early—about 1865—Castellani version of a necklace similar to this one.[2] He apparently kept it and later retailed it at his shop in London that he opened in Piccadilly in 1874, just two years after the ancient necklace was purchased for the British Museum.[3] Similarly, Castellani jewelry appeared at Hancocks & Co., a London jewelry retailer.[4]

London was not the only place to admire Castellani's work. Many of the wealthy clients for this necklace would have been those who traveled to Italy, sometimes to study antiquity; others might have seen the original in the London World's Fair of 1872 or in the British Museum. By the 1850s, the Castellani shop was a destination for predominantly French and English visitors to Rome. Among them was the English Arts and Crafts architect and designer William Burges (1827–81), who might seem an unlikely admirer of classically styled jewelry, considering how much he embraced medieval design in his desire to escape the Industrial Revolution and neoclassical architecture. However, he appreciated the interest in the handcrafting Castellani jewelry displayed when, in 1853, he visited its premises in Rome, enough to publish an account of ancient jewelry ten years later and to produce an ancient-style necklace design.[5]

Early on Castellani saw the benefits of exhibiting at world's fairs, where the firm's jewelry, including versions of the Melos necklace, enjoyed a broad visibility in the diverse European and American venues of these well-attended events. While Castellani did not exhibit in the Crystal Palace exhibition in London in 1851, the firm exhibited in Paris in 1867, London in 1872 (showing a version of the Melos necklace), and notably, in Vienna in 1873, where their exhibition played an influential role in dispersing designs such as the Melos necklace and techniques such granulation to other decorative arts.[6] The Castellani version, published in catalogs of the exhibition,[7] inspired copies by other jewelers, such as examples by the Viennese firm Josef Bacher & Sohn, an ornate version of which was acquired directly by the Österreichisches Museum für angewandte Kunst (The Austrian Museum for Applied Arts, now known as MAK) in 1878.[8] Bacher's interpretation was not as innovative as another use of the design—this time by Ludwig Lobmeyr in a totally different medium—glass, which appeared well before Bacher's necklace. One of the founders and professors at the Applied Arts design school in Vienna, Ludwig Lobmeyr was head of the J&L Lobmeyr glass firm. He appreciated the pattern and varying textures of the necklace and understood the transferability of pattern and texture from one medium to another, using it to create his own personal glass table service in 1873 **(0582)**, along with porcelain and table linens to match.

For its adaptive use of designs from antiquity, its high level of craftsmanship—including the requirement of difficult techniques—its visual impact, and its influence on design in various media throughout Europe and the United States, Castellani's Melos necklace is a design icon. **SDC**

1 Elizabeth Simpson, "'A Perfect Imitation of the Ancient Work'—Ancient Jewelry and Castellani Adaptations," in *Castellani and Italian Archaeological Jewelry*, ed. Susan Soros et al. (New Haven, CT: Published for the Bard Graduate Center by Yale University Press, 2005), 209, 210 212, 217.

2 Diana Scarisbrick, "Archaeological Jewelry in the Orbit of Castellani," in Soros, *Castellani and Italian Archaeological Jewelry*, 324.

3 Geoffrey Munn, *Castellani and Giuliano: Revivalist Jewellers of the 19th Century* (New York: Rizzoli, 1984), 57.

4 Ibid., 53.

5 Shirley Bury, "Alessandro Castellani and the Revival of Granulation," *The Burlington Magazine* 117, no. 871 (October 1975): 667.

6 Susan Weber Soros, "'Under the Great Canopies of Civilization': Castellani Jewelry and Metalwork at the International Exhibitions," in Soros, *Castellani and Italian Archaeological Jewelry*, 258–59, 262.

7 Welt-Ausstellung, *L'Esposizione Universale di Vienna del 1873 illustrata*, Vol. 2 (Milano, 1873–74), 336, which states that a necklace having a description much like Cooper Hewitt's was acquired by the "Museo Artistico di Vienna," although the MAK does not now have this in its collection. See Soros, *Castellani*, 263 and 281.

8 Hugh Tait, ed., *The Art of the Jeweller: A Catalogue of the Hull Grundy Gift to the British Museum: Jewellery, Engraved Gems, and Goldsmiths' Work* (London: British Museum, 1984), 154, no. 973 and fig. 81, depicting a detail of a similar Melos necklace by Castellani from Welt-Ausstellung, *L'Esposizione Universale di Vienna del 1873 illustrata*, 254.

0582. Tableware, glasses, Pattern No. 168, Lobmeyr's Gentlemen's Dinner Service, 1871, Ludwig Lobmeyr

Porca Miseria! hanging lamp, 2000
Ingo Maurer (German, b. 1932)
Manufactured by Ingo Maurer GmbH (Munich, Germany)
Glazed molded porcelain adhered to metal rods, stainless steel, halogen light source
Gift of Peter Norton, 2010-16-1

The Porca Miseria! lamp is among the most recognizable and expressive of lighting designer Ingo Maurer's works. Fascinated by what he calls the "magical and mystical" properties of light, Maurer constructs lighting forms and systems that play with conventional ideas about brightness, shadow, color, and ambiance.[1] Trained as a typographer and graphic artist, Maurer worked as a designer in the United States between 1960 and 1963. He returned to Europe in 1963, where he was active as a graphic designer. Maurer's shift to lighting design was sparked by his fascination with the lightbulb as the "perfect union of technology and poetry."[2] Since then, he has created more than two hundred different lights and lighting systems for many settings, including public buildings and monuments, and private commissions. Combining unexpected materials and found objects with various light sources, Maurer is a pioneer in the use of new lighting technologies and imaginative production techniques. Having a humorous and poetic sensibility, his choice of unconventional materials invites the user to question the relationship of form and function, and the nature of light.

Porca Miseria! came about through a 1990 private commission to design light sculptures for the owners of a villa on Lake Constance in Germany. Among Maurer's final pieces was the dining-table lamp for the contemporary kitchen, the social center of the house. Considering his first effort, made of paper, to have been unsuccessful, Maurer eventually created an object made of smashed ceramic tableware seemingly caught in midflight. The resulting form created an intricate play of light, shadow, and a sense of chaotic energy as an antidote to the stark space. The then-unnamed lamp, evocative of an explosion in a china cabinet, was constructed of fragments of white dishes, cups, and cutlery attached to a structure composed of metal rods radiating from a central lighting element. About four years later, in 1994, Maurer created a more complex and dynamic version, which he showed at the Euroluce lighting exposition in Milan. A fan of cinematic explosions, Maurer first named the lamp Zabriskie Point, after the 1970 movie in which director Michelangelo Antonioni blew up a castle in slow motion. When one Italian visitor saw the chaotic mass of shards and flatware, he exclaimed, "Porca miseria!" (literally "Miserable pig," an Italian expression meaning "What a disaster!"). This delighted Maurer so much that he changed the lamp's name.[3]

Despite the spontaneous look of the Porca Miseria!, it takes hours of exacting labor to fabricate one. There is a limited production of about ten per year, and no two are alike. Each example requires about seven days of intensive work by several people. Ceramic tableware is dropped or smashed with a hammer, then the pieces, some as is, others further broken and smoothed to more appropriate sizes and shapes, are arranged and mounted on the ends of thin metal rods that are joined to a metal armature housing the halogen light source and wiring. The rods have some give, allowing the fragile ceramics and cutlery to waver and clink, playing with light, sound, and heightening the sense of wonder and apprehension in the observer. Each lamp is a singular version of Maurer's riotous design. **CT**

0583. Porca Miseria! hanging lamp, Germany, 2000, Ingo Maurer

1 Kim Hastreiter, et al, *Provoking Magic: Lighting of Ingo Maurer* (New York: Cooper-Hewitt, National Design Museum, Smithsonian Institution, 2007), 1.

2 Jochen Eisenbrand, "Ingo Maurer—Light: Reaching for the Moon," Institut Valencia d'Art Modern, accessed January 8, 2014, www.ivam.es/images/exhibition_attachments/3761/original/Maurer_en.pdf.

3 Bernard Dessecker, "Porca Miseria!," in *Ingo Maurer: Designing with Light/Gestalten mit Licht*, ed. Bernard Dessecker, trans. Roderick O'Donovan (Munich: Prestel, 2008), 165.

Further References

Designophy. "Porca Miseria!" Accessed August 16, 2012. www.designophy.com/designpedia/design-product-1000000113-porca-miseria.htm.

Museum of Modern Art. "Ingo Maurer. Porca Miseria! Chandelier, 1994." Accessed August 16, 2012. www.moma.org/interactives/exhibitions/1998/projects66/i07.htm.

Vegesack, Alexander von, et al. *Ingo Maurer, Light—Reaching for the Moon*. Weil am Rhein: Vitra Design Museum, 2004.

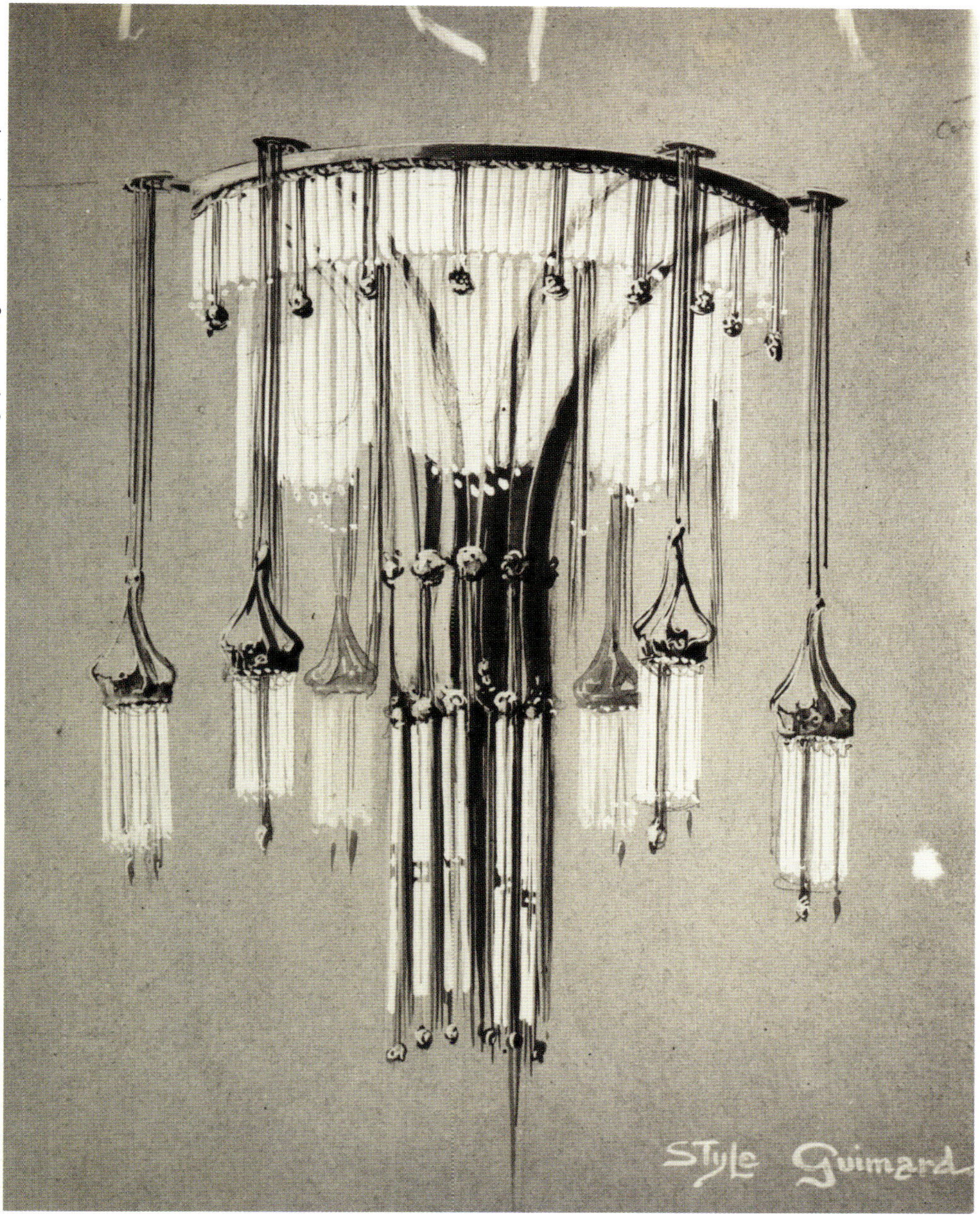

0584. Photograph, Drawing of Chandelier, ca. 1905, Hector Guimard

0585. Chandelier, possibly Netherlands, 15th–16th century

0586. PH Artichoke hanging lamp, Denmark, 1958, manufactured 1983, Poul Henningsen

0587. Tassel, Italy, 17th century
0588. Tassel, Italy, 17th century
0589. Tassel, Italy, 17th century

0590. Hanging lamp, Italy, 1914–20, Vetreria Fratelli Toso or Barovier & Toso

Sidewall, Memory Wallpaper, 2003–04
Cynthia Hathaway (Canadian, active Netherlands, b. 1965)
Eindhoven, Netherlands
Adhesive vinyl with cutouts
Gift of Cynthia Hathaway, 2004-10-1

Memory Wallpaper was created by Cynthia Hathaway for an exhibition sponsored by Mother, a Canadian design collective of product and graphic designers. The exhibition focused on the iconic log cabin. Memory wallpaper is **die cut** on a walnut-grain adhesive vinyl. Hathaway chose this material because the wood-grain pattern is reminiscent of log cabins. The material has become ubiquitous worldwide; the hanging instructions are printed in thirteen languages. Hathaway took the basic wallcovering a step further: the roll was die cut with five motifs—a cuckoo clock, a rack of souvenir spoons, a lantern, canoe paddles, and a Canadian Mountie—which the designer felt were all cabinesque. The placement of the motifs is designed to align with the typical placement of those objects on the wall. The user can decide on the placement of motifs on the wall. Hathaway has a strong interest in the recyclability of materials and ideas and does not think the past should be obscured by the present. When this wallcovering is applied over existing wallpaper, the cutouts give the old surface an automatic link to the present.
In 1947, after nine years of research and development, United Wallpaper, Inc., introduced the first vinyl wallcovering, called Varlar. By 1948 Varlar was available in ninety-three patterns. Varlar was the first truly scrubbable wallcovering, able to withstand twenty-five thousand consecutive rubs in the same spot, as opposed to tests of earlier washable papers, which withstood only twenty-five rubs.
Vinyl is the common name for polyvinyl chloride (PVC), invented by a German chemist in the 1870s. Pure PVC is rigid, but in 1926 American chemists discovered they could make it flexible with the addition of plasticizers, greatly expanding the material's uses. Early vinyl wallcoverings consisted of two types: vinyl laminates and vinyl coated. Vinyl laminates have a dyed polyvinyl chloride film that is heat-laminated to a fabric or paper backing for stability. A design would be printed before heat lamination; **embossing** would be done during lamination. Vinyl-coated wallcoverings are produced by coating a fabric or paper backing with a layer of liquid vinyl, then thermally fusing them. The wallcovering is then ready to be printed or embossed.
The use of vinyls developed rapidly during World War II, but with rationing, they were generally not available for home use. The first self-adhesive vinyl was patented under the brand Con-Tact in 1954. Developed by Cohn-Hall-Marx in conjunction with the Monsanto Chemical Company, Con-Tact was 100 percent plastic with a pressure-sensitive adhesive back. It was meant to revolutionize the wallpaper industry. Designed for the do-it-yourself market, it was inexpensive (59 cents per yard,1954; $5.23 per yard, 2014), nearly indestructible, and the only tool needed to hang it was a pair of scissors. It was initially available in patterns of wood grains, marbles, stripes, solids, and kitchen and nursery prints. Born in Ontario, Hathaway studied at the Emily Carr Institute of Art and Design in Vancouver, British Columbia, and graduated in 2000 with a degree in architectural design from the Akademie voor Beeldende Kunst in Enschede, Netherlands. Her master's degree in product design is from the Design Academy in Eindhoven. She was a director of the masters program FunLab at the Eindhoven Academy, and taught at the Rietveld Academy and Academie van Bouwkunst in Amsterdam before starting her own Amsterdam firm, Hathaway Designs. **GH**

0591. Sidewall, Memory Wallpaper, 2003–04, Cynthia Hathaway

0592. Sidewall, France, 1835

0593. Drawing, Design for a Damask Textile, France, 1850–75

0594. Drawing, Design for a Gold and Cabochon Gem Brooch, ca. 1855, Alexis Falize

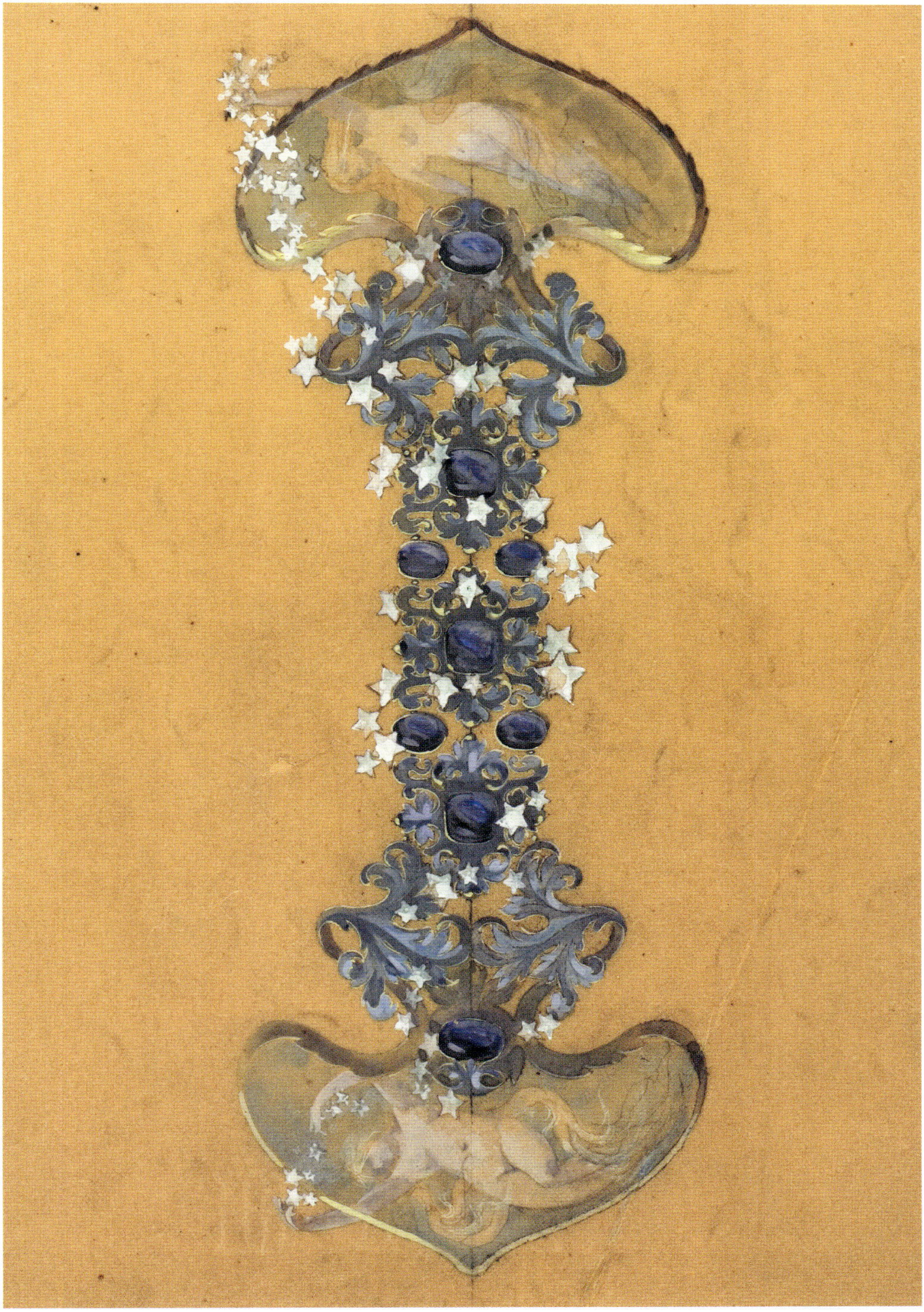

0595. Drawing, Design for a Corsage Ornament: Night, ca. 1900, René Lalique

Surtout de Table (Table centerpiece), France, ca. 1810
Pierre-Philippe Thomire (French, 1751–1843)
Cast and gilded bronze with hand engraving, cut glass, silvered mirrored glass
Bequest of the Reverend Alfred Duane Pell, 1991-31-1-a/ww

The changing fashions in dining, ranging from the time of day of the main meal, to its location, who was included, and how people entertained all contributed to the creation of a vast array of vessels and table decorations from the late seventeenth through the nineteenth centuries. In the seventeenth century, a large house normally would have a great hall with a long refectory table. The social hierarchy of the household and guests determined who ate where, with the house owner or lord sitting at one end and the staff either at the other end or at another table in the same hall. Entertaining was usually in the form of a dessert banquet, where sugar sculptures and other fancy sweets were arranged in elaborate patterns on the banqueting table, generally a long, straight table. Royalty dined at such tables, facing people who were invited to observe them.

After the death of Louis XIV in France in 1715, the younger court of the Regency period and Louis XV spent far more time in the more intimate spaces of Paris than in Versailles. With the increased emphasis on privacy and smaller domestic spaces in the early eighteenth century came the dining room, with smaller, often oval, tables. The objects that sat on these tables would have featured dishes of arranged food for the main course as the primary decoration along with possible sugar or porcelain figurines; silver, brass, or porcelain candlesticks or candelabra; flatware; and glasses. With the French Revolution of 1789, dining changed again. The intimacy of the private dining room became negatively associated with the frivolity of lifestyle attributed to the ancien régime. Once again, longer rectangular tables came back into fashion. By this time, the idea of eating in staggered courses, known as *service à la russe*, was coming into fashion, enabling the table to have more room for inedible display objects and lighting. The most elaborate of table display objects was the *surtout de table*, which was a large centerpiece, with mirrored plateaus and numerous candelabra and other possible display pieces on top, all to reflect and give more light and sparkle to an important occasion.

In a painting of the sumptuous wedding of Napoleon and his second wife Marie-Louise in 1812 **(0597)**, the surtout de table is arranged much as the one in Cooper Hewitt's collection **(0596)**. This not only gives an idea of how this object was used, but the level of the commission. Indeed, the history that was passed down from the donor is that this surtout was a present from Napoleon to his stepson Eugène de Beauharnais. This is a plausible story, not only because Pierre-Philippe Thomire, the designer and maker of this gilt-bronze work,[1] became "Gilt bronze maker to the Emperor" in 1809, but because he is responsible for several similar examples made for Napoleon to give to his mother, sisters, and a few of his marshals.[2] Recent examinations of Eugène's inventories have revealed more than one surtout among his possessions.[3] In 1816 house accounts under "extraordinary and unexpected expenses," are costs for moving two large "surtouts de table" to his house in Munich. The surtouts had been sent to Thomire Duterme and Ciev from Eugène's house in Paris for regilding, missing pieces, and other furnishings including artificial flowers at a cost of 2816 Francs.[4]

Although Thomire learned his bronze-working skills from his father in the foundry and his **chasing** and **gilding** from Louis XVI's chief bronze maker Pierre Gouthière

(1732–1813), he survived the change in patronage caused by the French Revolution by allying himself with both furniture makers for whom he made mounts in the neoclassical style favored by Napoleon, and by purchasing a decorating firm that was a supplier to Napoleon's palaces. The motifs used appear elsewhere in Napoleonic interiors as well as in other fashionable articles. The Three Graces, seen holding a basket for fruit **(0596)**, are adapted from ancient Greek models, or Roman interpretations of them. These comparisons to antiquity greatly appealed to Napoleon as he looked for models to compare himself with the emperors and rulers of ancient eras. **SDC**

1 D. H. Cohen, "Pierre Thomire-Unternehmer und Künstler," *Vergoldete Bronzen*, II, Hans Ottomeyer (München: Klinkhardt & Biermann, 1986).

2 Sir Pierson Dixon, "French Empire Clocks in the British Embassy at Paris," *Connoisseur* Vol. 150 (January 1968): 2–9. The embassy was formerly the house of Napoleon's sister Pauline Borghese, from whom the Duke of Wellington arranged to purchase the house and contents for the British as an embassy in 1814 after the abdication of Napoleon. The one made for her remained there.

3 I am indebted to Ulrich Leben for this information, as I am for the citation in endnote 4.

4 (0643/B 120) Maison du Prince Eugène, Eugène de Beauharnais papers, Firestone Library, Princeton University.

0596. Surtout de Table (Table centerpiece, detail), France, ca. 1810, Pierre-Philippe Thomire *(see pp. 406–07 for full image)*
0597. Painting, The Wedding Banquet of Napoleon I and Marie-Louise in the Grand Salon of the Tuileries Palace, 2 April 1810, 1812, Alexandre-Benoit-Jean Dufay, Casanova, Musée National du Château de Fontainebleau

0598. Pair of earrings, probably France, ca. 1860

0599. Ornament, Décor Chasse et Peche, 1859–65, Desfossé et Karth

0600. Drawing, Design for a Reliquary of the Holy Cross (detail), ca. 1540, Attributed to Luzio Romano

Drawing, Design for a Candlestick, ca. 1520–30
Michelangelo Buonarroti (Italian, 1475–1564)
Black chalk, brush and brown wash, incised lines and compass points on cream laid paper, lined
Museum purchase through gift of Mrs. John Innes Kane, 1942-36-4

This black-chalk drawing of a candlestick, first recognized in 2002 as a masterwork by Michelangelo, is an exquisite example of the artist's inventive exploration of ornamental vocabulary in his architectural design.[1] The drawing is probably an early conception for the paired marble candlesticks atop the altar of the New Sacristy in San Lorenzo, Florence, the Medici funerary chapel recognized as one of the artist's greatest sculptural ensembles. Michelangelo first submitted designs for the New Sacristy in 1520, and the work was completed in 1533, after his departure for Rome. Several sketches by Michelangelo have been associated with the New Sacristy commission, in which he experimented with the proportions of the architectural components of the wall tombs and the location of their sculptural figures.[2] This is the only drawing associated with the sacristy altar and is distinguished by its meticulously detailed articulation of the components of the central shaft of the candlestick.

The attribution of the drawing to Michelangelo is confirmed by various physical characteristics. The **laid paper** has a **watermark** of an anchor within an oval, surmounted by a six-pointed star, a watermark that is evident in numerous autograph drawings by the artist. Of particular significance is the construction of the drawing, in which the artist has first used a dull **stylus** with a compass and straightedge to incise a preliminary line. The black chalk is drawn on the incised surface, and the modeling is articulated with dark brown wash. This method of construction is consistent with many of Michelangelo's design drawings, both in architecture and for decorative objects.

The candlestick is composed of three sections. The base stands on lion's feet and is decorated with a scene of ancient sacrifice that would have been rendered in low relief. The graphic style of this scene, with its delicate facility of line and figural shorthand, is perhaps most immediately recognizable as Michelangelo's draftsmanship.

The central portion of the candlestick shaft consists of a rectangular block articulated with a pair of scalloped niches, each hung with a garland draped over a herm.

The base is supported by muscular seraphim, also characteristic of Michelangelo's ingenuity. The upper corners terminate with ornate rams' heads holding dense festoons. The uppermost portion of the candlestick is more traditional in design, and is surmounted by a bell form, covered with fish scales, that terminates in the baluster supporting the candle pricket and drip pan.

At the lower right of the sheet, two sketched ground plans for the candlestick, designating its upper and lower portions, are clearly marked with units of measure. The plinth supported by the seraphim is eight units square and the central rectangular block is five units square. Extrapolating from these markings, the candlestick itself is thirty-two units high. The unit of measurement is most likely the Florentine soldo, which results in a height of two to three feet. This corresponds to the extant marble candlesticks on either side of the New Sacristy altar. Only the candlestick on the right was completed contemporaneously. Its carving is attributed to Silvio Cosini, one of Michelangelo's most gifted assistants on this project. The completed work does not duplicate the design of the chalk drawing, but there is close correspondence, for example, in the rams' heads bearing festoons and the lion's claws

0601. Drawing, Design for a Candelabrum, 1520–30, Michelangelo Buonarroti

at the base. Other ornamental details, such as the fish-scaled surfaces, are echoed throughout the chapel's decoration and figural sculpture. The candlesticks on the altar are a significant focal point of the chapel, and Michelangelo's meticulously detailed drawing indicates his attention to their design as an elegant synthesis of the essential ornamental vocabulary applied throughout the architectural space. **SEL**

1 Timothy Clifford, "A Candelabrum by Michelangelo: A Discovery at the Cooper-Hewitt, National Design Museum in New York," *Apollo* vol. 156, 486 (September 2002): 30–40.

2 Cammy Brothers, *Michelangelo, Drawing, and the Invention of Architecture* (London: Yale University Press, 2008), 141–44.

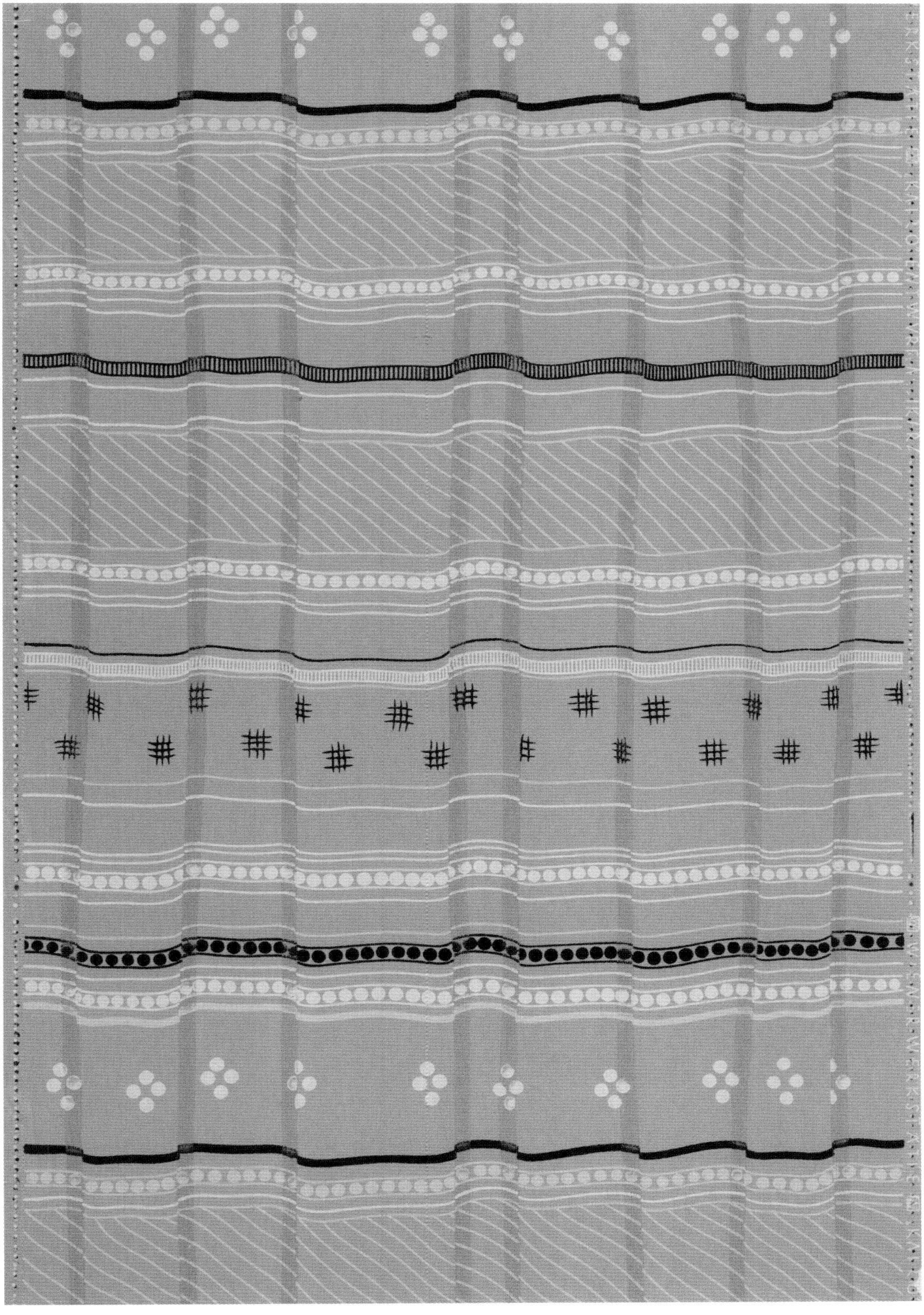

0602. Sidewall, Cairo, 1929, Maria Strauss Likarz

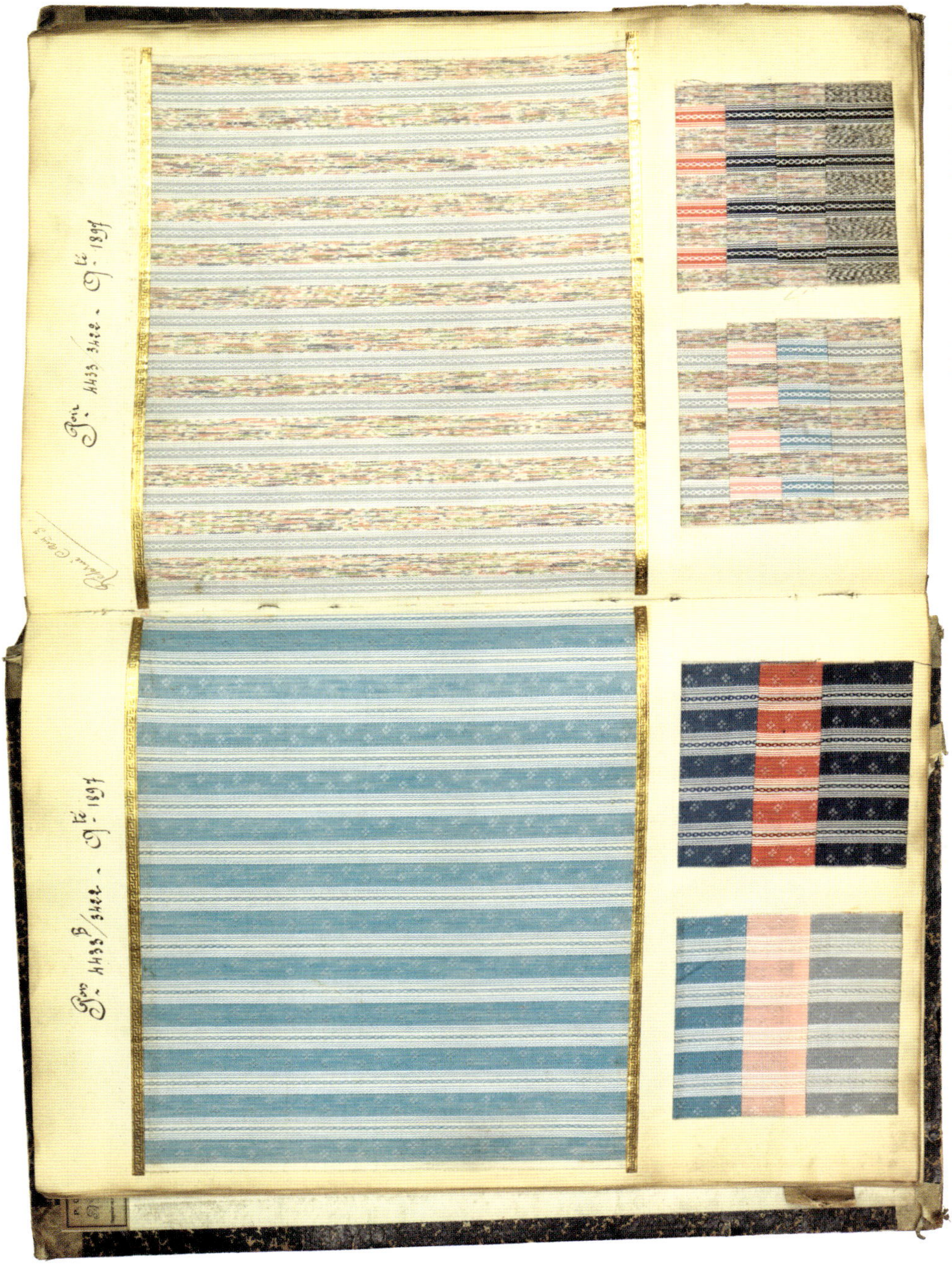

0603. Sample book, France, 1904–06, Hamill & Barker

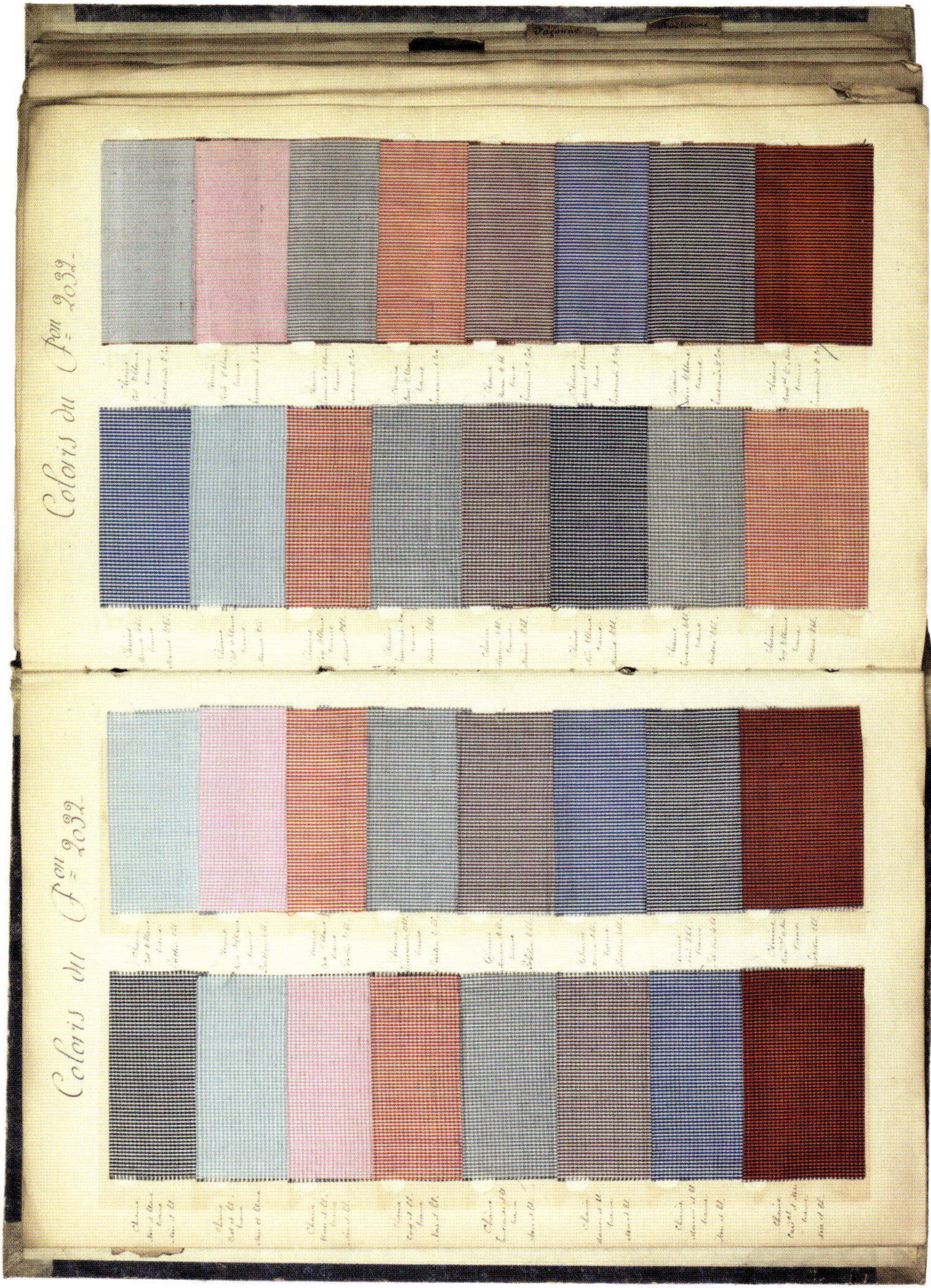

0604. Sample book, France, 1905–06

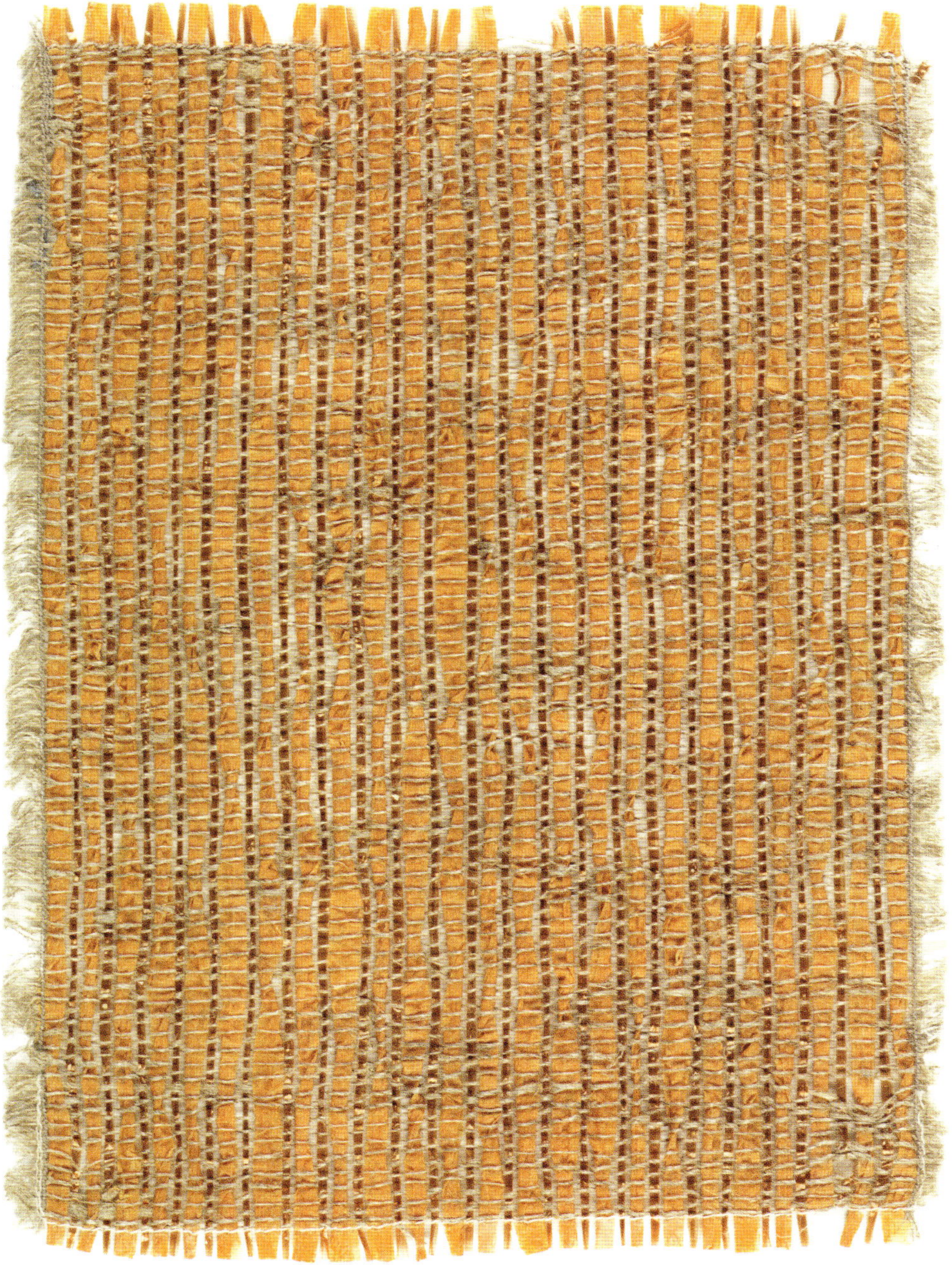

0605. Handwoven sample for a wallcovering, USA, ca. 1945, Anni Albers

0606. Window blind sample, USA, 1956, Dorothy Wright Liebes

0607. Ewe prestige cloth (detail), Ghana, early 20th century

0608. Textile, Causeway, 1967, Lucienne Day

0609. Drawing, Temple Rodef Sholom, San Rafael, California, USA: Design for an Ark Curtain, 1963–64, Trude Guermonprez

0610. Textile, Temple Rodef Sholom ark curtain trial, 1963–64, Trude Guermonprez

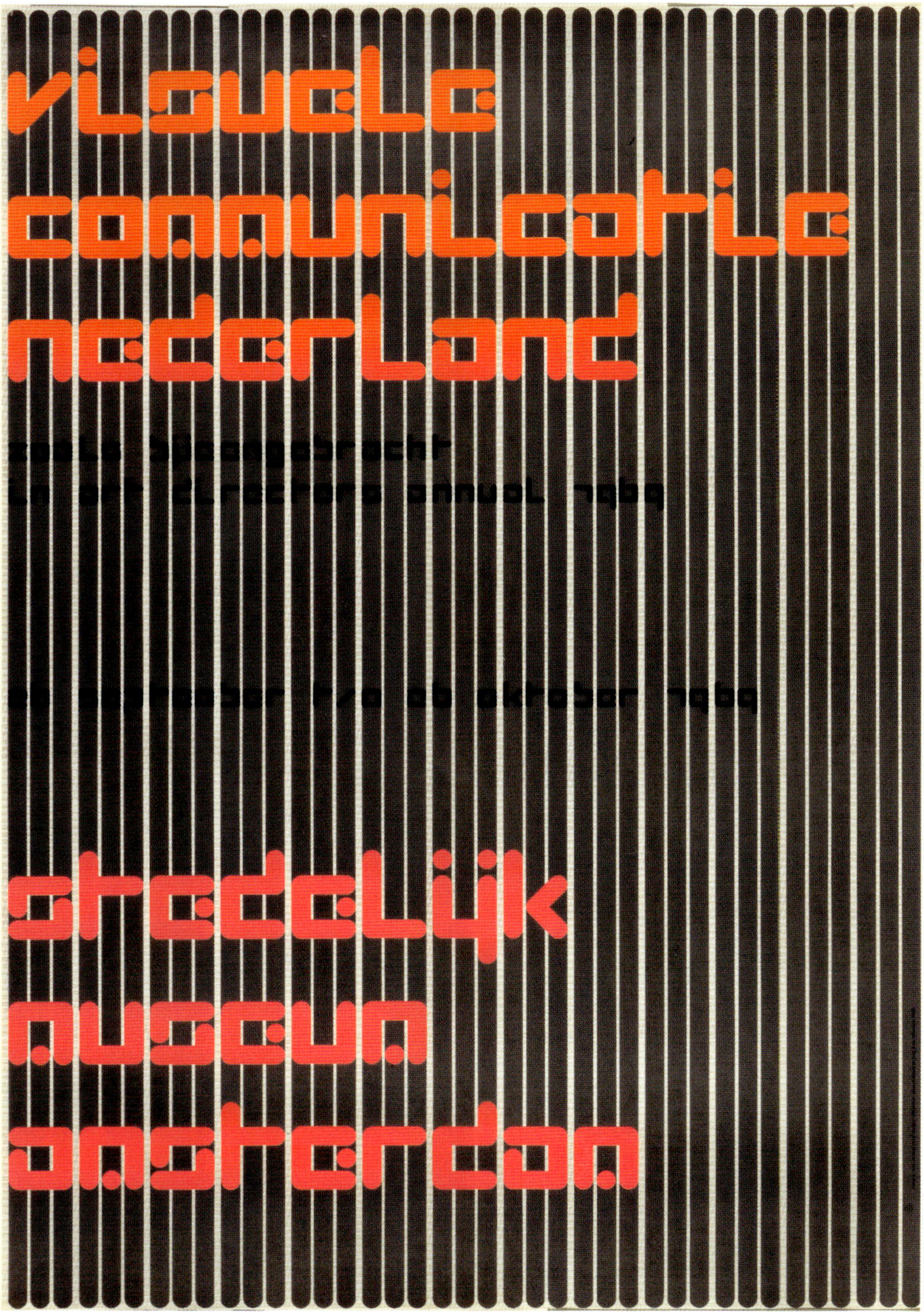

0611. Poster, Visuele Communicatie Nederland, Stedelijk Museum (Netherlands), 1969, Wim Crouwel

0612. Textile, Rivers, ca. 1972, Gretl and Leo Wollner

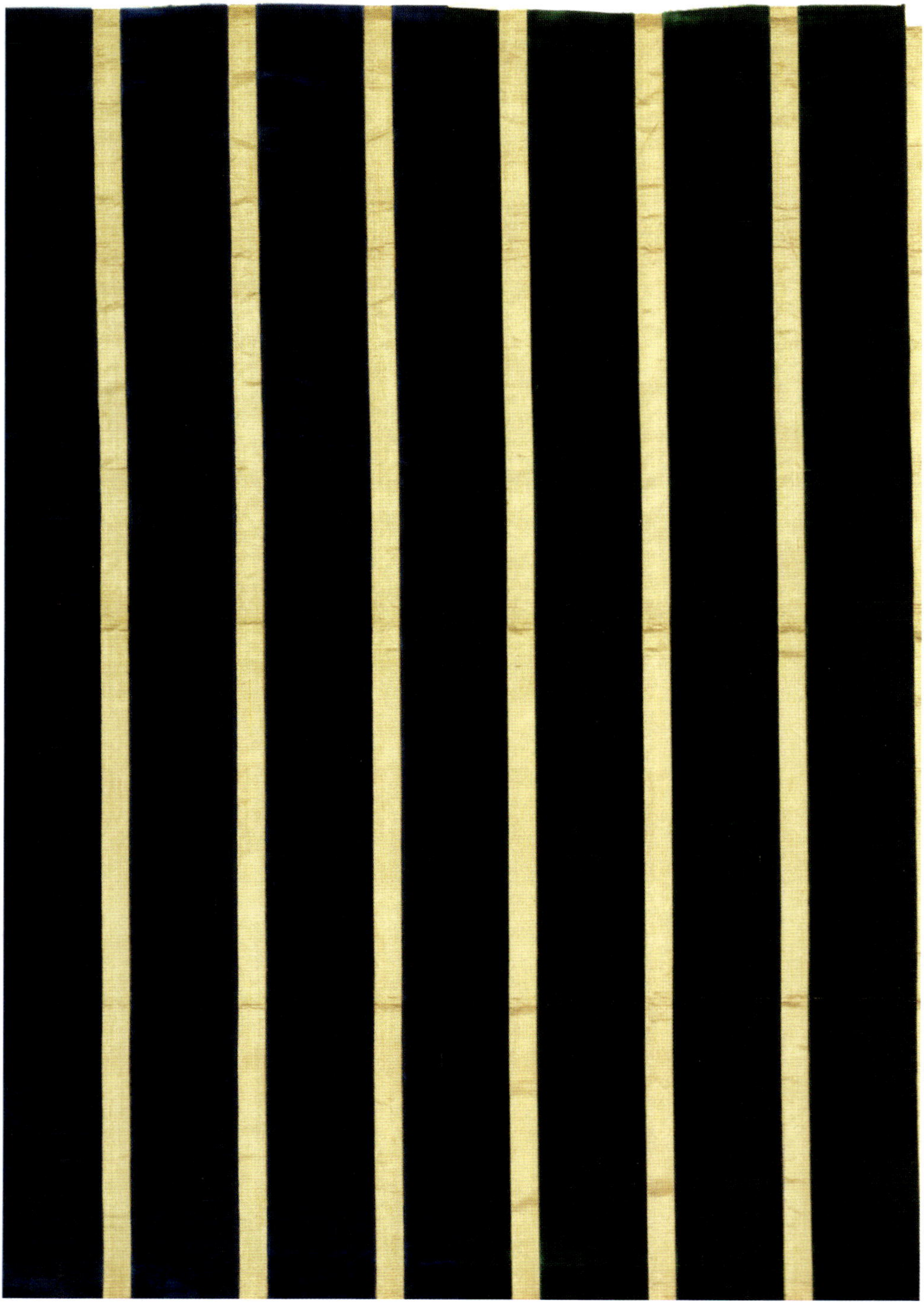

0613. Textile, France, ca. 1920, Herman A. Elsberg

0614. Sidewall, 1860, Dufour et Leroy
0615. Textile, Faruk, 1952, Armi Ratia

0616. Textile, Remoulade, 1956, Jack Lenor Larsen

0617. Sidewall, Newsworthy, 2010, Lori Weitzner

0618. Hand-woven sample, USA, before 1948, Anni Albers

0619. Hand-woven sample, USA, ca. 1945, Anni Albers

0620. Book illustration (detail), *Encyclopédie, ou, Dictionnaire raisonné des sciences, des arts et des métiers*, ca. 1769, Denis Diderot

0621. Side chair, France, ca. 1939, René Drouet
0622. Mark Hopkins House side chair, USA, ca. 1878–80, Herter Brothers

0623. DCM side chairs, USA, 1946, Charles and Ray Eames

0624. Sandows No. 5 side chair, France, 1929, René Herbst
0625. B5 side chair, Germany, 1926–27, Marcel Breuer

0626. Lounge chair, USA, 1939, Henrik Van Keppel and Taylor Green

0627. Barcelona chair, Germany, 1929, Ludwig Mies van der Rohe

0628. Trade catalog cover, DESTA tubular steel furniture, ca. 1930, DESTA Stahlmöbel

0629. Book illustration, DESTA tubular steel furniture, ca. 1930, DESTA Stahlmöbel

0630. Drawing, Design for a Dining Chair with Arms, 1955, Finn Juhl

0631. Small Diamond chair, USA, ca. 1957, Harry Bertoia

Model number 41 armchair, designed 1931–32
this example manufactured ca. 1935–40
Alvar Aalto (Finnish, 1898–1976)
Manufactured by Huonekalu-ja Rakennustyötehdas (Turku, Finland)
Bent birch plywood, solid birch
Museum purchase through gift of Linda and Irwin Berman and from General Acquisitions Endowment Fund, 2008-5-1

The Model 41 (Paimio) armchair is among architect Alvar Aalto's most recognized furniture forms, and has become an icon of twentieth-century design. Aalto was born in 1898 in Kuortane, Finland, and studied architecture at the Helsinki University of Technology from 1916 to 1921. He opened his own architectural practice in 1923. His first major project, the design of the Viipuri Library (1927–33), provided Aalto with many ideas that coalesced in his design of the Paimio Sanatorium (constructed 1928–32), a tuberculosis isolation facility named for the town in southwest Finland. From 1929 to 1933 Aalto carefully studied the needs of pulmonary tuberculosis patients. Before the advent of antibiotics and modern treatment methods in the mid-twentieth century, tuberculosis patients would have spent months or years in a sanatorium, often located in the countryside or mountains, where they could breathe fresh air and rest continually in an effort to cure the painful, wasting disease. Aalto designed the Paimio facility and its furnishings, exemplifying modernist ideals of an all-encompassing design program. His stamp on modernism is characterized by the use of natural materials and organic forms that were minimal, functional, and that emphasized the human side of design. His intention was to create furniture more comfortable than the new tubular metal furniture considered suitable for institutional use, created by contemporaries such as Marcel Breuer, Ludwig Mies van der Rohe, and Charlotte Perriand. Aalto was influenced by these designers and owned some of their furniture, but felt that although chromed tubular steel was sanitary and durable, "psychophysically [it was] not good for the human being. The sanatorium needed furniture that . . . was better for the human touch and more suitable as the general material for the long and painful life in a sanatorium." [1]

The Model 41 armchair **(0632)** was used in the sanatorium's lecture room (**0634**). The chair's back was angled to aid breathing, while the horizontal slits at the top provided ventilation for the sitter's neck since sporadic sweating was a tubercular symptom. There was no leg support, since the chair was intended for indoor use, so a patient's legs did not have to be raised off the ground to avoid cold drafts. The curved, flat armrests provided an easy grip and stable support for a weak patient rising from a seated position.

The Model 41 chair is a culmination of Aalto's early experimentation with **laminated** wood. From the late 1920s he experimented with plywood and wood strips, working with Otto Korhonen, the technical director of the furniture manufacturer Huonekalu-ja Rakennustyötehdas, in Turku, near Paimio. After extensive testing, they solved the difficult technical problems in producing the bending ribbonlike laminated strips and plywood sheet forms, while maintaining the materials' resilience and strength. Huonekalu-ja Rakennustyötehdas became the first manufacturer of the chair.

The form was achieved by **bending** the laminated and solid-wood elements in hot metal presses.

The Model 41 chair's one-piece seat suspended in its own frame displayed a structural rationalism essential to modernist design. The juxtaposition of the flowing curved

0632. Model Number 41 armchair, Finland, ca. 1935–40, Alvar Aalto

0633. Long chair, Estonia and England, 1936, Marcel Breuer

lines of the frame and the broad scrolling plane of the seat in warm, natural wood expresses an inviting, organic quality. Aalto said the chair was the first "resilient" plywood chair and "though buoyant as a spring cushion, the seat back is virtually unbreakable." Early examples of the chair include color variations such as seat and frame in natural wood finish or a black lacquered seat in a plain wood frame. In 1933 the Model 41 chair was shown in England at an exhibition of Finnish design sponsored by *The Architecture Review*, and by 1934 it was marketed there by the just-founded British importer and distributor Finmar. With his **bentwood** designs gaining popularity in international markets, Aalto, his wife the architect and designer Aino Marsio Aalto, art historian Nils-Gustav Hahl, and the Finnish industrialists Harry and Marie Gullichsen established the firm Artek in 1935 to produce and distribute Aalto's furniture. Artek has been active from that time to the present, and the Model 41 chair is still in production. **CT**

1 Alvar Aalto, "The Humanizing of Architecture," *Technology Review* vol. 43, no. 1 (November, 1940): 14-16, quoted in "Excerpts from Alvar Aalto's Articles on Interior and Furniture Design," in *Alvar Aalto Furniture*, ed. Juhani Pallasmaa (Cambridge, MA: MIT Press, 1985), 118.

Further References

Alvar Aalto Foundation. *Alvar Aalto: Designer*. Helsinski: Alvar Aalto Museum, 2005.
The Architectural Review, 1933, Vol 74.
Campbell, Margaret. "From Cure Chair to 'Chaise Longue': Medical Treatment and the Form of the Modern Recliner." *Journal of Design History* 12, no. 4 (1999): 327–43. www.jstor.org/stable/1316241.
Dachs, Sandra, Patricia de Muga, and Laura García Hintze, eds. *Alvar Aalto: Objects and Furniture Design*. Barcelona: Ediciones Polígrafa, 2007.
Davies, Kevin. "Finmar and the Furniture of the Future: The Sale of Alvar Aalto's Plywood Furniture in the UK, 1934–1939." *Journal of Design History* 11, no. 2 (1998): 145–46.
Hiesinger, Kathryn and George Marcus. *Landmarks of Twentieth-Century Design: An Illustrated Handbook*. New York: Abbeville Press, 1993.
Miller, William C. "Furniture, Painting, and Applied Designs: Alvar Aalto's Search for Architectural Form." *The Journal of Decorative and Propaganda Arts* 6 (Autumn 1987): 6–25. www.jstor.org/stable/1503910.
Juhani Pallasmaa, ed. *Alvar Aalto Furniture*. Cambridge, MA: MIT Press, 1985.
Pelkonen, Eeva-Liisa. *Alvar Aalto: Architecture, Modernity, and Geopolitics*. New Haven, CT: Yale University Press, 2009.

0634. Photograph, Model 41 (Paimio) armchairs in the lecture room of the Paimio Sanatorium, 1928–32, Gustav Welin, Alvar Aalto Museum

0635. Zig-Zag chair, Netherlands, ca. 1934, Gerrit Rietveld

0636. S chair, England, 1988, Tom Dixon

0637. Drawing, Design for Vegetal Chair (detail), 2005, Erwan and Ronan Bouroullec

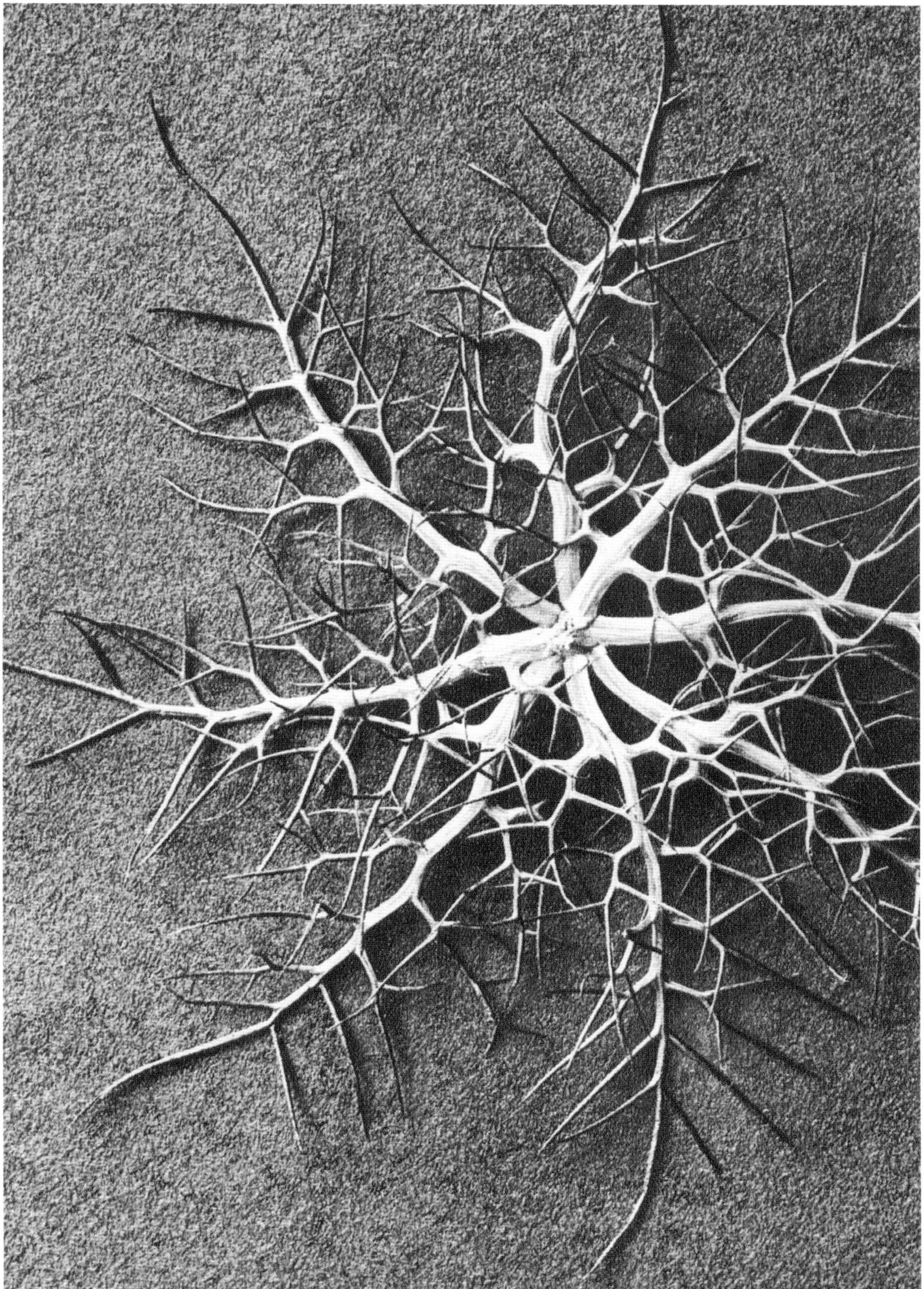

0638. Book illustration, *Art Forms in Nature*, Second Series, 1932, Karl Blossfeldt

Solid C2 chair, 2009
Patrick Jouin (French, b. 1967)
Manufactured by Materialise NV (Leuven, Belgium)
Stereolithography-formed epoxy resin
Museum purchase from the Members' Acquisitions Fund of Cooper-Hewitt, National Design Museum, 2009-8-1

The Solid C2 chair by French designer Patrick Jouin is a notable addition to the museum's growing collection of twenty-first-century **digital**ly designed and produced work. The Solid C2 was manufactured by what is known as rapid, or **additive**, manufacturing, which is more commonly called 3D printing. The specific technique used to create the Solid C2 is called **stereolithography**, in which a computer-controlled laser heats and solidifies a photosensitive epoxy resin upon contact. This process builds up a form, layer by minuscule layer, to create a single complete object, including any moving parts with joints or hinges. This method is a leap from traditional handcrafting and conventional mass-production methods such as **carving**, **molding**, and assembling parts.[1]

The technology enables designers to create forms that cannot be achieved with predigital techniques. The forms can be mass produced, or customized and made as limited editions or unique works just by altering the digital files. Rapid manufacturing is still a young and often costly technology, but it can enhance a designer's freedom to create, and, as it advances, will offer an alternative to older mass-production methods that rely on standardization to achieve easily manufactured, low-cost objects.

Since the 1980s, when it was first developed, **rapid manufacturing** has mainly been used to produce items such as automobile parts, industrial components, and architectural models. In 2004, Belgium-based Materialise NV, a firm specializing in such manufacturing, invited several architects and designers, including Jouin, to use the technology to create furniture, lighting, and other functional objects geared for the interior and domestic use.

Jouin started the Solid C2 design process by **sketching** by hand. His drawing was converted into digital code, then the digital file was uploaded to a computer that guided the laser that "printed" the design onto the successive thin layers of resin. Jouin took poetic inspiration for the Solid C2's structure from close observations of nature—grass in particular. The chair resembles the complex, organic patterns and texture of bent, overlapping, and intersecting blades of grass that seem to grow and fold over onto themselves to form the legs, seat, and back. This effect creates a highly sculptural yet functional form that appears light and airy. The juxtaposition of solid and void, created by the many angled bladelike elements and irregular spaces, heightens the dramatic impact of the chair. Jouin would have found it extremely challenging, if even possible, to achieve such an intricate structure using conventional furniture-manufacturing techniques.

Three-D printing is rapidly evolving. The technology has reached the stage at which a designer can design an object, write the design to a digital file, then send the file to a manufacturer, who can print the object and deliver it directly to the end user. Small 3D printers suitable for use in design studios are becoming more widely available and affordable. Manufacturers are expanding the range of "printable" materials, applying rapid manufacturing technology to metals, ceramics, and more. Over the last forty years, successive waves of digitization have disrupted the previous analog technology: word processing on computers replaced both manual and

0639. Solid C2 chair, Belgium, 2009, Patrick Jouin

electric typewriters; Internet publication and distribution replaced desktop publishing; and most recently, wireless distribution has enabled global publication of e-books directly to tablets, displacing hard-copy books, magazines, and newspapers.
3D printing builds on each of these previous innovations.
The impact of 3D printing is not likely to be limited to disrupting existing technologies. As with each of the previous waves of digitized technologies, the ability to make exact copies of copyrighted works (such as texts, sound recordings, and images) not only makes infringement (deliberate or inadvertent) quick and easy to do, but also difficult to stop. As the use of 3D printing becomes more widespread, the potential for conflict between users of this new technology and owners of copyrighted designs that can be infringed quickly and easily is also likely to increase. **CT**

1 Cara McCarty, *Currents 101: Patrick Jouin* (Saint Louis: Saint Louis Art Museum, 2007), unpaginated.

Further References
Weinberg, Michael. *It Will Be Awesome if They Don't Screw It Up: 3D Printing, Intellectual Property, and the Fight Over the Next Great Disruptive Technology*. Washington, DC: Public Knowledge, 2010. https://www.publicknowledge.org/news-blog/blogs/it-will-be-awesome-if-they-dont-screw-it-up-3d-printing.
Weinberg, Michael. *What's the Deal with Copyright and 3D Printing?* Washington, DC: Public Knowledge, 2013. www.publicknowledge.org/news-blog/blogs/whats-the-deal-with-copyright-and-3d-printing.

0640. Knotted chair, Italy, designed 1996, made 2008, Marcel Wanders

0641. Drawing, Study for Osso Chair, 2011, Erwan and Ronan Bouroullec

0642. Drawing, Designs for Three Chairs, ca. 1990–93, Karim Rashid

0643. Vermelha chair, Italy, designed 1998, manufactured 2007, Fernando and Humberto Campana

0644. Cabbage chair, Japan, 2008, Oki Sato and Nendo

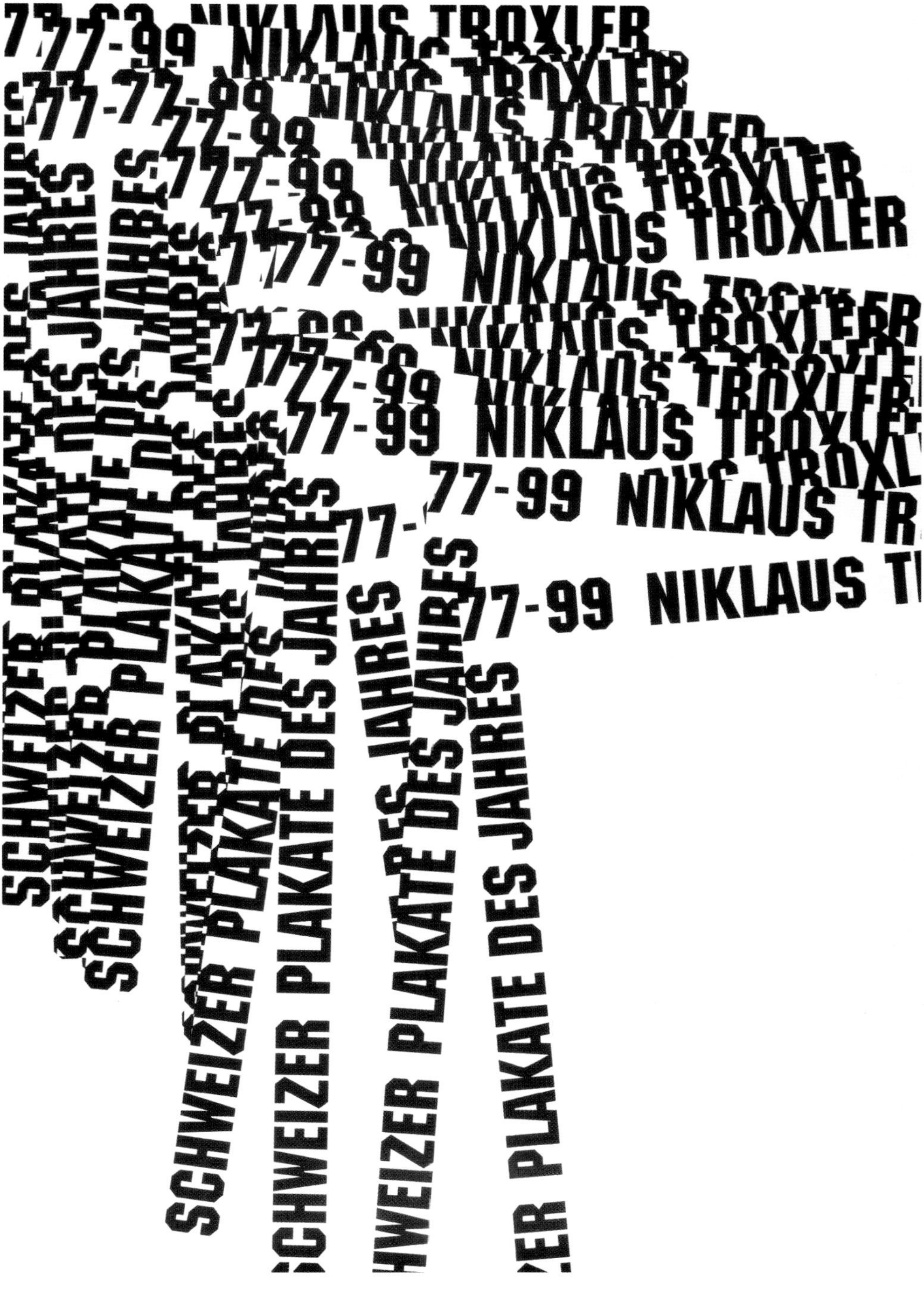

0645. Poster, Niklaus Troxler, Schweizer Plakate des Jahres 77–99, 2001, Niklaus Troxler

0646. Reclining rocking chair, Italy, ca. 1905, Antonio Volpe

0647. Rocking Chair No. 4, Austria, ca. 1860, Gebrüder (Brothers) Thonet

0648. DCW side chair, USA, 1946, Charles and Ray Eames

0649. Chair, England, ca. 1750–60
0650. Side chair, probably Northern Italy, ca. 1785, style of Michelangelo Pergolesi
0651. Chair, USA, ca. 1840, attributed to Duncan Phyfe

0652. Side chair, USA, 1901, Charles Rohlfs
0653. Scarsdale side chair, England, 1724–36, attributed to Thomas How
0654. Chair, England, 1844

0655. Armchair, England, ca. 1765
0656. Armchair, China (for export), ca. 1815
0657. Side chair, Germany, 1902, Peter Behrens

Causeuse d'Encoignure

Bois noir et Cuivres dorés.

Publié par D. Guilmard, r. de Lancry 2 Paris

0658. Book illustration, *Le garde-meuble*, 1841–51

0659. Writing desk, Italy, ca. 1902, Carlo Zen

0660. Argyle Tea Rooms armchair, Scotland, 1897, Charles Rennie Mackintosh

0661. Norman bar stools, England, 1997, Tom Dixon

0662. Bowls, China, late 19th–early 20th century

0663. Gloves, Italy, 1600–50

0664. Poster, Bayerische Staatsoper: *Rodelinda, Regina de' Longobardi*, Georg Friedrich Händel, 2003, Pierre Mendell

0665. Poster, He Who Stops Being Better Stops Being Good, IBM Excellence Plus, 1985, Paul Rand

0666. Up 1 chair, Italy, 1969, Gaetano Pesce

0667. Pastilli rocking chair, Finland, 1968, Eero Aarnio

0669. Salt and pepper shakers, Denmark, ca. 1975, Arne Petersen

0668. Colorstone salt and pepper shakers, USA, 1986, Lella and Massimo Vignelli with David Law

0670. Iroquois Casual stacking salt and pepper shakers, USA, 1947, Russel Wright

0671. Salt and pepper shakers, Germany, 1953, Wilhelm Wagenfeld

0673. Arc Touch flexible computer mouses with transceivers, USA, 2010, Microsoft Hardware User Experience Design Team

0672. Sinus bowls, Germany, ca. 1985–86, Lino Sabattini

0674. Paro goblets, Italy, 1983, Achille Castiglioni

THE "DOLPHIN."

Plate 123-G.

Plate 124-G.

For description, see opposite page.

0675. Book illustration, *Catalogue G*, 1888, J. L. Mott

0676. Vases, France, ca. 1905, Hector Guimard

0677. Stacking tea service, Italy, ca. 1970, Gabbianelli

FD-5

0678. Poster, FD-5: Flocking Diplomats New York: Time of Violation, 2008, Catalogtree

0679. Drawing, Paper Sample, Red, England, n.d.

0680. R-72 portable radio, Japan, ca. 1970, National Panasonic Radio, Matushita Electrical Industrial Co., Ltd.

0681. Pair of child's chairs with table insert, Denmark, 1957, Kristian Vedel

0682. Kobenstyle casserole and lid, Denmark, 1956, Jens H. Quistgaard

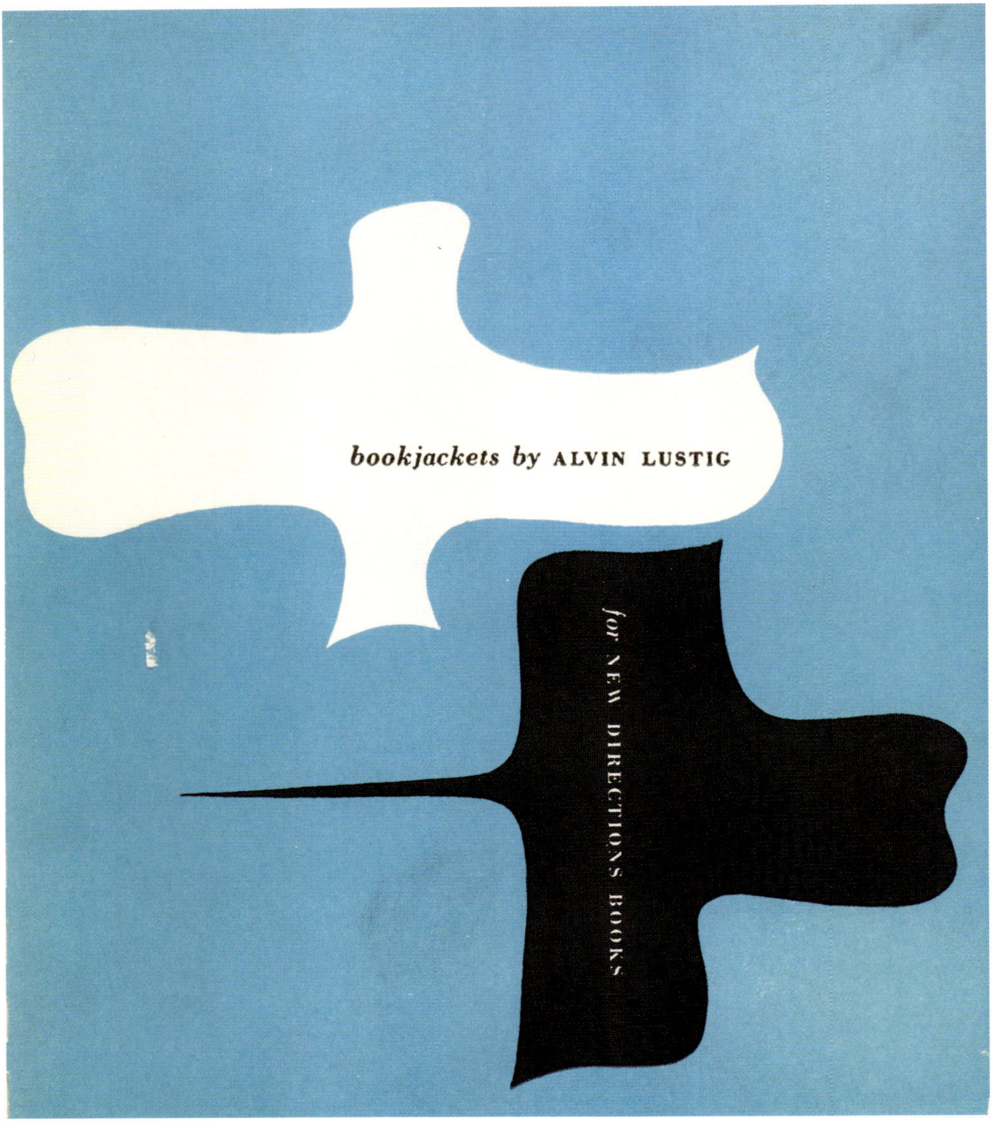

0683. Book cover, *Bookjackets by Alvin Lustig* for New Directions Books, 1947, Alvin Lustig

0684. Chest for Stereo, USA, 1973, Wendell Castle

Balcony grille, Paris, France, 1909–11
Hector Guimard (French, 1867–1942)
Manufactured by Saint Dizier Foundry (St. Dizier, Champagne, France)
Cast iron
Museum purchase from the Members' Acquisitions Fund of
Cooper-Hewitt, National Design Museum, 2011-28-1

Hector Guimard, considered one of the most prominent innovators of the art nouveau style, developed his commitment to this style in many media. Active in Paris from 1885 to 1938, when he moved to New York, Guimard designed myriad decorative objects from ceramics to furniture to create complete art nouveau interiors. Although best known as the designer of the iconic Paris Métro station metalwork, a public work, his architectural design production was more focused on domestic buildings—from private residences to apartment buildings. His designs for interiors included the fittings such as fireplace surrounds and decorative metalwork like doorplates, as well as his furniture designs—generally elongated tall-backed chairs with curvilinear cresting and legs—ceramics, picture frames, and other accessories, examples of which are in Cooper Hewitt's collections.

Guimard designed residential buildings developing art nouveau not only as an architectural style but as part of a business project. The building facades relate to their inventive interiors through their curving, sinuous art nouveau forms and related detail elements, including **cast-iron** balcony grilles like Cooper Hewitt's example **(0685)**. The design of this grille appears in multiple Guimard constructions, including an ensemble of buildings built from 1909 to 1911 in Paris's sixteenth arrondissement (district). The buildings at 17, 19, and 21 Rue La Fontaine and 8 and 10 Rue Agar, from which this example comes, featured a variety of harmonizing designs of balconies and grilles. Produced in collaboration with the Saint Dizier Foundry, the Guimard ironwork designs represent early mass production. The process used to achieve larger production volume started with Guimard's drawings followed by cast-iron models with hand-finished decoration such as one now in Cooper Hewitt's collection **(0686)**. From this model, developers and other clients could place orders with Saint Dizier for ironworks in a variety of sizes. From private French residences to small Parisian apartments, such cast-iron works appear in a variety of exterior schemes. Guimard's grilles represent a collaboration between designer and industry that resulted in more widely available and visible products that played an important role in early twentieth-century visual culture.

Cooper Hewitt has a substantial collection of Guimard-designed domestic objects, including ceramics, gilt-bronze and other metals, furniture, textile designs for his wife, and a large number of drawings, including one showing the building with balcony grilles **(0687)**. All were donated by his widow to the museum in 1942 after his death in New York. **SDC**

0685. Balcony grille, France, 1909–11, Hector Guimard

0686. Model for Grillework, France, 1909-11, Hector Guimard

0687. Drawing, Societé Immobilière de la rue Moderne, No. 6, Paris, France: Design for the Façade, 1909, Hector Guimard

0688. Photograph, Apartment Building (No. 3), 1911, Hector Guimard

0689. Drawing, A.H. Barney Residence, USA: Design for Mermaid Window, 1882, Elihu Vedder

0690. Textile, Femme à Marguerite, 1898–1900, Alphonse Maria Mucha

0691. Print, Der Kuss, from *Pan*, 1898, Peter Behrens

0692. Textile, Honeysuckle, 1876, William Morris

0693. Clock, Netherlands, ca. 1910, Arnhem Faience Factory

0694. Paris Métro medallion, France, 1900, Hector Guimard

0695. Poster, Tropon est l'aliment le plus concentré, 1898, Henry van de Velde

0696. Teapot and lid, USA, 1988, Chunghi Choo

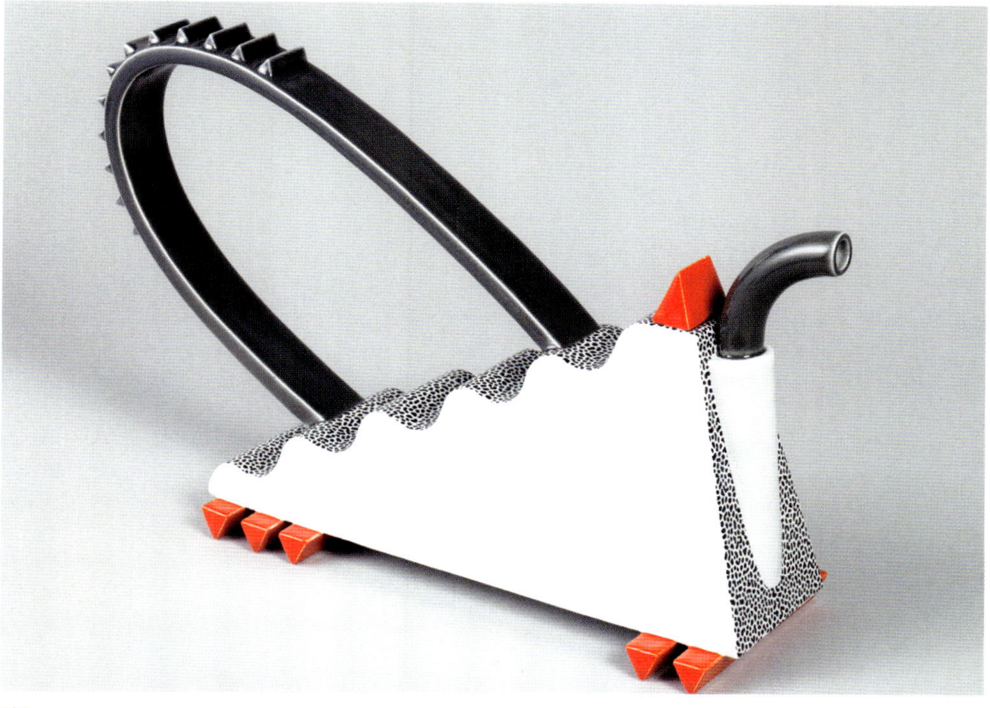

0697. Corvus Corax teapot and lid, Italy, 1982, Matteo Thun

0698. Book illustration, *Urformen der Kunst*, 1929, Karl Blossfeldt

0699. Footed bowl, USA, 1905–16, Louis Comfort Tiffany

0700. Print, Design for Cartouche with Fountain and Sea Putti, 1738/1745, Jean-François Cuvilliés

0701. Print, Winged Griffon on a Rocaille Bracket, 1745, Alexis Peyrotte

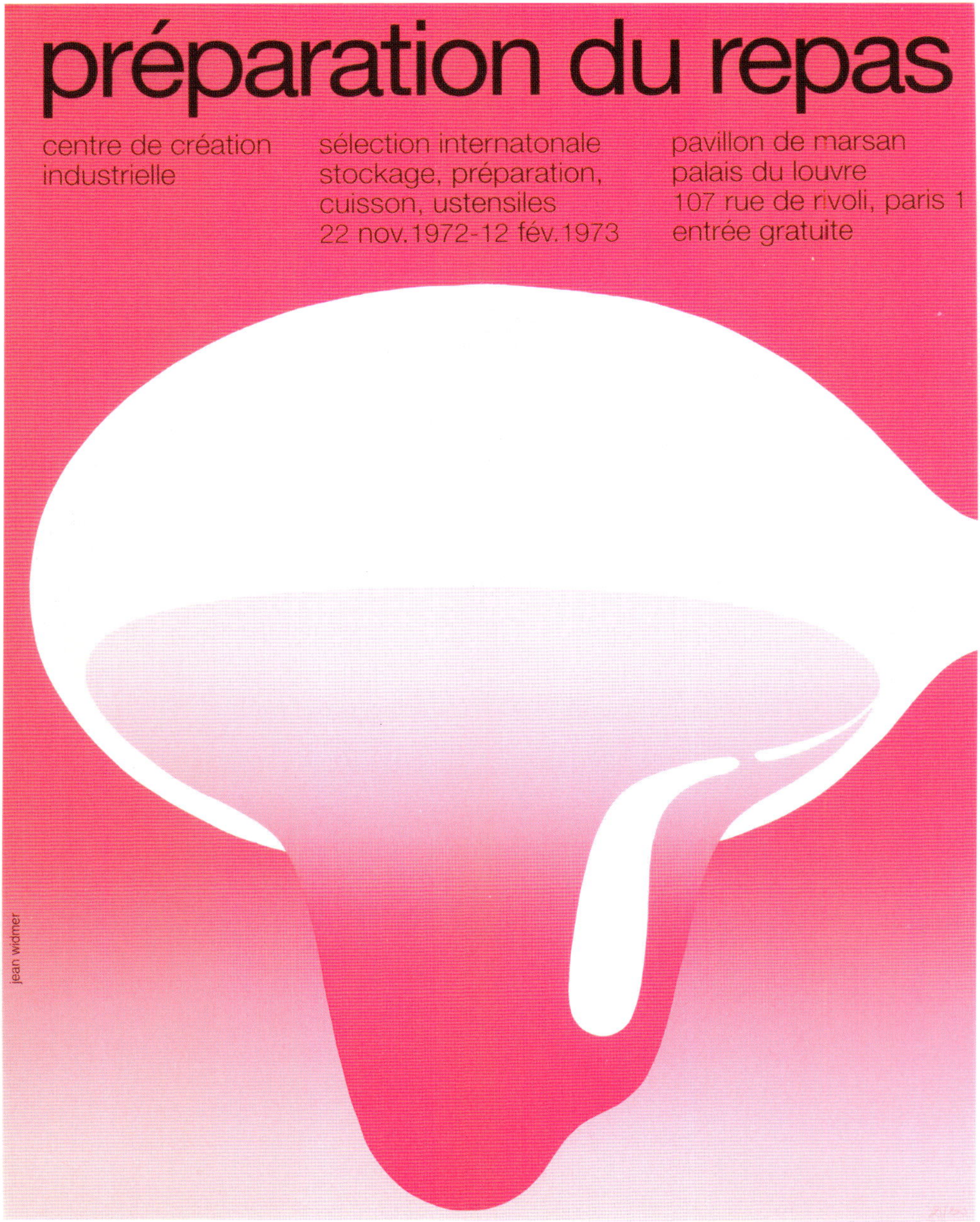

0702. Poster, Préparation du repas, sélection international stockage, préparation, caisson, utensiles, France, 1972, Jean Widmer, Louvre (Paris, France)

0703. Ashtray, USA, 1949, Russel Wright

0704. Powder compact, USA, 1978, Elsa Peretti

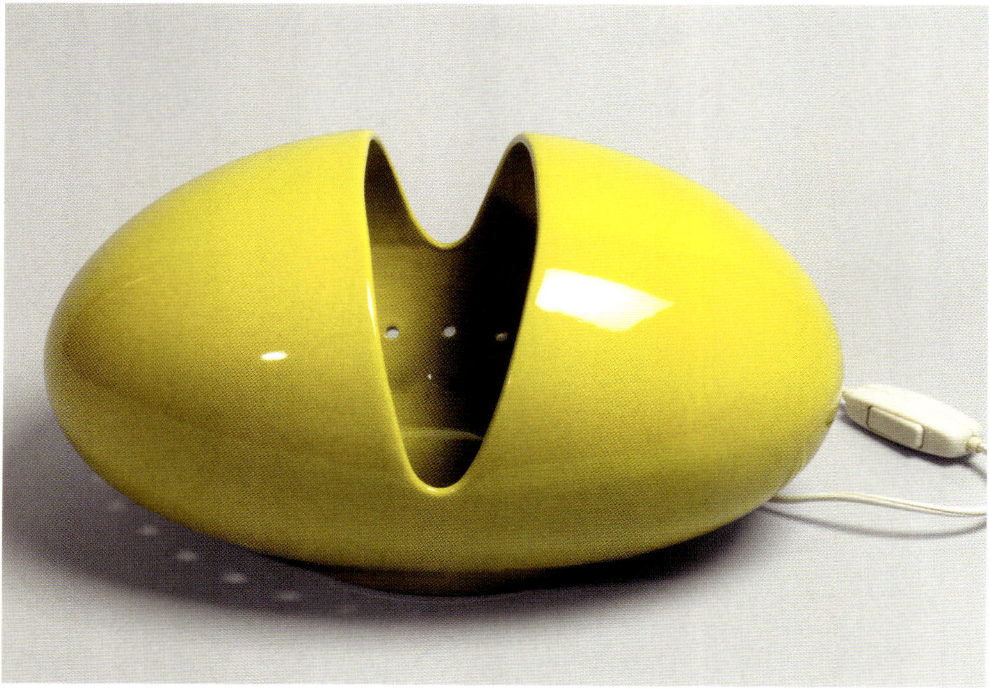

0705. Uovo Orizzontale (Horizontal Egg) table lamp, Italy, 1967, Cesare Casati

0706. American Modern cream boat, USA, 1937, Russel Wright

0707. American Modern celery dish, USA, 1937, Russel Wright

0708. Iroquois Casual butter dish and lid, USA, 1947, Russel Wright

Photograph, Ceiling fixture, Rockefeller Center, 1932
Designed by Caldwell and Company (New York, New York, USA, 1895–ca. 1944)
Smithsonian Libraries, NK2115.5.L5 S54

This photograph of a Rockefeller Center pendant light is one of almost fifty thousand photographs and drawings in the Smithsonian Design Library's Edward F. Caldwell Collection. Caldwell and Company was a premier designer and manufacturer of custom lighting fixtures and fine metalwork from the late nineteenth to the mid-twentieth centuries. This immense visual resource is one of the largest such archives of a single American lighting company.

The firm was founded in 1895 in New York City by Edward F. Caldwell and his partner Victor F. von Lossberg, who had met while working at the lighting firm Archer and Pancoast. Caldwell had achieved great success at Archer and Pancoast working on commissions for the architectural firm McKim, Mead and White that included the New York State Building at the 1893 World's Columbian Exposition. He developed a lasting relationship with Stanford White, resulting in Caldwell and Company's securing numerous commissions, most notably the White House renovation in 1902. Many of their magnificent chandeliers, wall sconces, and torchieres continue to be prominent features throughout the White House, including the East Room ballroom and State Dining Room. Their work still graces many of New York City's best known public and private buildings, as well as others throughout the country and beyond. Working with many of the most renowned architects of their day, including Warren and Wetmore, Carrere and Hastings, and Cass Gilbert, they designed fixtures for most of the grand Beaux Arts mansions, including the homes of Henry Clay Frick, John Jacob Astor, J. Pierpont Morgan, Frederick W. Vanderbilt, and Andrew Carnegie. Public building commissions included Grand Central Terminal, the New York Public Library, and the magnificent art deco chandeliers and wall sconces for Radio City Music Hall. Visitors to Cooper Hewitt will see a series of bronze and alabaster ceiling fixtures in the Great Hall that leads to a massive chandelier illuminating the grand staircase—these are all original 1901 Caldwell designs for Andrew Carnegie's mansion.

The craftsmanship of Caldwell and Company also transferred to modernism, as seen in this cosmic ceiling fixture **(0709)** the firm designed in 1932 for the art deco icon Rockefeller Center. Built from 1930 to 1939 by a team of top architects led by Raymond Hood, Rockefeller Center consisted of fourteen buildings within three city blocks, making a mini city within a city of skyscrapers a reality for the first time. This commission was one of the largest and most prestigious a lighting manufacturer could achieve, and Caldwell was the obvious choice for the job. Each piece was custom designed and manufactured in their foundry at 36–40 West 15th Street, where they employed over a thousand people during the height of their operations. At a time when American manufacturing was at its peak, Caldwell and Company were masters at pairing design and craftsmanship with new electrical technologies, establishing a golden age of art lighting. The Edward F. Caldwell Collection, part of the Smithsonian Design Library archive and available online, is a valuable resource for historic preservationists, architectural scholars, lighting designers, and collectors. Because these fixtures are often found unmarked, disassembled, incomplete, or separated from their original locations, this archive is often the only source for identifying a Caldwell fixture in its original state. Browsing the archive also reveals the wide variety of tastes and styles that were rapidly developing and changing during an incredible time of growth in America. **JCB**

0709. Photograph, Ceiling fixture, Rockefeller Center, 1932, Caldwell and Company

0712. Drop teapot, sugar bowl, and cream pitcher, Germany, 1971, Luigi Colani

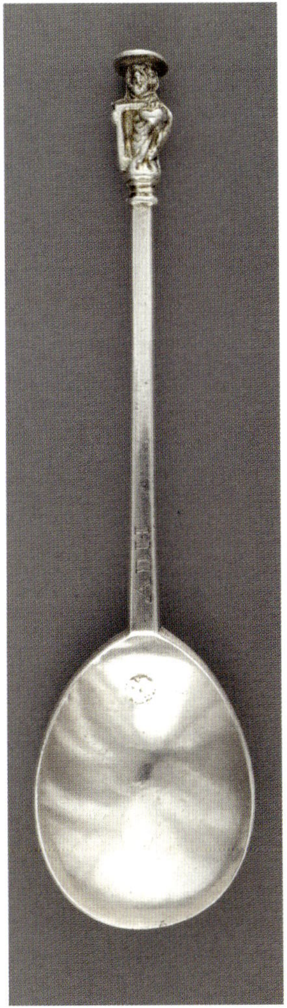

0710. St. Thomas or St. Matthew spoon, England, ca. 1661
0711. Fork and spoon, Germany, ca. 1600–30

0713. American Modern tableware and Pinch flatware, USA, 1937–50, Russel Wright

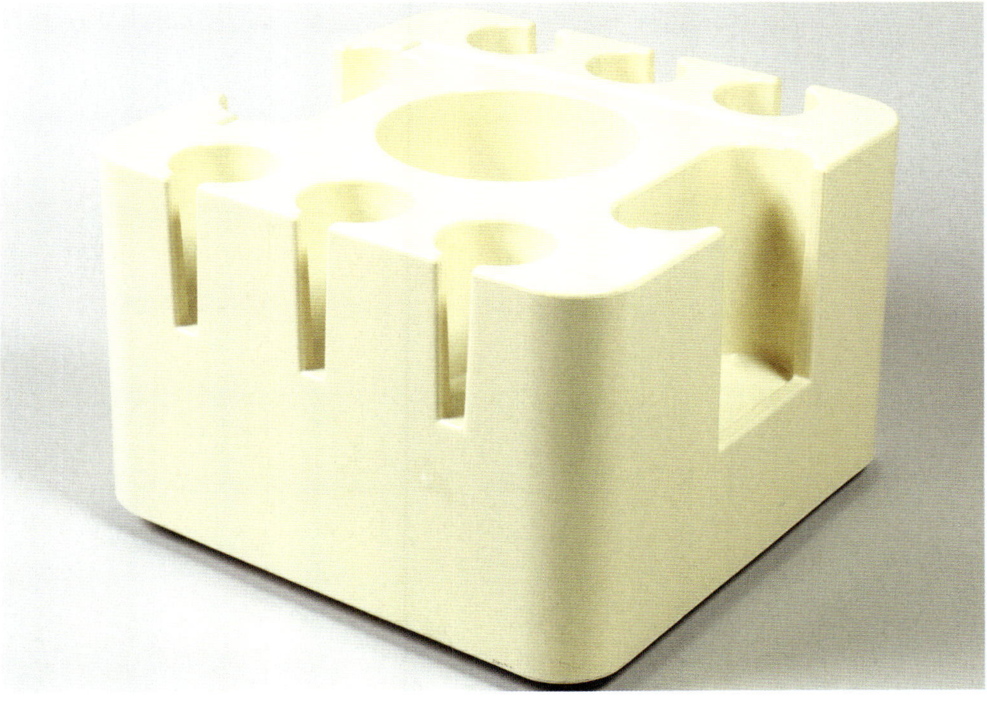

0714. Bacco cocktail cabinet, Italy, 1967–69, Sergio Mazza

Trade catalog, Specimens of Silver, Engraved, Oxidized and Gold Inlaid Ware, 1884
Designed by the firm of Reed & Barton
From *Reed & Barton, artistic workers in silver & gold plate : Reed & Barton trade mark. Sales & exhibition rooms, 37 Union Square, New York, and at their factories, Taunton, Mass., U.S.A., where all communications should be addressed*, p. 292
Illustrations by John A. J. (John Angel James) Wilcox (American, b. 1835)
Color lithograph on paper
Gift of Reed & Barton, ca. 1990, Smithsonian Libraries, f 046780

Manufacturers' trade catalogs offer important insight into the history of business, technology, marketing, consumption, and design, and are a valuable research tool because they are often the primary or only source that documents products and designs from a given time or place. Published in 1884 at the height of the Victorian era, this Reed & Barton catalog **(0715)** illustrates the styles and taste of an important era in American history and material culture. It demonstrates the complex dining and entertaining customs, the variety of design, and the growing consumerism of the period. It has beautifully engraved illustrations, with several color plates, and every object and plate number is identified, indexed, and on a price list.

The roots of the still-operating Reed & Barton go back to 1824, although it has seen several different ownerships. The firm's high-quality goods could compete with European and British silvers and established a reputation for well-crafted and beautifully designed sterling silver tableware. They were a pioneer in silver plating in the 1850s. When the famous Comstock Lode of silver was discovered in Nevada in the 1850s, silver became more widely available, greatly increasing the domestic manufacture and accessibility of sterling silver and silverlike tableware for many American families. Reed & Barton took advantage of the new technology of electroplating, in which a layer of silver is deposited on a cheaper metal, making goods of silver or gold more affordable to the growing American middle class. Ninety categories of products are listed in the index. The catalog contains 2,300 gold and silver items in sterling, silver plate, and gold plate: tea sets, pickle casters, grape shears, revolving butter dishes, toothpick holders, soup tureens, and candelabra. They made the complicated sets of flatware, beverage, and dinner services, with many specific-use components often used in the Victorian era, when dining could be an elaborate and complicated ritual. If dining at home without guests, dinner was five or six courses; when entertaining, as many as thirteen to twenty courses could be served. Four knives, a soup spoon, and four forks were standard place settings, with specialized cutlery and table accessories laid out as required for each course. As more specialized tableware was needed, so was the desire for a wider selection of styles. Employing the most skillful artisans, under the highest designing talent, Reed & Barton were able to create items ranging from traditional and historical patterns to more exotic designs of the Near East, the Aesthetic movement, and the Japonesque. This catalog is a great document of the eclectic tastes of the Victorian era. **EB**

0715. Trade catalog, Specimens of Silver, Engraved, Oxidized and Gold Inlaid Ware, 1884, Reed & Barton

BUCK & LINDNER, LITH. CENTRE cor. of WALKER ST. N.Y.

SPECIMENS OF SILVER ENGRAVED, OXIDIZED, AND GOLD INLAID WARE.

For Prices in other Styles of Finish, or in cases, see Spoon and Fork Price Lists, Pages 316-319, 324 & 325.

(CUTS FULL SIZE)

292 a.

0716. Book illustration, Artistic Workers in Silver & Gold Plate,1884, Reed & Barton

0718. Drawing, Design for Highlight / Pinch Flatware (detail), 1948, Russel Wright

0717. Drawing, Design for Knife, Fork, and Spoon (detail), 1950–70, Tommi Parzinger

REED & BARTON
SILVER AND GOLD PLATE.

PATENTED.
No. 1365. Chased, 1 No. 110 Bottle, $9.00. (ENDITE)

No. 1510. 1 No. 130 Bottle, $6.50. (LINEN)

No. 1235. 2 No. 120 Bottles, $9.50. (ENDLESS)

No. 1520. 1 No. 148 Bottle, $9.50. (LINGUAL)

No. 1160. 1 No. 95 Bottle, $17.00. (LINGUIST)
No. 1160. 1 No. 90 Bottle, 16.00. (LINIMENT)
Gold and Oxidized, $5.00 extra.

No. 1485. Hammered, 1 No. 125 Bottle, $8.75. (LINGER)
Gold-lined, 9.75. (LINGO)

PATENTED.
No. 1272. Chased, 1 No. 100 Bottle, $7.75. (ENCOMPASS)

No. 1170. 1 No. 37 Bottle, $8.00. (ENDORSER)

No. 1175. 1 No. 82 Bottle, $10.00. (EMULATOR)

No. 1250. Chased, 1 No. 100 Bottle, $6.00. (EXIT)

PICKLE CASTERS.

(CUTS ONE-THIRD SIZE.)

—163—

REED & BARTON.

No. 3166. FLUTED AND ORIENTAL CHASED TEA SET.

No. 3166. Set of Six Pieces, $75.00. (REGIMES) With Bell Slop, 77.00. (REGION) Coffee. $17.00. Tea, 6 half-pints. $16.00. Water, 5 half-pints. $15.50. Sugar. $10.00. Cream, gold-lined. $10.00. Bowl, gold-lined, $6.50. With Bell, 8.50. Set, without gold lining. $4.00 less.

No. 3166. Urn, 12 half-pints, $40.00. (REGISTER) Kettle, 8 half-pints, $32.00. (REIGN) Spoon Holder, gold-lined, $9.50. (REGRESS) Butter Dish, $12.50. (REGRET) Sirup, $11.50. (REHEARSE) No. 456. Waiter, 24 inch, $62.00. (REGULATE)

(CUT ONE-THIRD SIZE.)

—7—

0721. Garbo wastebasket, USA, 1996, Karim Rashid

0722. Vase, Italy, 1968–69, Lüsi Beckman

Radio Nurse intercom speaker, 1937–38
Isamu Noguchi (American, 1904–88)
Manufactured by Zenith Radio Corporation (Chicago, Illinois, USA)
Molded Bakelite, metal
Gift of Mel Byars, 1991-59-61

A fascinating confluence of design, art, technology, utility, and economic, social, and cultural influences is embodied in the Radio Nurse. It was part of a wireless microphone and speaker system manufactured by the Zenith Radio Corporation in 1938, conceived as a baby monitor and aid for home or hospital. The system consists of a highly sculptural transmitter called the Radio Nurse, designed by sculptor Isamu Noguchi, and a boxlike receiver called the Guardian Ear.

Noguchi designed the Nurse component as an abstract headlike form. The simple ovoid shape, with speaker grille in front, resembles *kendo* masks that Noguchi wore during his childhood years in Japan; it also recalls the shape of a woman's head framed by the scarflike headdress worn by many nurses in the 1930s. While metal housings were more typical for early-twentieth-century electrical devices, the Radio Nurse was made of the new substance: Bakelite, a thermal plastic that could be **molded** into any shape, resulting in a hard, durable housing ideal for such devices since it was nonconductive and heat resistant. The softly curved, mottled brown form of the Nurse transmitter could pass as a fashionable accent in a contemporary living room, while the small, white metal Guardian Ear receiver could be placed discretely in the nursery or bedroom to be monitored **(0724)**.

The idea for the product grew out of the need of E. F. McDonald, Jr., president of Zenith, to monitor the nursery of his infant daughter. The Commander, as McDonald was known, was a navy veteran of World War I who had specialized in the young technologies of sound recording and radio. After a successful career in automobile finance, he became interested in the radio business, a burgeoning new enterprise. Having funds but lacking a patent license for manufacture, in 1921 he partnered with the founders of the Chicago Radio Laboratory (Z-nith), who held such a license. Two years later the partnership was formally incorporated as Zenith Radio Corporation, with McDonald as general manager. He positioned Zenith as a high-end radio manufacturer, but with the stock market crash of 1929 and the Great Depression, Zenith's sales declined. Under McDonald's leadership the company adapted, developing low-cost product lines that restored profits by 1933. McDonald would go on to lead the company for more than thirty years.

McDonald was skilled at finding practical applications for radio technology. He and his family lived aboard the *Mizpah*, his 185-foot yacht moored in Chicago's harbor when not sailing. More than a home, the vessel was outfitted with an array of radio equipment and served as a floating laboratory for Zenith. In 1937, five years after the infamous kidnapping and murder of aviator Charles Lindbergh's twenty-month-old son, and just one year after the kidnapper was convicted in the "trial of the century," the partially deaf McDonald, concerned for his young daughter's safety, decided to engineer a listening apparatus. Drawing on Zenith's new developments in wireless radio, McDonald started to experiment, rigging a microphone in the yacht's nursery and placing speakers "scattered about the boat." [1]

Adept at marketing, McDonald realized that the intercom system could be developed into a commercial product. He commissioned Noguchi to create a stylish housing for the transmitter. To generate income during the Depression, Noguchi, who had studied in the late 1920s with Constantin Brancusi in Paris, took commissions to

0723. Radio Nurse intercom speaker, USA, 1937–38, Isamu Noguchi

sculpt portrait heads in his distinctive minimalist style. However, by 1937 he had tired of this work: "I was willing to do almost anything to get out of my rut—to find the means to practice an art I did not have to sell. . . . That year I did my only strictly industrial design called 'The Radio Nurse,' a device for listening in to other rooms within a house, as a precaution against kidnapping." [2]

The Radio Nurse and Guardian Ear intercom system debuted in March 1938. As a result of the Lindbergh case, there was a concern for kidnapping, but it was also a time of decreasing dependence on domestic help and changing ideas about child rearing—that encouraged parents to leave babies unattended for periods of time. According to Zenith's product brochure, "Radio Nurse enables you to leave the nursery, yet guard your baby. . . . Be modern! Keep an 'ear' on your children!" Retailing for $29.95, costly for a radio device, the Nurse was still far less than an original Noguchi sculpture. The phrase "Designed by Noguchi" is clearly molded into the back of the Bakelite form. As aesthetically appealing as it was functional, in November, 1938, Radio Nurse won first place in the Household Product category of *Modern Plastics Magazine*'s Modern Plastics Competition, and in 1939, was shown in the Whitney Museum of American Art's annual sculpture exhibition. **CT**

1 Larry Wolters, "A 'Radio Nurse' Is Newest Thing for the Home: Idea, Born on a Yacht, Is to Be Marketed," *Chicago Daily Tribune*, March 2, 1938.

2 Isamu Noguchi, *A Sculptor's World* (New York: Harper and Row, 1968), 24.

Further References

Altschuler, Bruce. "Isamu Noguchi Indoors: Home Furnishings and Interior Design." In *Isamu Noguchi: Sculptural Design*, edited by Jochen Eisenbrand, Alexander von Vegesack, and Kararina V. Posch, 109–53. Heimerdingen: Grafisches Zentrum Drucktechnik, 2001.

Codex99. "The Radio Nurse: Noguchi as Industrial Designer." Last modified September 28, 2009. www.codex99.com/design/41.html.

Harris, Ruth Green. "Art in Our Daily Lives: Esthetic Considerations that Reach Out into Housing, Utilities, and Other Fields." *New York Times*, May 1, 1938.

Olds, Andrew. "Archives: Noguchi's Bakelite Nanny." *I.D.* (January/February 1992): 22.

"Plastics Awards Given: Developers of New Industrial Uses Are Honored." *New York Times*, November 16, 1938.

"Radio Nurse." Modern Plastics (June 1938): 24.

Wilson, Richard Guy, et al. *The Machine Age in America, 1918–1941*. New York: Brooklyn Museum and Harry N. Abrams, 1986.

The Zenith Story: A History From 1918–1954. Glenview, Illinois: Zenith Electronics Corporation, 1954.

"Zenith's Radio Nurse." *Radio News* 19 (June 1938): 30.

0724. Radio Nurse advertisement brochure, ca. 1938, Courtesy of Zenith Electronics LLC

0725. ALPS Interactive PS Gamepad video game controller, USA, 1996, Scott Henderson, Smart Design, Inc.

0726. Ericofon telephone, designed Sweden, manufactured USA, ca. 1956, L. M. Ericsson Company, Hugo Blomberg, Ralph Lysell, and Hans Gösta Thames

0727. Steam-O-Matic iron, USA, ca. 1939, Steam-O-Matic Corporation

0728. Sunny Suzy child's iron, USA, ca. 1955

0729. Model 302 telephone, USA, ca. 1937, Henry Dreyfuss

0730. Travel iron, Denmark, ca. 1950, O & N

0731. Silver Streak iron, USA, 1942–46, Saunders Machine & Tool Corp. and Corning Glass Works

0732. Sunbeam Mixmaster mixer (detail), Model 11C, USA, ca. 1955, Ivar Jepson

0733. GRiD Compass laptop computer prototype, USA, 1981, Bill Moggridge

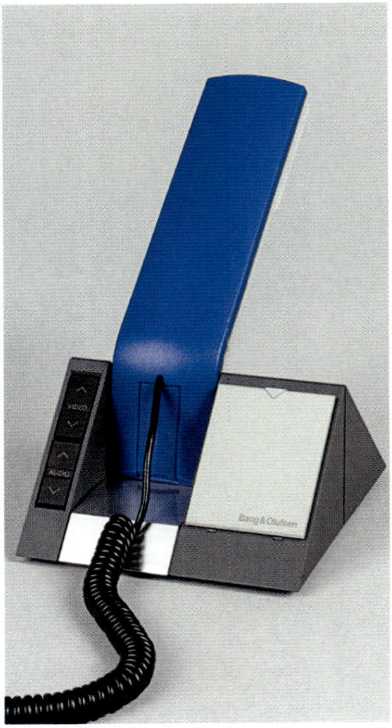

0734. Vertu MMII cellular telephone, England, 2002, Frank Nuovo
0735. BeoCom 1500 telephone and base, Denmark, 1994, Martin Iseli

0736. iPhone mobile telephone, USA 2007, Jonathan Ive and Apple Industrial Design Team
0737. StarTAC™ cellular telephone, USA, 1996, Al Nagele and Leon Soren

0738. BeoCom Copenhagen telephone, Denmark, 1986, Lininger-Lowy

0739. Enorme telephone, Italy, 1986, Ettore Sottsass, Jr. and Marco Zanini
0740. Folle 26 stapler, Denmark, 1977, Henning Andreasen

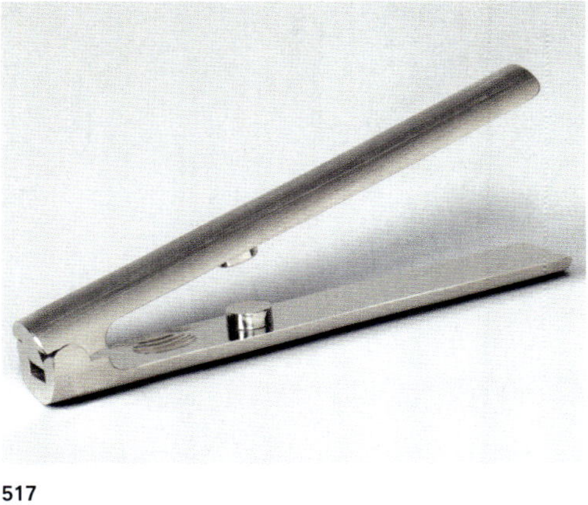

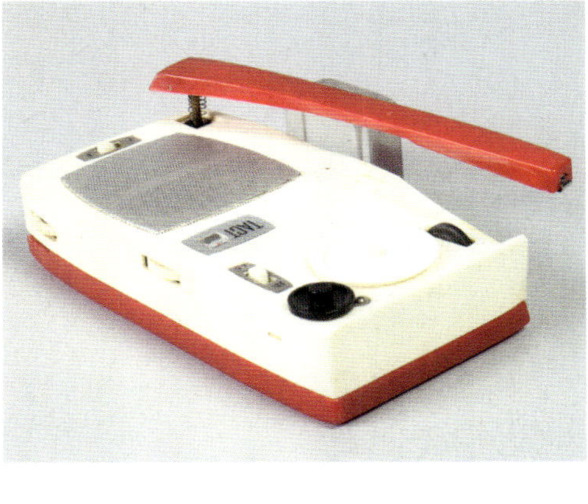

0741. Nutcracker, Italy, ca. 1987, Cini & Nils
0742. Transistor Phonoradio portable phonograph-radio, Japan, ca. 1962

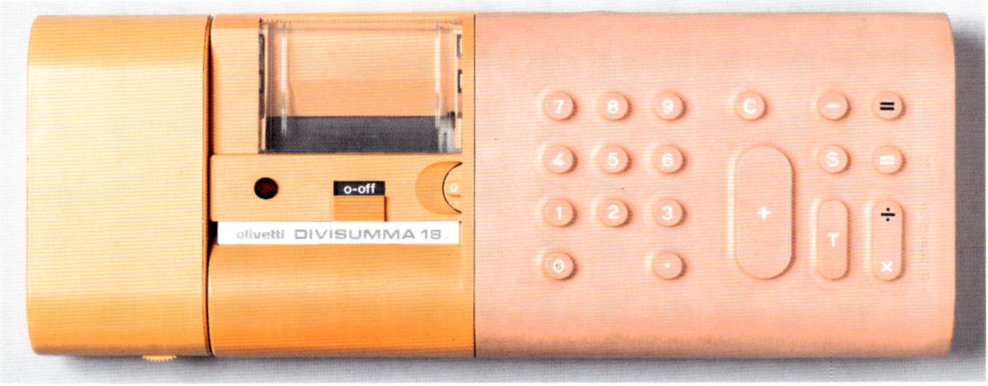

0743. Divisumma 18 calculator, Italy, 1973, Mario Bellini

0744. Logos 59 calculator, Italy, 1973, Mario Bellini

0745. T52 Clairtone portable radio, Germany, 1961, Dieter Rams

0746. Kindle (left) and Kindle 2 (right) electronic reading devices, USA, 2007, 2009, Amazon.com

0747. iPod Nano digital media player, USA, 2009, Jonathan Ive and Apple Industrial Design Team
0748. iPod digital music player, USA, 2001, Jonathan Ive and Apple Industrial Design Team

0749. Macintosh personal computer, USA, 1984, Jerrold Clifford Manock

0750. iMac personal computer, USA, 1999, Jonathan Ive and Apple Industrial Design Team

0751. Poster, Adler Typewriter (detail), 1909–10, Lucian Bernhard

0752. Valentine typewriter and case, Italy, ca. 1969, Ettore Sottsass, Jr. and Perry A. King

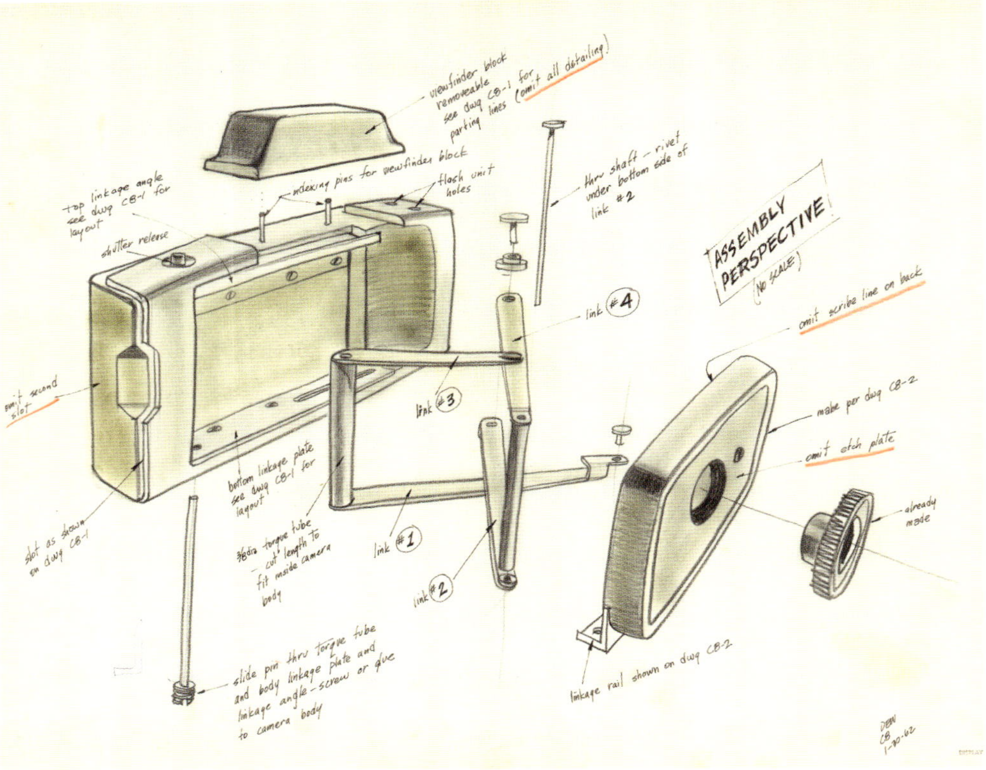

0753. Drawing, Assembly Perspective for Polaroid Automatic 100, 1962, Henry Dreyfuss

0754. Purma Special camera, England, 1937, Raymond Loewy

0755. Swinger camera, USA, 1965, Henry Dreyfuss
0756. Plus 126 camera, Austria, ca. 1970

0757. Big Shot camera, USA, 1971, Henry Dreyfuss

0758. Kodak Pocket Instamatic 10 camera, USA, 1973–76, Eastman Kodak

0759. Textile, Grey on Grey, ca. 1943, Marianne Strengell

0760. Textile, Origami Pleat, 2002–03, Reiko Sudo

Sidewall, In the White Room, 2008
Tracy Kendall (British)
London, England
Cut and sewn paper on paper support
Gift of Tracy Kendall, 2008-11-1

British designer Tracy Kendall began designing wallpapers in 1996 and has been a seminal figure in the renewed vogue for handmade wallpapers. She began by creating panels of unique oversize images of cutlery, feathers, and plant stems. She moved into the realm of the third dimension in 2002 with the introduction of her custom-constructed wallpapers. Cut, stitched, and tagged, she added a whole new concept to the field of handmade papers. While she still prints these earlier panels today, she has added a line of repeating and stacking patterns, and more than twenty custom papers that sparkle, flutter, and zip. The White Room has no printed design, contrasting stitching, or color; varying-sized squares of white paper are hand stitched in evenly spaced horizontal rows on a white paper backing, creating a layered composite that interacts with the environment. Changes in humidity and lighting cause slight fluctuations in the curl and shadows, making ever-changing textural patterns on the wall. Subtle in its lack of color and pattern, the paper exudes much energy in the strength of the curls and the latent shadows. This paper is available in several versions: one with text containing words of Shakespeare printed in large black type, Tyvek for outdoor use, and with interspersed splashes of color. **GH**

0761. Sidewall, In the White Room, 2008, Tracy Kendall

0762. Hand-woven sample, USA, before 1953, Anni Albers

0763. Hand-woven sample, USA, before 1953, Anni Albers

0764. Honey-Pop chair, Japan, 2001, Tokujin Yoshioka

0765. Book, *No. 5 Culture Chanel*, 2013, Irma Boom

0766. Hanging, Prayer Wall, 2012, Sheila Hicks

0767. Sidewall, Zed, 1992, Bořek Šipek
0768. Sidewall, Arabia Felix, 1992, Ettore Sottsass, Jr.

0769. Sidewall, Drop, 2011, J. Abbott Miller

Staircase model, France, early 19th century
Cut, joined, and inlaid mahogany, ebony, pear or sycamore, oak, molded biscuit porcelain (busts)
Gift of Eugene V. and Clare E. Thaw, 2007-45-12

The staircase model reached its zenith as an art form in eighteenth- and nineteenth-century France, thanks to a formalized system known as *compagnonnage* (society of companions), an association of journeyman workers that existed in France, parts of Germany, and western Switzerland. Its main purpose was to allow any man (women were barred from guilds and the compagnonnage societies) the privilege of learning specific crafts based on a meritocratic system with stages of exams in design and execution.

Apprentices in carpentry, **cabinetmaking**, and **joinery** honed their skills in the workshops of acknowledged masters by day and took courses in the art of geometrical design drawing (*l'art du trait*) in the evenings, including basic concepts of staircase design. The apprentices were taught the skills necessary to execute their designs in three-dimensional form as models to be judged for proficiency. In order to prove himself worthy of being taken on as an apprentice in one of the guildlike specialty societies, a young man first produced an acceptance work. If admitted, he then made a "tour de France," working and studying under different master designer–craftsmen in major French cities such as Tours, Marseille, and Lyon. In each studio, the apprentice had to prove his competence in drawing and workmanship before he was able to go on to the next location. At the end of a successful tour—which normally took four to seven years—the apprentice produced a "reception masterpiece" showing a high level of comprehension and execution of the complicated designs and specialties he had learned from multiple teachers. The last step in the compagnonnage process to attain the title of master was the production of a maîtrise, or masterwork, exhibiting a level of design and craftsmanship beyond what was required for the reception work.

This model **(0770)**—with its sophisticated use of materials, including Sèvres porcelain busts and the humorous juxtaposition of the two great French philosophers of the eighteenth century, Voltaire and Rousseau—reveals itself as the work of a master, and a showpiece, or *chef d'oeuvre*. It also is a design tour de force demonstrating the skill required to produce a double stair that spirals as it revolves around a central space, resolving itself into a central staircase that reverse-curves up to another level—all of which is self-supporting.

The use of curved line and the trompe l'oeil effect in the veneers to simulate banded carpet on the curved and molded staircase risers show its creator to be a master **ébéniste**—a cabinetmaker capable of veneering (known as a **menuisier**) in ebony—the highest grade of cabinetmaker. The remarkably delicate spindles on the balustrade show skill as a master turner; its construction shows mastery of joinery too. The delicacy and lack of carving are characteristic of the neoclassical style that was in fashion when both Voltaire and Rousseau died in 1778. However, this does not mean the model dates to their lifetimes. They continued to be widely admired and read long after their deaths. The Sèvres Porcelain Manufactory started to market miniature busts in the first years of the nineteenth century, the staircase's likely date. The staircase seems to be intended to rise toward the busts of Voltaire and Rousseau but never reaches their elongated, lofty plinths from which the philosophers look down on all who ascend the staircase, the kind of conceit a thoroughly proficient

0770. Staircase model, France, early 19th century

master could do for his own or someone else's pleasure. Although their interactions were often contentious, Voltaire and Rousseau espoused some similar ideals. Thus, the pedestals of two pillars of French philosophy who tangled with tradition and each other had an additional meaning—for the viewer who would have been aware of Voltaire and Rousseau's sparring.

Compagnonnage artisans were likely to agree with ideals from outside the traditional guild system that had been favored by the pre-Revolution monarchy. One of the most articulate of the compagnonnage masters and leaders starting in the 1820s was Agricole Perdiguier (1805–75), who tried to lead three rival groups of compagnonnage organizations into becoming one more effective union. Perdiguier—a master ébéniste himself, whose staircase model served as an example for purity of form—thought Rousseau's *Social Contract* to be one of the three most important books in his library.[1] It is likely that the maker of this model was of a similar mind. Before the Revolution, both Voltaire and Rousseau were, at times, exiled from Paris due to their antimonarchical writings—which also happened to many compagnonnage workers who attempted to practice their trades outside the royal guild system. While life improved for these workers after the French Revolution, the Parisian guilds still held strong against "intruders," even though there was no longer a royal patronage system left to protect. Sèvres, the source of the busts on this model, is in the outskirts of Paris. The master who produced this may indeed have lived near Paris, as he had the high skill level to benefit from that market, and where he might have located the busts from a factory newly severed from its royal patronage and looking to work within the Revolution's ideals.

This model both conveys the concept of the model as a work of art, and satisfies the requirements that Eugene Thaw asked of the pieces he and his wife Clare collected: "Are they pleasing to the eye? Do they possess a sweep, a kind of flare? And that they can be displayed as art, without need of any special skill or historical knowledge?"[2] **SDC**

1 Edgar Leon Newman, "This Historian as Apostle: Romanticism, Religion, and the First Socialist History of the World," *Journal of the History of Ideas* 56, no. 2 (April 1995): 240, 242.

2 Eugene Thaw, interview conducted at Cooper Hewitt, Smithsonian Design Museum, June 22, 2006, quoted in "Reflections on the Staircase Collection," in *Made to Scale, Staircase Masterpieces: The Eugene and Clare Thaw Gift* (Cooper-Hewitt, National Design Museum, Smithsonian Institution, New York, 2006), 3.

0771. Staircase model, France, ca. 1820–40

0772. Plumen 001 lightbulb, England, 2010, Samuel Wilkinson

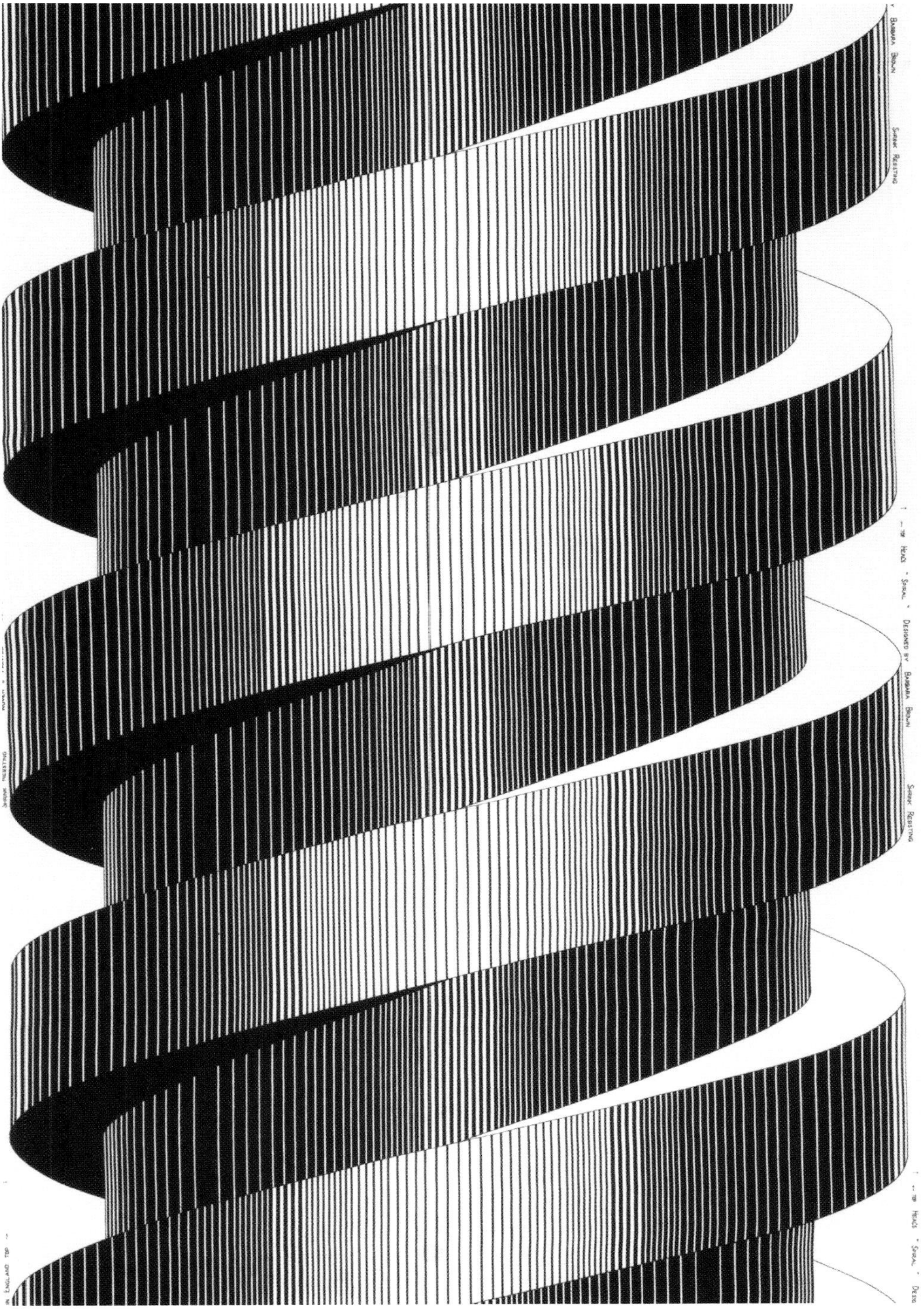

0773. Textile, Spiral, 1969, Barbara Brown

0774. Poster, Olivetti Divisumma, 1953, Herbert Bayer

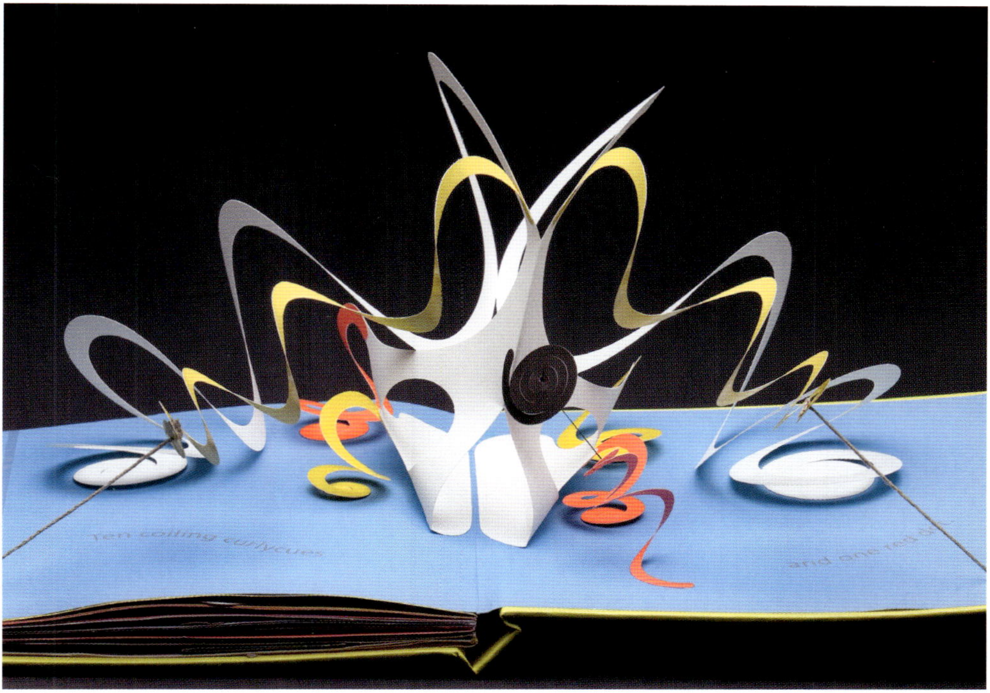

0775. Paper Construction, *One Red Dot*, 2005, David A. Carter

0776. Frieze, Serpentine, 1958–70, Barbara White

0777. Pair of curtain panels, Blond, 2002, Nicolette Brunklaus

0778. Wood chair, Italy, 1988, Marc Newson

0779. Bubbles chaise longue, USA, ca. 1988, Frank O. Gehry

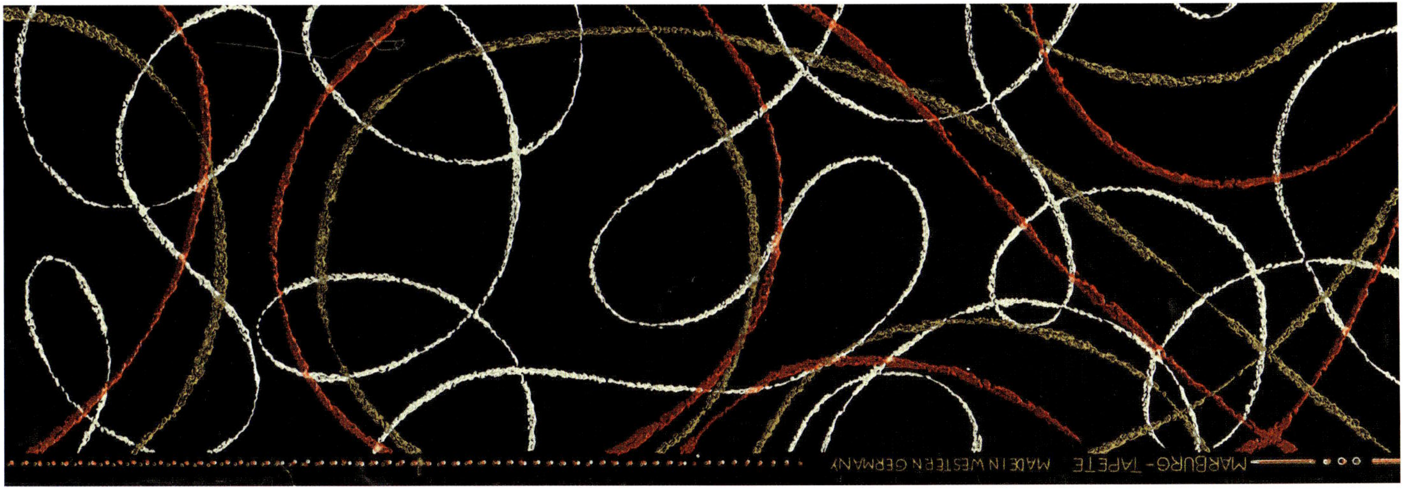

0780. Poster, Cinema Afrika, Filmpodium, Filmtage (detail), 2006, Ralph Schraivogel

0781. Sidewall, Germany, 1956–57, Marburger Tapetenfabrik
0782. Poster, Design Ignites Change, 2008, Marian Bantjes

0783. Print, Writing Example from *Spieghel der Schrijfkonste, tweede deel* (detail), 1609, Jan van de Velde I

0784. Heatwave radiator (detail), Belgium, 2007, Joris Laarman

0785. Paper construction, *[2,3]*, 2010, Tauba Auerbach

0786. Drawing, Textile Design: Bow Motif,1950–70, Tommi Parzinger

0787. Book cover, *Siddhartha* by Hermann Hesse, 1951, Alvin Lustig

0788. Poster, Wozzeck, 1964, Jan Lenica

0789. Braniff Airways Model 66310 armchair, USA, ca. 1968, Alexander Hayden Girard

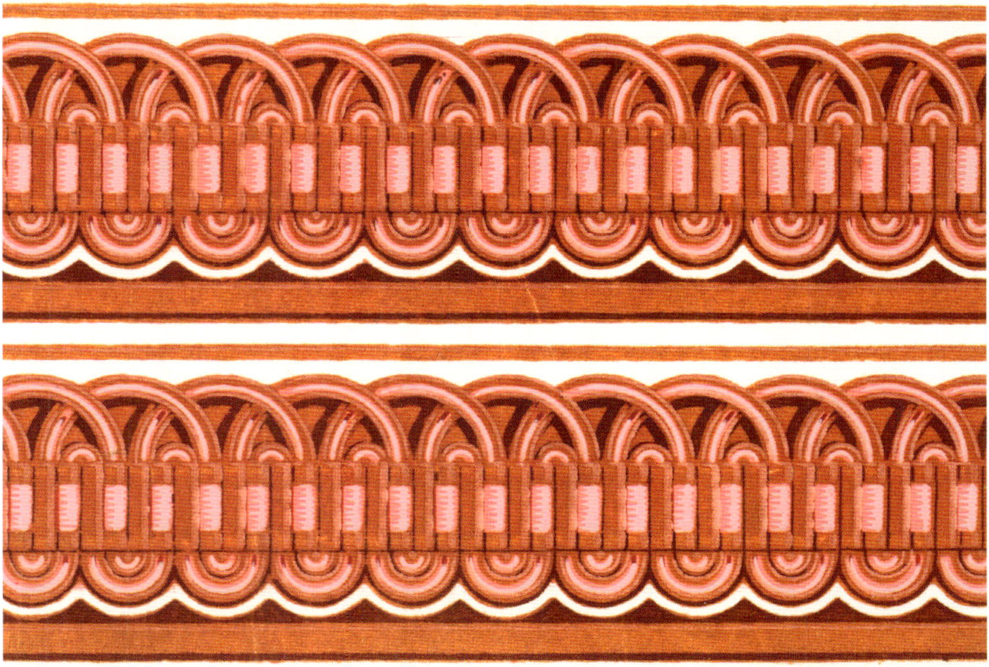

0790. Border, France, 1835–50

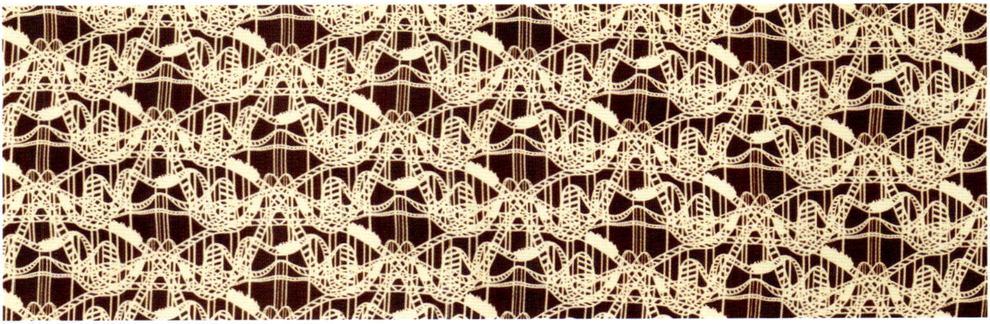

0791. Band, Italy, late 16th–early 17th century

0792. Textile, Thrill, 1925, Dwight Taylor

0793. Poster, Internationale Economisch-Historische Tentoonstelling: Tentoonstelling, Schilderijen, Miniaturen, Gobelins, Documenten, Modellen, Grafiek Enz, Stedelijk Museum (Amsterdam, Netherlands), 1929, Hendrikus Theodorus Wijdeveld

0796. Textile, Design 107, Taliesin Line, 1957, Frank Lloyd Wright

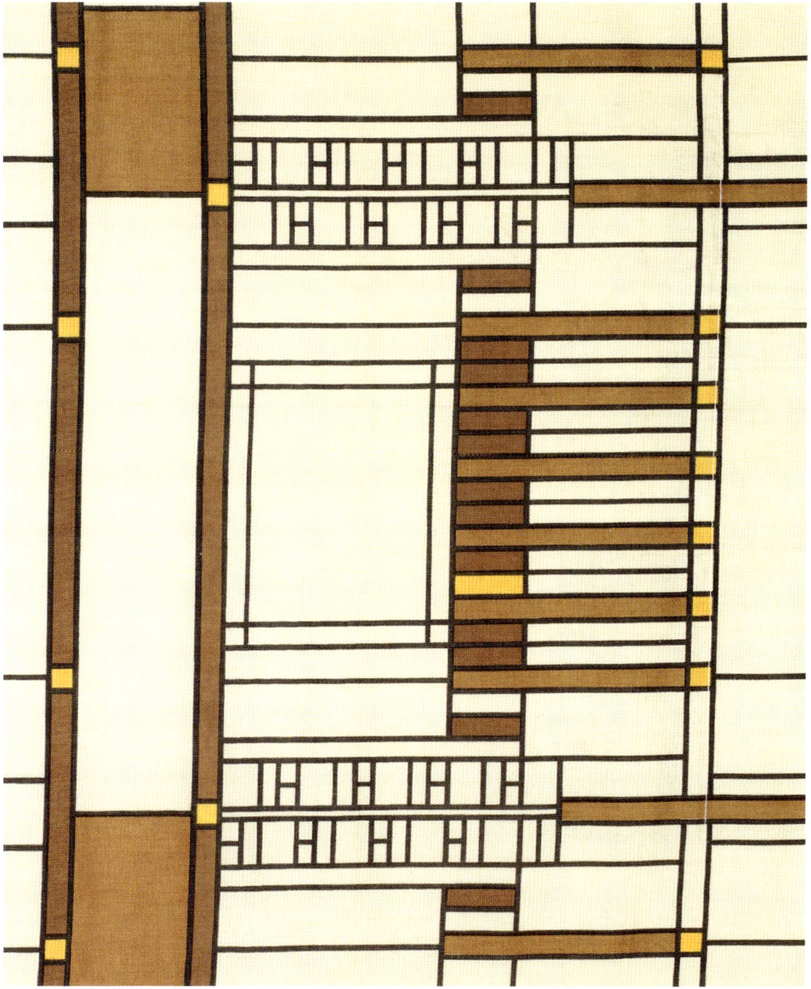

0794. Sidewall, Design 105, 1957, Frank Lloyd Wright
0795. Textile, Design 105, Taliesin Line, 1956, Frank Lloyd Wright

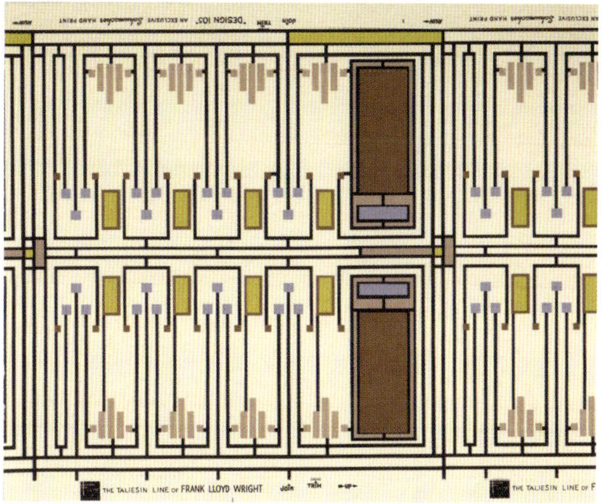

0797. Miao baby carrier (mei tai), Guizhou, China, 1950–2000

0798. Mantle fragment, coastal Tiahuanaco, 8th–10th century

0799. Textile, Design 103, Taliesin Line, 1955, Frank Lloyd Wright
0800. Textile, Notschrei, 1904, Josef Hoffmann

0801. Poster, Schweizerische Städtebau-Ausstellung, 1928, Niklaus Stoecklin

0802. Poster, Jean Prouvé: Architekt und Konstrukteur, 1978, Siegfried Odermatt

0803. Poster, American Airlines to New York, ca. 1948, Edward McKnight Kauffer

0804. Textile, Big City, 1960s, Arthur Sanderson & Sons, Ltd.

Drawing, Design for Sportshack, 1940
Designed by Donald Deskey (American, 1894–1989)
New York, New York, USA
Brush and gouache, airbrush over stencil, black ink, graphite on illustration board
Gift of Donald Deskey, 1988-101-1515

The need for affordable housing through prefabrication has challenged architects and consumers since the late nineteenth century. In the 1920s through the 1940s, European architects such as Le Corbusier, Walter Gropius, and Jean Prouvé experimented with types of prefabricated housing and materials. During the pre–World War II period in the United States, inventor Buckminster Fuller and architects George Fred Keck and Frank Lloyd Wright among others constructed their prefabrication prototypes. US Government subsidies during and after World War II infused new funds and energy into other prefabrication projects, including those by Sears, Roebuck & Company and General Housing,[1] as well as by industrial designers and architects including Fuller, Walter Dorwin Teague, Norman Bel Geddes, and Henry Dreyfuss. Donald Deskey, who had earlier collaborated on an experimental prefabricated steel-paneled house for the 1933 Chicago Century of Progress International Exposition, introduced his own proposal at the Metropolitan Museum of Art's Contemporary American Industrial Art: 1940 exhibition from April 29 through September 15, 1940. The installation Sportshack included a model of a three-room shed roof structure with an open-plan convertible living room/dining room/bedroom room, sliding picture window, kitchen, bathroom, and deck with grill. Accompanying the model was a full-scale mock-up of the living and dining areas. As the name implies, the house, advertised as sleeping six people, was pitched to the second-home market for "gentlemen's relaxation," hunting, fishing, and beaching. It was estimated to cost around $1,285 equipped and furnished (without construction and the land) and to be produced by Deskey's new company, Week-End Cabins. Anticipating the hesitant response by a conservative public and thinking pragmatically of how he could market two projects simultaneously, Deskey incorporated in Sportshack a striated plywood that he had recently invented and developed with U.S. Plywood, called Weldtex. According to Deskey, this distressed, rustic-looking wood product, manufactured in panels and used on both the exterior and interior walls, would automatically convey the warm comfort of a traditional house in this spare, modern structure. While on exhibition at the Metropolitan Museum of Art, another complete and full-scale example of Sportshack was set up in the second year of the New York 1939–40 New York World's Fair in the America at Home section. World War II prevented the manufacture of Weldtex, but at the war's conclusion, Deskey officially resumed his prefabrication efforts to meet the emergency deman for homes by returning veterans. In 1946 he created Shelter Industries to market and manufacture two- or three-bedroom homes based on the Sportshack model with the addition of a prefabricated utility core, which Deskey designed for Ingersoll Steel, that included heating, plumbing, laundry, kitchen, and bathroom facilities. The two-bedroom model was to sell for under $7,000. Despite the promise and press coverage for the Shelter Industries home (two examples were constructed without the utility core, which was not yet in production) in Linden, New Jersey, and in Connecticut, this project, like many prefabrication projects across the country, failed to catch on with the public.

This design for Sportshack **(0805)** was probably used as presentation material for the Metropolitan Museum of Art and World's Fair exhibitions and/or in preparation for the project's reproduction in the August 1940 issue of *Esquire*.[2] Like many 1930s and 1940s design drawings, it was executed by hand in brush and gouache with airbrush. **Airbrush** is an adjustable spray technique, first patented in the nineteenth century, that allows an even flow of paint to mist over a substrate, producing a smooth, almost machinelike appearance. Sometimes, as here, it is used with a **stencil** to cover a surface not meant to be painted or to be airbrushed with another color. The technique was especially popular in the late 1930s, as it helped to convey the speed and slickness of the modern streamline style. **GSD**

1 Barry Bergdoll and Peter Christensen, *Home Delivery, Fabricating the Modern Dwelling* (New York: Museum of Modern Art, 2008), 17–93.
2 Robert W. Marks, "Donald Deskey's Sportshack..." *Esquire* vol. 14 (August, 1940): 69.

0805. Drawing, Design for Sportshack (detail), 1940, Donald Deskey

0806. Drawing, Museum of American Folk Art, USA: Collage Perspective, 1997, Billie Tsien

0807. Print, New Urban Ground, Proposal for Rising Currents Exhibition, Museum of Modern Art, USA, 2009, Architectural Research Office and DLandstudio

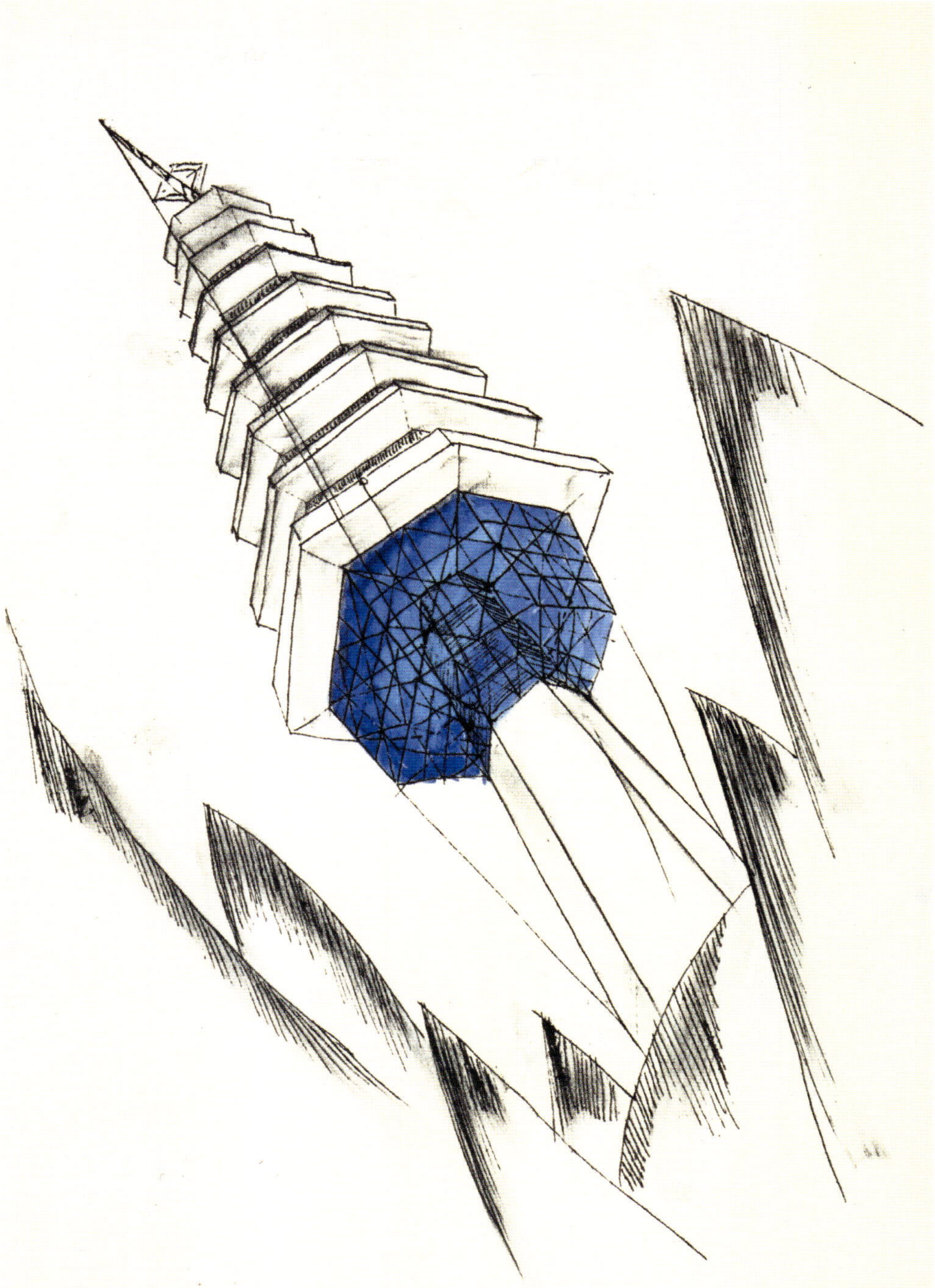

0808. Print, Design for Ten-Deck House, 1928, R. Buckminster Fuller

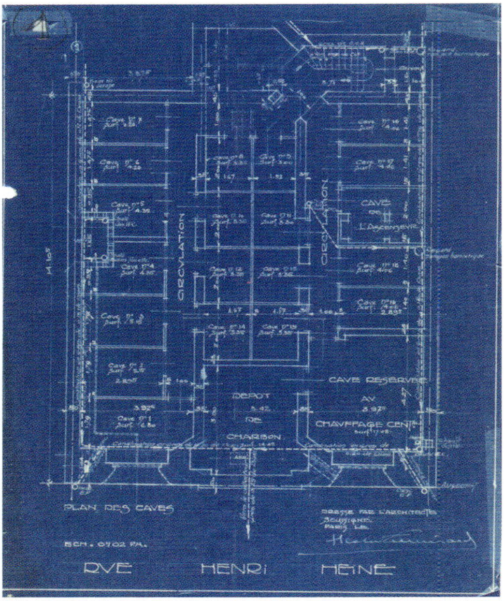

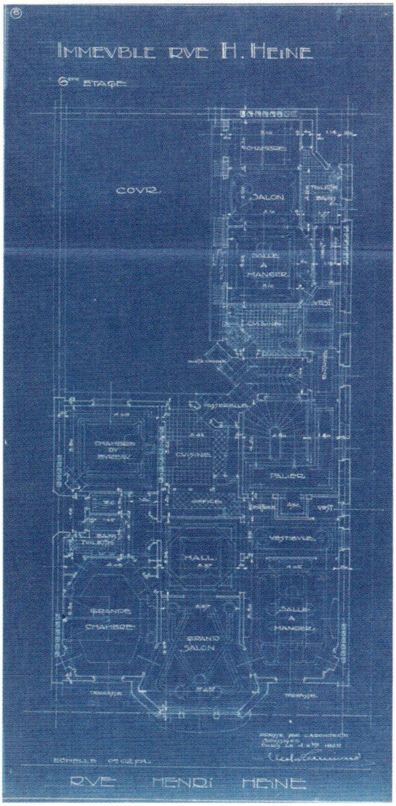

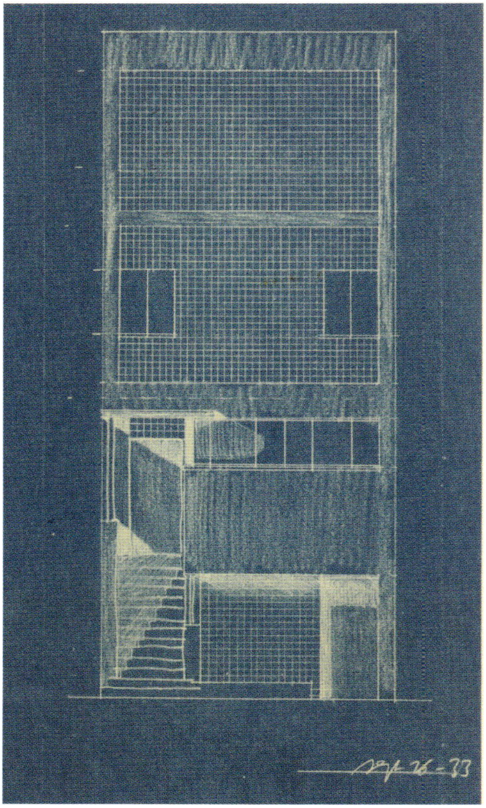

0809. Blueprint, Propriété de Monsieur Hemsy, France: Principal Façade, 1913, Hector Guimard
0810. Blueprint, Immeuble, Rue Heine, France: Plan des Caves, 1925, Hector Guimard
0811. Blueprint, Immeuble, Rue Heine, France: Plan du 6e Étage, 1925, Hector Guimard
0812. Blueprint, Townhouse, 211 East 48th Street, USA: Elevation, 1933, William E. Lescaze

0813. Sidewall, Views of Paris, 1946–50, Saul Steinberg

0814. Photostat, Immeuble, Rue Heine, France: Façade sur Rue, 1925, Hector Guimard

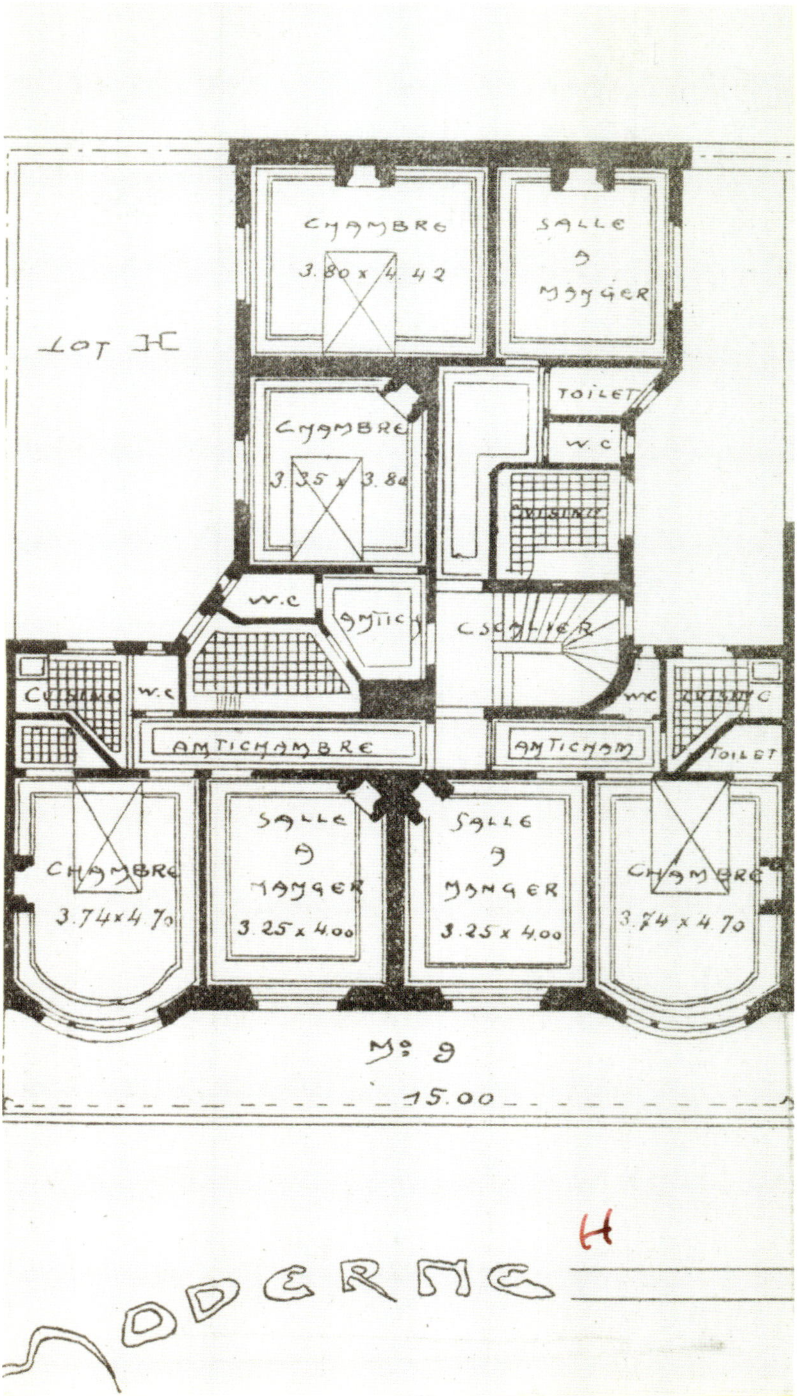

0815. Photograph, Floor Plan for an Apartment Building, 1911, Hector Guimard

0816. Kubus stacking storage container set, Germany, 1938, Wilhelm Wagenfeld

0817. Poster, NOH: UCLA Asian Performing Arts, 1981, Takenobu Igarashi

0818. Collage, Maquette of Book Cover Design: *Portrait of the Artist as a Young Dog* by Dylan Thomas, ca. 1955, Alvin Lustig

0819. Book illustration (detail), *A Treatise of Japaning [sic] and Varnishing*, 1688, John Stalker and George Parker

0820. Drawing, Design for a Skyscraper, 1930, Ely Jacques Kahn
0821. Drawing, Study after a Bronze Chandelier, Kaid Bey Mosque, Egypt, 1856–66, Alfred Normand

0822. Cabinet, Italy, 1890–1900, Carlo Bugatti
0823. Birdcage, England, ca. 1765

Jewel Cabinet on Stand, 1824–26
Designed by Jean-Charles-François Leloy (French, active 1816–44)
Designed and produced by Alexandre Brongniart (French, 1770–1847)
for King Charles X of France (reign 1824–30)
Primary porcelain painting by Pierre Huard (French, active 1811–47, d. 1857)
Designed by Alexandre Évariste Fragonard (French, 1780–1850)
Mounts by Louis-Honoré Boquet (French, active Sèvres 1815–ca. 1860)
Porcelain gilding by Boullemier le jeune (the younger), probably Antoine-Gabriel Boullemier (French, 1781–1842), and Boullemier l'ainé (the elder), probably François-Antoine Boullemier (French, 1773–1838)
Porcelain burnished by Madame Boullemier le jeune, Geneviève Boullemier (French, b. 1781)
Additional painting by Pierre Riton (French, active 1821–60), Antoine Béranger (French, 1785–1867), Godin (probably the younger) (French, active late 18th/early 19th centuries)
Production directed by Vicomte (Sostène) de La Rochefoucauld (French, 1785–1864), for Sèvres Porcelain Manufactory (Sèvres, France)
Casework of molded hard-paste porcelain with enamel-painted and fired decoration, with gilding in gold leaf and platinum, mounted in gilt bronze, joined mahogany drawers, gilt metal
Gift of Alfred Duane Pell, 1991-31-2 (by transfer)

This cabinet represents a rare confluence of technical innovation, superb skills in design and execution, artistic inspiration, royal patronage, diplomacy, and political impact. A jewel cabinet on stand was described on its design drawings variously as armoire à bijoux and as secrétaire à bijoux, made of porcelain with **gilt-bronze** mounts represents an innovation: porcelain as the carcass of a piece of furniture, and not porcelain applied to one. This unexpected choice of medium for furniture was made possible by technical developments in porcelain making that evolved at the Sèvres Porcelain Manufactory in the early nineteenth century, thanks to the guidance of its head, Alexandre Brongniart. Hired in 1800, Brongniart took an interest in every aspect of Sèvres's production in his aim to make it the preeminent porcelain factory in the world. During his tenure, both Napoleon and monarchies reigned, making it necessary for the firm to remain popular with both types of regimes as he exploited porcelain to claim cultural and scientific superiority for France's business and diplomatic ends. Decoration and form could change to suit taste, but if Sèvres led in style, innovation, and quality, then the world would want it.

The Sèvres factory, founded in 1740 in Vincennes, moved to Sèvres on the outskirts of Paris in 1756. It became a royal manufactory in 1759, when Louis XV became its primary shareholder and patron, encouraged by his mistress Madame de Pompadour. Sèvres lost its royal patronage and underwriting during the French Revolution. During the ancien régime the fashion for Sèvres porcelain led to its inclusion as plaques set into wooden furniture by makers such as Martin Carlin. The smooth surfaces of the neoclassical style popular after the French Revolution contributed to the fashion for **hard-paste porcelain** plaques as Sèvres looked for new clients. Although hard-paste porcelain existed at Sèvres from the late 1760s, it was not until Brongniart closed the **soft-paste** factory in 1802 that hard-paste ensured a new identity. Crisper definition, durability from higher firing temperatures, and new brighter colors available in hard-paste porcelain combined with larger kilns and more even temperatures that made large plaques possible.

0824. Jewel Cabinet on Stand, France, 1824–26, Jean-Charles-François Leloy, Alexandre Brongniart, et al.

Napoleon also wanted Sèvres to support itself as a profit-making business.
The resulting governmental decree included a letter from the minister: "You must never lose sight of the fact that if Sèvres becomes inimitable in the matter of luxury objects, it must serve as a model for all ordinary objects." Production was to be divided into two categories: "ordinary products intended for sale," whose costs would be covered by receipts; and luxury objects reserved for the government to be produced in an *atelier de perfectionnement* to be subsidized by six thousand francs per month. [1]

This cabinet clearly belonged to the latter category. It was so complex and detailed it took almost two years to complete. The marks of adorsed Cs enclosing an X for King Charles X on the versos of the plaques date from his reign (1824–30). Although the cabinet became his royal gift to Francis I of Naples in 1830, its beginnings in 1824 antedate Charles's reign. Its completion in late 1826 and display in the showroom in January 1827 without a patron's name indicate that it was unlikely to have started out with out an intended recipient. [2]

Brongniart picked highly skilled artist-designers, as is seen in the quality of the **drawings** at the Sèvres archives and on the actual cabinet. [3] The drawings range from pencil **sketches** on full-size templates to detailed **watercolors** by Jean-Charles-François Leloy, a draftsman and painter specializing in ornament who probably created the composition of the cabinet to Brongniart's specifications. Although the cabinet's lilac color was suggested during the final design-approval process in March 1825 by the Vicomte de La Rochefoucauld, Charles X's Director General of Fine Arts, the creation of the actual color was almost certainly directed by Brongniart. [4] The lilac would have been applied first, as colors on hard-paste porcelain were applied from lighter to darker to minimize the number of firings needed, thereby reducing the possibility of cracking.

Brongniart's pursuit of the best materials, methods, and people took him to other factories, including Meissen, where he collected ceramics that became the basis of the Sèvres Museum he founded in 1803. [5] He even gave questionnaires to ceramic makers canvassing their reactions to the media and methods they used. Through his father's artistic connections he made useful friends, such as the sculptor Houdon, who helped expand the design and sculptural resources for the factory. [6]

Leloy, while talented as a draftsman and colorist, does not seem to have been the real designer of this cabinet's iconography. Lists of his drawings appear in July 1825 and July 1826 records, well after the designs were approved, suggesting some were for presentation, which their style bears out. Brongniart's own entries show his depth of involvement from 1824 to 1826, corroborating that while Leloy may have composed suggested motifs, the original concept is most likely to have been Brongniart's. [7]

The rich iconography of the jewel cabinet portrays symbols of love mixed with jewels, perhaps as tokens of love. Antiquity is mixed with early-nineteenth-century jewelry styles and horticulturally up-to-date renditions of flowers, many of which were chosen for their symbolism in connection to ancient mythology, a dominant theme in the cabinet's decoration. The large panels display central medallions of Venus and Psyche at their toilettes, done from drawings supplied by Alexandre Évariste Fragonard.

On the side with Venus, the Roman goddess of love, Venus is shown putting on an earring while winged putti attend her with a mirror, jewel casket, and ribbons. [8] **(0826)**
The dove on her footstool is another of her attributes. The smaller medallions around her represent other mythological figures related to the theme of Venus and love, each

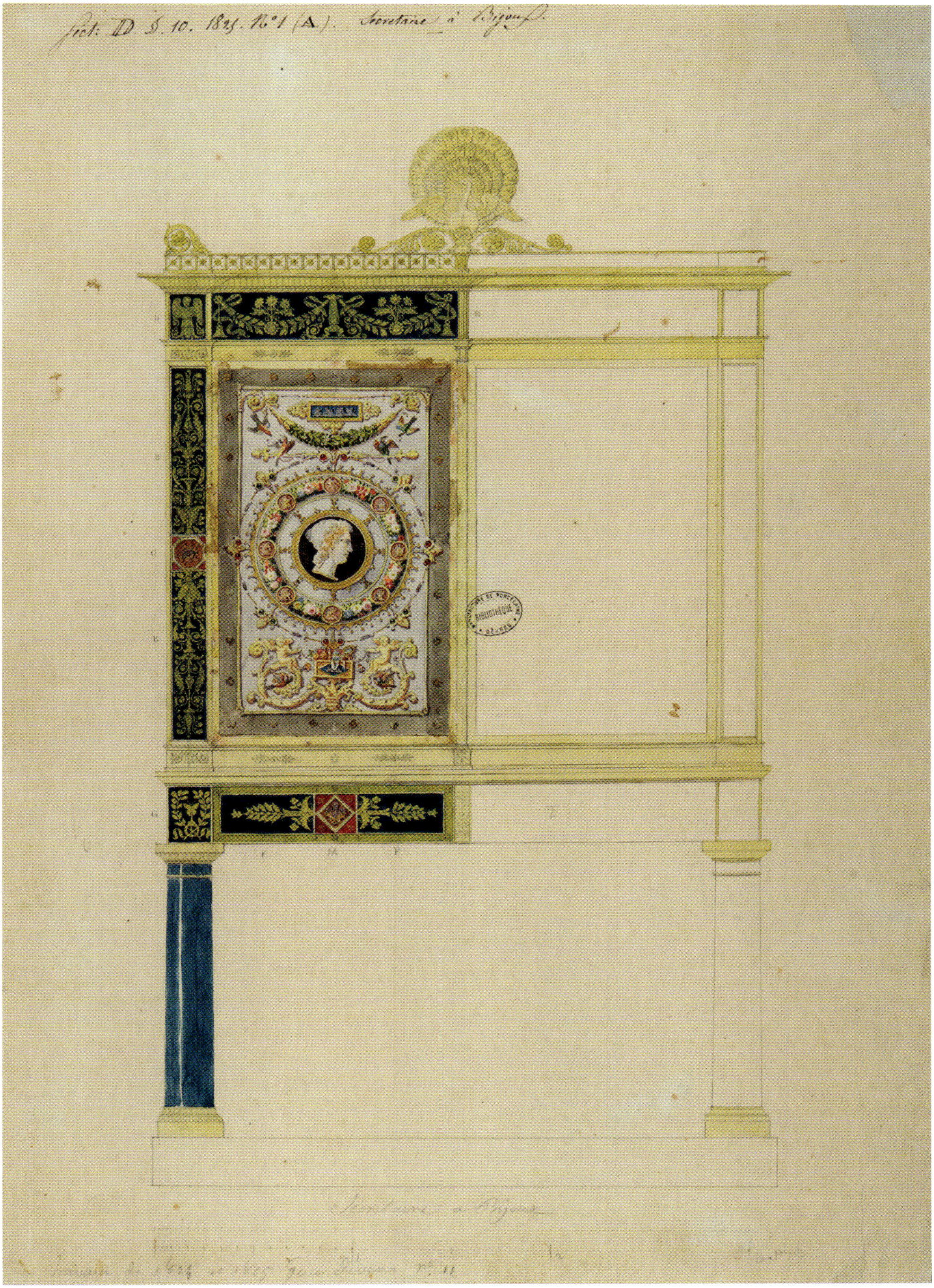

0825. Drawing, Presentation Watercolor Drawing Front of Cabinet, France, 1826 , Jean-Charles-François Leloy

with an attribute. The Psyche panel is similarly surrounded with a circle of related gods and goddesses. On both doors the encircling ovals intersperse medallions with roses, traditionally associated with Venus. The alternating of cameo images based on antiquity, possibly painted by Antoine Béranger, with trompe l'oeil flowers reflects the mix of neoclassicism with naturalism that pervades this period.[9]

This cabinet, unlike the few others which were secretaries, was planned from the outset of the decoration as a jewel cabinet, evident from the choice of detail motifs.[10] Venus is shown with a jewelry casket and scent bottle; square and lozenge-shaped plaques depict jewelry and luxury objects such as necklaces, bracelets, rings, and a gold étui (a small, usually narrow box) arranged artfully in colorful displays, resulting in a trompe l'oeil effect of objects that might be inside **(0826, 0827)**. One such drawing describes the articles as "a scent bottle in crystal and gold, an ivory souvenir [case for a dance card or mementos], and a necklace in gold and colored enamel."[11]

Brongniart recognized the economic benefits of first-rights outsourcing to sought-after independent artists for figure, flower, or cameo **painting**, but retained overall design supervision. This maestro approach is responsible for the longest object description in the museum's collection, with Leloy, who signed the detailed presentation drawings **(0825)** listed as a designer in addition to Brongniart. The other artists were specialty painters: Alexandre Évariste Fragonard, an artist in his own right; Pierre Huard, who was listed first in the accounting page, and was the primary creator of the underdrawings and much of the overall painting including the small trompe l'oeil medallions of jewelry;[12] Antoine Béranger, a painter also known for his imitation of cameos, who did the four putti on the front doors; Pierre Riton, who painted some foundation color, the brownish-purple color, and some of the platinum; Godin (probably the younger), who produced the blue foundation color;[13] and Madame Boullemier the younger, who **burnished** the **gilding** of the porcelain along with several others.[14] Huard provided an estimate to produce the large plaques, and on July 20 Brongniart noted, "the two front and side plaques are painted in the rough and are being fired today,"[15] with fees suggesting that Huard did much of the initial painting.[16] The Boullemiers specialized in painting gilded decoration on porcelain and burnishing it, usually late in the process, with little or no firing. But nowhere could the need to lock in specialized skills be seen more notably than in Brongniart's contracts for gilt-bronze mounts.

The mount maker, Louis-Honoré Boquet (or Bocquet), was accorded very special status.[17] Due to the danger and cost of transferring porcelain to outside mount makers over rough streets, Sèvres established workshops on-site. Boquet signed an initial agreement in 1815 to direct this workshop for Sèvres. He became a permanent staff member in 1823, producing bronze elements such as framing, handles, bases, and joints until about 1860.[18]

The archives' templates served as actual models to create the plaques, and generally have penciled-in decoration for design but not coloration. Occasional pieces of paper glued over an earlier or alternate design show final selection. The templates also show the gilt-bronze designs and placement, including the ormolu peacock surmounting the top, of key importance for the firing, the decorator, and Boquet's mounting. Templates could enable replacement pieces to be made in the event of faulty firing or damage in transit, in addition to their potential use for future commissions. The resulting cabinet produced by a multimaker process and led by an impassioned impresario combined art, science, and business to create this extraordinary statement. **SDC**

0826. Jewel Cabinet, detail showing jewelry and objects of the toilette, France, 1824–26, Jean-Charles François Leloy, Alexandre Brongniart, et al.
0827. Jewel Cabinet, detail showing an étui, 1824–26, Jean-Charles François Leloy, Alexandre Brongniart, et al.

1 Since this cabinet was published, in David McFadden and Deborah Sampson Shinn "A Royal Gift: the 1826 Porcelain Jewel Cabinet," *The Magazine Antiques* 146, no. 3 (Sept 1994), 300–07, several important works have appeared. Three, written by or with substantial portions by Tamara Préaud have provided significant scholarship on Brongniart, so that this cabinet now can be seen as the triumph of his leadership in design and commerce and friendship for artists and artisans, while balancing financial demands. These works form a useful bibliography: D. Ostergaard, ed., *The Sèvres Porcelain Manufactory: Alexandre Brongniart and the Triumph of Art and Industry* (New Haven: Yale University Press), in conjunction with an exhibition at The Bard Graduate Center for the Decorative Arts, October 17, 1997–February 1, 1998; Marcelle Brunet and Tamara Préaud, *Sèvres des origines à nos jours* (Paris: Office du Livre, 1978) and *Un Âge d'or des arts décoratifs* (Paris: Éditions de la Réunion des Musées Nationaux, 1991). We are extremely grateful for Ms. Préaud's generosity in providing some of her unpublished scholarship and introductions to the Sèvres Archives for the author's research on this cabinet. In addition, special thanks are due to Jean-Gerald Castex and Coralie Coscino of the Sèvres Archives for making available the original templates, drawings, and documents related to the cabinet. Sèvres Archives, Sèvres, Carton T1, liasse 3, dossier 1, letter signed August 4, 1802, as cited by Tamara Préaud, "Brongniart as Administrator," in *The Sèvres Porcelain Manufactory: Alexandre Brongniart and the Triumph of Art and Industry, 1800–1847*, ed. Tamara Préaud (New Haven, CT: Yale University Press, 1997), 44, note 18.

2 The Registers document is organized by the name of the artisan, the date, and the nature of the work performed. Sèvres Archives:
Carton Pb 5, Appréciations 1826 "Feuille d'appréciation: a recapitulation of expenses to establish the sale price when it entered the shop: Secrétaire à bijoux (Jewel secretary)

Background	325
Gilt ornament, decoration: Boullemier the younger and Boullemier the elder	648
Gold or platinum and gold leaf	149.70
Ornamental painting M Huard	3600
Figure painting by Riton	272
Figure painting by Béranger	240
Burnishing	18.20
Total direct costs	5252.90
Incidental costs	1751.20
Value of the blank porcelain before decorating according to the cost list	1248
Value of the plaques, column, undecorated, with background color	240
Mounting and bronze decoration	9600
Fabrication cost	18,091
Price for sale	24,000

3 Sèvres Archives, 2012.1.557 (former number Section D.S. 10.1825. No 1 (A), "Inventaire 1825," "Sécretaire à Bijoux"

4 Carton Pb 5, liasse 2, dossier 1, Meubles 1823–1824–1825, dossier sur le Secrétaire à bijoux. In 1824, only the templates and size of the plaques are noted. According to Brongniart in the 1824 dossier, one template was remitted by Leloy on August 28, 1824. But on March 10, 1825, Brongniart noted that Leloy's drawing, remitted with variants, "was submitted today in my office to 'Mr. De La Rochefoucauld' and to de Turpin, who decided on the variant with the lilac base [background] color."

5 Préaud, "Brongniart as Administrator," 49.

6 Tamara Préaud, "Alexandre Brongniart: Scholar and Member of the Institut de France," in *Tamara Préaud, The Sèvres Porcelain Manufactory: Alexandre Brongniart and the Triumph of Art and Industry, 1800–1847*, 25. His father's many friendships included Talleyrand, who served kings and Napoleon, and the painter Jean-Baptiste Isabey and sculptor Claude Michel, known as Clodion.

7 Sèvres Archives; Travaux des décorateurs, Registre Vj' 32 (1825), fol. 1ff; Registre Vj' 33 (1826), fol. 1ff, where there are long lists of drawings furnished by Leloy in July 1825 and July 1826.

8 Registre Vj' 33 (1826), folio 181, "January: two drawings for the jewel cabinet, subjects of Venus, 120 francs."

9 Registre Vj' 33 (1826), folios 12 ff: Béranger received the two doors in July for the first painting of four figures of children.

10 See Brunet and Préaud, *Sèvres des origines à nos jours*; and *Un Âge d'or des arts décoratifs*. These pieces, from Versailles and the Sèvres Museum, are different in having wider proportions, and they each have a mechanically driven lowering mechanism that pulls the whole front slab of porcelain down behind the central plaque of the stands, but for which the solid slab in the stand gives support. While the stands are almost identical, the upper portions have gilt-bronze mounts whose motifs relate to the themes of the cabinets, and thus are individually designed for the specific subjects in the porcelain.

11 Archives de Sèvres, 2012.1.572.

12 Registre Vj' 32 (1825), folio 42 and Registre Vj' 33 (1826), folios 42 ff, "July 7, received 4 little plaques . . . painting of the jewels."

13 Registre Vj' 33 (1826), folios 54 ff.

14 The following burnishers appear in reference to this cabinet: Madame Bougon (Vj' 33, fol. 223ff); Madame Boullemier jeune (ibid., fol.133ff); Madame Bouvrain (ibid., fol. 251ff); Madame Godin jeune (ibid., fol. 148ff); Madame Lapierre (ibid., fol.165ff), Madame Micaud (ibid., fol. 157ff) and Madame Troyon (ibid., fol. 124ff). I am grateful to Madame Préaud for the information on the others beyond Madame Boullemier.

15 Travaux des décorateurs, Registre Vj' 31 (1824), "Pièces diverses no. 11, Secrétaire à bijoux," includes the following page written by Brongniart, who describes the project thus: "Program: a table surmounted by a small armoire of two doors opening on the side. Plan to make a large design to make the template from the labeled plaques, research the plaques, glue the large design drawing on a wood cabinet that represents the piece of furniture, and color it full-scale. Try the plaques cut by Bocquet before giving them to Huard." This shows how deeply Brongniart was involved as the principal supervisor and even designer of the cabinet.

16 Huard's accounts are listed in Registre Vj' 32 (1825), folio 42:"Received April 13 one plaque for one of the doors . . . for first painting of the ornaments, figure, flowers etc." C Registre Vj' 33 (1826), folios 42ff. "March, received a second door for the first painting"; July 7 received "4 little plaques . . . painting of the jewels." These records give a clear indication of the division of the labor.

17 Sèvres Archives, Carton Pb 5, liasse 2, dossier 1, Meubles 1823–1824–1825, includes detailed estimates from Boquet for the models and execution of the bronzes, to which was added on September 20 the framing of the blue plaques that cover the top of the cabinet and the front of the base, a sketch of the ensemble, and front and side views with the plaques and columns numbered.

18 Préaud, "Brongniart as Technician," 51–63.

0828. Sidewall, Opera, 1953, Saul Steinberg

0829. Drawing, Place de la Concorde, France: Elevation of the Maritime Fountain, 1839, Jacques Ignace Hittorff

0830. Renaissance-Style Baptistry architectural model, Italy, 1782

0831. Bandbox and Lid, USA, ca. 1830

0832. Drawing, Aqua Tower, USA: Study Exploring Chromatic Strata, ca. 2005, Jeanne Gang

0833. Photograph, Staircase Construction of a Mass-Produced House (No. 43), 1921, Hector Guimard

0834. Digital print, Tel Aviv Museum of Art (TAMA), Israel: Lightfall I, 2003, Preston Scott Cohen

0835. Oil Sketch, Parthenon, from the Northwest (Illuminated Night View), 1869, Frederic Edwin Church

0836. Textile, Pokeri, 1967, Maija Isola

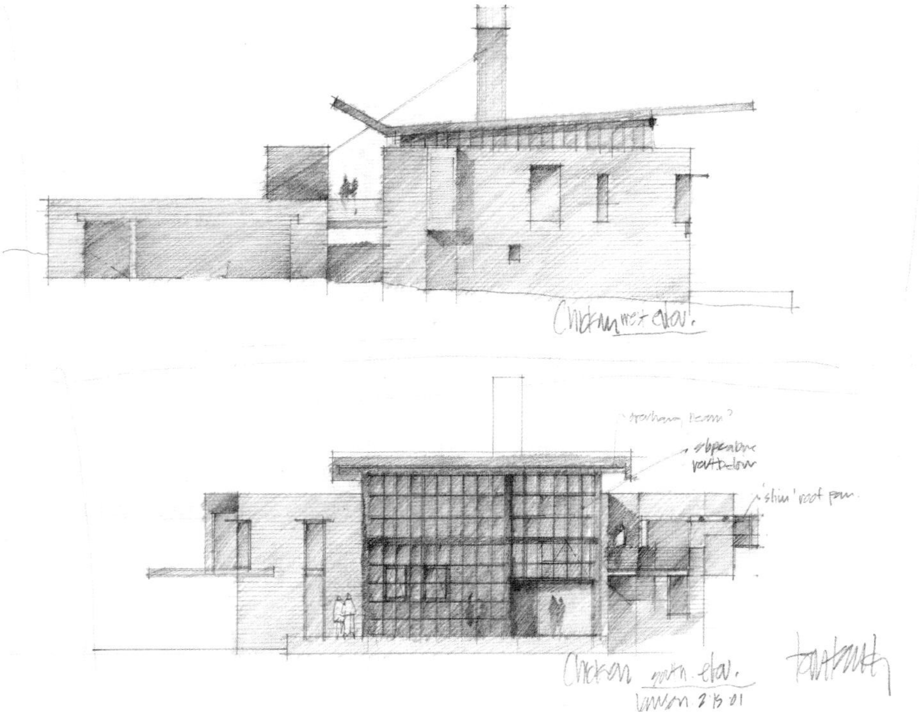

0837. Drawing, Chicken Point Cabin, USA: West and South Elevations, 2001, Tom Kundig

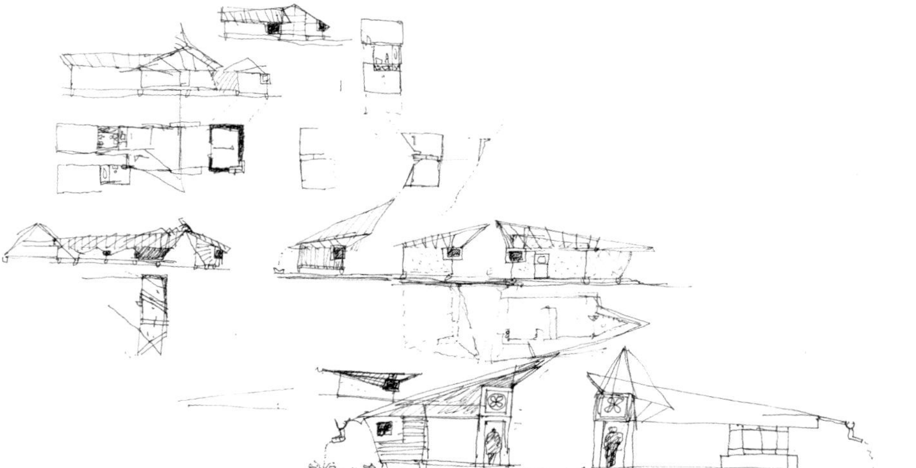

0838. Drawing, Butterfly House, USA: Concept Sketches, 1997, Samuel Mockbee

Drawing, Phillips Exeter Library, Exeter, NH, USA: Sketch of Plan with Elevations, ca. 1967
Louis I. Kahn (American, b. Estonia, 1901–74)
Graphite on yellow tracing paper
Museum purchase through gift of Anonymous Donors, Architectural Research Office, and Susan and Mark Stumer and from Drawings & Prints Council, General Acquisitions Endowment and Krieg Funds, 2012-22-1

The Phillips Exeter Academy Library in Exeter, New Hampshire, ranks among the most celebrated buildings by twentieth-century architect Louis I. Kahn. This early design for the Library, Sketch Plan with **Elevations**, probably from May 1967, is the only Kahn drawing documenting the Exeter project in a New York public collection. It also provides a major 1960s anchor for the Cooper Hewitt's architectural drawings collection.

Born in Kingisepp, Saaremaa, in Estonia, of Jewish ancestry, Kahn absorbed the idea that a divine spirit exists in people and the world from his Jewish roots; he carried this same conviction to architecture, that it could reveal the divine in the world. Having spent 1950 as a fellow at the American Academy in Rome, where he was able to study the great classical ruins and Renaissance structures and absorb their use of Platonic geometric forms, Kahn developed his ideas regarding structural mass, using brick and concrete to create thick and powerful buildings. He adopted the Renaissance ideal of geometry as an expression of the divine and the circle being the most divine of forms.

The Exeter Library embodies the midcentury philosophy of geometry and spiritual awareness. The Cooper Hewitt drawing **(0839)** records the beginning of Kahn's design process of the central plan building: a square atrium is surrounded by two square ambulatories, or what he called "donuts." The inner donut was to hold the books, while the outer one, only suggested in the sketch, contained student carrels. The drawing also includes, on the right side, two perspective designs for the elevation of the central atrium with double circular openings (like the dormitories at Dacca, which he was designing at the same time) and an ambulatory below, which Kahn would adapt for the library's ground floor.

To support his idea of study carrels near the windows of the building yet interconnected with the books, Kahn cited the monastic library at England's Durham Cathedral, where the monks read at desks in the cloister's daylight—which in his design Kahn equated with spiritual light—while books rested in cabinets against the wall of the church. Monastic references are also apparent on the elevations, in the austerity of the symmetrical, unadorned brick cube, each side 111 by 111 feet, broken only by vertical rectangular windows. Standing virtually isolated in the middle of a large quadrangle, Kahn's building marks the soul of the Exeter campus.

The reverence that Kahn expressed in the library dovetailed with the Library Committee's philosophy, outlined in June 1966, a year and a half after Kahn received the commission. They wanted the modern library to be "a quiet retreat for study, reading, and reflection, the intellectual center of the community . . . such a library [should] affirm the regard at the Academy for the work of the mind and the hands of man." [1]

Throughout the design process, Kahn and the Library Committee were in continual dialogue. Each change that resulted from the collaboration made the design more compact and unified. Initially, as seen in the plan, Kahn placed two towers on the north entrance–side corners to contain service spaces, stairs, bathrooms, and

0839. Drawing, Phillips Exeter Library, USA: Sketch of Plan with Elevations, ca. 1967, Louis I. Kahn

elevators. At the request of the committee and the Library Board, he reduced the size of the corner towers and eventually eliminated them altogether, withdrawing the service spaces into the square footprint of the building. This opened up the exterior of the library stacks layer and allowed the brick facade to float like a separate screen, achieving one of the building's most successful features. Visitors to the building's atrium are struck with respect and awe. In one dramatic moment they feel the power of the books and are humbled by the centuries of wisdom they contain. **GSD**

1 Rodney Armstrong, Elliot G. Fish, and Albert C. Ganley, *Proposals for The Library at The Phillips Exeter Academy* (Exeter, NH: Phillips Exeter Academy, 1966), 1.

0840. Exterior of Philips Exeter Library

0841. Interior of Philips Exeter Library

0842. Sudbury Hall architectural model, England, 1660–90

0843. Bookcase, USA, ca. 1875, Herter Brothers

0844. Drawing, Brighton Pavilion, England: Design for a Chinese Pavilion, 1815–22, Frederick Crace

0845. Drawing, Concert Room of Sanssouci Palace, Germany, 1852, Eduard Gaertner

0846. Book illustration, *Household Furniture and Interior Decoration*, 1807, Thomas Hope

0847. Book illustration, *Farbige Räume und Bauten*, ca. 1929, Wilhelm Jöker

0848. Drawing, Grand Central Terminal, USA: Design for Façade (detail), 1910, Whitney Warren, Jr.

0849. Scarf, Trains (detail), 1951, Saul Steinberg

0850. Book illustration, *Architectural Designs for Model Country Residences*, 1861, John Riddell

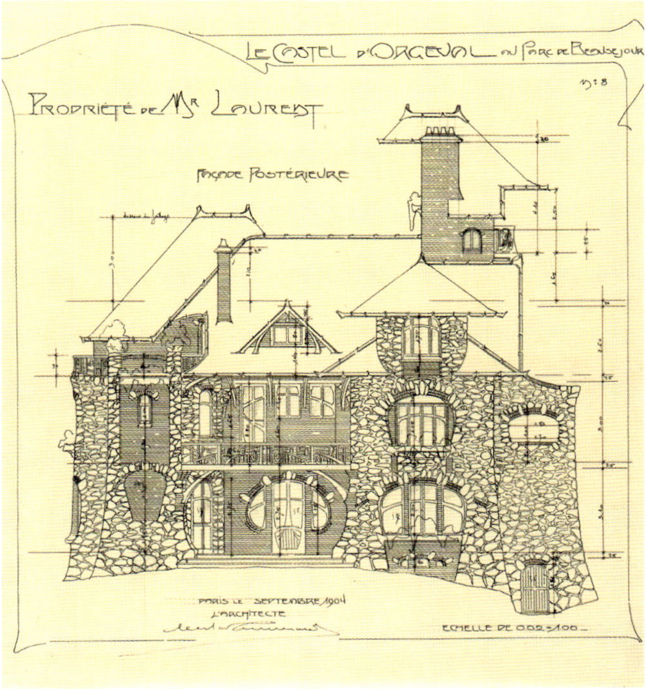

0851. Drawing, Castel d'Orgeval, France: Design for Rear Elevation, 1904, Hector Guimard

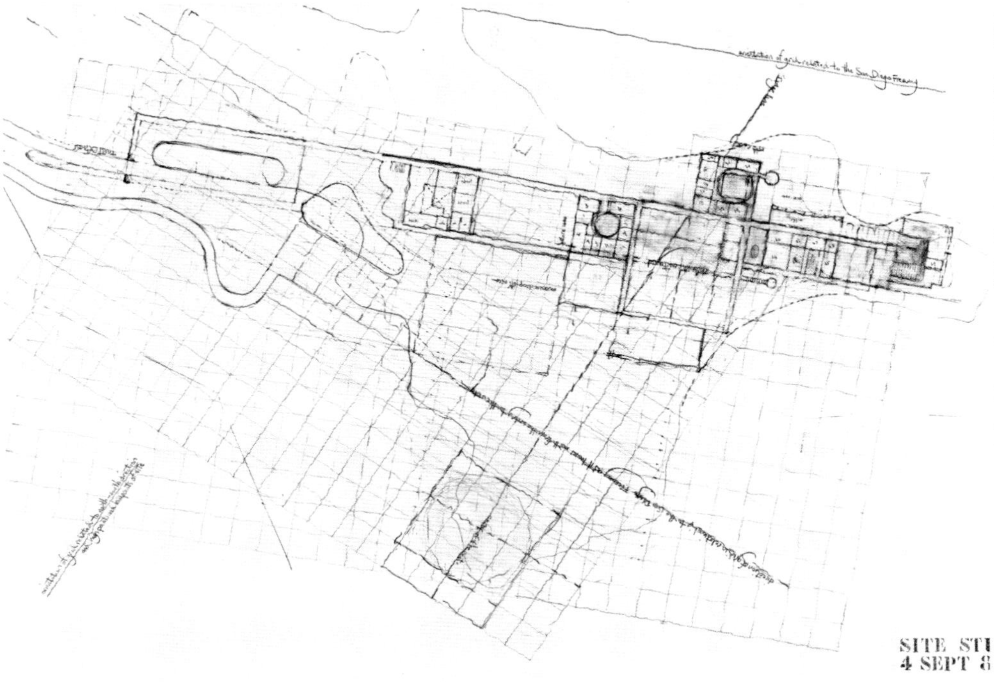

0852. Drawing, J. Paul Getty Center, USA: Site Study 1, 1986, Richard Meier

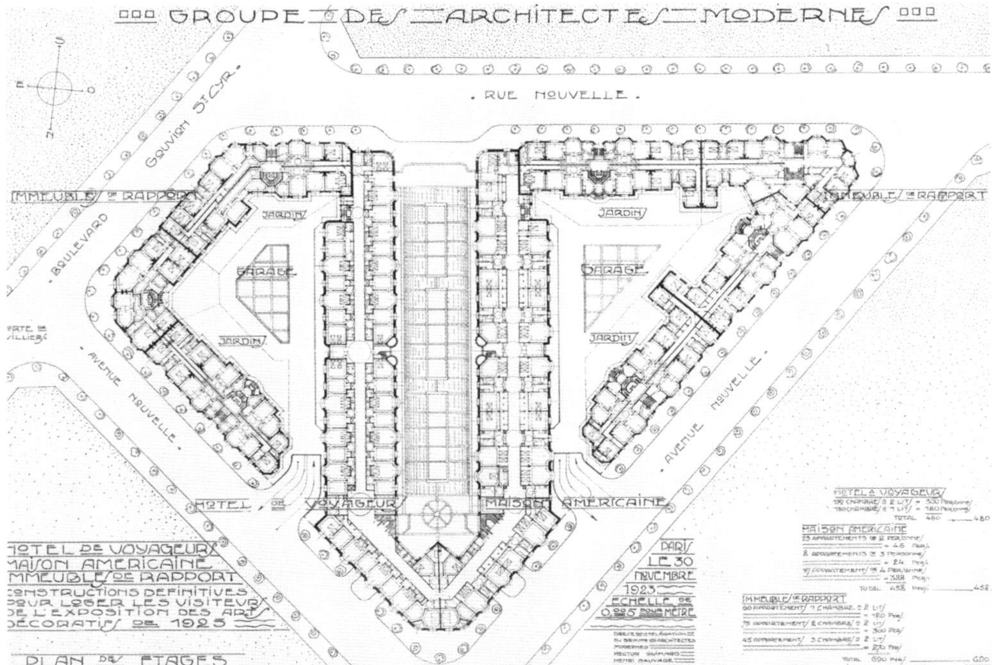

0853. Photostat, Hôtel de Voyageur, Maison Americaine, 1925 Exposition, France: Proposal, 1923, Hector Guimard

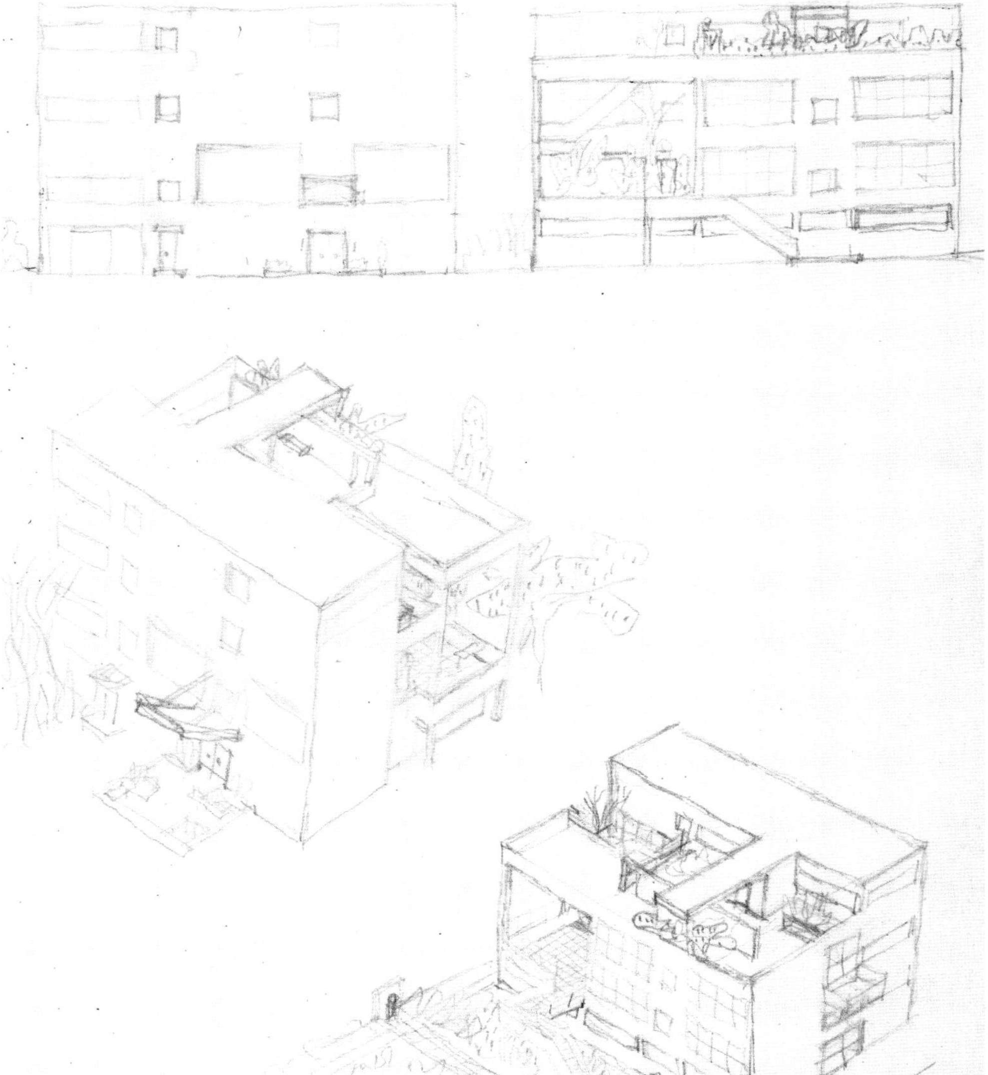

0854. Drawing, Villa Stein-de Monzie, France: First Studies, 1926, Le Corbusier

0855. Birdcage, USA, mid-19th century

0856. Rialto Bridge birdcage, Italy, late 19th–early 20th century

0857. Drawing, Galician Center of Contemporary Art, Spain: Concept Sketches, 1988–93, Álvaro Joaquim de Melo Siza Vieira

Paper construction, Miniature theater depicting a garden scene with dancers
Attributed to engraver and print seller Martin Engelbrecht, (Augsbourg, Germany, 1684–1756)
Published in Augsburg, c. 1740
Illustrations by Jeremiastet Wachsmuth (German) and David Nessenthaler (German)
Purchase, Smithsonian Libraries, GV1521.E54 1740

This miniature theater, a book form also known as a peepshow, diorama, or tunnel book, consists of six intricately cut, hand-colored cards picturing aristocratic figures dancing in a Versailles-like formal garden setting. These cardboard scenes, placed evenly spaced one behind the other in a viewing box, create a delightful, dramatic, multilayered perspective view into a lively garden party.

This tunnel book demonstrates the high craftsmanship, intricacy, and innovativeness of Martin Engelbrecht's designs, as he cleverly transformed two-dimensional illustrations into a whimsical three-dimensional curiosity. Delicate **cutpaper** figures, engaged in courtly leisure and flirtatious dance, emerge from the stage. They build up layers of depth at each set of stage wings representing French or Italianate formal gardens, in a system that imitates in miniature the baroque stage, at a high point of theater and opera in the first half of the eighteenth century.

Although tunnel books as optical experiments date back to the Renaissance, they were made popular in the seventeenth century as so-called peepshow boxes depicting complex theatrical, historical, and religious scenes at traveling fairs throughout Europe. A century later, smaller versions of tunnel books were printed in greater numbers for home entertainment.

Martin Engelbrecht and his brother Christian managed a printing firm in Augsburg (in Bavaria) that was known for the large-scale book productions for works as diverse as Ovid's *Metamorphoses* and a series *Assemblage Nouveau des Manouvries Habilles* (New Assembly of Working Clothing)—the latter a book of plates, showing peasant and tradesmen's clothes that are "assembled" from collagelike pictures of the "working" tools or products of their industry. They also produced more than sixty six- to eight-panel peepshows from about 1740 to 1770, making them one of the earliest, most prolific, and most innovative creators of this type of book. Engelbrecht employed skilled artists such as Wachsmuth and Nessenthaler to illustrate the scenes, which were etched onto copper plates, printed on thin paper, hand colored, and adhered to cardboard before being cut and assembled by the printer, merchant, or buyer. Unlike later tunnel books whose panels were attached by paper or cloth, Engelbrecht's tunnel books required viewing boxes with slots to fit and support each panel.

Images of foreign lands, biblical scenes, famous shipwrecks and battles, as well as pastoral, sporting, and courtly scenes appealed to an elite leisure class seeking novel forms of parlor entertainment. They were beautifully crafted, luxurious artifacts—the finest examples of paper engineering of the day.

Engelbrecht's tunnel books are the forerunners of the peepshow books popularized by Dean & Son of London during the mid-nineteenth century and inspired photographers and cinematographers for their early optical effects. **SVD**

0858. Paper construction, Miniature theater depicting a garden scene with dancers, ca. 1740, Martin Engelbrecht

Print, Projet de Sculpture en Argent d'un Grand Surtout de Table et les Deux Terrines . . . Executée pour Millord Kingston [sic] en 1735 (Design for Centerpiece and Two Tureens Executed for the Duke of Kingston in 1735), plate 115 in Œuvre de Juste-Aurèle Meissonnier, 1748
Designed by Juste-Aurèle Meissonnier (French, 1695–1750)
Etched by Gabriel Huquier (French, 1695–1772)
Paris, France
Etching on white laid paper
Purchased for the Museum by the Advisory Council, 1921-6-212-72

The silver table centerpiece (*surtout de table*) depicted in an **etching** by Gabriel Huquier was the most celebrated achievement of Juste-Aurèle Meissonnier, the French rococo designer and silversmith. Its swirling lines and swelling volumes are perfectly expressed by the etching process, which enabled the printmaker to draw freely and calligraphically on the wax-covered surface of a copper plate before it was dipped in acid that bite into the metal surface, permitting the lines to catch the ink for printing. Commissioned by Evelyn Pierrepont, second Duke of Kingston (1712–73) in 1734, this fabulous confection comprised two elaborate tureens (surviving today in the Cleveland Museum of Art and in a private collection) for serving soup or ragouts whose shell-formed bodies and covers, including fowl, fish, crustaceans, and vegetables, were all made from **castings** after the real objects. These foodstuffs presumably were ingredients in the soups or stews served in the vessels.
Ragouts of different types were a relatively recent dining fad in the early eighteenth century, and the *grand oille*, dating back to the kitchen of Louis XIII, is usually cited as the soup intended to be served in the Kingston tureens. This dish, which is plated in two parts with the clear broth separated from the meats, would have made good use of the two tureens, one part in each. However, early recipes for this special ragout contained pigeons or other fowl, beef, mutton, and vegetables including carrots, mushrooms, as well as cabbage, but no crayfish, crab, or eels, all of which are also represented on the tureen covers. It appears, therefore, that Meissonnier could have chosen to include on each tureen ingredients for at least two types of popular soups/ragouts, one containing fowl, meat, and vegetables (*oille*), and the other some kind of fish stew like a bouillabaisse.
In between the two *pots à oille* (tureens), as they are called colloquially, is a large centerpiece fantasy featuring two children frolicking on a dolphin fountain whose rough, tufa-like crevasses support cruets for oils, vinegars, and other accoutrements. This centerpiece design, which was never executed, differs from Meissonnier's initial concept for the surtout, as represented in a drawing in the Bibliothèque Nationale de France, of two women luxuriating on a similar fountain. It is likely that the entire centerpiece also included four candlesticks (one of which survives in the Les Arts Décoratifs, Paris). The swirling lines, encompassing all the elements including the tureen platters, gave the *surtout* what has been called "a dynamic unity"[1] and likened to "a boat tossed upon the brim of a swelling wave, the ornaments on [the lids] loosely scattered as if by a storm."[2]
Meissonnier's preoccupation with the natural world should be seen in light of the eighteenth-century fascination with the eccentricities of nature, such as shell formations. In France, the educated public collected shells and other bizarre curi-osities of nature, which they displayed on side tables or on top of commodes and small cabinets in their living quarters or in separate rooms, known as cabinets of curiosities. Beautifully illustrated publications by respected scholars and paintings

0859. Print, Project de Sculpture en argent d'un grand surtout de table et les deux terrines . . . executée pour Millord Kingston en 1735, 1742–48, Juste-Aurèle Meissonnier

dealers stimulated the public's interest in collecting the extraordinary products of the natural world.

If Meissonnier's print and the entire Œuvre publication served, among other functions, to promote Meissonnier's singular design abilities as a silversmith, architect, and interior designer, it also served a second function of showing contemporary metal-smiths and other artisans who were among Meissonnier's many admirers, how such complicated metal constructions were to be fabricated in three dimensions. The surtout print covers a double folio sheet in the artist's Œuvre.

This monographic publication was the concept of the printmaker and important print publisher Gabriel Huquier, who also produced most of the etchings for the Œuvre. Containing nearly 140 prints after Meissonnier's designs, some of which the designer published himself initially in fascicules of six, eight, or ten prints before Huquier's bound book of ca. 1748, the publication served as a wellspring of ideas for candle-sticks, tobacco boxes, sword hilts, watch cases, wall paneling, religious objects, and furniture. The Œuvre collection was influential within France, where the designs were copied or inspired different variations by French designers, and in Germany, where the Meissen factory produced a ceramic version of one of the French silversmith's candlestick designs.[3] Undoubtedly the Œuvre de Juste-Aurèle Meissonnier, including the surtout for the Duke of Kingston, transformed Meissonnier into a design celebrity throughout the Western world. **GSD**

1 Peter Fuhring, *Juste-Aurèle Meissonnier: Un Génie du Rococo 1695–1750*, vol. 1 (Turin: Umberto Allemandi & C., 1999), 91.

2 Peter Fuhring, *The Thyssen Meissonnier Silver Tureen Made for the 2nd Duke of Kingston* (New York: Sotheby's, 1998), 34.

3 Gail S. Davidson, "Ornament of Bizarre Imagination...," in *Rococo, the Continuing Curve, 1730–2008*, Sarah Coffin et al. (New York: Smithsonian Cooper-Hewitt, National Design Museum, 2008), 46–47, fig. 8.

0860. Drawing, First Design for Centerpiece and Two Tureens for the Duke of Kingston, 1733–34, Juste-Aurèle Meissonnier

0861. Drawing, The Japanese Salon, Villa Hügel, Hietzing, Austria, 1855, Rudolf von Alt

0862. Book illustration, *Haus eines Kunst-freundes*, 1902, Mackay Hugh Baillie-Scott and Emil Hochdanz

0863. Drawing, Design for a Dining Room, USA, 1934, Donald Deskey

0864. Print, Vue perspective de la chambre à coucher du Cit[oyen] V à Paris, 1812, Charles Percier and Pierre-François-Léonard Fontaine

Drawing, Sir Lawrence Alma-Tadema's Study, Townshend House, London, 1884
Anna Alma-Tadema (British, 1865–1943)
London, England
Brush and watercolor, gouache, pen and ink, graphite on white paper
Thaw Collection, 2007-27-72

In 1911, Hallie Eustace Killick Miles wrote in her book *The Ideal Home and Its Problems*: "Everything in a human dwelling is bathed in personality . . . everything has a voice that speaks of the character and individuality of the person to whom the room belongs." [1] Today we take for granted the idea that our interiors express who we are and what we value, but at the time this concept was barely thirty years old—dating to a time of the Aesthetic Movement's critiquing of industrialization and the promotion of beauty, individual expression, and craft in the home in England, and an interest in the salubrious effects of beauty and craft in the home.
The study interior depicted in this drawing **(0865)** belonged to the Dutch-born painter Sir Lawrence Alma-Tadema, who in 1869 moved with his second wife and two daughters to London, where he became enormously successful as a painter of ancient Roman daily life scenes. In 1870 he acquired a modest home, Townshend House, which he began to renovate as a combination studio home, popular at the time among British and European painters. Like Leighton House, the lavish Kensington studio home that Sir Frederic Leighton had built just three years earlier, Alma-Tadema's home and plan, with its first-floor study just off the front door, was featured in several contemporary publications, where his fashionably individualistic taste was heartily praised: "Alma-Tadema's house is but another work of art from his own hand, planned and decorated after his own designs, and his boldly original taste, free from any taint of conventionality, is everywhere evident." [2]
This radiant, light-filled watercolor drawing, by his fifteen- or sixteen-year-old daughter Anna, shows the cozy study and renders the textures of his eclectic furnishings: the mass-produced bentwood Thonet-type desk chair, with Dutch oak cabinetry on the rear wall at the right, tatami matting on the floor, Indonesian batik on the lower part of the walls, a Japanese fan or parasol on the ceiling at the left, and a fur-covered daybed and bronze chandelier, both designed by Alma-Tadema. Anna made watercolor drawings of at least two other rooms in her family's home, the Drawing Room (1885, Royal Academy, London) and the Interior of the Gold Room (ca. 1883, Nelson Atkins Museum of Art, Kansas City, Missouri), [3] probably as mementos before 1886, when the family moved to a larger home on Grove End Road that had been previously owned by the painter James Tissot. **GSD**

1 Hallie Eustace Killick Miles, *The Ideal Home and its Problems* (London: Methuen and Co., 1911), 514.
2 Helen Zimmern, "The Home of Alma-Tadema," *The Art Amateur* vol. 10, no. 3 (Feb. 1884): 71.
3 Charlotte Gere, *Artistic Circles, Design & Decoration in the Aesthetic Movement* (London: V&A Publishing, 2010), 188–89, figs. 190 and 191. See discussion of Townshend House, 195–200.

0865. Drawing, Sir Lawrence Alma-Tadema's Study, Townshend House, England, 1884, Anna Alma-Tadema

0866. Book illustration, *Raisons des forces mouvantes* (detail), 1615, Salomon de Caus

0867. Drawing, View of a Masquerade Ball, 1770–80, Jean-Charles Delafosse

0868. Drawing, Theater Design: A Town Square, ca. 1719, Francesco Galli Bibiena

0869. Scenic panel, Reconciliation of Venus and Psyche, 1923, Desfossé et Karth

0870.Book illustration, Design for a State Bedchamber,
from *Second Livre d'Appartements*, ca. 1702, Daniel Marot

Desk, France, ca. 1935
Jean-Michel Frank (French, 1895–1941)
Joined wood, cut, pressed and dyed shagreen, carved ivory
Gift of Mr. and Mrs. Forsythe Sherfesee, 1968-144-13-a/g

This desk is part of a group of objects designed by Jean-Michel Frank in the 1930s for Villa Bontoc, the residence of Mr. and Mrs. William Forsythe Sherfesee, American clients in Saint-Jean-Cap-Ferrat, in the maritime Alps of the French Riviera. Comprising five armchairs, two side chairs, three desks, three tables, a removable tabletop covered in parchment, several lamp bases and shades, a leather bed, and two decorative ornaments, these items were given to the museum as a group in 1968, in the name of both the original owners, by Mr. Sherfesee some years after his wife's death. Together the objects represent elements of a unified interior treatment in the modern fashion that was emblematic of both its designer and the impact of the unified interiors shown in the Exposition des Arts Décoratifs in Paris in 1925.
Jean-Michel Frank produced interiors, furniture, and accessories that were influential on domestic spaces and the social scene in Europe and America from the mid-1920s up to his untimely death in 1941, at the age of forty-six. His nearly two-decade career coincided with a vibrant period for the arts in Paris. His family and business connections led him to work with such high-profile clients as fashion designer Elsa Schiaparelli, the Viscount and Viscountess Charles and Marie-Laure de Noailles, and the American composer and lyricist Cole Porter.[1] Two American projects were the 1929 San Francisco penthouse for millionaire art enthusiast Templeton Crocker, called at the time by *Vogue* the first truly modern apartment in the United States, [2] and, ten years later, the Nelson Rockefeller apartment at the top of Rockefeller Center in New York. In the Crocker space, Frank included walls and ceilings upholstered in parchment or straw, and furniture made of cast bronze, or covered in materials like leather and straw marquetry.
Frank's work could be considered a hybrid. His designs combined elements suggestive of the decorative approach based in a tradition of fine craftsmanship, as seen in the work of contemporaries like Émile-Jacques Ruhlmann and Süe et Mare's use of luxurious materials, voluptuous forms, and rich surface treatments that suggested the ancient régime of the late eighteenth century. Yet they also showed an understanding of and appreciation for the modern. While Frank did not deeply investigate innovative industrial materials of the time, such as tubular steel, his forms were very functional, often stripped to the minimum, emphasizing proportion and line for interest. This is also seen in the work of modernist contemporaries such as Eileen Gray and René Herbst, for example. Frank also used humble substances such as straw or plaster in concert with the more lavish surface treatments as he sought texture in the overall scheme.
The mixture of textures is characteristic of the Sherfesee ensemble, which includes shagreen (sharkskin) on this desk **(0871)** and a side chair; a **lacquered painted** surface on another desk with chair; straw and striated wood **veneers** on some of the chairs and tables; others with parchment and painted textured gesso surfaces; pigskin leather on the club chairs and bed; glass decorative ornamental disks; and rock and crystal for the lamp bases with mica and shell shades, the last, no doubt, a topical reference to Saint-Jean-Cap-Ferrat's location near the Mediterranean Sea. This unique combination of simple, clean-lined modernism and a lavish art deco style meant Frank's style and commissions worked well with skyscrapers, Paris

0871. Desk, France, ca. 1935, Jean-Michel Frank

0872. Snapshot of raffia-covered writing table and chair at Villa Bontoc taken in 1962

apartments, and seaside casual environments, varying the blend and balance of austere forms combined with elegant, luxurious-looking surface treatments, depending on the client and locale.

While much of Frank's work has been documented so that it is easy to see that this desk and the other pieces are his, less documented are the Sherfesees, an unusual but by all accounts well-suited couple. Forsythe Sherfesee was a graduate of the Yale School of Forestry who went on to become assistant director of the Philippines Bureau of Forestry and a financial advisor to China. There he met Emily Borie Ryerson, a widow nineteen years his senior, who was visiting the country in 1927; they were married in December that year. In 1912, she and her first husband had been aboard the ill-fated Titanic, after a vacation in France. While she survived, her husband perished. As a widow, she not only raised her children but did charity work abroad, including so much for the French wounded in World War I that she was awarded the Croix de Guerre. So the choice of the south of France may have been initially hers, but clearly Sherfesee was no stranger to life abroad. They settled in Cap-Ferrat not long after their villa, named Villa Bontoc, was completed during their extended honeymoon travels that lasted a year starting in December 1927.

Her wealth had been enough to send a plane for her fiancé to St. Paul, Minnesota, from Chicago to get him there for the wedding when snowstorms delayed his return, but he too had collected in his foreign postings. Thus, Chinese carpets and ceramics found their way, along with modern paintings, into the interiors that Frank designed. Clearly the couple was wealthy and sophisticated, having built their villa in a place frequented by an elegant and international coterie, and next door to Somerset Maugham.

It may have been Frank's 1929 visit to Pierre Drieu, who had a house in Cap Ferrat, who introduced Frank to the Sherfesees. It appears that the Frank furnishings at the Villa Bontoc may have been later augmented with pieces from Eyre de Lanux's 1929 interiors for the Sherfesee's Paris apartment, including some by Frank and some by Eyre de Lanux. [3]

The desk and other furniture pieces may well have been produced by Chanaux & Company, the interior design firm Frank co-owned with decorator-craftsman Adolphe Chanaux. As design director there, Frank was responsible for over thirty workers assigned to his projects, and he taught as well. The collaboration enabled him to use proficient draftsmen and other skilled members of the firm rather than draw himself. Also while at Chanaux in the 1930s, Frank developed what came to be known as the Parsons table, a simple rectilinear form consisting of a thin square tabletop on four slim legs, through a design exercise he devised for students at the Paris Atelier (now Parsons Paris School of Art and Design). [4] The Sherfesee ensemble features this sort of table with a parchment surface, not associated with this design classic today.

Frank collaborated with artists of his day to create accessories, including plaster vases and wall sconces, and **cast** and **gilt-bronze** floor lamps by the sculptor Alberto Giacometti; this ensemble features objects he designed, such as the disks. Although Frank did not design for mass industrial production per se, he understood that his furniture could be marketed on its own, not just part of a specific interior. This desk, while part of a larger ensemble, could work well in almost any interior of his day, as well as with the classic lines of the late eighteenth century.

Despite its luxury status, the desk may have inspired others, as his firm sometimes

produced variations of a model to hold as inventory for use in later commissions or to be sold individually. Frank also sold his designs through his own boutique established in 1935, in French department stores, from 1924 at Hermès, licensed through design firms in England and Argentina, and in the United States.
World War II brought both Frank's and the Sherfesees' flight from France, the former in 1940, and the latter in 1939. Frank went to Argentina, and thence to New York, where he committed suicide in 1941. The Sherfesees also went to South America, where, while traveling, Emily Sherfesee died of a heart attack that year. Her husband, known as Forsythe, returned to France after the war, during which time the house had been commandeered by the Germans and many of the furnishings dispersed. However, he was able to retrieve or buy back most of them, and continued to entertain the Anglo-French community and visitors until his death in 1971. In 1968 he arranged through a decorator friend, William Pahlmann, to donate the Frank furniture and an accompanying carpet to Cooper Hewitt, where this desk and its companions give insight into Frank's style, an era, and the taste of his clients. **SDC, CT**

1 Peirre-Emmanuel Martin-Vivier, *Jean-Michel Frank: The Strange and Subtle Luxury of the Parisian Haute-Monde in the Art Deco Period* (New York: Rizzoli International Publications, Inc., 2008).

2 Mary Ashee Miller, "A Twentieth Century Apartment," *Vogue,* August 3, 1929, 30–35, 94.

3 "Records and drawings exist by American-born designer Eyre de Lanux for the Sherfesee's apartment, in the Archives of American Art. Some of the pieces appear in images of the Paris apartment (cf Madge Garland, "Interiors by Eyre de Lanux," *Creative Art* (April 1930): 263–65), which, along with the drawings, appear to indicate that she both placed Franks's furnishings and used her own. These pieces later may have been taken to the Villa Bontoc. We are grateful to Mitchell Owens for these references, including, Louis-Géraud Castor and Willy Huybrechts, *Eyre de Lanux: Une Décoratrice Américaine à Paris* (Paris: Norma Éditions, 2013), 154–56, and the Eyre de Lanux papers at the Archives of American Art, http://www.aaa.si.edu/collections/eyre-de-lanux-papers-6668.

4 "Frank Alvah Parsons: Leader in Franco-American Education Exchange," American Center France, accessed January 13, 2014, www.americancenterfrance.org/front/index. php?&lvlid=37&dsgtypid= 10&artid=48&pos=1&lang=en.

0873. Dressing table and bench, USA, ca. 1929, after a design by Léon Jallot

0874. Architect's table, Germany, 1780–95, David Roentgen

0875. Drawing, Henry J. Allen Residence, USA: Piano Bench and Taboret (detail), 1917, Frank Lloyd Wright

0876. Desk, USA, ca. 1933, Paul T. Frankl

0877. Print, Deux diferents desseins de comodes, 1745–55, Jean-François Cuvilliés

0878. Buffet, France, ca. 1905, Louis Majorelle

Cabinet on stand, probably England, 1675–1700
Marquetry inlaid, veneered, and joined oak, deal, walnut, and other wood, bone, brass
Bequest of Mrs. John Innes Kane, 1926-22-43

This cabinet on stand represents the convergence of art and design, function and display, technique and statement. It was made as elegant storage and was probably part of a unified scheme. Its display of flowers marquetry inlaid into the surface is like seventeenth-century Dutch still-life paintings, with the overall pattern of floral textiles of the period.

Most likely intended for the bedroom of a wealthy woman, the cabinet was probably originally part of a suite with a table, and two candle stands. Made to hold precious objects—jewelry and larger fine accessories, such as lace—its exterior was expected to be at least as splendid as its contents. It dates to a time when the noble and wealthy started to consider furniture as furnishings, rather than as pieces that moved with their owners. In fact, in most European languages other than English, the words for furniture—mobile, *meubles, Möbel*—are based on its mobility.

An increasingly wealthy merchant class patronized local top-level craftsman-designers, especially in the Netherlands and England, where the East India companies enriched many from trading with Asia. New forms of decoration may have resulted from competition from imported wares such as Asian black lacquer cabinets, which often rested on lavish European stands. European craftsmen also responded by creating jewel-like details in bone and mixed-wood **inlays** and **veneers** combined with sophisticated cabinetry techniques. One such technique is **dovetailing**, a relatively new skill adopted by top **cabinetmakers** at the time when it appears in this cabinet was made.

Floral decoration, especially incorporating tulips, was in demand throughout Europe, partially inspired by "tulip mania," the obsession with the bulbs that appeared in Europe in the late sixteenth century, generally thought to have arrived from the Ottoman Empire through Vienna. By 1636 the tulip bulb became the fourth-leading export product of the Netherlands.[1] Augsburg and especially Antwerp and Amsterdam, all centers for tulip bulb distribution, were also centers of cutting, including **marquetry** cabinetry panels—in wood, metal, tortoiseshell, and hardstones —*pietre dure*—as well as gemstones. The proximity of wood- and stoneworkers suggests that some cutters may have applied their cutting skills to both materials.

These centers were sources of craftsmen for King Louis XIV of France (reign 1643–1715).The popularity in England of this cabinet's style is probably due to the time Charles II (reign 1660–85) spent absorbing new developments in style while exiled in the Netherlands and France in the 1650s. Two of the greatest marquetry artists of the court of Louis XIV were creating lavish and expressive works then: Pierre Gôle (1620–85), originally from Bergen in Holland, and André Charles Boulle, although Frenchborn, the son of a "journeyman ebony **joiner**" from the duchy of Guelders (now in Germany and the Netherlands).[2] Boulle studied **painting** and **drawing** before applying his skills to marquetry. Although renowned for geometric patterns in tortoiseshell and metal-inlaid pieces, his wood marquetry resembling painting in wood impacted taste.

In England the diarist and collector John Evelyn, who traveled extensively to France and Italy from 1643 to 1652, had a cabinet made in England to hold his collection of medals. It incorporated pietre dure panels he bought in Florence in 1644[3] that feature

0879. Cabinet on stand, probably England, 1675–1700

small arrangements of flowers and birds, arranged on small drawers much like the interior of the Cooper Hewitt's cabinet. In his 1664 work *Silva* Evelyn recorded the presence in London of specialty cabinetmakers proficient in applying veneer and, in a later edition of 1670, added specific descriptions of the staining, coloring, and shading of various woods by inlay specialists there: "when they would imitate the natural turning of Leaves in their curious Compartiments and bordures of Flower-works, they effect it by dipping the pieces (first cut into shape and ready to In-lay) so far into hot Sand, as they would have the shadow and the heat of the Sand darkens it so gradually without detriment or burning the thin Chip, as one would conceive it to be natural." [4]

The techniques of naturalistic marquetry were based on those of Continental Europe, but English cabinetmakers specialized in **veneering** bands around the edges of the decorative panels as a way to frame them like a picture, but also to avoid the damaging effects of opening doors to the intricate marquetry. If a piece of edging came off, it could be readily matched to the band and not the jigsaw puzzle effect of floral marquetry. The presence of this technique on the Cooper Hewitt's cabinet suggests that the marquetry specialist, possibly Dutch, provided these panels to an English workshop that created the structure.

The high quality of marquetry work on the doors continues on their interiors and to the drawers, each element adding to the cost and to the visual impression created for someone privileged enough to own and use it. The patron also would have known how costly the striped tulips in the design were, the added difficulty of depicting them in marquetry, and could have been familiar with the floral bouquets of the decorative **prints** and paintings by Jean-Baptiste Monnoyer (French, 1636–99), who is the likely design source. Monnoyer, who studied flower painting in Antwerp and worked under Charles Le Brun at Versailles, was brought to England by the first Duke of Montagu to create floral bouquet–painted overdoors in the redecoration of his London house in the 1690s, probably under Daniel Marot. Some of his prints were issued in Amsterdam, so not surprisingly, his designs relate to Dutch marquetry as well as Delft ceramic decoration **(0879)**.

Three cabinets with marquetry apparently by the same hand include this one at Cooper Hewitt and an extremely similar one in Museum of Applied Arts (Oslo, Norway) **(0880)**. It has been suggested that the marquetry may be by the Dutch specialist Jan van Mekeren (1658–1733) when he was young. [5] Van Mekeren may have been in England early in his career. While his early style is not known, and it is likely that he would have produced his marquetry from within the workshop of a master cabinetmaker or marquetry specialist, the quality of the work on this cabinet is such that even if his name is not identifiable securely, it suggests someone of van Mekeren's sphere based on technical style and motifs. **SDC**

0879. Cooper Hewitt's Cabinet on stand with open doors

0880. Marquetry Cabinet, probably England, ca 1690, Museum of Applied Arts (Oslo, Norway)

1 Peter M. Garber, "Tulipmania," *Journal of Political Economy* 97, no. 3 (1989): 535–60, doi:10.1086/261615.

2 Adriana Turpin, "Floral Marquetry in Late Seventeenth-century England and Holland," in *Dutch and Flemish Artists in Britain, 1550–1800*; Juliette Roding (Leiden: Primavera Pers, 2003), 226, note 27. London, British Library Add MS 36781, Household of Charles II; Adrian Bolte is listed as a cabinetmaker.
Also as cited ibid., 226, note 29: J.-P. Samoyault traced the family of André Charles Boulle via his father Jean Bolt in Paris, and suggested it was a common name in Gelders. See *J.-P. Samoyault, André-Charles Boulle et sa Famille* (Geneva: Droz, 1979), 5.

3 Victoria and Albert Museum, V&A W.38-1983.

4 Monique Riccardi-Cubitt, *The Art of the Cabinet* (London: Thames & Hudson, 1992), 86; Reiner Baarsen, *17th-Century Cabinets*, trans. John Rudge (Amsterdam: Rijksmuseum, Waanders, Uitgevers, 2000), 53–55; Adam Bowett, *English Furniture 1660–1714: From Charles II to Queen Anne* (Woodbridge, England: Antique Collectors Club, 2002), 55.

5 Turpin, "Floral Marquetry in Late Seventeenth-century England and Holland," 228, bases this attribution on a cabinet with floral marquetry in a private collection in Alkmaar; its provenance connects it to the Van Mekeren almshouses, illustrated in H. Lunsingh Scheuleer, "Jan van Mekeren, een Amsterdamsche meubelmaker uit het end der 17de en begin der 18de eeuw," *Oud Holland* 58 (1941): 178–88.

0881. Cabinet on stand, left door (detail), probably England, 1675–1700
0882. Cabinet on stand, right door (detail), probably England, 1675–1700

0883. Print, Basket with Flowers on a Table, ca. 1680, France, Jean-Baptiste Monnoyer

0884. Book illustration, *Urformen der Kunst*, 1932, Karl Blossfeldt

0885. Sidewall, England, 1848–60, A. W. N. Pugin

0886. Sidewall, City Park, 2007, Dan Funderburgh

0887. Sampler (detail), China, ca. 1930

0888. Purse, England, early 17th century

0889. Textile, Nigeria, mid-20th century
0890. Fragment (detail), Spain, 15th century

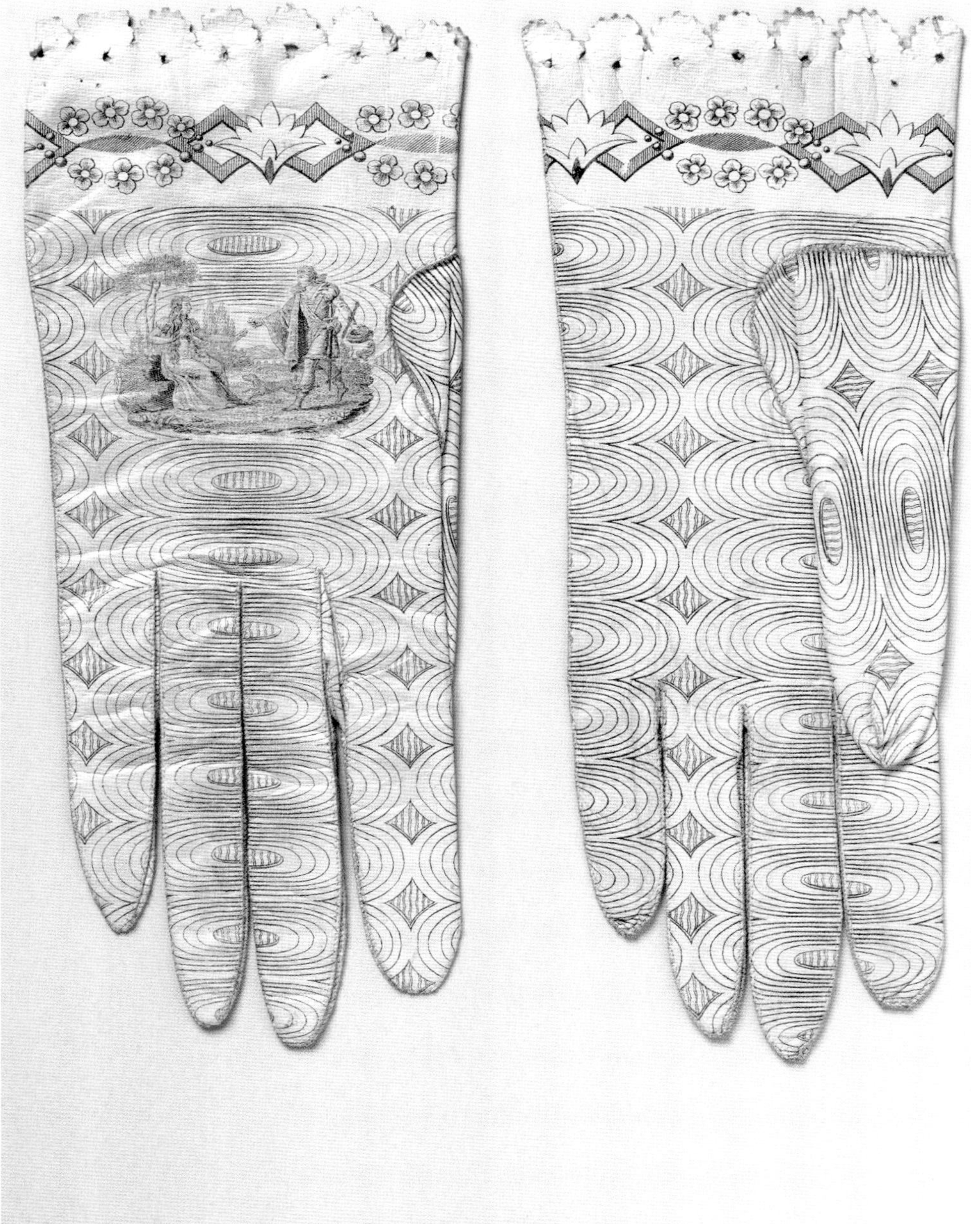

0891. Woman's gloves, Spain, 1800–20

0892. Table cover, USA, ca. 1900, Sybil Carter Indian Mission and Lace Industry Association

Textile, Gold Ripple-Wave, ca. 1956
Probably designed by Marianne Strengell (Finnish, active United States, 1909–98)
Manufactured by Chatham Manufacturing Company for Ford Motor Company (USA)
Jacquard woven cotton, rayon, and Lurex
Museum purchase from Smithsonian Institution Collections Acquisition Program Fund, 1998-56-1

When is the last time you were dazzled by a car's upholstery? Leather seems to be the only luxury option today, but custom woven fabrics used to be an important part of a car's interior styling. Gold Ripple-wave—with its lustrous fibers, lemon-yellow color, and sparkling silver accents—was a luxury interior option on Ford's 1957 Fairlane 500 Club and Town Victoria—and was offered only in this distinctive yellow and black color combination to match the two-tone exterior paint finish. The interior was also fitted with a white-and-black pin-dot hood liner and black rayon vinyl trim.[1] According to *American Fabrics* magazine, the design was very on-trend for 1957: "Both jacquards and tweeds frequently include the use of metallic yarns. The aim is to make the fabric harmonize visually with the chrome . . . . There is a natural leaning toward two-tone color treatment that harmonizes with the exterior paint work."[2]

In the 1950s, cars were being marketed aggressively to women, especially the rapidly increasing numbers living in the suburbs, who needed cars to fulfill their household duties. Some manufacturers experimented with a fashion approach to auto interiors —in 1955 Ford even made driving coats and umbrellas to match their car interiors— but in selling directly to consumers, automobile manufacturers were taking on a much larger financial risk in their styling choices. "If the color combinations used in the trim and upholstery of automobiles today bear a definite resemblance to the fashions well-dressed women are wearing, it is no accident. The top styling directors in Detroit study the public's taste and preferences in clothes today more closely and scientifically perhaps than many manufacturers in the apparel field."[3] Car makers needed to be attentive to long-term fashion and color trends, but avoid seasonal fads. Textures, tweeds, and small-scale abstract patterns were embraced because lead times for automobile manufacture were two to three years, as opposed to a few months for apparel. Automobiles also posed technical challenges for textile designers, especially constant sun exposure. Designers needed to experiment with new synthetic materials and dyes to ensure resistance to fading. Interior fabrics were rigorously tested to prove resistance to wear and fading. "Directions in Automobile Upholstery" was a regular feature in *American Fabrics* magazine through the 1950s, advising designers on slick fibers with "the right amount of slide" to prevent dresses and hosiery from snagging on seats, and the need to develop durable and colorful fabrics to stand up to the new fadeless auto body paints—also synthetic polyesters.

Gold Ripple-wave was manufactured for Ford by the Chatham Manufacturing Company, and most likely designed by Marianne Strengell. The work of individual designers was not acknowledged by the car companies, but Strengell worked with Chatham from 1954 to 1960, and according to a contemporary magazine account, a large percentage of the automotive fabrics chosen by Ford for its 1957 automobiles were "Strengell-designed and Chatham-woven."[4]

Strengell, who was head of the Department of Weaving and Textile Design at Cranbrook Academy, had several connections to the automobile industry. While teaching at Cranbrook, she also held a number of outside consulting positions and worked on commissions for architects, including the interior fabrics for Eero

0893. Textile, Gold Ripple-Wave, ca. 1956, probably Marianne Strengell

Saarinen's General Motors Technical Center, as well as for the private office of Harley Earl, GM's vice president in charge of styling.[5] She created upholstery fabrics for Ford Motor Company, General Motors Corporation, Chrysler, and American Motors, as well as for United Airlines. She was a pioneer in the use of synthetic fibers and helped Chatham to develop equipment for the mass production of fabrics using synthetic fibers, which were so essential to the automobile industry.[6] **SB**

1 "Ford Factory Color and Upholstery Book," Ford Motor Company, www.1957ford.com/interior/.
2 "Trends in Automobile Upholstery Fabrics," *American Fabrics* 39 (Winter 1956–57): 70.
3 "General Motors: A Fashion Factor in the United States," *American Fabrics* 37 (Summer 1956): 112–15.
4 Karen Kehoe, "She Works in Detroit," *Charm Magazine,* April 1956, 169. With special thanks to Leslie S. Edwards, Head Archivist, Cranbrook Archives, for providing this reference.
5 Ibid.
6 Ibid.

0894. Collar, Italy, 1650–75

0895. Apron, Italy, 1906–10, Aemilia Ars

0896. Cravat end, France, 1670–85

0897. Cravat end, Flanders (present-day Belgium), 1700–50

0898. Border, Italy, early 17th century

0899. Border, France, 18th century

0900. Print, Garden of Love (detail), ca. 1500, Israhel van Meckenem

0901. Print, Design for Cover Paper: Floral Motif (detail), France or England, 1825–50

Cravat end, France, ca. 1695
Linen needle lace
Bequest of Richard Cranch Greenleaf in memory of his mother, Adeline Emma Greenleaf, 1962-50-18-a

In 1962, Cooper Hewitt was the fortunate recipient of an exceptional bequest—mostly costume and textiles—belonging to Richard Cranch Greenleaf (1887–1961). He collected only the best, and to the present day, these objects are considered highlights of the Textiles Department. That his primary interest was lace can be seen in the detailed catalogs he compiled during a lifetime of collecting. From the Greenleaf Collection is an important cravat end **(0902)** made to celebrate the marriage of the Duke of Burgundy (1682–1712) to Marie-Adélaïde of Savoy (1685–1712) in 1697. The cravat end marks the culmination of a considerable effort, begun in the 1660s, by the French royal government under Louis XIV (1638–1715) and Jean-Baptiste Colbert (1619–83) to develop a lace industry that rivaled the high-quality laces made in Venice and Flanders. By the end of the seventeenth century, the French were producing fine **needle lace** that was markedly different from their early imitative efforts of foreign styles. Meticulously conceived designs were small, delicate, and complex. Pattern and contrast, skillfully rendered in linen thread, produced designs that were highly readable as visual expressions of the French royal aesthetic. Refinements in structure and technique made the new designs possible. Lace makers employed a twisted buttonhole stitch to create light, open lace that was a departure from the padded, three-dimensional Venetian lace of the past. Raised foundation threads outlined areas rendered with a variety of patterned filling stitches, while pinholes lightened densely worked areas of the design. A buttonholed hexagonal mesh decorated with tiny knobs called picots was used to connect discrete areas of the design. Initially, all needle and **bobbin laces** produced under Colbert were known as *point de France*, but by the eighteenth century the term identified only the needle lace technique used in this cravat end. With broader changes taking place in fashion, the stylistic and technical developments insured the success of French needle lace, as its open, delicate quality lent itself to the soft gathers that were becoming fashionable. France increasingly set the new standard for European styles, which at the turn of the eighteenth century were worn with flounces, aprons, scarves, and cravats made of lightweight lace.

The rectangular man's cravat **(0902)** allowed lace designers to incorporate pictorial and narrative elements, and was especially suitable for expressing the artistic refinements achieved under the French system. A royal wedding was a politically significant event and presented an opportunity to depict royal personages and symbols of French power. Louis XIV enlisted several royal designers to create his aesthetic vision, notably Charles Le Brun (1619–90) and Jean Bérain (1640–1711), whose influence is most evident here. Bérain's designs for furniture, interiors, theater sets, and costumes were fanciful and whimsical, employing many arabesques and free-floating architectural elements such as draped canopies. His costumes for theater frequently featured Roman warriors with elaborately plumed helmets. With characteristic restraint, designs by Bérain tend to align and separate various motifs along a vertical axis so the numerous figures, heraldic symbols, and architectural flourishes retain an elegant balance.

A royal wedding is suggested in a typically Bérainesque arrangement of symmetrical elements. The design shows a central figure of a warrior outfitted in Greco-Roman

0902. Cravat end, France, ca. 1695

armor with a helmet in the form of a double-headed eagle. Above him is a large closed crown flanked by cherubs. A symbol of sovereignty, the closed crown reveals that the central character is very likely the Duke of Burgundy, grandson of Louis XIV. Crouched on either side of him are his brothers, the Duke of Anjou and the Duke of Berry. At the top, two pairs of addorsed dolphins offer further evidence of the marriage of the heir apparent or Dauphin of France. Bacchus, who straddles a barrel with a raised glass, symbolizes the celebratory nature of the occasion. The marriage came on the heels of the Treaty of Turin, in which the Duke of Savoy promised his allegiance to France in the Nine Years' War and agreed that his daughter, Marie-Adélaïde, would marry the grandson of Louis XIV. Cooper Hewitt's cravat end is believed to be part of a set made specially to celebrate their union. **KR**

0902. Cravat end (detail), France, ca. 1695

0903. Textile, Marigold, 1875, William Morris

0904. Tapestry square, Egypt, 3rd–4th century

0905. Textile, France, ca. 1919, Herman A. Elsberg

0906. Fragment, Italy or Spain, 15th century

Woodblock print, *Kaigara Danmen Zuan*, 1913
Written by Yoichirō Hirase (Japanese, 1859–1925)
Illustrated by Jun Nishikawa
Published by Unsōdō, Kyoto
Ink on paper
Purchased by the Mary Stuart Book Fund, Cooper Union Library, Smithsonian Libraries, q N8243.S4 H57

Most design pattern books published by Unsōdō were based on flora and fauna motifs that move through and divide spaces in contrasting ways. While some may see that these works share some superficial characteristics of the European art nouveau—organic designs, curved lines, and flattened forms of colored planes with bold outlines—these compositions have deep roots in the traditional Japanese Rinpa style, a courtly aesthetic with origins in the early seventeenth century. This style experienced a resurgence at the turn of the twentieth century, during Japan's design education reform. Studying European design books along with reexamining Japanese design traditions led to a revival of beautifully crafted designs that explore the traditions of Rinpa through modern eyes.

This composition was published by Unsōdō in 1913, at the end of Japan's design reform movement. While its bold lines, sweeping curves, and organic forms are characteristic of Rinpa, they were derived by a scientist, not a designer. Yoichirō Hirase, a prominent mollusk biologist in Japan, collected over thirty-five hundred shells, one thousand of which were new discoveries. Hirase explained in the introduction of the book that he is not a designer or artist, but that he came up with the idea for the book while researching shells and cutting them at various angles. He found the cross sections so strange and interesting that he used **seal ink** to stamp them on paper. He further explored these interesting patterns with illustrator Jun Nishikawa. The result of their efforts, *Kaigara Danmen Zuan*, has over fifty pages of designs based on the cross sections of twelve different shells. Over a century later, these designs still embody a timeless and modern sensibility that continues to inspire new creations. **JCB**

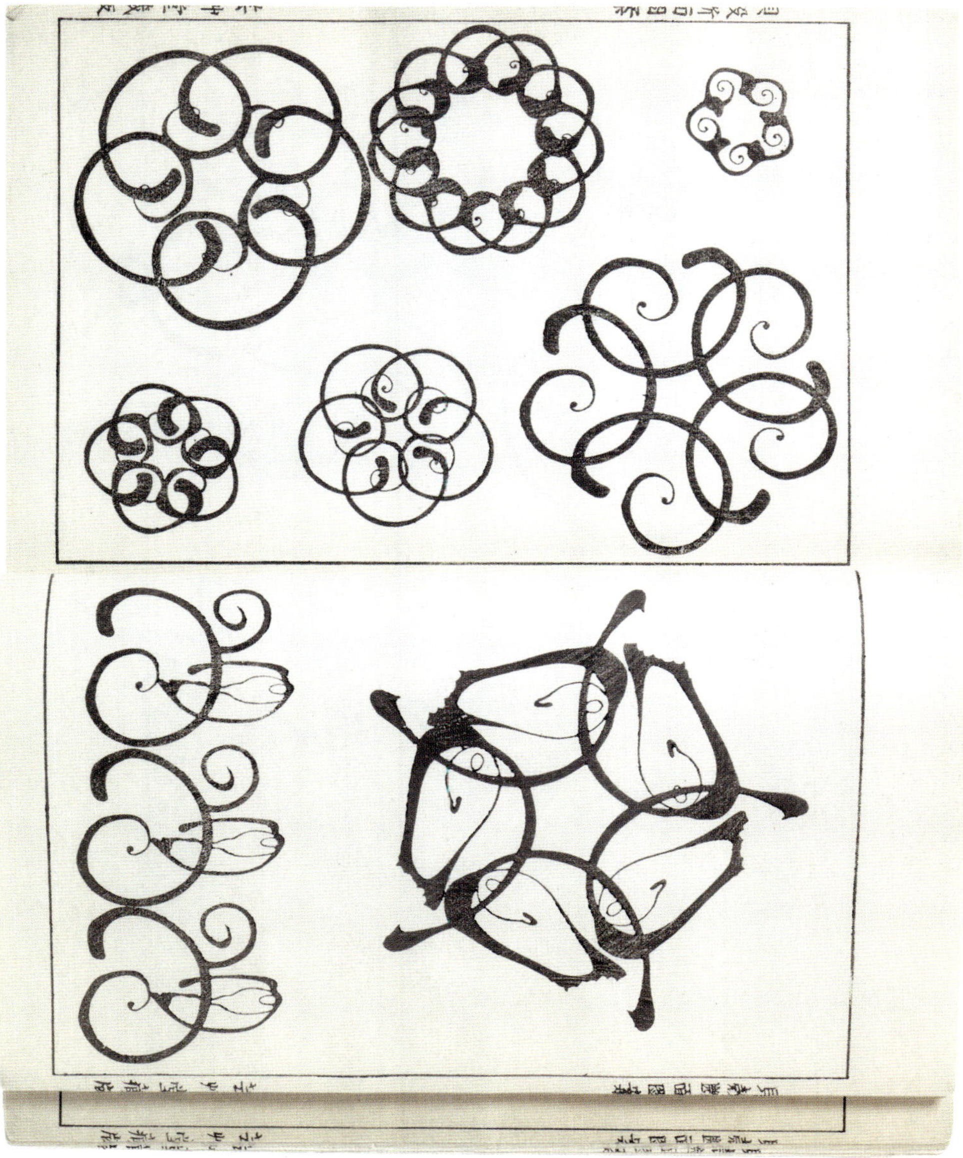

0907. Woodblock print, *Kaigara Danmen Zuan*, 1913, Yoichirō Hirase

0908. Trade catalog, The Armstrong Pattern Book, 1939, Armstrong Cork Company

0909. Sidewall, PHE-06, 2011, Piet Hein Eek

0910. Panel, Interlacings (detail), 1984, Ethel Stein

0911. Sidewall, PHE-02, 2011, Piet Hein Eek

0912. Shawl, India for European market, mid-19th century

0913. Man's head cloth (tzute), Guatemala, before 1962

0914. Drawing, Design for a Painted Ceiling (detail), 1815–22, Frederick Crace

0915. Drawing, Wallpaper Design (detail), France, 1815–30

0916. Tile, Ottoman Empire (present-day Syria), late 16th–early 17th century
0917. Chalice cover, Italy, early 18th century

0918. Floor tile, possibly Portugal, 16th–early 17th century
0919. Portable equatorial sundial and compass, Germany, 1748, Jacob Emanuel Laminit

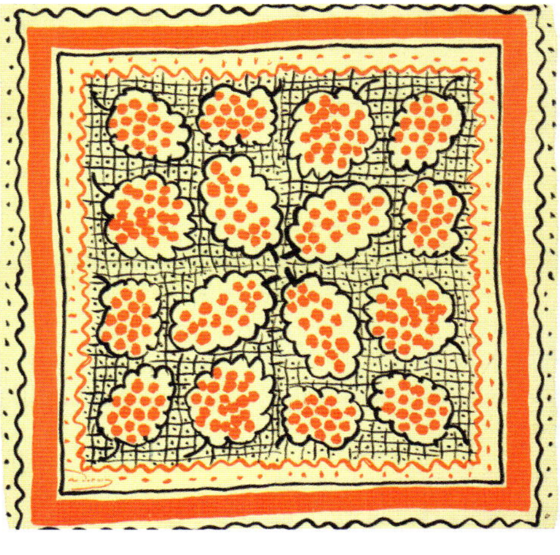

0920. Sampler, Germany, 19th century
0921. Square, Grapes, 1947, André Derain

0922. Textile (detail), France, 1934

0923. Textile, Guatemala, early 20th century

0924. Drawing, Design for Double Woven Cloth (detail), ca. 1926, Adelgunde (Gunta) Stölzl

0925. Textile, Kilometer 177½, 2002–03, Sheila Hicks

0926. Pezzato vase, Italy, 1950–51, Fulvio Bianconi

0927. Hand-woven sample, USA, before 1953, Anni Albers

0928. Sample, USA, 1949, Anni Albers
0929. Textile, Peru, Late Central Coast, 1000–1450

0930. Book-form flask, Switzerland, 18th century

0931. Stackable drinking glass, Finland, ca. 1952, Saara Hopea-Untracht

0932. Textile, Peach Fuzz, 1986, Junichi Arai

0933. Guaranty Building doorplate, Buffalo, New York, USA, ca. 1895, Louis Henry Sullivan
0934. Textile, Les Jets d'Eau, 1925, Édouard Bénédictus

0935. Coverlet, USA, early 19th century

0936. Book illustration, ca. 1780, Birmingham Brass Company

Drawing, Study for Maximum Mass Permitted by the 1916 New York Zoning Law, Stage 4, 1922
Hugh Ferriss (American, 1889–1962)
Black crayon, paper stump, pen and black ink, brush and black wash, and varnish on illustration board
Gift of Mrs. Hugh Ferriss, 1969-137-4

During the 1920s, architects and critics debated the architectural future of New York City in popular magazines and newspapers, including the *Saturday Evening Post*, *Architectural Forum*, and the *New York Times*, where articles seemed to either optimistically proclaim the skyscraper as the unique expression of American energy and power, or else warn of overcongestion, bad air, and potential danger to the city. As the **renderer** for the architect Harvey Wiley Corbett, who actively promoted the commercial advantages of skyscrapers, Hugh Ferriss produced dramatic images of real and visionary buildings that would accompany articles by Corbett and others. His unique drawings gave form to the new modern skyscraper building type.
While the controversy over tall buildings originated in the late nineteenth century, it was enflamed by the passage of New York's 1916 zoning law governing the mass and height of future city structures. According to the law, buildings could rise only to a specified height in relation to the width of the street, and above that, they had to slope or stairstep back in a fixed proportion in relation to the street wall. In addition, a tower could be constructed to any height provided it did not occupy more than one-quarter of the lot. An illustrated article by Ferriss, "The New Architecture" (the *New York Times*, March 19, 1922), argued that, with new glass-and-steel construction replacing masonry-supported buildings, the unadorned, unornamented skyscraper was the only truthful architectural solution for future development. Ferriss illustrated his article with futuristic drawings, of which this is one, demonstrating four possible orchestrations of a building's mass based on the 1916 zoning law. Following his typical drawing process, he worked first in a greasy crayon, which allowed him to achieve the densest blacks, to block out the forms and mark the deep shadows. Then he worked a paper **stump** (like a cardboard pencil, for smudging) to pull tone off of the darkest areas to lighten the shadows. He would then erase pigment to bring out the highlights. Finally, the drawing was varnished. This process imbued his images with powerful emotional force and moody romance.
The first of his Maximum Mass drawings **(0938)** illustrates a building that fills an entire city block in a district that permitted a mass twice the width of the street. **Sketch** two **(0939)** shows a building in which light courts are cut into the structure with the mass sloped backward, producing an impractical interior space solution. In the third stage **(0940)**, the sloping areas are squared off in a stepped pattern to achieve more usable commercial space with setbacks every two floors. Finally, in the fourth stage **(0937)**, a central tower of about seventy stories is flanked by setbacked wings of about half the building's height—what Ferriss called a "pyramid . . . sculpted in three dimensions." The entire pyramidal mass is dramatically lit from behind by radiating beams of light, as if declaring this solution to be the winning submission in the architectural contest.
Ferriss compiled his Maximum Mass drawings with additional renderings of actual and visionary structures in the celebrated 1929 book *The Metropolis of Tomorrow*. Through this volume, along with his newspaper images and contemporary exhibitions of his work, Ferriss influenced the architecture of art deco skyscrapers during the 1920s and early 1930s. In our age of computer-driven architectural renderings, architects today marvel at Ferriss's masterful handling of light and shade. **GSD**

0937. Drawing, Study for Maximum Mass Permitted by the 1916 New York Zoning Law, Stage 4, 1922, Hugh Ferriss

0939. Study for Maximum Mass Permitted by the 1916 New York Zoning Law, Stage 2, New York City, 1922, Hugh Ferriss

0940. Study for Maximum Mass Permitted by the 1916 New York Zoning Law, Stage 3, 1922, Hugh Ferriss

0938. Drawing, Study for Maximum Mass Permitted by the 1916 New York Zoning Law, Stage 1, New York City, 1922, Hugh Ferriss

0941. Shoehorn, England, 1604

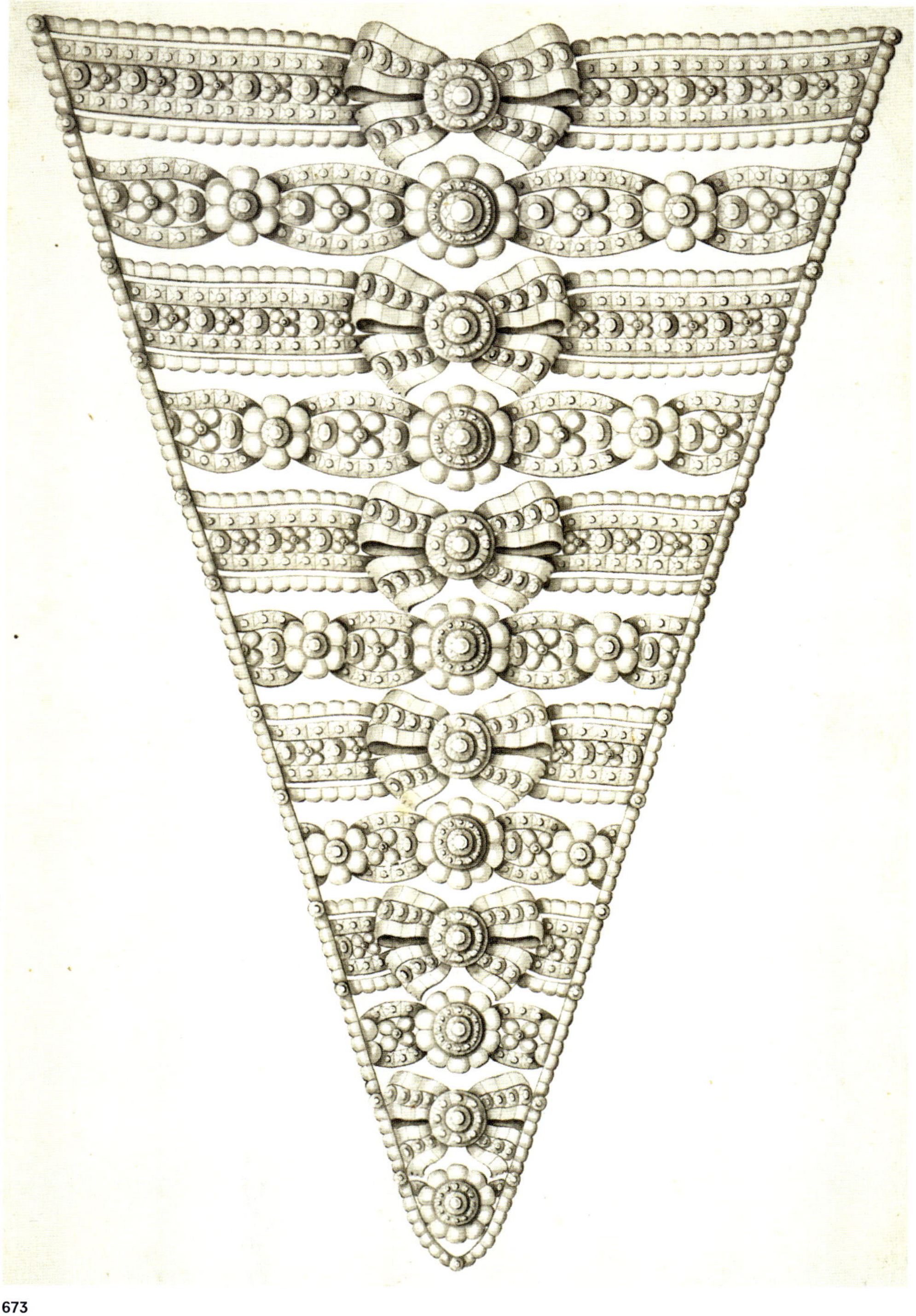

0942. Drawing, Design for a Jeweled Stomacher, Italy(?), 1775–1800

0943. Book illustration, *New Illustration of the Sexual System of Carolus von Linnaeus*, 1807, Robert John Thornton

0944. Print, Trial Proof for a Printed Textile, France, 1790–1800

0945. Palampore, India, mid–late 18th century

0946. Book illustration, *Metamorphosis insectorum Surinamensium*, 1730, Maria Sibylla Merian

0947. Print, Ornamental Design, after 1775, Anne Allen after Jean-Baptiste Pillement

0948. Textile, England, 1760–80, Ollive and Talwin

0949. Drawing, Design for a Printed Vertical Border, France, 18th century

0950. Textile, Iguanus, 1990, Timorous Beasties

0951. Sidewall, 1817–27, Robert Jones
0952. Ceiling paper, USA, 1880–1900, Cresswell & Washburn Ltd.

0953. Sidewall, Graduated Net, 1953–55, Bent Karlby

0954. Drawing, Paper Sample, Yellow, England, n.d.

0955. Sidewall, England, 1840–60

0956. Book illustration, *Icones lignorum exoticorum*, 1773–78, Jan Christian Sepp

0957. Drawing, Design for a Mirror Frame with Monogram of Marie-Antoinette, 1787–90, Richard de Lalonde

0958. Drawing, Design for a Cartel Clock Case, 1715–25, Gilles-Marie Oppenord

0959. Drawing, Wall Elevation for an Antechamber or Salon, ca. 1785, Louis-Gustave Taraval

0960. Drawing, Textile Design: Indian Heads, 1943, Angelo Testa

0961. Sidewall, Acorn, 2000, Francesco Simeti

0962. Border, France, ca. 1810

0963. Border, France, 1820–40

0964. Border, France, 1810–20
0965. Dado, France, 1820–30

0966. Dado, France, 1820–30
0967. Border corner, England, 1850–60

0968. Border, France, ca. 1850
0969. Border, France, 1830–60
0970. Border, France, ca. 1850

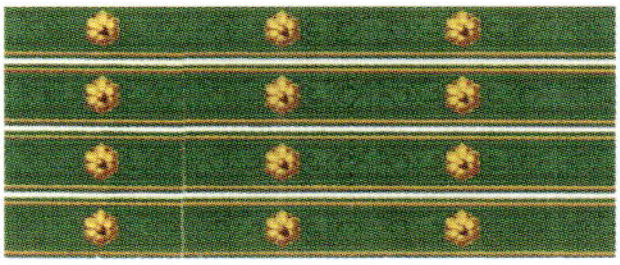

0971. Border, France, 1825–45, Jean Louis Mery

0972. Window shade, USA, 1875–1900

0973. Sidewall, France, ca. 1860

0974. Chasuble back, England, 15th century
0975. Window shade, USA, ca. 1860

Sidewall, The House that Jack Built, 1886
Walter Crane (British, 1845–1915)
Manufactured by Jeffrey & Company (London, 1836–1930)
Machine printed on paper
Gift of Grace Lincoln Temple, 1938-62-57

Wallpaper has been used in interior decoration for about three hundred years, but wallpapers designed for children's rooms were introduced only in the second half of the nineteenth century. Several social changes and technological advances made wallpapers for children a viable product. The nineteenth century witnessed an increased awareness placed on the value of childhood, and youth was finally viewed as a normal stage of development. The founding of public schools, child welfare agencies, child labor laws, and the emergence of pediatrics as a medical specialty all helped make the world a more hospitable place for children.

Beginning around 1840, advances in technology and the development of inexpensive wood-pulp paper made wallpapers affordable. These major changes greatly increased production and lowered the cost for the consumer. The developing train system allowed the papers to be quickly transported great distances. Additionally, in 1870 the British developed a surface that could be wiped clean, a key advance for papers designed for use in children's rooms.

While designed in a decorative fashion, early wallpapers for children were meant to educate. Two of the earliest children's papers in Cooper Hewitt's collection, Pilgrim's Progress and Robinson Crusoe, printed in the 1870s, illustrate these popular tales of moral discipline and adventure.

Both papers are **intaglio prints**, roller printed in oil colors with engraved copper rollers, in monochrome shades of brown. They were the first wallpapers with wipeable surfaces. A later intaglio wallpaper that was printed in colors in1893 using designs by book illustrator Kate Greenaway also stressed the importance of good behavior by showing children properly coiffed and accessorized. Wallpapers generally were not designed to amuse children with humorous and fantastic designs until early in the twentieth century.

Walter Crane was the first well-known artist to design children's wallpaper, and also the first to create designs that would delight and engage children by illustrating familiar people, places, and animals in a whimsical fashion. Crane began illustrating children's books in the 1860s and quickly became a favorite of both children and adults. This popularity earned him a commission to design wallpapers for children beginning in 1875, and working exclusively for Jeffrey & Company in London, he designed six nursery papers over the course of his career.

From the beginning, all of his children's wallpapers were printed in colors, distinguishing them from the earlier monochrome prints. While all of Crane's papers created for the general market were **wood block printed** with larger repeats, his nursery papers were **machine printed**, which made them more affordable for this niche market.

The House that Jack Built illustrates the popular nursery rhyme line by line and is drawn in the Aesthetic style. It is printed in tertiary colors on an off-white ground. While symmetrical in format, the design is full of pattern. All the different elements of the house, the church, the costumes, even the background, contain intricate patterns, leaving few voids in the surface design. Potted sunflowers fill in the niches on the porch. There is no sense of depth, as the colors are all contained within heavy

0976. Sidewall, The House that Jack Built, 1886, Walter Crane

outlines with no attempt at creating highlights and shadows. All of these elements reflect the artistic style Crane portrayed in the beautifully detailed interiors of his children's **book illustrations**.

Crane's wallpapers were displayed by Jeffrey & Company at major expositions and won awards at several, including the Centennial International Exhibition in Philadelphia in 1876, and the Paris Expositions Universelles in 1878 and 1889. As machine-printed papers were seen as a lesser form of printing through most of the nineteenth century, it is noteworthy that The House that Jack Built was the only machine-printed wallpaper shown at the World's Columbian Exposition in Chicago in 1893. Crane designed wallpapers until 1908.

The purpose of decorating a room with children's paper was to identify it as belonging to a child. The idea was to create a room the child could call his or her own that expressed their personality, both in scale and aesthetics. Wallpaper friezes and pictures were hung lower to make them more accessible, and furniture was produced in a smaller scale to fit the child. This all but ended with the Depression in 1929. From then on, parents and decorators designed rooms that could grow with the child, and used simple striped and plaid wallpapers. The elements that defined the room as a child's were relegated to pictures and accessories, which could be easily and cheaply replaced as the child grew. **GH**

0977. May Tree frieze, 1896, Walter Crane

0978. Sidewall, Golden Relief, 2014, David Nosanchuk

0979. Kimono length, Japan, late 19th–early 20th century

0980. Fine Binding, *Wine, Women, and Song*, 1907, Sangorski & Sutcliffe

0981. Photograph, Storefront of Printer and Bookbinder Brodard & Taupin, ca. 1924, M. Thérèse Bonney

Color lithograph print depicting De la Rue's Stationery Stand and Envelope Machine
By Edwin Thomas Dolby (fl. 1849–70)
From *Recollections of the Great Exhibition*, 1851
Published by Lloyd Brothers & Co., & Simpkin Marshall & Co. (London, 1851)
Smithsonian Libraries, fT690.C1 R43 1851

World's fairs (known also as international expositions or exhibitions), primarily in the nineteenth and early twentieth centuries, were important means of displaying and promoting the arts, rare natural specimens, culture, inventions, and hand-crafted and manufactured items of many nations at a single venue. These monumental events additionally featured pavilions with innovative and nationalist styles and sites that became the foundation for urban centers and parks. On the one hand, they were arenas of fierce industrial, commercial, and national competition and, on the other hand, they were forums for an international exchange of ideas and education.
Recollections of the Great Exhibition, 1851 includes twenty-five hand-colored **lithographs** depicting scenes at the first international fair held in Hyde Park, London in 1851. This lavishly illustrated commemorative—complete with images of cluttered displays and Victorian era-clad visitors—provides a flavor of the overall experience of being at the event.
The Great Exhibition of the Works of Industry of All Nations of 1851 was remarkable in many ways. The exhibition hall (known as the Crystal Palace), designed by Joseph Paxton, consisted of three thousand prefabricated sheets of glass and iron, and was erected on the site in less than nine months. More than one hundred thousand objects by nearly fourteen thousand exhibitors from many countries were seen by more than six million visitors at this fair—making it the most extensive display of decorative arts and manufactured items at any single event to date.
Recollections of the Great Exhibition, 1851, as well as more detailed commissioner's reports and juries published for the Crystal Palace fair and subsequent expositions that followed, provides valuable data and insight to the manufacture, design, and marketing of decorative arts objects and inventions worldwide. Illustrated commemoratives like this, along with planning manuals, souvenir guides, pamphlets, and contemporary histories, were the major way new ideas on design and innovative inventions were introduced internationally. These publications no doubt were an inspiration for the creation of later world's expositions in America and Europe.
The image of De la Rue's Stationery Stand and Envelope Machine includes a display of the firm's designs for colorful, printed, and **embossed** cards, writing papers, box tops, tickets, book covers, playing cards, and envelopes. Postal reforms in England in the late 1830s standardized and facilitated the efficiency and growth of mail service, resulting in the need for the mass production of printed paper items. The firm also responded to Victorian taste and modes of correspondence with their designs for wedding invitations, mourning and personalized calling cards, and ornate book covers. Demonstrations of an envelope-folding apparatus, invented by Edwin Hill and Warren De la Rue, were also a major attraction of the display. This machine reportedly operated at a rate of folding twenty-seven hundred envelopes per hour—far more efficient than the manual output of three thousand envelopes per day. **SVD**

0982. Color lithograph, Scene of De la Rue's Stationery Stand and Envelope Machine, 1851, Edwin Thomas Dolby

0983. Sidewall, Antoinette with Black Stripe, ca. 1956, Elsbeth Kupferoth

0984. Casket, England, 1654, Frances Basnet

0985. Matchsafe, Russia, 1882–96

0986. Mural miniature (detail), El Sol, 1948, Joan Miró

0987. Textile, USA, 1950–59, Paul László

0988. Fragment, Spain, 11th–12th century

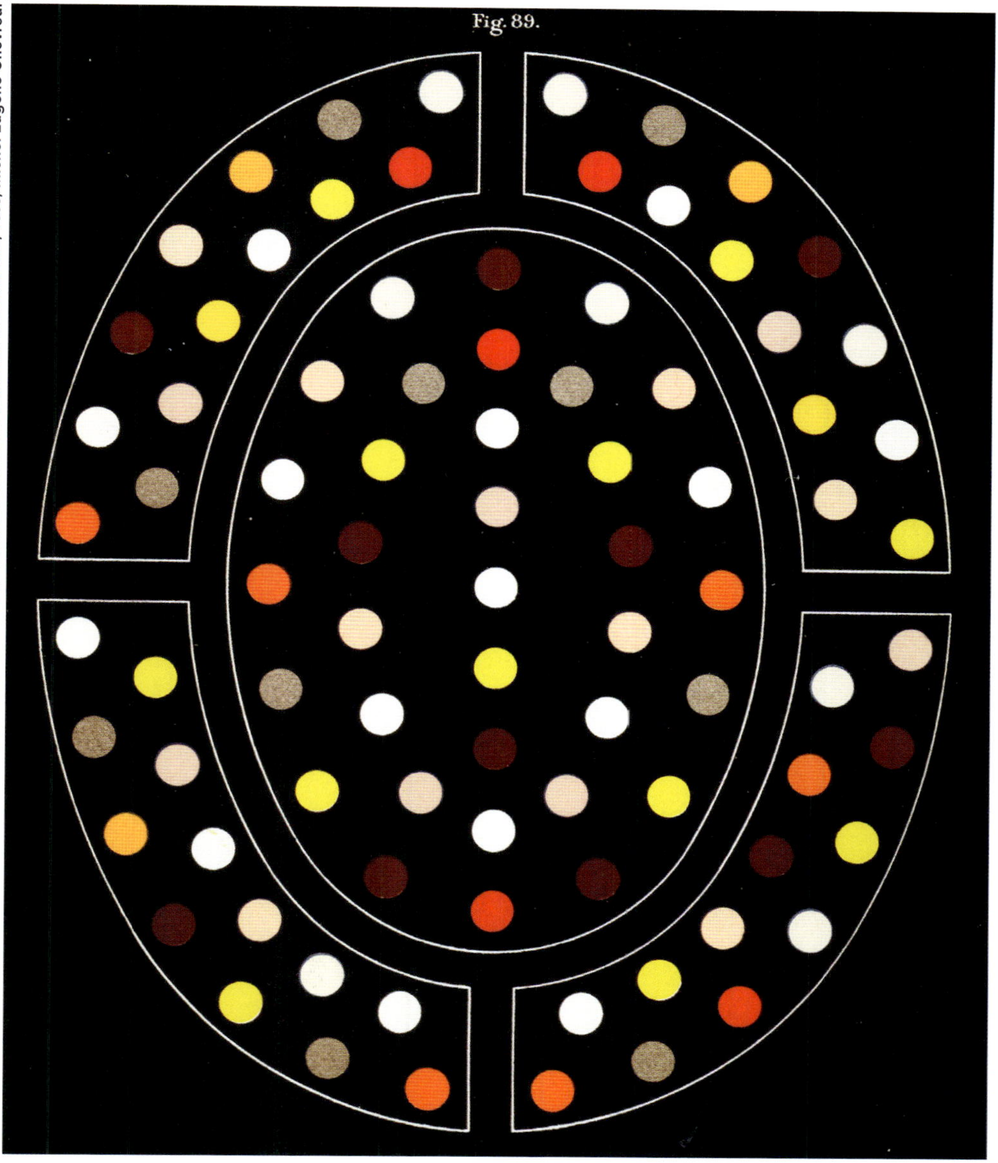

0989. Book illustration, *De la loi du contraste simultané des couleurs*, 1889, Michel Eugène Chevreul

Textile, Bioimplantable device for reconstructive shoulder surgery, 2004
Designed by Prof. Simon Frostick and Dr. Alan McLeod, textile designed by Peter Butcher
Developed by Ellis Developments Ltd., 2003
Manufactured by Pearsalls Ltd. (England)
Machine-embroidered polyester (base cloth dissolved)
Cooper Hewitt, Smithsonian Design Museum, 2004-15-1

Technical textiles are some of the purest and most innovative examples of design. The high performance and functionality of these super fabrics are their sole reason for being, yet the final product often fortuitously reveals an extraordinary beauty. Every field—architecture, transportation, agriculture, civil engineering, sports, and medicine—has benefited from advances in technical textiles, whose designs are more successful from cross-disciplinary innovations.

This surgical implant, developed after a close collaboration between physicians and textile engineers, was designed for a patient who had a tumor removed from his shoulder and needed extensive reconstruction two years later. The surgeon had requested a wide range of possible attachment points so he could use all of the tissue he found in the patient at implantation. This design, made from advanced medical imaging technologies and a **computer-aided design (CAD)** program, uses machine **embroidery** to create a scaffold (or structure) to which the surgeon can attach the metal replacement bone and healthy tissue. Embroidery also allows elements such as eyelets to be integrated into the design to accommodate attachment points and to create open areas for tissue ingrowth.[1]

When designing a surgical implant, it is essential that it fits perfectly in order to give maximum benefit to the patient. Most implants, however, are available only in limited sizes, and adapting them to the patient during surgery is not feasible. In addition, many are woven traditionally, with fibers at right angles to one another, rather than oriented to maximize the implant's strength. A woven implant will also fray when cut, compromising it and ultimately contributing to failure.

Julian Ellis and his collaborators at Pearsalls found that machine embroidery could overcome these problems. Embroidery could mimic the natural fibrous arrays of ligaments and form a scaffold for new growth. It can also be cut without fraying.[2] With modifications to modern lace-embroidery software, Ellis and his team can produce customized surgical implants almost as easily as monograms for baseball caps. The initial specifications or rough sketch from the surgeon can be converted into an embroidery design, emailed to Pearsalls, and manufactured within a few hours.[3] The same embroidery machine that can produce decorative trimmings can turn out durable, utilitarian medical implants of astonishing strength, delicacy, and beauty. **MM**

1 Susan Brown, "Textiles: Fiber, Structure, and Function," in *Extreme Textiles: Designing for High Performance*, ed. Matilda McQuaid (New York: Princeton Architectural Press 2005), 50–51.
2 Julian Ellis, "Embroidery for Engineering," April 2000, presentation transcript, Textile Institute World Conference in Manchester, www.ellisdev.co.uk/embroide2.html.
3 Julian Ellis, "Embroidered Surgical Implants," Ellis Developments Limited, www. ellisdev.co.uk/site1.html.

0990. Bioimplantable device, England, 2004, Ellis Developments Ltd. and Pearsalls Ltd.

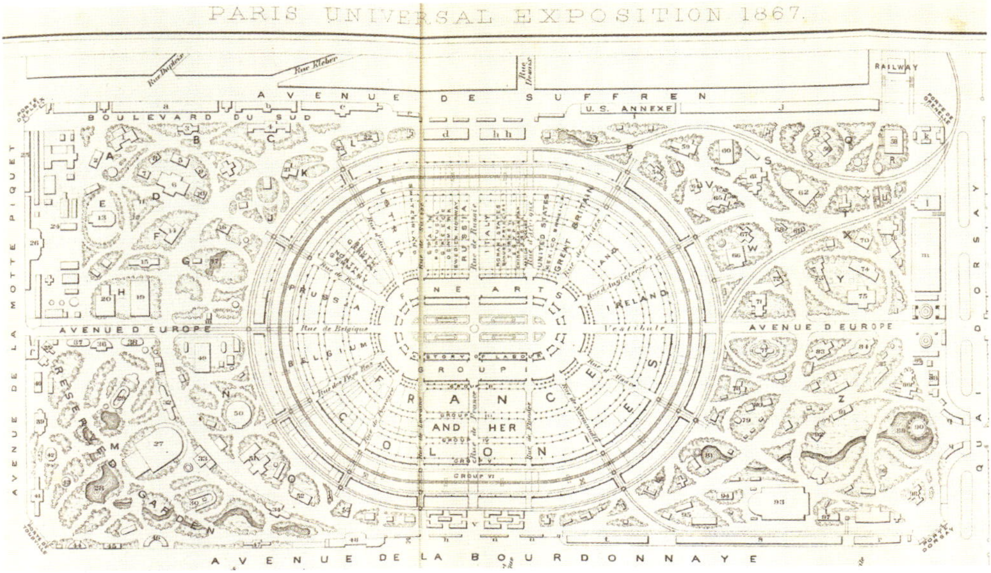

0991. Foldout, 1867 Paris Universal Exposition floor plan, 1870

0992. Textile, Turkey, 18th century

0993. Cabaret service (detail), France, 1813, attributed to Alexandre Brongniart

0994. Fashion plate, *Gazette du bon ton*, 1924, Jeanne Lanvin and Georges Lepape

0995. Roasting pan and lid, probably USA, ca. 1935

0996. Cylinda ashtray, Denmark, 1967, Arne Jacobsen

0997. ConferenceMaster Audio teleconferencing system, 1993, Walter Dorwin Teague Associates

0998. Colorstone tableware, USA, 1986, Lella and Massimo Vignelli with David Law

0999. Pedestal stool, USA, 1957, Eero Saarinen

1002. Sidewall tile, V2, 2004, MIO

1000. Sidewall, Lagoon, 1929, Edward Bawden
1001. Sidewall, Austria or Switzerland, 1925–30, Josef Hillerbrand

1003. Bowl, USA, ca. 1930, George Sakier

1004. Jar and lid, Czechoslovakia, ca. 1915–20, Moser Glass Factory

1005. Photograph, Castel d'Orgeval, France, 1904, Hector Guimard

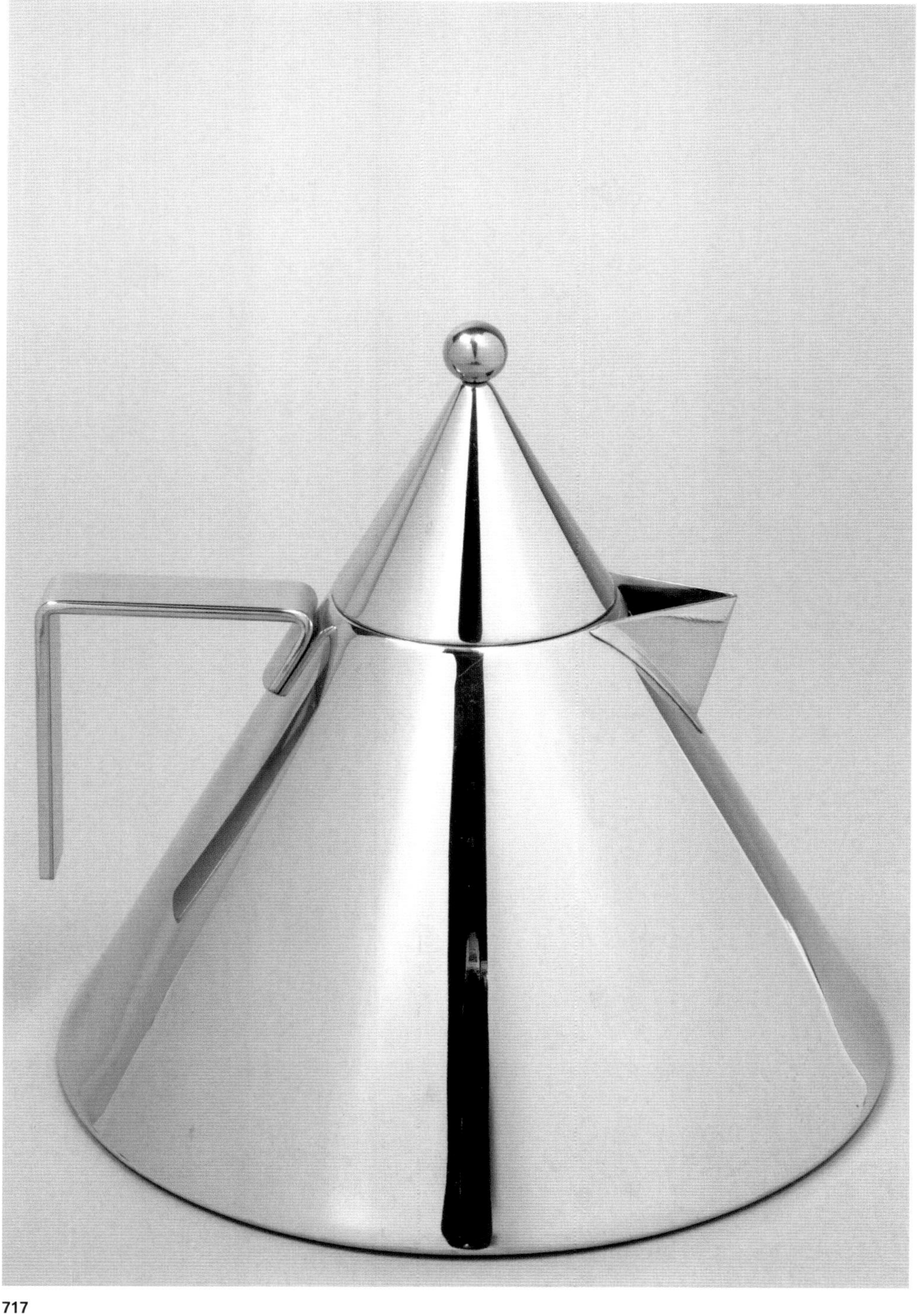

1006. Il Conico kettle, Italy, 1986, Aldo Rossi

Drawing, Designs for Bowls, Vases, Candlesticks, and Teapots, ca. 1928
Ilonka Karasz (American, b. Hungary, 1896–1981)
New York, New York, USA
Graphite on tracing paper
Museum purchase from General Acquisitions Endowment Fund, 2006-16-1

This essay on geometric form by the American modernist designer Ilonka Karasz develops the triangle into a family of eighteen tabletop objects. While depicted as a series of flat planes, these designs were meant to be fabricated with conical bodies on X-shaped cruciform bases. The various object types include vases of different sizes and proportions, candlesticks, covered and uncovered bowls, sugar bowls and creamers, teapots, and coffeepots. Some of the examples have inverted triangular or cone-shaped knops; some have square tube or columnar handles. A few pieces have handles consisting of flat, rectangular planes with semicircular finger openings. Two pieces, the large vase and creamer on the lower part of the sheet, have rims that taper out to the shoulder of the bodies.[1]

This very significant drawing counts among the rare extant design drawings documenting the explorations of an American designer working in the 1920s and 1930s who reinterpreted the European modernist style into an American modern aesthetic. The sheet also represents the contribution of one of the few woman designers whose work and talent were considered equal to those of her male counterparts, including Paul Frankl, Kem Weber, Winold Reiss, Eugene Schoen, and Walter von Nessen.

Ilonka Karasz was born in 1896 in Budapest, where she trained at the Royal School of Arts and Crafts. After settling in New York in 1913, she became part of a lively community of young émigré artists and designers. She initially worked as a graphic designer, creating covers for the *New Yorker* and advertisements for New York shops, as well as textile and wallpaper designs. By the late 1920s, Karasz's textiles, metalwork, and furniture were shown in modern design exhibitions in New York and around the country. She was also a leader in the important organizations of designers working in the modern style. Her work was featured in the 1928 Macy's International Exposition of Art in Industry that traveled to ten cities. She became part of the alliance of modern designers known as AUDAC (American Union of Decorative Artists and Craftsmen) and exhibited in the two AUDAC exhibitions of 1930 and 1931 at the Grand Central Palace and the Brooklyn Museum, respectively. She also showed work at the 1928 and 1929 American Designers Gallery exhibitions, for which she was on the executive committee and designed the catalogs. For the 1929 installation she created a modern dining room with furniture characterized by simple rectilinear shapes and flat planes. A photograph of the installation reveals, on the sideboard, an uncovered conical bowl resting on a cruciform base corresponding to the sketch at the center left of the Cooper Hewitt's drawing. This bowl, like the related coffee and tea services, vases, candlesticks, and bowls, was meant to appeal to progressive young apartment dwellers, devotees of the latest avant-garde styles. The bowl and some of the forms in the drawing were fabricated in electroplated nickel silver by Paye and Baker Manufacturing Company in North Attleboro, Massachusetts. A vase, candlestick, and small bowl (candy dish) as well as the creamer and sugar bowl from this group are represented in Cooper Hewitt's collection.

The relationship of Karasz's conical forms on cruciform bases to the1924 series of geometrically based teapots, tea infusers, and ashtrays on cruciform bases by the Bauhaus designer Marianne Brandt is often cited, though no proof that Karasz knew

1007. Drawing, Designs for Bowls, Vases, Candlesticks, and Teapots, ca. 1928, Ilonka Karasz

Brandt's metal objects has been found. Brandt's pieces were published in several German periodicals, including *Dekorative Kunst* (1928), and in two exhibition catalogs, which Karasz probably saw on her own or in the collection of her German-born colleagues, including Paul Frankl. However, Karasz made essential alterations to the body and base of Brandt's objects that demonstrate her insights into harmony and proportion. Karasz changed Brandt's hemispherical forms into conical bodies and, most importantly, enlarged the cruciform bases so they reached approximately half the height of the body. Each base becomes a major design feature, both a support and an alternative geometry to the conical body. Karasz's objects developed from this sheet of designs represent the most austere, geometrically radical examples of modern American metalwork in the 1920s. **GSD**

1 Jewel Stern, *Modernism in American Silver* (New Haven, CT: Yale University Press, 2006), 84.

1008. Photograph, Dining Room, Exhibition of American Designer's Gallery Inc., 1929, The Art Institute of Chicago
1009. Tea Infuser, designed 1925, Marianne Brandt, The British Museum

1010. Candlestick, bowl, and vase, USA, 1928, Ilonka Karasz

1011. Half Teacup, USSR, 1923, Kazimir Severinovich Malevich (form) and Ilia Grigorevich Chasnik (decoration)

1012. Bambu vase from the Pasta Vitrea Series, Italy, 1998, Yoichi Ohira

1014. Flaches Modell (Flat Model) dessert fork and knife, Austria, 1903, Josef Hoffmann

1013. Dinner plate, France, ca. 1937, Jean Luce

1015. Cruet set and stand, Italy, ca. 1987, Roberto Sambonet

1016. TōFU lamp, Japan, 2000, Tokujin Yoshioka

1017. Prototype for domestic space heater, England, 1973, Bill Moggridge

1018. Lytro camera, USA, 2012, Lytro, Inc.

1019. Via Portico d'Ottavia vase, France, 1988–91, Gaetano Pesce

1020. One of a pair of pier tables (detail), Ireland, ca. 1785, attributed to William Moore

Signs for the 5 groups of men

PICTURE 15

47

1021. Book illustration, *International Picture Language*, 1936, Otto Neurath and Gerd Arntz

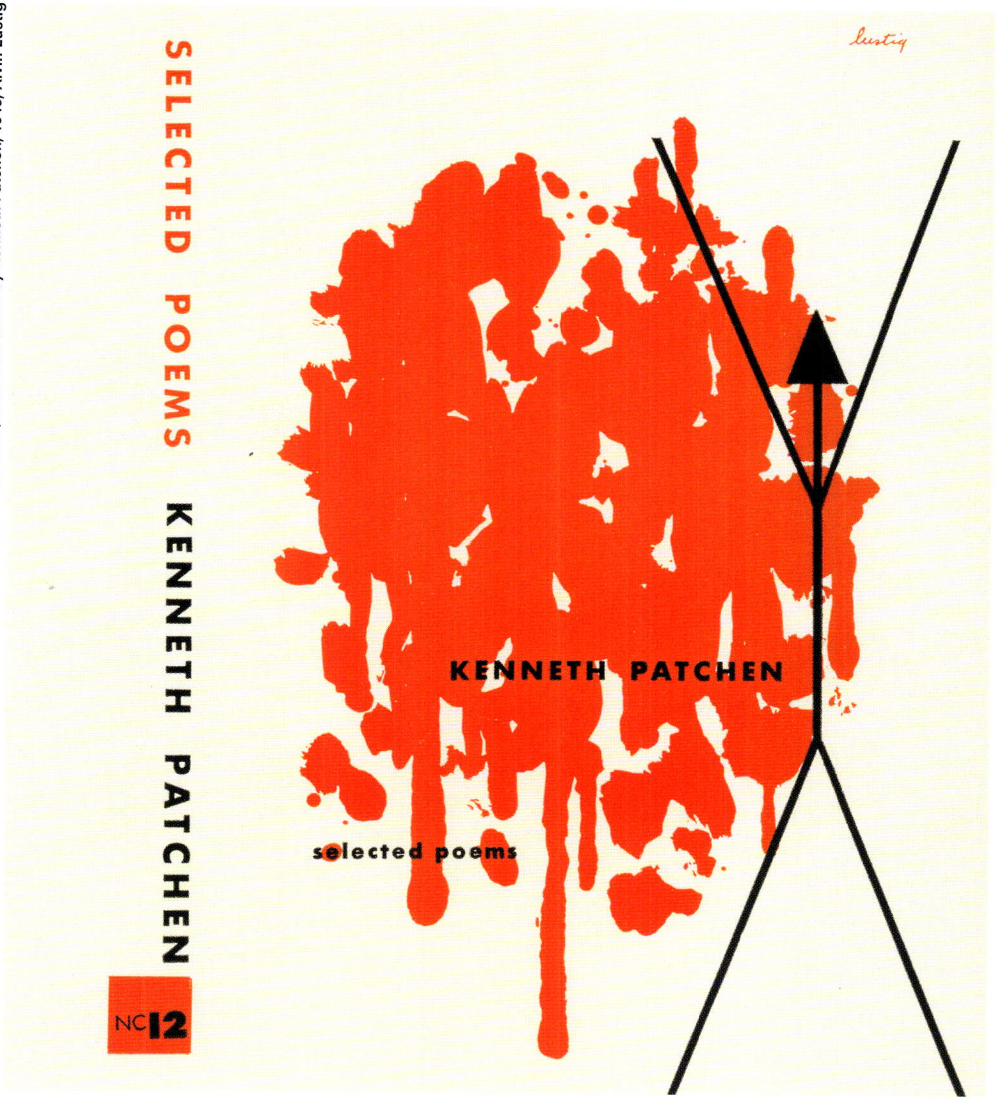

1022. Book cover, *Selected Poems by Kenneth Patchen*, 1946, Alvin Lustig

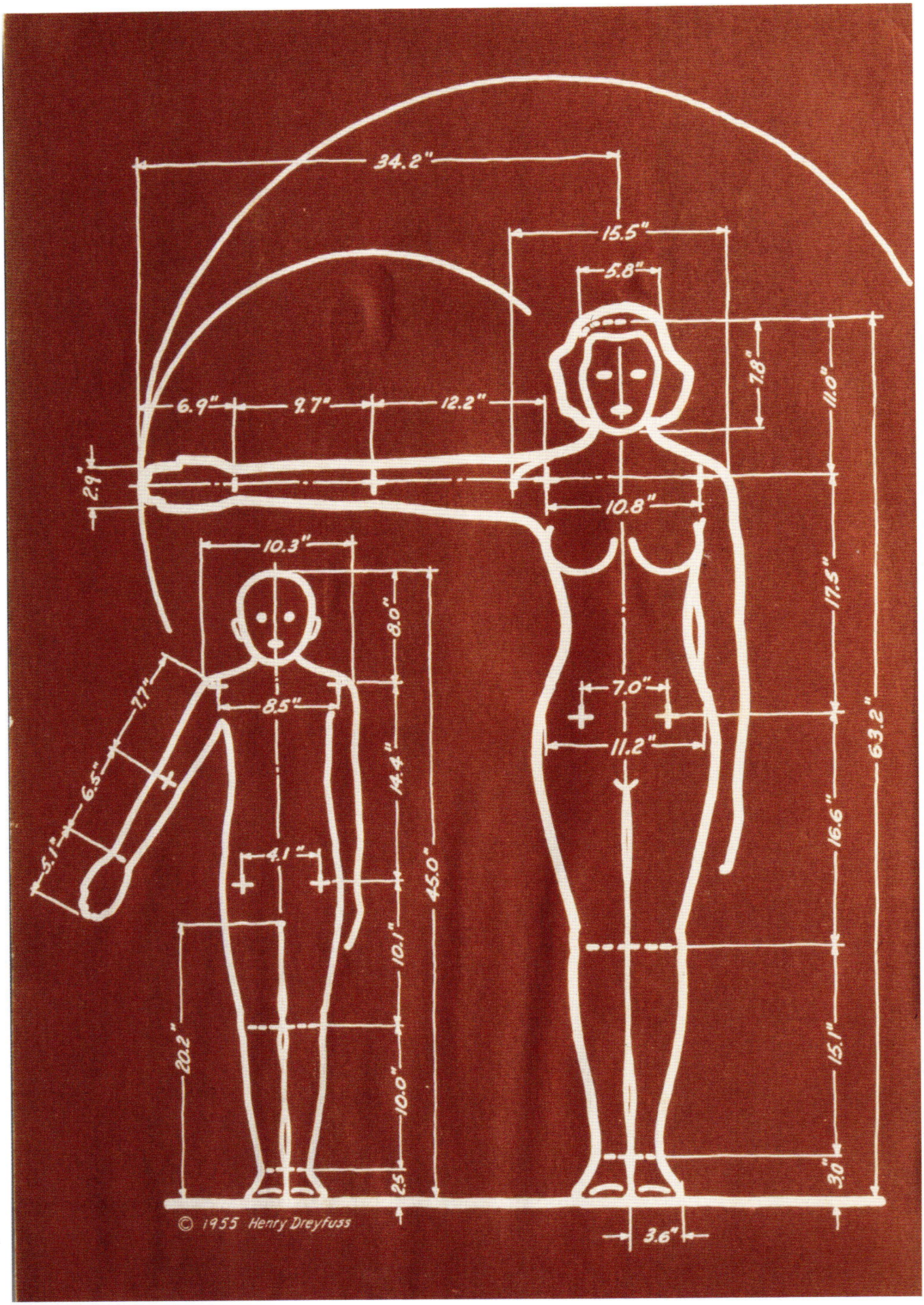

1023. Endpapers, *Designing for People*, 1955, Henry Dreyfuss

1024. Poster, International Women Workers Day, 1930, Valentina N. Kulagina

1025. Textile, La Moisson, ca. 1922, Raoul Dufy

1026. The Reds and the Whites chess set, USSR, 1922–32, Natalya Yakovlevna Danko

1027. Poster, Graphic Design China 2005 (GDC 05), 2005, Bi Xue Feng

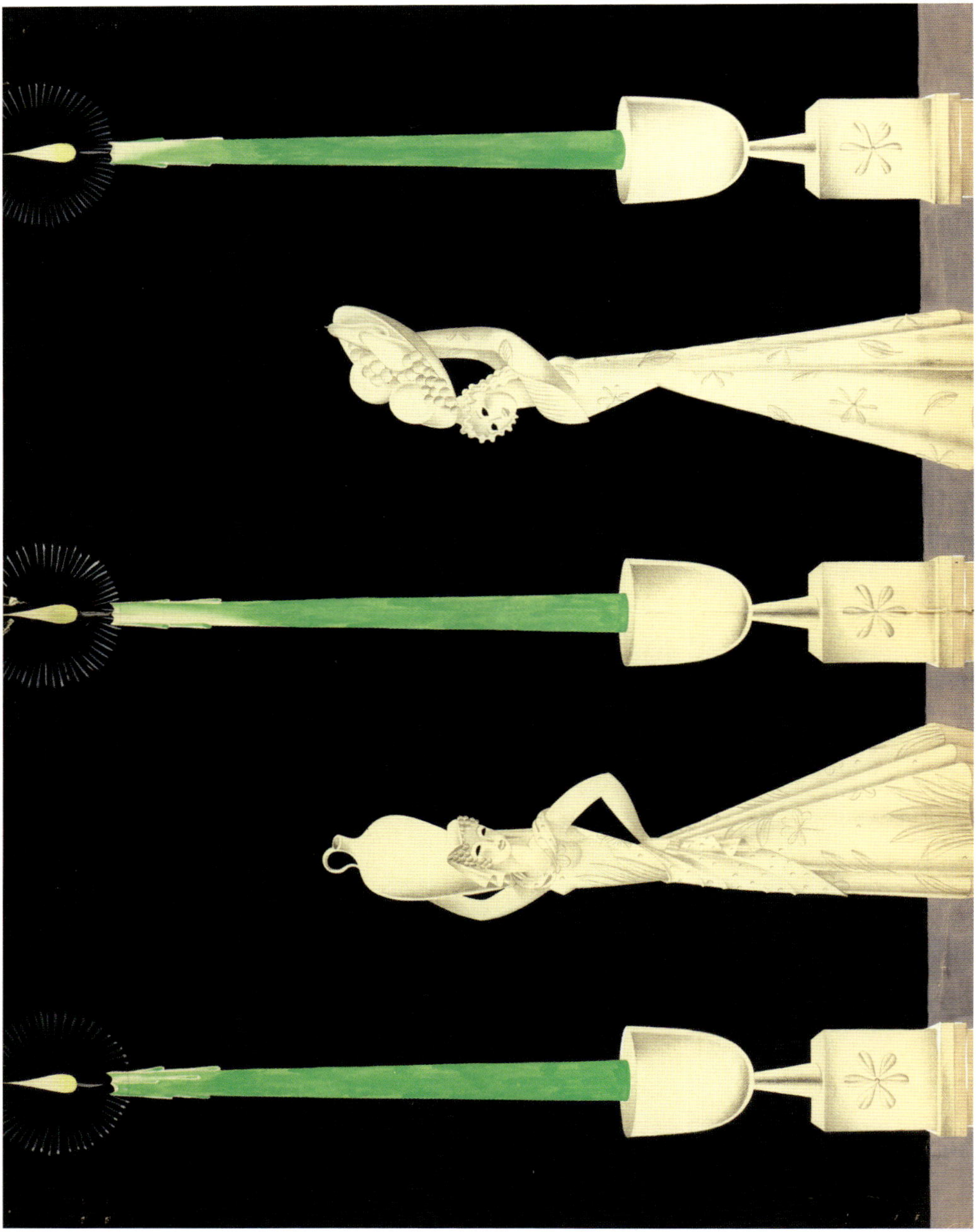

1028. Drawing, Design for Candlesticks with Figurines, 1950–70, Tommi Parzinger

1029. Book cover, *Three Lives* by Gertrude Stein, 1947, Alvin Lustig

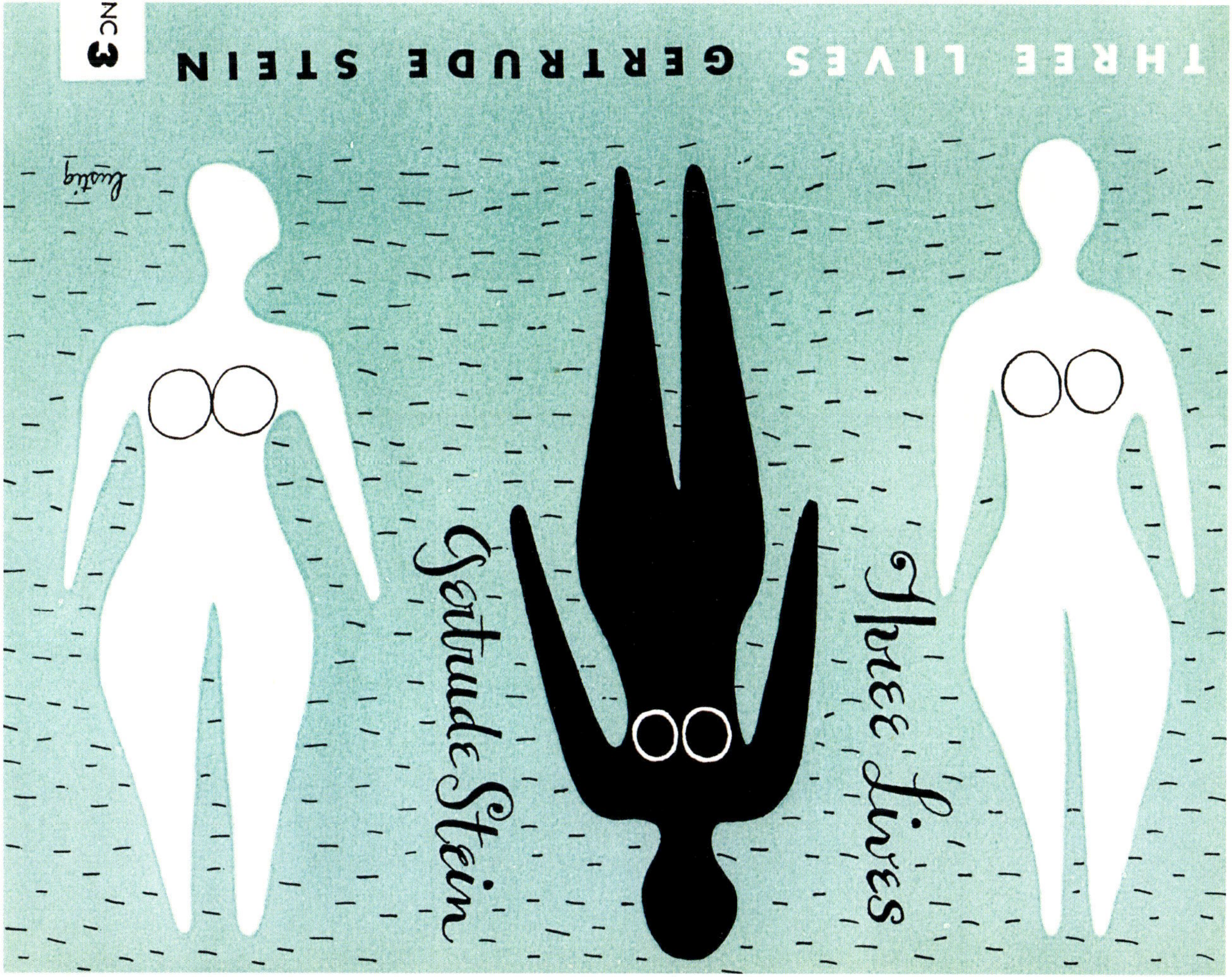

1030. Sidewall, Nana, 1971–72, Niki de St. Phalle

LA DANSEUSE AUX JETS D'EAU

ROBE DE DANSE, DE WORTH

1031. Fashion plate, *Gazette du Bon Ton*,1924–25, House of Worth, George Barbier

1032. Poster, 1999 Season, Ballet Tech, 1999, Paula Scher

Design: Pentagram, Photo: © Lois Greenfield

1033. Figurine, England, early 19th century, after a design by Johann Joachim Kändler

1034. Allegorical Figure of America from the Four Continents, Germany, 19th century

1035. Sidewall, Nofretari, 1951, Peter Mijer

1036. Panel (detail), Spain or Portugal, ca. 1600

1037. Plaque, England, possibly 1909, Marc-Louis Emmanuel Solon

1038. Print, Woman Bathing Her Feet at a Brook, 1658, Rembrandt Harmensz. van Rijn

1039. Furniture mount, France, 19th century

1040. Frontispiece (detail), *The Wood Beyond the World*, 1894, Edward Burne-Jones

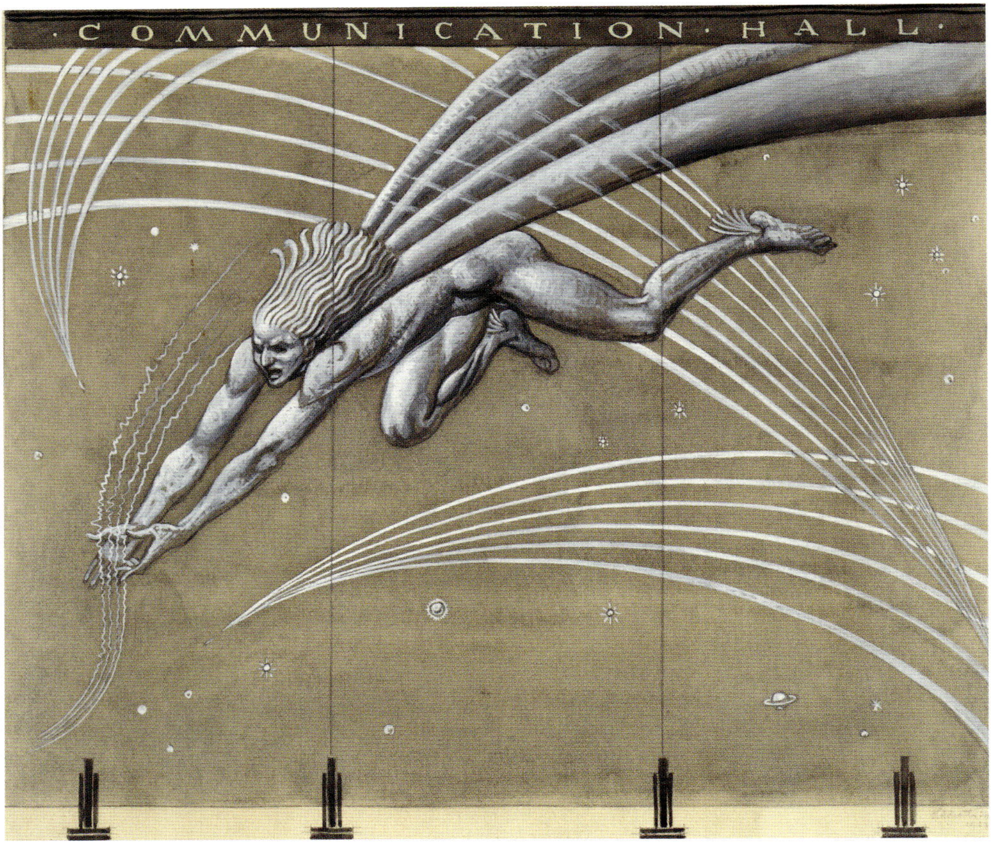

1041. Drawing, Design for Sandblasted Glass Mural: Mercury Gathering Air Waves amidst Planets and Stars, 1932, Hildreth Meière

1042. Overdoor, France, 1800–10

1043. Sidewall, France, 1925–30, André Groult

Safavid Velvet, Persia (present-day India or Iran), ca. 1640
Velvet, cut and voided, with silk- and metal-wrapped silk threads
Gift of Anonymous Donor, 1977-119-1

In this spectacular and enigmatic **velvet**, four opulently attired women stand in a setting filled with fantastic blossoms.[1] Wearing garments that whimsically blend Persian and European elements, the four figures form two pairs, each facing inward across a small pond. From right to left—the direction in which Persian is written—the first couple is equipped for hunting, and the second is furnished with food and drink for feasting. The woman with spear and hound represents the coursing hunt, while her counterpart, wearing a lure on her belt and hooding the falcon on her gloved hand, represents the flying hunt. Carrying a Persian wine ewer, a European pitcher, a serving bowl, and a lapful of fruit, the left pair suggests the celebratory repast following a successful hunt. This velvet is an extraordinary work of art and an exceedingly rare historical document. It represents the culmination of **weaving** techniques developed in Iran during the reign of the Safavid dynasty (1501–1722) and offers a unique glimpse of cultural interplay between Iran and Europe.

As this and many other velvets attest, the Safavids presided over one of history's most brilliant periods for silk weaving. For about a century beginning in 1550, velvet was the luxury weave of choice for the Safavid court. Safavid velvets are remarkable for the beauty of their designs, the extravagant use of gold and silver threads, and the unusually large number of pile colors. The eighteen pile colors used in this velvet are randomly distributed in the pattern by means of pile warp substitution, a labor-intensive technique that is the hallmark of the finest Safavid velvets.[2]

Seventeenth-century sources particularly praise Iran's gold and "curled" velvets.[3]

In modern terminology, the velvet with four women would be designated as cut and voided: the pile loops are all cut to form surface pile; and parts of the design are deliberately left void of pile. Safavid velvet weavers always covered the voided sections entirely in supplementary silk **wefts** that had been wrapped barber-pole fashion with flattened metallic strips. In this velvet, gold wefts fill the background of the pattern. Supplementary silver wefts appear in two guises—woven flat for a smooth, shining surface, as in the little shimmering ponds; and brought to the surface in twisted loops or curls to create accents of sparkling, three-dimensional texture.

The city of Isfahan in south-central Iran was a particularly important center for velvet weaving in the Safavid period and served as the dynasty's capital from 1598 to 1722. Most Safavid rulers were enthusiastic supporters of the arts, and under their patronage, artists developed a recognizable style of figural representation. This velvet's large, swaying figures; schematic landscape elements; and calligraphic line demonstrate the Isfahan style. Following the court's outward-looking tendencies and coinciding with the rise of the European trading companies, Isfahan was highly cosmopolitan, hosting diplomats, adventurers, missionaries, and merchants from across Eurasia. The influx brought new elements into Safavid art. European prints and paintings circulated in Isfahan, and Dutch artists are known to have served at the Safavid court.[4]

While the city served as their capital, the Safavids transformed Isfahan with urban planning and architectural programs on a grand scale that included gardens and numerous palaces and pleasure pavilions for the royal family and members of the court. This velvet probably served as a furnishing fabric, perhaps for a private pavilion. It might have been used as a wall hanging or as skirting for the base of a *takht*, a rectangular platform raised above the ground on which one or two people could sit or recline on carpets and cushions. Islamic paintings depict a variety of activities taking place upon a *takht*: holding audience, reading poetry, feasting, entertaining, or engaging in amorous play.

This last activity—amorous play—would beautifully suit the pattern of the velvet with four women, for its pictorial program weaves together ideas and images of love drawn from both Persian and European sources.[5] In Persian art and poetry, images of a beautiful youth in a flowering landscape embody a wealth of overlapping iconographic traditions linking gardens, lovers, and paradise. The leftmost figure, wearing a conical hat and bearing a wine ewer in her outstretched arm, brings together two popular strands of Persian imagery: the *saqi*, or wine bearer, suggests the intoxication caused by wine as well as love; the domical hat miniaturizes a type of headgear characteristic of dervishes, or religious mystics, thereby reminding the viewer that God can be approached through the contemplation of physical beauty. This velvet taps an equally rich vein of European iconographic traditions concerning love. The quasiclassical costume elements, *contrapposto* stance of the figures, and certain motifs suggest knowledge of emblem books, a pictorial-literary genre of immense popularity throughout Western Europe in the seventeenth century. Emblem literature constructs metaphors and allegories both erudite and earthy by combining symbolic images with explanatory text. The genre was especially popular in the Low Countries, and at least one of the Dutch artists who served at the Safavid court was conversant with emblem literature.[6] Emblematists fully exploited the self-evident connections between hunting and amorous pursuit and capture. For example, a hooded falcon may appear as an emblem of the heart subjugated by love. Dogs occur frequently in emblems, often referring to affairs of the heart. Fighting dogs, such as the snarling pair beside the spear carrier, can symbolize the jealous lover who will tolerate no rival.

Although drawing on diverse sources, the pattern of this velvet could not have been constructed by mere copyists. The rhythmic design imaginatively integrates Persian and European imagery into an artistic whole. A work of open-minded intelligence, it suggests an informed, even playful, sharing of traditions. One can only speculate for whom it was created, but the enormous cost of its production suggests the very highest level of court patronage. It may have been commissioned for private use, or as a magnificent gift to the shah from a state official, or from the shah to a foreign ruler. As a tributary culture, the giving of gifts was part of Safavid court protocol, and the quality of a gift reflected the prestige of both recipient and donor.[7] Whatever the circumstances of its manufacture, this velvet could only have been appreciated by viewers familiar with Persian poetry and matters of the hunt, and interested at least to some degree in European art and culture. One of the more promising candidates to have commissioned or received this velvet is the seventh Safavid ruler, Shah `Abbas II (reign 1642–66). Known for his hospitality to European visitors and for indulging his favorite pastimes of drinking and hunting, the young monarch had learned the art of drawing from two Dutchmen.[8]

One of the foreign visitors who enjoyed the shah's hospitality, the French merchant Jean-Baptiste Tavernier, left a fascinating description of a very long day spent talking, feasting, and drinking in company with `Abbas II in January 1665. In addition to discussing international politics, the shah evinced an interest in European women's fashions and in different ideals of female beauty. Tavernier's seventeen-hour visit concluded when he delighted the shah with a French drinking song.[9] While we cannot fully reconstruct what this eclectic velvet represented to its creators or owners, it opens a window onto late Safavid Iran and the types of exchanges that were possible in Isfahan's cultural milieu. **MMcW**

1 There are four other known pieces of the same velvet: (1) The Keir Collection, Dallas Museum of Art (112 x 71.5 cm); (2) New Delhi, The National Museum of India; (3) Toronto, Royal Ontario Museum, 1960.257 (222 x 74.5 cm); (4) Sotheby's Doha, Arts of the Islamic World, 19 March 2009, lot 301 (approximately 74 x 107 cm).

2 Sonday, "Patterns and Weaves: Safavid Lampas and Velvet," in Bier, *Woven from the Soul,* 79–81.

3 Chardin, *Sir John Chardin's Travels in Persia*, 277–78.

4 An excellent examination of Dutch artists in Safavid Iran is presented in Schwartz, "Between Court and Company: Dutch Artists in Persia."

5 The Persian and European iconographic sources are explicated more fully in McWilliams, "Allegories Unveiled," and McWilliams, "Three Figural Velvets from Safavid Iran," 22–27.

6 Before working as an artist at the court of Shah `Abbas II, the Dutch artist Phillips Angel (1616–c. 1683) had published a small pamphlet, "Praise of the Art of Painting" (Leiden, 1642), that was illustrated with an allegorical figure of the Art of Painting in Holland. Angel's text demonstrates his familiarity with emblem literature.

7 Matthee, "Between Aloofness and Fascination," 243.

8 A more nuanced and multifaceted portrait of `Abbas II is presented in Matthee, "The Career of Mohammed Beg."

9 Tavernier, *The Six Voyages of John Baptista Tavernier,* 181–83.

References (for known fragments)

Bier, Carol, ed., *Woven from the Soul, Spun from the Heart: Textile Arts of Safavid and Qajar Iran, 16th–19th Centuries*, exh. cat., Washington, DC: Textile Museum, 1987, 78–79, 40–41 (New York).
Kahlenberg, Mary, "A Mughal Personage Velvet," *Burlington Magazine* 115, no. 848 (November 1973) 721–25, 727 (Toronto).
McWilliams, Mary, "Allegories Unveiled: European Sources for a Safavid Velvet," *Textiles and Trade*, Proceedings of the Second Conference of the Textile Society of America, Washington, DC, 1990, 136–48, fig. 1 (New York).
McWilliams, Mary, "Three Figural Velvets from Safavid Iran," *Hadeeth ad-Dar: The Journal of the Dar al-Athar al-Islamiyyah*, 14, 2003, 22–27, fig. 2 (New York).
Scott, Philippa, *The Book of Silk*, London: Thames and Hudson, 1993, 138–39 (detail of huntress, Toronto).
Spuhler, Friedrich, *Islamic Carpets and Textiles in the Keir Collection*, London: Faber and Faber, 1978, cat. no. 108, 18–89, illus. 184 (Dallas).
Vollmer, John E., et al. *Silk Roads, China Ships*, Toronto: Royal Ontario Museum, 1983, 230, illus. p.141 and cover (Toronto).

Additional bibliography

Chardin, Sir John. *Sir John Chardin's Travels in Persia*. London, Argonaut Press, 1927.
Matthee, Rudi. "Between Aloofness and Fascination: Safavid Views of the West," *Iranian Studies* 31, no. 2 (1998): 219–46.
Matthee, Rudi. "The Career of Mohammad Beg, Grand Vizier of Shah `Abbas II (r. 1642–1666)," *Iranian Studies* 24, no. 1 (1991): 17–36.
Schwartz, Gary. "Between Court and Company: Dutch Artists in Persia," in *The Fascination of Persia. The Persian-European Dialogue in Seventeenth-Century Art & Contemporary Art of Teheran*, ed. Axel Langer, 152–167, Zurich, Museum Rietberg, 2013.
Sonday, Milton. "Patterns and Weaves: Safavid Lampas and Velvet," in *Woven from the Soul, Spun from the Heart: Textile Arts of Safavid and Qajar Iran, 16th–19th Centuries*, ed. Carol Bier, 79–81. Washington, DC: Textile Museum, 1987.
Tavernier, Jean-Baptiste. *The Six Voyages of John Baptista Tavernier, a Noble Man of France Now Living, through Turky into Persia, and the East-Indies, Finished in the Year 1670....* Translated by J. Phillips. London, 1678.

1044. Safavid velvet, Persia (present-day India or Iran), ca. 1640

1045. Print, Nemesis, 1501–2, Albrecht Dürer

1046. Ornament, Mother and Child, France, ca. 1850

1047. Print, Four Nude Women or The Four Witches, 1497, Albrecht Dürer

Poster, Levi's, The Strongest Thread, 2009
Art directed by Stefan Sagmeister (Austrian, b. 1962)
Designed by Joe Shouldice (Canadian), Richard The
Photographed by Tom Schierlitz Photography
Offset lithograph on coated wove paper
Gift of Stefan Sagmeister, 2011-34-1

Commissioned to celebrate Levi's iconic 501 jeans, Stefan Sagmeister decided to take the product apart, breaking it down into its physical components: rivets, zippers, snaps, and thread (lots and lots of thread). A small tag sewn inside the jeans triggered the idea: "This is a Pair of Levis Sewed with the Strongest Thread." Sagmeister's team battled warp and woof to transform the tough denim fabric into soft mounds of thread in two shades of indigo. Laying out the salvaged hardware and thread on the floor, they reassembled them into a graphic interpretation of the famous jeans. To produce the final image for reproduction, Sagmeister and his design team would pack up the materials and put them back together in a professional photo studio, where the image was shot at high resolution by Tom Schierlitz. The completed poster offers up an uncanny collision of realism and representation, a metacommentary on the processes of making and unmaking.

Building graphic images out of physical materials is a hallmark of Sagmeister's work. To produce an album cover for Lou Reed, he drew words directly on the musician's face. To create a lecture poster for Cranbrook Academy of Art, he asked his assistant to carve the poster's text into his own naked torso with an Xacto knife **(1050)**; the final poster is a photograph of the resulting carnage. In a series of projects with no client or commission, Sagmeister used ordinary materials to spell out simple messages about art and life; the materials merged with the environment and changed over time. Photographs of these installations appear in Sagmeister's book *Things I Have Learned in My Life So Far* (2008), where they are preserved and disseminated in print and have inspired many designers to think about new methods and contexts for creating graphic design.

While the Levi's poster is a commercial commission, Sagmeister approached this project as if it were a work of art, granting no promotional message to the piece that hadn't been directly sewn, stamped, or stitched into the product itself. The posters were printed by **offset lithography** (the standard method for commercial design) and distributed to lucky recipients at the American Rag stores in Los Angeles and San Francisco. They became instant collector's items. Their richly textured materiality invites viewers to encounter a familiar object in a new way. **EL**

1048. Poster, Levi's, The Strongest Thread, 2009, Stephen Sagmeister

1049. Drawing, Design for a Candlestick, 1820–30, Joseph Anton Seethaler II

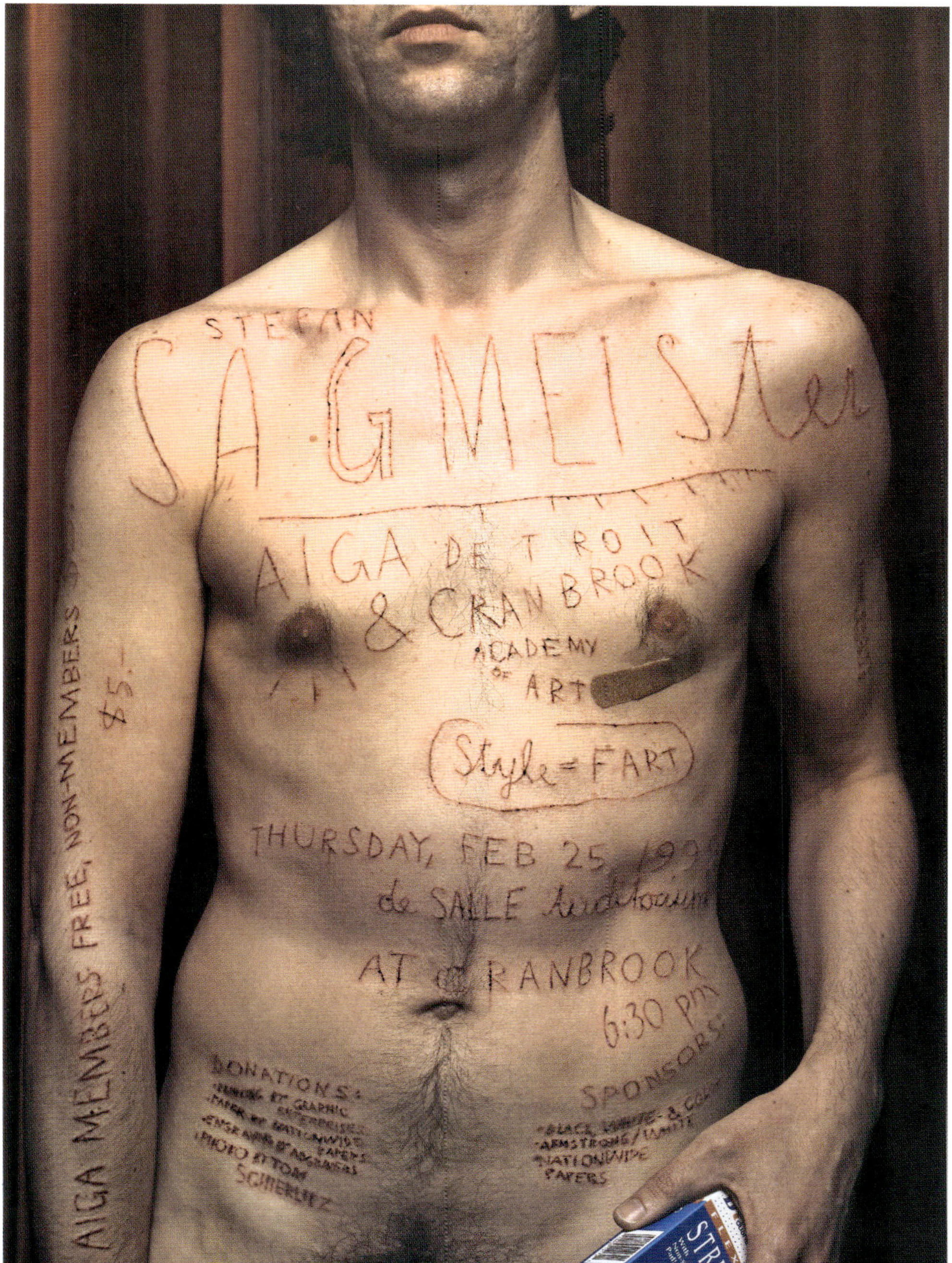

1050. Poster, Stefan Sagmeister AIGA Program, USA, 1999, Stefan Sagmeister

Textile, Attush robe, 19th century
Ainu culture, Hokkaido, Japan
Woven elm bark (*attush*),
appliquéd and embroidered with cotton
Gift of Alice Boney, 1962-67-1

I did not know
what sort of creature
I was;
as time went on
I gradually became aware.

Then each day,
day after day,
I remained staring
after the many needle paths,
after the countless needle paths,
and in the paths of my needle
there would take form
many swirling patterns,
countless swirling patterns.
The upper clothing racks
and the lower clothing racks
would bend down under the weight
of the beautiful robes
which I had embroidered.[1]

Ainu culture in Japan has some of the oldest continuing creative traditions in the world, dating to at least twelve thousand years ago.[2] Vital to their tradition and ethnic identity is the woven elm bark (*attush*) robe, one of the Ainu's most stunning public art forms. Often included in epic narratives (*yukar*), like this example above, attush robes are highly prized by both wearer and maker. Before beginning the robe, the maker contemplated all aspects of the wearer, visualizing the person in the robe, and then designed a suitable decorative pattern. An Ainu woman put her soul into each stitch, believing that a garment made without a purpose would not have a soul.[3] Textile making in general was reserved for women, and men helped to procure the animal skin, plant fiber, and tree barks for processing. The elm tree was the primary source for the bark fiber, which went through an extremely laborious process to make thread (*ohyo*) or cord for use in weaving or basketry. The men carefully stripped the elm of its bark, retaining enough on the tree to protect it. The women then separated the outer and inner bark and soaked the softer inner layers in water for several days to loosen the fibers, which were then split into long, narrow strips and dried. These strands could be twisted to make thread or cord, and either left its natural golden color or dyed with vegetable dyes. The thread was then ready to be woven into strips of cloth fourteen to eighteen inches wide on a **backstrap loom** or *izaribata*, and these strips were finally sewn together to form the robe.[4] The entire process—from initial gathering of the bark to the woven cloth—took more than two months, yet it was only at this point that the robe was ready to receive the **embroidery** and **appliqué** that made it so distinctive and highly valued.

1051. Textile, Attush robe (back view), Ainu culture, Japan. 19th century

Embroidery was stitched directly on cotton cloth (rather than on the robe). Until the early twentieth century cotton fabric was imported and quite expensive, and it often took a woman several years to accumulate enough remnants to complete a more complicated attush robe. The embroidered pieces were then appliquéd to the robe at strategic locations around the neck, front opening, sleeves, and hem in order to protect the wearer from evil spirits. Often the most decorative area was on the back, believed to be the most vulnerable spot where evil spirits could enter a person. This concept of spiritual protection is believed to derive from the rope that Ainu women used to encircle their sleeping children in order to safeguard them while the mothers worked in the mountains or fields.[5]

Design motifs were passed down from mother to daughter; girls practiced dutifully by drawing in the sand or leftover ashes. The most prized designs were original, imaginative reinterpretations and arrangements of traditional motifs. Approximately nineteen different motifs have been identified, including patterns with thorns (bracket-like forms) and *whori* (spiral shapes), represented in this robe.[6] Tattooing on the backs of women's hands and around their arms employed similar curvilinear designs as protection from evil spirits. Inspired by nature, the embroidered designs never referenced animals for fear that it would anger the gods if they saw animals (or humans) trapped inside a design.[7] Controversy still remains over the exact meaning of the designs, but recent scholarship reflects that patterns were made simply to protect the wearer and to please the gods, which embodied both the animate and inanimate worlds. **MM**

1 Recited by Shikata Shimaukano, recorded by Kubodera, August 19, 1940, "Song of a Human Woman," in *Songs of Gods, Songs of Humans: The Epic Tradition of the Ainu*, ed. and trans. Donald L. Philippi (Tokyo: University of Tokyo Press, 1979), 254.

2 Chisato O. Dubreuil, "Ainu Art on the Backs of Gods: Two Exquisite Examples in the DIA Collection," *Bulletin of the Detroit Institute of Arts* no. 1/2 (2002): 6.

3 Chisato O. Dubreuil, "Ainu Art: The Beginnings of Tradition," in *Ainu: Spirit of a Northern People*, ed. William W. Fitzhugh and Chisato O. Dubreuil (Washington, DC: Arctic Studies Center, National Museum of Natural History, Smithsonian Institution, in association with University of Washington Press, 1999), 291.

4 Mari Kodama, "Clothing and Ornamentation," in Fitzhugh and Dubreuil, *Ainu: Spirit of a Northern People*, 314.

5 Dubreuil, "Ainu Art: The Beginnings of Tradition," 293.

6 Kodama, "Clothing and Ornamentation," 321.

7 Dubreuil, "Ainu Art: The Beginnings of Tradition," 292.

1051. Textile, Attush robe (front view), Ainu culture, Japan, 19th Century

1052. Noh robe (detail), Japan, ca. 1800

1053. Child's dress, England, early 18th century

1054. Sidewall, Modernistic, 1927, Charles Burchfield

1055. Textile, Wonda ya chi, Zomo ya chi gudu, mid-20th century, Heinrich Habig Aktiengesellschaft Stoffdruckerei

1056. Child's dress, Europe of Indian fabric, late 18th century

1057. Bed hanging (detail), France, 1730–70

1058. Waistcoat, England, 1770–80

1059. Tekke woman's mantle (chyrpy), Turkmenistan, 19th century

1060. Coat, France, ca. 1790

1061. Petticoat, India for European market, 1700–50

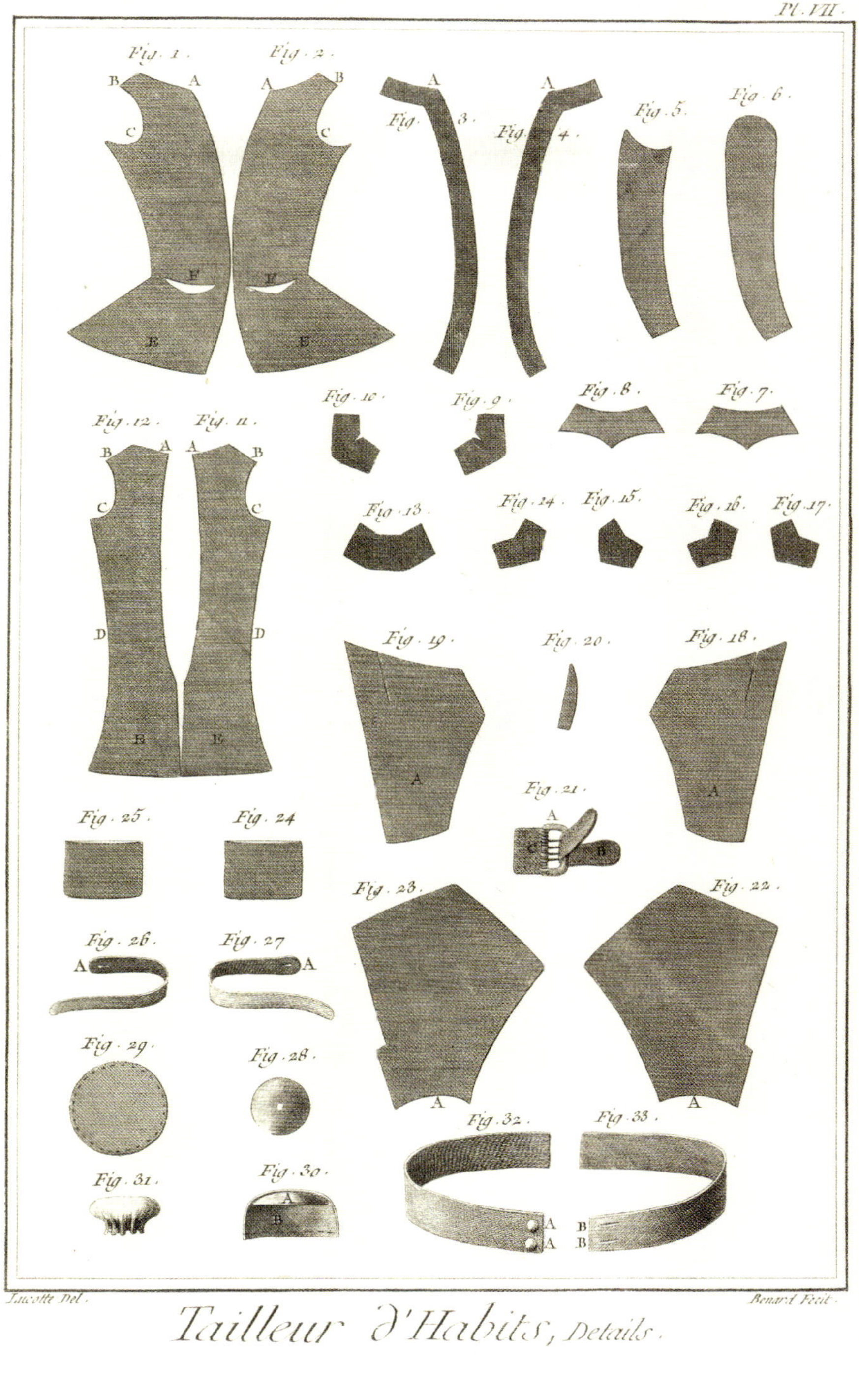

1062. Print, Tailleur d'Habits (detail), 1763, Denis Diderot

1063. Daoist priest's robe, China, 19th century

1064. Robe, Turkestan region, 19th century

1065. Robe for statue, China, late 18th century

1066. Book illustration, *The Goblin Spider*, ca. 1900, Lafcadio Hearn

1067. Drawing, Costume Design: Two Pirates, for *Daphnis et Chloé*, 1913, Léon Nikolajewitsch Bakst

1068. Book illustration (detail), *Kyūgi sōshoku jūrokushiki zufu*, 1903, Kōrin Furuya

1069. Textile, Japan, early 20th century

1070. Print, Great Wave at Satta Beach, Suruga, 1858, Ando Hiroshige

1071. Print, Seki, Early Departure (detail), ca. 1834, Ando Hiroshige

1072. Print, Hakone Lake, ca. 1834, Ando Hiroshige

1073. Print, Ejiri, View over Mio-no-Matsu-bara, ca. 1834, Ando Hiroshige

1074. Mural miniature, Arches, 1948, Ilonka Karasz

1075. Frontispiece, *Architectural Iron Works*, 1865, Daniel D. Badger

1076. Clock, France, 1807–10, Antoine-André Ravrio

1077. Mural miniature, Arabian Nights, 1948, Ilonka Karasz

1078. Frieze, England, 1850–60

Scenic wallpaper, Psyche Bringing Venus a Goblet of Water from the Fountain of Youth, from Les Amours de Psyché, ca. 1820
Designed by Merry-Joseph Blondel (French, 1781–1853)
Made by Joseph Dufour et Cie (Paris, 1752–1827)
Paris, France
Block printed on handmade paper
Gift of Elizabeth Werter and Henry Trevor, 2013-9-1

Scenic wallpapers, the epitome of nineteenth-century **block printing**, were designed to emulate landscape painting. By visually eliminating the boundaries of the walls, they greatly enlarged the perceived size of a room. Scenics usually contained twenty to thirty-two panels with no repeat within a set; each set could require thousands of woodblocks to print. First produced in 1804, scenic papers remained popular with new designs introduced, until 1865. Les Amours de Psyché, first printed by the Parisian firm Dufour et Cie in 1816, was considered the firm's masterpiece. After Dufour's death, the woodblocks were sold to the firm of Desfosse & Karth, who by 1931 had printed five more editions. The printing blocks were badly damaged during World War II, and no more sets have been produced since.

The Psyche wallpaper **(1079)** is unique in two ways: It was designed to be hung in sections rather than as a continuous scene, with each scene surrounded by a border. It is also the only scenic paper whose major scenes are set indoors. The full set contains twenty-six panels showing twelve different scenes, which range in width from one to four panels. The full set required 1,245 wood blocks to print.

The scenes are based on episodes from La Fontaine's 1869 novel *Les Amours de Psyché et de Cupidon* (*The Loves of Psyche and Cupid*), itself based on *Metamorphoses*, Apuleius's second-century account of the Roman myth of great mortal beauty, love, and jealousy.[1] This scene shows a kneeling Psyche offering Venus a goblet of water from the fountain of youth, the offering being one of the last feats Psyche was asked to perform by Venus in order for her to be reunited with her love, Cupid. After the successful completion of her feats Psyche marries Cupid, is made a goddess, and lives happily ever after. This wallpaper example is especially vibrant as it is an early printing.

While scenic papers were costly, there was a great variation in pricing so they were not produced exclusively for the wealthy. The cost was dependent on several factors, including the number of panels and printed colors. Monochromatic papers, such as this *grisaille* (in shades of gray, imitating traditional grisaille wall painting), required fewer blocks to print and were normally available at a lower cost. For most wallpapers, one block is necessary to print each color, but given the large size and lack of repeat on scenic papers numerous blocks could be required for each color. The designs for scenic papers tended to come from existing prints, from which artists would meld together the elements needed for the desired scenes. While the completed drawings for this scenic wallpaper were a collaboration among Louis Lafitte (1770–1828), Merry-Joseph Blondel (1781–1853), and Zavier Mader (1789–1830), half of the scenes were clearly inspired by François Gérard's illustrations for La Fontaine's *Amours de Psyche et de Cupidon* published in 1798.[2] In 1815 Blondel created drawings for two of the remaining scenes, including this one, which Cooper Hewitt acquired in 1996. **GH**

1 Bernard Jacqué and Christine Woods, *The Story of Cupid and Psyche* (Manchester: Whitworth Art Gallery, University of Manchester, 1995), 1.

2 Odile Nouvel-Kammerer, *French Scenic Wallpapers, 1795–1865* (Paris: Musée des Arts Décoratifs, 2000), 141.

1079. Scenic wallpaper, Psyche Bringing Venus a Goblet of Water from the Fountain of Youth, ca. 1820, Merry-Joseph Blondel

1080. Drawing, Bathroom and Boudoir Interior, 1807, Jean-Claude Rumeau

1081. Drawing, Sepulcher in Egyptian Style with Sphinxes and an Owl, 1779–84, Louis-Jean Desprez

1082. Sample book, France, 1785–95, Jean-Baptiste Réveillon
1083. Sidewall, Sacred to Washington, ca. 1800, Ebenezer Clough

Sidewall, ca. 1750
England
Block printed and flocked on handmade paper, varnished
Gift of Josephine Howell, 1972-42-187-a

Wallcoverings have long been imitative in nature and have traditionally copied more exotic and expensive materials. **Flocked** papers, introduced by the late seventeenth century, generally copied patterns for **damasks** and cut velvets. The better flocked papers usually contained a large repeat, and their greater expense usually determined their use in public rooms. Eighteenth-century flocked papers from England were considered the finest available and were widely exported. Flocked wallpapers are making a resurgence today as designers experiment with the tactile nature of this material.

This wallpaper, containing slightly more than one repeat, is printed in deep yellow flock on a yellow ground and imitates a cut-velvet fabric. The designer has rendered the motifs in a rather gestural fashion, and the minimal detailing found in the drapery swags, cording, and tassels is quite expressive, creating a nice rhythm in the folds and twists of the motifs. This wallpaper was printed on joined sheets of handmade paper with a deckle edge still visible on the right side.

Historically, flock consisted of minute particles of wool, linen, or silk, which provided a reuse of textile industry by-products as well as existing rags. As mentioned in Robert Dossie's *Handmade to the Arts* (London, 1764), flock could be made by chopping cloth either by hand or using horse-powered machines. The paper being flocked was **block printed** with varnish, then drawn into a flock-filled trough with a taut, drumlike bottom. The bottom was then beaten with sticks, which caused the flock to rise up and settle in the wet varnish. **GH**

1084. Sidewall, England, ca. 1750

1085. Drawing, Embroidery Design Commemorating the Marriage of Napoleon I and Marie-Louise of Austria, ca. 1810, attributed to Jean-François Bony

1086. Textile, Turkey, 19th century

1087. Textile, Tulip and Rose, 1876, William Morris for Morris & Co.

1088. Textile, France, ca. 1924, Herman A. Elsberg

1089. Sidewall, Versailles, 1951, Piazza Prints, Inc.
1090. Leather, Netherlands, ca. 1750

1091. Brooch, Italy, ca. 1898, Fortunato Pio Castellani & Sons

1092. Drawing, Design for Woven Fabric with Neoclassical Motifs, France, ca. 1820
1093. Sidewall, Crystals, 1953, Janice Hart White

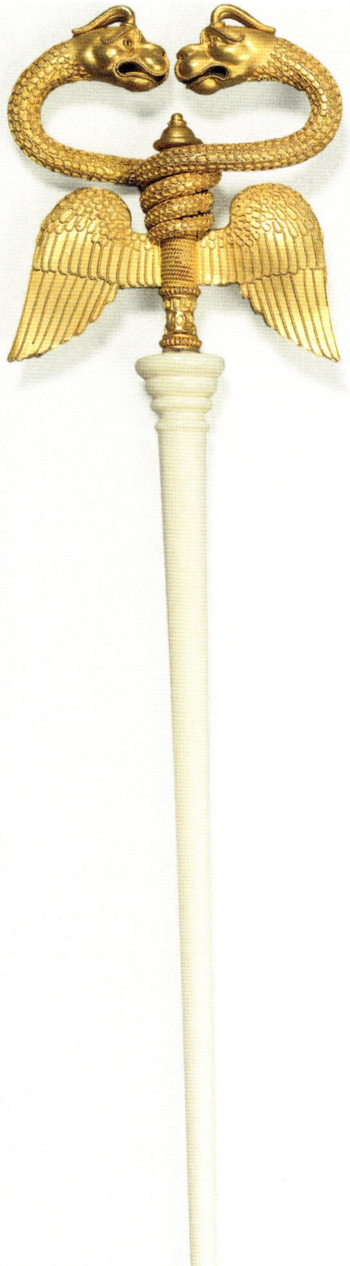

1094. Caduceus-form hair ornament, Italy, ca. 1875, Fortunato Pio Castellani & Sons
1095. Stick pin, France, ca. 1867

1096. Cuff buttons, probably France, ca. 1860

1097. Buckle, France, ca. 1900, attributed to Edward Colonna

Sidewall, Lincrusta-Walton, 1884
Attributed to Christopher Dresser (British, 1834–1904)
England
Painted and gilded Lincrusta
Gift of John Davison Rockefeller, Jr. 1937-57-3

Significant urban growth during the late nineteenth century led authorities to question whether appropriate sanitary measures were being taken to safeguard people's well-being. On the domestic front, this raised concerns about the safety of wallpapers due to the fact they could not be cleaned. Until 1934, wallpapers were printed with water-soluble colors where washing would smear pigments.
For this reason, critics claimed wallpapers harbored germs and were unsanitary. Additionally, many homeowners and landlords did not remove old wallpapers before applying a new one, allowing multiple layers of old papers to build up on the wall. This practice was strongly condemned by the sanitation commission of New York City, which in the 1890s included a measure in the Tenement House Bill stating only one layer of wallpaper could be on the walls at a time.
Manufacturers had begun searching for formulas for washable papers in the 1850s but did not find a feasible solution until the 1870s, with **intaglio** prints. These designs were printed in oil colors using engraved copper rollers, which created a very smooth surface that could be wiped clean. Varnished tile papers were also introduced as a sanitary option; however, no wallcoverings on the market matched the sanitary qualities of Lincrusta-Walton (Lincrusta). Impermeable to moisture and completely waterproof, it could be scrubbed with soap and water. Created in England in 1877 by Frederick Walton, the inventor of linoleum, Lincrusta contained oxidized linseed oil and wood pulp, among other materials. The name is a derivation *linum*—flax, from which linseed oil is obtained—and *crusta*—meaning relief. It was based on the linoleum formula already known for its water-resistant and washable properties. Lincrusta applied these same qualities to the wall adding a relief surface, created by running the pulp under rollers that embossed the surface. Lincrusta was produced in several shades of tan and brown, and could be left in its natural state or painted to resemble plasterwork or embossed leather. It cost the same as the finer grades of wallpaper, but was less expensive than other relief materials.
Many well-known designers—including Christopher Dresser, Lewis F. Day, Hector Guimard, and the Herter Brothers—employed Lincrusta. This sample **(1098)** was formerly used in the John D. Rockefeller dining room on West 54th Street in New York City, and at one time was thought to be a Dresser design. The base material is a dark brown; after installation it was painted to resemble gilt leather. The entire surface was covered with a metallic gold pigment, with the recessed areas then painted a deep red. The original backing appears to be paper, indicating a slightly later production, as the original patterns were backed with canvas. Lincrusta had a range of uses and the canvas proved to be too stiff for many applications. In 1887 the rigid fabric backing was replaced with a light waterproof paper.
Lincrusta was called one of the most valuable decorative materials ever introduced, and its popularity continued to grow. Marketing of Lincrusta in the United States began in 1879 with limited success. In August 1883 Frederick Beck & Co. purchased the patent rights and began production at its factory in Stamford, Connecticut, leading to increased sales in the United States. In 1880, a French concern bought patent rights, leading to its European production and worldwide popularity. **GH**

1098. Sidewall, Lincrusta-Walton, England, 1884, attributed to Christopher Dresser

1099. Sidewall, Aesop's Fables, 1952, Herndon Papers

1100. Suite of micro-mosaic jewelry, Italy, 1800–25

1101. Dish, France, ca. 1920, Jean Cros

Panel for a cabinet door, France or Flanders (present-day Belgium), late 16th–early 17th century
Silk embroidered with silk, metal threads, and coral beads
Gift of Marian Hague, 1959-144-1

This tiny scene, painstakingly built up from **embroidered** stitches, commands attention with its astonishing depth and detail. The tree with its twisting branches and leaves that seem to rustle, the lizard and snakes with sparkling silver skins and glittering black eyes, draw us into a realm of complex symbolic imagery. Whether the designer intended to captivate the eye with extravagant materials and workmanship or to invite moral and spiritual contemplation, an abundance of detail supports either pursuit.
Panels of this type were made as part of sets for the interior doors and drawers of jewel cabinets. Intact cabinets are rare, but examples in the collections of the Kunstindustrimuseet in Copenhagen and the Musées Royaux d'Art et d'Histoire in Brussels, as well as others sold at auction, reveal that panels like this one formed a center door that would have been surrounded by ten to twelve small drawers, frequently embroidered with real and fantastical animals. The casework was often ebony or dark-stained wood, with a hinged lid that concealed a mirror, two doors that opened to reveal the embroidered interior, and sometimes the addition of legs to make a standing cabinet.[1]
The virtuosity of the stitching suggests that this panel was made in a workshop by professional embroiderers and, perhaps more notably, a maker of metal threads. There are dozens of unique threads and other metal elements. These include strips in various widths; filé, in which a thin strip of metal is wrapped around a core of silk floss, sometimes covering it entirely and sometimes wrapped loosely to reveal the color of the silk; and purl, round or flattened wire wrapped tightly around a small rod to form a coil. These were used in seemingly endless combinations to create the heavy, ornate framework; the trunk and branches of the tree; and the salamander at its base. Although the effect today is of tarnished silver, the threads were originally silver, gold, or silver and gold in combination, designed to reflect light in myriad ways. The tree, with its raised trunk and three-dimensional branches, is made from filé couched down over bundles of tightly wrapped silk cords. In couching, the costly metal threads stay on the surface, and are secured to the foundation with silk. Each leaf on the tree is individual and three-dimensional, made from silk floss loosely wound with wire. In contrast to the richly textured foreground, the background is decorated with encroaching satin stitches in pale shades of silk for a watercolor effect and the illusion of distance.
Although Adam and Eve are not represented in the image, the story of the Fall of Man and the expulsion from the Garden of Eden are implicit in the tree that dominates the composition. The snake in that narrative is the symbol of temptation and evil. The salamander, which is said to thrive in flames rather than be destroyed by them, is typically used as a symbol of regeneration. In combination with the discarded crutches and votive offering of a wax leg, seen hanging from the branches of the tree, the salamander is a symbol of healing with the snakes in the four corners taking on Renaissance associations of knowledge and the practice of medicine. **SB**

1 Vibeke Woldbye, "Sharloth's Curious Cabinet," *Furniture History* 21 (1985): 70.

1102. Panel for a cabinet door, France or Flanders (present-day Belgium), late 16th–early 17th century

1103. Sampler (detail), USA, 1734, Ann Peartree

1104. Embroidered picture (detail), England, late 17th century

1105. Embroidered picture, USA, 1760–70
1106. Sampler, USA, 1828, Ann E. Kelly

1107. Adoration of the Magi figural group, Flanders (present-day Belgium), ca. 1525
1108. Adoration of the Magi plaque (detail), France, 1500–50

1109. Drawing (detail), Wallpaper Design: Reconciliation of Venus and Psyche, 1815, Merry-Joseph Blondel
1110. Tapestry fragment (detail), Spain, 13th century

1111. Vase, Austria, 1923, Dagobert Peche

1112. Print, Design for a Footed Vase, ca. 1700, Daniel Marot

1113. Locket, Russia, 1899–1908, workshop of Fabergé, August Hollming, workmaster

1114. Print, Pendant Design with the Temptation, from *Pendants with the Virtues*, 1615–23, Jan Theodor de Bry after Daniel Mignot

One of a pair of candelabra, Paris, France, 1739
Made by Claude Ballin II the Younger (French, 1661–1754)
Cast and chased silver with traces of gilding
Gift of Anonymous Donor, 1949-131-2-a/c

This pair of candelabra is a rare surviving example of Parisian eighteenth-century rococo silver. Most of the important silver commissioned by French clients during the rococo period was melted down during the French Revolution. However, impressive French rococo silver was created for foreigners. Some of these commissions survive, displaying the glories of craftsmanship, design, and display characteristic of great French rococo silver. The sinuous S-curve of the stem spirals onto the base like a swirling ball gown, and the organic, asymmetrical branches of the arms epitomize the freedom of rococo design in the 1730s. The style, called the Style Louis XV in France, came in reaction to the more bombastic classicism of Louis XIV's court at Versailles. This stylistic change did not occur immediately after Louis XIV's death in 1715 during the Régence, when the Duc d'Orléans reigned for the child Louis XV.
But the minute Louis XV was of age to be monarch without a regent and got married, the new style—an anticlassical rebellion—became fashionable. Louis XV's 1725 wedding to Maria Leczinscka, the daughter of Stanislas, King of Poland, a great patron of rococo design in his own right, produced early rococo commissions, including from Juste-Aurèle Meissonnier, the primary introducer of the style in Paris. Meissonnier normally would have been outside the Paris corporation of silver and goldsmiths, having been trained by his father in Turin, but Louis XV gave him a royal decree as goldsmith, commissioned him to produce the sword hilts given as presents by the young couple to gentlemen of her father's household, and snuffboxes, confirming the new style as the royal preference. By 1740, around the time these candelabra were made, the style was at its peak, and Claude Ballin was a royal silversmith supplying not only the French crown, but other courts of Europe.
Rococo, as the style is generally known outside of France, is based on barocco and rocaille, for baroque combinations of shells and rockwork of grottoes. This pair of candelabra use stylized shell designs at the base and at the knop of the stem. Their subtlety is what helps distinguish them from some of the foreign interpretations. The style as interpreted in other countries was usually inspired by Paris, but the execution might reflect local skill levels or stylistic preferences in the details. These candelabra, or others of the same model, were possibly made for Charles III, King of Spain, whose successor commissioned replicas from his court silversmith, Juan de Fauri (active 1740–70) in 1762.[1] De Fauri's have less delicate **chasing** of lines but the design is essentially the same. Another set of this model of candelabra must have been in Dresden, where Christian Heinrich Ingermann (German, active 1732–98) created a version similar in style, although not as faithful a replica as de Fauri's, in about 1750.[2] Ingermann's were less restrained than Cooper Hewitt's Ballin examples, having more all over ornament on the stems, but with less curvaceous and not as precisely detailed chasing and cutting in the forms of the branches.
All of these candelabra did more than light the dining table. Boldly **cast**, chased, and **engraved** spiraling forms and textured surfaces produced a playful dancing light, reflecting the candles, creating the rococo aesthetic that they embody. Their design was an important ambassador of this style to other countries. **SDC**

1 Sarah Coffin, et al, *Rococo: The Continuing Curve 1730–2008* (New York: Cooper-Hewitt, National Design Museum, 2008), 116. This pair of candelabra is in a private collection

2 Ibid. This set is in the collection of the Museum of Fine Arts Boston, 1984.186.

1115. One of a pair of candelabra, France, 1739, Claude Ballin II, the Younger

1116. Print, Ewer with Handle (detail), 1548, Cornelis Floris II

1117. Bratina (ceremonial vessel), stand, and tcharkas (cups), Russia, 1884, Pavel Akinov Ovchinnikov

1118. Panel (detail), France, 18th century

Drawing, Design for Two Andirons and Sconce of Gilt Bronze, 1777–90
Jean-Démosthène Dugourc (French, 1749–1825)
Pen and black ink, brush and watercolor on paper, lined, framed with brown paper, pen, and black ink lines
Purchased for the Museum by the Advisory Council, 1921-6-61

Traditionally, when designers received a commission for decorative arts, they would begin the design process with simple hand sketches, from which they would work up more detailed studies, ending with highly finished presentation drawings to be approved by the client. This **presentation drawing** shows designs for a pair of andirons (log holders), one with sphinxes and the other with griffons, and a wall fixture in the neoclassical style, popular in Europe and America in the late eighteenth and early nineteenth centuries.

The inscription in the lower margin, "Bélanger," refers to the architect and landscape designer François-Joseph Bélanger, who would have been contracted by the client for this commission. Following normal procedure, however, Bélanger would have employed assistants to execute designs for him. In this case, the drawing and the inscription were executed by his brother-in-law, Jean Démosthène Dugourc, who early in his career assisted Bélanger on projects for the court of Louis XVI. In addition to commissions for the king and his wife, Marie-Antoinette, Dugourc worked under Bélanger on architectural commissions for, among others, Louis XVI's brother, Charles-Philippe, Comte d'Artois (later King Charles X). According to his autobiography, Dugourc assisted Bélanger on the Comte d'Artois's residences in and around Paris, including palaces at Vincennes, Saint-Germain, Maisons, and at the small "pleasure palace" called Bagatelle.

Historically, the Cooper Hewitt drawing has been associated with Bagatelle (1777–86),[1] for which the Comte d'Artois commissioned the architecture and interior furnishings, along with an extensive garden in the English style. The Bagatelle project originated in a wager between d'Artois and his close friend and sister-in-law, Marie-Antoinette, that this former hunting lodge could be designed, built, and furnished in one summer, in time for a fall 1777 celebration. The bet would explain d'Artois's tribute to the queen by adding her monogram, "MA", to one of the andiron designs.

A group of drawings is known showing variations on the designs on Cooper Hewitt's Dugourc drawing. The sheet coming from a suite of fireplace designs by Bélanger, in the Bibliothèque Nationale de France,[2] shows a fireplace concept with andirons of a similar model as in the Cooper Hewitt drawing on the left, except the sphinxes are without trappings, and instead of monograms there are two portrait busts. Additional versions of the sphinx and griffon andirons on the Cooper Hewitt sheet come from an archive of Dugourc drawings that was purchased at auction after the designer's death by the Lyon textile firm Grand Brothers, formerly Pernon, for whom Dugourc contributed textile designs. The archive descended to the successor firm Tassinari et Chatel, which auctioned the contents in 1988.[3] Several of the 215 drawings auctioned include designs related to the Cooper Hewitt sheet. One sketch, now in the Musée des Tissus et des Arts Décoratifs, Lyon, shows an andiron with sphinxes, with one paw resting on a cannonball, like that in the Cooper Hewitt drawing, with the initials of Louis-Stanislaus-Xavier, Comte de Provence, the older brother of the Comte d'Artois.[4] A second drawing (present location unknown) repeats the andiron with griffons also with the monogram of the Comte de Provence.[5] Finally, there is a drawing for eight wall sconces belonging to the Louvre that in the upper right

1119. Drawing, Design for Two Andirons and Sconce of Gilt Bronze, 1777–90, Jean-Démosthène Dugourc

contains a sketch repeating the wall sconce seen in the middle of the Cooper Hewitt drawing.[6] This wall sconce design also appears in a sketchbook of Dugourc drawings in Les Arts Décoratifs, Paris.[7]
All of these sheets combined tell us something about the standard pragmatic working method of eighteenth-century French designers. The Bibliothèque Nationale drawing appears to show Bélanger's earlier concept for the andirons, which Dugourc worked up in a detailed variation for Bagatelle in Cooper Hewitt's presentation drawing, as well as variations on the andirons in two other sheets for the Comte de Provence. This study of the Bélanger/Dugourc team illustrates how designers exploited successful designs for various clients and contexts, merely by changing the motifs, monograms, or portraits. This workshop practice created stylistic cohesion and expediency in the studio production.[8] **GSD**

1 Richard Paul Wunder, "Bagatelle and Two Drawings by Belanger in the Cooper Union," *Connoisseur* CXLVIII, no. 586 (October 1961): 171–74.
2 Livre des cheminées, Bibliothèque Nationale de France, Cabinet des Estampes, Ha 58f, p.15.
3 Sale Drouot, Paris, J. D. Dugourc (1749–1825), Friday, June 3, 1988.
4 Christian Baulez, *De Dugourc a Pernon: nouvelles acquisitions graphiques pour les musées* (Lyon: Musée historiques des Tissus, 1990), 50, no. 3.
5 Dugourc Sale, p. 37, no. 84, Projet de feu à griffons.
6 Baulez, 55–56, no. 6, Louvre RF 41599.
7 Dugourc Album, Les Arts Décoratifs, Gift of David David-Weil, 1924 GF 23, F4, CD 2709, Neuf projets du lustres et de pendules (Nine projects for lighting and clocks).
8 I want to thank Peter Fuhring for sharing his thoughts about the significance of these drawings. The Cooper Hewitt collection includes a second Dugourc presentation drawing, Design for Two Chandeliers (1921-6-62), one of which has been connected to the salon de parade in the Camenoïstrof Palace commissioned by the Comte du Nord, the future Emperor Paul I of Russia. See Peter Fuhring, *Design Into Art, Drawings for Architecture and Ornament, the Lodewijk Houthakker Collection,* 2 vols. (London: Philip Wilson Publishers Ltd., 1989), vol. 1, 380–82, no. 596.

1121. Project for Eight Lighting Fixtures and Clocks, 1777–90, Jean-Démosthène Dugourc

1120. Drawing, Project for a Fireplace with Sphinx Andirons from Projets de Cheminées, 1777–90, François-Joseph Bélanger, Biblitèque Nationale de France

1122. Project for Andiron with Sphinxes and the Monogram of the Comte de Provence, ca. 1780, Jean-Démosthène Dugourc

1123. Sidewall, Oakleaf, 2004, Marthe Armitage

1124. Sidewall, Angela, 1953, Gene McDonald

1125. Textile, England, 1750–59
1126. Scenic wallpaper, China, 1800–30

1127 A & B. Textiles, France, ca. 1919, Herman A. Elsberg

1128. Drawing, Textile Design: Tropical Flowers, 1912–13, Raoul Dufy

1129. Tulip dish and lid, Germany, 1760–90, probably Volkstedt
1130. Drawing, Honeysuckle and Hollyhocks, 1897–98, Alphonse Maria Mucha

1131. Sidewall, France, 1925–30, André Groult

1132. Sidewall, Geraniums, 1938–40, The DeAndrado's

1133. Drawing, Design for a Printed Border, France, 1810–20

1134. Purse, France, 1820–40

1135. Reticule, France, late 18th century

1136. Textile, Germany, ca. 1928, Ruth Hildegard Geyer-Raack

1137. Letter case, France, 18th century
1138. Letter case, France, 18th century

1139. Letter case, France, late 18th century
1140. Letter case, England or Netherlands, 19th century

1141. Letter case, Spain, 18th century
1142. Letter case, Spain, 18th century

1143. Hanging, Röd crocus, 1945, Ann-Mari Forsberg

1145. Hanging, Syrian Pomegranate Tree (detail), 1919–26, Lydia Bush-Brown

1144. Drawing, Three Studies of Poppies, before 1907, Sophia L. Crownfield

1146. Textile, Japan, 1936

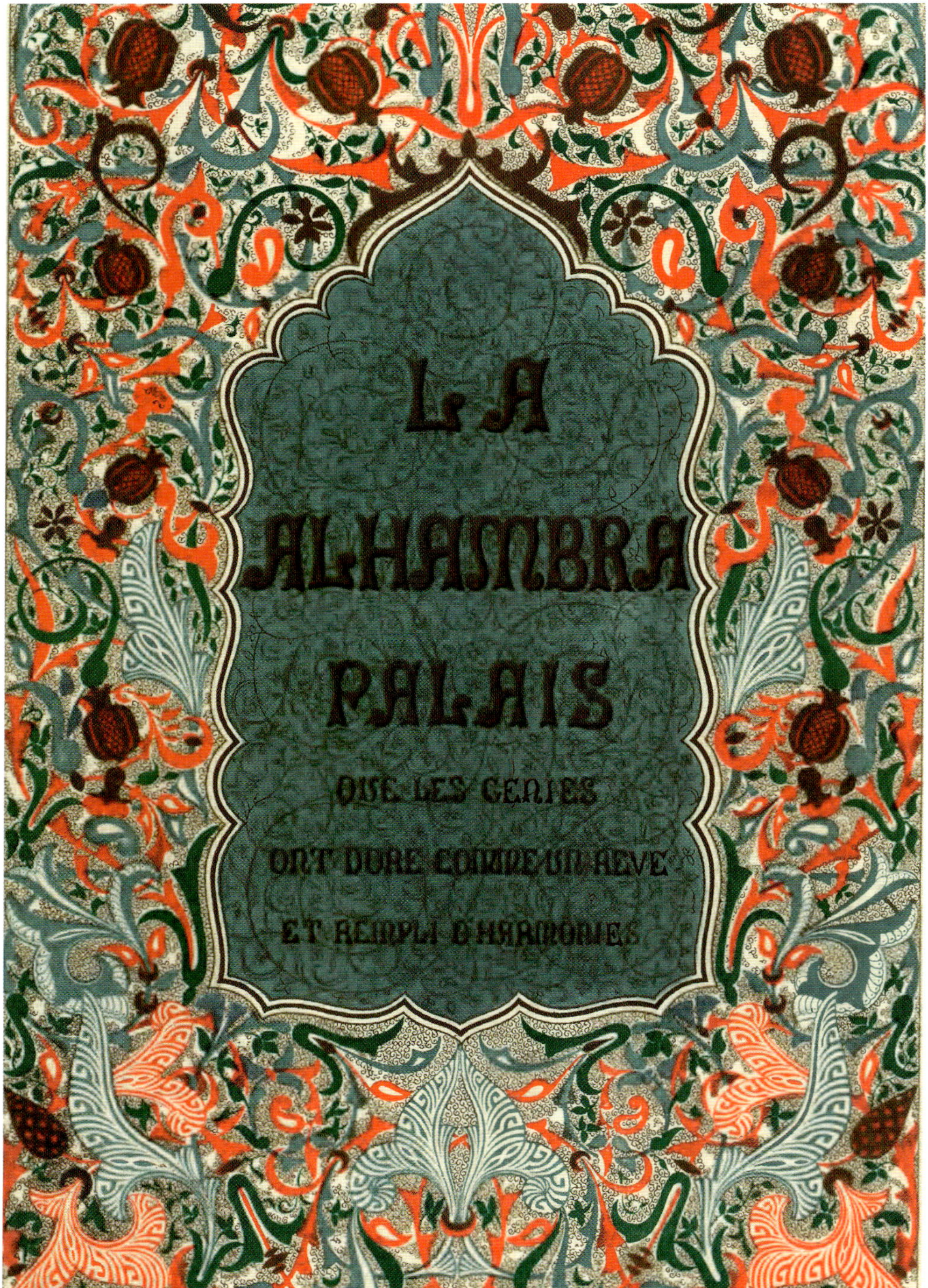

1147. Title page (detail), *La Alhambra Palais*, 1842–45, Jules Goury and Owen Jones

1148. Sidewall and attached border, République Française Liberté Égalité, France, ca. 1792

1149. Border, France, 1775–99

1150. Man's mantle (hinggi), Indonesia, 19th century
1151. Ceremonial cloth (pewo), Indonesia, late 19th–early 20th century

1152. Sidewall, Le Marin, 1920–30, Jean-Émile Laboureur

1153. Sidewall, Blutengarten, 1913–32, Felice Rix-Ueno

1154. Sidewall, Kolibri, ca. 1920, Josef Hillerbrand

1155. Textile, England, 1774–1811, Bromley Hall

1156. Sidewall, USA, 1934–40, Imperial Wallcoverings, Inc.

1157. Textile, USA, 1930s, S. Kahn

1158. Sidewall, Robinson Crusoe, ca. 1875

1159. Box, France, 1858, Louis Toussaint

1160. Sidewall, Japonaiserie, 1883–85, W. N. Peak
1161. (Overleaf) Paper construction, *Alice's Adventures in Wonderland: A Pop-Up Book*, 1980, John Strejan

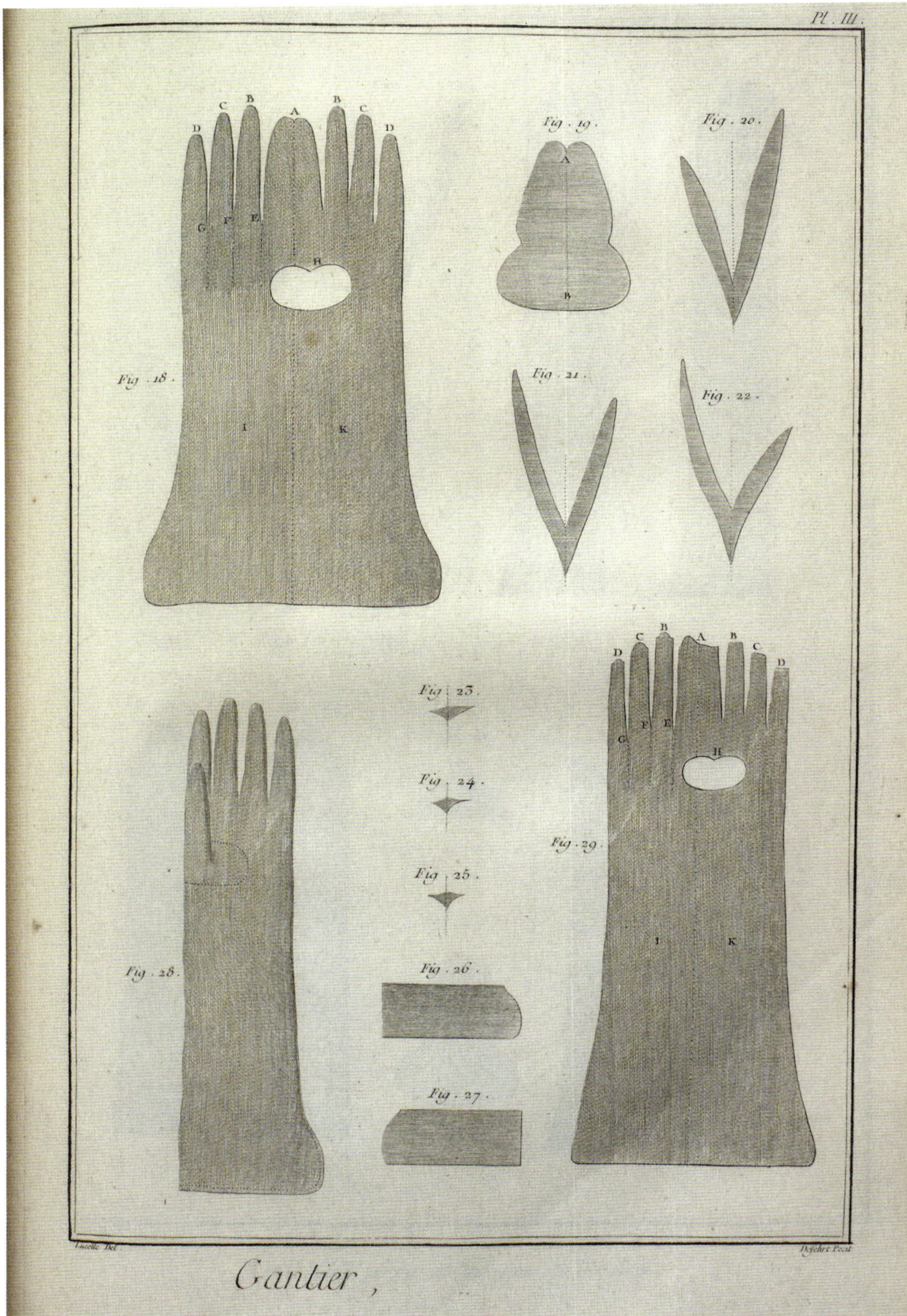

1162. Book Illustration (detail), *Encyclopédie, ou, Dictionnaire raisonné des sciences, des arts et des métiers*, 1751–65, Denis Diderot

3D printing
plastic, other materials
See **additive manufacturing**.

additive manufacturing
plastic, other materials
An additive process for making a three-dimensional object of virtually any shape from a digital model. Successive layers of material build up the form, as opposed to conventional subtractive machining techniques that generally remove material by methods such as cutting or drilling. The process is also known as rapid manufacturing, **rapid prototyping**, **3D printing**, and **stereolithography**.
See **0448**

airbrushing
paper
An adjustable spray technique, first patented in the nineteenth century, that allows an even flow of paint to mist over a substrate, producing a smooth, almost machinelike appearance. Sometimes used with a stencil to cover a surface not meant to be painted or to be airbrushed with another color. The technique was especially popular in the late 1930s as it helped to convey the speed and slickness of the modern streamline style.
See **0805**

amberina glass
glass
Technique used for producing a gradation of colors from amber to red by reheating one end of a glass object before it is fully cooled.
See **0430**

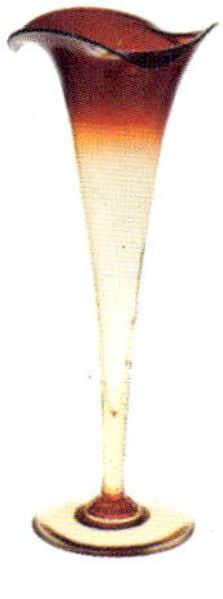

annotation
paper
An annotation is a comment, explanation, presentational mark-up, or other inscription attached to a text or image (e.g., inscribed on or pasted to the sheet or artwork).
See **0340**, **0753**

anodizing
metal
A method of electroplating metal to resist corrosion and abrasion, and provide a decorative finish. An oxide film is electrically deposited from an aqueous solution onto the surface of a metal, oftenaluminum.
See **0696**

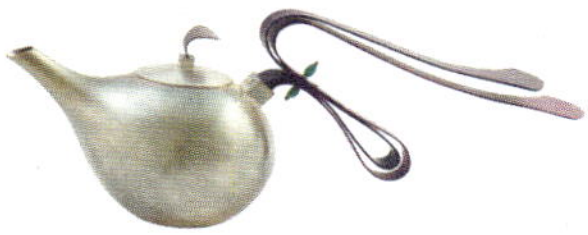

appliqué
textile
A technique of applying cutout pieces of a textile to a ground material by sewing invisibly or decoratively, forming a design.
See **1051**

backstrap loom
textile
A backstrap, or body tension, loom has two loom bars holding the **warp**. One is attached to a stationary device, such as a tree, and the other to the backstrap, a belt around the weaver's waist. The weaver leans backward and forward to pull or ease the tension, opening the sheds for inserting the **weft**.

bentwood
wood
Bentwood is made using various techniques, including steam, to bend the flexible and strong grain of dowels or sheets of wood, such as veneer or plywood, into a form instead of sawing or carving it. Kerfing is the method of cutting partway through or notching the timber so it can be malleable around a form or while clamped.
See **0647**

binary code
Represents text or computer processor instructions using two binary digits, 0 and 1. It is the basis of all computer code.

block print
paper, textile
A print from one or more hand-carved blocks of wood or other material, such as linoleum. Fine lines can be added with metal strips or pins. If printing in two or more colors is required, many techniques can be applied: the block can by inked and printed in one impression, printed in two or more impressions, or two or more blocks can be cut. See **woodcut**.
As a method of decorating wallcoverings or textiles, as opposed to smaller sheets or artistic works, repetitions of the design must be controlled rigorously for color registration. This is achieved through a series of registration guides, called pitch pins. Each printing block is dipped onto a color tray before being impressed onto the paper or cloth. The entire length is printed with one color at a time and then allowed to dry before the subsequent color is introduced. The pattern is stamped on the fabric using the handle of a small heavy hammer, or maul, to aid even penetration of the pasty ink.
See **0022**, **0190**, **0173**

blueprint
paper
Reproductive prints of architectural plans, maps, mechanical drawings, and other technical drawings, characterized by having white images on blue backgrounds and produced by the cyanotype process.
See **0812**

bobbin lace
textile
Lace made by braiding and twisting together a number of threads wound on small bobbins and secured at the upper ends to a pillow. The lace is worked over a paper pattern, and the work is held in place by pins as it progresses.
See **0353**

book illustration
paper
Pictures or diagrams that clarify or provide an example or visualization, usually to accompany a text.
See **0559**

bookplate
paper
A label inside a book to identify its owner. It is usually printed or engraved, frequently with a distinctive personalized design, and usually pasted to the inside of the front cover. Bookplates may simply give the name of the owner with the expression *ex libris* ("from the books"), or they can have elaborate heraldic emblems or insignia.

bright-cutting
metal
Bright-cut engraving, which was introduced around 1770 by silversmiths in London, involves cutting facets in a metal surface to create a sparkling effect. This was done by tilting the graver (a hand tool), which enabled the workman to cut with the polished side of the tool, producing a much broader cut that resembled the facet of a jewel. See also **engraving**.
See **0598**

brocade
textile
A fabric in which a design is created with supplementary **wefts** that are used only where a particular color or pattern is called for in the design.
See **0196**

cabinetmaking
wood
The manufacture of mobile furniture. The term was first used in the late seventeenth century to distinguish the craftsmen specializing in **veneering** and **marquetry** from the joiners who were otherwise responsible for the manufacture of furniture.
See **0843**

CAD
paper
CAD (computer-aided design), once reserved for the most complex and expensive forms of design where precision is paramount, such as architecture and engineering, is now used within a wide range of design fields, as well as by amateurs at varying levels of proficiency. It can also be used to reconstruct fragmentary objects and environments of the past, as well as to forecast and speculate changes in fields such as urban and environmental design.
See **0807**

caning
wood
The process of weaving rattan palm fibers. The technique originated in Asia and was used in England after the 1650s for chair seats and backs. In the late nineteenth and early twentieth centuries there was a worldwide demand for furniture constructed entirely of the lightweight but tough, fibrous core of the rattan palm.
See **0646**

carving
wood, glass
The act of cutting and incising wood, stone, glass, or another material with blades, chisels, and rasps. In decorative arts such as furniture, it refers to a craftsman's decorative treatments of, for example, chair backs, decorative corbels, or chimneypieces. In a different sense, carving is also a fine-art process in sculpture indicating, for example, working in marble, as opposed to terra cotta or plaster, for bronze casts.
See **0649**
See **0649**

casting
metal
The process of forming an object by pouring a liquid or molten material into a mold and allowing it to solidify.
See **0685**

champlevé enameling
metal
In champlevé enameling, a metal is carved out to form pits for enamel and ridges that form the metal outlines of the design. Colored enamels are inserted into the small cavities, the object is fired, and the designs are cleaned and polished.
See **0985**

charcoal
paper
The drawing medium made from burned plant material and available in varying densities and shades of gray and black. Its tones are modulated by **stumping**.
See **0937**

chasing
metal
The tooling of a metal surface by denting or hammering with specialized instruments. In traditional bronze casting, a statue was chased to smooth the work after casting to eliminate unwanted textures, such as seams and imperfections, from the lost wax. Chasing techniques can be used to apply numerous decorative textures and effects in various types of sculpture, decorative metalwork, and jewelry.
See **0472**

chiaroscuro
paper
From the Italian for "light-dark." The contrasting of pools of light and dark in an image to give a deeply shadowed, often moody quality, in which areas are alternately clarified and obscured.

chiaroscuro woodcut
paper
A **woodcut** developed in the sixteenth century with enhanced tonal range from printing from more than one block.

chintz
textile
Traditionally, Indian cotton fabrics where mordants (metallic salts that enable dyes to bind to fibers) are applied by hand before dyeing; the colors are expressed only where the mordants allow the dyes to bind. Usually combined with resist-dyeing and hand-painting techniques.
See **1061**

coated paper
paper
Paper or board that is coated with a clay, adhesive, varnish, or numerous other substances to give a smoother or more durable finish, or a better ability to take inks, depending on its function.

collector's mark
paper
An inked or uninked stamp on a print or drawing impressed by its owner. Originating in the seventeenth century, such marks often play a crucial role in reconstructing provenance.
See **0944**

color lithography
paper
Printing by **lithography** using a separate stone or plate for each color.
See **0265**

compression molding
plastic
The earliest method for molding plastics, by which the molten or softened material is formed into a mold by a hydraulic press.
See **1017**

computer-aided design
See **CAD**

Conté crayon
paper
A brand of fabricated graphite and clay crayon, first made in the mid-nineteenth century in France, that was a popular artists' drawing medium.
See **0937**

copperplate printing
textile
A method of textile printing in which an image is engraved or incised into a metal plate. The printing ink is applied to it, the surface is wiped clean, and the ink remaining in the incised lines is transferred onto cloth in a printing press.
See **0948**

crepe paper
paper
Paper with a crinkled texture.
See **1066**

crochet
textile
A construction in which a length of yarn is manipulated with a hook to form a series of interworked loops and chains.
See **0569**

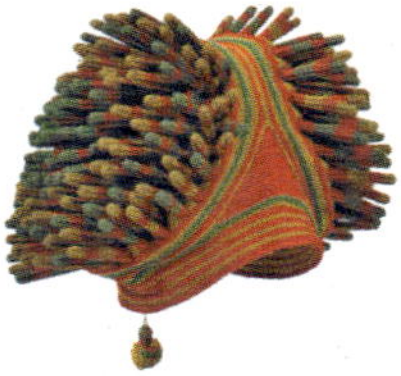

cross-hatching
paper
A toning technique for drawings and prints in which a network of crossed lines creates a darker value.
See **0320**

cross-section drawing
paper
An orthographic drawing that depicts a building, object, or site as if cut transversely or longitudinally, parallel to the structure.
See **0837**

cuenca technique glazing
ceramics
For tiles: originating in Cuenca, Spain. Outlines are drawn on a surface using manganese mixed with a greasy substance to prevent the colored glazes from mingling. Resulting tiles have deeply impressed patterns with compartments filled with colored glazes, often with lustre pigments.
See **0336**

cut glass
glass
A technique used since antiquity, but refined in the eighteenth century, by which the surface of glass is cut into facets, grooves, and depressions with the aid of a large rotating iron, carborundum, or diamond-coated wheel cooled with water or wet sand.
See **0497**

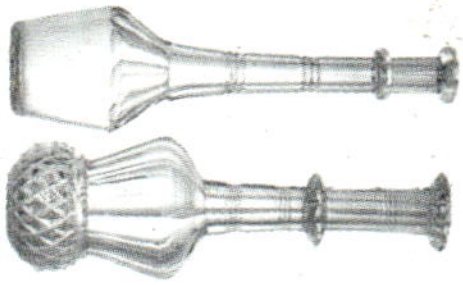

cut paper
paper
Designs created by removing small portions from a piece of paper.
See **0352**, **0785**, **0367**

damask
textile
A weaving technique that uses a single set of warps and wefts to create a typically monochromatic pattern by contrasting the surface texture of the face and reverse of a weave structure.
See **1053**

diazo lithography
paper
A printing process using light-sensitive diazonium compounds.

diazotype
paper
Prints, usually technical drawings, made by exposing diazonium-sensitized materials to light.

die cutting
paper
The use of a die, or sharp stamp, to cut shaped patterns or motifs in a sheet of material such as leather, cloth, or paper.
See **0098**, **0099**

digital printing
paper, textile
The process of utilizing a digital image, whether scanned, photographed, or digitally generated, and printing by various digital means, including inkjet, laser, electrostatic, thermal transfer, and dry transfer. All colors are printed simultaneously.
See **0165**, **0176**

digitizing
Converting sound, motion pictures, images, or other analog data to binary form for computer storage, alteration, or other use.

discharge printing
textile
A method of applying a design to dyed fabric by printing a color-destroying agent to bleach out a white or light pattern on the darker-colored ground. In color-discharge printing, a dye impervious to the bleaching agent is combined with it, producing a colored design instead of white on the dyed ground.
See **0005**

doublecloth
textile
A weaving technique in which there are two structures, each with its own set of **warp**s and **weft**s, with an open pocket between the layers. The layers are connected only where layers exchange places for patterning purposes, usually from one solid color to another.
See **0309**

drafting
paper
Drawing technical graphic representations of structures, machines, or other objects to indicate the size and interrelationship of their component parts for the use of a craftsman.

drypoint
paper
An **intaglio** process in which a sharp needle or **stylus** scratches the metal plate, pulling up a tiny particle or roll of the metal, called a burr. The printmaker can clean off the burr for a crisp line or leave it on the plate to create a velvety line or richly nuanced **cross-hatching**.

dyeing
various materials
The process of applying a coloring matter that is in a solution or fine dispersion, often with various mordants, acids, or other additives to help the dye react chemically and more permanently with the material, such as a leather, fiber, or textile.
See **0871**

ébénisterie
wood
The art of cabinetmaking using **veneering**, a more sophisticated skill level of **menuiserie**. The term derives from the seventeenth-century use of ebony as a material for veneering.

ebonizing
wood
Staining wood black. Employing various stains, vapors, and solutions to imitate ebony. See image for **cabinetmaking**.
See **0843**

Eisengarn
textile
German for "iron yarn." A strong twisted cotton that is waxed for durability, which Marcel Breuer used in the Bauhaus in the 1920s for the seats and backs of his bent-metal furniture.
See **0625**

elevation drawing
paper
A drawing of the vertical elements of the exterior of a building or its interior walls, parallel to the picture surface, as a direct projection to a vertical plane.
See **0829**

embossing
paper
Producing raised letters or designs on any number of sheet and surface types, typically by stamping or molding one or both sides of the surface.
See **0837**, **0848**

embroidery
textile
Decorative surface stitching executed with a needle and thread. Embroidery may be counted (where the stitches are aligned with the warp and weft of the foundation fabric) or uncounted (threads move freely over the surface). Embroidery executed in wool yarns is called crewel.
See **1102**

enameling
metal
The fusing of a ground vitreous frit (ground glass) to metal, ceramic, glass, or other surfaces in a kiln or furnace to create a smooth, hard, colored surface.
The ground frit is made into a paste with water or oil, and applied to a prepared metal surface, then fired at a low temperature in an enameling oven.
See also **champlevé enameling**
See **0341**

endpapers
paper
The sheets placed in the front and back of a book between its covers and text block. Originally used to hold the text block to the covers and to relieve strain on the sewn binding.
See **1023**

engine turning
metal
Engraving of symmetrical decorative patterns on metal by turning on a lathe.
See **1113**

engraving
paper, metal
An **intaglio** process in which the lines are created with a burin, a steel graver with a V-shaped point, on a metal plate, usually of copper. The engraver modulates the depth and ink-holding capacity of the lines by applying varying pressure on the tool. The plate is then inked and skillfully wiped to leave crisp lines in some areas and inkier lines in others. With the pressure of the press, the ink is drawn up into the paper above it.
In engraved metalwork and jewelry, a design is often carved mechanically, using high-speed tools or a diamond point.
See **1007**, **0919**

etching
paper
The etching process starts with a metal plate painted with a waxy or tarlike acid-resistant ground. The artist creates the design in the plate with a **stylus**, scraping away a line of the protective ground.
The plate is then covered with acid, which bites into the metal lines, creating the **intaglio** plate, with tiny channels where the line is to ink and print. As with **engraving** and **drypoint**, the etcher's artistry is evident not only in the subtle variations of lines and **cross-hatching**s, but with the skill of inking the plate. With etching, sections of the plate are protected or retreated with acid to create nuanced variations of shadowy tone and crisper clarity on the same plate.
See **0701**

fashion plate
paper
A print in a periodical or sheet with fashion illustration, often promoting new styles, designers, makers, or shops. In the early twentieth century, many colored fashion plates were **pochoirs**.
See **0994**

felting
textile
A process for forming fabric by matting and shrinking animal hair (usually sheep's wool) under conditions of heat, moisture, and friction.

fine binding
various materials
A book's binding produced for a special edition using hand techniques rather than machine automation.
See **0930**

flashing
glass
The process of taking a piece of hot glass and coating it in colored molten glass. The outer layer can be cut through for further ornamentation.
See **0374**

flocking
paper
A technique for achieving a softly textured or brocadelike finish on paper. A design is applied to the paper in adhesive. The flocking—chopped wool, silk, or other fiber—is sprinkled on and sticks to the glued areas.
See **0119**

foldout
paper
In bookbinding, a page that is larger than the trim size of the book and is folded. It is either prepared within the signature (large sheet folded into pages) before binding and cutting or tipped (pasted) into the bound book.
See **0076**

folly
stone, various materials
An often whimsical or historical-looking building or false ruins built in a park or on private grounds.

foreshortening
paper
Rendering certain parts of an object or figure with smaller dimensions to suggest they are receding in perspective.
See **0864**

forging
metalwork
The process of hammering a cold or (usually) hot metal to shape it and to improve its strength and ductility (ability to be formed). Forging is often done after casting a general shape to refine and strengthen the piece, especially for functional objects.
See **0627**

frontispiece
paper
An illustration on the first verso page of a book, usually facing the title page.
See **1040**

gilding
metal, various materials
The application of gold or another metal to a surface in leaf (a tissuelike sheet), ground gold, ground metal mixed with a binder, electroplating, or other form to approximate the effect of solid or inlaid metal. For porcelain and glass, gilding is generally applied at the end of the manufacturing process, sometimes with low firing in porcelain, so as not to change the previous glazes. There are several different gilding techniques.

Fire gilding is an ancient and very durable method of gilding achieved by applying a milled 1:8 amalgam of gold and mercury. When the paste is applied and heated in a kiln or crucible, the mercury vaporizes to leave a thin layer of gold. Because the substrate must be able to withstand the melting point of gold, fire gilding is only employed on metals (prepared with a surface of silver or copper), ceramics, and glass. It is the method associated with armor and ormolu mounts for ceramics, but has since been abandoned due to mercury's toxicity. In *oil gilding*, a sizing, often containing linseed oil, is applied to the cleaned surface. Gold leaf is applied, smoothed carefully with a brush, and the excess removed. *Water gilding* is a technique used for objects that are not exposed to water, such as frames. The surface is first covered with several coats of gesso; bole (a red clay compound) and a sizing of rabbitskin glue are applied next. Then, water is brushed on, and gold leaf is applied to conform to the surface decoration. The surface can be burnished for more shine. See also **plating**.
See **0551**, **1076**

glass blowing
glass
See **mouth blowing** and **mold blowing**.

glazing
ceramics
A substance high in silica is applied to a ceramic and fired, forming a hard, glass-like surface. Various minerals and elements in the mixture provide distinctive color and quality to the glaze. The substances may also be mixed directly with the clay.
See **0467**

gold tooling
leather
In leatherwork and bookbinding, the process of lettering and/or decorating the spine and covers of a book with gold leaf impressed into the leather by means of a heated letter, lettering pallet, or finishing tool.

gouache
paper
A matte, opaque water-based paint typically using **gum arabic**, gum senegal, or dextrin as a binder. Gouache paints use opaque pigments and chalk or other fillers rather than the transparent pigments used in **watercolor** paints. Gouache was used for miniature paintings from the sixteenth to the eighteenth centuries, and for decorative painting on paper or other supports for the immediacy of watercolor combined with opacity.
See **0145**

granulating
metal
A technique for decorating jewelry, used since antiquity, whereby a metal surface is covered with minute gold or silver granules and heated so they adhere and form a textured surface. A gold alloy is cut up, dispersed in a crucible filled with ground charcoal, and heated until the metal melts and contracts to granules. The granules are applied to a surface of an identical alloy and fused either by heat, a colloidal (or chemical) solder, or an organic adhesive.
See **0579**

graphite
paper
A crystalline form of carbon, graphite is opaque, soft, greasy to the touch, and ranges from steel gray to iron black in color. Artist's graphite pencils may be mixed with clays, oils, or waxy substances.
See **1007**

grisaille
various materials
Images created in monochrome (usually gray tones) that would normally be in full color if executed in other media.
See **0869**

gum arabic
paper
A water-soluble gum exuded by two species, *Senegalia senegal* and *Vachellia seyal*, which were formerly classified under the genus *Acacia*. Gum arabic is used in inks and paints, notably in gum arabic transfers, a type of **lithography**.
See **0535**

hand coloring
paper
The technique of adding color to a black-and-white image.
See **0316**

hard-paste porcelain
ceramics
True porcelain is hard-paste porcelain, the two most important ingredients of which are kaolin (china clay) and petuntse (China stone). When fired to a temperature of

1,250 to 1,350°C (2,282 to 2,462 °F), the body fuses to a glassy matrix and becomes hard, white, and translucent. It is usually covered with a feldspar **glaze**, then fired. The method originated in China, where it has been practiced for over 2,000 years. Compare **soft-paste porcelain.**
See **0556**

india ink
paper
A very black ink, enriched with a suspension of lampblack, used for drawing with a nib or quill or for diluting into washes.

inlay
wood
A design formed by inserting a decorative material (such as wood, bone, or stone) into another—often contrasting—material to create a pattern or design. Inlay techniques are used in **enamel**work, furniture decoration, **lacquer**work, and metalwork. See **intarsia**, **marquetry**.
See **1020**

instructional drawing
paper
A functional or didactic drawing or diagram produced to aid carrying out a specific procedure.

intaglio
paper
A category of printing in which the plate is recessed in the places that are to print the line. Unlike relief methods such as **woodcut** or **letterpress**, which are stamped from above, in intaglio processes the plate lies beneath the paper and cut lines hold minute ridges of ink; these are pressed from above. Aquatint, **drypoint**, **engraving**, **etching**, **mezzotint**, **photogravure**, and **stipple engraving** are intaglio processes.
See **0870**

intarsia
wood
In wood and furniture making, the inlay of woods of different shapes, grains, and colors, sometimes with bone, ivory, or other materials, to form a design.

iridizing
glass
Ancient Roman glass has an iridescence from the natural deterioration of the glass and organic material buried with it. This effect, prized by nineteenth-century collectors, was imitated in 1877, when Thomas Wilkes Webb of Stourbridge, England, devised an iridizing method whereby hot glass in a kiln was exposed to fumes or sprays from evaporating tin and other metals.
See **0429**

iron-gall ink
paper
An ink prepared by binding carbon particles in gall extract (from an abnormal growth on oak trees) that, when applied to paper, darkens to brown- or purple-black by **oxidation**.
See **0379**

isometric drawing
paper
A technical drawing indicating three dimensions, with none of the three planes parallel to the picture plane.

jacquard
textile
Fabrics created by means of the Jacquard loom attachment, which allows warp threads to be raised independently in complex woven patterns. Originally the warps were manipulated with a series of punched cards; today the warps are computer controlled.
See **0893**

joinery
wood
A *mortise and tenon* joint connects two perpendicular pieces of wood. Usually working with the strength of the grain, a tenon, or tongue, is inserted into a mortise, or slot. *Dovetail* joining is one of the many variations of this basic join, in which a triangular tab and corresponding notch are cut so that two pieces of wood can lock tightly together at the point of stress; the joints are sometimes left visible since they can be decorative.
See **0651** (mortise and tenon), **0874** (dovetail)

knitting
textile
A looped construction in which a length of yarn is manipulated with two to five needles (or a row of hooks, if by machine) to form successive rows of open loops, each loop engaging the corresponding one in the previous row, to form an elastic fabric either horizontally or vertically.
See **0570**

lacquer
wood
A durable, water-resistant **resin** finish made from the sap of the *Rhus verniciflua* tree, native to East Asia. After annual collection, the sap is purified and prepared. It can be diluted with spirits and built up in many thin coats—often dozens of layers—to make a shiny and durable finish that can either protect decoration underneath, or can be finely carved itself, as in traditional Chinese lacquer wares. Japanese for "sprinkled picture," *maki-e* is a highly developed lacquering technique that encompasses various methods of applying gold and silver particles to damp lacquer. *Wajima-nuri* is a method named for the Japanese town or its origin; fine *jinoko*, made from a baked local diatomaceous earth, is mixed with lacquer for enhanced durability and various precious metals decorations are incorporated.
See **0517**, **051**

laid paper
paper
Paper usually produced by handmade techniques whereby a fiber pulp is pushed into a screened frame, leaving the screen's long, fine, horizontal parallel lines as a faint pattern, visible when held up to the light. Sometimes it also has a distinctive **watermark**, embossed or visible on the paper. Compare **wove paper**.
See **0601**

laminating
wood; furniture
For wood, the process of bonding several **veneers** or plies of wood for strength, economy, or for bending and shaping. Also, bonding another finish or layer, such as a plastic, to the wood.
See **0633**

lampas
textile
A weaving technique that produces a figured textile whose pattern is created by a supplementary pattern weft, held in place by its own binding warp, on a ground weave produced by the foundation warp and weft.
See **0574**

letterpress
paper
Printing from raised and inked type used in printing some books and sheets. Letterpress, a relief printing process, is characterized by distinctive impressed letters on the printed page. Compare **lithography**, **intaglio**.

lithography
paper
A planographic printing process in which a design is printed from a flat stone or plate rather than a dimensional plate or block to either hold the ink in intaglio grooves (compare **etching**, **engraving**) or stamp it (e.g., **block printing**). Lithography uses the principle of water and grease resist to make a surface that can be printed many times and immediately cleaned and used for something else. Invented in 1796 as a means of cheap reproduction and flourishing in the nineteenth century for its subtle, evocative, painterly graphic possibilities, the artist's method is still similar: an image is drawn with a special greasy pencil or inks onto the plate. Water is used in the process so the untreated areas of the paper remain white. Developed later and popular in the twentieth century, four-color lithography produces a finished print that has much of the immediacy of a **gouache**.
See also **offset lithography**.
See **0126**, **0545**

longitudinal section drawing
paper
An architectural or technical drawing of a cross-section of the longest axis.

lustering
ceramics, glass
The process of giving a metallic or reflective surface to ceramic or glass. For ceramics, salts of silver, gold, or copper (depending on the desired color) are dissolved and applied to the glaze. When fired in low heat, the salts are burned away, leaving a fine metallic film. To achieve the effect in glass, metallic oxides are dissolved in acid and added to an oily medium. The glass is painted with this and then fired, fusing the metals to the surface. Also see **iridizing**.
See **0344**

macramé
textile
Interknotting cords in various styles of knots to make various meshlike, or lacelike textiles.
See **0888**

marquetry
wood; furniture
The craft of **inlay**ing **veneers** of wood, bone, horn, and various precious materials in **intarsia** designs on furniture. Fine patterns and borders can be made by cross-cutting layers of materials one or more times.
See **0879**

menuiserie
wood; furniture
The art of joining and basic cabinetmaking that does not include the use of **veneer** and **inlay**. Compare **ébénisterie**.
See **0879**

metal point
paper
A metal **stylus**, rod, or wire, often in a holder, used for drawing. See **drypoint**.

mezza filigrana (half filigree)
glass
A technique using a series of transparent glass rods with a central piece of colored glass. The rods are fire joined at 700°C (1,292 °F), shaped into a cylinder, and then modeled with a blowpipe.
See **0328**

mezzotint
paper
An **intaglio** printing process in which the surface of the plate is methodically roughened with a rocker to hold the ink and produce areas of shadow. This method somewhat mechanized the creation of tone and shadow (as did aquatint) that in **engraving**, **etching**, or **drypoint** would have been achieved with **cross-hatching**, although each of the later, faster methods could be used masterfully by artists and printmakers, and the uniform tonalities could be seen as more naturalistic than hatching. For its qualities of speed and a more easily learned skill, mezzotints were often used in reproductive prints, ephemera, and book and magazine illustration, especially throughout the eighteenth century, before being superseded by **lithography** in the nineteenth century.

mezzotone printing
paper
A printing method for wallcoverings developed by wallpaper manufacturer Katzenbach & Warren in 1947. The full-scale artwork is drawn in graphite and ink on linen then photographically captured; the wallpaper is a positive print of the blueprint negative. This technique allows the print to pick up all the intricacies and nuances of the original artwork.
See **1074**

mirroring
glass
For millennia, mirrors and mirrored surfaces were made by polished metals, then mercury- or foil-backed crystal or glass. In 1835, the process called silvering was developed in which a silver-ammonia is reduced and applied to the back of a piece glass, forming a mirrored surface on the other side.
See **0596**

mise en carte
paper
Layouts marked on a card or paper as patterns for weaving or lacemaking motifs.

mold blowing
glass
The technique of blowing molten glass into a mold has been practiced since antiquity. The glass hardens quickly as it touches the mold; depending on the specific technique, the inside can be blown, forming a vessel. Moldblowing is used to produce many examples of the same form with a minimum of skill and time. Molding also makes it possible to create forms and details not possible by traditional handblowing methods.
See **0510**

molding
various materials
The technique of filling an empty, three-dimensional form with a soft, particulate, or liquid substance. See **casting** (metal), hardened steel for molds for plastic materials, and plaster for various purposes. See also **compression molding**, **mold blowing**, **rotational molding**, and **wood molding**.
See **0366**, **0484**

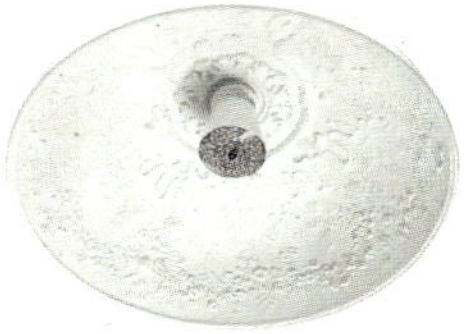

mosaic
various materials
A design formed by small pieces of stone, glass, metal, or shell (called tesserae) embedded into a binder.
See **1100**

mouth blowing
glass
A means—used since antiquity—of making hollow glass vessels in which a lump of molten glass on one end of a long metal tube is blown from the other end of the tube. The knob of soft glass is skillfully turned and blown until the vessel is formed and properly shaped. Blowing is often combined with colored glasses and **tooling** or **cutting** of the soft glass for aesthetics or function.

needle lace
textile
Lace made by building up an openwork structure of looped and twisted stitches made by a needle and thread.
See **0902**

negative print
paper
A print on paper, such as a cyanotype, with reverse coloring of the original design and void, as a negative film would have.

netting
textile
An open-mesh structure with openings of fixed dimensions secured by knots.
See **0327**

newsprint
paper
Inexpensive, low-quality wood-pulp paper used chiefly for printing newspapers. It is high in acid, which is used to break down the wood.

offset lithography
paper
A variation of **lithography** used for commercial printing that came to replace more labor-intensive **letterpress** methods in the last quarter of the nineteenth century. A plate is made with the book type or commercial material and design; the ink is transferred, or offset, onto a rubber roller, which prints the oily ink with water onto the press sheet.
See **1032**

openwork embroidery (cut, withdrawn, or deflected element work)
textile
A type of embroidery in which parts of the ground fabric are removed by cutting (cutwork) or pulling out individual **warp** and/or **weft** threads (withdrawn element or drawnwork); the openings are filled with needle lace.
See **0895**

orthogonal drawing
paper
A drawing that represents a three-dimensional object or diagram in two dimensions using parallel lines but without the use of any visual compensations of perspective, such as foreshortening.

overglaze decoration
ceramics
In ceramics, the technique of painting decorations in glazes over the primary glaze and then firing at a lower temperature.
See **0468**

oxidation
metal
The process or result of a substance combining with oxygen. In metals, this reaction often changes the color of the surface, as seen in the blackening of oxidized silver, the aqua-green **patination** of copper and bronze, or the rust of iron.

painted enameling (Limoges)
metalwork / jewelry
In this process, the object, usually copper, is covered with an opaque white enamel and fired; it is then decorated with colored enamels, each of which requires different firings. In Renaissance Limoges, the production of painted enamels superseded that of **champlevé enameling**.

painting
various materials
Applying a coating usually consisting of a pigment and binder.

paper construction
paper
The art of cut and folded paper such as those forming pop-ups and other paper mechanisms.

paper pulp
paper
A dispersion of vegetable, mineral, or man-made fibers in water, used as the raw material for pressing into paper.
See also **rag paper**, **wood pulp paper**.

papier mâché
paper
An inexpensive, malleable, and paintable mixture of paper pieces or pulp, sometimes reinforced with textiles, bound with an adhesive such as glue, starch, or paste.
See **0654**

pâte de verre
glass
A process to make glass resemble semi-precious stones by firing a paste of crushed glass bound with water and an organic gum. The technique originated in ancient Egypt and was revived in the 1880s by French sculptor Henri Cros.
See **1101**

pâte-sur-pâte
ceramics
French for "paste on paste." A porcelain decorating technique in which designs are built up in white porcelain **slip** on the fired piece and then refired in successive passes to form often delicate motifs in subtle relief.
See **1037**

patination
metal
The changes in color and surface to a metal because of **oxidation**, atmosphere, or applied chemicals or gases.
See **0694**

pen-and-ink lithograph
paper
A **lithograph** that uses a greasy pen instead of a crayon.

perspective drawing
paper
Drawing in three-point perspective, such as an architectural rendering, using **foreshortening** to indicate a three-dimensional form in two dimensions.
Compare **orthogonal drawing**, **elevation drawing**.

photo blow-up
paper
A greatly enlarged photographic print.

photocopy
paper
A light-sensitive one-to-one reproduction technique.
See **0637**

photograph
paper
An image made with light by means of photographic negatives, a direct positive process, or a digital process, usually by means of a camera and lenses. In traditional black-and-white photography, a negative image is impressed on the silver-based (light-sensitive) film. This is then usually enlarged and printed on treated paper as a positive of the image.
See **0833**

photogravure
paper
An **intaglio** process whereby a copper plate is given a gelatin-silver (light-sensitive) coating that has been exposed to a film positive, and then etched, resulting in a high-quality intaglio print that can reproduce the detail and continuous halftones of a photograph.

photolithograph
paper
Lithography that uses a photographic process to create the positive for the lithographic plate.

photomechanical process
paper
A relatively nonspecific term whereby a photographic process is used to create a printing matrix; this may be printed on various supports.
See **0638**

piercing
metalwork
Perforating a metal sheet to create a decorative pattern with the use of a chisel, piercing saw, or punch.
See **0462**

plain weave
textile
The most basic of fabric structures, in which one set of **warps** and one set of **wefts** interlace in alternating rows of over-one and under-one.
See **0462**

plate
paper
In printing, a piece of metal or similar material from which textual or pictorial images are printed.

plating
metal, various materials
In metalwork, the thin coating of a more desirable metal on a more functional or cheaper one, such as gold-plated bronze. Plating can be done mechanically, chemically, and electrolytically.
See **0235**

pochoir
paper
French for "stencil." A way of mass producing hand-colored illustrations with the guidance of multiple stencils for each color area.
See **0319**

polishing
glass
Using friction and various combinations of felt, wood, acid, or pumice, or other powdered materials to achieve a shiny surface on blown or molded glass.

polychromy
various materials
The practice of painting, especially sculpture or architectural decoration, in several colors. The term is usually used for art objects one would expect to be one color, such as bronze or marble sculpted decoration.

pop-up
paper
See **paper construction**.

positive print
paper
A print with dark and light forms that imitate the original subject.

presentation drawing
paper
A finished rendering of a project such as a building, a monument, or an ambitious smaller work of art or furnishing, on which the artist has filled in practical details and often the context, so the client can understand, approve, and fund the various steps to completion. A presentation drawing or model might be created by someone other than the main designer in order to present a finished product that the client can easily comprehend and appreciate.
See **1119**

rag paper
paper
Paper made of linen or cotton fiber instead of wood pulp broken down by acids. The rag material is boiled, shredded, and beaten to a smooth pulp, which is laid into a screen frame, dried, and pressed. Rag paper has a characteristic hand, texture, and longevity.

raising
metalwork / jewelry
The process of forming an object, such as a hollow vessel, from a flat sheet of metal by alternately heating and hammering.
See **0495**

rapid manufacturing
plastic, other materials
See **additive manufacturing**

rapid prototyping
plastic, other materials
See **additive manufacturing**

recto
paper
The front or obverse sides of a leaf; the right-hand pages of an open book or manuscript.

relief halftone
paper
A method of reproducing images, especially photographs, for the popular press, particularly from the 1880s to the 1950s. In this method, halftones can be successfully reproduced as images having only solid black. A work is rephotographed to create a copy negative and then printed on a coated plate through screens so the halftones will be shaded with increasingly large dots. The unexposed areas remain soluble after development and are washed away; then, the plate is acid etched, inked, and printed.

rendering
paper
A drawing such as of architecture, to show a work fully in its context rather than as an abstracted technical drawing or study. Details in an architectural rendering can include passersby and users, landscaping, and everyday occurrences such as diners, visitors, etc., with coloring for added realism.

repoussé
metal
Hammered or punched metal, such as copper, worked from the back to create a relief design on the front. It enjoyed great popularity with the late nineteenth- and twentieth-century craft movements.
See **0454**

resin
paper
Natural resins are plant or animal secretions, such as conifer sap, that can be thinned in mineral spirits to make a waterproof coating, such as lacquer, shellac, and inks. Artificial resins can include various polymers. See **shellac**.
See **0595**

roller printing
textile
In fabric printing, a method of printing cloth from a rotating cylinder. The design is typically engraved on a metal roller. The roller is inked and wiped and the remaining ink is transferred to the cloth by forcing it between the engraved top and a bottom roller.
See **1055**

rose cutting
gemstones
A faceting style with a wide unfaceted base and a domed top with triangular facets, forming a point at the highest part of the stone.
See **0420**

rotational molding
plastic
In this process, powdered or fine pelleted polymer is put into a mold, which spins under constant heat, often on two

axes at once, allowing the molten material to work into the small details of the mold and create an object that is variously hollow, according to the amount of material that was put into the mold.
See **0157**

s-spun yarn
textile
Plied yarn twisted to the right during spinning. Compare **z-spun yarn.**

sample book
paper
A book or collection of commercial samples, such as fabric swatches.

sanguine
paper
A drawing medium made from natural red clay containing iron ocher (anhydrous iron oxides from hematite). The color ranges from blood red to reddish brown and was traditionally used in academic drawings to build up subtle fleshlike tones.

satin weave
textile
A weave formed by a **warp** with long floats, spanning several **weft** threads. Generally, each warp end passes over four or more adjacent weft picks and under the next one, providing a smooth, lustrous surface.

screenprinting
textile
A type of stencil printing in which the first step is to stretch and attach a woven fabric (originally silk, but now more commonly of synthetic material) tightly over a wooden frame. Areas of the screen that are not part of the image are blocked out with a variety of stencil-based methods, including painting out with varnish, or exposure of photographic emulsion. A squeegee is then used to press ink through the unblocked areas of the screen directly onto fabric. In industry, so-called *flatbed printing* has largely been replaced by *rotary screenprinting*, in which the screens are typically metal mesh, not fabric.
See **0305**, **0121**

seal ink
paper
A pasty, oil-based red ink originating in the Far East and used for stamping with a carved wooden stamp on paintings or for sealing documents. It is made of vermillion or cinnabar, oil, and the spongy decayed leaf of the moxa herb, which forms something like a spongy stamp pad for the wooden seal, which is carved with the characters to be inked.

selective laser sintering (SLS)
plastic
An **additive manufacturing** technique used in prototyping in which a laser is used to sinter—bind a substance such as powdered polymer—with heat without melting.

sepia ink
paper
An ink made from the brown pigment derived from the ink of cuttlefish. The ink has been used for drawing and brown washes since ancient Rome.

shellac
wood
A **resin** of the female lac bug in the forests of India and Thailand, which can be thinned with ethanol to make a durable sealer and wood finisher that can be plastic, melted, and carved.

silkscreening
paper
See **screenprinting**

sketch
paper
A summary drawing expressing what an artist sees or imagines, whether a few lines or something approaching a full drawing.
See **0256**

slip
ceramics
A very dilute, fine clay used variously for finishing, decorating, or as a paste for ceramics.

soft-paste porcelain
ceramics
An artificial porcelain made with white clay and ground glass frit to give it a translucence that imitates **hard-paste porcelain**, but without the superior qualities of kaolin clay.

squaring
paper
A method for enlarging, reducing, or copying a design, as from a working drawing to a wall for mural painting.

stack laminating
wood
A process by which wood boards or planks are stacked and glued together to form a mass, which can then be carved into a shape. The method, traditionally used to make duck decoys, was refined in the twentieth century as a furniture-making technique by American designer-craftsman Wendell Castle.
See **0684**

stamped metal foil printing
paper
The process of stamping paper with a metal die to emboss the paper and apply a layer of metal leaf.
See **0973**

stencil printing
textile
A printing process that uses a stencil cut from paper or metal. Ink paste or resist paste can be applied through the stencil.
See **0307**

stereolithography (SLA)
plastic
One of the best-known methods of **additive manufacturing**. Driven by a **CAD** file, a form is produced as a laser scans a vat of photopolymer, building the form by converting the light-sensitive liquid to solid in thin layers.
See **0639**

stipple engraving
paper
An **intaglio** printmaking process that achieves tonal areas by directly engraving short flicks or dots, usually in conjunction with engraved or etched lines.

stippling
wood
Inking or punching groups of dots for a decorative effect such as to fill zones of a pattern.

stitched resist
textile
A type of resist-dye patterning in which selected areas of fabric are protected from the dye by being stitched with water-resistant thread. After dyeing, these emerge as negative patterns on the dyed ground.

stumping
paper
In drawing, the act of blending **charcoal**, pastels, chalks, or other soft media with a pencil-shaped roll of paper or other material. It may be used for simple toning effects, or for great finish in shadows and color.
See **0937**

stylus
paper
Any small pencil-shaped instrument with a hard point, usually metal; used for incising lines on a soft surface or for transferring drawings. See **drypoint**, **metal point**.

surface printing
paper
A type of **roller printing** in which the cylinders bear the design to be printed in relief. The raised surface of the roller can be formed from wood, metal strips and pins, or metal outlines packed with a compressible material such as felt.
See **0091**

tapestry weave
textile
A **weft**-faced **plain weave** in which the wefts are discontinuous, turning back at the boundries of each color area instead of continuing selvedge to selvedge. The handling of the meeting of two color areas further defines the technique as *slit* tapestry (each weft turns back, leaving an open slit), *dovetailed* (wefts from adjacent color areas each wrap in alternation around a common **warp** before turning back), or *interlocked* (wefts from adjacent areas wrap around each other).
See **1143**

thumbnail sketching
paper
A small conceptual sketch made at the beginning of a project summarizing an idea, usually forming a cluster of such possible visual ideas that are posited and considered.

tied resist
textile
A type of resist-dye patterning where selected areas of fabric are tied with strips or cords of water-resistant material. After dyeing, these protected areas emerge as undyed negative patterns on the dyed ground. If the design is tied into the warp or weft threads prior to weaving, this technique is called *ikat* and may be specified warp *ikat*, *weft ikat*, or *double ikat*.
See **0220**

title page
paper
The page of the book, usually on the **recto** of its second leaf, displaying the full title, author, edition, publisher and, sometimes, publication date.
See **1147**

tooling
leather, other materials
In bookbinding, the process of decorating and lettering a binding using a variety of small tools or type. The design or lettering can be accentuated by using heat to darken, or foils and leaf to **gild** the letters.

trade catalog
paper
A catalog produced by a manufacturer or dealer to present products for purchase.
See **0675**

transfer printing
ceramics, glass, textile
A method of applying a decoration to a surface. In glass and ceramics, the term refers to transfer prints made for decorating objects, first used in England in the mid-eighteenth century. The print is made using a special ink and transferred while still wet or by using heat.
See **0358**

turning
wood; furniture
The use of a lathe to produce rounded items, usually of wood, such as spindles, rails, furniture legs, and wooden vessels. A mechanical or motorized apparatus spins a length of wood and the turner tools it to grind away material so it conforms to the profile of the longitudinal section of the design.

twill weave
textile
A diagonal weave formed by passing the **weft** under one **warp** and over two or more warps, and offsetting each successive row, creating a pattern of short floats that run diagonally along the length of the fabric.
See **1052**

upholstering
furniture
Affixing soft paddings and textile or leather coverings to furniture for comfort and decoration.
See **0789**

vellum
paper
True vellum is a parchment—a prepared fine paperlike leather from a young animal—made from calfskin and used since antiquity for manuscripts, illuminations, and for binding books. In modern times, the terms *vellum* and *parchment* both apply to types of paper that imitate the smoothness of these leather skins.
See **0378**

velvet
textile
A weave structure in which a supplementary (nonessential) warp is used to create a raised-pile surface. During weaving, pile rods are inserted to create **warp** loops on the surface of the fabric, which may subsequently be cut (*cut pile*) or left as loops (*uncut pile*). If pile appears only in select pattern areas, the structure is referred to as *voided velvet*.
See **1044**

veneering
wood
The use of thin sheets of decorative wood or ivory, tortoiseshell, or brass, to cover the surface of furniture constructed of coarser or more common wood.

verre églomisé
glass
In this process, gold leaf is attached to the back of glass, then a design is engraved, removing the gold. Colored pigment can then be applied, so from the front, a design shows against a gold ground.
See **0653**

verre fixe
glass
Painting on the reverse of glass, or affixing a painting to the reverse of glass. Also known as *fixé sous verre*.
See **0376**

verso
paper
The reverse of a sheet of paper; the left page of an open book. Compare **recto**.

volvelle
paper
Devices made of independently rotating discs mounted together to enable mathematical and scientific calculations, including the prediction of moon phases and rising tides. Often made of paper, cardboard, or vellum and attached to the page with string, volvelles first appeared in the thirteenth century and are widely considered to be the earliest example of movable paper construction in books.

warp
textile
A set of threads mounted under tension to a loom.

watercolor
paper
A transparent **paint** consisting of pigment suspended in water. Compare **gouache**.
See **1130**

watermark
paper
Faint designs or devices incorporated into paper when made that show up as a translucent design when held up to light. A watermark can indicate a paper's manufacturer or personal or official seals.
See **0944**

wax resist / paste resist
textile
A type of resist-dye patterning where selected areas of fabric are protected from the dye by the application of a starch paste or wax. This can be applied by hand or with a carved block or stencil. After dyeing, these protected areas emerge as undyed negative patterns on the dyed ground. To create multicolored designs, the paste must be removed and reapplied in different areas before each dye bath.
See **0211**

weaving
textile
The process of creating a woven structure on a loom that has a mechanism to lift warps in a specific predetermined order to allow for the passage of the weft threads.

weft
textile
The element that interlaces with the **warp** on a loom in a perpendicular fashion to form a woven structure.

welding
metal
The process of joining two pieces of metal by melting both surfaces, sometimes with a filler material or pressure. *Hammer welding*, achieved without heat, attaches two flat pieces of gold, silver, lead, or platinum face-to-face by hammering alone.
See **0636**

wet processing
paper
The process in which a print is immersed in a bath during development, fixing, or rinsing. The liquid raises the paper fibers, creating a matte surface.

wood molding
wood
The process of creating a shaped run of milled lumber or wood pulp. For milled lumber, this is accomplished through the use of a router to gouge out the wood in a preset measured pattern. For wood pulp, the process is achieved through the creation of a reverse form into which the particulate paste is pressed and set.

wood-pulp paper
paper
Paper made of wood pulp broken down by acids, a process patented in 1854 and used in the popular press. See **newsprint**.
See **0793**

woodcut
paper
A relief process in which the design is cut into and printed from the plank side of a woodblock. See **block print**.
See **0691**

wove paper
paper
A paper made by pressing the pulp into a wire or fabric mesh screen. Wove paper, with its characteristic even weave evident when held up to light, is distinguished from **laid paper**, which has a longer grid pattern.

wrought iron
metal
A ductile and corrosion-resistant iron alloy formed by melting white cast iron, passing an oxidizing flame over it, and rolling.
See **0419**

z-spun yarn
textile
A yarn that is created by drawing together and twisting fibers to the left, when held vertically. Compare **s-spun yarn**.

Long Captions by Sequence

Unless otherwise noted, all Cooper Hewitt collection photography is by Matt Flynn © Smithsonian Institution.

0001. Sidewall, Harlequin, 1953; Timely Service, Inc. (USA); Screenprinted on paper; 83 x 77 cm (32 11/16 x 30 5/16 in.); Gift of B.H. Hellman, 1954-21-10

0002. Pinocchio vase, 2011; Philipp Bruni (Austrian, b. 1982); Manufactured by Neue Wiener Porzellanmanufaktur GmbH & Co KG (Augarten, Vienna, Austria); Molded and weighted hard-paste porcelain; 30.5 x 10.2 cm diam. (12 x 4 in.); Neue Wiener Porzellanmanufaktur GmbH & Co KG, 2011-48-1

0003. Sidewall, Japan, 1990–95; Paper molded from blue and white pulp; 196 x 98 cm (77 3/16 x 38 9/16 in.); Gift of Susumu Sakane, 1998-79-1

0004. Sidewall, Tile, 1958; Barbara White (American); Hand-folded and dyed Japanese paper; 45.7 x 61 cm (18 x 24 in.); Gift of Barbara White, 2000-64-10; © Barbara White

0005. Textile, Van Dyke Squares, ca. 1953; Philip Johnson (American, 1906–2005); Produced by Arundell Clarke Ltd. (New York, New York, USA); Screenprinted with discharge on cotton; 4.40 m x 132.1 cm (14 ft. 5 1/4 in. x 52 in.), repeat: 74 cm (29 1/8 in.); Gift of Arundell Clarke, 1956-150-8

0006. Drawing, Textile Design: Optical Black and White, 1930s; Donald Deskey (American, 1894–1989); Brush and gouache on illustration board; 50.8 x 38 cm (20 x 14 15/16 in.); Gift of Donald Deskey, 1988-101-1494

0007. Poster, Ontwerpen van Tanaka, Ikko (Ikko Tanaka Graphics), 1965; Pieter Brattinga (Dutch, 1931–2004); Offset lithograph on white paper; 62.9 x 38.1 cm (24 3/4 x 15 in.); Gift of Pieter Brattinga, 2000-75-1; © Pieter Brattinga

0008. Zebra cup and saucer, 1955; Eugen Trost (Swedish, 1898–1983); Manufactured by Gefle Porslinsfabrik (Gävle, Sweden); Molded, glazed, and enameled porcelain; 8.3 x 15.9 cm (3 1/4 x 6 1/4 in.); Gift of Dorothy T. Globus, 1992-95-1-a,b; Photo by Ellen McDermott © Smithsonian Institution

0009. Footed bowl, Austria, ca. 1914; Michael Powolny (Austrian, 1871–1954); Johannes Loetz Witwe Glass (Klostermühle, Bohemia and Austria,1852–1948); Mold blown internally decorated white and overlaid opaline and black glass; 14.1 x 21.2 cm (5 9/16 x 8 3/8 in.); Gift of Daniel Morris and Denis Gallion, 1993-134-8; Photo by Ellen McDermott © Smithsonian Institution

0010. Hand-woven sample for drapery material, USA, ca. 1945; Anni Albers (American, b. Germany, 1899–1994); Cotton, rayon, and metallic doublecloth; 26 x 20 cm (10 1/4 x 7 7/8 in.); Museum purchase through gift of Mrs. John Innes Kane, 1948-85-5; © Josef and Anni Albers Foundation

0011. Sidewall, Mauer, ca. 1959; Le Corbusier (Swiss, b. Charles-Édouard Jeanneret-Gris, active France, 1887–1965); Made by Salubra (Switzerland); Machine printed on paper; 217.8 x 78.8 cm (7 ft. 1 3/4 in. x 31 in.); Gift of Marilyn Hapgood, 1992-191-7

0012. Sidewall, Japan, 1990–95; Printed design on ingrain paper, applied fiber; 196 x 98 cm (77 3/16 x 38 9/16 in.); Gift of Susumu Sakane, 1998-79-14

0013. Textile, Campagna, 1948; Angelo Testa (American, 1921–84); Manufactured by Angelo Testa and Company (Chicago, Illinois, USA); Screenprinted cotton; 130.8 x 95.6 cm (51 1/2 x 37 5/8 in.); Gift of Angelo Testa and Company, 1948-119-5

0014. Red White vase, 1998; Hella Jongerius (Dutch, b. 1963); Manufactured by Koninklijke Tichelaar Makkum (Makkum, Netherlands); Molded porcelain with applied automotive paint; 41 x 16 cm diam. (16 1/8 x 6 5/16 in.); Gift of Hella Jongerius, 2014-17-1

0015. Hand-woven sample for drapery material, USA, ca. 1948; Anni Albers (American, b. Germany, 1899–1994); Silk, cotton, and metallic doublecloth; 32.1 x 44.1 cm (12 5/8 x 17 3/8 in.); Gift of Anni Albers, 1953-208-3; © Josef and Anni Albers Foundation

0016. Sidewall, Zeppelin, 1998; Elizabeth Dow Ltd. (American); Hand-painted paper; 243.8 x 101.6 cm (96 x 40 in.); Gift of Elizabeth Dow Ltd., 1998-66-3; © Elizabeth Dow Ltd.

0017. Coverlet fragment, Harris or Meriwether County, Georgia, USA, ca. 1850; Cotton with wool supplementary weft patterning; 85.1 x 42.2 cm (33 1/2 x 16 5/8 in.); Gift of Mrs. Sara Muschel, 1956-173-1

0018. Textile, Central Asia, 19th century; Silk velvet, warps tie-dyed before weaving (ikat); 34 x 32.5 cm (13 3/8 x 12 7/8 in.); Gift of Clara Waldeck, 1969-170-9

0019. Book cover, *The Artwork of Louis C. Tiffany*, 1914; Louis C. Tiffany (American, 1848–1933); *The Artwork of Louis C. Tiffany* (New York: Doubleday, Page & Company); Gold over a red ground papier-mâché binding; 32 x 25.5 x 4.5 cm (12 1/2 x 10 x 1 3/4 in.); Gift of Louis C. Tiffany, 1915, Smithsonian Libraries, fN6537. T5A78 1914

0020. Textile, South China Sea, 1972; Jack Lenor Larsen (American, b. 1927); Produced by Jack Lenor Larsen Inc. (New York, New York, USA); Screenprinted with discharge on dyed silk; 187.3 x 100.3 cm (73 3/4 x 39 1/2 in.), repeat: 91.4 cm (36 in.); Gift of Jack Lenor Larsen, 1973-54-1-a; © Cowtan & Tout

0021. Katagami, Water Pattern, Japan, late 19th–early 20th century; Cut mulberry paper treated with persimmon tannin and silk thread; 41.3 x 28 cm (16 1/4 x 11 in.); Gift of Helen Snyder, 1976-103-111

0022. Print, Trial Proof for Printed Textile, ca. 1759–1815; Oberkampf & Cie. Workshop (Jouy-en-Josas, France, 1759–1815); Woodcut on cream laid paper, lined; 35.7 x 31 cm (14 1/16 x 12 3/16 in.), irregular; Museum purchase through gift of Brunschwig & Fils and James Amster and from General Acquisitions Endowment and Friends of Drawings and Prints Funds, 1989-65-13

0023. Scenic, Les Vues d'Italie (Views of Italy), ca. 1830; Dufour et Leroy (Paris, France); Block printed on joined sheets of handmade paper; 2.21 x 14.40 m (7 ft. 3 in. x 47 ft. 3 in.); Museum purchase from Sarah Cooper-Hewitt, Pauline Cooper Noyes, and General Acquisitions Endowment Funds, 2000-29-1-a/mm

0024. Drawing, Villa Albani, Rome, Italy: Design for a Fountain with Pegasus, ca. 1750; Carlo Marchionni (Italian, 1702–86); Pen and brown ink, brush and gray wash, graphite on cream laid paper; 31.9 x 35.1 cm (12 9/16 x 13 13/16 in.); Museum purchase through gift of various donors, 1901-39-2102

0025. Cooper Union; Photo © Smithsonian Institution

0026. Class of Women's Art School, ca. 1900; Photo © Smithsonian Institution

0027. Katagami, Arrow Design Imitating Warp Ikat (Kasuri), Japan, late 19th–early 20th century; Cut mulberry paper treated with persimmon tannin and silk thread; 46.7 x 34 cm (18 3/8 x 13 3/8 in.); Gift of Helen Snyder, 1976-103-289

0028. Purse, USA, early 19th century; Linen canvas embroidered in wool in counted stitches (bargello); 16.2 x 12.7 cm (6 3/8 x 5 in.); Museum purchase from Pauline Riggs Noyes Fund, 1954-160-1

0029. Textile, Manchester, England, for African market, early 20th century; Cotton, wax printed by engraved roller; 243.8 x 62.9 cm (8 ft. x 24 3/4 in.); Gift of Elizabeth Riefstahl, 1953-90-6-a,b

0030. Purse, USA, ca. 1880; Silk embroidered with silk ribbon and wool yarns, cotton lining; 12 x 14 cm (4 3/4 x 5 1/2 in.); Gift of Mrs. William P. Treadwell, 1916-33-178

0031. Sidewall, Japan, 1954; Grasscloth, cotton, paper; 181.5 x 88 cm (71 1/4 x 34 5/8 in.); Gift of S. Stanley Sogg, 1955-88-1

0032. Sidewall, Checks and Balances, 1998; Elizabeth Dow Ltd. (American); Hand-painted paper; 243.8 x 101.6 cm (96 x 40 in.); Gift of Elizabeth Dow Ltd., 1998-66-4; © Elizabeth Dow Ltd.

0033. Sidewall, Edo, 1967; William Justema (American, 1905–87); Made by James D. Gaffney (New York, New York, USA) Screenprinted on paper; 182.5 x 76 cm (71 7/8 x 29 15/16 in.); Gift of William Justema, 1969-70-2

0034. Sidewall, Frames, 2004; Craig Wood (British) and Chris Taylor (British); Made by Graham & Brown Inc. (Blackburn, Lancashire, England); Screenprinted on paper; 10 m x 52 cm (33 ft. x 20 1/2 in.); Gift of Graham & Brown Inc., 2005-31-1; Frames design © Taylor & Wood 2000

0035. Textile, Staccato, 1951; Angelo Testa (American, 1921–84); Manufactured by Angelo Testa and Company (Chicago, Illinois, USA); Screenprinted cotton; 288.9 x 121 cm (113 3/4 x 47 5/8 in.); Museum purchase from Au Panier Fleuri Fund, 2001-1-1

0036. Sample, Matrix, 1973; Jack Lenor Larsen (American, b. 1927); Produced by Jack Lenor Larsen Inc. (New York, New York, USA); Wool doublecloth; 62.9 x 62.2 cm (24 3/4 x 24 1/2 in.), repeat H: 25.4 cm (10 in.); Gift of Jack Lenor Larsen Inc., 1973-67-1; © Cowtan & Tout

0037. Mural miniature, Quadrati, from *Kaleidoscope, Vol. I* sample book, 1971; James Seeman Studios Inc. (Long Island, New York, USA); Screenprinted on vinyl; 63.5 x 43.2 x 2.5 cm (25 x 17 x 1 in.); Gift of Vincent Scalia, 1982-35-3-7

0038. Textile, Landis II, 1973; Richard Landis (American, b. 1931); Produced by Jack Lenor Larsen Inc. (New York, New York, USA); Linen and polyester doublecloth; 284.5 x 128.9 cm (112 x 50 3/4 in.), repeat: 111.1 x 61 cm (43 3/4 x 24 in.); Gift of Jack Lenor Larsen, Inc., 1977-67-6; © Cowtan & Tout

0039. Textile, Suora (Straight), 1980; Markku Piri (Finnish, b. 1955); Manufactured by Marimekko Oy (Helsinki, Finland); Screenprinted cotton; 134 x 138.1 cm (52 3/4 x 54 3/8 in.); Gift of David R. McFadden, 1986-67-3; © Marimekko Oy

0040. Textile, Mexican Plaid, ca. 1938; Dorothy Wright Liebes (American, 1897–1972); Twill-woven wool, cotton, silk, synthetic, and Lurex; 311.2 x 126 cm (10 ft. 2 1/2 in. x 49 5/8 in.); Gift of the Estate of Dorothy (Liebes) Morin, 1972-75-1

0041. Sample book, Paris, France, 1822–30; Jacquemart & Benard (France); Block printed, gilded, and flocked on handmade paper; 49 x 66 x 10.5 cm (19 5/16 x 26 x 4 1/8 in.); Museum purchase from General Acquisitions Endowment and Decorative Arts Association Acquisitions Funds and through gift of Anonymous Donor and Bequest of Mary Hayward Weir, 1986-34-2-1/1364; Photo by Ken Pelka © Smithsonian Institution

0042. The Weighing of the Heart brooch in art form holder, England, ca. 1998; Kevin Coates (British, b. 1950); Gold, faience (ceramic frit amulet fragment, Egyptian, probably 7th–5th century BC), turquoise, carnelian, ebony, silver (brooch); mixed media on slate, joined and painted wood, Plexiglass (holder); 38.4 x 31.1 x 6.5 cm (15 1/8 x 12 1/4 x 2 9/16 in.); Gift of Linda Lichtenberg Kaplan, 2011-15-1,2-a,b; © Courtesy of the Artist and Mobilia Gallery

0043. Hand-woven sample, USA, 1948; Anni Albers (American, b. Germany, 1899–1994); Woven cotton, jute, and Lurex; 18.4 x 23.5 cm (7 1/4 x 9 1/4 in.); Gift of Anni Albers, 1948-93-1; © Josef and Anni Albers Foundation

0044. Textile, New York, New York, USA, 1930–31; Donald Deskey (American, 1894–1989); Screenprinted linen; 236.9 x 124.5 cm (93 1/4 x 49 in.), repeat: 60 x 30.5 cm (23 5/8 x 12 in.); Museum purchase through bequest of Ida C. McNeil in memory of Lincoln C. McNeil and Catherine McNeil, 1989-86-1

0045. Sample, Bedspread for Harvard Graduate Center double bedroom, 1949; Anni Albers (American, b. Germany, 1899–1994); Plain-woven cotton and linen; 44.1 x 33.7 cm (17 3/8 x 13 1/4 in.); Gift of Anni Albers, 1953-208-4; © Josef and Anni Albers Foundation

0046. Darning sampler, Germany, 1841; S. Hille, student of C. Keiber; Cotton embroidered in silk and wool in running (pattern darning) stitches and cross-stitches; 33 x 40 cm (13 x 15 3/4 in.); Bequest of Gertrude M. Oppenheimer, 1981-28-322

0047. Sewing sampler, Germany, late 19th century; Sewn and embroidered cotton, wool, silk, and linen; 26.7 x 50.8 cm (10 1/2 x 20 in.); Bequest of Gertrude M. Oppenheimer, 1981-28-315

0048. Darning sampler, Netherlands, 1711; Linen embroidered in silk in running (pattern darning) stitches and cross-stitches; 80 x 64.1 cm (31 1/2 x 25 1/4 in.); Gift of Mrs. Montgomery Hare, 1937-75-1

0049. Darning sampler, Netherlands or Denmark, early 19th century; Linen embroidered in silk in running, satin, buttonhole, and eyelet stitches with overcasting and withdrawn element work; 30.5 x 31.1 cm (12 x 12 1/4 in.); Bequest of Gertrude M. Oppenheimer, 1981-28-207

0050. Darning sampler, England, 1800; Hannah Walne (British); Linen embroidered in silk in counted running (pattern darning) stitches, paper backing; 36.2 x 36.2 cm (14 1/4 x 14 1/4 in.); Gift of Harvey Smith, 1968-50-3

0051. Darning sampler, Netherlands, 1767; Linen embroidered in silk in running (pattern darning) and eyelet stitches; 47.6 x 41 cm (18 3/4 x 16 1/8 in.); Bequest of Gertrude M. Oppenheimer, 1981-28-249

0052. Darning sampler, Netherlands, 1735; Linen embroidered with silk in running (pattern darning) and eyelet stitches; 43.8 x 41.3 cm (17 1/4 x 16 1/4 in.); Bequest of Gertrude M. Oppenheimer, 1981-28-234; Photo © Smithsonian Institution

0053. Fragment of a garment, Iran or Iraq, 10–11th century; Plain-weave cotton with printed and gilded inscription; 19.1 x 29.8 cm (7 1/2 x 11 3/4 in.); Museum purchase from Au Panier Fleuri Fund, 1959-105-9

0054. Mending sampler, Germany, 1869; Silk embroidery and stitching in a variety of patching and mending techniques on plain-weave linen foundation; 43.2 x 43.2 cm (17 x 17 in.); Bequest of Gertrude M. Oppenheimer, 1981-28-311

0055. Darning sampler, Netherlands, 1814; Silk pattern darning, cross-stitch, and withdrawn element work on plain-weave cotton foundation; 41.9 x 41.3 cm (16 ½ x 16 1/4 in.); Bequest of Gertrude M. Oppenheimer, 1981-28-253

0056. Sampler, Spain, 1753; Marie Claerejo; Linen embroidered in silk cross-stitch; 50.5 x 31.1 cm (19 7/8 x 12 1/4 in.); Bequest of Marian Hague, 1971-50-169

0057. Tea towels, Index Collection, 2012; Raw Color (Amsterdam, Netherlands, 2008); Woven by TextielMuseum (Tilburg, Netherlands); Damask woven organic cotton; 67.3 x 55.9 cm (26 1/2 x 22 in.); Gift of Raw Color, 2013-22-2-1/3; © Raw Color

0058. Drawing, Design for a Jacquard Woven Textile, ca. 1927; Adelgunde (Gunta) Stölzl (German, 1897–1983); Brush and watercolor, white gouache, pen and black ink on off-white wove paper; 38.9 x 23.4 cm (15 5/16 x 9 3/16 in.); Museum purchase from General Acquisitions Endowment Fund, 2011-4-1

0059. Sidewall, Pindespil, 1970; Screenprinted on Mylar; 74 x 73.5 cm (29 1/8 x 28 15/16 in.); Gift of Various Donors, 1980-78-13-b

0060. Sampler, Germany or Denmark, 1739; Cotton embroidered in silk in satin, chain, cross-, stem, and buttonhole stitches with deflected element work; 29.2 x 25.4 cm (11 1/2 x 10 in.); Bequest of Gertrude M. Oppenheimer, 1981-28-266

0061. Sampler, Mexico, 19th century; Linen embroidered in silk in withdrawn element work with satin and overcasting stitches; 36.2 x 51.8 cm (14 1/4 x 20 3/8 in.); Bequest of Gertrude M. Oppenheimer, 1981-28-365

0062. Sampler, probably Mexico, 20th century; Silk gauze embroidered in silk and mercerized cotton in running, satin, and couching stitches; 54.6 x 44.5 cm (21 1/2 x 17 1/2 in.); Bequest of Gertrude M. Oppenheimer, 1981-28-344

0063. Huipil (uncut), Cobán, Alta Verapaz, Guatemala, early 20th century; Plain-woven cotton with supplementary weft patterning; 96.5 x 95.9 cm (38 x 37 3/4 in.); Gift of Alan L. Wolfe, 1962-233-26

0064. Coif, England, late 16th–early 17th century; Linen embroidered with silk and metallic yarns in stem, coral, leaf, chain, and detached looping stitches; 22.2 x 21 cm (8 3/4 x 8 1/4 in.); Bequest of Richard Cranch Greenleaf in memory of his mother, Adeline Emma Greenleaf, 1962-53-4

0065. Purse, Germany, 1815–40; Knitted silk with glass beads, metal bar, and chain closure; 9 x 7 cm (3 5/8 x 2 3/4 in.); Gift of Mrs. Albert Blum, 1953-106-15

0066. Sampler, Italy, 19th century; Linen, embroidered in wool in herringbone, cross-, cross-variation, long-armed cross-, and satin stitches; 39.4 x 62.9 cm (15 1/2 x 24 3/4 in.); Bequest of Gertrude M. Oppenheimer, 1981-28-32

0067. Sampler, Mexico, 19th century; Linen embroidered in silk and linen in deflected and withdrawn element work and needle lace stitches; 74 x 99 cm (29 1/8 x 39 in.); Bequest of Marian Hague, 1971-50-160

0068. Sampler, Austria or Germany, 19th century; Cotton embroidered in silk in cross-, back-, straight, running, scotch, and tent stitches; 38.1 x 40 cm (15 x 15 3/4 in.); Bequest of Marian Hague, 1971-50-156

0069. Poster, Zürcher Theater Spektakel (Zurich Theater Spectacle), 1996; Benker & Steiner Werbeagentur AG (Switzerland, 1996–2000); Offset lithograph on wove paper; 128 x 90.5 cm (50 3/8 x 35 5/8 in.); Gift of Sara and Marc Benda, 2010-21-91

0070. Sidewall, Star Dots, 1969–70; Barbara White (American); Hand-folded and dyed Japanese paper; 46 x 65.6 cm (18 1/8 x 25 13/16 in.); Gift of Barbara White, 2000-64-29; © Barbara White

0071. Textile, Discus, ca. 1955; Arundell Clarke Ltd. (New York, New York, USA); Screenprinted cotton; 4.62 m x 121.9 cm (15 ft. 2 in. x 48 in.); Gift of Arundell Clarke, 1956-150-12

0072. Purkersdorf Sanatorium side chair, Austria, 1904–06; Josef Hoffmann (Czech, 1870–1956, active Germany and Austria, 1891–1955); Manufactured by J & J Kohn, for Purkersdorf Sanatorium (Vienna, Austria); Beechwood, leather, metal; 98.8 x 44.2 x 47.3 cm (38 7/8 x 17 3/8 x 18 5/8 in.); Museum purchase from Combined Funds and through gift of Crane and Co., 1968-6-1; Photo by Dave King © Smithsonian Institution

0073. Textile, Golf Magic, ca. 1953; Brian Connelly (American, 1926–62); Produced by Associated American Artists (New York, New York, USA); Screenprinted cotton; 182.9 x 89.5 cm (72 x 35 1/4 in.); Museum purchase through gift of Mrs. William Goulding, 2002-23-1

0074. Textile, Kivet, 1956; Maija Isola (Finnish, 1927–2001); Manufactured by Marimekko Oy (Helsinki, Finland); Screenprinted cotton; 351.2 x 135 cm (11 ft. 6 1/4 in. x 53 1/8 in.), repeat: 64 cm (25 3/16 in.); Gift of Marimekko, Inc., 1979-89-3; © Marimekko Oy

0075. Border, France, 1800–20; Block printed on handmade paper; 93 x 57.5 cm (36 5/8 x 22 5/8 in.); Gift of Josephine Howell, 1972-42-168-a

0076. Foldout, Color chart, 1839; Michel Eugène Chevreul (French, 1786–1889), engraved by H. Legrand; From Michel Eugène Chevreul, *De la loi du contraste simultané des couleurs* (*The Principles of Harmony and Contrast of Colors*), (Paris: Pitois-Levrault), plates 6, 7, 8; Hand-colored engraving on paper; 27 x 71.5 cm (10 1/2 x 28 in.); Purchase, Cooper Union Museum, 1960, Smithsonian Libraries, ND1488.C52 1839

0077. Textile, Repeat Dot Print, 2002; Hella Jongerius (Dutch, b. 1963); Produced by Maharam (New York, New York, USA); Jacquard-woven and screenprinted cotton, rayon, and polyester; 445.1 x 144.1 cm (175 1/4 x 56 3/4 in.); Gift of Maharam, 2003-13-1; © Maharam

0078. Sidewall, 1950; Manufactured by J. Line & Sons (England); Machine-printed; 37 x 57 cm (14 9/16 x 22 7/16 in.); Gift of Donald D. MacMillan, 1950-78-1

0079. Hanging, Rush Hour 2/Shangahi, 2012; Grethe Sørensen (Danish, b. 1947); Woven by TextielMuseum (Tilburg, Netherlands); Jacquard-woven cotton; 162 x 283.2 cm (63 3/4 x 9 ft. 3 1/2 in.); Museum purchase through gift of Wolf-Gordon and Maleyne M. Syracuse and Michael Trenner in memory of Richard M. Syracuse and from General Acquisitions Endowment Fund, 2014-15-1

0080. Stencil, Katagami, Pine Needle Clusters, Japan, 1877–83; Cut mulberry paper treated with persimmon tannin and silk thread; 44.2 x 30 cm (17 3/8 x 11 13/16 in.); Gift of Helen Snyder, 1976-103-56

0081. Tile, 1877–83; Manufactured by J. & J. G. Low Art Tile Works (Chelsea, Massachusetts, USA); Molded glazed earthenware; 11 x 11 x 1.8 cm (4 5/16 x 4 5/16 x 11/16 in.); Gift of Mrs. Florence Barnes, 1981-56-42; Photo by Ellen McDermott © Smithsonian Institution

0082. Sidewall, Dandelion, 1952–53; Denst and Soderlund (American); Screenprinted; 100.5 x 55 cm (39 9/16 x 21 5/8 in.); Gift of The Wallpaper Magazine, 1953-198-1

0083. Panel, Study for Ford Foundation wall panels, 1967; Sheila Hicks (American, b. 1934), architect: Warren Platner (American, 1919–2006); Linen embroidered in linen; 72 x 72 cm (28 3/8 x 28 3/8 in.); Gift of Sheila Hicks, 1969-25-1; © Sheila Hicks

0084. Sidewall, Pause, 2004; 2x4 (founded 1994); Manufactured by KnollTextiles (New York, New York, USA); Screenprinted on vinyl; 2.99 m x 137.2 cm (9 ft. 9 1/2 in. x 54 in.); Gift of KnollTextiles, 2006-25-1

0085. Drawing, Textile Design: Abstract Snow Flake, 1950–70; Tommi Parzinger (American, b. Germany, 1903–81); Brush and gouache, graphite on cream paper; 53 x 45.3 cm (20 7/8 x 17 13/16 in.); Gift of Donald Cameron, 1998-19-144

0086. Textile, Abacus, 1946; Paul Rand (American, 1914–96) for L. Anton Maix, Inc. (New York, New York, USA); Screenprinted linen; 290.8 x 130.2 cm (114 1/2 x 51 1/4 in.), repeat: 102.9 cm (40 1/2 in.); Museum purchase through gift of Mrs. William Goulding, 2003-7-1

0087. Textile, Armour, ca. 1955; Joseph Provato (American); Manufactured by Creative Looms Inc. (New York, New York, USA); Screenprinted linen; 118.7 x 65.4 cm (46 3/4 x 25 3/4 in.); Gift of Joseph Provato, 1957-171-2

0088. Sidewall, Paris, France, ca. 1872; Block printed on embossed paper; 146 x 50.5 cm (57 1/2 x 19 7/8 in.); Gift of Edith and Maude Wetmore, 1939-45-6-a

0089. Frieze, USA, 1905–20; Machine printed on machine-made paper; 92 x 49.5 cm (36 1/4 x 19 1/2 in.); Gift of Victorian Collectibles, 1979-91-447

0090. Frieze, 1905–20; Carey Bros. Wall Paper Manufacturing Co. (Philadelphia, Pennsylvania, USA); Machine printed on paper; 91.5 x 49.5 cm (36 x 19 1/2 in.); Gift of Victorian Collectibles, 1979-91-437

0091. Sidewall, Efeu/Ivy, 2006; Thomas Demand (German, b. 1964); Made by Anstey (Loughborough, England); Machine printed on paper; 10 m x 52 cm (32 ft. 9 11/16 in. x 20 1/2 in.); Museum purchase from General Acquisitions Endowment Fund, 2007-19-1

0092. Sidewall, sample, USA, 1906–08; Machine printed on paper; 69 x 49 cm (27 3/16 x 19 5/16 in.); Gift of Dorwin L. Starr, 1985-19-78

0093. Sidewall, France, 1850–60; Desfossé et Karth; Block printed on continuous paper; 60.5 x 46.5 cm (23 13/16 x 18 5/16 in.); Gift of Harvey Smith, 1968-111-87

0094. Sidewall, possibly England, 1770–80; Block printed on handmade paper; 152 x 50.5 cm (59 13/16 x 19 7/8 in.); Gift of Mrs. Luke Vincent Lockwood, 1935-6-1

0095. Sidewall, Fernery, 1967–69; Woodson Wallpapers, Inc. (New York, New York, USA); Screenprinted on paper; 140.5 x 76 cm (55 5/16 x 29 15/16 in.); Gift of Woodson Wallpapers, Inc., 1969-54-11

0096. Sidewall and frieze, USA, 1905–15; M. H. Birge & Sons Co. (Buffalo, New York, USA); Machine printed on paper; 97 x 56 cm (38 3/16 x 22 1/16 in.); Gift of Philadelphia Museum of Art, 1971-58-8-a,b

0097. Dish, 1749–60; Longton Hall (near Newcastle-under-Lyme, Staffordshire, England); Glazed porcelain; 4.1 x 19.8 cm diam. (1 5/8 x 7 13/16 in.); Gift of Wendy Vanderbilt Lehman, 1992-5-3; Photo by Ellen McDermott © Smithsonian Institution

0098. Border, Germany, 1905–15; Embossed and die-cut paper, airbrushed; 46 x 36.5 cm (18 1/8 x 14 3/8 in.); Gift of Mary P. Race, 1979-45-3

0099. Border, Germany, 1905–15; Embossed and die-cut paper, airbrushed; 45 x 37 cm (17 11/16 x 14 9/16 in.); Gift of Mary Race, 1979-45-10

0100. Textile, Austria or Germany, early 20th century; Jacquard-woven silk; 55.9 x 51.4 cm (22 x 20 1/4 in.); Museum purchase through General Acquisitions Endowment Fund, 1985-52-4

0101. Sidewall, Rixheim, Alsace, France, 1830–31; Zuber & Cie; Block printed on polished ground; 60.5 x 48.5 cm (23 13/16 x 19 1/8 in.); Gift of Harvey Smith, 1968-111-14

0102. Sidewall, England, 1765; Block printed on handmade paper; 260.5 x 66.5 cm (102 9/16 x 26 3/16 in.); Museum purchase from Friends of the Museum Fund, 1952-52-11

0103. Sidewall, England, ca. 1848; A. W. N. Pugin (British, 1812–52); Made by William Woolams and Co.; Block printed on paper; 57.5 x 57 cm (22 5/8 x 22 7/16 in.); Gift of Cole and Son, Ltd., 1953-134-2

0104. Border, France, 1840–45; Block printed on paper; 157 x 51 cm (61 13/16 x 20 1/16 in.); Museum purchase from Friends of the Museum Fund, 1952-52-17

0105. Sidewall, Leafstalk, 1967–69; Woodson Wallpapers, Inc. (New York, New York, USA); Screenprinted on paper; 147 x 76 cm (57 7/8 x 29 15/16 in.); Gift of Woodson Wallpapers, Inc., 1969-54-10

0106. Textile, Vågorna, 1949; Stig Lindberg (Swedish, 1916–82); Manufactured by NK Textilkammare (Stockholm, Sweden); Screenprinted linen; 364.5 x 135.6 cm (11 ft. 11 1/2 in. x 53 3/8 in.), repeat: 57.2 cm (22 1/2 in.); Gift of Anonymous Donor, a-t-837

0107. Textile, Fibra, 1953; Eszter Haraszty (American, b. Hungary, 1920–94); Produced by KnollTextiles (New York, New York, USA), printed by Printex (USA); Screenprinted linen; 416.6 x 129.5 cm (13 ft. 8 in. x 51 in.); Gift of Larry Weinberg, 2011-20-1; © Knoll, Inc.

0108. Sidewall, Overlay, 1953; Gene McDonald (New York, New York, USA); Screenprinted on paper; 89 x 76 cm (35 1/16 x 29 15/16 in.); Gift of The Wallpaper Magazine, 1953-198-2

0109. Textile, Bloomfield Hills, Michigan, USA, ca. 1950; Marianne Strengell (Finnish, active USA, 1909–98); Hand-printed at Cranbrook Academy of Art; Screenprinted cotton; 302.3 x 137.2 cm (119 x 54 in.); Gift of Marianne Strengell, 1984-111-75

0110. Textile, Filc, 1942; Angelo Testa (American, 1921–84); Produced by KnollTextiles (New York, New York, USA); Screenprinted cotton; 79.4 x 62.9 cm (31 1/4 x 24 3/4 in.); Gift of Mae Lamar Festa, 1991-157-8; Photo by Andrew Garn © Smithsonian Institution

0111. Sidewall, 1080 Cadires, 2010; Javier Mariscal (Spanish, b. 1950); Made by Tres Tintas Barcelona (Barcelona, Spain); Machine printed on paper; 10 m x 53 cm (32 ft. 9 11/16 in. x 20 7/8 in.); Gift of Tres Tintas Barcelona, 2010-29-1; © Tres Tintas Barcelona

0112. Sidewall, Sound Waves, 1948; Multiplex Display Fixture Co.; Screenprinted on paper; 83 x 76 cm (32 11/16 x 29 15/16 in.); Gift of Edward F. McGuiness, 1949-25-1

0113. Drawing, Textile Design: The Dance, 1950s; Angelo Testa (American, 1921–84); Pen and black ink on paper; 34 x 42.2 cm (13 3/8 x 16 5/8 in.); Museum purchase through gift of Eleanor and Sarah Hewitt, 2001-9-1

0114. Sample, Lines, 1952; Alexander Hayden Girard (American, 1907–93); Produced by Herman Miller Fabrics (Zeeland, Michigan, USA); Screenprinted linen, 61 x 60 cm (24 x 23 5/8 in.); Gift of Alexander H. Girard, 1969-165-155; © 1952 Girard Studios, LLC, all rights reserved

0115. Sample, Pepitas, 1952; Alexander Hayden Girard (American, 1907–93); Produced by Herman Miller Fabrics (Zeeland, Michigan, USA); Screenprinted linen and cotton; 29.2 x 29.8 cm (11 1/2 x 11 3/4 in.); Gift of Alexander H. Girard, 1969-165-137; © 1952 Girard Studios, LLC, all rights reserved

0116. Sidewall, *The Architect's Book of One Hundred Wallpapers*, 1954–55; Designed by Lucienne Day (British, 1917–2010); Made by The Wall Paper Manufacturers Limited (London, England); Machine printed on paper; 25.5 x 40.5 cm (10 1/16 x 15 15/16 in.); Gift of Eric A. Entwisle, 1954-63-1-51; Photo © Smithsonian Institution; © Robin and Lucienne Day Foundation

0117. Sidewall, London, 1953–54; Arthur Sanderson & Sons, Ltd.; Machine printed on paper; 54 x 55.5 cm (21 1/4 x 21 7/8 in.); Gift of W. H. S. Lloyd and Co., Inc., 1954-49-4-d

0118. Textile, Incantation, 1947; Alvin Lustig (American, 1915–55); Produced by Laverne International, Ltd. (New York, New York, USA); Screenprinted cotton, 236.2 x 381 cm (7 ft. 9 in. x 12 ft. 6 in.); Gift of Max Finkelstein, 1973-9-1; © Elaine Lustig Cohen

0119. Sidewall, Listen and Record, 2009; Ilias Fotopoulos (Australian, b. 1966); Screenprinted and flocked on paper; 10 m x 71.2 cm (32 ft. 10 in. x 28 1/16 in.); Gift of Ilias Fotopoulos, 2010-27-1; © Ilias Fotopoulos

0120. Textile, Stilts, 1951; Angelo Testa (American, 1921–84); Manufactured ed by Angelo Testa and Company (Chicago, Illinois, USA); Screenprinted cotton; 285.4 x 124.5 cm (112 3/8 x 49 in.); Museum purchase from Au Panier Fleuri Fund, 2001-1-2

0121. Textile, Eclat, 1975; Anni Albers (American, b. Germany, 1899–1994); Produced by Knoll International (New York, New York, USA); Screenprinted cotton; 411.5 x 135.9 cm (13 ft. 6 in. x 53 1/2 in.); repeat: 43.8 x 44.5 cm (17 1/4 x 17 1/2 in.); Museum purchase through gift of the Josef and Anni Albers Foundation and from General Acquisitions Endowment Fund, 2011-41-1; © Josef and Anni Albers Foundation

0122. Screenprint, PO I, 1973; Anni Albers (American, b. Germany, 1899–1994); Screenprint and photo offset on Arches paper; 73 x 56 cm (28 3/4 x 22 in.); Josef and Anni Albers Foundation, Bethany, Connecticut; JAAF: 1994.11.33; © 2007 The Josef and Anni Albers Foundation / Artists Rights Society (ARS), New York

0123. Drawing from a Notebook, ca. 1970; Anni Albers (American, b. Germany, 1899–1994); Pencil on paper; 25.4 x 19.69 cm (10 x 7 3/4 in.); Josef and Anni Albers Foundation, Bethany, Connecticut; JAAF: 1994.10.117; © 2007 Josef and Anni Albers Foundation / Artists Rights Society (ARS), New York

0124. Sample, Celtic Fret, 1969; Ted Hallman (American, b. 1933) and Larsen Design Studio (New York, New York, USA); Produced by Jack Lenor Larsen, Inc. (New York, New York, USA); Twill-woven wool, 62.9 x 62.9 cm (24 3/4 x 24 3/4 in.), repeat: 30.5 cm (12 in.); Gift of Jack Lenor Larsen, Inc., 1973-67-4; © Cowtan & Tout

0125. Sidewall, Japan, 1935–39; Grasscloth; 46.5 x 43 cm (18 5/16 x 16 15/16 in.); Gift of William R. Osmun, 1954-150-1

0126. Poster, HorseProjectSpace Presents: Ritual Tendencies, 2007; Michiel Schuurman (Dutch, b. 1974); Offset lithograph on white wove paper; 117.8 x 73 cm (46 3/8 x 28 3/4 in.); Gift of Michiel Schuurman, 2008-22-3; © Michiel Schuurman

0127. Textile, Unikko, 1965; Maija Isola (Finnish, 1927–2001); Manufactured by Marimekko Oy (Helsinki, Finland); Screenprinted cotton; 302.3 x 137.2 cm (119 x 54 in.); Gift of Marimekko, Inc., 1979-89-7; © Marimekko Oy

0128. Sidewall, Poppies, ca. 1968; Ben Morris; Made by Hubbell Pierce Wallpapers (New York, New York, USA); Screenprinted on paper; 120 x 76.5 cm (47 1/4 x 30 1/8 in.); Gift of Philip Graf, 1969-53-7

0129. Sidewall, Muguet, 1967–69; Woodson Wallpapers, Inc. (New York, New York, USA); Screenprinted on paper; 138.5 x 76.5 cm (54 1/2 x 30 1/8 in.); Gift of Woodson Wallpapers, Inc., 1969-54-5

0130. Sidewall, Pasture Flowers, 1960–66; Phoebe Hyde (1917–67); Made by Louis W. Bowen, Inc. (New York, New York, USA); Screenprinted on paper; 75 x 66 cm (29 1/2 x 26 in.); Gift of Mrs. Kolbert Leonard, 1967-80-2-a/g

0131. Sidewall, Ramona, 1965–68; Don Elmer; Made by Piazza Prints, Inc. (New York, New York, USA); Screenprinted on vinyl; 99 x 75.5 cm (39 x 29 3/4 in.); Gift of Piazza Prints, Inc., 1969-56-2; © F. Schumacher & Co., all rights reserved

0132. Textile, Collage, 1967; Wolf Bauer (German, 1938–90); Produced by Knoll International (New York, New York, USA); Printed by Pausa AG (Mössingen, Germany); Screenprinted cotton velveteen; 254 x 124.5 cm (100 x 49 in.); Museum purchase through gift of Knoll, Inc. and Laurence N. Strenger, 2011-6-1; © Knoll, Inc.

0133. Sidewall, Orleans, ca. 1968; Eaglesham Accessories; Screenprinted; 134.5 x 76 cm (52 15/16 x 29 15/16 in.); Gift of Philip Graf, 1969-53-6

0134. Sidewall, Poppies, 1912; Paul Poiret (French, 1879–1944); Made by Paul Dumas (Paris, France); Machine printed on machine-made paper; 83 x 75 cm (32 11/16 x 29 1/2 in.); Gift of Cincinnati Art Museum, 1990-129-24

0135. Sidewall, France, ca. 1920; René Crevel (French, 1900–35); Made by C. H. H. Geffroy for Nancy McClelland, Inc.; Block printed on paper; 71 x 51 cm (27 15/16 x 20 1/16 in.); Gift of Nancy McClelland, 1945-3-4

0136. Textile, Punchinello, 1960; Contessa Friedlinde di Colbertaldo Dinzl (Austrian, active Italy); Manufactured by Edinburgh Weavers (Carlisle, England); Screenprinted cotton; 101.6 x 119.1 cm (40 x 46 7/8 in.); Gift of Mr. Eddie Squires, 1993-70-1-a

0137. Drawing, Textile Design: Butterfly Motif, France, 19th century; Brush and gouache, graphite on cream paper; 42.8 x 39.9 cm (16 7/8 x 15 11/16 in.); Gift of Harvey Smith, 1968-107-25

0138. Sampler, Mexico, early 19th century; Cotton embroidered with silk in cross-, stem, satin, long-armed cross-, threaded running, Roumanian, fern, and buttonhole stitches; 38.6 x 36.5 cm (15 3/16 x 14 3/8 in.); Bequest of Gertrude M. Oppenheimer, 1981-28-341

0139. Wrapping cloth (bojaggi), Korea, ca. 1900; Pieced and sewn silk; 85.1 x 101.6 cm (33 1/2 x 40 in.); Museum purchase from Roy and Niuta Titus Foundation Fund, 1994-22-2

0140. Textile, Bows, ca. 1960; Josef Frank (Austrian, active Sweden, 1885–1967); Screenprinted linen and cotton; 294.6 x 130.2 cm (116 x 51 1/4 in.); Museum purchase from General Acquisitions Endowment Fund, 2011-41-2; © Backhausen

0141. Sample, Rain, 1954; Alexander Hayden Girard (American, 1907–93); Screenprinted linen; 60 x 60 cm (23 5/8 x 23 5/8 in.); Gift of Alexander H. Girard, 1969-165-75

0142. Textile, Pythagoras, 1953; Sven Markelius (Swedish, 1889–1972); Manufactured by KnollTextiles (New York, New York, USA); Printed by Ljungbergs Textiltryck AB (Floda, Sweden); Screenprinted on 60% linen, 40% cotton; 459.7 x 130.2 cm (181 x 51 1/4 in.); Gift of Knoll Associates, Inc., 1956-123-1

0143. Book illustration, Fabric design, ca. 1929; Sonia Delaunay (French, 1885–1979); From *Tapis et tissus* (*Carpets and Fabrics*), *L'art international d'aujourd'hui* no. 15. (Paris: Editions d'Art Charles Moreau), plate 13; Pochoir on paper; 34 x 25 cm (13 1/2 x 9 7/8 in.); Cooper Union Museum Library 1950, Smithsonian Libraries, qNK28849.D34 1929

0144. Textile, Pythagoras, 1953; Sven Markelius (Swedish, 1889–1972); Produced by KnollTextiles (New York, New York, USA); Screenprinted cotton; 280 x 126 cm (9 ft. 2 1/4 in. x 49 5/8 in.), repeat: 144.1 cm (56 3/4 in.); Gift of August Boj, 1982-54-1; © Knoll, Inc.

0145. Drawing, Textile Design: Alternating Triangular Forms, 1930–31; Donald Deskey (American, 1894–1989); Brush and white and blue gouache on gray illustration board; 50.6 x 38.3 cm (19 15/16 x 15 1/16 in); Gift of Donald Deskey, 1975-11-28

0146. Book illustration, Geometric designs, 1930; Édouard Benedictus (French, 1879–1930); From Édouard Benedictus, *Relais: quinze planches donnant quarante-deux motifs décoratifs* (*Relay: Fifteen Plates Giving Forty-Two Decorative Motifs*), (Paris: Éditions Vincent, Freal et Cie), plate 13; Pochoir print on paper; 47.5 x 38 cm (18 5/8 x 15 in.); Smithsonian Libraries, fNK1535.B46R16

0147. Sidewall, Brighton, 1960–70; Joe Martin; Screenprinted on vinyl; 81 x 75 cm (31 7/8 x 29 1/2 in.); Gift of John Bulica Nicholson, 2001-3-4; Reproduced with permission © John Bulica Nicholson

0148. Textile, Zebra, 1971; Sven Fristedt (Swedish, b. 1940); Manufactured by Borås Wäfveri AB (Gothenburg, Sweden); Screenprinted cotton, 125.7 x 144.8 cm (49 1/2 x 57 in.), repeat: 87.6 cm (34 1/2 in.); Gift of Boras Wafveri Aktiebolag, 1974-51-3; © Brand New Homes TXT AB

0149. Textile, Enku, 1965; Hans Krondahl (Swedish, b. 1929); Printed by Ljungbergs Textiltryck AB (Floda, Sweden); Screenprinted cotton velveteen; 383.2 x 133 cm (150 7/8 x 52 3/8 in.); Gift of Hans Krondahl, 1997-116-1

0150. Purse, USA, 18th century; Hemp canvas embroidered in wool in counted stitches (flame stitch), wool binding, silk lining; 13.5 x 20 cm (5 3/8 x 7 7/8 in.); Gift of Marian Hague, 1954-100-1

0151. Drawing, Textile Design: Colorways for Montezuma, designed 1910–12; Josef Hoffmann (Czech, 1870–1956, active Germany and Austria, 1891–1955) for Wiener Werkstätte (Vienna, Austria); Brush and gouache, pen and black ink, graphite on paper; 5.7 x 20.3 cm (2 1/4 x 8 in.); Museum purchase from Smithsonian Collections Acquisition and Decorative Arts Association Acquisition Funds, 1988-62-199/206; Photo © Smithsonian Institution

0152. Panel, USA, 1952; Mariska Karasz (American b. Hungary, 1898–1960); Linen embroidered in wool and cotton in feather stitches; 63.5 x 46 cm (25 x 18 1/8 in.); Gift of Elizabeth Gordon, 1964-35-14; © Mariska Karasz

0153. Sidewall, Sahara, 1928; Edward Bawden (British, 1903–89); Lithograph from linocut on paper; 70.5 x 53.5 cm (27 3/4 x 21 1/16 in.); Museum purchase from Smithsonian Institution Collections Acquisition Program and Pauline C. Noyes Funds, 1996-32-6

0154. Textile, Motus, 1970; Gaetano Pesce (Italian, b. 1939); Manufactured by Expansion; Screenprinted on cotton velveteen; 411.5 x 130.8 cm (162 x 51 1/2 in.); Gift of The Lake St. Louis Historical Society, 2001-30-1

0155. Sample, Ribbons, 1957; Alexander Hayden Girard (American, 1907–93); Produced by Herman Miller Textiles (Zeeland, Michigan, USA); Screenprinted on 66% cotton, 34% linen; 59.1 x 60 cm (23 1/4 x 23 5/8 in.); Gift of Alexander H. Girard, 1969-165-66; © 1957 Girard Studios, LLC, all rights reserved

0156. Sidewall, Crazy Key, 1967; William Justema (American, 1905–87); Screenprinted on paper; 94 x 77 cm (37 x 30 5/16 in.); Gift of William Justema, 1969-70-6

0157. Spun chair, 2010; Thomas Heatherwick (British, b. 1970); Manufactured by Magis S.p.A. (Italy); Produced by Herman Miller Furniture Company (Zeeland, Michigan, USA); Rationally molded polyethylene; 66 x 91.4 cm diam. (26 x 36 in.); Gift of Herman Miller, Inc., 2012-18-1; Photo by Ellen McDermott © Smithsonian Institution

0158. Sidewall, Compendium, 1968; Rosemary Newson (British); Made by The Wall Paper Manufacturers Limited (London, England); Screenprinted on paper; 92 x 50.5 cm (36 1/4 x 19 7/8 in.); Gift of Arthur Sanderson & Sons, Ltd., 1970-1-14

0159. Sidewall, Stitched Vertical, 2008; David Rockwell (American, b. 1956); Made by Maya Romanoff; Hand-stitched and dyed paper; 274.3 x 76.2 cm (9 ft. x 30 in.); Gift of Maya Romanoff, 2008-26-2; © David Rockwell

0160. Sidewall, Citadel, 1959–60; Jack Lenor Larsen (American, b. 1927); Made by Karl Mann Associates (New York, New York, USA); Screenprinted on paper; 183 x 76 cm (72 1/16 x 29 15/16 in.); Gift of Karl Mann Associates, 1960-91-2

0161. Sidewall, Yvonne Coordinate, 1950–56; Elsbeth Kupferoth (German, b. 1920); Made by Marburger Tapetenfabrik (Kirchhain, Germany); Machine printed on paper; 107.5 x 56 cm (42 5/16 x 22 1/16 in.); Gift of Marburger Tapetenfabrik, 1957-116-12; © Marburg

0162. Sidewall, Early Eighties, 1992; Matteo Thun (Italian, b. 1952); Made by Rasch & Company (Bramsche, Germany); Screenprinted on paper-backed vinyl; 1005 x 53.5 cm (395 11/16 x 21 1/16 in.); Gift of Gebr. Rasch GmbH & Co., 1995-163-26; © Rasch

0163. Sample book, Bauhaus, 1929–30; Rasch & Company (Bramsche, Germany); Machine printed on paper; 16 x 23.7 x 3.3 cm (6 5/16 x 9 5/16 x 1 5/16 in.); Gift of Jacqueline Fowler, 1992-2-1, © Rasch

0164. Sample book, Bauhaus, 1929–30; Rasch & Company (Bramsche, Germany); Machine printed on paper; 16 x 23.7 x 3.3 cm (6 5/16 x 9 5/16 x 1 5/16 in.); Gift of Jacqueline Fowler, 1992-2-1, © Rasch

0165. Installation, Dutch Clouds, 2011; Karel Martens (Dutch, b. 1939); Made by Maharam (New York, New York, USA); Digital print on cellulose/latex/nylon substrate; 243.8 x 406.4 cm (8 ft. x 13 ft. 4 in.); Gift of Maharam, 2012-11-2-1/5; © 2009 Karel Martens, Maharam under license

0166. Poster, Specimen, 2008; Fanette Mellier (French, b. 1977); Offset lithograph on paper; 175 x 118.6 cm (5 ft. 8 7/8 in. x 46 11/16 in.); Gift of Fanette Mellier, 2013-18-1; © Fanette Mellier

0167. Blanket, Index Collection, 2012; Raw Color (Amsterdam, Netherlands); Woven by TextielMuseum (Tilburg, Netherlands); Woven organic cotton and merino wool; 170.2 x 200 cm (5 ft. 7 in. x 6 ft. 6 3/4 in.); Gift of Raw Color, 2013-22-1; © Sheila Hicks

0168. Hand-woven sample, USA, before 1953; Anni Albers (American, b. Germany, 1899–1994); Plain-woven silk and cotton; 17.5 x 27 cm (6 7/8 x 10 5/8 in.); Gift of Anni Albers, 1953-180-4; © Josef and Anni Albers Foundation

0169. Textile, Squares, 1950–55; Arundell Clarke Ltd. (New York, New York, USA); Screenprinted on plain-woven spun silk; 344.2 x 116.8 cm (135 1/2 x 46 in.); Gift of Arundell Clarke, 1956-150-7

0170. Textile, Tiiliskivi, 1952; Armi Ratia (Finnish, 1912–79); Manufactured by Marimekko Oy (Helsinki, Finland); Screenprinted cotton; 311.8 x 137.5 cm (10 ft. 2 3/4 in. x 54 1/8 in.), repeat: 24 cm (9 7/16 in.); Gift of Marimekko, Inc., 1979-89-1; © Marimekko Oy

0171. Textile, Interferens, 2007; Grethe Sørensen (Danish, b. 1947); Produced by Kvadrat (Copenhagen, Denmark); Jacquard-woven wool; 299.7 x 142.2 cm (9 ft. 10 in. x 56 in.); Gift of Kvadrat, 2010-18-2; Photo by Andrew Garn © Smithsonian Institution; © Kvadrat

0172. Textile, Ghana, 20th century; Dyed and stamped cotton (*adinkra*); 179.1 x 109.2 cm (70 1/2 x 43 in.); Bequest of Mary Kirby, 1962-123-1

0173. Textile, Regenbogen (Rainbow), 1919; Dagobert Peche (Austrian, 1887–1923); Produced by Wiener Werkstätte (Vienna, Austria); Dyed by Clavel & Lindenmeyer, Wasservogel (Basel, Switzerland); Block-printed silk; 243.2 x 91.4 cm (95 3/4 x 36 in.); Gift of Frances Cogan, 1988-40-1

0174. Photograph, Wolko Gartenberg apartment: Living room, 1921; MAK – Austrian Museum of Applied Arts / Contemporary Art

0175. Photograph, Wolko Gartenberg apartment: Corner seating in the living room, 1921; MAK – Austrian Museum of Applied Arts / Contemporary Art

0176. Textile, Auden, 2009; Kate Mulleavy (American, b. 1979) and Laura Mulleavy (American, b. 1980), Rodarte (Los Angeles, California, USA); Produced by Knoll Luxe (New York, New York, USA); Digitally printed ramie and polyester; 299.7 x 147.3 cm (118 x 58 in.); Gift of KnollTextiles, 2010-7-2; © Rodarte for Knoll Luxe

0177. Sidewall, t.e.124, 2012; Irma Boom (Dutch, b. 1960); Made by Eijffinger (The Hague, Netherlands); Digital print on non-woven paper; 901.7 x 74.9 cm (29 ft. 7 in. x 29 1/2 in.); Gift of Thomas Eyck, 7632.1.2012

0178. Sample, USA, 1959; Produced by Jack Lenor Larsen Inc. (New York, New York, USA); Plain-woven cotton, leather, and synthetic leather; 47.6 x 113.7 cm (18 3/4 x 44 3/4 in.); Museum purchase from Au Panier Fleuri Fund, 1959-98-4; © Cowtan & Tout

0179. Textile, Sherman, 2013; Irma Boom (Dutch, b. 1960) for KnollTextiles (New York, NY, USA); Plain woven 33% acrylic, 30% cotton, 21% alpaca, 8% nylon; 302.3 x 137.2 cm (9 ft. 11 in. x 54 in.); Gift of Knoll Textiles, 2014-3-1; © Knoll Textiles

0180. Sidewall, 1950–56; Elsbeth Kupferoth (German, b. 1920); Made by Marburger Tapetenfabrik (Kirchhain, Germany); Machine printed on paper; 107 x 56 cm (42 1/8 x 22 1/16 in.); Gift of Marburger Tapetenfabrik, 1957-116-10; © Marburg

0181. Ornament—pilaster, Palm, 1947–51; Denys Fitzpatrick; Made by Katzenbach and Warren, Inc. (New York, New York, USA); Screenprinted on paper; 160 x 76.5 cm (63 x 30 1/8 in.); Gift of Katzenbach & Warren, Inc., 1953-41-1-b; © Katzenbach & Warren

0182. Sidewall, Cord #1, 2003; Petra Blaisse (Dutch, b. London, 1955); Manufactured by Wolf-Gordon Inc. (Long Island City, New York, USA); Rotogravure printed on vinyl; 293.4 x 137.2 cm (9 ft. 7 1/2 in. x 54 in.); Gift of Wolf-Gordon Inc., 2004-26-1; © Petra Blaisse 2003 for Wolf-Gordon Inc.

0183. Sidewall, Thorny Stripe, 1993; Christine Tarkowski (American, b. 1968); Screenprinted on paper; 309.9 x 66 cm (10 ft. 2 in. x 26 in.); Museum purchase from Sarah Cooper-Hewitt and Friends of Wallcoverings Funds, 1996-104-1; © Christine Tarkowski

0184. Egyptian Story bangle bracelet, 2012; Stefan Hemmerle (German, b. 1946); Made by Gebrüder Hemmerle (Munich, Germany); Carved pockwood, cut and polished turquoises and tsavorites, oxidized silver, white gold; 7 x 8 x 2.5 cm (2 3/4. x 3 1/8 in. x 1 in.); Gift of Fiona Druckenmiller, 2013-27-1; Photo by Ellen McDermott © Smithsonian Institution; © Hemmerle

0185. Sidewall, Folded Stripe, 1965–69; Barbara White (American); Hand-folded and dyed Japanese paper; 66.0 x 94.0 cm (26 x 37 in.); Gift of Barbara White, 2000-64-21; © Barbara White

0186. Book cover, *The Hero with a Thousand Faces* by Joseph Campbell, 1955; Alvin Lustig (American, 1915–55) for Meridian Books (New York, New York, USA); Lithograph on white shiny wove paper; 22 x 29.1 cm (8 11/16 x 11 7/16 in.); Gift of Tamar Cohen and Dave Slatoff, 1993-31-186; © Elaine Lustig Cohen

0187. Sidewall, Baroque Stripe, 1959–60; Jack Lenor Larsen (American, b. 1927); Made by Karl Mann Associates (New York, New York, USA); Screenprinted on paper; 175.5 x 76.5 cm (69 1/8 x 30 1/8 in.); Gift of Karl Mann Associates, 1960-91-1

0188. Sidewall, der Spitz (Lace), 1921–22; Dagobert Peche (Austrian, 1887–1923); Made by Flammersheim & Steinmann (Germany); Machine printed on machine-made paper; 109 x 54.5 cm (43 x 21 7/16 in.); Gift of Cincinnati Art Museum, 1990-129-7

0189. Textile, Manchester, England, ca. 1795; Cotton printed by engraved plate; 208 x 71.1 cm (6 ft. 9 7/8 in. x 28 in.); Museum purchase from Au Panier Fleuri Fund, 1957-49-1

0190. Sidewall, Rixheim, Alsace, France, 1901–06; Harry Wearne (American, b. London, 1852–1929); Made by Zuber & Cie; Block printed on paper; 102 x 50 cm (40 3/16 x 19 11/16 in.); Gift of James J. Rorimer, 1950-111-7

0191. Textile, France, 1710–15; Woven silk with silk and metallic brocade, 96.5 x 54 cm (38 x 21 1/4 in.); Museum purchase from Au Panier Fleuri Fund, 1960-72-6

0192. Textile, France or Italy, 1700–05; Silk damask brocaded with silk and metallic yarns; 110 x 54 cm (43 5/16 x 21 1/4 in.); Museum Purchase from Au Panier Fleuri and Smithsonian Institution Collections Acquisition Program Funds, 2000-23-1

0193. Sidewall, Acanthus, ca. 1925; William Morris (British, 1834–96); Made by Jeffrey & Company (London, England, 1836–1930); Block printed on paper; 64 x 57.3 cm (25 3/16 x 22 9/16 in.); Gift of Robert W. Friedel, 1941-74-20-a,b

0194. Sidewall, Tulip, 1893–95; Charles Francis Annesley Voysey (British, 1857–1941); Block printed on paper; 91.5 x 56 cm (36 x 22 1/16 in.); Gift of Dr. Francis J. Geck, 1980-73-32

0195. Textile, France or Italy, ca. 1700; Silk satin damask with silk and metallic brocading; 91.4 x 48.3 cm (36 x 19 in.); Gift of John Pierpont Morgan, 1902-1-900-a

0196. Textile, Spitalfields, England, ca. 1740; Silk brocaded with metallic yarns; 109.2 x 54.9 cm (43 x 21 5/8 in.), repeat: 74.9 cm (29 1/2 in.); Museum purchase through gift of various donors, 1990-150-2

0197. Sidewall, USA, 1828–50; Block printed on paper; 44.5 x 24 cm (17 1/2 x 9 7/16 in.); Gift of Harvey Smith, 1972-22-5-b,e,f

0198. Textile, Compton, 1896; John Henry Dearle (British, 1860–1932); Manufactured by Morris & Company, Decorators Ltd. (Merton Abbey, England); Block-printed cotton; 85.1 x 77.2 cm (33 1/2 x 30 3/8 in.); Gift of Robert W. Friedel, 1951-103-18-a

0199. Textile, France, ca. 1785; Oberkampf & Cie. (Jouy-en-Josas, France); Block printed on linen warp, cotton weft; 41.9 x 61 cm (16 1/2 x 24 in.), repeat: 30.5 cm (12 in.); Gift of Josephine Howell, 1973-51-85

0200. Textile, Juin (June), 1930; Paul Poiret (French, 1879–1944); Produced by F. Schumacher & Co. (New York, New York, USA); Cotton printed by engraved roller; 278.1 x 80.6 cm (109 1/2 x 31 3/4 in.); Museum purchase from Sarah Cooper-Hewitt Fund, 1994-115-1; © F. Schumacher & Co., all rights reserved

0201A. Sidewall, Meadow, 1967; William Justema (American, 1905–87); Made by James D. Gaffney (New York, New York, USA); Screenprinted on paper; 155 x 76 cm (61 x 29 15/16 in.); Gift of William Justema, 1969-70-4

0201B. Sidewall, Meadow, 1967; William Justema (American, 1905–87); Made by James D. Gaffney (New York, New York, USA); Screenprinted on paper; 285 x 76 cm (112 3/16 x 29 15/16 in.); Gift of William Justema, 1969-70-5

0202. Bed cover (suzani), Anadolu, Turkey, 19th century; Cotton, embroidered in silk in chain and Bokhara couching stitches; 248.9 x 182.9 cm (8 ft. 2 in. x 6 ft.); Gift of Provident Securities Company from the Estate of Mr. and Mrs. William H. Crocker, 1955-133-18

0203. Textile, France, ca. 1792; Oberkampf & Cie. (Jouy-en-Josas, France); Block-printed cotton; 50.8 x 40 cm (20 x 15 3/4 in.), repeat: 26.7 cm (10 1/2 in.); Gift of Josephine Howell, 1973-51-148

0204. Sidewall, Tree of Wisdom, 1952; Kakegawa Grasscloth Manufacturing Co. and Orientex, Ltd. (Japan); Screenprinted on grasscloth; 91 x 77 cm (35 13/16 x 30 5/16 in.); Gift of S. Stanley Sogg, 1955-88-2-a

0205. Sidewall, Love in Bloom, 1968; The Jack Denst Designs, Inc. (Chicago, Illinois, USA); Screenprinted in enamel inks on foil; 14.63 m x 76.2 cm (48 ft. x 30 in.); Gift of The Jack Denst Designs, Inc., 2004-19-1; © 2014 Jack Denst, all rights reserved

0206. Sidewall, England or USA, 1880–1900; Machine printed; 107 x 55.5 cm (42 1/8 x 21 7/8 in.); Gift of Deerfield Academy, 1972-51-9

0207. Textile, Primavera, 1959; Don Wight (American, 1924–99) and Larsen Design Studio (New York, New York, USA); Produced by Jack Lenor Larsen Inc. (New York, New York, USA); Printed by Taunus Textildruck Zimmer (Oberursel, Germany); Screenprinted cotton velvet; 143.5 x 142.2 cm (56 1/2 x 56 in.), repeat: 91.4 x 121.9 cm (36 x 48 in.); Gift of Jack Lenor Larsen, 1973-54-2; © Cowtan & Tout

0208. Sidewall, USA, 1938–40; Screenprinted on paper; 88 x 65 cm (34 5/8 x 25 9/16 in.); Gift of D. Lorraine Yerkes, 1940-117-25

0209. Sidewall, France, ca. 1920; René Crevel (French, 1900–35); Made by C. H. H. Geffroy for Nancy McClelland, Inc.; Block printed on paper; 71 x 51 cm (27 15/16 x 20 1/16 in.); Gift of Nancy McClelland, 1945-3-6

0210. Textile, England or Netherlands for African market, 1960s; Screenprinted cotton; 198.1 x 113 cm (78 x 44 1/2 in.); Gift of Milton Sonday, 1972-31-2

0211. Textile, Fan, 1985; Theo Maas for Vlisco (Helmond, Netherlands); Wax-resist printed cotton; 548.6 x 120 cm (18 ft. x 47 1/4 in.); Gift of Vlisco, 5808.8.2014

0212. Textile, 2012; Nico Verbart for Vlisco (Helmond, Netherlands); Wax-resist printed cotton; 548.6 x 120 cm (18 ft. x 47 1/4 in.); Gift of Vlisco, 5808.17.2014

0213. Sidewall, Folded Stripe, 1965–69; Barbara White (American); Hand-folded and dyed Japanese paper; 66 x 94 cm (26 x 37 in.); Gift of Barbara White, 2000-64-20; © Barbara White

0214. Textile, Melooni, 1963; Maija Isola (Finnish, 1927–2001); Manufactured by Marimekko Oy (Helsinki, Finland); Screen-printed cotton; 421.6 x 137.8 cm (13 ft. 10 in. x 54 1/4 in.); Gift of Marimekko, Inc., 1979-89-6; © Marimekko Oy

0215. Textile, Kyoto, 1965; Hans Krondahl (Swedish, b. 1929); Printed by Ljungbergs Textiltryck AB (Floda, Sweden); Screenprinted cotton velveteen; 311.8 x 134.6 cm (122 3/4 x 53 in.); Gift of Hans Krondahl, 1997-116-2

0216. Sidewall, Tie Dye, 1958; Barbara White (American); Hand-dyed and folded Japanese paper; 45.7 x 61 cm (18 x 24 in.); Gift of Barbara White, 2000-64-2; © Barbara White

0217. Sidewall, Asters, 1959–65; Barbara White (American); Hand-folded and dyed Japanese paper; 66 x 94 cm (26 x 37 in.); Gift of Barbara White, 2000-64-16; © Barbara White

0218. Sidewall, Roses, 1959–65; Barbara White (American); Hand-folded and dyed Japanese paper; 66 x 94 cm (26 x 37 in.); Gift of Barbara White, 2000-64-12; © Barbara White

0219. Tea ceremony rug (mosen), China for Japanese market, late 19th century; Felted and tie-dyed wool; 200.7 x 127 cm (79 x 50 in.); Museum purchase from General Acquisitions Endowment Fund, 2005-2-1

0220. Textile, Felsenhuhn, 1910–12; Wilhelm Martens (Austrian); Produced by Wiener Werkstätte (Vienna, Austria); Printed by Neunkirchner Druckfabrik (Austria); Block-printed linen; 105.7 x 71.1 cm (41 5/8 x 28 in.), repeat: 38.1 x 24.1 cm (15 x 9 1/2 in.); Gift of Jessie Poesch, 2003-8-1

0221. Sidewall, Homestead, 1962–69; William Justema (American, 1905–87); Made by James D. Gaffney (New York, New York, USA); Screenprinted on paper; 124.5 x 76 cm (49 x 29 15/16 in.); Gift of William Justema, 1969-70-8

0222. Sidewall, France, 1810–20; Block printed on handmade paper; 76 x 51.5 cm (29 15/16 x 20 1/4 in.); Gift of Eleanor and Sarah Hewitt, 1928-2-110

0223. Textile, Santana, 1984; Johan Sleegers for Vlisco (Helmond, Netherlands); Wax-resist printed cotton; 548.6 x 120 cm (18 ft. x 47 1/4 in.); Gift of Vlisco, 5808.6.2014

0224. Poster, Knoll International, 1967; Massimo Vignelli (Italian, 1931–2014); Offset lithograph on white wove paper; 81.3 x 120.7 cm (32 x 47 1/2 in.); Gift of Lella and Massimo Vignelli, 2009-42-1; © Vignelli Designs

0225. Textile, Istuva Harka (Sitting Bull), 1967; Maija Isola (Finnish, 1927–2001); Manufactured by Marimekko Oy (Helsinki, Finland); Screenprinted cotton; 460.1 x 136.2 cm (181 1/8 x 53 5/8 in.), repeat: 74.6 cm (29 3/8 in.); Gift of Marimekko, Inc., 1979-89-8; © Marimekko Oy

0226. Print, Invitation for Alvin Lustig: An Exhibition of His Work, Frank Perls Gallery, Beverly Hills, California, USA, 1949–50; Alvin Lustig (American, 1915–55); Lithograph on white wove paper; 12.7 x 17.7 cm (5 x 6 15/16 in.); Gift of Tamar Cohen and Dave Slatoff, 1993-31-155; © Elaine Lustig Cohen

0227. Sidewall, Pennants, 1953; James Kemble Mills, Inc. (San Francisco, California, USA); Screenprinted on paper; 88.5 x 76 cm (34 13/16 x 29 15/16 in.); Gift of The Wallpaper Magazine, 1953-198-4

0228. Poster, Nippon Good Design Show, 1963; Taï Tsuge (Japanese); Lithograph on wove paper; 102.5 x 68.8 cm (40 3/8 x 27 1/16 in.); Gift of Sara and Marc Benda, 2009-12-20

0229. Sidewall, To the Point, ca. 1970; Perceptive Concepts, Inc. (New York, New York, USA); Screenprinted on vinyl; 137 x 75.5 cm (53 15/16 x 29 3/4 in.); Gift of Joy Wolf, 1981-64-1

0230. Book cover, *Under Western Eyes* by Joseph Conrad, 1951; Alvin Lustig (American, 1915–55) for New Directions (New York, New York, USA); Offset lithograph on thin glossy paper; 18.4 x 13 cm (7 1/4 x 5 1/8 in.); Gift of Susan Lustig Peck, 2001-29-13; © Estate of Susan Lustig Peck

0231. Book cover, *Selected Poems* by Ezra Pound, 1948; Alvin Lustig (American, 1915–55) for New Directions (New York, New York, USA); Lithograph on thin glossy paper; 18.4 x 18.4 cm (7 1/4 x 7 1/4 in.); Gift of Susan Lustig Peck, 2001-29-7; © Estate of Susan Lustig Peck

0232. Poster, Exhibition Grammo-Grafik (Recorded Music Graphics); Kunstgewerbemuseum, Zürich, Switzerland, 1957; Gottlieb Soland (Swiss, 1928–2011); Lithograph on wove paper; 100 x 69.9 cm (39 3/8 x 27 1/2 in.); Gift of Sara and Marc Benda, 2009-12-19

0233. Poster, Alberto Flammer / Flavio Paolucci, Museo Cantonale d'Arte, Lugano, Italy, 1988; Bruno Monguzzi (Swiss, b. 1941); Offset lithograph on paper; 128 x 90.5 cm (50 3/8 x 35 5/8 in.); Gift of Elaine Lustig Cohen, 2002-15-3; © Elaine Lustig Cohen

0234. Book illustration, Aviation exposition, 1909; Created by André Granet (French, 1881–1974), photographed by Studio Chevojon; From *Décors éphémères: Les expositions jeux d'eau et de lumière* (*Ephemeral Decorations: Exhibitions of Fountains and Light*), (Paris: E. Desfossés, 1948); Photograph on paper; 36 x 26 cm (14 x 10 1/2 in.); Gift of Paula Michtom, Smithsonian Libraries, TK4148.F8G73 1948

0235. Bulb lamp, 1966; Ingo Maurer (German, b. 1932); Manufactured by Ingo Maurer GmbH (Munich, Germany); Mold-blown glass, chrome-plated metal, incandescent bulb; 29.2 x 20.3 cm diam. (11 1/2 x 8 in.); Gift of Ingo Maurer, 2008-16-1-a,b; Photo by Ellen McDermott © Smithsonian Institution; © Ingo Maurer GmbH

0236. Printed packaging, 100 Watt Soft White Bulbs, ca. 1968; Paul Rand (American, 1914–96) for Westinghouse (USA); Offset lithograph on white cardboard; 12 x 9.8 x 6.7 cm (4 3/4 x 3 7/8 x 2 5/8 in.); Gift of Marion S. Rand, 2002-11-43; © Marion S. Rand

0237. Poster, Nouveaux Espaces, Pesce/Quasar (New Spaces, Pesce/Quasar), 1970; Jean Widmer (Swiss, b. 1929) for Centre de Création Industrielle (Paris, France); Screenprint on wove paper; 64.8 x 49.8 cm (25 1/2 x 19 5/8 in.); Gift of Sara and Marc Benda, 2009-12-21

0238. Poster, The Geography of Oil, 1943; Ladislav Sutnar (Czech-American, b. Pilsen, Bohemia, 1897, d. New York, New York, USA, 1976) for Standard Oil Company (New Jersey, USA); Offset lithograph on white wove paper; 101.8 x 76.2 cm (40 1/16 in. x 30 in.); Gift of Anonymous Donor, 1994-109-1

0239. Poster, Yale University School of Art Graduate Program: 1991–1992, 1991; Paul Rand (American, 1914–96) for Yale University (New Haven, Connecticut, USA); Offset lithograph on white paper; 27.9 x 76.5 cm (11 x 30 1/8 in.); Gift of Marion S. Rand, 2002-11-38; © Marion S. Rand

0240. Book illustration, *Catalog Designs*, 1944; Knud Lönberg-Holm (Danish, 1895–1972, active USA, 1924–72) and Ladislav Sutnar (Czech-American, b. Pilsen, Bohemia, 1897, d. New York, New York, USA, 1976); From *Catalog Design* (New York: Sweet's Catalog Service, 1944); Photomechanical process on paper; 21.5 x 30.5 cm (8 1/2 x 12 in.); Smithsonian Libraries, HF5862.L6X 1944

0241. Poster, Yale University School of Art, 1988; Paul Rand (American, 1914–96) for Yale University (New Haven, Connecticut, USA); Offset lithograph on white paper; 43.8 x 22.2 cm (17 1/4 x 8 3/4 in.); Gift of Marion S. Rand, 2002-11-4; © Marion S. Rand

0242. Envelope, *Industrial Design* magazine, 1953; Alvin Lustig (American, 1915–55); Lithograph on off-white wove paper; 32.8 x 25.6 cm (12 15/16 x 10 1/16 in.); Gift of Tamar Cohen and Dave Slatoff, 1993-31-170; © Elaine Lustig Cohen

0243. Poster, Seduction, for the Yale School of Architecture Symposium, 2006–07; Marian Bantjes (Canadian, b. 1963); Offset lithograph on white wove paper; 86.4 x 81.3 cm (34 x 32 in.); Gift of Marian Bantjes, 2007-25-2; © Marian Bantjes and Michael Bierut

0244. Poster, PhotoGraphie Zeit: Raum M. Mathys, 1973; Wolfgang Weingart (Swiss, b.1941); Screenprint on black wove paper; 59.1 x 43.8 cm (23 1/4 x 17 1/4 in.); Gift of Ken Friedman, 1997-19-410; © Wolfgang Weingart.

0245. Drawing, Design for Numerals for a Thermostat, ca. 1950; Henry Dreyfuss (American, 1904–72); Text printed, graphite on white paper; 22.9 x 29.1 cm (9 x 11 7/16 in.); Gift of Honeywell, Inc., 1997-10-26

0246. Poster, LIGHT/YEARS, for the Architectural League's Beaux-Arts Ball, 1999; Michael Bierut (American, b. 1957); Offset lithograph on white wove paper; 59.7 x 97.8 cm (23 1/2 x 38 1/2 in.); Gift of Michael Bierut, 2007-12-2; © Michael Bierut/Pentagram

0247. Book cover, *Catalog Design*, 1944; Knud Lönberg-Holm (Danish, 1895–1972, active USA, 1924–72) and Ladislav Sutnar (Czech-American, b. Pilsen, Bohemia, 1897, d. New York, New York, USA, 1976); From *Catalog Design* (New York: Sweet's Catalog Service, 1944); Photomechanical process on paper; 21.5 x 30.5 cm (8 1/2 x 12 in.); Smithsonian Libraries, HF5862.L6X 1944

0248. Print, Citibank Golden Passbook Deposit Slip, ca. 1975; Dan Friedman (American, 1945–95); Offset lithograph on paper; 9 x 19.7 cm (3 9/16 x 7 3/4 in.); Gift of Ken Friedman, 1997-19-66

0249. Poster, Herman Miller Inc., Textiles & Objects, 1961; John Neuhart (American, 1928–2011) and Alexander Hayden Girard (American, 1907–93) for Herman Miller Inc. (Zeeland, Michigan, USA); Screenprint on textured off-white paper; 66.4 x 50.8 cm (26 1/8 x 20 in.); Gift of Marilyn and John Neuhart, 2004-13-1

0250. Printed packaging, 60 Watt Extra Life* Bulbs, 1960s; Paul Rand (American, 1914–96); Offset lithograph on cardboard; 12.1 x 10.8 x 7 cm (4 3/4 x 4 1/4 x 2 3/4 in.); Gift of Marion S. Rand, 2002-11-44; © Marion S. Rand

0251. Booklet, 2 pittori, 3 scultori, XXVII Biennale, Venice, 1954; Alvin Lustig (American, 1915–55); Lithograph on handmade off-white paper; 17 x 13.4 cm (6 11/16 x 5 1/4 in.); Gift of Tamar Cohen and Dave Slatoff, 1993-31-168; © Elaine Lustig Cohen

0252. Poster, Jazz Willisau: Charles Gayle Solo, 2009; Niklaus Troxler (Swiss, b. 1947); Offset lithograph on paper; 128.1 x 90.6 cm (50 7/16 x 35 11/16 in.); Gift of Niklaus Troxler, 2009-3-1; © Niklaus Troxler

0253. Poster, Fucking A, The Public Theater, 2003; Paula Scher (American, b. 1948); Screenprint on paper; 116.8 x 76.2 cm (46 x 30 in.); Gift of Paula Scher, 2013-25-5

0254. Book illustration, *Catalog Designs*, 1944; Knud Lönberg-Holm (Danish, 1895–1972, active USA, 1924–72) and Ladislav Sutnar (Czech-American, b. Pilsen, Bohemia, 1897, d. New York, New York, USA, 1976); From *Catalog Design* (New York: Sweet's Catalog Service, 1944); Photomechanical process on paper; 21.5 x 30.5 cm (8 1/2 x 12 in.); Smithsonian Libraries, HF5862.L6X 1944

0255. Sample, Alphabet, 1960; Alexander Hayden Girard (American, 1907–93); Produced by Herman Miller Textiles (Zeeland, Michigan, USA); Screenprinted cotton; 60 x 60 cm (23 5/8 x 23 5/8 in.); Gift of Alexander H. Girard, 1969-165-164; © 1960 Girard Studios, LLC, all rights reserved

0256. Drawing, Design for Public Theater Flyer, 1994; Paula Scher (American, b. 1948) for The Public Theater (New York, New York, USA); Color pencil and graphite on paper; 27.8 x 21.6 cm (10 15/16 x 8 1/2 in.); Gift of Paula Scher, 6817.39.2013; © Paula Scher

0257. Alphabet border, 1993; William Wegman (American, b. 1943); Screenprinted on paper; 967 x 34.5 cm (380 11/16 x 13 9/16 in.); Gift of A/D Gallery, 1996-53-1; © William Wegman

0258. 'Ultima II' LOVE ring, ca. 1972; After Robert Indiana (American, b. 1928); Manufactured by Charles Revson, Inc.; Gilt cast metal; 1.8 x 2.2 cm diam. (11/16 x 7/8 in.); Museum purchase from Sarah Cooper Hewitt Fund, 1992-103-3; Photo by Ellen McDermott © Smithsonian Institution

0259. Poster, Shakespeare in the Park 2007: Romeo and Juliet/ A Midsummer Night's Dream, The Public Theater, 2007; Paula Scher (American, b. 1948); Offset lithograph on varnish-coated paper; 119.4 x 172.7 cm (47 in. x 5 ft. 8 in.); Gift of Paula Scher, 2013-25-9; © Paula Scher

0260. Book illustration, Letters, ca. 1870; Friedrich Christmann (German) and Hermann Junker (German, 1838–99); From Friedrich Christmann and Hermann Junker, *Alphabete = Alphabets . . .* (Frankfurt am Main: B. Dondorf), p. 37; Color lithograph on paper; 25.5 x 62 cm (10 x 24.5 in.); Smithsonian Libraries, Q NK3600.C55 1870z

0261. Book illustration, The Letter A, 1922; Frederic W. Goudy (American, 1865–1947); From Frederic W. Goudy, *The Alphabet: Fifteen Interpretative Designs Drawn and Arranged with Explanatory Text and Illustrations* (New York: Mitchell Kennerley), p. 46; Engraving on paper; 33 x 24.5 cm (13 x 9.6 in.); Gift of Robert W. Chanler, 1933, Smithsonian Libraries, q NK3631. G68 A4 1922x

0262. Sampler, England, 19th century; Jane Hall; Linen embroidered with glass beads; 13.7 x 12.1 cm (5 3/8 x 4 3/4 in.); Bequest of Mrs. Henry E. Coe, 1941-69-216

0263. Print, Invitation for Knoll, ca. 1945; Herbert Matter (Swiss, 1907–84); Lithograph on white wove paper; 17.7 x 12.6 cm (6 15/16 x 4 15/16 in.); Gift of James Fraser, 1997-76-2; © Alex Matter

0264. Print, Exhibition Announcement for "Tom E. Lewis," 1940; Alvin Lustig (American, 1915–55) for Stendahl Galleries (Los Angeles, California, USA); Lithograph on light gray wove paper; 15.9 x 31.6 cm (6 1/4 x 12 7/16 in.); Gift of Tamar Cohen and Dave Slatoff, 1993-31-154; © Elaine Lustig Cohen

0265. Book cover, USA, for XXXII International Biennial Exposition of Art, Venice, Italy, 1964; Elaine Lustig Cohen (American, b. 1929); Offset lithograph on paper; 27.8 x 43.2 cm (10 15/16 x 17 in.); Gift of Tamar Cohen and Dave Slatoff, 1993-31-62; Photo by Dennis Cowley © Smithsonian Institution; © Elaine Lustig Cohen

0266. Poster, Typografie Piet Zwart (The Typography of Piet Zwart), 1960; Pieter Brattinga (Dutch, 1931–2004); Offset lithograph on paper; 62.9 x 38.1 cm (24 3/4 x 15 in.); Gift of Pieter Brattinga, 2000-75-8; © Pieter Brattinga

0267. Poster, Max Bill: Werbegrafik und Buchgestaltung 1930–55 (Max Bill: Graphics and Book Design), 1998; Robert & Durrer (Switzerland, founded 1977); Offset lithograph on wove paper; 128.2 x 89.8 cm (50 1/2 x 35 3/8 in.); Gift of Sara and Marc Benda, 2010-21-112

0268. Poster, Alles Falsch: Imitationen, Nachahmung und Modell: von der Lust am Falschen (Everything is Fake: Imitation, Emulation and Copies: From Lust to Counterfeit), ca. 1989; Michael Schirner (German, b. 1941) for Museum für Gestaltung, Zürich, Switzerland; Screenprint on wove paper; 128.3 x 89.8 cm (50 1/2 x 35 3/8 in.); Gift of Sara and Marc Benda, 2010-21-34

0269. Poster, Jazz Willisau: McCoy Tyner Sextet, 1980; Niklaus Troxler (Swiss, b. 1947); Offset lithograph on paper; 128.1 x 90.6 cm (50 7/16 x 35 11/16 in.); Gift of Niklaus Troxler, 2009-3-4; © Niklaus Troxler

0270. Poster, Exposicion Litografias, Galeria de Arte de la Universidad Nacional (Exhibition of Lithographs, National University Art Gallery), 1939; Francisco Dosamantes (Mexican, b. 1911); Lithograph on newsprint; 45.1 x 59.7 cm (17 3/4 x 23 1/2 in.); Museum purchase from General Acquisitions Endowment Fund, 2000-34-1; © El Taller de Gráfica Popular

0271. Print, Andrew Good, 1939; Alvin Lustig (American, 1915–55); Lithograph on light gray laid paper; 6.5 x 6.8 cm (2 9/16 x 2 11/16 in.); Gift of Tamar Cohen and Dave Slatoff, 1993-31-157; © Elaine Lustig Cohen

0272. Poster, IBM Rebus, ca. 1992; Paul Rand (American, 1914–96); Offset lithograph on paper; 99.1 x 34.9 cm (39 x 13 3/4 in); Gift of Marion S. Rand, 2002-11-26; © Marion S. Rand

0273. Sidewall, Space Stations and Rockets, ca. 1950; Machine printed on paper; 77 x 49 cm (30 5/16 x 19 5/16 in.); Gift of Suzanne Lipschutz, 1991-89-133

0274. Sidewall, Constellation, 1938; Marion Dorn Kauffer (American, active England, 1896–1964); Made by Cole and Son, Ltd.; Screenprinted on machine-made paper; 46 x 55 cm (18 1/8 x 21 5/8 in.); Gift of Richard E. Thibaut, Inc., 1946-74-11

0275. Poster, Organs of the United Nations, 1946; Ladislav Sutnar (Czech-American, b. Pilsen, Bohemia, 1897, d. New York, New York, USA, 1976); Offset lithograph on paper; 55.9 x 86.4 cm (22 x 34 in.); Gift of Anonymous Donor, 1994-109-13

0276. Book illustration, the Marmon Sixteen Five-Passenger Close-Coupled Sedan, 1930; From The Marmon Motor Car Company, *The Marmon Sixteen*—enclosed booklet by Walter Dorwin Teague (American, 1883–1960), *The Marmon Sixteen From the Notes of the Designer, Walter Dorwin Teague* (Indianapolis: Marmon Motor Car Company); Photomechanical process on paper; 16 x 12 cm (6 1/4 x 4 3/4 in.); Gift of Herbert Kleist, Smithsonian Libraries, TL215.M352

0277. Book cover, *Des canons, des munitions?* (*Guns and Ammunition?*), 1938; Le Corbusier (Swiss, b. Charles-Édouard Jeanneret-Gris, active France, 1887–1965); From *Des canons, des munitions?* (*Guns and Ammunition?*), (Boulogne, France: Éditions de l'Architecture d'aujourd'hui); Photomechanical process on paper; 24 x 30 cm (9 1/2 x 11 7/8 in.); Gift of Hester Diamond, ca. 2000, Smithsonian Libraries, qNA9030.L43 1938

0278. Poster, Vorm en Luchtfoto (Form in Aerial Photography), 1960; Pieter Brattinga (Dutch, 1931–2004); Offset lithograph on paper; 62.9 x 38.1 cm (24 3/4 x 15 in.); Gift of Pieter Brattinga, 2000-75-5; © Pieter Brattinga

0279. Business card, K2 Snowboards, 1994; Robynne Raye (American, b. 1964) for Modern Dog (Seattle, Washington, USA); Offset lithograph on card stock; 6 x 10 cm (2 3/8 x 3 15/16 in.); Gift of Robynne Raye, 1996-5-11

0280. Drawing, Textile Design: Plane Motif, 1950–70; Tommi Parzinger (American, b. Germany, 1903–81); Brush and gouache, graphite on paper, lined; 11.5 x 11.5 cm (4 1/2 x 4 1/2 in.); Gift of Mr. Donald Cameron, 1992-51-30; © Parzinger Originals

0281. Drawing, Yellow Submarine Film Celluloid, 1967–68; Heinz Edelmann (German, 1934–2009) for United Artists; Made by King Features Production, for Apple Films; Brush and acrylic paint, pen and ink on two sheets of cellulose acetate; 31.9 x 41 cm (12 9/16 x 16 1/8 in.); Museum purchase through gift of Erskine Hewitt, 1969-73-1; Photo by Scott Hyde © Smithsonian Institution; © Subafilms Ltd.

0282. Poster, Paul Newman, Filmpodium Zürich, 2001; Ralph Schraivogel (Swiss, b. 1960); Screenprint and lithograph on white wove paper; 128 x 90.4 cm (50 3/8 x 35 9/16 in.); Gift of Anonymous Donor, 2010-8-1

0283. Poster, Tadanori Yokoo, Stedelijk Museum, Amsterdam, Netherlands, 1974; Tadanori Yokoo (Japanese, b. 1936); Offset lithograph on white wove paper; 95.2 x 63.3 cm (37 1/2 x 24 15/16 in.); Gift of Sara and Marc Benda, 2009-12-6

0284. Poster, ITF Internationale tentoonstelling op filmgebied (International Film Exhibition), 1928; Piet Zwart (Dutch, 1885–1977); Lithograph on wove paper; 85 x 61 cm (33 7/16 x 24 in.); Museum purchase through gift of Susan Hermanos, Judith and Charles Bergoffen, Cathy Nierras, and Anonymous Donors and from Drawings and Prints Council and General Acquisitions Endowment Funds, 2013-20-1

0285. Poster, Oskar Schlemmer, Les Noces, Igor Stravinsky, 1988; Bruno Monguzzi (Swiss, b. 1941) for Museo Cantonale d'Arte (Lugano, Switzerland); Offset lithograph on white paper; 128 x 90.5 cm (50 3/8 x 35 5/8 in.); Gift of Elaine Lustig Cohen, 2002-15-2; © Elaine Lustig Cohen

0286. Poster, The Chap-Book (Blue Lady), August 1894; William Henry Bradley (American, 1868–1962); Color zincograph on thin cream wove paper; 50.8 x 35.6 cm (20 x 14 in.); Museum purchase through gift of Mrs. Gilbert W. Chapman and Ely Jacques Kahn, 2003-6-1

0287. Poster, *Exodus*, 1960; Saul Bass (American, 1920–96); Offset lithograph on wove paper; 104 x 68.5 cm (40 15/16 x 26 15/16 in.); Gift of Sara and Marc Benda, 2010-21-16; © Metro-Goldwyn-Mayer Media

0288. Magazine cover, Wendingen: Frank Lloyd Wright, 1925; Hendrik Wijdeveld (Dutch, 1885–1987); From Frank Lloyd Wright (American, 1867–1959), contributing author, *Wendingen: maandblad voor bouwen en sieren (Turning: Monthly for Building and Adorning)*, vol. 7, no. 4, (Santpoort, Netherlands: C. A. Mees); Photo-mechanical process on paper; 34 x 34 cm (13 3/8 x 13 3/8 in.); Purchase, 2013, Smithsonian Libraries, fN5.W469

0289. Poster, Power—*The Nerve Centre of London's Underground*, 1930; Edward McKnight Kauffer (American, active in England, 1890–1954); Lithograph on white wove paper mounted on board; 101.6 x 61.4 cm (40 x 24 3/16 in.); Gift of Mrs. E. McKnight Kauffer, 1963-39-45; Photo by Ken Pelka © Smithsonian Institution; © TfL from the London Transport Museum Collection

0290. Trade catalog, front and back cover, *Livery, MDCCCXCIX*, ca. 1899; Designed and printed by Will Bradley (American, 1868–1962); (Cambridge, MA: University Press for Rogers, Peet & Company); Offset lithograph on paper; 17 x 18 cm (6 3/4 x 7 in.); Gift of Roy Young, Smithsonian Libraries, TT626.R64 1899

0291. Printed blotter, Lijstwerk; de grootste en de kleinste partij direct uit voorraad, maart 1935 (Moldings; The Largest and the Smallest Parts Available in Stock, March 1935), 1935; Piet Zwart (Dutch, 1885–1977); Offset lithograph on white wove paper, mounted on blue blotting paper; 9.2 x 20.8 cm (3 5/8 x 8 3/16 in.); Museum purchase through gift of Eleanor and Sarah Hewitt, 2004-1-2

0292. Textile, Nuno me Gara (Cloth-patterned cloth), 1981; Junichi Arai (Japanese, b. 1932); Cotton doublecloth; 259.1 x 120 cm (102 x 47 1/4 in.), repeat: 60 cm (23 5/8 in.); Gift of Junichi Arai, 1985-31-1

0293. Poster, Vivo in Typo, 2008; Philippe Apeloig (French, b. 1962); Screenprint on coated paper; 175 x 118 cm (5 ft. 8 7/8 in. x 46 7/16 in.); Gift of Philippe Apeloig, 2013-16-2; © Philippe Apeloig

0294. Poster, Rural Industries, 1947; Lester Beall (American, 1909–69); Screenprint on paper; 101.6 x 76.2 cm (40 x 30 in.); Museum purchase through gift of Mrs. Edward C. Post and from Friends of Drawings and Prints, General Acquisition Endowment, Sarah Cooper Hewitt, and Smithsonian Institution Collections Acquisition Program Funds, 1995-106-1; Photo by Ken Pelka © Smithsonian Institution

0295. Poster, Semana de Cine Cubano en Boliva (Cuban Cinema Week in Bolivia), 1985; Nestor (Cuban, b. 1948); Screenprint on wove paper; 75.6 x 50.2 cm (29 3/4 x 19 3/4 in.); Museum purchase from Smithsonian Institution Collections Acquisition Program Fund and through gift of Anonymous Donors, 1994-65-7; Photo © Smithsonian Institution

0296. Poster, Symphony of a Big City, 1928; Georgii Augustovich Stenberg (Russian, 1900–33) and Vladimir Augustovich Stenberg (Russian, 1899–1982); Lithograph on off-white wove paper; 106.7 x 70.5 cm (42 x 27 3/4 in.); Museum purchase from Drawings and Prints Council and General Acquisitions Endowment Funds, 2008-1-1

0297. Print, Wandbehang die Reifezeit (Harvest Time Wall Hanging), from Die Quelle: Flächen Schmuck (The Source: Ornament for Flat Surfaces), 1901, plate 7; Koloman Moser (Austrian, 1868–1918); Lithograph on paper; 24.9 x 29.5 cm (9 13/16 x 11 5/8 in.); Gift of Jerrol E. Golden, 1999-41-1-8

0298. Poster, Schule für Gestaltung Bern, 1998; Ralph Schraivogel (Swiss, b. 1960); Printed by Albin Uldry Workshop (Switzerland); Screenprint on white wove paper; 100 x 70.6 cm (39 3/8 x 27 13/16 in.); Gift of Ralph Schraivogel, 2007-15-1; Reproduced with permission © Ralph Schraivogel

0299. Poster, Tanzstudio Wulff, Basel. Relâche, Parade, Ariadne, 1931; Max Bill (Swiss, 1908–94); Offset lithograph on white wove paper; 64.1 x 90.8 cm (25 1/4 x 35 3/4 in.); Museum purchase through gift of Eleanor and Sarah Hewitt, 2004-1-1

0300. Poster, Bicycle, Public, 2012; Paula Scher (American, b. 1948); Digital offset lithograph on paper; 91.4 x 68.6 cm (36 x 27 in.); Gift of Paula Scher, 2013-25-10

0301. Poster, California Institute of the Arts, 1978; Design and typography by April Greiman (American, b. 1948), creative direction, design, and photography by Jayme Odgers (American, b. 1939); Lithograph on paper; 29 x 118 cm (11 7/16 x 46 7/16 in.); Gift of Various Donors, 1981-29-25; © 1979 Jayme Odgers, April Greiman

0302. Poster, Spitzen der Wiener Werkstätte (Wiener Werkstätte Lacework), ca. 1919; Dagobert Peche (Austrian, 1887–1923, active Vienna 1911–23); Lithograph on off-white paper; 57.2 x 45.7 cm (22 1/2 x 18 in.); Museum purchase through gift of George A. Hearn, 2002-19-1

0303. Poster, Engelberg, Trübsee, Switzerland, 1936; Herbert Matter (Swiss, 1907–84); Two-color gravure on white wove paper; 101.9 x 63.7 cm (40 1/8 x 25 1/16 in.); Museum purchase from General Acquisitions Endowment Fund, 2006-15-1; © Alex Matter

0304. Textile, Futsu Crisscross, 2009; Reiko Sudo (Japanese, b. 1953); Manufactured by NUNO Corporation (Tokyo, Japan); Raw silk, kibiso, and cotton doublecloth; 308 x 21.6 cm (121 1/4 x 8 1/2 in.); Gift of NUNO, 2009-48-3; © NUNO Corporation

0305. Sidewall, Hexagon, 2004; Marcel Wanders (Dutch, b. 1963); Screenprinted on non-woven paper; 100 x 115.5 cm (39 3/8 x 45 1/2 in.); Gift of Marcel Wanders, 2009-11-1; © Wonders Holding BV / Marcel Wanders

0306. Album, Woven Paper Designs, 1902–04; Margarete Riessen (German, 1884–1980); Blue, white paper, various colored thread, stitched, pricked or mounted on brown wove paper, graphite, ink-drawn notations; lithograph; covered paperboard and brown ribbon (portfolio); 27 x 47 cm (10 5/8 x 18 1/2 in.); Gift of Marie-Luise Bensel, 1997-25-1-1/54

0307. Kimono, Japan, Taisho period, 1926–45; Silk, stencil-printed in warp and weft (meisen); 147.3 x 123.2 cm (58 x 48 1/2 in.); Museum purchase from Friends of Textiles and General Acquisitions Endowment Funds, 2013-15-1

0308. Poster, Dylan, 1966; Milton Glaser (American, b. 1929); Offset lithograph on white wove paper; 84 x 55.9 cm (33 1/16 x 22 in.); Gift of Richard Kusack, 2007-24-1; © Milton Glaser

0309. Hanging, Binary Traces: Kay, 2005; Lia Cook (American, b. 1942); Jacquard-woven cotton doublecloth; 142.2 x 129.5 cm (56 x 51 in.); Museum purchase from General Acquisitions Endowment Fund, 2007-33-1; © 2005 Lia Cook

0310. Poster, Chambers Brothers Band, Neon Rose #12, 1967; Victor Moscoso (American, b. Spain, 1936); Lithograph on wove paper; 50.2 x 35.7 cm (19 3/4 x 14 1/16 in.); Gift of Sara and Marc Benda, 2009-12-23

0311. Poster, Hoffnung und Widerstand (Hope and Resistance), ca. 1998; Cornel Windlin (Swiss, b. 1964) for Museum für Gestaltung, Zürich, Switzerland; Offset lithograph; 127.9 x 89.6 cm (50 3/8 x 35 1/4 in.); Gift of Sara and Marc Benda, 2010-21-109

0312. Square, Egypt, 5th–7th century; Wool slit tapestry; 15.3 x 14.6 cm (6 x 5 3/4 in.); Gift of John Pierpont Morgan, 1902-1-72; Photo by Andrew Garn © Smithsonian Institution

0313. Print, Self-Portrait, Rembrandt with Plumed Hat and Lowered Sabre, 1634; Rembrandt Harmensz. van Rijn (Dutch, 1606–69); Etching on laid paper; 13.7 x 11.7 cm (5 3/8 x 4 5/8 in.); Gift of Leo Wallerstein, 1950-131-145

0314. Sidewall, Bullies, 1992; Virgil Marti (American, b. 1962); Screenprinted and rayon flock on Tyvek; 574 x 138.5 cm (18 ft. 10 in. x 54 1/2 in.); Museum purchase from General Acquisitions Endowment and Friends of Wallcoverings Funds through gift of the Raymond Family in honor of Paul Raymond, 2002-4-1; © Virgil Marti 1992

0315. Sidewall, Bachelor's Wall Paper, 1969; Charles Dana Gibson (American, 1867–1944); Made by M. H. Birge & Sons Co. (Buffalo, New York, USA); Screenprinted on paper; 79 x 76.5 cm (31 1/8 x 30 1/8 in.); Gift of Philadelphia Museum of Art, 1971-58-3-b

0316. Fashion plate, Modes de Paris (Paris Fashions), Bonnet designs, 1829; From *Petit courrier des dames: annonces des modes, des nouveautés et des arts* (*Little Post for Ladies: Fashion News, Novelties, and Arts*), 9th year, vol. 17, no. 31 (December 5, 1829), no. 69/686; Hand-colored engraving on paper; 21 x 14 cm (8 1/4 x 5 1/2 in.); Smithsonian Libraries, TT500.P4X 1829-30

0317. Book illustration, Woman with curled hairstyle, 1768; Sieur Legros de Rumigny (French, 1710–70); From *L'art de la coëffure des dames françoises* (*The Art of French Ladies' Hairstyles*), (Paris: Antoine Boudet), plate 12; Hand-colored engraving on paper; 22 x 16 cm (8 5/8 x 6 3/8 in.); Cooper Union Museum 1969, Smithsonian Libraries, TT956.L519 1768

0318. Sidewall, Beauty, 1972; Werner Berges (German, b. 1941); Made by Marburg (Kirchhain, Germany); Screenprinted on paper; 58 x 53 cm (22 13/16 x 20 7/8 in.); Museum purchase from Sarah Cooper-Hewitt Fund, 1992-110-5; © Marburg

0319. Book illustration, Woman in a turban, 1911; Illustrated by Georges Lepape (French, 1887–1971), fashion by Paul Poiret (French, 1879–1944); From *Les choses de Paul Poiret vues par Georges Lepape* (*Items by Paul Poiret as Seen by George Lepape*), (Paris: Paul Poiret par Maquet), plate 6; Pochoir print on paper; 36 x 34 cm (14 x 13 3/8 in.); Purchased by the J. Pierpont Morgan Book Fund, Smithsonian Libraries, fGT513 L59 1911

0320. Print, Portrait of Albrecht of Brandenburg, 1524; Albrecht Dürer (German, 1471–1528); Engraving on laid paper; 14.8 x 10 cm (5 13/16 x 3 15/16 in.); Gift of Leo Wallerstein, 1949-29-20

0321. Poster, De Man achter de Vormgeving van de P.T.T. (The Man Behind the Design for the Dutch Post Office), 1960; Pieter Brattinga (Dutch, 1931–2004); Offset lithograph on paper; 62.9 x 38.1 cm (24 3/4 x 15 in.); Gift of Pieter Brattinga, 2000-75-7; © Pieter Brattinga

0322. Embroidered picture, England, ca. 1840; Cotton embroidered in wool and silk in counted stitches; 21 x 16.5 cm (8 1/4 x 6 1/2 in.); Gift of Anonymous Donor from the Fraser/Martin Collection, 1974-100-20

0323. Sidewall, Paris, France, 1918–23; Émile-Jacques Ruhlmann (French, 1879–1933); Produced by Desfossé et Karth; Machine printed on paper; 100 x 50 cm (39 3/8 x 19 11/16 in.); Museum purchase from General Acquisition Endowment Fund, 2003-9-1

0324. Textile, Crossing Colors, 2013; Sheila Hicks (American, b. 1934) for Momentum Textiles (Irvine, California, USA); Jacquard-woven 81% cotton, 19% solution-dyed nylon; 355.9 x 142.5 cm (11 ft. 8 1/8 in. x 56 1/8 in.); Gift of Momentum Group, 2013-36-3; © Sheila Hicks

0325. Textile, Gazebo, 1960s; Win Anderson (American, 1922–2009); Produced by Jack Lenor Larsen Inc. (New York, New York, USA); Screenprinted linen; 275.6 x 121.9 cm (9 ft. 1/2 in. x 48 in.); Gift of Anonymous Donor, 1967-9-2; © Cowtan & Tout

0326. Fungo table lamp, 1956; Massimo Vignelli (Italian, 1931–2014); Manufactured by Venini Glassworks (Murano, Venice, Italy); Blown and cased glass, metal, plastic; 33.3 x 23 cm diam. (13 1/8 x 9 1/16 in.); Gift of Lella and Massimo Vignelli, 1986-111-1; Photo by Ellen McDermott © Smithsonian Institution; © Vignelli Designs Inc.

0327. Encircling fishing net, designed 1996, manufactured 2003; Manufactured by Toray Industries, Inc. (Japan); Polyester knotless net with heat finishing treatment; 18.69 m x 4 cm (61 ft. 4 in. x 1 9/16 in.); Gift of Toray Industries, Inc., 2003-22-1

0328. Vase, Model 3461, ca. 1934; Carlo Scarpa (Italian, 1906–78); Made by Venini Glassworks (Murano, Venice, Italy); Hand-molded glass set with fire-joined turquoise canes (mezza-filigrana), gold leaf inclusions; 40 x 16.5 cm diam. (15 3/4 x 6 1/2 in.); Museum purchase from the Members' Acquisitions Fund of Cooper-Hewitt National Design Museum, 2013-11-1; © Venini S.p.A.

0329. Textile, Sticks, 1957; Joseph Provato (American); Manufactured by Creative Looms Inc. (New York, New York, USA); Screenprinted linen; 77.5 x 62.5 cm (30 1/2 x 24 5/8 in.); Gift of Joseph Provato, 1957-171-3

0330. Sidewall, Razzmatazz, 1967; William Justema (American, 1905–87); Made by Stamford Wallpaper Co. (Bloomfield, New Jersey, USA); Screenprinted and flocked on machine-made paper; 247 x 76 cm (97 1/4 x 29 15/16 in.); Gift of William Justema, 1969-70-3

0331. Textile, Obelisk, 1958; Jack Lenor Larsen (American, b. 1927); Produced by Jack Lenor Larsen Inc. (New York, New York, USA); Screenprinted linen; 156.5 x 126.4 cm (61 5/8 x 49 3/4 in.), repeat: 121.9 cm (48 in.); Gift of Jack Lenor Larsen, Inc., 1960-170-1; © Cowtan & Tout

0332. Sidewall, Japan, 1954; Grasscloth, cotton, paper; 181 x 88 cm (71 1/4 x 34 5/8 in.); Gift of S. Stanley Sogg, 1955-88-3

0333. Sidewall, Chopped Herringbone, 1971; Alan Buchsbaum (American, 1936–87); Made by Norton Blumenthal, Inc.; Screenprinted on vinyl; 135 x 75 cm (53 1/8 x 29 1/2 in.); Gift of Alan Buchsbaum, 1980-66-1-a/e

0334. Poster, Architektur und Kinder, 1995; Peter Frey (Swiss, b. 1959) for Museum für Gestaltung, Zürich, Switzerland; Printed by Serigraphie Uldry AG (Switzerland); Screenprint on wove paper; 128 x 96 cm (50 3/8 x 37 13/16 in.); Gift of Sara and Marc Benda, 2010-21-115

0335. Sidewall, Testura Grafica, 1971–72; Getulio Alviani (Italian, b. 1939); Made by Marburg (Kirchhain, Germany); Flexograph printed on ribbed paper; 30 x 53 cm (11 13/16 x 20 7/8 in.); Museum purchase from Sarah Cooper-Hewitt Fund, 1992-110-7; © Marburg

0336. Tile, Spain, 17th century; Glazed molded earthenware (cuenca technique); 5.4 x 5.3 x 1.3 cm (2 1/8 x 2 1/16 x 1/2 in.); Gift of Eleanor and Sarah Hewitt, 1929-17-20-a,b; Photo by Ellen McDermott © Smithsonian Institution

0337. Sidewall, France, ca. 1800; Block printed on handmade paper; 49 x 104 cm (19 5/16 x 40 15/16 in.); Gift of Eleanor and Sarah Hewitt, 1928-2-70

0338. Coverlet fragment, USA, early 19th century; Wool and cotton doublecloth; 33 x 30.5 cm (13 x 12 in.); Gift of Ohio State Museum, 1953-114-3

0339. Magazine title page with fabric samples, England, 1810; Rudolph Ackermann, compiler (British, 1764–1834); from *The Repository of Arts, Literature, Commerce, Manufactures, Fashions and Politics*, series.1, vol. 3, no.14 (February 1810), (London: Printed for R. Ackermann); Engraving, fabric samples, paper; 23.5 x 15 cm (10 1/4 x 6 7/8 in.); Purchase Friends of the Museum, Smithsonian Libraries, AP4.R425

0340. Drawing, Leaf Table, 2010; Joris Laarman (Dutch, b. 1979); Graphite, brush and white gouache, on white paper pre-printed with digital code; 100.4 x 70 cm (39 1/2 x 27 9/16 in.); Gift of Marc Benda, courtesy of the artist, 2013-24-9; © Joris Laarman Labs

0341. Plate, China (for export), ca. 1830; Enameled copper, brass; 3.1 x 21.3 cm (1 1/4 x 8 3/8 in.); Gift of Samuel P. Avery, 1903-1-18

0342. Plate, Moustiers, France, 1760–80; Molded, tin-glazed earthenware; 3.5 x 22.5 x 22.7 cm (1 3/8 x 8 7/8 x 8 15/16 in.); Gift of Eugene V. and Clare E. Thaw, 2008-40-1

0343. Kremlin Service dessert plate, ca.1830; Fedor Grigorievich Solntsev (Russian, 1801–92); Made by Imperial Porcelain Manufactory (St. Petersburg, Russia); Gilt and glazed hard-paste porcelain; 3.2 x 22.2 cm diam. (1 1/4 x 8 3/4 in.); Museum purchase from General Acquisitions Endowment Fund, 2005-6-1; Photo by Andrew Garn © Smithsonian Institution

0344. Platter, 1888–98; William Frend De Morgan (British, 1839–1917); Made by Sand's End Pottery (London, England); Lustered and glazed earthenware; 5 x 43 cm diam. (1 15/16 x 16 15/16 in.); Museum purchase through bequest of Dona Guimaraes, 1992-124-1; Photo by Eric Baum © Smithsonian Institution

0345. Plate, The Reign of Workers and Peasants Will Be Without End, 1920; Sergei Vasilievich Chekhonin (Russian, 1878–1936); Made by State Porcelain Factory (Leningrad, USSR); Enameled, gilt, glazed, and molded porcelain; 3.2 x 24 cm diam. (1 1/4 x 9 7/16 in.); The Henry and Ludmilla Shapiro Collection; Partial gift and partial purchase through the Decorative Arts Association Acquisition and Smithsonian Collections Acquisition Program Funds, 1989-41-14; Photo John Parnell © Smithsonian Institution

0346. Plate, ca. 1901; Peter Behrens (German, 1868–1940); Manufactured by Gebrüder Bauscher (Weiden, Bavaria, Germany); Glazed and molded porcelain; 1.3 x 19.1 cm diam. (1/2 x 7 1/2 in.); Gift of Daniel Morris and Denis Gallion, 1993-134-13; Photo by Dennis Cowley © Smithsonian Institution

0347. Poster, el atomo para la paz (Atoms for Peace), General Dynamics, 1955; Erik Nitsche (Swiss, 1908–98) for General Dynamics Corporation (USA); Offset lithograph on paper; 128.5 x 91.6 cm (50 9/16 x 36 1/16 in.); Gift of Arthur Cohen and Daryl Otte in memory of Bill Moggridge, 2013-42-1; © General Dynamics Corporation

0348. Buffaloware sample plate, 1950s; Manufactured by Oneida (Buffalo, New York, USA); Molded and glazed earthenware; 2.8 x 23 cm diam. (1 1/8 x 9 1/16 in.); Museum purchase from General Acquisitions Endowment, 2005-11-3; Photo by Ellen McDermott © Smithsonian Institution

0349. Sample plate, 1887; A. Lacroix & Cie (France); Porcelain; 2.8 x 23 cm diam. (1 1/8 x 9 1/16 in.); Museum purchase from General Acquisitions Endowment, 2005-11-1; Photo by Ellen McDermott © Smithsonian Institution

0350. Textile, Spectrum, 1950–55; Rolf Middelboe (Danish, 1917–95); Screenprinted cotton sateen; 4.46 m x 128 cm (14 ft. 7 3/8 in. x 50 3/8 in.); Gift of Jack Lenor Larsen Inc., 1960-170-2

0351. Print, Interlace Pattern with White Medallion, before 1521; Albrecht Dürer (German, 1471–1528); Woodcut on off-white laid paper; 27.4 x 21.2 cm (10 13/16 x 8 3/8 in.); Museum purchase through gift of Eleanor and Sarah Hewitt, 1944-37-1-b

0352. Cut paper, Noah's Ark, 1982; Ernst Oppliger (Swiss, b. 1950); Cut black paper; 60.3 cm (23 3/4 in.); This acquisition was made possible through the Louis Comfort Tiffany Foundation, 1985-22-1; © Ernst Oppliger CH

0353. Hanging, Four Seasons, 1964; Luba Krejci (Czech, 1925–2005); Linen bobbin lace; 100.3 cm diam(39 1/2 in.); Gift of Dr. and Mrs. Herbert Paskow, 1982-9-1

0354. Drawing, Perspective Design for a Painted Dome and Cupola of a Church, 1700–25; After Andrea Pozzo (Italian, 1642–1709; active Rome, 1681–1702, Vienna, 1703–09); Pen and black ink, brush and gray wash on off-white laid paper; 43.5 x 43.2 cm (17 1/8 x 17 1/16 in.); Museum purchase through gift of various donors and from Eleanor G. Hewitt Fund, 1938-88-3461; Photo by Ken Pelka © Smithsonian Institution

0355. Skirt, China, 1950–60; Hemp, hand-drawn starch resist, indigo-dyed; 55.9 x 431.8 cm (22 x 170 in.) at lower edge; Museum purchase from General Acquisitions Endowment Fund, 2009-36-3

0356. Tsuba (sword guard), Kyoto, Japan, 1830–43; Iron, gold, nunome zogan (cloth inlay), gold leaf hammered into cross-hatches on surface, material: tetsu, surface: migaki; 7.7 x 7 x 0.4 cm (3 1/16 x 2 3/4 x 3/16 in.); Bequest of George Cameron Stone, 1936-4-1142

0357. Lock, Spain, late 16th– early 17th century; Cast and engraved steel, iron; 1.2 x 24.5 cm diam. (1/2 x 9 5/8 in.); Gift of anonymous donor, 1952-161-134-a/e

0358. Sample plate, France, ca. 1875; Enameled, gilt, and glazed porcelain; 6.1 x 44.5 cm (2 3/8 x 17 1/2 in.); Museum purchase from Decorative Arts Association Acquisition Fund, 1990-152-1

0359. Poster, Sutnar: Visual Design in Action, The American Institute of Graphic Arts, 1961; Ladislav Sutnar (Czech-American, b. Pilsen, Bohemia, 1897, d. New York, New York, USA, 1976); Offset lithograph on heavy, coated white wove paper; 61 x 45.7 cm (24 x 18 in.); Gift of Unknown Donor, 1980-32-1119

0360. Plate, France, ca. 1870; Designed and made by Léon Parvillée (French, 1830–85); Enamel-painted, glazed, and gilt earthenware; 6.8 x 62 cm diam. (2 11/16 x 24 7/16 in.); Museum purchase from Charles E. Sampson Memorial and Decorative Arts Association Acquisition Funds, 1987-79-1; Photo by John Parnell © Smithsonian Institution

0361. Volvelle, *Astronomicum Caesareum* (*The Astronomy of the Caesars*), 1540; Originally written and published by Peter Apian (German, 1495–1552); Facsimile edition by Diedrich Wattenberg; From *Astronomicum Caesareum* (*The Astronomy of the Caesars*), (New York: McGraw-Hill, 1969, c1967); Offset lithography, paper; 45.7 x 32.6 x 5.2 cm (18 x 12 13/16 x 2 1/16 in.); Smithsonian Libraries, Gift from the Margery Masinter Foundation Endowment for Illustrated Books, f QB41. A64 1540ab; Photo: Ellen McDermott © Smithsonian Institution

0362. Plate, USA, ca. 1905; Raised copper with silver overlay; 1.9 x 20.8 cm diam. (3/4 x 8 3/16 in.); Gift of Anonymous Donor, 1967-48-105; Photo by Ellen McDermott © Smithsonian Institution

0363. Argenta ware plate, ca. 1940; Wilhelm Kåge (Swedish, 1889–1960); Manufactured by Gustavsberg Ceramic Factory (Gustavsberg, Sweden); Glazed stoneware inlaid with raised silver; 3.8 x 29.9 cm (1 1/2 x 11 3/4 in.); Museum purchase from General Acquisitions Endowment, 1982-8-1; Photo by Ellen McDermott © Smithsonian Institution

0364. Plate, 1753–58; Made by Chelsea Porcelain Manufactory (London, England); Glazed porcelain with overglaze decoration; 3.9 x 22.7 cm diam. (1 9/16 x 8 15/16 in.); Gift of Irwin Untermyer, 1957-11-12

0365. Ianvarivs (January) plate, Limoges, France, 1565–75; Martial Courteys (French, d. 1592); Grisaille enamel, flesh tones, touches of color, and gold on modeled copper; 1.8 x 18.4 cm diam. (11/16 x 7 1/4 in.); Gift of Mrs. Howard J. Sachs and Mr. Peter G. Sachs in memory of Miss Edith L. Sachs, 1978-168-65; Photo by Ellen McDermott © Smithsonian Institution

0366. Swan Service charger, 1737–41; Modeled by Johann Joachim Kändler (German, 1706–75); Made by Meissen Porcelain Factory (Meissen, Saxony, Germany); Production directed by Count Henrich Graf Brühl (German, 1700–63); Glazed, enameled, gilt, and molded porcelain; 6.6 x 38.2 cm diam. (2 5/8 x 15 1/16 in.); Museum purchase through gift of Commander Henry H. Gorringe, 1950-130-1

0367. Five buttons from a set of ten, France, 1775–80; Cut paper on silk set in copper with glass covers; 3.8 cm diam.(1 1/2 in.); Bequest of Sarah Cooper Hewitt, 1931-6-3-a/j

0368. Fountain, Nevers, France, early 18th century; Lead-glazed earthenware; 37 x 24.5 cm (14 9/16 x 9 5/8 in.); Gift of Mrs. George T. Bliss, 1907-23-1; Photo by Ellen McDermott © Smithsonian Institution

0369. Cooling pail, Rouen, France, ca. 1740; Enameled and lead-glazed sculpted earthenware; 17.7 x 21.7 x 25.3 cm (6 15/16 x 8 9/16 x 9 15/16 in.); Gift of Mrs. George T. Bliss, 1907-23-6; Photo by Ellen McDermott © Smithsonian Institution

0370. Nest Learning thermostat, 2011; Tony Fadell (American, b. 1969) and Matt Rogers (American); Manufactured by Nest Labs, Inc. (Palo Alto, California, USA); Stainless steel, plastic; 3.8 x 8.3 cm diam. (1 1/2 x 3 1/4 in.); Gift of Nest Labs, Inc., 2013-19-1; Photo by Ellen McDermott © Smithsonian Institution; © Nest Labs, Inc.

0371. Big Ben Chime Alarm clock, ca. 1944; Henry Dreyfuss (American, 1904–72); Manufactured by Westclox (La Salle, Illinois, USA); Enameled metal, brass, blued steel (hands), printed paper; 14 x 13 x 7 cm (5 1/2 x 5 1/8 x 2 3/4 in.); Gift of Henry Dreyfuss, 1972-88-185; Photo by Ellen McDermott © Smithsonian Institution

0372. Box and lid with portrait miniature, France, ca. 1770; Horn, watercolor painted on ivory, carved ivory, red fabric backing, gold; 1.4 x 3.2 cm (9/16 x 1 1/4 in.); Bequest of Sarah Cooper Hewitt, 1931-6-75-a,b; Photo by Ellen McDermott © Smithsonian Institution

0373. Box and lid with portrait miniature of a gentleman, England, 1793; Villers (French, active ca. 1781–93); Horn, glass, gold, watercolor painted on ivory, carved ivory, engine-turned foil backing paper, brass, paper; 2.5 x 7.2 cm (1 x 2 13/16 in.); Bequest of Sarah Cooper Hewitt, 1931-6-85-a,b; Photo by Ellen McDermott © Smithsonian Institution

0374. Vase, ca. 1925; Moser Glass Factory (Austria); Etched blown glass; 17.6 x 21 cm diam. (6 15/16 x 8 1/4 in.); Gift of Mrs. John Rolph from the collection of, and in memory of, her sister, Mrs. Evsei Belousoff, 1961-113-2; Photo by Ellen McDermott © Smithsonian Institution

0375. Box, probably Italy, early-mid-18th century; Gold horn box technique; 3.5 x 6.4 cm (1 3/8 x 2 1/2 in.); Bequest of Sarah Cooper Hewitt, 1931-6-4; Photo by Ellen McDermott © Smithsonian Institution

0376. Button, West Indies, late 18th century; Attributed to Agostino Brunias (Italian, ca. 1730–96); Gouache paint verre fixé, ivory (backing), glass, gilt metal; 3.7 x 3.7 x 1 cm (1 7/16 x 1 7/16 x 3/8 in.); Gift of R. Keith Kane from the Estate of Mrs. Robert B. Noyes, 1949-94-9

0377. Vase, Paris, France, ca. 1925; Designed and made by Jean Dunand (French, b. Switzerland, 1877–1942); Raised brass, hand-painted lacquer, applied nickel (rim); 15.3 x 17 cm diam. (6 x 6 11/16 in.); Gift of Linda Lichtenberg Kaplan, 2004-21-1; Photo by Andrew Garn © Smithsonian Institution

0378. Drawing, Design for Woven Silk and Embroidery: Woman Swallowed by Fish and Head of Christ Surrounded by Seraphim (verso), Italy, late 14th century; Pen and brown ink on vellum; 11.6 x 15 cm (4 9/16 x 5 7/8 in.); Museum purchase through gift of various donors and from Friends of Textiles Fund, 1993-119-1

0379. Drawing, Ceiling Design: Iris and the Rainbow, 1810–25; Felice Giani (Italian, 1758–1823); Pen and brown ink, brush and watercolor on off-white laid paper; 33.5 x 30.8 cm (13 3/16 x 12 1/8 in.); Museum purchase through gift of various donors, 1901-39-1807

0380. Drawing, Design for Acratherm Gauge, May 19, 1943; Henry Dreyfuss (American, 1904–72) for Honeywell Inc. (Minneapolis, Minnesota, USA); Rendered by Roland Stickney (American, 1892–1975); Brush and gouache, graphite, pen and black ink on illustration board; 27.9 x 21.6 cm (11 x 8 1/2 in.); Gift of Honeywell, Inc., 1997-10-6

0381. T-86 Round thermostat, 1953; Henry Dreyfuss (American, 1904–72); Manufactured by Honeywell, Inc. (Minneapolis, Minnesota, USA); Metal and molded plastic; 4.5 x 8 cm diam. (1 3/4 x 3 1/8 in.); Gift of Honeywell, Inc., 1994-37-1

0382. Drawing, Design for Chronotherm, June 28, 1938; Henry Dreyfuss (American, 1904–72) for Honeywell, Inc. (Minneapolis, Minnesota, USA); Rendered by Roland Stickney (American, 1892–1975); Brush and gouache, pen and black ink, graphite on illustration board; 22.6 x 29.1 cm (8 7/8 x 11 7/16 in.); Gift of Honeywell, Inc., 1997-10-3

0383. Print, Honeywell Advertisement from *Life* magazine for the T-86 "Honeywell Round" Thermostat, November 9, 1953; Henry Dreyfuss (American, 1904–72) and Carl Kronmiller (American, 1889–1968); Manufactured by the Minneapolis-Honeywell Regulator Co. (Minneapolis, Minnesota, USA); Offset lithography, paper; Purchase Smithsonian Libraries

0384. Beadwork picture, France, early 19th century; Cotton embroidered with glass and ceramic beads; 17.5 x 12 cm (6 7/8 x 4 3/4 in.); Gift of Mrs. Harley Lord Stowell, 1944-57-3

0385. Drawing, Textile Design: No. 8359, January 24, 1918; Robert M. Davidson for Orinoka Mills (Philadelphia, Pennsylvania, USA); Published by F. Jones & Co. (USA); Brush and gouache, graphite on pre-printed graph paper; 45.3 x 58.2 cm (17 13/16 x 22 15/16 in.); Gift of Orinoka Mills, 1971-57-1-a

0386. Drawing, Textile Design: No. 8672, May 24, 1924; M. K. Ayling (American) for Orinoka Mills (Philadelphia, Pennsylvania, USA); Published by F. Jones & Co. (USA); Brush and gouache, graphite on pre-printed graph paper; 58.2 x 45.6 cm (22 15/16 x 17 15/16 in.); Gift of Orinoka Mills, 1971-57-2-c

0387. Drawing, Textile Design: Floral Motif, France, 19th century; Brush and gouache, graphite on blue paper; 25.9 x 25.8 cm (10 3/16 x 10 3/16 in.); Gift of Harvey Smith, 1968-107-51

0388. Textile, 1920–30; Josef Frank (Austrian, active Sweden, 1885–1967), probably Wiener Werkstätte (Vienna, Austria); Printed linen; 57.2 x 56.5 cm (22 1/2 x 22 1/4 in.), repeat: 20 cm (7 7/8 in.); Gift of Edward J. Wormley, 1963-36-1; © Svenskt Tenn AB

0389. Drawing, Textile Design: Floral Motif, France, 19th century; Brush and gouache on blue paper; 34.3 x 40.7 cm (13 1/2 in. x 16 in.); Gift of Harvey Smith, 1968-107-79

0390. Sidewall, Field Flowers, 1952; Winifred Mury; Made by Piazza Prints, Inc. (New York, New York, USA); Screenprinted on paper; 95 x 76 cm (37 3/8 x 29 15/16 in.); Gift of B. H. Hellman, 1953-84-3; © F. Schumacher & Co., all rights reserved

0391. Sidewall, France, 1840–70; Block printed on handmade paper; 87 x 49.5 cm (34 1/4 x 19 1/2 in.); Gift of Josephine Howell, 1972-42-202-a

0392. Sidewall, Paris, France, 1788; Jean-Baptiste Réveillon (French, 1725–1811); Block printed, hand painted, and gilded on handmade paper; 10.87 m x 60 cm (35 ft. 8 in. x 23 5/8 in.); Museum purchase from General Acquisitions Endowment Fund, 1985-26-1

0393. Ornament—panel, Paris, France, 1856–57; Jules Desfossé; Block printed on machine-made paper; 182 x 69 cm (71 5/8 x 27 3/16 in.); Gift of Alan Moss, 1992-156-18

0394. Scenic panel, Le Jardin d'Armide (The Garden of Armida), 1854; Edouard Muller (French); Manufactured by Desfossé et Karth (Paris, France); Block printed on paper; 3.81 m x 130.2 cm (12 ft. 6 in. x 51 1/4 in.); Gift of Arthur V. Stanley, 1953-158-4

0395. Sidewall, France, ca. 1875; Machine printed on embossed paper; 5.29 m x 50 cm (17 ft. 4 1/4 in. x 19 11/16 in.); Museum purchase from Sarah Cooper-Hewitt Fund, 2000-31-11

0396. Sidewall, Le Printemps from Les Quatre Saisons, ca. 1785; Jean-Baptiste Réveillon (French, 1725–1811); Block printed on handmade paper; 247.5 x 53.7 cm (97 7/16 x 21 1/8 in.); Museum purchase from the Smithsonian Institution Collections Acquisition Program, General Acquisitions Endowment, Eleanor G. Hewitt, and Pauline Cooper Noyes Funds, 1994-101-12-a

0397. Drawing, Hôtel de Salm, Paris, France: Panel of Arabesques, 1785; Jean-Guillaume Moitte (French, 1746–1810); Pen and black ink, brush and gouache, black chalk on toned paper, lined; 43 x 10.1 cm (16 15/16 x 4 in.); Purchased for the Museum by the Advisory Council, 1911-28-219

0398. Ornament, Decor Pastoral, 1851–64; Jules Desfossé (French); Block printed on paper; 245.1 x 69.9 cm (96.5 x 27.5 in.; Museum purchase from Friends of the Museum Fund, 1955-12-2

0399. Drawing, Design for a Bowl with Enamel Cover, 1950–70; Tommi Parzinger (American, b. Germany, 1903–81); Brush and gouache, graphite on tracing paper, lined; 18 x 21.3 cm (7 1/16 x 8 3/8 in.); Gift of Donald Cameron, 1998-19-113; © Parzinger Originals

0400. Sidewall, France, ca. 1800; Block printed on handmade paper; 59 x 48 cm (23 1/4 x 18 7/8 in.); Gift of Harvey Smith, 1968-111-11

0401. Sidewall fragment, France, 1855–70; Block printed on paper; 51.5 x 42 cm (20 1/4 x 16 9/16 in.); Gift of Dr. Francis J. Geck, 1980-73-4

0402. Sidewall, Daphnis, ca. 1921; Dagobert Peche (Austrian, 1887–1923, active Vienna 1911–23); Machine printed on paper; 35.5 x 55.5 cm (14 x 21 7/8 in.); Gift of Teresa Kilham, 1958-80-1

0403. Sidewall, Daphnis, ca. 1921; Dagobert Peche (Austrian, 1887–1923, active Vienna 1911–23); Machine printed on paper; 35.5 x 55.5 cm (14 x 21 7/8 in.); Gift of Frankl Galleries, 1958-80-1

0404. Pair of doors with handles, Paris, France, 1925–26; Designed by Seraphin Soudbinine (French, b. Russia, 1870–1944); Executed by Jean Dunand (French, b. Switzerland, 1877–1942); Carved, joined, and lacquered wood, eggshell, mother-of-pearl, gold leaf, cast bronze; 271.2 x 65.9 x 30 cm (8 ft. 10 3/4 in. x 25 15/16 in. x 11 13/16 in.); Gift of Mrs. Solomon R. Guggenheim, 1950-104-1-a,b,-2-a,b

0405. Book illustration, Photograph of the Court of Pacifica at night, Golden Gate International Exposition, 1939–40; Gabriel Moulin (American, 1872–1945); From *Magic in the Night: Official Souvenir, Golden Gate International Exposition* (San Francisco: Crocker Company, 1940); Photomechanical processes on paper; 23 x 31 cm (9 1/16 x 12 3/8 in.); Gift of Bernard Rosenfeld 2010, Smithsonian Libraries, F869.S37M34 1939

0406. Window shade, New York Crystal Palace, USA, 1853; Machine printed on continuous paper; 153 x 90 cm (60 1/4 x 35 7/16 in.); Museum purchase through gift of Eleanor and Sarah Hewitt, 1944-66-1

0407. Oil sketch, Niagara from Goat Island, Winter, March 1856; Frederic Edwin Church (American, 1826–1900); Brush and oil paint, graphite on paperboard; 29.3 x 44 cm (11 9/16 x 17 5/16 in.); Gift of Louis P. Church, 1917-4-765-a; Photo by Scott Hyde © Smithsonian Institution

0408. Drawing, Fisherman in Quebec, 1895; Winslow Homer (American, 1836–1910); Brush and black, gray wash, white gouache, charcoal on gray-green wove paper; 30.5 x 50.6 cm (12 x 19 15/16 in.); Gift of Charles Savage Homer, Jr., 1912-12-89

0409. Frieze, Hoboken, New Jersey, USA, ca. 1900; Hobbs, Benton & Heath; Machine printed on paper; 121 x 51 cm (47 5/8 x 20 1/16 in.); Gift of Paul F. Franco, 1938-50-16

0410. Indian Encampment vase,1909; Decorated by Edward Timothy Hurley (American, 1869–1950); Manufactured by Rookwood Pottery (Cincinnati, Ohio, USA); Glazed stoneware; 34.7 x 16.5 cm diam. (13 11/16 x 6 1/2 in.); Gift of Marcia and William Goodman, 1984-84-1; Photo © Smithsonian Institution

0411. Drawing, Floral Design for a Printed Project, France, 1820–40; Pen and ink, brush and watercolor on paper; 11.2 x 8.5 cm (4 7/16 x 3 3/8 in.); Purchased for the Museum by the Advisory Council, 1924-38-167

0412. Collar, China, 19th century; Silk embroidered with silk; 41.9 x 38.1 cm (16 1/2 x 15 in.); Bequest of Marian Hague, 1971-50-150

0413. Drawing, Brighton Pavilion, Brighton, England: Design for the West Wall of Music Room, ca. 1817; Frederick Crace (British, 1779–1859); Brush and watercolor, gouache over graphite traces on white wove paper; 33.6 x 51.1 cm (13 1/4 x 20 1/8 in.); Museum purchase through gift of Mrs. John Innes Kane, 1948-40-9-a,b

0414. Poster, Aeron Chair, 2012; Kam Tang (British, b. Hong Kong, 1971) for Herman Miller Furniture Company (Zeeland, Michigan, USA); Inkjet print on paper; 175.3 x 121 cm (5 ft. 9 in. x 47 5/8 in.); Gift of Herman Miller, 7448.1.2014

0415. Book illustration, Ostrich feather samples, 1888; Alexander Paul (American); From Alexander Paul, *The Practical Ostrich Feather Dyer*, revised and corrected by Dr. M. Frank (Philadelphia: Mrs. Dr. M. Frank), p. 64a; Dyed feather samples on paper; 17 x 14 cm (6 5/8 x 5 1/2 in.); Purchased by the Mary Stuart Book Fund, 1954, Smithsonian Libraries, TP908.P32X 1888

0416. Scarf, San Francisco, California, USA, 1975; Alan Grinberg (American, b. 1949); Screenprinted and airbrush-painted silk; 84 x 81 cm (33 1/16 x 31 7/8 in.); Gift of Mrs. Richard Lederer, Jr., 1983-74-1; © Alan Grinberg

0417. Drawing, Textile Design: Purpurnelke (Purple Carnation): Red with Teal and Brown, 1924; Felice Rix-Ueno (Austrian, 1893–1967) for Wiener Werkstätte (Vienna, Austria); Brush and gouache, graphite on paper; 35.1 x 29.8 cm (13 13/16 x 11 3/4 in.); Museum purchase from Smithsonian Collections Acquisition and Decorative Arts Association Acquisition Funds, 1988-62-893; Photo by Ken Pelka © Smithsonian Institution; © The National Museum of Modern Art, Kyoto

0418. Paper construction, Pyramid, 2010; Tauba Auerbach (American, b. 1981); From *[2,3]*, (New York: Tauba Auerbach and Printed Matter, Inc.); Cut paper; 51 x 82 x 40 cm (20 1/8 x 32 1/4 x 15 1/2 in.); Purchase, 2011, Smithsonian Libraries, fN7433.4.A94 B73 2010X; Photo by Ellen McDermott © Smithsonian Institution

0419. Pair of gates from the Chanin Building, New York, New York, USA, 1928; René Paul Chambellan (American, 1893–1955); Wrought iron, bronze; 1: 189.2 x 114.3 x 11.4 cm (74 1/2 x 45 x 4 1/2 in.), 2: 189.2 x 114.3 x 11.4 cm (74 1/2 x 45 x 4 1/2 in.); Gift of Marcy Chanin, 1993-135-1, 2; Photo by Dennis Cowley © Smithsonian Institution

0420. Brooch, England or France, 1750–1800; Rose-cut diamonds, cut silver, gold wire; 5.1 x 7.4 x 1.2 cm (2 x 2 15/16 x 1/2 in.); Gift of Gertrude Sampson, 1962-26-1; Photo by Dennis Cowley © Smithsonian Institution

0421. Fan, USA, ca. 1905; Carved and incised mahogany sticks, printed silk gauze leaf; 24.5 x 38.1 cm (9 5/8 x 15 in.); Gift of Mrs. John Innes Kane, 1920-19-39

0422. Brisé fan, China, 1710–20; Pierced and painted ivory blades with leather ribbon, tortoise thumb guard, and glass rivet; 19 x 30.5 cm (7 1/2 x 12 in.); Bequest of Miss Elizabeth d'Hauteville Kean, 1923-24-3

0423. Folding fan, England or France, 1800–10; Carved and pierced ivory sticks, painted paper leaf with parchment backing; 33.6 x 17.8 cm (13 1/4 x 7 in.); Gift of Anonymous Donor, 1952-161-240

0424. Folding fan, USA, 1890–1910; Painted paper leaf, gilt metal sticks and guards with applied enamel plaques and cut marcasites; 3 x 38.5 cm (8 x 15 1/8 in.); Gift of Anonymous Donor, 1952-161-227-a,b

0425. Fan, possibly France, 1830–50; Carved and drilled bone sticks with applied metal spangles, pricked paper blades, guards inlaid with turquoise and mother-of-pearl; 24 x 45 cm (9 7/16 x 17 11/16 in.); Bequest of Miss Elizabeth d'Hauteville Kean, 1923-24-7

0426. Fan, France, 1885–90; Alouise van de Voorde (Paris, France); Pierced and carved ivory sticks, cotton bobbin lace leaf backed with silk; 28 x 54 cm (11 x 21 1/4 in.); Gift of Mrs. Robert B. Noyes, 1942-34-9-a

0427. Drawing, Floral Design, France, late 19th century; Brush and gouache on cream paper, mounted on cream paper; 40 x 25.3 cm (15 3/4 x 9 15/16 in.); Gift of Friends of Drawings and Prints with special assistance from Theodore E. Stebbins, Jr. and Phyllis Dearborn Massar, 1975-73-1-10

0428. Fan, Austria or Germany, early 20th century; Carved and painted wood sticks, painted silk ribbon, mother-of-pearl rivet; 23.5 x 40.6 cm (9 1/4 x 16 in.); Gift of Mrs. Max Farrand, 1953-143-21

0429. Peacock vase, ca. 1901; Louis Comfort Tiffany (American, 1848–1933); Produced by Tiffany Studios (Corona, New York, USA); Mold-blown and iridized glass; 33.7 x 25 x 14 cm (13 1/4 x 9 13/16 x 5 1/2 in.); Gift of Stanley Siegel, from the Stanley Siegel Collection, 1975-32-11; Photo by Dave King © Smithsonian Institution

0430. Vase, 1883–88; Manufactured by New England Glass Company (East Cambridge, Massachusetts, USA); Blown amberina glass; 39.5 x 15 cm diam. (15 9/16 x 5 7/8 in.); Gift of Paul F. Walter, 2010-6-3

0431. Drawing, Designs for Colored Glass Vases, Bohemia, Czechoslovakia, ca. 1850; Brush and rose and green watercolor, gold paint, graphite on white wove paper; 40.7 x 31 cm (16 x 12 3/16 in.); Gift of Virginia Hamill, 1953-82-2

0432. Vase, Nancy, France, late 19th–early 20th century; Émile Gallé (French, 1846–1904); Blown, cased, acid-etched glass; 41.7 x 13.3 cm diam. (16 7/16 x 5 1/4 in.); Gift of the Estate of Max Kobre, 1996-45-17; Photo by Ellen McDermott © Smithsonian Institution

0433. Decanter and stopper, Model 5929S, 1959; Wayne Husted (American, b. 1927); Manufactured by Blenko Glass Company (Milton, West Virginia, USA, 1921–2012); Blown glass; 56.4 x 18.4 cm diam. (21 1/2 x 7 1/4 in.); Gift of William Agle, 2013-26-1-a,b;
Photo by Ellen McDermott © Smithsonian Institution

0434. Bud vase, France, ca. 1900; Émile Gallé (French, 1846–1904); Mold-blown and carved glass; 31.5 x 11 cm diam. (12 3/8 x 4 5/16 in.); Gift of Jacqueline Rea in memory of Dr. Robert Roux-Delimal, 1974-105-1; Photo by Ellen McDermott © Smithsonian Institution

0435. Solifleur, Clutha series vase, ca. 1890; Christopher Dresser (British, 1834–1904); Manufactured by James Couper & Sons (Glasgow, Scotland); Mold-blown glass; 48.3 x 10.2 cm diam. (19 x 4 in.); Museum purchase from General Acquisitions Endowment Fund, 2012-7-1; Photo by Ellen McDermott © Smithsonian Institution

0436. Vase, ca. 1900; Louis Comfort Tiffany (American, 1848–1933); Manufactured by Tiffany Studios (Corona, New York, USA); Mold-blown favrile glass; 31.2 x 10.8 cm (12 5/16 x 4 1/4 in.); Bequest of Joseph L. Morris, 1966-55-35; Photo by Ellen McDermott © Smithsonian Institution

0437. Scent bottle, England, ca. 1750; Agate, gold; Overall 7.5 x 3 x 1.5 cm (2 15/16 x 1 3/16 x 9/16 in.); Gift of the Panwy Foundation, from the collection of Maria Wyman, 1994-129-1

0438. Vase, Delft, Netherlands, 1875–1900; Tin-glazed and painted earthenware; 25 x 13 x 13 cm (9 13/16 x 5 1/8 x 5 1/8 in.); Bequest of Walter Phelps Warren, 1986-61-40; Photo by Ellen McDermott © Smithsonian Institution

0439. Vase, probably for S. A. Weller Theater, ca. 1902; Decorated by Jacques Sicard (French, 1865–1923); Made by Weller Pottery (Zanesville, Ohio, USA); Glazed earthenware; 63.8 x 35.6 cm diam. (25 1/8 x 14 in.); Gift of Marcia and William Goodman, 1984-84-25; Photo © Smithsonian Institution

0440. Jeux de Fonds—Astronomie vase, 1951; Rabaey (French, active mid-20th century); Modeled by Maurice Gensoli (French, active ca. 1921–57); Decorated by Andrée Kiefer (French, active mid-20th century); Made by Sèvres Porcelain Manufactory (Sèvres, France); Glazed and gilded porcelain; 40.5 x 17 cm diam. (15 15/16 x 6 11/16 in.); Museum purchase from Charles E. Sampson Memorial Fund, 2000-32-1; Photo by Ellen McDermott © Smithsonian Institution

0441. Lotus-shaped cup, Egypt, ca. 1100 BC; Colored faience (ceramic frit); 8 x 5 cm diam. (3 1/8 x 1 15/16 in.); Museum purchase through gift of Eleanor and Sarah Hewitt, 1960-29-1; Photo © Smithsonian Institution

0442. Vase, Switzerland, 18th century; Handblown and tooled glass; 15.3 x 6 cm diam. (6 x 2 3/8 in.); Gift of the C. Helme and Alice B. Strater Collection, 1976-1-72; Photo by Ellen McDermott © Smithsonian Institution

0443. Border, England, 1800–20; Block printed and flocked on handmade paper; 18.7 x 82.3 cm (7 3/8 x 32 3/8 in.); Gift of Cowtan and Sons, Ltd., 1907-5-27

0444. Cravat end, Italy, mid–late 16th century; Linen needle lace; 29.2 x 162 cm (11 1/2 x 63 3/4 in.); Gift of Frances Morris, 1951-111-72-a

0445. Ewer, Shape No. 469, 1894; Pitts Harrison Burt (American, 1837–1906); Decorated by Matthew Andrew Daly (American, 1860–1937); Made by Rookwood Pottery (Cincinnati, Ohio, USA) (ewer); Gorham Manufacturing Company (Providence, Rhode Island, USA) (silver); Glazed thrown earthenware, enamel-painted and fired decoration, pierced and engraved silver overlay; 54.6 x 21.3 cm diam. (21 1/2 x 8 3/8 in.); Gift of Marcia and William Goodman, 1984-84-9

0446. Drawing, Design for a Crystal Urn with Silver Mounts, ca. 1827–35; Joseph Anton Seethaler II (German, 1799–1868); Pen and black ink, brush and wash, green watercolor on paper; 47.3 x 37.5 cm (18 5/8 x 14 3/4 in.); Purchased for the Museum by the Advisory Council, 1911-28-330

0447. Water pitcher, 1913–14; Karl Massanetz (Czech, 1890–1918); Manufactured by J. & L. Lobmeyr GmbH (Vienna, Austria) at Karlsbader Kristallglasfabriken A. G (Klostermühle, Bohemia); Mouth-blown colorless glass, black ink feather-pen drawing with gilding; 24.7 x 15.5 cm diam. (9 3/4 x 6 1/8 in.), 24.7 x 15.5 x 9 cm (9 3/4 x 6 1/8 x 3 9/16 in.); Museum purchase through gift of Dale and Doug Anderson, Anonymous Donor, Arthur Liu, and Prairie Pictures, Inc and from General Acquisitions Endowment Fund, 2009-18-86; Photo by Andrew Garn © Smithsonian Institution

0448. Tall Green Bloom urn, England, 2012; Michael Eden (British, b. 1955); 3D printed nylon; 41 x 18 cm (16 1/8 x 7 1/16 in.); Museum purchase through gift of Elizabeth and Lee Ainslie and from General Acquisitions Endowment Fund, 2013-53-1; Photo by Ellen McDermott © Smithsonian Institution

0449. Pitcher, Klostermühle, Bohemia, Austro-Hungarian Empire, ca. 1905; Johann Lötz Witwe; Mold-blown glass; 17.1 x 22.9 cm (6 3/4 x 9 in.); Gift of Elizabeth Ainslie, 2012-25-1; Photo by Ellen McDermott © Smithsonian Institution

0450. Flask, Netherlands, mid-18th century; Blown glass; 14.7 x 6.5 x 10.6 cm (5 13/16 x 2 9/16 x 4 3/16 in.); Anonymous Gift, 1947-69-4; Photo by Ellen McDermott © Smithsonian Institution

0451. Purse, USA, 1830–60; Knitted silk with metal beads; 10.2 x 5.1 cm (4 x 2 in.); Gift of Eleanor and Sarah Hewitt, 1925-2-343

0452. Ewer, possibly Ireland, ca. 1810; Cut blown glass; 29.2 x 18.5 x 12.5 cm (11 1/2 x 7 5/16 x 4 15/16 in.); Bequest of Walter Phelps Warren, 1986-61-144; Photo by Ellen McDermott © Smithsonian Institution

0453. Flagon, Philadelphia, Pennsylvania, USA, 1860–80; Peter L. Krider (American, 1821–95); Spun and engraved silver; 33.7 x 15.2 cm diam. (13 1/4 x 6 in.); Gift of Brian Tolle and Brian Clyne, 2013-28-1; Photo by Ellen McDermott © Smithsonian Institution

0454. Standing cup and cover, Nuremberg, Germany, ca. 1650; Georg Kraudi (German, active 1643–76); Parcel-gilt repoussé and chased raised silver; 24.5 x 7.5 cm diam. (9 5/8 x 2 15/16 in.); Museum purchase through gift of Annie I. Kane, 1959-15-1-a,b; Photo by Ellen McDermott © Smithsonian Institution

0455. Ewer, Iran, 17th–18th century; Blown glass, applied glass decoration; 17.9 x 15.5 x 8.8 cm (7 1/16 x 6 1/8 x 3 7/16 in.); Gift of Rodman Wanamaker, 1919-24-86; Photo by Ellen McDermott © Smithsonian Institution

0456. Drawing, Design for Majolica Pitcher, Italian, 18th century; Black chalk, pen and black-brown ink, brush and sepia, blue wash on paper; 18.9 x 11.7 cm (7 7/16 x 4 5/8 in.); Museum purchase through gift of various donors, 1901-39-908

0457. Vintage jug, London, England, 1854–55; Joseph Angell III (ca. 1816–ca. 1891); Raised, cast, and applied gilt silver; 31.5 x 12.5 x 12.5 cm (12 3/8 x 4 15/16 x 4 15/16 in.); Gift of Louise B. Scott, 1936-21-1

0458. Pomander and case, Dijon, France, 1682–83; Cast, chased, engraved, and raised silver, gilt silver; sharkskin, wood, silver (case); 6.8 x 4 cm diam. (2 11/16 x 1 9/16 in.); Bequest of Joan W. Leidesdorf, 1997-62-23; Photo by Ellen McDermott © Smithsonian Institution

0459. Painting, Lady Frances Sidney of Sussex, ca. 1570–75; By permission of the Master and Fellows of Sidney Sussex College, Cambridge

0460. Drawing, Design for a Sauce Boat, 1827–35; Joseph Anton Seethaler II (German, 1799–1868); Graphite, pen and black ink, brush and wash on paper; 26.9 x 32.1 cm (10 9/16 x 12 5/8 in.); Purchased for the Museum by the Advisory Council, 1911-28-342

0461. Drawing, Design for a Boat-Shaped Vessel, Possibly for a Festival Float, 1524–46; Giulio Romano (Italian, 1499–1546); Pen and brown ink, brush and brown wash, black chalk on off-white laid paper; 35.2 x 30.1 cm (13 7/8 x 11 7/8 in.); Purchased for the Museum by the Advisory Council, 1911-28-169

0462. Cake basket, London, England, 1758; Thomas Heming (English, active 1745–73); Raised, cast, and pierced silver; 26.3 x 28 x 33 cm (10 3/8 x 11 x 13 in.); Gift of Mrs. J. A. Q. Franks, 1977-62-6; Photo by Ellen McDermott © Smithsonian Institution

0463. Cream pitcher, France, 19th century; Raised and stamped gilt silver, carved wood (handle); 15.6 x 12 x 6.9 cm (6 1/8 x 4 3/4 x 2 11/16 in.), Gift of Arthur Ross, 1980-76-3; Photo by Ellen McDermott © Smithsonian Institution

0464. Ewer, 1686–1701; Made by Adriaen Kocx (Greek, d. 1701), for Griekschе A [de] (the Greek A factory) (Delft, Netherlands); Tin-glazed earthenware; 23 x 25.4 x 13.8 cm (9 1/16 x 10 x 5 7/16 in.); Bequest of Walter Phelps Warren, 1986-61-53; Photo by John Parnell © Smithsonian Institution

0465. American Modern pitcher, 1937; Russel Wright (American, 1904–76); Manufactured by Steubenville Pottery Company (Steubenville, Ohio, USA); Glazed, molded earthenware; 26 x 19 x 16 cm (10 1/4 x 7 1/2 x 6 5/16 in.); Gift of Paul F. Walter, 1991-30-39; Photo by Ellen McDermott © Smithsonian Institution; © Russel Wright is a registered trademark by Russel Wright Studios, LLC

0466. Jug, 1880–82; Christopher Dresser (British, 1834–1904); Manufactured by Linthorpe Pottery (Yorkshire, England); Glazed earthenware; 21.5 x 12 x 13.4 cm (8 7/16 x 4 3/4 x 5 1/4 in.); Gift of David Schafer, 1986-42-2; Photo by Scott Hyde © Smithsonian Institution

0467. Teapot and lid, Czechoslovakia, ca. 1932; Ladislav Sutnar (Czech-American, b. Pilsen, Bohemia, 1897, d. New York, New York, USA, 1976); Manufactured by EPIAG (Loket, Czechoslovakia) for Družstevní práce; Glazed, molded porcelain; 15.2 x 22.9 x 15.2 cm (6 x 9 x 6 in.); Museum purchase through gift of Estate of Ladislav Sutnar, 2011-10-1-a,b

0468. Teapot and lid, Berlin, Germany, ca. 1770; Berlin Porcelain Factory (Berlin, Prussia); Glazed and gilt porcelain with overglaze decoration; a, b: 10.6 x 18 x 10.4 cm (4 3/16 x 7 1/16 x 4 1/8 in.); Bequest of Erskine Hewitt, 1938-57-651-a,b; Photo by Ellen McDermott © Smithsonian Institution

0469. Chocolate pot and lid, mid-18th century; Meissen Porcelain Factory (Meissen, Saxony, Germany); Enameled and glazed porcelain; 24 x 16.2 cm (9 7/16 x 6 3/8 in.), a: 18.4 x 12.5 x 16.2 cm (7 1/4 x 4 15/16 x 6 3/8 in.), b: 5.7 x 12.5 x 7.1 cm (2 1/4 x 4 15/16 x 2 13/16 in.); Gift of Mrs. Edward Luckemeyer, 1912-13-1-a, b

0470. Chocolate pot and lid, Meissen, Saxony, Germany, ca. 1735; Gilt and glazed porcelain; 19.8 x 11.4 x 3.1 cm (7 13/16 x 4 1/2 x 1 1/4 in.); Bequest of Erskine Hewitt, 1938-57-633; Photo by Ellen McDermott © Smithsonian Institution

0471. Chrysanthemum Teapot, 1891–1902; Tiffany and Co. (New York, New York, USA); Raised, cast, chased, and engraved silver; 16 x 27.8 x 17 cm (6 5/16 x 10 15/16 x 6 11/16 in.); Gift of Mrs. Roswell Miller, 1978-6-3; Photo by Ellen McDermott © Smithsonian Institution

0472. Teapot, Baltimore, Maryland, USA, ca. 1845; Samuel Kirk (American, 1793–1872); Raised, repoussé, chased, and cast silver, ivory; 21.5 x 28 x 16.3 cm (8 7/16 x 11 x 6 7/16 in.); Gift of Allyn Cox, 1976-109-1-a

0473. Book illustration, Specimens of Silver, Engraved, Oxidized and Gold Inlaid Ware, 1884; The firm of Reed & Barton, illustrations by John A. J. (Angel James Wilcox, b. 1835); From *Reed & Barton, Artistic Workers in Silver & Gold Plate* (Taunton, Massachusetts: Reed & Barton, 1884), p. 7; Color lithograph on paper; Gift of Reed & Barton, ca. 1990, Smithsonian Libraries, f 046780

0474. Teapot and lid, ca. 1925; Franz von Zülow (Austrian, 1883–1963); Manufactured by Wiener Porzellan Manufaktur (Augarten, Vienna, Austria); Glazed and gilt molded porcelain; Overall, a, b: 21 x 19 x 13.5 cm (8 1/4 x 7 1/2 x 5 5/16 in.); Gift of the Estate of Edgar Sachs, from the Collection of Hilda G. and Edgar Sachs, 2008-42-1-a,b; Photo by Ellen McDermott © Smithsonian Institution

0475. Catalog illustration, Specimens of Silver, Engraved, Oxidized and Gold Inlaid Ware, 1884; The firm of Reed & Barton, illustrations by John A. J. (Angel James Wilcox, b. 1835); From *Reed & Barton, Artistic Workers in Silver & Gold Plate* (Taunton, Massachusetts: Reed & Barton, 1884), p. 292; Color lithograph on paper; Gift of Reed & Barton, ca. 1990, Smithsonian Libraries, f 046780

0476. Kayserzinn tureen, 1902–04; Hugo Leven (German, 1874–1956); Manufactured by J. P. Kayser & Sohn (Krefeld, Germany); Cast pewter; H x W x D: 33 x 29.2 x 32.4 cm (13 x 11 1/2 x 12 3/4 in.); Gift of Gerald G. Stiebel and Penelope Hunter-Stiebel, 2013-49-3-a/c; Photo by Ellen McDermott © Smithsonian Institution

0477. Bowl, Roman Syria, 1st century; Blown and tooled glass; 7.3 x 11.9 cm diam. (2 7/8 x 4 11/16 in.); Gift of Mrs. Leo Wallerstein, 1961-88-9; Photo © Smithsonian Institution

0478. Kilta sugar bowl and lid, 1952; Kaj Franck (Finnish, 1911–89); Manufactured by Arabia (Helsinki, Finland); Glazed, molded earthenware; 8.3 x 9.5 cm diam. (3 1/4 x 3 3/4 in.); Gift of Harry Blomster, 1985-55-8-a,b; Photo by Ellen McDermott © Smithsonian Institution

0479. Fruit basket and cover, 1890–1910; Manufactured by Belleek (Northern Ireland); Iridized, glazed, hand-rolled, cut, and assembled porcelain; 17.1 x 31.1 x 22.5 cm (6 3/4 x 12 1/4 x 8 7/8 in.); Gift of Suzanne W. Todd in Memory of William & Beatrice Votaw, 2011-37-1-a,b; Photo by Ellen McDermott © Smithsonian Institution

0480. Mamluk cap, Egypt, late 13th or early 14th century; Quilted and embroidered silk with gilded parchment; 11.4 x 15.2 cm (4 1/2 x 6 in.); Museum purchase through gift of Anonymous Donor, 1949-64-7

0481. Jazz punch bowl, 1931; Viktor Schreckengost (American, 1906–2008); Made by Cowan Pottery Studio (Rocky River, Ohio, USA); Glazed, molded earthenware; 29.9 x 42.2 cm diam. (11 3/4 x 16 5/8 in.), foot: 17.5 cm diam. (6 7/8 in.); Gift of Mrs. Homer Kripke, 1980-21-7; Photo by Dave King © Smithsonian Institution

0482. Cap, England, 17th century; Linen, embroidered in silk, needle lace trim; 23.5 x 17.8 cm (9 1/4 x 7 in.); Bequest of Marian Hague, 1971-50-115

0483. Cache-pot, Pont-aux-Choux or Creil, France, ca. 1765; Tin-glazed molded earthenware; 13 x 17.7 cm (5 1/8 x 6 15/16 in.); Gift of Catharine Oglesby, 1958-119-10; Photo by Ellen McDermott © Smithsonian Institution

0484. Skygarden hanging lamp, 2011; Marcel Wanders (Dutch, b. 1963); Manufactured by Flos (Brescia, Italy); Aluminum, plaster, halogen light source; 45 x 90 cm diam. (17 11/16 x 35 7/16 in.); Museum purchase from General Acquisitions Endowment Fund, 2011-27-1; Photo by Ellen McDermott © Smithsonian Institution

0485. Kylix, Attica, Greece, 6th century BC; Attributed to the Heidelberg Painter; Black-figured earthenware; 13.6 x 32.5 x 26 cm (5 3/8 x 12 13/16 x 10 1/4 in.); Gift of Anonymous Donor, 1921-1-1; Photo by Dennis Cowley © Smithsonian Institution

0486. Skyphos (drinking cup), Etruria (present-day Italy), 6th century BC; Terracotta; 14 x 16.8 x 25.1 cm (5 1/2 x 6 5/8 x 9 7/8 in.); Gift of Charles W. Gould, 1915-11-31; Photo by Eric Baum © Smithsonian Institution

0487. Ecuelle and cover, 1872–88; Manufactured by Charles Thieme Saxonian Porcelain Company (Potschappel, Saxony, Germany); Enamel-painted and glazed, molded and hand-carved hard-paste porcelain; 10.2 x 16 cm diam. (4 x 6 5/16 in.); Gift of Wendy Vanderbilt Lehman, 1992-5-10-a,b; Photo by Ellen McDermott © Smithsonian Institution

0488. Scholten family tureen, lid, and stand, China for the Dutch market, ca. 1775–95; Glazed porcelain; a, b: tureen and cover, 18.6 x 36 x 18.3 cm (7 5/16 x 14 3/16 x 7 3/16 in.), c: stand, 3.2 x 36.3 x 21.2 cm (1 1/4 x 14 5/16 x 8 3/8 in.); Bequest of Erskine Hewitt, 1938-57-354-a/c

0489. Pot and lid, USA, 1930–40; Russel Wright (American, 1904–76); Spun aluminum, wood; 13 x 27 x 24 cm (5 1/8 x 10 5/8 x 9 7/16 in.); Gift of Paul F. Walter, 1991-30-1-a,b; Photo by Ellen McDermott © Smithsonian Institution; © Russel Wright is a registered trademark by Russel Wright Studios, LLC

0490. Madame de Pompadour (née Poisson) covered tureen and stand, 1990; Cindy Sherman (American, b. 1954); Produced by Artes Magnus; Manufactured by Ancienne Manufacture Royale de Limoges (Limoges, France); Glazed, molded porcelain with photo-transfer (silkscreen) and painted-platinum decoration; a,c: 30 x 56.1 x 37 cm (11 13/16 x 22 1/16 x 14 9/16 in.); Museum purchase from Charles E. Sampson Memorial Fund, 2003-4-1-a/c; © Artes Magnus

0491. Monte Santo bowl, 1924–25; Gio Ponti (Italian, 1891–1979); Manufactured by Richard-Ginori (Doccia, Italy, founded as Ginori); Glazed, slip-cast porcelain; 10.9 x 21.3 cm diam. (4 5/16 x 8 3/8 in.); Museum purchase from General Acquisitions Endowment, 1968-146-2; Photo by Ellen McDermott © Smithsonian Institution

0492. Bowl, ca. 1900; Produced by Louis Comfort Tiffany (American, 1848–1933); Manufactured by Tiffany Studios (Corona, New York, USA); Mold-blown favrile glass; 6.7 x 18 cm diam. (2 5/8 x 7 1/16 in.); Bequest of Joseph L. Morris, 1966-55-22; Photo by Ellen McDermott © Smithsonian Institution

0493. Sidewall, USA, 1936–56; Machine printed on paper; 132 x 52 cm (51 15/16 x 20 1/2 in.); Gift of Suzanne Lipschutz, 1991-89-110

0494. Rock crystal style flower bowl, 1923–24; Marianne Rath (Austrian, 1904–85); Manufactured by J. & L. Lobmeyr GmbH (Vienna, Austria); Mouth-blown glass, exact shape cut, half-polished surface cutting; 16.3 x 37.6 x 24.6 cm (6 7/16 x 14 13/16 x 9 11/16 in.); Museum purchase through gift of Dale and Doug Anderson, Anonymous Donor, Arthur Liu, and Prairie Pictures, Inc. and from General Acquisitions Endowment Fund, 2009-18-65; Photo by Andrew Garn © Smithsonian Institution

0495. Bowl, 1917; Josef Hoffmann (Czech, 1870–1956, active Germany and Austria, 1891–1955); Produced by Wiener Werkstätte (Vienna, Austria); Raised and engraved silver; 21.7 x 39 x 34.4 cm (8 9/16 x 15 3/8 x 13 9/16 in.); Gift of Ely Jacques Kahn, 1962-227-1; Photo by John White © Smithsonian Institution

0496. Sidewall, Batterie de Cuisine, 1965–68; Piazza Prints, Inc. (New York, New York, USA); Screenprinted on vinyl; 114 x 75 cm (44 7/8 x 29 1/2 in.); Gift of Piazza Prints, Inc., 1969-56-4; © F. Schumacher & Co., all rights reserved

0497. Toddy lifters (syphons), Ireland or England, 18th–19th century; Cut glass; -149: 16 x 4.3 cm diam. (6 5/16 x 1 11/16 in.), -150: 17.1 x 4.7 cm diam. (6 3/4 x 1 7/8 in.); Bequest of Walter Phelps Warren, 1986-61-149,150; Photo by Ellen McDermott © Smithsonian Institution

0498. Cup and saucer, Sazava, Czechoslovakia, 1932; Ladislav Sutnar (Czech-American, b. Pilsen, Bohemia, 1897, d. New York, New York, USA, 1976); Manufactured by Kavalier Glassworks; Blown glass; a, cup: 5.6 x 13.3 x 11.3 cm (2 3/16 x 5 1/4 x 4 7/16 in.), b, saucer: 1.4 x 15.6 cm diam. (9/16 x 6 1/8 in.); Museum purchase from Decorative Arts Association Acquisitions Fund, 1993-113-4-a,b; Photo by Ellen McDermott © Smithsonian Institution

0499. Decanters and stoppers, Ireland, ca. 1800; Cut and engraved blown glass; -177-a,b: 16.2 x 10.5 cm diam. (6 3/8 x 4 1/8 in.), -178-a,b: 17.5 x 10.5 cm diam. (6 7/8 x 4 1/8 in.); Bequest of Walter Phelps Warren, 1986-61-177-a,b, -178-a,b; Photo by Ellen McDermott © Smithsonian Institution

0500. Footed vase, 1910–14; Josef Hoffmann (Czech, 1870–1956, active Germany and Austria, 1891–1955); Manufactured by Meyr's Neffen, Adolf for J. & L. Lobmeyr GmbH (Vienna, Austria); Mouth-blown, cut, and polished glass; 17.8 x 14.7 cm diam. (7 x 5 13/16 in.); Museum purchase through gift of Dale and Doug Anderson, Anonymous Donor, Arthur Liu, and Prairie Pictures, Inc. and from General Acquisitions Endowment Fund, 2009-18-75; Photo by Andrew Garn © Smithsonian Institution

0501. Decanter and stopper, Waterford, Ireland, 1st half 19th century; Cut blown glass; 38.8 x 9 cm (15 1/4 x 3 9/16 in.); Bequest of Mrs. John Innes Kane, 1926-22-496-a,b; Photo by Ellen McDermott © Smithsonian Institution

0502. Four Continents goblet, Bohemia, 1750–70; Engraved, cut, and gilt glass; a, b: 28.9 x 10.2 cm (11 3/8 x 4 in.); Gift of the Estate of James Hazen Hyde, 1960-1-81-a,b

0503. Candlestick and drip pan, England, 1760–90; Cut blown glass; 28 x 13 cm (11 x 5 1/8 in.); Bequest of Mrs. John Innes Kane, 1926-37-44-a/c; Photo by Ellen McDermott © Smithsonian Institution

0504. Pinch drinking glass, 1950; Russel Wright (American, 1904–76); Manufactured by Imperial Glass Corporation (Bellaire, Ohio, USA); Molded glass, 12.2 x 9.1 cm diam. (4 13/16 x 3 9/16 in.); Gift of Imperial Glass Corporation, 1950-105-3; Photo by Ellen McDermott © Smithsonian Institution; © Russel Wright is a registered trademark by Russel Wright Studio, LLC

0505. Ambassador vase, 1925–27; Oswald Haerdtl (Austrian, 1899–1959); Manufactured by J. L. Lobmeyr GmbH (Vienna, Austria) at Karlsbader Kristallglasfabriken A. G. (Klostermühle, Czechoslovakia); Mouth-blown crystal ("muslin glass"); 53.3 x 12.7 cm diam. (21 x 5 in.) Museum purchase through gift of Georgiana L. McClellan, 1958-98-42

0506. Drawing, Design for Tall Flower Glasses, Ashtrays, Table Ornament, ca. 1926; Flower Glasses designed by Oswald Haerdtl; Ashtrays designed by Stefan Rath; Table Ornament designed by O. E. Wagner with Franz Cizek; Manufactured by J. L. Lobmeyr GmbH (Vienna, Austria); Graphite on tracing paper, lined; 60 x 37.5 cm (23 5/8 x 14 3/4 in.); Gift of Frederick G. Weisser, 1958-77-1-a

0507. Sculptural vessel, Amsterdam, Netherlands, 1985; Toots Zynsky (American, b. 1951); Fused and thermo-formed glass threads (filet-de-verre); 14 x 29.2 x 31.8 cm (5 1/2 x 11 1/2 x 12 1/2 in.); Museum purchase through gift of Anonymous Donor, Carol B. Brener and Stephen W. Brener, Mr. and Mrs. Max B. Furman, Mrs. John Innes Kane, James M. Osborn and Thornet Industries, Inc., 1986-20-1; Photo by John White © Smithsonian Institution; © Toots Zynsky

0508. Drawing, Concept Design for Air Jordan XIII Sneaker, 1996; Tinker Hatfield (American, b. 1952) for Nike (Beaverton, Oregon, USA); Black and color marking pens, turquoise, blue crayon on tracing paper; 27.9 x 43.2 cm (11 x 17 in.); Gift of Nike, 2002-1-1; © Nike, Inc. 1996

0509. Handkerchief vase, 1955; Fulvio Bianconi (Italian, 1915–96); Made by Venini Glassworks (Murano, Venice, Italy); Blown and cased glass; 21 x 23 x 22 cm (8 1/4 x 9 1/16 x 8 11/16 in.); Gift of Christian Rohlfing, 1969-46-1; © Venini S.p.A.

0510. Savoy vase, ca. 1936–37; Alvar Aalto (Finnish, 1898–1976); Manufactured by Karhula Glass Works (Karhula, Finland); Mold-blown glass; 15 x 28.3 x 24.2 cm (5 7/8 x 11 1/8 x 9 1/2 in.); Gift of Harmon Goldstone, 1990-61-2; Photo by John White © Smithsonian Institution; © Iittala Group Oy Ab

0511. Collage, The Gates, Project for Central Park, New York, New York, USA, 2003; Christo (b. Christo Vladimirov Javacheff, American, b. Bulgaria 1935); Brush and enamel paint, wax crayon, graphite, collaged fabric sample over photocopied map, photograph (Wolfgang Volz) on white paper; 43.2 x 55.9 cm (17 x 22 in.); Museum purchase from General Acquisitions Endowment Fund, 2004-2-1; © Christo 2003

0512. Drawing, Design for a Verrière (Monteith), 1765–75; Painted by Jacques-François Micaud (French, ca. 1732–1811) for Sèvres Porcelain Manufactory (Paris, France); Pen and brown ink, brush and watercolor on off-white laid paper; 27.1 x 41.4 cm (10 11/16 x 16 5/16 in.); Museum purchase through gift of various donors and from Eleanor G. Hewitt Fund, 1938-88-8316

0513. Kuba woman's ceremonial skirt, Democratic Republic of the Congo, early 20th century; Woven raffia, embroidered in buttonhole, stem, and pile stitches with openwork; 68.6 x 149.9 cm (27 x 59 in.); Museum purchase through gift of Anonymous, Dr. and Mrs. Lewis Balamuth, Mr. and Mrs. Dewitt Clinton Cohen, Gertrude Crownfeld, Valerie Dreyfus, Norvin Hewitt Green, Rodman A. Heeren, Misses Hewitt, Sarah Cooper Hewitt, Florence N. Levy, Mrs. Paul C. Pennoyer, Mrs. Harry T. Peters, Mrs. Bernard Reis, Mrs. William Jay Schieffelin, and Mr. and Mrs. Stephens B. Stanton, 1990-133-3

0514. Kuba loom, Democratic Republic of the Congo, early 20th century; Wood, raffia; 91.4 x 96.5 cm (36 x 38 in.); Museum purchase from Au Panier Fleuri Fund, 1957-110-15

0515. Book illustration, Designs inspired by insects, 1927; Eugène Alain Séguy (French, 1890–1985); From Eugène Alain Séguy, *Insectes* (*Insects*), (Paris: Chartre et Van Buggenhoudt), plate 7; Pochoir print on paper; 46 x 33.5 cm (18 1/8 x 13 in.); Smithsonian Libraries, fNK1555.S47

0516. Dragonfly and Cattail Pond Lily lamp, Model 1462 (shade), Model 225 (base), 1900–10; Clara Driscoll (American, 1861–1933); Design directed by Louis Comfort Tiffany (American, 1848–1933); Made by Tiffany Studios (Corona, New York, USA); Stained glass, lead, cut brass, gilt bronze; 54.5 x 53 cm diam. (21 7/16 x 20 7/8 in.); Gift of Mrs. Margaret Carnegie Miller, 1977-111-1-a/c; Photo by Dennis Cowley © Smithsonian Institution

0517. Hanakarakusa W brooch, France and Japan, 2007; Made by Van Cleef & Arpels (Paris, France); Lacquered by Junichi Hakose (Japanese, b. 1955); Gold powder, gold beads, eggshells, mother-of-pearl, colored lacquer, gray mother-of-pearl support on white gold, 9 round-cut diamonds: 0.26 ct; 4.1 x 5 x 0.5 cm (1 5/8 x 1 15/16 x 3/16 in.); Gift of Van Cleef & Arpels, 2011-42-2; © Van Cleef & Arpels

0518. Araiso U brooch, France and Japan, 2007; Made by Van Cleef & Arpels (Paris, France); Lacquered by Junichi Hakose (Japanese, b. 1955); Raised white gold, gold beads, eggshell lacquer on mother-of-pearl support on white gold, round-cut diamonds; 4.1 x 5 x 0.5 cm (1 5/8 x 1 15/16 x 3/16 in.); Gift of Van Cleef & Arpels, 2011-42-1; © Van Cleef & Arpels

0519. J. B. Schmetterling hanging lamp, 2011; Ingo Maurer (German, b. 1932) and Axel Schmid (German, b. 1971); Manufactured by Ingo Maurer GmbH (Munich, Germany); Mouth-blown glass, 3D printed (flexible free-formed) plastic, machined brass, halogen light source; 46 x 32 cm diam. (18 1/8 x 12 9/16 in.); Gift of Ingo Maurer GmbH and Graham Owen, 2014-7-1-a/c; © Ingo Maurer GmbH

0520. Textile, Farfalle, 1963; Harvey Smith (American, 1906–94) and Clayton Ryder (American); Manufactured by Patterson-Piazza, Inc. (New York, New York, USA); Screenprinted cotton velveteen; 269.2 x 139.7 cm (8 ft. 10 in. x 55 in.), repeat H: 108 cm (42 1/2 in.); Gift of Anonymous Donor, 1967-9-11; © F. Schumacher & Co., all rights reserved

0521. Sidewall, The Peacock, ca. 1890; Machine printed on paper; 105 x 56 cm (41 5/16 x 22 1/16 in.); Gift of Grace Lincoln Temple, 1938-62-56-a,b

0522. Drawing, Textile Design: Bird Motif, France, 19th century; Brush and gouache, graphite on cream paper; 35 x 39.8 cm (13 3/4 x 15 11/16 in.); Gift of Harvey Smith, 1968-107-3

0523. Sidewall, The Cedar Tree, 1910; Louis Stahl; Made by Arthur Sanderson & Sons, Ltd. (London, England); Block printed on machine-made paper; 170.5 x 57 cm (67 1/8 x 22 7/16 in.); Gift of Harvey Smith, 1957-127-1

0524. Rooster figurine, England, ca. 1760; Possibly manufactured by Derby Porcelain Factory; Glazed porcelain; 10.4 x 11 x 6.5 cm (4 1/8 x 4 5/16 x 2 9/16 in.); Bequest of Mrs. John Innes Kane, 1926-22-479; Photo by Ellen McDermott © Smithsonian Institution

0525. Sidewall, Sommerfeld, 1917–28; Felice Rix-Ueno (Austrian, 1893–1967) for the Wiener Werkstätte (Vienna, Austria); Made by Salubra-Werke A. G. (Grenzach, Switzerland); Machine printed on machine-made paper; 451.5 x 77 cm (14 ft. 9 3/4 in. x 30 5/16 in.); Gift of Mrs. A. H. Jacobs, 1967-14-1-a/f; © The National Museum of Modern Art, Kyoto

0526. Drawing, Cartoon for Wallpaper and Textile: Peacock, 1960; Harvey Smith (American. 1906–94); Brush and gouache, bronze paint, graphite on white wove paper; 61 x 47.5 cm (24 x 18 11/16 in.); Gift of Harvey Smith, 1967-97-24-c

0527. Book illustration, Le Nébuleux, étalant ses parures (The nebulous spreads her ornaments), 1806; Illustrated by Jacques Barraband (French, 1767–1809); From François Le Vaillant (French, 1753–1824), *Histoire naturelle des oiseaux de paradis et des rolliers, suivie de celle des toucans et des barbus* (*Natural History of Birds of Paradise and Rollers: Followed by Toucans and Barbets*), (Paris: Chez Denné le jeune et chez Perlet), vol. 1, plate 16; Hand-colored engraving on paper; 56 x 40 cm (22 x 13 in.); Gift of Robert Winthrop Chanler, ca. 1930, Smithsonian Libraries, fQL674.L65 1806

0528. Sidewall, Tumtin, ca. 1967; Philip Graf Wallpapers, Inc. (New York, New York, USA); Screenprinted on paper; 137.5 x 76 cm (54 1/8 x 29 15/16 in.); Gift of Philip Graf, 1969-53-3

0529. Drawing, Textile Design: Birds, France, 19th century; Brush and gouache, graphite on cream paper; 41.8 x 38.3 cm (16 7/16 x 15 1/16 in.); Gift of Harvey Smith, 1968-107-20

0530. Rank badge (buzi), China, Ming dynasty, 1368–1644; Silk and metallic tapestry (kesi); 34 x 31.1 cm (13 3/8 x 12 1/4 in.); Gift of John Pierpont Morgan, 1902-1-433; Photo by Scott Hyde © Smithsonian Institution

0531. Sidewall, Celui qui aime ecrit sur les murs (One who loves writes on the walls), ca. 1924; Jean Lurçat (French, 1892–1966); Made by Pierre Chareau; Block printed on machine-made paper; 45.5 x 47.8 cm (17 15/16 x 18 13/16 in.); Gift of Mrs. Cornelius Sullivan, 1930-21-1-c

0532. Textile, Japan, 1936; Stencil-printed cotton; 57.1 x 33.6 cm (22 1/2 x 13 1/4 in.); Gift of American Council, Institute of Pacific Relations, 1937-69-29

0533. Poster, Levi's 501, The Button Fly, 2010; Sagmeister Inc. (New York, New York, USA); Stefan Sagmeister (Austrian, b. 1962), Richard The, and Joe Shouldice (Canadian) for Levi Strauss & Co. (San Francisco, California, USA); Offset lithograph with rainbow foil stamping on coated wove paper; 119.4 x 76.2 cm (47 x 30 in.); Gift of Stefan Sagmeister, 2011-34-2; © Stefan Sagmeister

0534. Book illustration, Macrocercus Aracanga (red and yellow macaw), 1832; Edward Lear (British, 1812–88); From *Illustrations of the Family of Psittacidœ, or Parrots* (London: E. Lear, 1832); Chromolithograph on paper; 56 x 37 cm (22 1/16 x 14 9/16 in.); Mary Stuart Book Fund, Smithsonian Libraries, fQL696. P7L43 1832

0535. Sidewall, Cat and Canary, 1958; John Rombola (American, b. 1933); Made by Harben Papers, Inc.; Screenprinted; 279 x 76 cm (109 13/16 x 29 15/16 in.); Gift of John Rombola, 1984-102-2

0536. Drawing, Dog Wallpaper, ca. 1956; Saul Steinberg (American, b. Romania, 1914–99); Pen and black ink on wove graph paper; 25.4 x 38.2 cm (10 x 15 1/16 in.); Gift of Harvey Smith, 1956-126-1

0537. Compact disc, Imaginary Day by Pat Methany, 1997; Stefan Sagmeister (Austrian, b. 1962); Printed cardboard and plastic; 12.7 x 14.3 cm (5 x 5 5/8 in.); Gift of Sagmeister, Inc., 2000-61-9-a/c

0538. Sidewall, Alice in Wonderland, 1968; John Rombola (American, b. 1933); Made by Piazza Prints, Inc. (New York, New York, USA); Screenprinted on vinyl; 77.8 x 74.5 cm (30 5/8 x 29 5/16 in.); Gift of The Museum at The Fashion Institute of Technology, 1998-75-180; © F. Schumacher & Co., all rights reserved

0539. Embroidered picture, USA, 1965; Cotton embroidered in cotton in cross-stitch; 36.2 x 45.1 cm (14 1/4 x 17 3/4 in.); Gift of Miss Alice DeLamar, 1966-21-1

0540. Sidewall, Cow, 1971; Andy Warhol (American, 1928–87); Made by Bob Miller's Wallpaper Studio (New York, New York, USA); Screenprinted on paper; 348.5 x 75.5 cm (137 3/16 x 29 3/4 in.); Gift of Andy Warhol, 1980-69-1

0541. Scenic panel, L'Orage, 1861; Eugene Ehrmann (French, 1804–96), after a painting by Robert Eberle (active Germany, 1815–60); Made by Zuber & Cie (Rixheim, Alsace, France); Block printed on paper; 235 x 194 cm (92 1/2 x 76 3/8 in.); Gift of Harvey Smith, 1968-130-13

0542. Sidewall, Zodiac, 1942; Marion Dorn (American, active England, 1896–1964); Made by Bassett & Vollum, Inc. (Galena, Illinois, USA); Screenprinted on paper; 6.0 m x 55.8 cm (19 ft. 8 1/2 in. x 21 15/16 in.); Gift of Anonymous Donor, 1967-49-1-a,b; © Bassett & Vollum, Inc.

0543. Sidewall, Animal Kingdom, 1950; Edgar Miller (American, 1899–1993); Made by Bassett & Vollum, Inc. (Chicago, Illinois, USA); Screenprinted on paper; 121 x 56 cm (47 5/8 x 22 1/16 in.); Gift of Donald D. MacMillan, 1950-78-10; © Bassett & Vollum, Inc.

0544. Drawing, Still Life with Fish and Parrot, 1740; Jean-Baptiste Oudry (French, 1686–1755); Black and white chalk on blue laid paper; 30.6 x 41.6 cm (12 1/16 x 16 3/8 in.); Museum purchase from Friends of the Museum Fund, 1938-66-1

0545. Scenic wallpaper, Sea Beauties, 1920–40; Ideal Wall Decoration (Germany); Manufactured by The P. Company; Lithograph on paper; 167.6 x 106.7 cm (5 ft. 6 in. x 42 in.); Gift of the family of Victor S. Robinson, Salem, New Jersey, 2004-16-1

0546. Textile, L'Eau (Water), ca. 1924; Yvonne Clarinval (French, 1884–1979); Manufactured by Tassinari & Chatel (Paris and Lyon, France); Mercerized cotton and rayon compound satin; 201.9 x 130.2 cm (79 1/2 x 51 1/4 in.); Gift of Anonymous Donor, 1931-1-1; © Tassinari & Chatel

0547. Frog paperweight, France, ca. 1910–20; François-Émile Décorchemont (French, 1880–1971); Molded, colored glass; 5.6 x 13.8 cm diam. (2 3/16 x 5 7/16 in.); Gift of Harold Lanzner, 1994-45-1; Photo by Ellen McDermott © Smithsonian Institution

0548. Ornament, France, 1850–60; Block printed and hand painted on combed background, paper support; 80 x 50.5 cm (31 1/2 x 19 7/8 in.); Gift of Eleanor and Sarah Hewitt, 1931-45-64

0549. Sidewall and frieze, 1928–29; J. Grantil Company (Châlons-sur-Marne, France); Machine printed and airbrushed on paper; 75 x 47 cm (29 1/2 x 18 1/2 in.); Gift of Carolle Thibaut-Pomerantz, 2010-31-19

0550. Print, The Rhinoceros, 1515; Albrecht Dürer (German, 1471–1528); Woodcut on laid paper; 24 x 30.4 cm (9 7/16 x 11 15/16 in.); Gift of Leo Wallerstein, 1950-5-24

0551. Inkwell, Germany, ca. 1735; Cast and gilt bronze; 24 x 10.2 x 28 cm (9 7/16 x 4 x 11 in.); Gift of Mr. and Mrs. Edward Pflueger, 1983-84-1-a/e

0552. Print, Lion and Hare Composed of Ornamental Leaf-Work, 1698; Wolfgang Hieronymus Von Bömmel (German, active 1660–1700); Engraving on off-white laid paper; 12.7 x 20 cm (5 x 7 7/8 in.); Museum purchase through gift of the Estate of David Wolfe Bishop, 1957-162-13

0553. The "Hunting" Frieze, 1905; Cecil Aldin (British, 1870–1935); Produced by Arthur Sanderson & Sons, Ltd. (London, England); Block printed on ingrain paper; 162 x 57.2 cm (5 ft. 3 3/4 in. x 22 1/2 in.); Gift of Standard Coated Products, 1975-2-5-a/g

0554. Frieze, Winnie the Pooh, after 1926; Block printed on ingrain paper; 12 m x 54.5 cm (39 ft. 4 7/16 in. x 21 7/16 in.); Gift of Standard Coated Products, 1975-2-2

0555. Matchsafe, 1905–15; Manufactured by Theodore B. Starr (New York, New York, USA); Gold, diamonds, emeralds, rubies; 5.1 x 3.7 x 1 cm (2 x 1 7/16 x 3/8 in.); Gift of Stephen W. Brener and Carol B. Brener, 1978-146-464-a,b

0556. Allegorical Figure of America from the Four Continents, late 18th–early 19th century; Manufactured by Meissen Porcelain Manufactory (Meissen, Saxony, Germany); Polychromed, gilt, and glazed porcelain; 14 x 13.7 x 17.8 cm (5 1/2 x 5 3/8 x 7 in.); Gift of the Estate of James Hazen Hyde, 1960-1-38-d; Photo by Ellen McDermott © Smithsonian Institution

0557. Frieze, Kindergarten Cut-Outs, 1907; The Schmitz-Horning Co. (Cleveland, Ohio, USA); Chromolithograph on paper; 50.2 x 78.1 cm (19 3/4 x 30 3/4 in.); Gift of Wallpaper Council, Inc., 1960-163-36

0558. Frieze, Jungle Cut-Outs, 1907–10; The Schmitz-Horning Co. (Cleveland, Ohio, USA); Chromolithograph on paper; 50.2 x 78.1 cm (19 3/4 x 30 3/4 in.); Gift of Wallpaper Council, Inc., 1960-163-37

0559. Book illustration, Rabbits and babies eating berries, ca. 1900–20; Illustrated by Sibylle von Olfers (German, 1881–1916); From Marie Hildebrandt (Dutch, 1881–1947), *Mapje en Papje in het Hazenbosch* (*Folder and Paste in the Hadden*), (Amsterdam: van Holkema & Warendorf), plate 4; Color lithograph on paper; 29 x 23 cm (11 3/8 x 9 in.); Gift from Mary Stuart Book Fund, ca. 1931, Smithsonian Libraries, PZ14.H55 1900

0560. Book illustration, Two grotesque dado rails, 1876; Christopher Dresser (Scottish, 1834–1904, active England, 1854–1904); From Christopher Dresser, *Studies in Design* (London: Cassell, Petter and Galpin), plate XIV; Color lithograph on paper; 42 x 29 cm (16 1/2 x 11 2/3 in.); Smithsonian Libraries, fNK1535.D77 1876

0561. Paper construction, Lion cage, ca. 1895; Ernest Nister (German 1842–1909); From Lucy L. Weedon, *The Model Menagerie: With Natural History Stories* (New York: E. P. Dutton); Color lithograph on folded and cut paper; 28 x 36 x 6 cm (11 x 14 x 2 1/2 in.); Gift of Dr. Daniel J. Mason, Smithsonian Libraries, QL791.W39 1895

0562. Mantle, Peru, 16th–17th century; Silk and metallic tapestry, 92.7 x 127 cm (36 1/2 x 50 in.); Gift of John Pierpont Morgan, 1902-1-782

0563. Book illustration, Designs inspired by insects, 1927; Eugène Alain Séguy (French, 1890–1985); From *Insectes* (*Insects*), (Paris: Chartre et Van Buggenhoudt, 1927), plate 14; Pochoir print on paper; 46 x 33.5 cm (18 1/8 x 13 in.); Smithsonian Libraries, fNK1555.S47;

0564. Drawing, Textile Design: Insect Motif, France, 19th century; Brush and gouache, graphite on cream paper; 40 x 47.8 cm (15 3/4 x 18 13/16 in.); Gift of Harvey Smith, 1968-107-28

0565. Book illustration, Squid, 1734–65; Albertus Seba (Dutch, 1665–1736); From *Locupletissimi rerum naturalium thesauri accurata description* (*Most Accurate Description of Natural Treasures*), (Amsterdam: Apud J. Wetstenium, & Gul. Smith, & Janssonio-Waesbergios); Hand-colored engraving on paper; 53 x 78 cm (20 3/4 x 30 3/4 in.); Gift of The Misses Hewitt, 1922, Smithsonian Libraries, f QH41.S44 1734

0566. Elefantenruesseltisch (Elephant trunk table), Vienna, Austria, ca. 1910; Adolf Loos (Austrian, 1870–1933); Made by Friedrich Otto Schmidt (table), Loetz-Witwe (glass tiles); Carved and veneered mahogany, molded and iridized glass, sheet brass; 63.5 x 81.3 cm diam. (25 x 32 in.); Museum purchase from General Acquisitions Endowment Fund, 2005-22-1

0567. Vase, ca. 1905–14; Louis Comfort Tiffany (American, 1848–1933); Manufactured by Tiffany Furnaces, Tiffany Studios (Corona, New York, USA); Glazed, molded earthenware; 27.7 x 29.2 cm diam. (10 7/8 x 11 1/2 in.); Gift of Marcia and William Goodman, 1984-84-32; Photo © Smithsonian Institution

0568. Drawing, Squid Costume Design for the Opera *Sadko* by Rimsky-Korsakov, ca. 1929; Serge Soudeikine (Russian, 1886–1946); Brush and gouache, graphite on paper; 36.4 x 28.3 cm (14 5/16 x 11 1/8 in.); Museum purchase from General Acquisitions Endowment Fund, 1984-65-2

0569. Man's hat (ashetu), Cameroon, after 1957; Crocheted cotton reinforced with wood; 19.1 x 35.6 cm (7 1/2 x 14 in.); Museum purchase through gift of Mrs. William Goulding, 2003-3-1; Photo by Ellen McDermott © Smithsonian Institution

0570. Cap, Spain, late 18th century; Knitted silk with knotted chenille tassel; 25.1 x 25.1 cm (9 7/8 x 9 7/8 in.); Tassel: 58.1 cm (22 7/8 in.); Gift of Richard C. Greenleaf, 1951-105-35

0571. Bowl, ca. 1893–1909; Designed and made by George E. Ohr (American, 1857–1918), Biloxi Art Pottery (Biloxi, Mississippi, USA); Glazed earthenware; 10.8 x 15.55 cm diam. (4 1/4 x 6 1/8 in.); Gift of Marcia and William Goodman, 1984-84-34

0572. Man's cap, England, late 16th century; Linen embroidered with silk and metallic yarns; 20 x 19 cm (7 7/8 x 7 1/2 in.); Bequest of Richard Cranch Greenleaf in memory of his mother, Adeline Emma Greenleaf, 1962-53-11

0573. Man's hat, France, 18th century; Linen and cotton foundation embroidered in wool in chain, buttonhole, and stem stitches, silk binding, silk and metallic tassel; 22.9 x 17.8 cm (9 x 7 in.); Gift of Richard C. Greenleaf in memory of his mother, Adeline E. Greenleaf, 1952-47-3

0574. Man's hat, France, ca. 1730; Silk and metallic lampas, embroidered with silk; 21 x 27.9 cm (8 1/4 x 11 in.); Gift of Richard C. Greenleaf, 1951-105-31

0575. Kuba man's hat (laket), Democratic Republic of the Congo, 19th century; Woven raffia; 14 x 15.9 cm (5 1/2 x 6 1/4 in.); Museum purchase from Au Panier Fleuri Fund, 1957-110-12

0576. Kuba man's hat (laket), Democratic Republic of the Congo, 19th century; Woven raffia; 16.5 x 23.5 cm (6 1/2 x 9 1/4 in.); Museum purchase from Au Panier Fleuri Fund, 1957-110-14

0577. Hat, France, 18th century; Silk embroidered in metallic yarns in satin and stem stitches; 24.1 x 25.4 x 27.9 cm (9 1/2 x 10 x 11 in.); Gift of Richard C. Greenleaf, 1951-105-30

0578. Bonbonnière, London, England, ca. 1755; Gold, carved gray agate, enamel decoration on gold; 4.5 x 3 cm diam. (1 3/4 x 1 3/16 in.); Gift of the Panwy Foundation, from the collection of Maria Wyman, 1994-129-3; Photo by Richard Goodbody © Smithsonian Institution

0579. Melos necklace, ca. 1873; Fortunato Pio Castellani & Sons (Rome, Italy); Enameled, granulated, and rolled gold; Clasped: 16.6 x 0.6 cm (6 9/16 x 1/4 in.); Museum purchase through gift of Anonymous Donor, Annie Schermerhorn Kane, and various donors, 1969-40-17

0580. Necklace, France, ca. 1930; René Lalique (French, 1860–1945); Molded and carved glass, white metal; leather, silk, brass (case); H x diam.: 4 x 21.3 cm (1 9/16 x 8 3/8 in.); Gift of Jacques Jugeat, 1968-163-1-a,b; Photo by Ellen McDermott © Smithsonian Institution

0581. Necklace, Oslo, Norway, 1983; Tone Vigeland (Norwegian, b. 1938); Hammered steel nails, raised gold, silver, mother-of-pearl; Clasped: 21 x 23 cm (8 1/4 x 9 1/16 in.) ; Museum purchase from Decorative Arts Association Acquisition Funds and General Acquisition Endowment, 1984-83-1; Photo by John White © Smithsonian Institution

0582. Tableware, glasses, Pattern No. 168, Lobmeyr's Gentlemen's Dinner Service, 1871; Ludwig Lobmeyr (Austrian, 1829–1917); Manufactured for J. & L. Lobmeyr GmbH (Vienna, Austria); Mouth-blown crystal, facet-cut and polished; Museum purchase through gift of Dale and Doug Anderson, Anonymous Donor, Arthur Liu, and Prairie Pictures, Inc., and from the General Acquisitions Endowment Fund, 2009-18-42/47

0583. Porca Miseria! hanging lamp, 2000; Ingo Maurer (German, b. 1932); Manufactured by Ingo Maurer GmbH (Munich, Germany); Glazed, molded porcelain adhered to metal rods, stainless steel, halogen light source; 114.3 x 101 x 82.6 cm (45 x 39 3/4 x 32 1/2 in.); Gift of Peter Norton, 2010-16-1; Photo by Ellen McDermott © Smithsonian Institution; © Ingo Maurer GmbH

0584. Photograph, Drawing of Chandelier, ca. 1905; Hector Guimard (French, 1867–1942); Printed ink on sensitized paper; 25.3 x 20.2 cm (9 15/16 x 7 15/16 in.); Gift of Unknown Donor, 1963-59-5

0585. Chandelier, possibly Netherlands, 15th–16th century; Bronze; H x diam.: 55.5 x 63 cm (21 7/8 x 24 13/16 in.); Gift of Irwin Untermyer, 1963-50-1-a,b; Photo by Ellen McDermott © Smithsonian Institution

0586. PH Artichoke hanging lamp, 1958, manufactured 1983; Poul Henningsen (Danish, 1894–1967); Manufactured by Louis Poulson & Co. A/S (Copenhagen, Denmark); Bent copper, steel, enameled metal; 69 x 84 cm diam. (27 3/16 x 33 1/16 in.); Museum purchase from General Exhibition Funds, 1983-16-1; Photo by Dave King © Smithsonian Institution

0587. Tassel, Italy, 17th century; Braided and knotted linen with bobbin lace; 41 x 8 cm (16 1/8 x 3 1/8 in.); Bequest of Richard Cranch Greenleaf in memory of his mother, Adeline Emma Greenleaf, 1962-51-28

0588. Tassel, Italy, 17th century; Braided and knotted linen; 17.8 x 9.5 cm (7 x 3 3/4 in.); Bequest of Richard Cranch Greenleaf in memory of his mother, Adeline Emma Greenleaf, 1962-51-14

0589. Tassel, Italy, 17th century; Braided and knotted linen; 13.5 x 4.5 cm (5 3/8 x 1 3/4 in.); Bequest of Richard Cranch Greenleaf in memory of his mother, Adeline Emma Greenleaf, 1962-51-13

0590. Hanging lamp, 1914–20; Glass made by Vetreria Fratelli Toso (Murano, Venice, Italy) or Barovier & Toso (Murano, Venice, Italy); Metal frame manufactured by Umberto Bellotto (Venice, Italy); Millefiori glass, wrought iron, enamel; 37.5 x 30.8 cm diam. (14 3/4 x 12 1/8 in.); Gift of Neil and Donna Weisman, 2012-9-1-a/j; Photo by Ellen McDermott © Smithsonian Institution

0591. Sidewall, Memory Wallpaper, 2003–04; Cynthia Hathaway (Canadian, active Amsterdam, Netherlands, b. 1965); Adhesive vinyl with cut-outs; 14.65 m x 70 cm (48 ft. 3/4 in. x 27 9/16 in.); Gift of Cynthia Hathaway, 2004-10-1; © Hathaway Designs

0592. Sidewall, France, 1835; Hand painted on machine-made paper; 64.5 x 49 cm (25 3/8 x 19 5/16 in.); Gift of Josephine Howell, 1972-42-209-a

0593. Drawing, Design for a Damask Textile, France, 1850–75; Brush and gouache on tracing paper; 55 x 42.2 cm (21 5/8 x 16 5/8 in.), irregular; Gift of Eleanor and Sarah Hewitt, 1909-13-95

0594. Drawing, Design for a Gold and Cabochon Gem Brooch, ca. 1855; Alexis Falize (French, 1811–98); Brush and gouache, gum varnish over graphite on tan wove paper; 45.7 x 35.6 cm (18 x 14 in.); Museum purchase through gift of Mrs. Gustav E. Kissel, 1950-6-1

0595. Drawing, Design for a Corsage Ornament: Night, ca. 1900; René Lalique (French, 1860–1945); Brush and watercolor, graphite, brush and gouache on brownish, translucent wove paper, possibly coated with resin; 21.9 x 27.9 cm (8 5/8 x 11 in.); Museum purchase from Drawings and Prints Council Fund through gift of The Florence Gould Foundation, 1998-50-1

0596. Surtout de Table (Table centerpiece), Paris, France, ca. 1810; Pierre-Philippe Thomire (French, 1751–1843); Cast and gilt bronze with hand engraving, cut glass, silvered-mirrored glass; Assembled: 76.2 x 327.7 x 77.5 cm (30 x 129 x 30 1/2 in.); Bequest of the Reverend Alfred Duane Pell, 1991-31-1-a/ww; Photo by Ellen McDermott © Smithsonian Institution

0597. Painting, The Wedding Banquet of Napoleon I and Marie-Louise in the Grand Salon of the Tuileries Palace, 2 April 1810, 1812; Alexandre-Benoit-Jean Dufay, Casanova (French, 1770–1844); Oil on canvas; Musée National du Château de Fontainebleau; Photo by Gérard Blot © RMN

0598. Pair of earrings, probably France, ca. 1860; Bright-cut engraved aluminum, gold; b: 6.4 x 1.9 x 1.1 cm (2 1/2 x 3/4 x 7/16 in.), c: 6.5 x 1 x 1.9 cm (2 9/16 x 3/8 x 3/4 in.); Gift of Mrs. Gustav E. Kissel, 1928-5-4-b,c; Photo by John Parnell © Smithsonian Institution

0599. Ornament, Décor Chasse et Peche, 1859–65; Desfossé et Karth (Paris, France); Block printed on machine-made paper; 2.39 m x 70 cm (7 ft. 10 1/8 in. x 27 9/16 in.); Museum purchase from Friends of the Museum Fund, 1955-12-10-a

0600. Drawing, Design for a Reliquary of the Holy Cross, ca. 1540; Attributed to Luzio Romano (Italian, active 1528–75); Black chalk, brush and brown wash, pen and brown ink on cream paper, lined; 32.8 x 16.1 cm (12 15/16 x 6 5/16 in.); Museum purchase through gift of Mrs. John Innes Kane, 1942-36-2

0601. Drawing, Design for a Candelabrum, 1520–30; Michelangelo Buonarroti (Italian, 1475–1564); Black chalk, brush and brown wash, incised lines and compass points on cream laid paper, lined; 43.4 x 25.4 cm (17 1/16 x 10 in.); Museum purchase through gift of Mrs. John Innes Kane, 1942-36-4

0602. Sidewall, Cairo, 1929; Maria Strauss Likarz (Austrian, 1893–1971); Made by Wiener Werkstätte (Vienna, Austria); Machine printed on paper; 92 x 55.5 cm (36 1/4 x 21 7/8 in.); Gift of Harrison Cultra, 1971-62-6

0603. Sample book, *Fabrique de registres toile soie 1904 – 1905 – 1906* (*Factory record of silk fabrics*), 1904–06; Woven silk samples, affixed paper pages, cardboard covers; 50.2 x 35.6 x 10.2 cm (19 3/4 x 14 x 4 in.); Gift of Hamill & Barker, 1968-63-2

0604. Sample book, *Fabrique de registres nouveautes Teint en Fils* (*Factory record of yarn-dyed novelties*), 1905–06; Samples of dyed silk pasted to paper pages; 49.5 x 33.7 x 9.5 cm (19 1/2 x 13 1/4 x 3 3/4 in.); Gift of Hamill & Barker, 1968-63-3

0605. Hand-woven sample for a wallcovering, USA, ca. 1945; Anni Albers (American, b. Germany, 1899–1994); Plain-woven linen, cellophane, and paper; 12.1 x 15.9 cm (4 3/4 x 6 1/4 in.); Museum purchase through gift of Mrs. John Innes Kane, 1948-85-2; © Josef and Anni Albers Foundation

0606. Window blind sample, USA, 1956; Dorothy Wright Liebes (American, 1897–1972); Woven by Ralph Higbee (American); Plain-woven synthetic, metallic, and wood; 46 x 117.5 cm (18 1/8 x 46 1/4 in.); Gift of the Estate of Dorothy (Liebes) Morin, 1972-75-9

0607. Ewe prestige cloth, Ghana, early 20th century; Strip-woven cotton; 317.5 x 193 cm (125 x 76 in.); Museum purchase from General Acquisitions Endowment Fund, 2007-8-1

0608. Textile, Causeway, 1967; Lucienne Day (British, 1917–2010); Produced by Heal Fabrics (London, England); Screenprinted cotton crepe; 228.6 x 116.8 cm (90 x 46 in.); Museum purchase from General Acquisitions Endowment Fund, 2007-5-1; © Robin and Lucienne Day Foundation

0609. Drawing, Temple Rodef Sholom, San Rafael, California, USA: Design for an Ark Curtain, 1963–64; Trude Guermonprez (American, b. Germany, 1910–76); Brush and gouache on gold-patterned Chinese paper; 51 x 35.6 cm (20 1/16 x 14 in.); Gift of Mr. Eric and Mrs. Sylvia Elsesser, The Trude Guermonprez Archives, 1993-121-68

0610. Textile, Temple Rodef Shalom ark curtain trial, 1963–64; Trude Guermonprez (American, b. Germany, 1910–76); Silk, brocaded with silk and synthetic metallic yarns; 193 x 94 cm (76 x 37 in.); Gift of Mr. Eric and Mrs. Sylvia Elsesser, The Trude Guermonprez Archives, 1993-121-5

0611. Poster, Visuele Communicatie Nederland (Visual Communication in the Netherlands), Stedelijk Museum (Amsterdam, Netherlands), 1969; Wim Crouwel (Dutch, b. 1928); Offset lithograph on wove paper; 94.6 x 64.7 cm (37 1/4 x 25 1/2 in.); Museum purchase from General Acquisitions Endowment Fund, 2009-13-1; © Wim Crouwel

0612. Textile, Rivers, ca. 1972; Gretl Wollner (Austrian, 1920–2006) and Leo Wollner (Austrian, 1925–95); Produced by KnollTextiles (New York, New York, USA): Printed by Pausa AG (Mössingen, Germany); Screenprinted cotton velveteen; 261.6 x 123.2 cm (103 x 48 1/2 in.); Gift of Cindia Cameron, 2011-21-2; © KnollTextiles

0613. Textile, Lyon, France, ca. 1920; Herman A. Elsberg (American, 1869–1938); Silk and metallic cut and voided velvet; 98.5 x 80.6 cm (38 3/4 x 31 3/4 in.); Anonymous bequest in memory of Albert and Rebecca Elsberg, 1938-82-195-a

0614. Sidewall, France, 1860; Dufour et Leroy; Block printed on continuous paper; 183 x 50 cm (72 1/16 x 19 11/16 in.); Gift of Josephine Howell, 1972-42-225-a

0615. Textile, Faruk, 1952; Armi Ratia (Finnish, 1912–79); Manufactured by Marimekko Oy (Helsinki, Finland); Screen-printed cotton; 311.2 x 138.1 cm (10 ft. 2 1/2 in. x 54 3/8 in.), repeat H: 14 cm (5 1/2 in.); Gift of Marimekko, Inc., 1979-89-2; © Marimekko Oy

0616. Textile, Remoulade, 1956; Jack Lenor Larsen (American, b. 1927); Produced by Jack Lenor Larsen Inc. (New York, New York, USA); Plain-woven wool, linen, cotton, silk, jute, rayon, metallic yarns, and mohair, with warp and weft float patterning; 78.7 x 87 cm (31 x 34 1/4 in.); Museum purchase from Au Panier Fleuri Fund, 1959-98-1; © Cowtan & Tout

0617. Sidewall, Newsworthy, 2010; Lori Weitzner (American, b. 1961); Coiled newspaper woven with nylon filaments, paper backing; 457.2 x 123.8 cm (15 ft. x 48 3/4 in.); Gift of Lori Weitzner, 2010-15-1

0618. Hand-woven sample, USA, before. 1945; Anni Albers (American, b. Germany, 1899–1994); Plain and gauze woven cotton, linen, and metallic yarns; 64.8 x 64.1 cm (25 1/2 x 25 1/4 in.); Museum purchase through gift of Mrs. John Innes Kane, 1948-85-7; © Josef and Anni Albers Foundation

0619. Hand-woven sample, USA, ca. 1945; Anni Albers (American, b. Germany, 1899–1994); Plain-woven wool; 16.2 x 19 cm (6 3/8 x 7 1/2 in.); Museum purchase through gift of Mrs. John Innes Kane, 1948-85-14; © Josef and Anni Albers Foundation

0620. Book illustration, Tapissier, Suite de la Facon d'un Fauteuil (Upholstery, the steps in making an armchair), ca. 1769; From *Encyclopédie, ou, Dictionnaire raisonné des sciences, des arts et des métiers* (*Encyclopaedia, or a Systematic Dictionary of the Sciences, Arts, and Crafts*) vol. 8, plate 9; Denis Diderot (French, 1713–84) and Jean le Rond d'Alembert (French 1717–83), editors (Paris: Antoine-Claude Briasson, Michel Antoine David, André Le Breton, Laurent Durand, ca. 1769); Engraving on paper; 40 x 26.5 cm (15 3/4 x 10 7/16 in.); Gift of Marion Hague, Smithsonian Libraries, fAE25.E53X 1751

0621. Side chair, France, ca. 1939; Designed by René Drouet; Textile designed by Madeline Luka (1894–1989); Tapestry made by Aubusson; Lacquered and gilt wood; 79.5 x 53 x 49.5 cm (31 5/16 x 20 7/8 x 19 1/2 in.); Bequest of Faie J. Joyce, 1989-23-1

0622. Mark Hopkins House side chair, ca. 1878–80; Herter Brothers (New York, New York, USA); Rosewood, inlaid and veneered with various woods, silk (of the period but not original); 88.9 x 43.2 x 44.5 cm (35 x 17 x 17 1/2 in.); Museum purchase from General Acquisitions Endowment Fund, 2010-5-1

0623. DCM side chairs, 1946; Charles Eames (American, 1907–78) and Ray Eames (American, 1912–88); Manufactured by Evans Products Company (Detroit, Michigan, USA) for Herman Miller Furniture Company (Zeeland, Michigan, USA); Molded laminated plywood, bent tubular steel, metal, molded rubber; Each chair: 74.5 x 49 x 51 cm (29 5/16 x 19 5/16 x 20 1/16 in.); Gift of Olive Emslie, 1990-112-1,2; Photo by Ellen McDermott © Smithsonian Institution; © Courtesy of Herman Miller, Charles and Ray Eames Designers

0624. Sandows No. 5 side chair, France, 1929; René Herbst (French, 1891–1982); Manufactured by Van Keppel-Green (Los Angeles, California, USA); Bent chromium-plated tubular steel, fiber, rubber; 78.5 x 42.5 x 48 cm (30 7/8 x 16 3/4 x 18 7/8 in.); Museum purchase through gift of Esme Usdan and from General Acquisitions Endowment Fund, 2006-17-1

0625. B5 side chair, 1926–27; Marcel Breuer (American, b. Hungary, 1902–81); Manufactured by Standard-Möbel (Dessau, Germany); Bent chrome-plated tubular steel, Eisengarn (paraffin treated cotton canvas); 84 x 47 x 62.5 cm (33 1/16 x 18 1/2 x 24 5/8 in.); Museum purchase from General Acquisitions Endowment Fund, 2007-9-1

0626. Lounge chair, 1939; Henrik Van Keppel (American, 1914–87) and Taylor Green (American, 1914–91); Manufactured by Van Keppel-Green (Los Angeles, California, USA); Enameled bent tubular steel, cotton cord; 52.3 x 53 x 87.2 cm (20 9/16 x 20 7/8 x 34 5/16 in.); Gift of Powell/Kleinschmidt, 1997-111-1; Photo by Ellen McDermott © Smithsonian Institution

0627. Barcelona chair, 1929; Ludwig Mies van der Rohe (American, b. Germany, 1886–1969); Fabricated by Berliner Metallgewerbe (Berlin, Germany); Metal worked by Joseph Muller (German); Hand-forged steel, hemp; 78.3 x 65.5 x 83 cm (30 13/16 x 25 13/16 x 32 11/16 in.); Museum purchase from Smithsonian Institution Collections Acquisition Program, General Acquisitions Endowment, and Decorative Arts Association Acquisition Funds and through gift of Torsten Bršhan, Mr. and Mrs. Samuel A. Dix, Anne McDonnell Ford, Eleanor and Sarah Hewitt, Mrs. John Innes Kane from the estate of and in memory of her sister Mrs. Samuel W. Bridgeham, Mrs. Paul Moore, Neil Sellin, Unknown Donor and through bequest of Mrs. John Innes Kane, Ruth Vollmer, and Mary Hayward Weir, 2000-12-1-a,b

0628. Trade catalog cover, DESTA Tubular Steel Furniture, ca. 1930; From *DESTA Stahlmöbel* (Berlin, Germany), (Berlin: Desta Stahlmöbel); Offset lithograph on paper; 21 x 14.75 cm (8 1/4 x 5 5/8 in.); Purchase, Cooper Hewitt Museum Library, ca. 1997, Smithsonian Libraries, NK2554.D47D47 1930z

0629. Book illustration, DESTA Tubular Steel Furniture, ca. 1930; From *DESTA Stahlmöbel* (Berlin, Germany), (Berlin: Desta Stahlmöbel); Offset lithograph on paper; 14.75 x 42 cm (5 5/8 x 16 1/2 in.); Purchase, Cooper Hewitt Museum Library, ca. 1997, Smithsonian Libraries, NK2554. D47D47 1930z

0630. Drawing, Design for a Dining Chair with Arms, 1955; Finn Juhl (Danish, 1912–1989) for Baker Furniture Incorporated (Grand Rapids, Michigan, USA); Brush and blue watercolor on pre-printed white wove paper; 41.9 x 58.3 cm (16 1/2 x 22 15/16 in.); Museum purchase through gift of George A. Hearn, 2002-20-2; © The Wilhelm Hansen Foundation

0631. Small Diamond chair, ca. 1957; Harry Bertoia (Italian, 1915–78) (chair) and Antoinette Lackner Webster (American, 1909–98) (textile); Manufactured by Knoll Associates, Inc. (East Greenville, Pennsylvania, USA) (chair) and Louisville Textiles (textile); Bent plastic-coated metal wire, woven cotton upholstery, foam rubber; 77.5 x 88.9 x 74.9 cm (30 1/2 x 35 x 29 1/2 in.); Gift of the Bard Graduate Center: Decorative Arts, Design History, Material Culture, 2011-22-1

0632. Model Number 41 armchair, ca. 1935–40; Alvar Aalto (Finnish, 1898–1976); Manufactured by Huonekalu-ja Rakennustyštehdas (Turku, Finland); Bent birch plywood, solid birch; 63.5 x 60.5 x 83 cm (25 x 23 13/16 x 32 11/16 in.); Museum purchase through gift of Linda and Irwin Berman and from General Acquisitions Endowment Fund, 2008-5-1

0633. Long chair, Estonia and London, England, 1936; Marcel Breuer (American, b. Hungary, 1902–81); Manufactured by Isokon Furniture Company (London, England); Bent birch (frame), bent and molded birch-faced plywood (seat); 74 x 62.6 x 136 cm (29 1/8 x 24 5/8 x 53 9/16 in.); Museum purchase through gift of George R. Kravis II, Anonymous Donor, and Judy Francis Zankel, 2013-17-1

0634. Photograph, Model 41 (Paimio) armchairs in the lecture room of the Paimio Sanatorium, 1928–32; Photo by Gustav Welin, Alvar Aalto Museum, 1930s

0635. Zig-Zag chair, Netherlands, ca. 1934; Gerrit Rietveld (Dutch, 1888–1964); Joined and painted elm; 73.8 x 36.8 x 42.5 cm (29 1/16 x 14 7/16 x 16 3/4 in.); Museum purchase from Decorative Arts Association Acquisition Fund, 1994-60-1; Photo by Dave King © Smithsonian Institution

0636. S chair, England, 1988; Tom Dixon (English, b. 1959); Recycled automobile rubber tire inner tube, steering wheel, welded steel (frame); 109.2 x 47 x 55.9 cm (43 x 18 1/2 x 22 in.); Museum purchase from General Acquisitions Endowment Fund, 2006-4-2; © Tom Dixon

0637. Drawing, Design for Vegetal Chair, 2005; Erwan Bouroullec (French, b. 1976) and Ronan Bouroullec (French, b. 1971); Photocopy, black marking pen on white wove paper; 20 x 29.6 cm (7 7/8 x 11 5/8 in.); Museum purchase from General Acquisitions Endowment Fund, 2011-30-1; © Ronan & Erwan Bouroullec

0638. Book illustration, Phacelia congesta (Phacelia), 1932; Karl Blossfeldt (German 1865–1932); From *Art Forms in Nature,* Second Series, (New York: E. Weyhe, 1932), plate 41; Photomechanical process on paper; 32.5 x 52.5 cm (12 3/4 x 20 5/8 in.); Purchased by the Mary Stuart Book Fund, Smithsonian Libraries, qNK1560. B52x

0639. Solid C2 chair, 2009; Patrick Jouin (French, b. 1967); Manufactured by Materialise NV (Leuven, Belgium); Stereolithography-formed epoxy resin; 76.8 x 40 x 54 cm (30 1/4 x 15 3/4 x 21 1/4 in.); Museum purchase from the Members' Acquisitions Fund of Cooper-Hewitt, National Design Museum, 2009-8-1; © C2 Chair, Solid Collection, Patrick Jouin iD

0640. Knotted chair, designed 1996, made 2008; Marcel Wanders (Dutch, b. 1963); Produced by Cappellini (Arioso, Italy); Rope (aramid fibers over carbon core; macramé knotting technique), soaked in epoxy resin, dried; 70.8 x 53.3 x 63.5 cm (27 7/8 x 21 x 25 in.); Gift of Cappellini, 2008-23-1; Photo by Ellen McDermott © Smithsonian Institution; © Cap Design S.p.A. / Wonders Holding BV

0641. Drawing, Study for Osso Chair, 2011; Erwan Bouroullec (French, b. 1976) and Ronan Bouroullec (French, b. 1971); Purple marking pen, graphite on white paper; 17.8 x 25 cm (7 x 9 13/16 in.); Gift of Erwan and Ronan Bouroullec, 2014-18-1; © Ronan & Erwan Bouroullec

0642. Drawing, Designs for Three Chairs, ca. 1990–93; Karim Rashid (Canadian, b. Egypt, 1960) for Plycraft (Lawrence, Massachusetts, USA); Pen and black ink on vellum; 43.2 x 35.6 cm (17 x 14 in.); Gift of Karim Rashid, 2000-50-11; © Karim Rashid

0643. Vermelha chair, designed 1998, manufactured 2007; Fernando Campana (Brazilian, b. 1961) and Humberto Campana (Brazilian, b. 1953); Manufactured by Edra S.p.A. (Pisa, Italy); Bent epoxy-coated steel, hand-woven dyed cotton rope, aluminum; 76.2 x 85.1 x 67.3 cm (30 x 33 1/2 x 26 1/2 in.); Gift of Edra S.p.A., Italy, 2007-39-1; Photo by Andrew Garn © Smithsonian Institution

0644. Cabbage chair, 2008; Oki Sato (Canadian, b. 1977) and Nendo (Tokyo, Japan); Pleated resin-coated paper, rolled, cut, and peeled to form layers; 78.7 x 74.9 x 68.6 cm (31 x 29 1/2 x 27 in.); Gift of Friedman Benda, New York and Nendo, 2009-9-1

0645. Poster, Niklaus Troxler, Schweizer Plakate des Jahres 77–99 (Swiss Posters from 1977–1999), 2001; Niklaus Troxler (Swiss, b. 1947); Offset lithograph on paper; 128.1 x 90.6 cm (50 7/16 x 35 11/16 in.); Gift of Niklaus Troxler, 2009-3-13; © Niklaus Troxler

0646. Reclining rocking chair, ca. 1905; Antonio Volpe (Italian); Manufactured by Societa Anonima Antonio Volpe (Udine, Italy); Bent beechwood, woven caning; 102.9 x 73.7 cm (40 1/2 x 29 in.); Museum purchase from the Members' Acquisitions Fund of Cooper-Hewitt, National Design Museum, 2007-7-1-a/c

0647. Rocking Chair No. 4, Vienna, Austria, ca. 1860; Made by Gebrüder (Brothers) Thonet (Vienna, Austria); Bent beechwood, woven caning; 97 x 56 x 80 cm (38 3/16 x 22 1/16 x 31 1/2 in.); Museum purchase through gift of American Institute of Interior Designers, 1969-103-2; Photo © Smithsonian Institution

0648. DCW side chair, 1946; Charles Eames (American, 1907–78) and Ray Eames (American, 1912–88); Manufactured by Herman Miller Furniture Company (Zeeland, Michigan, USA); Molded and bent plywood, rubber; 72.5 x 46 x 58 cm (28 9/16 x 18 1/8 x 22 13/16 in.); Gift of Anonymous Donor, 1963-22-1; © Courtesy of Herman Miller, Charles and Ray Eames Designers

0649. Chair, probably Birmingham, England, ca. 1750–60; Carved and joined red walnut, silk damask (reproduction); 95.5 x 62 x 57.5 cm (37 5/8 x 24 7/16 x 22 5/8 in.); Museum purchase from General Acquisitions Endowment Fund, 2006-5-1

0650. Side chair, probably Northern Italy, ca. 1785; Style of Michelangelo Pergolesi (Italian, active ca. 1760–1801); Carved, polychromed, gilt wood; 100 x 46.5 x 41.5 cm (39 3/8 x 18 5/16 x 16 5/16 in.); Gift of the Countess Costantini, 1924-6-1; Photo by Andrew Garn © Smithsonian Institution

0651. Chair, New York, New York, USA, ca. 1840; Attributed to Duncan Phyfe (American, 1768–1854); Turned, carved, and joined mahogany (legs and back), mahogany veneer (frame), oak, maple, ash (secondary wood in frame), brass (casters); 90.1 x 55.7 x 57.1 cm (35 1/2 x 21 15/16 x 22 1/2 in.); Bequest of Mrs. John Innes Kane, 1926-22-487

0652. Side chair, Buffalo, New York, USA, 1901; Charles Rohlfs (1853–1936); Joined and carved oak, leather cushions (reproduction); 122.5 x 51 x 59 cm (48 1/4 x 20 1/16 x 23 1/4 in.); Museum purchase from Mary Blackwelder Memorial Fund, 1976-22-1-a,b; Photo by Andrew Garn © Smithsonian Institution

0653. Scarsdale side chair, England, 1724–36; Attributed to Thomas How; Walnut and beechwood, gilt pewter, gilt-painted glass, verre églomisé panel, mortise-and-tenon construction; 104.1 x 55 x 57 cm (41 x 21 5/8 x 22 7/16 in.); Bequest of Mrs. John Innes Kane, 1926-22-58; Photo by Ellen McDermott © Smithsonian Institution

0654. Chair, probably Birmingham, England, 1844; Molded papier-mâché, inlaid with mother-of-pearl, painted and gilt wood; 90.5 x 63 x 60.1 cm (35 5/8 x 24 13/16 x 23 11/16 in.); Gift of Mr. and Mrs. Arthur Wiesenberger, 1967-66-1; Photo by Ellen McDermott © Smithsonian Institution

0655. Armchair, England, ca. 1765; Joined and turned mahogany; 87 x 59.5 x 49 cm (34 1/4 x 23 7/16 x 19 5/16 in.); Gift of George A. Hearn, 1900-25-14; Photo by Andrew Garn © Smithsonian Institution

0656. Armchair, China (for export), ca. 1815; Cut and stained bamboo, woven caning, varnish; 84.5 x 49 x 52 cm (33 1/4 x 19 5/16 x 20 1/2 in.); Gift of Mrs. William Pedlar, 1962-75-1; Photo by Andrew Garn © Smithsonian Institution

0657. Side chair, Berlin, Germany, 1902; Peter Behrens (German, 1868–1940); Made by Anton Blüggel; Distributed by Wertheim Department Store; Joined oak, pine, woven-rush caning; 98.4 x 55 x 45 cm (38 3/4 x 21 5/8 x 17 11/16 in.); Museum purchase from General Acquisitions Endowment Fund, 1985-121-1; Photo by Dennis Cowley © Smithsonian Institution

0658. Book illustration, Causeuse d'encoignure (Corner love seat), 1841–51; Désiré Guilmard, compiler (French, b. 1810); From *Le garde-meuble* (Furniture Depository), (Paris: D. Guilmard), book 68, plate 392; Color lithograph on paper; 36 x 26 cm (14 x 10 1/4 in.); Purchase, Smithsonian Libraries, f NK2547.Z8 G96

0659. Writing desk, Milan, Italy, ca. 1902; Carlo Zen (Italian, 1851–1918); Joined, bent, and turned fruitwood, inlaid with brass, white metal, mother-of-pearl, leather; 104.1 x 64.8 x 63.5 cm (41 x 25 1/2 x 25 in.); Gift of John Goodwin, 1963-29-1

0660. Argyle Tea Rooms armchair, Glasgow, Scotland, 1897; Charles Rennie Mackintosh (Scottish, 1868–1928); Made by Francis Smith & Son; Joined oak; 82.5 x 52 x 47 cm (32 1/2 x 20 1/2 x 18 1/2 in.); Gift of David Byrne and Adelle Lutz, 1994-52-1

0661. Norman bar stools, 1997; Tom Dixon (Bristish, b. 1959); Manufactured by Eurolounge (England); Molded polyethylene; each: 49.5 x 56.8 x 53.3 cm (19 1/2 x 22 3/8 x 21 in.); The Linda and Irwin R. Berman Stool Collection, 2008-32-6, S-A-252; Photo by Ellen McDermott © Smithsonian Institution; © Tom Dixon

0662. Bowls, China, late 19th–early 20th century; Carved molded glass; a: 6.2 x 15.2 cm diam. (2 7/16 x 6 in.), b: 6.1 x 15.2 cm diam. (2 3/8 x 6 in.); Gift of Paul Manheim, 1968-155-14-a,b; Photo by Ellen McDermott © Smithsonian Institution

0663. Gloves, taly, 1600–50; Leather glove with silk satin cuff, embroidered with metallic yarns, woven silk fringe; 36.2 x 22.2 cm (14 1/4 x 8 3/4 in.) each; Gift of Mrs. John Innes Kane, 1941-86-1-a,b

0664. Poster, Bayerische Staatsoper (Bavarian State Opera), *Rodelinda, Regina de' Longobardi*, Georg Friedrich Händel, 2003; Pierre Mendell(German, 1929–2008); Offset lithograph on paper; 119 x 84 cm (46 7/8 x 33 1/16 in.); Gift of Sara and Marc Benda, 2009-20-35; © Pierre Mendell Design Studio

0665. Poster, He Who Stops Being Better Stops Being Good, IBM Excellence Plus, 1985; Paul Rand (American, 1914–96) for IBM (Armonk, New York, USA); Offset lithograph on paper; 32.9 x 25.2 cm (12 15/16 x 9 15/16 in.); Gift of Marion S. Rand, 2002-11-32; © Marion S. Rand

0666. Up 1 chair, 1969; Gaetano Pesce (Italian, b. 1939); Produced by Cassina and Busnelli Italia (C & B) (Como, Italy); Molded polyurethane foam, stretch-fabric upholstery; 63 x 93 x 78 cm (24 13/16 x 36 5/8 x 30 11/16 in.); Gift of the Estate of Frederick N. Babbish, 1991-94-5; Photo by Ellen McDermott © Smithsonian Institution

0667. Pastilli rocking chair, 1968; Eero Aarnio (Finnish, b. 1932); Manufactured by Asko Oy (Lahti, Finland); Molded fiber-glass-reinforced polyester; 52 x 92 cm diam. (20 1/2 x 36 1/4 in.); Gift of The Lake St. Louis Historical Society, 2001-31-2; Photo by Ellen McDermott © Smithsonian Institution

0668. Colorstone salt and pepper shakers, 1986; Lella Vignelli (Italian, b. 1934) and Massimo Vignelli (Italian, 1931–2014) with David Law (American, b. 1937); Manufactured by Sasaki (Japan); Glazed molded stoneware; Each: 5.5 x 5 cm diam. (2 3/16 x 1 15/16 in.); Gift of Lella and Massimo Vignelli, 1990-2-5,6; Photo by Ellen McDermott © Smithsonian Institution; © Vignelli Designs, 1986

0669. Salt and pepper shakers, ca. 1975; Arne Petersen (Danish, b. 1922); Manufactured by Georg Jensen Sølvsmedie (Copenhagen, Denmark); Press-formed stainless steel; Each: 3.5 x 6 cm diam. (1 3/8 x 2 3/8 in.); Gift of Mel Byars, 1991-59-36,37; Photo by Ellen McDermott © Smithsonian Institution

0670. Iroquois Casual stacking salt and pepper shakers, 1947; Russel Wright (American, 1904–76); Manufactured by Iroquois China Company (Syracuse, New York, USA); Glazed, molded porcelain, cork; -26-a,b: 3.4 x 7.1 cm diam. (1 5/16 x 2 13/16 in.), -27-a,b: 4.5 x 7 cm (1 3/4 x 2 3/4 in.); Gift of the Brooklyn Museum of Art, Paul F. Walter Collection, 1999-42-26-a,b, 27-a,b; Photo by Ellen McDermott © Smithsonian Institution; © Russel Wright is a registered trademark by Russel Wright Studios, LLC

0671. Salt and pepper shakers, 1953; Wilhelm Wagenfeld (German, 1900–90); Manufactured by Württembergische Metallwarenfabrik (WMF) (Geislingen, Germany); Molded glass, pierced stainless steel; H x diam.: 6.7 x 5.5 cm (2 5/8 x 2 3/16 in.); Gift of Christian Rohlfing, 1979-63-1-a,b; Photo by Ellen McDermott © Smithsonian Institution

0672. Sinus bowls, ca. 1985–86; Lino Sabattini (Italian, b. 1925); Manufactured by Rosenthal Glas und Porzellan Aktiengesellschaft (Selb/Bayern, Germany); Glazed molded porcelain; -1: 6.5 x 34 x 12 cm (2 9/16 x 13 3/8 x 4 3/4 in.); -2: 4.5 x 24 x 8.5 cm (1 3/4 x 9 7/16 x 3 3/8 in.); Gift of Lino Sabattini, 1987-38-1,2; Photo by Ellen McDermott © Smithsonian Institution

0673. Arc Touch flexible computer mouses with transceivers, 2010; Microsoft Hardware User Experience Design Team; Manufactured by Microsoft (Redmond, Washington, USA); Molded ABS plastic, polycarbonate, silicone, metal; 1a,b (flat): 1.6 x 5.7 x 13 cm (5/8 x 2 1/4 x 5 1/8 in.), 2a,b (curved): 3.2 × 5.7 × 10.8 cm (1 1/4 × 2 1/4 × 4 1/4 in.); Gift of Microsoft, 2011-60-1-a,b, 2a,b; Photo by Ellen McDermott © Smithsonian Institution

0674. Paro goblets, 1983; Achille Castiglioni (Italian, 1918–2002); Manufactured by Danese Milano (Milan, Italy); Glass; a, b, each: 20.6 x 8.2 cm diam. (8 1/8 x 3 1/4 in.); Gift of Bruno Danese snc, 1986-36-1, 2

0675. Book illustration, Dolphin Toilet, 1888; J. L. Mott (American, 1829–1915); From *Catalogue G* (New York: The J. L. Mott Iron Works), p. 72; Color lithograph on paper; 35.5 x 28 (14 x 11 in.); Gift of Calvin S. Hathaway, 1956, Smithsonian Libraries, fTH6255.J615 1888

0676. Vases, France, ca. 1905; Hector Guimard (French, 1867–1942); Gilt bronze; 26 x 12.6 x 12.6 cm (10 1/4 x 4 15/16 x 4 15/16 in.); Gift of Mme Hector Guimard, 1948-114-3; Photo © Smithsonian Institution

0677. Stacking tea service, ca. 1970; Manufactured by Gabbianelli (Milan, Italy); Molded and glazed earthenware, metal; a/f assembled: 22.5 x 24.5 x 15.2 cm (8 7/8 x 9 5/8 x 6 in.); Gift of George and Louise Beylerian, 1991-168-2-a/f; Photo by Ellen McDermott © Smithsonian Institution

0678. Poster, FD-5: Flocking Diplomats New York: Time of Violation, January 2008; Catalogtree (Arnhem, Netherlands); Offset lithograph on white wove paper; 100.2 x 68.9 cm (39 7/16 x 27 1/8 in.); Gift of Joris Maltha and Daniel Gross, 2009-30-5; © Joris Maltha & Daniel Gross (Catalogtree)

0679. Drawing, Paper Sample, Red, England, n.d.; Red printed laid paper; 6.5 x 17.3 cm (2 9/16 x 6 13/16 in.), irregular; Museum purchase through gift of Mrs. John Innes Kane, 1948-40-191-a

0680. R-72 portable radio, ca. 1970; Manufactured by National Panasonic Radio, Matushita Electrical Industrial Co., Ltd. (Japan); Molded ABS plastic, metal; Closed: 7 x 15.2 cm diam. (2 3/4 x 6 in.); Gift of Jacqueline Loewe Fowler, 2007-37-5; Photo by Ellen McDermott © Smithsonian Institution

0681. Pair of child's chairs with table insert, 1957; Kristian Vedel (Danish, 1923–2003); Manufactured by Torben Ørskov & Co. (Copenhagen, Denmark); Painted, bent-beech plywood; 40.3 x 44.1 x 32.1 cm (15 7/8 x 17 3/8 x 12 5/8 in.); Gift of Jacqueline Loewe Fowler, 2007-37-1, 2; © Kristian Vedel Design

0682. Kobenstyle casserole and lid, designed in Denmark, 1956, manufactured in France, ca. 1970; Jens H. Quistgaard (Danish, 1919–2008); Manufactured by Dansk International Designs, Ltd.; Enameled steel; 13 x 29 x 23 cm (5 1/8 x 11 7/16 x 9 1/16 in.); Gift of Dansk Designs, Ltd., 1975-57-3-a,b; Photo by Ellen McDermott © Smithsonian Institution

0683. Book cover, *Bookjackets by Alvin Lustig* for New Directions Books, 1947; Alvin Lustig (American, 1915–55) for New Directions (New York, New York, USA); Lithograph on white wove paper; 18.8 x 18.9 cm (7 3/8 x 7 7/16 in.); Gift of Tamar Cohen and Dave Slatoff, 1993-31-165-15; © Elaine Lustig Cohen

0684. Chest for stereo, Scottsville, New York, USA, 1973; Wendell Castle (American, b. 1932); Stack-laminated and carved walnut, metal, leather, stereo components; Closed: 113.3 x 109.2 x 55.9 cm (44 5/8 x 43 x 22 in.); Gift of Linda and Irwin R. Berman, 2005-9-1-a/e; Photo by Ellen McDermott © Smithsonian Institution; © Wendell Castle, Inc.

0685. Balcony grille, 1909–11; Hector Guimard (French, 1867–1942); Manufactured by Saint Dizier Foundry (St. Dizier, Champagne, France); Cast iron; 50.8 x 83.8 x 4 cm (20 in. x 33 in. x 3/4 in.); Museum purchase from the Members' Acquisitions Fund of Cooper-Hewitt, National Design Museum, 2011-28-1; Photo by Ellen McDermott © Smithsonian Institution

0686. Model for Grillework, 1909–11; Hector Guidmard (French, 1867–1942); Made by Saint Dizier Foundry (St. Dizier, Champagne, France); Cast iron; 12.1 x 121.3 cm (4 ¾ x 47 ¾ in.); Gift of Harry C. Sigman, 2013-21-7

0687. Drawing, Societé Immobilière de la rue Moderne, No. 6, Paris, France: Design for the Façade, 1909; Hector Guimard (French, 1867–1942); Pen and black ink, graphite on heavy tracing paper; 61.9 x 46.7 cm (24 3/8 x 18 3/8 in.); Gift of Mme Hector Guimard, 1950-66-12

0688. Photograph, Apartment Building (No. 3), 1911; Hector Guimard (French, 1867–1942); Photographic print on sensitized paper; 17.8 x 11.5 cm (7 x 4 1/2 in.); Gift of Mme Hector Guimard, 1951-160-1-3

0689. Drawing, A.H. Barney Residence, New York, New York, USA: Design for Mermaid Window, 1882; Elihu Vedder (American, 1836–1923) for Louis C. Tiffany & Co. (USA); Color crayon, brush, and gold paint on off-white wove paper; 22.7 x 8.1 cm (8 15/16 x 3 3/16 in.); Gift of the American Academy of Arts and Letters, 1955-38-2-a

0690. Textile, Femme à Marguerite (Woman with Daisy), 1898–1900; Alphonse Maria Mucha (Czech, 1860–1939); Printed cotton velvet; 70.2 x 78.1 cm (27 5/8 x 30 3/4 in.); Museum purchase from General Acquisitions Endowment Fund, 2004-6-2

0691. Print, Der Kuss (The Kiss), from *Pan*, vol. 4, no. 2, 1898; Peter Behrens (German, 1868–1940); Woodcut on thin buff Japan paper; 27.2 x 21.6 cm (10 11/16 x 8 1/2 in.); Museum purchase from General Acquisitions Endowment Fund, 2005-13-1

0692. Textile, Honeysuckle, designed 1876; William Morris (British, 1834–96); Manufactured by Morris & Co. (Merton Abbey, England); Block printed on cotton warp, linen weft; 274.3 x 95.3 cm (108 x 37 1/2 in.); Gift of Robert W. Friedel, 1951-103-53-a

0693. Clock, ca. 1910; Arnhem Faience Factory (Arnhem, Netherlands); Glazed earthenware, molded, cast, gilt, and enameled metal; 22.7 x 13.1 cm (8 15/16 x 5 3/16 in.); Gift of Justin G. Schiller, 1993-120-3-a/c; Photo by Ellen McDermott © Smithsonian Institution

0694. Paris Métro medallion, Paris, France, 1900; Hector Guimard (French, 1867–1942); Painted and patinated cast iron; 73.7 x 61 cm (29 x 24 in.); Gift of Harry C. Sigman, 2013-21-6

0695. Poster, Tropon est l'aliment le plus concentré (Tropon Is the Most Concentrated Food Supplement), 1898; Henry van de Velde (Belgian, 1863–1957); Lithograph on wove paper, lined; 111.8 x 77.5 cm (44 x 30 1/2 in.); Museum purchase through gift of Mr. and Mrs. Lee S. Ainslie III, Marilyn Friedman, and Nancy Marks; General Acquisitions Endowment; Drawings & Prints Council Fund, 2007-2-1

0696. Teapot and lid, Iowa City, Iowa, USA, 1988; Chunghi Choo (American, b. Korea, 1938); Silver-plated electroformed copper, anodized aluminum, onyx; 17.3 x 45.5 x 11 cm (6 13/16 x 17 15/16 x 4 5/16 in.); Purchase in memory of Mildred Rosenberg, Gift of her Family, 1992-33-1-a,b

0697. Corvus Corax teapot and lid, 1982; Matteo Thun (Italian, b. 1952); Manufactured by Alessio Sarri Ceramiche (Florence, Italy) for Anthologie Quartett; Glazed molded porcelain; 21.3 x 35.6 cm (8 3/8 x 14 in.); Museum purchase from General Acquisition Endowment, 1984-70-1-a,b; Photo by Ellen McDermott © Smithsonian Institution

0698. Book illustration, Adiantum pedatum Haarfarn (Maidenhair fern), 1929; Karl Blossfeldt (German 1865–1932); From *Urformen der Kunst* (*Art Forms in Nature*), (Berlin: Ernst Wasmuth, 1929), plate 55; Photomechanical process on paper; 32 x 49.5 cm (12 5/8 x 19 3/8 in.); Purchase J. Pierpont Morgan Book Fund, 1942, Smithsonian Libraries, qNK1560. B65

0699. Footed bowl, 1905–16; Louis Comfort Tiffany (American, 1848–1933); Made by Tiffany Studios (Corona, New York, USA); Molded iridized glass; 19.2 x 22.8 cm diam. (7 9/16 x 9 in.); Gift of Stanley Siegel, from the Stanley Siegel Collection, 1975-32-14; Photo by John White © Smithsonian Institution

0700. Print, Design for Cartouche with Fountain and Sea Putti, from *Livre nouveau de morceaux de fantaisie* (*Book of New Fantasy Designs*), 1738/1745; Jean-François Cuvilliés (Flemish, active Germany, 1695–1768); Engraved and etched by Charles-Albert Lespilliez (Flemish, active Germany, 1723–96); Engraving, etching on laid paper; 38.9 x 27.9 cm (15 5/16 x 11 in); Purchased for the Museum by the Advisory Council, 1921-6-282-18

0701. Print, Winged Griffon on a Rocaille Bracket, from *Divers ornemens, première partie* (*Various Ornament Designs, Part One*), 1745; Alexis Peyrotte (French, 1699–1769); Etched and published by Gabriel Huquier (French, 1695–1772); Etching on white laid paper; 47.9 x 32.8 cm (18 7/8 x 12 15/16 in.); Purchased for the Museum by the Advisory Council, 1921-6-213-6

0702. Poster, Préparation du repas, sélection international stockage, préparation, caisson, utensiles (Preparation of Meals, Storage, Housing, Utensils), Centre de Création Industrielle (Center of Industrial Creation), Paris, France, 1972; Jean Widmer (Swiss, b. 1929); Screenprint on wove paper; 64.4 x 50 cm (25 3/8 x 19 11/16 in.); Gift of Sara and Marc Benda, 2009-12-22

0703. Ashtray, 1949; Russel Wright (American, 1904–76); Manufactured by Sterling China Company (Wellsville, Ohio, USA); Glazed, molded porcelain; 3.2 x 15.5 cm diam. (1 1/4 x 6 1/8 in.); Gift of the Brooklyn Museum of Art, Paul F. Walter Collection, 1999-42-38; Photo by Ellen McDermott © Smithsonian Institution; © Russel Wright is a registered trademark by Russel Wright Studios, LLC

0704. Powder compact, 1978; Elsa Peretti (Italian, b. 1940); Manufactured by Max Factor for Halston Enterprises, Inc. (New York, New York, USA); Cast, silver-plated metal, mirror; 1.8 x 9.8 x 7.2 cm (11/16 x 3 7/8 x 2 13/16 in.); Gift of Halston Enterprises, Inc., 1978-123-2; Photo by Ellen McDermott © Smithsonian Institution

0705. Uovo Orizzontale (Horizontal Egg) table lamp, 1967; Cesare Casati (Italian, b. 1936); Manufactured by Ceramic Franco Pozzi (Gallarate, Italy); Glazed, molded earthenware, metal; 16 x 31 x 21 cm (6 5/16 x 12 3/16 x 8 1/4 in.); Museum purchase from General Acquisitions Endowment Fund, 2007-16-1; Photo by Ellen McDermott © Smithsonian Institution

0706. American Modern cream boat, 1937; Russel Wright (American, 1904–76); Manufactured by Steubenville Pottery Company (Steubenville, Ohio, USA); Glazed, molded earthenware; 7.9 x 18.3 x 8.3 cm (3 1/8 x 7 3/16 x 3 1/4 in.); Gift of Mark Kaminski, 1993-63-13; Photo by Ellen McDermott © Smithsonian Institution; © Russel Wright is a registered trademark by Russel Wright Studios, LLC

0707. American Modern celery dish, 1937; Russel Wright (American, 1904–76); Manufactured by Steubenville Pottery Company (Steubenville, Ohio, USA); Glazed, molded earthenware; 3 x 33 x 8.5 cm (1 3/16 x 13 x 3 3/8 in.); Gift of Max Pine, 2010-2-1; © Russel Wright is a registered trademark by Russel Wright Studios, LLC

0708. Iroquois Casual butter dish and lid, 1947; Russel Wright (American, 1904–76); Manufactured by Iroquois China Company (Syracuse, New York, USA); Glazed, molded porcelain; a, b overall: 6.5 x 19 x 10.5 cm (2 9/16 x 7 1/2 x 4 1/8 in.); Gift of the Brooklyn Museum of Art, Paul F. Walter Collection, 1999-42-32-a,b; Photo by Ellen McDermott © Smithsonian Institution; © Russel Wright is a registered trademark by Russel Wright Studios, LLC

0709. Photograph, Ceiling fixture, Rockefeller Center, 1932; Caldwell and Company (New York, New York, USA, 1894–ca. 1944); Photograph on paper; 15 x 15 cm (6 x 6 in.); Smithsonian Libraries, NK2115.5.L5 S54

0710. St. Thomas or St. Matthew Spoon, Exeter, England, ca. 1661; Cast and molded parcel gilt silver; 18.6 x 4.9 cm (7 5/16 x 1 15/16 in.); Museum purchase through gift of Joseph Holtzman and from General Acquisitions Endowment Fund, 2006-7-1

0711. Fork and spoon, Nuremburg, Germany, ca. 1600–30; Carved coral, cast and chased gilt silver; Fork: 19 x 1.7 cm (7 1/2 x 11/16 in.), spoon: 19.5 x 4.9 cm (7 11/16 x 1 15/16 in.); The Robert L. Metzenberg Collection, gift of Eleanor L. Metzenberg, 1985-103-81,82

0712. Drop teapot, sugar bowl, and cream pitcher, 1971; Luigi Colani (German, b. 1928); Manufactured by Rosenthal Glas Und Porzellan Aktiengesellschaft for Studio-Line (Division of Rosenthal) (Selb, Germany); Molded and glazed porcelain; Teapot: 10.5 x 25 x 19.6 cm (4 1/8 x 9 13/16 x 7 11/16 in.); Gift of Rosenthal Glas und Porzellan AG, 1985-3-9-a,b,10,11; Photo by Ellen McDermott © Smithsonian Institution

0713. American Modern tableware and Pinch flatware, 1937–50; Russel Wright (American, 1904–76); Manufactured by Steubenville Pottery Company (Steubenville, Ohio, USA) (ceramics), Morgantown Glass Guild (Morgantown, West Virginia, USA) (glassware), Hull Cutlery (Meriden, Connecticut, USA) (flatware); Glazed, molded earthenware, molded glass, forged stainless steel; Gift of Russel Wright, 1976-15-4a/e, 5c/e, 6a/d; Photo by © Smithsonian Institution; © Russel Wright is a registered trademark by Russel Wright Studios, LLC.

0714. Bacco cocktail cabinet, 1967–69; Sergio Mazza (Italian, b. 1931); manufactured by Artemide S.p.A. (Milan, Italy); Molded ABS plastic; 42 x 61.5 x 61.5 cm (16 9/16 x 24 3/16 x 24 3/16 in.); Gift of The Lake St. Louis Historical Society, 2001-31-3; Photo by Ellen McDermott © Smithsonian Institution

0715. Trade catalog, Specimens of Silver, Engraved, Oxidized and Gold Inlaid Ware, 1884; The firm of Reed & Barton, illustrations by John A. J. (Angel James Wilcox, b. 1835); From *Reed & Barton, Artistic Workers in Silver & Gold plate* (Taunton, Massachusetts: Reed & Barton, 1884), p. 292; Color lithograph on paper; Gift of Reed & Barton, ca. 1990, Smithsonian Libraries, f 046780

0716. Book illustration, Specimens of Silver, Engraved, Oxidized and Gold Inlaid Ware, 1884; The firm of Reed & Barton, illustrations by John A. J. (Angel James Wilcox, b. 1835); From *Reed & Barton, Artistic Workers in Silver & Gold Plate* (Taunton, Massachusetts: Reed & Barton, 1884), p. 300–01; Color lithograph on paper; Gift of Reed & Barton, ca. 1990, Smithsonian Libraries, f 046780

0717. Drawing, Design for Knife, Fork, and Spoon, 1950–70; Tommi Parzinger (American, b. Germany, 1903–81); Brush and silver paint, white gouache, graphite on heavy cream paper; 25 x 19.2 cm (9 13/16 x 7 9/16 in.); Gift of Donald Cameron, 1998-19-51

0718. Drawing, Design for Highlight / Pinch flatware, for John Hull Cutlers Corporation, February 20, 1948; Russel Wright (American, 1904–76); Brush and green, white gouache, black ink, wash, black chalk, graphite on chartreuse paper mounted on board; 53.1 x 48.2 cm (20 7/8 x 19 in.); Gift of Russel Wright, 1976-15-9; Photo by Ken Pelka © Smithsonian Institution, © Russel Wright is a registered trademark by Russel Wright Studios, LLC.

0719. Book illustration, Specimens of Silver, Engraved, Oxidized and Gold Inlaid Ware, 1884; The firm of Reed & Barton, illustrations by John A. J. (Angel James Wilcox, b. 1835); From *Reed & Barton, Artistic Workers in Silver & Gold Plate* (Taunton, Massachusetts: Reed & Barton, 1884), p. 168; Color lithograph on paper; Gift of Reed & Barton, c. 1990, Smithsonian Libraries, f 046780

0720. Book illustration, Specimens of Silver, Engraved, Oxidized and Gold Inlaid Ware, 1884; The firm of Reed & Barton, illustrations by John A. J. (Angel James Wilcox, b. 1835); From *Reed & Barton, Artistic Workers in Silver & Gold Plate* (Taunton, Massachusetts: Reed & Barton, 1884), p. 7; Color lithograph on paper; Gift of Reed & Barton, ca. 1990, Smithsonian Libraries, f 046780

0721. Garbo wastebasket, 1996; Karim Rashid (Canadian, b. Egypt, 1960), Karim Rashid Industrial Design; Manufactured by Umbra (Buffalo, New York, USA); Molded polypropylene; 43.1 x 34.2 x 34 cm (16 15/16 x 13 7/16 x 13 3/8 in.); Gift of Anonymous Donor, 1999-9-1; Photo by Ellen McDermott © Smithsonian Institution

0722. Vase, 1968–69; Lüsi Beckman; Manufactured by Gabbianelli (Milan, Italy); Glazed, molded earthenware; 22.5 x 28.5 x 13 cm (8 7/8 x 11 1/4 x 5 1/8 in.); Gift of George and Louise Beylerian, 1991-168-7; Photo by Ellen McDermott © Smithsonian Institution

0723. Radio Nurse intercom speaker, 1937–38; Isamu Noguchi (American, 1904–88); Manufactured by Zenith Radio Corporation (Chicago, Illinois, USA); Molded Bakelite, metal; Without cord: 19.8 x 17 x 16 cm (7 13/16 x 6 11/16 x 6 5/16 in.); Gift of Mel Byars, 1991-59-61; Photo by John White © Smithsonian Institution

0724. Brochure, Radio Nurse advertisement brochure, ca. 1938; Courtesy of Zenith Electronics LLC

0725. ALPS Interactive PS Gamepad video game controller, 1996; Scott Henderson (American, b. 1966), Smart Design, Inc.; Manufactured by Alps Electric Co., Ltd. (Japan); Molded plastic, electronic components; 5.3 x 19 x 15.5 cm (2 1/16 x 7 1/2 x 6 1/8 in.); Gift of Smart Design, 1997-182-1; Photo by Ellen McDermott © Smithsonian Institution

0726. Ericofon telephone, designed 1949–54, this example ca. 1956; L.M. Ericsson Company (Sweden), Hugo Blomberg (Swedish, b. 1897), Ralph Lysell (Swedish, b. 1907), Hans Gösta Thames (Swedish, b. 1916); Manufactured by North Electric Company (Galion, Ohio, USA); Molded ABS plastic, nylon, rubber, metal, printed paper; 20.5 x 9 x 11 cm (8 1/16 x 3 9/16 x 4 5/16 in.); Museum purchase from General Acquisitions Endowment and through gifts of Charlton M. Theus, Jr., and Mrs. Paul Moore, 1998-36-1; Photo by Ellen McDermott © Smithsonian Institution

0727. Steam-O-Matic iron, ca. 1939; Steam-O-Matic Corporation (Milwaukee, Wisconsin, USA); Cast aluminum, painted wood; 16.2 x 28 x 13 cm (6 3/8 x 11 x 5 1/8 in.); Gift of Ms. Carole Krohn, 1993-126-15; Photo by Ellen McDermott © Smithsonian Institution

0728. Sunny Suzy child's iron, ca. 1955; Wolverine Supply & Mfg. Co. (Pittsburgh, Pennsylvania, USA); Cast metal, painted metal and wood, fabric (cord); 8.8 x 16.5 x 8 cm (3 7/16 x 6 1/2 x 3 1/8 in.); Gift of Ms. Carole Krohn, 1993-126-7; Photo by Ellen McDermott © Smithsonian Institution

0729. Model 302 telephone, ca. 1937; Henry Dreyfuss (American, 1904–72); Manufactured by Western Electric Manufacturing Company for Bell Telephone Company (USA); Cast and enamel-coated metal, steel, printed paper, rubber-sheathed cord; 14 x 23 x 18.5 cm (5 1/2 x 9 1/16 x 7 5/16 in.); Museum purchase from the Decorative Arts Association Acquisition Fund, 1994-73-2; Photo by Dave King © Smithsonian Institution

0730. Travel iron, ca. 1950; Manufactured by O & N (Denmark); Cast metal, molded plastic, fabric (cord); 5.5 x 12 x 5.2 cm (2 3/16 x 4 3/4 x 2 1/16 in.); Museum purchase from Eleanor G. Hewitt Fund, 1998-9-1; Photo by Ellen McDermott © Smithsonian Institution

0731. Silver Streak iron, 1942–46; Manufactured by Saunders Machine & Tool Corp. (Yonkers, New York, USA) and Corning Glass Works (Corning, New York, USA) (glass); Molded Pyrex glass, metal, molded plastic, rubber, fabric (cord); 13.8 x 9.8 x 23 cm (5 7/16 x 3 7/8 x 9 1/16 in.); Museum purchase from Decorative Arts Association Acquisition Fund, 1996-39-1; Photo by Hiro Ihara © Smithsonian Institution

0732. Sunbeam Mixmaster mixer, Model 11C, ca. 1955; Ivar Jepson (American, b. Sweden, 1903–65); Manufactured by Sunbeam Corporation (Chicago, Illinois, USA); Chrome-plated metal, molded glass, molded plastic; 32 x 25 x 34 cm (12 5/8 x 9 13/16 x 13 3/8 in.); Museum purchase from Decorative Arts Association Acquisition Fund, 1993-150-1-a/h; Photo by Ellen McDermott © Smithsonian Institution

0733. GRiD Compass laptop computer prototype, 1981; Bill Moggridge (British, 1943–2012); Manufactured by GRiD Systems Corp. (Mountain View, California, USA); Die-cast magnesium, injection-molded plastic; 25.4 x 29.2 x 37.9 cm (10 x 11 1/2 x 14 15/16 in.); Gift of Bill Moggridge, 2010-22-1

0734. Vertu MMII cellular telephone, 2002; Mr. Frank Nuovo (American, b. 1961); Manufactured by Vertu Ltd. (England); Platinum, sapphire crystal, ceramic, leather; 12.2 x 4.2 x 1.6 cm (4 13/16 x 1 5/8 x 5/8 in.); Gift of Vertu, Ltd., 2004-9-1-a,b; © Vertu, Ltd.

0735. BeoCom 1500 telephone and base, 1994; Martin Iseli (Swiss, b. 1952); Manufactured by Bang & Olufsen (Copenhagen, Denmark) for ASCOM Business Systems AG; Molded plastic, metal; 18 x 15 cm (7 1/16 x 5 7/8 in.); Gift of Bang & Olufsen, Telephone Division, 1995-126-1-a,b; Photo by Ellen McDermott © Smithsonian Institution

0736. iPhone mobile telephone, 2007; Jonathan Ive (British, b. 1967) and Apple Industrial Design Team; Manufactured by Apple Computer, Inc. (Cupertino, California, USA); Molded ABS plastic and polycarbonate resin, polished stainless steel, oleophobic coated glass, aluminum; 11.4 x 6.1 x 1.2 cm (4 1/2 x 2 3/8 x 7/16 in.); Gift of Roland L. Trope, 2009-29-1; © Apple, Inc.

0737. StarTAC™ cellular telephone, 1996; Al Nagele (American, b. 1935) and Leon Soren (American, b. 1945); Manufactured by Motorola, Inc. (Libertyville, Illinois, USA); Injection-molded polycarbonate, metal, electronic components; 2.2 x 6 x 12.5 cm (7/8 x 2 3/8 x 4 15/16 in.); Gift of Motorola, Inc., 1999-56-1-a/c; Photo by Ellen McDermott © Smithsonian Institution; Motorola and the insignia logo are registered trademarks of Motorola, Inc. © Motorola, Inc., all rights reserved

0738. BeoCom Copenhagen telephone, 1986; Lininger-Lowy; Manufactured by Bang & Olufsen (Copenhagen, Denmark); Molded plastic, electronic components; 7.8 x 21 x 21.5 cm (3 1/16 x 8 1/4 x 8 7/16 in.); Gift of Arango Design Foundation, 1994-31-122-a/c; Photo by Ellen McDermott © Smithsonian Institution

0739. Enorme telephone, 1986; Ettore Sottsass, Jr. (Italian, 1917–2007), and Marco Zanini (Italian, b. 1954); Manufactured by Enorme (Italy) for Becker Inc.; Molded plastic, rubber, electronic components; 5.8 x 19.2 x 10.2 cm (2 5/16 x 7 9/16 x 4 in.); Gift of Becker Inc., 1987-91-1-a/d; Photo by Ellen McDermott © Smithsonian Institution

0740. Folle 26 stapler, 1977; Henning Andreasen (Danish, b. 1923); Manufactured by Folle APS (Denmark); Enameled steel, steel, iron; 4.2 x 15.5 x 3.8 cm (1 5/8 x 6 1/8 x 1 1/2 in.); Gift of Arango Design Foundation, 1994-31-75; Photo by Ellen McDermott © Smithsonian Institution

0741. Nutcracker, ca. 1987; Manufactured by Cini & Nils (Milan, Italy); Stainless steel; 16 x 2.5 cm diam. (6 5/16 x 1 in.); Gift of Dr. Richard Grant, 1987-95-3; Photo by Ellen McDermott © Smithsonian Institution

0742. Transistor Phonoradio portable phonograph-radio, ca. 1962; Manufactured by TACT Denici Co., Ltd. (Japan); Molded plastic, metal, electronics; 4 x 17.3 x 8.7 cm (1 9/16 x 6 13/16 x 3 7/16 in.); Gift of Arthur Lindo and Jay Loebel, 1991-92-1-a/d; Photo by Ellen McDermott © Smithsonian Institution

0743. Divisumma 18 calculator, 1973; Mario Bellini (Italian, b. 1935); Manufactured by Ing. C. Olivetti & C. S.p.A. (Ivrea, Italy); ABS plastic, melamine, rubber, metal; 4.6 x 30.9 x 12 cm (1 13/16 x 12 3/16 x 4 3/4 in.); Gift of Barry Friedman and Patricia Pastor, 1986-99-41; Photo by Matt Flynn © Smithsonian Institution

0744. Logos 59 calculator, 1973; Mario Bellini (Italian, b. 1935); Manufactured by Ing. C. Olivetti & C. S.p.A. (Ivrea, Italy); Molded plastic, metal; 12.3 x 42.2 x 33.2 cm (4 13/16 x 16 5/8 x 13 1/16 in.); Gift of Barry Friedman and Patricia Pastor, 1986-99-1; Photo by Ellen McDermott © Smithsonian Institution

0745. T52 Clairtone portable radio, 1961; Dieter Rams (German, b. 1932); Manufactured by Braun AG (Frankfurt, Germany); Molded plastic, metal; 5.8 x 22.8 x 14.5 cm (2 5/16 x 9 x 5 11/16 in.); Gift of Barry Friedman and Patricia Pastor, 1986-99-23; Photo by Ellen McDermott © Smithsonian Institution

0746. Kindle and Kindle 2 electronic reading devices, 2007, 2009; Amazon.com (Seattle, Washington, USA); Plastic, acrylic; 1: 20.3 × 13.5 × 1.8 cm (8 in. × 5 5/16 in. × 11/16 in.), 2: 20.3 x 13.5 x 0.9 cm (8 x 5 5/16 x 3/8 in.); Gift of Amazon.com, 2009-53-1, 2

0747. iPod Nano digital media player, 2009; Jonathan Ive (British, b. 1967) and Apple Industrial Design Team; Manufactured by Apple Computer, Inc. (Cupertino, California, USA); Molded ABS plastic and polycarbonate resin, polished stainless steel, aluminum; 9 x 4 x 1 cm (3 9/16 x 1 9/16 x 3/8 in.); Gift of Apple, 2010-34-3; © Apple, Inc.

0748. iPod digital music player, 2001; Jonathan Ive (English, b. 1967) and Apple Industrial Design Team; Manufactured by Apple Computer, Inc. (Cupertino, California, USA); Plastic, polycarbonate, stainless steel; 10.4 x 6.1 x 1.9 cm (4 1/8 x 2 3/8 x 3/4 in.); Gift of David and Kelly Theresa Linton, 2009-49-1; © Apple, Inc.

0749. Macintosh personal computer, 1984; Jerrold Clifford Manock (American, b. 1944); Manufactured by Apple Computer, Inc. (Cupertino, California, USA); Molded plastic, glass, electronic components; a, monitor: 33.8 x 24.3 x 27.7 cm (13 5/16 x 9 9/16 x 10 7/8 in.); Gift of Alan Plaut and Roland Trope, 1997-66-1-a/c; Photo by Ellen McDermott © Smithsonian Institution; © Apple Computer

0750. iMac personal computer, 1999; Jonathan Ive (British, b. 1967) and Apple Industrial Design Team; Manufactured by Apple Computer, Inc. (Cupertino, California, USA); Molded plastic, rubber, glass, metal, electronic components; a, computer/monitor: 38 x 38.5 x 42.5 cm (14 15/16 x 15 3/16 x 16 3/4 in.); Gift of Apple Computer, 2000-63-1-a/c; Photo by Ellen McDermott © Smithsonian Institution; © Apple Computer

0751. Poster, Adler Typewriter, 1909–10; Lucian Bernhard (German, 1883–1972); Printed by Hollerbaum & Schmidt (Germany); Lithograph on paper; 34.5 x 47 cm (13 9/16 x 18 1/2 in.); Gift of the Eric Kellenberger Collection, Switzerland and museum purchase from General Acquisitions Endowment, 2005-12-2

0752. Valentine typewriter and case, ca. 1969; Ettore Sottsass Jr. (Italian, 1917–2007) and Perry A. King (British, b. 1938); Manufactured by Ing. C. Olivetti & C. S.p.A. (Ivrea, Italy); Molded ABS plastic, metal, rubber; a, b: 11.5 x 34.5 x 35.5 cm (4 1/2 x 13 9/16 x 14 in.); Gift of Barry Friedman and Patricia Pastor, 1986-99-40-a,b; Photo by John White © Smithsonian Institution

0753. Drawing, Assembly Perspective for Polaroid Automatic 100, 1962; Henry Dreyfuss (American, 1904–72); Black, red crayon, pen and black ink, green pastel, blue ball-point pen on tracing paper; 45.7 x 60.8 cm (18 x 23 15/16 in.); Gift of Henry Dreyfuss, 1972-88-357

0754. Purma Special camera, 1937; Raymond Loewy (American, b. France, 1893–1986); Manufactured by Thomas De La Rue for Purma Cameras Ltd. (camera), Beck (lens) (England); Molded Bakelite, acrylic (lens), metal; 7 x 15.2 x 6.8 cm (2 3/4 x 6 x 2 11/16 in.); Gift of Barry Friedman and Patricia Pastor, 1986-99-24; Photo by Hiro Ihara © Smithsonian Institution

0755. Swinger camera, 1965; Henry Dreyfuss (American, 1904–72); Manufactured by Polaroid Corporation (Cambridge, Massachusetts, USA); Molded plastic, metal; 12.4 x 15 x 13 cm (4 7/8 x 5 7/8 x 5 1/8 in.); Museum purchase through gift of Neil Sellin, 1999-2-4; Photo by Ellen McDermott © Smithsonian Institution

0756. Plus 126 camera, Austria, ca. 1970; Molded plastic; 6.8 x 8.8 x 5 cm (2 11/16 x 3 7/16 x 1 15/16 in.); Gift of Barry Friedman and Patricia Pastor, 1986-99-25; Photo by Ellen McDermott © Smithsonian Institution

0757. Big Shot camera, 1971; Henry Dreyfuss (American, 1904–72); Manufactured by Polaroid Corporation (Cambridge, Massachusetts, USA); Molded plastic, metal; 21 x 15.5 x 26 cm (8 1/4 x 6 1/8 x 10 1/4 in.); Museum purchase through gift of Neil Sellin, 1999-2-3; Photo by Ellen McDermott © Smithsonian Institution

0758. Kodak Pocket Instamatic 10 camera, 1973–76; Eastman Kodak Company (Rochester, New York, USA); Molded plastic, metal, woven cord (strap); 2.7 x 11.4 x 5.6 cm (1 1/16 x 4 1/2 x 2 3/16 in.); Gift of Warren A. James, 1998-41-1-a; Photo by Ellen McDermott © Smithsonian Institution

0759. Textile, Grey on Grey, ca. 1943; Marianne Strengell (Finnish, active U.S.A., 1909–98); Screenprinted linen; 94.6 x 97.8 cm (37 1/4 x 38 1/2 in.); Gift of Marianne Strengell, 1984-111-73

0760. Textile, Origami Pleat, 2002–03; Reiko Sudo (Japanese, b. 1953); Manufactured by NUNO Corporation (Tokyo, Japan); Folded, transfer-printed, and permanently pressed polyester; 553.7 x 94 cm (18 ft. 2 in. x 37 in.), folded width: 7.6 cm (3 in.); Gift of the Nuno Corporation, 2004-18-1; © Nuno Corporation

0761. Sidewall, In the White Room, 2008; Tracy Kendall (British); Cut and sewn paper on paper; 371.3 x 55 cm (12 ft. 2 3/16 in. x 21 5/8 in.); Gift of Tracy Kendall, 2008-11-1; © Tracy Kendall

0762. Hand-woven sample, USA, before 1953; Anni Albers (American, b. Germany, 1899–1994); Plain-woven silk and wool; 17.8 x 27 cm (7 x 10 5/8 in.); Gift of Anni Albers, 1953-180-3; © Josef and Anni Albers Foundation

0763. Hand-woven sample, USA, before 1953; Anni Albers (American, b. Germany, 1899–1994); Plain-woven silk and cotton with paired wefts; 17.5 x 27 cm (6 7/8 x 10 5/8 in.); Museum purchase through gift of Gift of Anni Albers, 1953-180-1; © Josef and Anni Albers Foundation

0764. Honey-Pop chair, Japan, 2001; Tokujin Yoshioka (Japanese, b. 1967); Layered paper, partially glued, cut, and fanned open accordion style; Seat compressed by body of designer; 81.3 x 79.1 x 81.3 cm (32 x 31 1/8 x 32 in.); Museum purchase from Friends of Product Design and Decorative Arts Fund through gift of Lisa Roberts and David Seltzer, 2008-6-1; Photo by Matt Flynn © Smithsonian Institution; © Tokujin Yoshioka

0765. Book, 2013; Designed by Irma Boom (Dutch, b. 1960); From Jean-Louis Froment, *No. 5 Culture Chanel* (New York: Abrams, 2013); Embossed paper; 24.5 x 42 cm (9 3/4 x 16 5/8 in.); Smithsonian Libraries, Gift of Chanel, N7433.4.B64 N6 2013; Photo courtesy Irma Boom Office

0766. Hanging, Prayer Wall, 2012; Sheila Hicks (American, b. 1934); Cotton stitched with linen; 182.9 x 116.8 x 15.2 cm (72 x 46 x 6 in.); Gift of Momentum Group, 2013-48-1; Photo by © Smithsonian Institution; © Sheila Hicks

0767. Sidewall, Zed, 1992; Bořek Šipek (Czech, b. 1949); Manufactured by Gebr. Rasch GmbH & Co. (Germany); Vinyl and blown glass beads; 10.05 m x 53.5 cm (33 ft. x 21 1/16 in); Gift of Gebr. Rasch GmbH & Co., 1995-163-17; © Rasch

0768. Sidewall, Arabia Felix, 1992; Ettore Sottsass, Jr. (Italian, 1917–2007); Manufactured by Gebr. Rasch GmbH & Co. (Germany); Screenprinted on vinyl; 300 x 53 cm (118 1/8 x 20 7/8 in.); Gift of Gebr. Rasch Gmb H & Co., 1995-163-18; Reproduced with permission © Rasch

0769. Sidewall, Drop, 2011; J. Abbott Miller (American, b. 1963); Manufactured by KnollTextiles (New York, New York, USA); Screenprinted on vinyl, polyester backing; 304.8 x 132.1 cm (10 ft. x 52 in.); Gift of KnollTextiles, 2011-40-1; © Knoll, Inc.

0770. Staircase model, France, early 19th century; Cut, joined, and inlaid mahogany, ebony, pear or sycamore, oak, molded biscuit porcelain (busts); 68 x 48.3 x 31.1 cm (26 3/4 x 19 x 12 1/4 in.); Gift of Eugene V. and Clare E. Thaw, 2007-45-12; Photo by Ali Elai © Smithsonian Institution

0771. Staircase model, France, ca. 1820–40; Planed and jointed pearwood, walnut; 27 x 20 x 15.5 cm (10 5/8 x 7 7/8 x 6 1/8 in.); Gift of Eugene V. and Clare E. Thaw, 2007-45-21

0772. Plumen 001 lightbulb, 2010; Samuel Wilkinson (British, b. 1977); Manufactured by Hulger Design Ltd. (England); Glass, molded ABS plastic, wire, electronics; 19.2 x 10.5 x 10 cm (7 9/16 x 4 1/8 x 3 15/16 in.); Gift of Hulger, 2011-39-1; Photo by Ellen McDermott © Smithsonian Institution

0773. Textile, Spiral, 1969; Barbara Brown (English, b. 1932); Produced by Heal Fabrics (London, England); Screenprinted cotton; 264.2 x 127 cm (104 x 50 in.); Museum purchase from General Acquisitions Endowment Fund, 2007-5-3

0774. Poster, Olivetti Divisumma, 1953; Herbert Bayer (Austrian, active Germany and USA, 1900–85) for Olivetti (Ivrea, Italy); Offset lithograph on white wove paper; 67.9 x 47.9 cm (26 3/4 x 18 7/8 in.); Museum purchase through gift of James A. Lapides and from General Acquisitions Endowment Fund, 2009-1-1

0775. Paper construction, Pop-up illustration, 2005; David A. Carter (American, b. 1957); From *One Red Dot: A Pop-up Book for Children of All Ages* (New York: Little Simon); Offset lithograph on cut paper; 23.3 x 46 x 27 cm (9 1/8 x 18 1/8 x 10 5/8 in.); Gift of Sue Ellen Appleman, 2009, Smithsonian Libraries, QA113.C3779 2005

0776. Frieze, Serpentine, 1958–70; Barbara White (American); Hand-folded and dyed Japanese paper; 46.5 x 66 cm (18 5/16 x 26 in.); Gift of Barbara White, 2000-64-43; © Barbara White

0777. Pair of curtain panels, Blond, 2002; Nicolette Brunklaus (Dutch, b. 1959); Produced by Brunklaus Amsterdam (Netherlands); Digitally printed on cotton velvet; Two panels side by side: 300 x 280 cm (118 1/8 x 110 1/4 in.); Gift of Brunklaus Amsterdam, 2013-51-1-a,b; © Nicolette Brunklaus

0778. Wood chair, 1988; Marc Newson (Australian, b. 1963); Manufactured by Cappellini S.p.A. (Milan, Italy); Bent beechwood, metal screws; 69 x 83 x 100 cm (27 3/16 x 32 11/16 x 39 3/8 in.); Museum purchase from General Acquisitions Endowment Fund, 2006-4-3; © Marc Newson

0779. Bubbles chaise longue, ca. 1988; Frank O. Gehry (Canadian, b. 1929); Manufactured by New City Editions (Venice, California, USA); Layered and bent corrugated cardboard; 87.6 x 219.1 x 73.7 cm (34 1/2 in. x 7 ft. 2 1/4 in. x 29 in.); Museum purchase from the Members' Acquisitions Fund of Cooper-Hewitt, National Design Museum, 2012-3-1; Photo by Ellen McDermott © Smithsonian Institution; © Gehry Partners, LLC

0780. Poster, Cinema Afrika, Filmpodium, Filmtage, 2006; Ralph Schraivogel (Swiss, b. 1960); Screenprint on white wove paper; 128 x 90.3 cm (50 3/8 x 35 9/16 in.); Gift of Ralph Schraivogel, 2007-15-3; © Ralph Schraivogel

0781. Sidewall, Kirchhain, Germany, 1956–57; Made by Marburger Tapetenfabrik; Machine printed and plastic-coated paper; 108.5 x 56 cm (42 11/16 x 22 1/16 in.); Gift of Marburger Tapetenfabrik, 1957-116-2; Reproduced with permission © Marburger Tapetenfabrik

0782. Poster, Design Ignites Change, 2008; Marian Bantjes (Canadian, b. 1963); Laser-cut wove paper; 71.3 x 51 cm (28 1/16 x 20 1/16 in.); Gift of Marian Bantjes, 2013-23-1; © Marian Bantjes

0783. Print, Writing Example from *Spieghel der Schrijfkonste, tweede deel* (*The Mirror of Calligraphy, Second Part*), 1609; Jan van de Velde I (Netherlands, 1569–1623); Engraved by Simon Weynouts Frisius (Flemish, ca. 1580–1628); Engraving on laid paper; 20.4 x 31.1 cm (8 1/16 x 12 1/4 in.); Gift of William J. Donald, 1954-18-30

0784. Heatwave radiator, 2007; Joris Laarman (Dutch, b. 1979); Manufactured by Jaga, N. V. (Diepenbeek, Belgium); Molded polyconcrete (polyester concrete), aluminum; a/c: 104.5 x 209.6 x 15.2 cm (41 1/8 in. x 6 ft. 10 1/2 in. x 6 in.); Gift of Jaga, N.V., 2008-13-1-a/c; Photo by Ellen McDermott © Smithsonian Institution; © Joris Laarman Lab

0785. Paper construction, Möbius, 2010; Tauba Auerbach (American, b. 1981); From *[2,3]*; (New York: Tauba Auerbach and Printed Matter, Inc); Cut paper; 51 x 82 x 40 cm (20 1/8 x 32 1/4 x 15 1/2 in.); Purchase, 2011, Photo by Ellen McDermott © Smithsonian Libraries, fN7433.4.A94 B73 2010X

0786. Drawing, Textile Design: Bow Motif, 1950–70; Tommi Parzinger (American, b. Germany, 1903–81); Brush and gouache, graphite on paper, lined; 12 x 11.5 cm (4 3/4 x 4 1/2 in.); Gift of Mr. Donald Cameron, 1992-51-42; Reproduced with permission © Parzinger Originals

0787. Book cover, *Siddhartha* by Hermann Hesse, 1951; Alvin Lustig (American, 1915–55) for New Directions (New York, New York, USA); Lithograph on thin coated paper; 18.4 x 17.5 cm (7 1/4 x 6 7/8 in.); Gift of Susan Lustig Peck, 2001-29-25; © Estate of Susan Lustig Peck

0788. Poster, Wozzeck, 1964; Jan Lenica (Polish, 1928–2001); Offset lithograph on paper; 96.5 x 67.3 cm (38 x 26 1/2 in.); Museum purchase from Friends of Drawings & Prints Fund, 2013-30-1

0789. Braniff Airways Model 66310 armchair, ca. 1968; Alexander Hayden Girard (American, 1907–93); Manufactured by Herman Miller Furniture Company (Zeeland, Michigan, USA); Woven textile upholstery of cotton (46%), wool (33%), and nylon (21%), with vinyl, urethane foam, latex foam; molded plywood (body), cast aluminum (legs); 66 x 102.9 x 73.7 cm (26 in. x 40 1/2 in. x 29 in.); Gift of George R. Kravis II in honor of Caroline Baumann, 2013-37-1

0790. Border, France, 1830–50; Block printed and flocked on machine-made paper; 90.4 x 17.5 cm (35 9/16 x 6 7/8 in.); Gift of Josephine Howell, 1972-42-137-a

0791. Band, Italy, late 16th–early 17th century; Linen embroidered with silk in counted back- and stem stitches; 21.9 x 83.8 cm (8 5/8 x 33 in.); Bequest of Richard Cranch Greenleaf in memory of his mother, Adeline Emma Greenleaf, 1962-52-3; Photo by Andrew Garn © Smithsonian Institution

0792. Textile, Thrill, 1925; Dwight Taylor (American); Manufactured by Stehli Silk Corporation (New York, New York, USA); Screenprinted silk; 24.8 x 114 cm (9 3/4 x 44 7/8 in.); Gift of Marian Hague, 1937-1-1

0793. Poster, Internationale Economisch-Historische: Tentoonstelling, Schilderijen, Miniaturen, Gobelins, Documenten, Modellen, Grafiek Enz, Stedelijk Museum, Amsterdam (Exhibition of International Economic History: Pictures, Miniatures, Tapestries, Documents, Models, Graphics, Stedelijk Museum, Amsterdam), July 4–Sept. 15, 1929; Hendrikus Theodorus Wijdeveld (Dutch, 1885–1987); Block print, letterpress on cream wove paper; 64.6 x 50.4 cm (25 3/8 x 19 3/4 in); Museum purchase through gift of Eleanor and Sarah Hewitt and Jacob H. Schiff and through bequest of Mrs. John Innes Kane, 2001-7-1; © Eryen H. Th. Wijdeveld

0794. Sidewall, Design 105, 1957; Frank Lloyd Wright (American, 1867–1959); Made by F. Schumacher & Co. (New York, New York, USA, founded 1889); Screenprinted on paper; 117 x 76.5 cm (46 1/16 x 30 1/8 in.); Gift of Suzanne Lipschutz, 1991-89-201

0795. Textile, Design 105, Taliesin Line, 1956; Frank Lloyd Wright (American, 1867–1959); Produced by F. Schumacher & Co. (New York, New York, USA); Screenprinted linen; 120 x 57.5 cm (47 1/4 x 22 5/8 in.), repeat: 63.5 cm (25 in.); Gift of Mr. and Mrs. Burton Tremaine, 1967-90-1

0796. Textile, Design 107, Taliesin Line, 1957; Frank Lloyd Wright (American, 1867–1959); Manufactured by F. Schumacher & Co. (New York, New York, USA); Screen-printed cotton; 134.9 x 61.3 cm (53 1/8 x 24 1/8 in.), repeat H: 86.4 cm (34 in.); Gift of Mr. and Mrs. Burton Tremaine, 1967-90-2

0797. Miao baby carrier (*mei tai*), Guizhou, China, 1950–2000; Indigo-dyed cotton, appliquéd and embroidered with cotton in cross-stitch; 69.5 x 51.4 cm (27 3/8 x 20 1/4 in.); Museum purchase from General Acquisitions Endowment Fund, 2012-6-1

0798. Mantle fragment, coastal Tiahuanaco (present-day Bolivia or Peru), 8th–10th century; Tapestry woven with cotton warp and camelid weft; 59 x 44.5 cm (23 1/4 x 17 1/2 in.); Museum purchase from Pauline Riggs Noyes Fund, 1956-196-1

0799. Textile, Design 103, Taliesin Line, 1955; Frank Lloyd Wright (American, 1867–1959); Manufactured by F. Schumacher & Co. (New York, New York, USA); Screenprinted cotton, rayon, and mohair; 123.5 x 121 cm (48 5/8 x 47 5/8 in.); Gift of Mr. and Mrs. Burton Tremaine, 1967-90-3

0800. Textile, Notschrei (Cry for Help), 1904; Josef Hoffmann (Czech, 1870–1956, active Germany and Austria, 1891–1955); Manufactured by Johann Backhausen & Sohne (Austria); Woven wool; 100.3 x 61.3 cm (39 1/2 x 24 1/8 in.); Museum purchase through General Acquisitions Endowment Fund, 1985-52-2

0801. Poster, Schweizerische Städtebau-Ausstellung (Swiss City Planning Exhibit), 1928; Niklaus Stoecklin (Swiss, 1896–1982); Lithograph on white wove paper; 128.4 x 90.3 cm (50 9/16 x 35 9/16 in.); Museum purchase through gift of Eric Kellenberger Collection, Switzerland and from General Acquisitions Endowment Fund, 2008-33-1

0802. Poster, Jean Prouvé: Architekt und Konstrukteur, 1978; Siegfried Odermatt (Swiss, b. 1926) of Odermatt & Tissi (Swiss, founded 1968) for Museum für Gestaltung, Zürich, Switzerland; Printed by J. C. Müller AG (Switzerland); Offset lithograph on wove paper; 128 x 90.2 cm (50 3/8 x 35 1/2 in.); Gift of Sara and Marc Benda, 2010-21-44

0803. Poster, American Airlines to New York, ca. 1948; Edward McKnight Kauffer (American, active iEngland, 1890–1954); Lithograph on white wove paper; 101.4 x 76 cm (39 15/16 x 29 15/16 in.); Gift of Mrs. E. McKnight Kauffer, 1963-39-139; © American Airlines, Inc.

0804. Textile, Big City, 1960s; Arthur Sanderson & Sons, Ltd. (London, England); Screenprinted cotton; 182.9 x 125.7 cm (72 x 49 1/2 in.); Museum purchase from General Acquisitions Endowment Fund, 2007-5-2

0805. Drawing, Design for Sportshack, 1940; Donald Deskey (American, 1894–1989); Brush and gouache, black ink, airbrush (stenciled), graphite on illustration board; 55.8 x 76 cm (21 15/16 x 29 15/16 in.); Gift of Donald Deskey, 1988-101-1515

0806. Drawing, Museum of American Folk Art, New York, New York, USA: Collage Perspective, November 1997; Billie Tsien (American, b. 1949) for Tod Williams Billie Tsien and Associates (New York, New York, USA); Photo-offset and photo-collage, white and blue crayon on white paper; 64.8 x 94.6 cm (25 9/16 x 37 5/16 in.); Gift of Tod Williams Billie Tsien, 2001-18-5; © Billie Tsien Tod Williams

0807. Print, New Urban Ground, Proposal for Rising Currents Exhibition, Museum of Modern Art, New York, New York, USA, 2009; Architectural Research Office (New York, New York, USA), Stephen Cassell (American, b. 1963), Kim Yao (American, b. 1971), Adam Yarinsky (American, b. 1962) and DLandstudio (Brooklyn, New York, USA), Susannah Churchill Drake (American, b. 1965); Digital print on archival paper; 61 x 91.4 cm (24 x 36 in.); Museum purchase from Architecture Research Office and from General Acquisitions Endowment Fund, 2013-52-2; © ARCHITECTURE RESEARCH OFFICE AND DLANDSTUDIO PLLC

0808. Print, Design for Ten-Deck House, June 16, 1928; R. Buckminster Fuller (American, 1895–1983); Mimeograph print, brush and blue watercolor on white wove paper; 29 x 22.7 cm (11 7/16 x 8 15/16 in.); Museum purchase from Smithsonian Institution Collections Acquisition Program Fund, 1991-53-1; © Courtesy, The Estate of R. Buckminster Fuller

0809. Blueprint, Propriété de Monsieur Hemsy, St. Cloud: Façade Principale (Principal Façade), 1913; Hector Guimard (French, 1867–1942); Blueprint on white wove paper; 54.4 x 33 cm (21 7/16 x 13 in.); Gift of Mme Hector Guimard, 1950-66-24

0810. Blueprint, Immeuble (Apartment House), Rue Heine, Paris: Plan des Caves (Cellar Plan), 1925; Hector Guimard (French, 1867–1942); Blueprint on paper; 46 x 35.1 cm (18 1/8 x 13 13/16 in.), irregular; Gift of Mme Hector Guimard, 1950-66-32

0811. Blueprint, Immeuble (Apartment House), Rue Heine, Paris: Plan du 6e Etage (6thFloor Plan), 1925; Hector Guimard (French, 1867–1942); Blueprint on paper; 70 x 36.6 cm (27 9/16 x 14 7/16 in.), irregular; Gift of Mme Hector Guimard, 1950-66-40

0812. Blueprint, Townhouse, 211 East 48th Street, New York, New York, USA: Elevation, 1933; William E. Lescaze (American, b. Switzerland, 1896–1969); Blueprint; 36.2 x 18.2 cm (14 1/4 x 7 3/16 in.); Gift of William E. Lescaze, 1937-37-2; Photo by Andrew Garn © Smithsonian Institution; © Estate of William E. Lescaze

0813. Sidewall, Views of Paris, 1946–50; Saul Steinberg (American, b. Romania, 1914–99); Made by Piazza Prints, Inc. (New York, New York, USA); Screenprinted on paper; 114 x 76 cm (44 7/8 x 29 15/16 in.); Gift of Harvey Smith, 1950-126-4-a,b; © F. Schumacher & Co., all rights reserved

0814. Photostat, Immeuble (Apartment House), Rue Heine, Paris, France: Façade sur Rue (Street Façade), 1925; Hector Guimard (French, 1867–1942); Photostat and black ink on paper; 71.5 x 37.5 cm (28 1/8 x 14 3/4 in.), irregular; Gift of Mme. Hector Guimard, 1950-66-31

0815. Photograph, Floor Plan for an Apartment Building, 1911; Hector Guimard (French, 1867–1942); Photographic print on sensitized paper; 14.4 x 8 cm (5 11/16 x 3 1/8 in.); Gift of Mme. Hector Guimard, 1951-160-1-10

0816. Kubus stacking storage container set, 1938; Wilhelm Wagenfeld (German, 1900–90); Manufactured by Vereinigte Lausitzer Glaswerke AG (Weisswasser, Germany); Machine-molded and pressed glass; 1, dish: 18.1 x 18.1 x 7.9 cm (7 1/8 x 7 1/8 x 3 1/8 in.); Museum purchase from Sir Arthur Bryan and General Acquisitions Endowment Funds, 1990-4-1/18; Photo by John Parnell © Smithsonian Institution

0817. Poster, NOH: UCLA Asian Performing Arts, 1981; Takenobu Igarashi (Japanese, b. 1944); Offset lithograph on paper; 72.6 x 102.8 cm (28 9/16 x 40 1/2 in.); Gift of Takenobu Igarashi, 1981-69-2

0818. Collage, Maquette of Book Cover Design: *Portrait of the Artist as a Young Dog* by Dylan Thomas, ca. 1955; Alvin Lustig (American, 1915–55) for New Directions (New York, New York, USA); Printed on adhesive, pasted on photograph on thin board adhered to cardboard; 18.1 x 11.0 cm (7 1/8 x 4 5/16 in.); Gift of Susan Lustig Peck, 2001-29-3; © Estate of Susan Lustig Peck

0819. Book illustration, Japanese village, 1688; John Stalker (British) and John Parker (British, active 17th century); From *A Treatise of Japaning [sic]and Varnishing* (Oxford: Richard Woods); Engraving on paper; 37 x 24 cm (14 5/8 x 9/1/2 in.); Purchase, 1948, Smithsonian Libraries, TP938.S78 1688

0820. Drawing, Design for a Skyscraper, 1930; Ely Jacques Kahn (American, 1884–1972) for Buchman and Kahn (New York, New York, USA); Graphite with fixative on tracing paper mounted on cardboard; 62.5 x 40 cm (24 5/8 x 15 3/4 in.); Gift of Ely Jacques Kahn, 1952-15-13

0821. Drawing, Study after a Bronze Chandelier, Kaid Bey Mosque, Cairo, Egypt, 1856–66; Alfred Normand (French, 1822–1909); Pen and black ink, brush and gray wash, red, green watercolor on tracing paper mounted to heavy wove paper; 47.8 x 30.8 cm (18 13/16 x 12 1/8 in.); Museum purchase through the bequest of Ida C. McNeil in memory of Lincoln C. McNeil and Catherine McNeil, 1992-147-3

0822. Cabinet, Italy, 1890–1900; Carlo Bugatti (Italian, 1856–1940); Joined hardwood, sheet vellum, applied, cut, and molded copper ornaments, inlaid pewter, brass wire, sheet glass, textile tassels; 150.2 x 73 x 37 cm (59 1/8 x 28 3/4 x 14 9/16 in.); Museum purchase from Decorative Arts Association Acquisition Fund, 1982-22-1; Photo by Ellen McDermott © Smithsonian Institution

0823. Birdcage, England, ca. 1765; Carved and joined mahogany, metal wire, sheet metal; 77 x 39 x 39 cm (30 5/16 x 15 3/8 x 15 3/8 in.); Gift of Alfred G. Burnham, 1952-69-1; Photo © Smithsonian Institution

0824. Jewel cabinet on stand, 1824–26; Jean-Charles- François Leloy (French, active 1816–44), designed and produced by Alexandre Brongniart (French, 1770–1847) for King Charles X of France (r. 1824–30), primary porcelain painting by Pierre Huard (French, active 1811–47, d. 1857), designed by Alexandre Évariste Fragonard (French, 1780–1850), mounts by Louis-Honoré Boquet (or Bocquet) (French, active Sèvres 1815–ca. 1860), porcelain gilding by Boullemier le jeune (the younger), probably Antoine-Gabriel Boullemier (French, 1781–1842), and Boullemier l'aîné (the elder), probably François-Antoine Boullemier (French, 1773–1838), porcelain burnishing by Madame Boullemier le jeune (Geneviève Boullemier, French, b. 1781), additional painting by Pierre Riton (French, active 1821–60), Antoine Béranger (French, 1785–1867); Godin (probably the younger) (French, active late 18th/early 19th centuries), director of production: Vicomte (Sostène) de La Rochefoucauld (French,1785–1864), Sèvres Porcelain Manufactory (Sèvres, France); Casework of molded hard-paste porcelain with enamel-painted and fired decoration, with gilding in gold leaf and platinum, mounted in gilt bronze, joined mahogany drawers, gilt metal; Gift of Alfred Duane Pell, 1991-31-2 (by transfer); Photo by Dennis Cowley © Smithsonian Institution

0825. Drawing, Presentation Watercolor for Front of Cabinet, 1826; Jean-Charles-François Leloy (French, active 1816–44); Watercolor and ink on paper; 44.9 cm x 32.3 cm (19 1/2 x 12 1/4 in.); Archives of the Manufacture Nationale de Sèvres, Sèvres, France, 2012.1.557

0826. Detail of Jewel cabinet on stand, 1824–26; Jean-Charles- François Leloy (French, active 1816–44), designed and produced by Alexandre Brongniart (French, 1770–1847), et al (See **0824**); Gift of Alfred Duane Pell, 1991-31-2 (by transfer); Photo by Dennis Cowley © Smithsonian Institution

0827. Detail of Jewel cabinet on stand, 1824–26; Jean-Charles- François Leloy (French, active 1816–44), designed and produced by Alexandre Brongniart (French, 1770–1847), et al (See **0824**);Gift of Alfred Duane Pell, 1991-31-2 (by transfer); Photo by Dennis Cowley © Smithsonian Institution

0828. Sidewall, Opera, 1953; Saul Steinberg (American, b. Romania, 1914–99); Made by Greeff Fabrics Inc. (New York, New York, USA); Screenprinted on paper; 231.1 x 76.5 cm (7 ft. 7 in. x 30 1/8 in.); Gift of Mrs. Howard Adams, 1981-33-1; © F. Schumacher & Co., all rights reserved

0829. Drawing, Place de la Concorde, Paris, France: Elevation of the Maritime Fountain, 1839; Jacques Ignace Hittorff (German, 1792–1867); Pen and black ink, brush and watercolor, highlighted with white gouache on paper; 98.9 x 127.6 cm (38 15/16 x 50 1/4 in.); Museum purchase from Sarah Cooper-Hewitt and Smithsonian Institution Collections Acquisition Funds and through gift of Lucy Work Hewitt, 1997-1-1

0830. Renaissance-Style Baptistry architectural model, Italy, 1782; Ivory, wood; 68.6 x 43.2 cm diam. (27 x 17 in.); Gift of Eugene V. and Clare E. Thaw, 2013-3-2; Photo by Ellen McDermott © Smithsonian Institution

0831. Bandbox and lid, USA, ca. 1830; Block printed on paper, pasteboard support; 41.5 x 31.5 x 27.5 cm (16 5/16 x 12 3/8 x 10 13/16 in.); Gift of Mrs. James O. Green, 1913-12-4-a,b

0832. Drawing, Aqua Tower, Chicago, Illinois, USA: Study Exploring Chromatic Strata, ca. 2005; Jeanne Gang (American, b. 1964) for Studio Gang Architects (Chicago, Illinois, USA); Graphite, color pencil on white paper; 29 x 22.7 cm (11 7/16 x 8 15/16 in.); Gift of Studio Gang Architects, 2014-4-4

0833. Photograph, Staircase Construction of a Mass-Produced House (No. 43), 1921; Hector Guimard (French, 1867–1942); Photographic print on sensitized paper mounted on gray paper; 33.4 x 28.5 cm (13 1/8 x 11 1/4 in.); Gift of Mme Hector Guimard, 1951-160-2-43

0834. Digital print, Tel Aviv Museum of Art (TAMA), Tel Aviv, Israel: Lightfall I, 2003; Preston Scott Cohen (American, b. 1961); Digitally enhanced Fujiflex print, laminated and mounted on Plexiglass; 152.7 x 114 cm (60 1/8 x 44 7/8 in.); Museum purchase from Drawings and Prints Council Fund, 2005-4-1

0835. Oil sketch, Parthenon, from the Northwest (Illuminated Night View), April 1869; Frederic Edwin Church (American, 1826–1900); Brush and oil paint, black chalk on thin cream board; 32.8 x 41.4 cm (12 15/16 x 16 5/16 in.); Gift of Louis P. Church, 1917-4-671

0836. Textile, Pokeri, 1967; Maija Isola (Finnish, 1927–2001); Manufactured by Marimekko Oy (Helsinki, Finland); Screenprinted cotton; 353.1 x 137.2 cm (139 x 54 in.), repeat H: 140.3 cm (55 1/4 in.); Gift of Marimekko, Inc., 1979-89-9; © Marimekko Oy

0837. Drawing, Chicken Point Cabin, Hayden Lake Idaho, USA: West and South Elevations, 2001; Tom Kundig (American, b. 1954); Graphite on tracing paper; 45.7 x 60.9 cm (18 x 24 in.); Gift of Tom Kundig, 2010-10-1; Photo by Andrew Garn © Smithsonian; © Tom Kundig

0838. Drawing, Butterfly House, Auburn, Alabama, USA: Concept Sketches, 1997; Samuel Mockbee (American, 1944–2001); Pen and black ink on heavy cream paper; 35.5 x 43.0 cm (14 x 16 15/16 in); Museum purchase from General Acquisitions Endowment Fund, 2001-5-1; © Samuel Mockbee

0839. Drawing, Phillips Exeter Library, Exeter, New Hampshire, USA: Sketch of Plan with Elevations, ca. 1967; Louis I. Kahn (Estonian-American, 1901–74); Graphite on yellow tracing paper; 29 x 32 cm (11 7/16 x 12 5/8 in.); Museum purchase through gift of Anonymous Donor, Architectural Research Office, and Susan and Mark Stumer and from Drawings & Prints Council, General Acquisitions Endowment and Krieg Funds, 2012-22-1; © Estate of Louis I. Kahn

0840. Photograph, Exterior of Philips Exeter Academy Library; © Richard Howard

0841. Photograph, Interior of Philips Exeter Academy Library; Photo by Brian F. Crowley, courtesy of Philips Exeter Academy

0842. Sudbury Hall architectural model, Derbyshire, England, 1660–90; Stained pine; (base) 30.5 x 69.2 x 35.6 cm (12 x 27 1/4 x 14 in.); Gift of Eugene V. and Clare E. Thaw, 2013-3-5; Photo by Ellen McDermott © Smithsonian Institution

0843. Bookcase, ca. 1875; Herter Brothers (New York, New York, USA); Joined and inlaid walnut, ebonized cherry, marquetry of various woods, incised gilding, plate glass, cast brass hardware; (overall) 162.6 x 243.8 x 41.9 cm (5 ft. 4 in. x 8 ft. 16 1/2 in.); Gift of George P. Ververis Jr., 2013-12-1-a/mm; Photo by Matt Flynn © Smithsonian Institution

0844. Drawing, Brighton Pavilion, Brighton, England: Design for a Chinese Pavilion, 1815–22; Frederick Crace (British, 1779–1859); Brush and watercolor, gouache, pen and black ink on paper; 24.9 x 31.8 cm (9 13/16 x 12 1/2 in.); Museum purchase through gift of Mrs. John Innes Kane, 1948-40-88

0845. Drawing, Concert Room of Sanssouci Palace, Potsdam, Germany, 1852; Eduard Gaertner (German, 1801–1877); Brush and gouache, watercolor, graphite, gum arabic on white wove paper; 17.7 x 26.4 cm (6 15/16 x 10 3/8 in.); Thaw Collection, 2007-27-51

0846. Book illustration, Drawing room, 1807; Thomas Hope (Dutch, 1770?–1831, active England, 1794–1831); From Thomas Hope, *Household Furniture and Interior Decoration* (London: Longman, Hurst, Rees & Orme), plate VIII; Engraving on paper; 46.5 x 28 cm (18.3 x 11 in.); Gift of Calvin S. Hathaway, 1956, Smithsonian Libraries, fNK2115.5.F77H79 1807

0847. Book illustration, Axonometric drawing of an interior, ca. 1929; Wilhelm Jöker (German, 1871–1929); *Farbige Räume und Bauten* (*Color in Interior Decoration*) From (Stuttgart: G. Siegle & Co.), plate 30; Pochoir on paper; 26 x 37 cm (10.23 x 14.5 in.); Smithsonian Libraries, fNK2115.5.C6 F22 1929

0848. Drawing, Grand Central Terminal, New York, New York, USA: Design for Façade, 1910; Whitney Warren Jr. (American, 1864–1943); Pen and black ink, graphite on cream tracing paper; 25.4 x 32.8 cm (10 x 12 15/16 in.); Gift of Mrs. William Greenough, 1943-51-13

0849. Scarf, Trains, 1951; Saul Steinberg (American, b. Romania, 1914–1999); Manufactured by Piazza Prints, Inc. (New York, New York, USA); Screenprinted silk. 88.9 x 88.3 cm (35 x 34 3/4 in.); Gift of Harvey Smith, 1968-135-90; © F. Schumacher & Co., all rights reserved

0850. Book illustration, Villa no. 1, 1861; John Riddell (American, 1814–ca. 1871), lithograph by T. Sinclair; From *Architectural Designs for Model Country Residences* (Philadelphia: John Riddell, Lindsay & Blakiston); Color lithograph on paper; 38 x 46 x 2 cm (15 x 18 x 3/4 in.); Smithsonian Libraries, f NA7561.R54 1861 (top right)

0851. Drawing, Castel d'Orgeval, Parc Beauséjour, Paris, France: Design for Rear Elevation, 1904; Hector Guimard (French, 1867–1942); Pen and black, red ink, graphite on tracing paper; 53.1 x 47.6 cm (20 7/8 x 18 3/4 in.); Gift of Mme. Hector Guimard, 1950-66-5

0852. Drawing, J. Paul Getty Center, Los Angeles California, USA: Site Study 1, September 4, 1986; Richard Meier (American, b. 1934); Graphite on tracing paper; 61 x 94 cm (24 x 37 in.); Gift of Ana Meier, 2009-15-1; © Richard Meier

0853. Photostat, Hôtel de Voyageur, Maison Americaine (Center for American Visitors), 1925 Exposition, Paris, France: Proposal, 1923; Hector Guimard (French, 1867–1942); Photostat and black ink on paper; 43.7 x 59 cm (17 3/16 x 23 1/4 in.); Gift of Mme Hector Guimard, 1950-66-48

0854. Drawing, Villa Stein-de Monzie, Garches, France: First Studies, 1926; Le Corbusier (Swiss, b. Charles-Édouard Jeanneret-Gris, active France, 1887–1965); Graphite on white paperboard, mounted on canvas; 32.2 x 24.1 cm (12 11/16 x 9 1/2 in.); Museum purchase from James B. Ford and Peter Cooper Hewitt Estate Funds, 1936-60-2

0855. Birdcage, New York, New York, USA, mid-19th century; Turned, cut, and stained mahogany, cherry, pine, cut brass, wire, enamel-painted metal; a, b: 79 x 38 x 75.5 cm (31 1/8 x 14 15/16 x 29 3/4 in.); Gift of Eleanor and Sarah Hewitt, 1916-19-83-a, b

0856. Rialto Bridge birdcage, Venice, Italy, late 19th–early 20th century; Painted wood, bent metal wire, metal; 47.6 x 85.7 x 35.6 cm (18 3/4 x 33 3/4 x 14 in.); Gift of Eleanor and Sarah Hewitt, 1916-19-14

0857. Drawing, Galician Center of Contemporary Art, Santiago de Compostela, Spain: Concept Sketches, 1988–93; Álvaro Joaquim de Melo Siza Vieira (Portuguese, b. 1933); Black ballpoint pen on cream (loose-leaf) paper; 29.6 x 21 cm (11 5/8 x 8 1/4 in.); Museum purchase through gift of George A. Hearn, 2004-5-1; © Álvaro Joaquim de Melo Siza Vieira

0858. Paper construction, Miniature theater depicting a garden scene with dancers, ca. 1740; Attributed to engraver and print-seller Martin Engelbrecht (Augsbourg, Germany, 1684–1756), illustrations by Jeremiastet Wachsmuth (German) and David Nessenthaler (German); From Martin Engelbrecht, *Miniature theater depicting a garden scene with dancers* (Augsburg: Martin Engelbrecht, ca. 1740); Hand-colored etched prints, cut paper; 17 x 23 cm (6 11/16 x 9 1/16 in.); Purchase, Smithsonian Libraries, GV1521.E54 1740

0859. Print, Project de Sculpture en argent d'un grand surtout de table et les deux terrines . . . executée pour Millord Kingston en 1735 (Design for Centerpiece and Two Tureens for the Duke of Kingston in 1735); From Juste-Aurèle Meissonnier (French, 1695–1750); Etched by Gabriel Huquier (French, 1695–1772) from *Œuvre de Juste-Aurèle Meissonnier*, 1742–48, plate 115; Etching on off-white laid paper; 33.7 x 57.8 cm (13 1/4 x 22 3/4 in.); Purchased for the Museum by the Advisory Council, 1921-6-212-72

0860. Drawing, First Design for a Centerpiece and Two Tureens for the Duke of Kingston, 1733–34; Juste-Aurèle Meissonnier (French, 1695–1750); Black chalk, brush, and white gouache on blue laid paper; 30 x 63 cm (11 13/16 x 24 13/16 in.); Bibliothèque Nationale de France, Cabinet des Estampes Inv. B. 11 rés, fol. 4

0861. Drawing, The Japanese Salon, Villa Hügel, Hietzing, Vienna, Austria, 1855; Rudolf von Alt (Austrian, 1812 –1905); Brush and watercolor, gouache, graphite on white paper; 38.4 x 53.2 cm (15 1/8 x 20 15/16 in.); Thaw Collection, 2007-27-56

0862. Book illustration, Music Room, 1902; Mackay Hugh Baillie-Scott (British, 1865–1945), engraved by Emil Hochdanz (German, 1816–85); From Mackay Hugh Baillie-Scott, *Haus eines Kunst-freundes* (*House for an Art Lover*), (Darmstadt: Alex Koch), plate IX; Photomechanical process on paper; 39 x 52 cm (15 3/8 x 20 1/2 in.); Smithsonian Libraries, fNA997.S26A4 1902

0863. Drawing, Design for a Dining Room: New York, New York, USA, 1934; Donald Deskey (American, 1894–1989); Pen and black ink, graphite on white wove construction paper; 33.1 x 43.3 cm (13 1/16 x 17 1/16 in.); Gift of Donald Deskey, 1975-11-4

0864. Print, *Vue perspective de la chambre à coucher du Cit[oyen] V à Paris* (Perspective View of the Bedroom of Cit. V in Paris), from *Recueil de décorations intérieures* (Collection of Interior Decorations), 1812, plate 13; Charles Percier (French, 1764–1838) and Pierre-François-Léonard Fontaine (French, 1762–1853); Etching on cream laid paper; 27.3 x 40 cm (10 3/4 x 15 3/4 in.); Purchased for the Museum by the Advisory Council, 1921-6-377-14

0865. Drawing, Sir Lawrence Alma-Tadema's Study, Townshend House, London, England, 1884; Anna Alma-Tadema (British, 1865–1943); Brush and watercolor, gouache, pen and brown and black ink, graphite on white paper; 33 x 45 cm (13 x 17 11/16 in.); Thaw Collection, 2007-27-72

0866. Book illustration, Solar powered fountain, 1615; Salomon de Caus (French, 1576–1626); From *Raisons des forces mouvantes avec diverses machines tant utiles que plaisantes* (*Explanations of Motive Forces, with Various Machines as Useful as They are Pleasing*), (Frankfurt: Jan Norton, 1615), Livre premier, Problesme XV (First Book, Problem 15); Engraving on paper; 41 x 52 x 2.2 cm (16 1/8 x 20 3/8 x 7/8 in.); Smithsonian Libraries, f TJ144. C37 1615

0867. Drawing, View of a Masquerade Ball, 1770–80; Jean-Charles Delafosse (French, 1734–91); Pen and black ink, brush and gray wash, watercolor, black chalk on white laid paper; 30.8 x 40.1 cm (12 1/8 x 15 13/16 in.); Purchased for the Museum by the Advisory Council, 1911-28-38

0868. Drawing, Theater Design: A Town Square, ca. 1719; Francesco Galli Bibiena (Italian, 1659–1739); Pen and brown ink, brush and gray wash, blue and pale rose watercolor on white laid paper, lined; 28.7 x 42.4 cm (11 5/16 x 16 11/16 in.); Museum purchase through gift of various donors and from Eleanor G. Hewitt Fund, 1938-88-50; Photo by Scott Hyde © Smithsonian Institution

0869. Scenic panel, Reconciliation of Venus and Psyche, 1923; Louis Lafitte (French, 1770–1828) and Merry-Joseph Blondel (French, 1781–1853, active Paris, France, 1802–51); Manufactured by Desfossé et Karth (French, active 1923); Originally produced by Dufour et Leroy; Block printed on continuous paper; 181 x 51 cm (5 ft. 11 1/4 in. x 20 1/16 in.); Gift of Mr. and Mrs. Abraham M. Adler, 1974-109-11-a/c; Photo by Ken Pelka © Smithsonian Institution

0870. Book illustration, Design for a State Bedchamber, From *Second Livre d'Appartements* (*Second book on interiors*), ca. 1702; Daniel Marot (French, 1661–1752, active Netherlands and England); Etching, engraving on white laid paper; 33.8 x 22.2 cm (13 5/16 x 8 3/4 in.); Museum purchase from General Acquisitions Endowment Fund, 1988-4-53

0871. Desk, France, ca. 1935; Jean-Michel Frank (French, 1895–1941); Joined wood, cut, pressed, and dyed shagreen, carved ivory; 80.8 x 142 x 60 cm (31 13/16 x 55 7/8 x 23 5/8 in.); Gift of Mr. and Mrs. Forsythe Sherfesee, 1968-144-13-a/g

0872. Photograph, Snapshot of raffia-covered writing table and chair at Villa Bontoc, 1962; Photo © Smithsonian Institution

0873. Dressing table and bench, New York, New York, USA, ca. 1929; After a design by Léon Jallot (French, 1874–1967); Retailed by Lord & Taylor; Lacquered, joined wood, glass, metal; a: dressing table, 79.3 x 105.4 x 60.3 cm (31 1/4 x 41 1/2 x 23 3/4 in.), b: bench, 49.5 x 54.8 x 31.5 cm (19 1/2 x 21 9/16 x 12 3/8 in.); Gift of James M. Osborn, 1969-97-7-a/i

0874. Architect's table, Neuwied, Germany, 1780–95; David Roentgen (German, 1743–1807); Carved and joined mahogany, mahogany veneer, oak, walnut, pine, cherry, partially tooled and gilt leather, gilt bronze, cut brass, steel, and iron; 81 x 83.3 x 69.7 cm (31 7/8 x 32 13/16 x 27 7/16 in.); Gift of Anonymous Donor, 1952-160-1; Photo by Peter Zeray, The Metropolitan Museum of Art © Smithsonian Institution

0875. Drawing, Henry J. Allen Residence, Wichita, Kansas, USA: Piano Bench and Taboret, 1917; Frank Lloyd Wright (American, 1867–1959); Graphite, color pencil on cream tracing paper; 37 x 45 cm (14 9/16 x 17 11/16 in.); Museum purchase from Smithsonian Regents Collections Acquisition and Friends of Drawings and Prints Funds, 1983-1-3; Photo by Ken Pelka © Smithsonian Institution

0876. Desk, ca. 1933; Paul T. Frankl (American, 1886–1958); Manufactured by Frankl Galleries (New York, New York, USA); Lacquered wood, painted canvas, chromed metal; 76.2 x 121.9 x 53.3 cm (30 x 48 x 21 in.); Gift of Joel and Anne Ehrenkranz, 2006-24-1; Photo by Andrew Garn © Smithsonian Institution

0877. Print, Deux différents desseins de comodes (Designs for Two Commodes), from *Livre de diferents dessein de comodes* (*Book of Various Designs for Commodes*), 1745–55; Jean-François Cuvilliés (Flemish, active Germany, 1695–1768); Engraved and etched by Karl Albert von Lespilliez (German, 1723–96); Etching, engraving on off-white laid paper; 44 x 28.6 cm (17 5/16 x 11 1/4 in.); Purchased for the Museum by the Advisory Council, 1921-6-285-35

0878. Buffet, France, ca. 1905; Louis Majorelle (French, 1859–1926); Wood, marble, metal, glass; 157.5 x 124.5 x 47 cm (5 ft. 2 in. x 49 in. x 18 1/2 in.); Gift of Harry C. Sigman, 2013-21-8-a/d

0879. Cabinet on stand, probably England, 1675–1700; Marquetry-inlaid, veneered, and joined oak, deal, walnut, and other wood, bone, brass; 171.5 x 133 x 55.8 cm (67 1/2 x 52 3/8 x 21 15/16 in.); Bequest of Mrs. John Innes Kane, 1926-22-43

0880. Marquetry cabinet, probably England, ca. 1690; 175 x 123 cm; Oslo Museum of Applied Arts, accession number OK 5392

0881. Cabinet on stand (detail, left door), probably England, 1675–1700; Marquetry-inlaid, veneered, and joined oak, deal, walnut, and other wood, bone, brass; 171.5 x 133 x 55.8 cm (67 1/2 x 52 3/8 x 21 15/16 in.); Bequest of Mrs. John Innes Kane, 1926-22-43

0882. Cabinet on stand (detail, right door), probably England, 1675–1700; Marquetry-inlaid, veneered, and joined oak, deal, walnut, and other wood, bone, brass; 171.5 x 133 x 55.8 cm (67 1/2 x 52 3/8 x 21 15/16 in.); Bequest of Mrs. John Innes Kane, 1926-22-43

0883. Print, Basket with Flowers on a Table, plate 8 from the series Livres de Plusieurs Paniers de Fleurs (Flowers in a Basket), ca. 1680; Jean-Baptiste Monnoyer (French, 1636–99); Etching, engraving on off-white laid paper; 66.8 x 54.1 cm (26 5/16 x 21 5/16 in.); Gift of Norvin Hewitt Green, 1938-58-865

0884. Book illustration, *Phacelia congesta* (*Phacelia*), 1932; Karl Blossfeldt (German 1865–1932); From *Urformen der Kunst* (*Art Forms in Nature*), Second series, (New York: E. Weyhe, 1932), plate 41; Photomechanical process on paper; 32.5 x 52.5 cm (12 3/4 x 20 5/8 in.); Purchase Mary Stuart Book Fund, Smithsonian Libraries, qNK1560. B52x

0885. Sidewall, England, 1848–60; A.W.N. Pugin (English, 1812–52); Made by Scott and Co.; Block printed and flocked on paper; 118 x 58.5 cm (46 7/16 x 23 1/16 in.); Gift of Cole and Son, Ltd., 1953-134-3

0886. Sidewall, City Park, 2007; Dan Funderburgh (American, b. 1978); Printed by Flavor Paper (New Orleans, Louisiana, USA); Screenprinted on paper; 4.57 m x 76.2 cm (15 ft. x 30 in.); Gift of Flavor Paper and Dan Funderburgh, 2007-36-2; © Flavor Paper by Dan Funderburgh

0887. Sampler, China, ca. 1930; Cotton embroidered in silk in cross-, back-, and double-running stitches; 36.2 x 32.1 cm (14 1/4 x 12 5/8 in.); Bequest of Gertrude M. Oppenheimer, 1981-28-19

0888. Purse, England, early 17th century; Macramé in metallic yarns; 9 x 10.5 cm (3 9/16 x 4 1/8 in.); Museum purchase from Au Panier Fleuri, McNeil, and General Acquisitions Endowment Funds, 1989-30-1

0889. Textile, Nigeria, mid-20th century; Cotton patterned with resist paste and indigo dyed (adire); 196.2 x 175 cm (77 1/4 x 68 7/8 in.); Museum purchase from Textile Department Fund, 1979-23-3; Photo by Ken Pelka © Smithsonian Institution

0890. Fragment, Spain, 15th century; Silk and metallic lampas, 42.5 x 33 cm (16 3/4 x 13 in.); Gift of John Pierpont Morgan, 1902-1-251; Photo by Andrew Garn © Smithsonian Institution

0891. Woman's gloves, Spain, 1800–20; Printed kid leather; 22.9 x 9.2 cm (9 x 3 5/8 in.) each; Gift of Mrs. John Innes Kane, 1941-86-4-a,b

0892. Table cover, USA, ca. 1900; Made by Sybil Carter Indian Mission and Lace Industry Association; Cutwork and embroidered linen; 68 x 42.3 cm (26 3/4 x 16 5/8 in.); Gift of Mrs. William Bayard Cutting in memory of Mary E. Parsons, 1943-44-13

0893. Textile, Gold Ripple-Wave, ca. 1956; Probably Marianne Strengell (Finnish, active USA, 1909–98); Made for Ford Motor Company (Dearborn, Michigan, USA); Manufactured by Chatham Manufacturing Company (Elkin, North Carolina, USA); Jacquard-woven cotton, rayon, and Lurex; 187 x 154.9 cm (73 5/8 x 61 in.); Museum Purchase from Smithsonian Institution Collections Acquisition Program Fund, 1998-56-1

0894. Collar, Italy, 1650–75; Linen needle lace; 39.7 x 38.1 cm (15 5/8 x 15 in.); Bequest of Richard Cranch Greenleaf in memory of his mother, Adeline Emma Greenleaf, 1962-50-28

0895. Apron, Italy, 1906–10; Aemelia Ars (Bologna, Italy); Linen trimmed with needle lace; 109.5 x 90.5 cm (43 1/8 x 35 5/8 in.); Gift of Richard C. Greenleaf Esq. in memory of his mother, Adeline Emma Greenleaf, 1950-121-1

0896. Cravat end, France, 1670–85; Linen needle lace with raised details; 62.9 x 61 cm (24 3/4 x 24 in.); Gift of Richard C. Greenleaf Esq. in memory of his mother, Adeline Emma Greenleaf, 1950-121-36

0897. Cravat end, Flanders (present-day Belgium), 1700–50; Linen bobbin lace; 35.6 x 33 cm (14 x 13 in.); Gift of the Estate of Mrs. Robert B. Noyes in her memory, 1947-19-1; Photo by Andrew Garn © Smithsonian Institution

0898. Border, Italy, early 17th century; Linen and metallic needle lace; 29.9 x 15 cm (11 3/4 x 5 7/8 in.); Bequest of Richard Cranch Greenleaf in memory of his mother, Adeline Emma Greenleaf, 1962-50-210

0899. Border, France, 18th century; Linen needle lace; 140.8 x 18.8 cm (55 7/16 x 7 3/8 in.); Gift of Richard C. Greenleaf Esq. in memory of his mother, Adeline Emma Greenleaf, 1950-121-35

0900. Print, Garden of Love, ca. 1500; Israhel van Meckenem (German, ca. 1440–1503); Engraving on off-white laid paper; 17 x 24.2 cm (6 11/16 x 9 ½ in.); Gift of Mrs. Leo Wallerstein, 1957-30-12

0901. Print, Design for Cover Paper: Floral Motif, France or England, 1825–50; Block print on white paper; 35.4 x 22.6 cm (13 15/16 x 8 7/8 in.), irregular; Gift of Eleanor and Sarah Hewitt, 1925-2-588

0902. Cravat end, France, ca. 1695; Linen needle lace; 24.8 x 47.6 cm (9 3/4 x 18 3/4 in.); Bequest of Richard Cranch Greenleaf in memory of his mother, Adeline Emma Greenleaf, 1962-50-18-a

0903. Textile, Marigold, 1875; William Morris (British, 1834–96); Manufactured by Morris & Co. (Merton Abbey, England); Block-printed cotton; 61 x 46.7 cm (24 x 18 3/8 in.); Gift of Robert W. Friedel, 1951-103-56-a

0904. Tapestry square, Egypt, 3rd–4th century; Tapestry woven, linen warp, wool and linen weft; 14.9 x 14 cm (5 7/8 x 5 1/2 in.); Gift of John Pierpont Morgan, 1902-1-83

0905. Textile, Lyon, France, ca. 1919; Herman A. Elsberg (American, 1869–1938); Silk and metallic cut and voided velvet; 74 x 78.1 cm (29 1/8 x 30 3/4 in.); Anonymous bequest in memory of Albert and Rebecca Elsberg, 1938-82-200-d

0906. Fragment, Italy or Spain, 15th century; Silk voided velvet in satin foundation; 61 x 50.2 cm (24 x 19 3/4 in.); Gift of John Pierpont Morgan, 1902-1-388-a

0907. Woodblock print, *Kaigara Danmen Zuan,* 1913; Yoichirō Hirase (Japanese, 1859–1925), illustrated by Jun Nishikawa (Japanese); From Yoichirō Hirase, *Kaigara Danmen Zuan* (Kyoto, Japan: Unsōdō, 1913); Woodcut print on paper; Purchased by the Mary Stuart Book Fund, Cooper Union Library, Smithsonian Libraries, q N8243.S4 H57

0908. Book illustration, design for Armstrong's Quaker linoleum floor covering no. 2750, 1939; Armstrong Cork Company (Lancaster, Pennsylvania, USA); From *The Armstrong Pattern Book* (Lancaster, PA: Armstrong Cork Company, 1939), p. 281; Offset lithography on paper; 28 x 21.5 cm (11 x 8 1/2 in.); Gift of Elizabeth Broman, Smithsonian Libraries, TS1778.L5 A76

0909. Sidewall, PHE-06, 2011; Piet Hein Eek (Dutch, b. 1967); Manufactured by NLXL (Netherlands); Digital print on paper; 900 x 45 cm (29 ft. 6 5/16 in. x 17 11/16 in.); Gift of NLXL, 2013-4-1; © NLXL 2011

0910. Panel, Interlacings, 1984; Ethel Stein (American, b. 1917); Silk damask; 80 x 85 cm (31 1/2 x 33 7/16 in.); Museum purchase through gift of Anonymous Donor, 2005-16-1; © Ethel Stein

0911. Sidewall, PHE-02, 2011; Piet Hein Eek (Dutch, b. 1967); Manufactured by NLXL (Netherlands); Digital print on paper; 900 x 45 cm (29 ft. 6 5/16 in. x 17 11/16 in.); Gift of Scrapwood Wallpaper, 2013-4-3; © NLXL 2011

0912. Shawl, India for European market, mid-19th century; Wool twill tapestry with embroidery; 198 x 203 cm (78 x 80 in.); Bequest of Dorothy Franklin Rolph, 1980-38-1

0913. Man's head cloth (tzute), Chichicastengarga, Guatemala, before 1962; Cotton with silk weft patterning; 65.1 x 55.9 cm (25 5/8 x 22 in.); Gift of Alan L. Wolfe, 1962-233-21

0914. Drawing, Design for a Painted Ceiling, 1815–22; Frederick Crace (British, 1779–1859); Graphite, pen and black ink, and watercolor on laid paper; 29.9 x 23.6 cm (11 3/4 x 9 5/16 in.); Museum purchase through gift of Mrs. John Innes Kane, 1948-40-164

0915. Drawing, Wallpaper Design, France, 1815–30; Brush and gouache, graphite on paper; 38.3 x 54.9 cm (15 1/16 x 21 5/8 in.); Gift of Eleanor and Sarah Hewitt, 1924-15-22

0916. Tile, Ottoman Empire (present-day Syria), late 16th–early 17th century; Tin-glazed earthenware, underglaze decoration; 26.8 x 25.9 x 2.5 cm (10 9/16 x 10 3/16 x 1 in.); Gift of Mrs. Russell C. Veit, 1951-66-9; Photo by Ellen McDermott © Smithsonian Institution

0917. Chalice cover, Italy, early 18th century; Linen needle lace; 16.2 x 16 cm (6 3/8 x 6 5/16 in.); Bequest of Richard Cranch Greenleaf in memory of his mother, Adeline Emma Greenleaf, 1962-50-239

0918. Floor tile, possibly Portugal, 16th–early 17th century; Glazed and painted earthenware; 1.8 x 12.7 x 12.7 cm (11/16 x 5 x 5 in.); Gift of J. L. Arnemann, 1955-145-1; Photo by Ellen McDermott © Smithsonian Institution

0919. Portable equatorial sundial and compass, Augsburg, Germany, 1748; Jacob Emanuel Laminit (German, 1719–60); Gilt and engraved brass, cut and blued steel, glass; 2 x 6.4 x 6 cm (13/16 x 2 1/2 x 2 3/8 in.); Gift of the Estate of James Hazen Hyde, 1960-1-12

0920. Sampler, Germany, 19th century; Cotton needle lace backed with silk; 14 x 15.2 cm (5 1/2 x 6 in.); Bequest of Gertrude M. Oppenheimer, 1981-28-290

0921. Square, Grapes, 1947; André Derain (French, 1880–1954); Manufactured by Ascher Squares (London, England); Screenprinted silk; 90.2 x 90.2 cm (35 1/2 x 35 1/2 in.); Gift of Cooper Union Art School, 1950-143-5; © Ascher Studio

0922. Textile, France, 1934; Cotton velour; 45.7 x 128.9 cm (18 x 50 3/4 in.); Museum purchase from General Acquisitions Endowment Fund, 2006-6-1

0923. Textile, Guatemala, early 20th century; Cotton and wool compound weave; 118.1 x 111.1 cm (46 1/2 x 43 3/4 in.); Gift of Charles Iklé, 1955-44-6

0924. Drawing, Design for Double Woven Cloth, ca. 1926; Adelgunde (Gunta) Stölzl (German, 1897–1983); Brush and watercolor, pen and black ink on wove paper, mounted on off-white mat board; 17.9 x 22.4 cm (7 1/16 x 8 13/16 in.); Museum purchase from General Acquisitions Endowment Fund, 2011-3-1; Photo by Andrew Garn © Smithsonian Institution

0925. Textile, Kilometer 177½, 2002–03; Sheila Hicks (American, b. 1934); Slit tapestry in cotton, leather, silk, linen, and wool; 27 x 22.5 cm (10 5/8 x 8 7/8 in.); Museum purchase from General Acquisitions Endowment Fund, 2006-13-6; © Sheila Hicks

0926. Pezzato vase, 1950–51; Fulvio Bianconi (Italian, 1915–96); Made by Venini Glasswork (Murano, Venice, Italy); Fused colored glass squares, reheated, blown, and shaped; 22 x 13.5 x 12 cm (8 11/16 x 5 5/16 x 4 3/4 in.); Museum purchase from General Acquisitions Endowment in honor of Piera Maria Watkins, 1998-54-1; Photo by Ellen McDermott © Smithsonian Institution; © Venini S.p.A.

0927. Hand-woven sample, USA, before 1953; Anni Albers (American, b. Germany, 1899–1994); Twill-woven cotton and elastic cord; 19.1 x 27.6 cm (7 1/2 x 10 7/8 in.); Gift of Anni Albers, 1953-180-6; © Josef and Anni Albers Foundation

0928. Sample, Dividing curtain for Harvard Graduate Center double bedroom, 1949; Anni Albers (American, b. Germany, 1899–1994); Plain-woven cotton and bast fiber with single and grouped wefts; 29.5 x 45.1 cm (11 5/8 x 17 3/4 in.); Gift of Anni Albers, 1953-208-2; © Josef and Anni Albers Foundation

0929. Textile, Peru, Late Central Coast, 1000–1450; Plain weave of over-twisted cotton with warp float patterning; 39.1 x 32.2 cm (15 3/8 x 12 11/16 in.); Museum purchase through gift of Mrs. John Innes Kane, 1948-122-3

0930. Book-form flask, Switzerland, 18th century; Painted and glazed earthenware; 19 x 9.5 x 6.5 cm (7 1/2 x 3 3/4 x 2 9/16 in.); Gift of the C. Helme and Alice B. Strater Collection, 1976-1-149; Photo by Ellen McDermott © Smithsonian Institution

0931. Stackable drinking glass, ca. 1952; Saara Hopea-Untracht (Finnish, 1925–84); Manufactured by Nuutajärvi-Notsjö (Nuutajärvi, Finland); Mold-blown glass; 9.7 x 8.7 cm diam. (3 13/16 x 3 7/16 in.); Gift of Oppi Untracht, 1988-17-2; Photo by Ellen McDermott © Smithsonian Institution

0932. Textile, Peach Fuzz, 1986; Junichi Arai (Japanese, b. 1932); Manufactured by NUNO Corporation (Tokyo, Japan); Printed on uncut polyester and rayon velvet; 346.7 x 104.1 cm (136 1/2 x 41 in.); Museum purchase from Sarah Cooper-Hewitt Fund, 1987-12-1

0933. Doorplate from the Guaranty Building, Buffalo, New York, USA, ca. 1895; Louis Henry Sullivan (American, 1856–1924); Cast iron; 35.6 x 6.1 x 2.7 cm (14 x 2 3/8 x 1 1/16 in.); Gift of Roger G. Kennedy, 1979-77-9; Photo by Hiro Ihara © Smithsonian Institution

0934. Textile, Les Jets d'Eau (Fountains), 1925; Édouard Bénédictus (French, 1878–1930); Manufactured by Brunet-Meunié et Cie (Paris, France); Jacquard-woven cotton and viscose; 238.4 x 126 cm (93 7/8 x 49 5/8 in.), repeat: 151 x 62.1 cm (59 7/16 x 24 7/16 in.); Museum purchase from General Acquisitions Endowment Fund, 1990-29-2

0935. Coverlet, Pennsylvania, USA, early 19th century; Cotton and wool double-cloth; 222.3 x 205.7 cm (87 1/2 x 81 in.); Museum purchase from General Acquisitions Endowment Fund, 2010-9-1

0936. Book illustration, Commode knobs, ca. 1780; Birmingham Brass Company (England); From *Birmingham Brass Catalog* (Birmingham: Birmingham Brass Company), p. 38; Engraving on paper; 40.5 x 30 cm (16 x 11 3/4 in.); Gift of Eleanor G. Hewitt, 1919, Smithsonian Libraries, q048505

0937. Drawing, Study for Maximum Mass Permitted by the 1916 New York Zoning Law, Stage 4, 1922; Hugh Ferriss (American, 1889–1962); Black crayon, stumped, pen and black ink, brush and black wash, varnish on illustration board; 68 x 52 cm (26 3/4 x 20 1/2 in.); Gift of Mrs. Hugh Ferriss, 1969-137-4; Photo by Ken Pelka © Smithsonian Institution

0938. Drawing, Study for Maximum Mass Permitted by the 1916 New York Zoning Law, Stage 1, 1922; Hugh Ferriss (American, 1889–1962); Black crayon, stumped; brush and black ink over photostat, varnish on illustration board; 66.5 x 51.0 cm (26 3/16 x 20 1/16 in.); Gift of Mrs. Hugh Ferriss, 1969-137-1

0939. Drawing, Study for Maximum Mass Permitted by the 1916 New York Zoning Law, Stage 2, 1922; Hugh Ferriss (American, 1889–1962); Black crayon, stumped; brush and black ink over photostat, varnish on illustration board; 66.8 x 51cm (26 5/16 x 20 1/16 in.); Gift of Mrs. Hugh Ferriss, 1969-137-2

0940. Drawing, Study for Maximum Mass Permitted by the 1916 New York Zoning Law, Stage 3, 1922; Hugh Ferriss (American, 1889–1962); Black crayon, stumped and erased; brush and black wash over photostat, varnish, on illustration board; 67.3 x 51.6 cm (26 1/2 x 20 5/16 in.); Gift of Mrs. Hugh Ferriss, 1969-137-3

0941. Shoehorn, England, 1604; Heat and steam-shaped horn, with engraved and black-stained decoration; 18.4 x 5.4 x 3.5 cm (7 1/4 x 2 1/8 x 1 3/8 in.); Gift of Barbara Munves, 2011-31-1

0942. Drawing, Design for a Jeweled Stomacher, Italy (?), 1775–1800; Pen and black ink, brush and gray wash on laid paper; 34.3 x 21.1cm (13 1/2 x 8 5/16 in.); Museum purchase through gift of various donors and from Eleanor G. Hewitt Fund, 1938-88-868; Photo by Ken Pelka © Smithsonian Institution

0943. Book illustration, The Maggot-bearing Stapelia, 1807; Robert John Thornton (British, 1768–1837); From Robert John Thornton, *New Illustration of the Sexual System of Carolus von Linnaeus, and the Temple of Flora, or Garden of Nature* (London: Robert John Thornton with T. Bensley), vol. 2; Hand-colored engraving on paper; 57 x 46 cm (22 3/8 x 18 in.); Purchased by the Mary Stuart Book Fund, 1923, Smithsonian Libraries, fQK91. T49 1807

0944. Print, Trial Proof for a Printed Textile, France, 1790–1800; Woodblock, hand colored with brush and gouache on paper; 8 x 5.4 cm (3 1/8 x 2 1/8 in.); Gift of Eleanor and Sarah Hewitt, 1909-29-12

0945. Palampore, Pondicherry, Coromandel coast, India, mid–late 18th century; Cotton, mordant-printed, resist painted, and dyed; 335.3 x 236.2 cm (11 ft. x 7 ft. 9 in.); Museum purchase from Au Panier Fleuri Fund, 1952-118-1

0946. Book illustration, Papaya with caterpillars, 1730; Maria Sibylla Merian (Dutch, 1647–1717); From *Metamorphosis insectorum Surinamensium* (*Metamorphosis of Insects of Surinam*) (Amsterdam: Jean Frederic Bernard); Hand-colored engraving and etching on paper; 54 x 36.5 cm (21 5/16 x 14 3/8 in.); Gift of Robert W. Chanler, Smithsonian Libraries, f QL466. M57X D1730

0947. Print, Ornamental Design, from *Nouvelle suite de cahiers chinois a l'usage des dessinateurs et des peintres* (*New Suite of Chinese Ornament for the Use of Designers and Painters*), no. 3, after 1775; Anne Allen (British, active 1750s–60s) after Jean-Baptiste Pillement (French, 1728–1808); Etching à la poupée on off-white laid paper; 19.6 x 13.8 cm (7 11/16 x 5 7/16 in.); Purchased for the Museum by the Advisory Council, 1921-41-26

0948. Textile, England, 1760–80; Manufactured by Ollive and Talwin (Bromley Hall, England); Cotton printed by engraved copperplate; 200 x 70.2 cm (78 3/4 x 27 5/8 in.), repeat: 87.9 cm (34 5/8 in.); Museum purchase from Au Panier Fleuri Fund, 1960-55-1

0949. Drawing, Design for a Printed Vertical Border, France, 18th century; Graphite, brush and gouache on paper; 50.6 x 29.6 cm (19 15/16 x 11 5/8 in.); Gift of Eleanor and Sarah Hewitt, 1909-13-135

0950. Textile, Iguanus, 1990; Paul Simmons (Scottish, b. 1967) and Alistair McAuley (Scottish, b. 1967); Manufactured by Timorous Beasties (Glasgow, Scotland); Screenprinted linen; 311.2 x 151.1 cm (122 1/2 x 59 1/2 in.), repeat: 77.2 cm (30 3/8 in.); Museum purchase from General Acquisitions Endowment Fund, 1990-164-1; © Timorous Beasties

0951. Sidewall, England, 1817–27; Robert Jones (British); Made by Crace and Sons; Block printed and varnished on handmade paper; 99.5 x 59 cm (39 3/16 x 23 1/4 in.); Gift of Brighton Art Gallery and Museum, 1950-59-1

0952. Ceiling paper, 1880–1900; Cresswell & Washburn Ltd. (Philadelphia, Pennsylvania, USA); Machine printed on paper; 92 x 49.5 cm (36 1/4 x 19 1/2 in.); Gift of Victorian Collectibles, 1979-91-614

0953. Sidewall, Graduated Net, 1953–55; Bent Karlby (Danish, 1912–98); Manufactured by Dahls Tapetkunst (Copenhagen, Denmark); Machine printed on paper; 59.5 x 56 cm (23 7/16 x 22 1/16 in.); Gift of C. Krugers Tapetfabrik, 1956-9-18

0954. Drawing, Paper Sample, Yellow, England, n.d.; Yellow printed wove paper; 7.3 x 21.9 cm (2 7/8 x 8 5/8 in.), irregular; Museum purchase through gift of Mrs. John Innes Kane, 1948-40-191-b

0955. Sidewall, England, 1840–60; Machine printed on paper; 75.5 x 56 cm (29 3/4 x 22 1/16 in.); Museum purchase through gift of George Arnold Hearn, 1943-25-1

0956. Book illustration, Representations of inlay and nonnative woods, 1773–78; Jan Christian Sepp (Dutch, 1739–1811); From Jan Christian Sepp, *Icones lignorum exoticorum et nostratium Germanicorum: ex arboribus, arbusculis et fruticibus varii generis collectorum* (*Icons and exotic trees and our German, trees, young trees and shrubs of various kinds of collectors*), indexes by Martinus Houttuyn (Nuremberg: In Commission der Seeligmännischen Kunsthandlung), plate VI; Hand-colored engraving; 29 x 22 cm (11 3/8 x 8 5/8 in.); Purchase ca. 1980s, Smithsonian Libraries, qSD385.S47 1773

0957. Drawing, Design for a Mirror Frame with Monogram of Marie-Antoinette, 1787–90; Richard de Lalonde (French, 1735–1808); Pen and black ink, brush and gray, yellow wash, graphite on paper; 49.8 x 32.2 cm (19 5/8 x 12 11/16 in.); Purchased for the Museum by the Advisory Council, 1911-28-207; Photo by Ken Pelka © Smithsonian Institution

0958. Drawing, Design for a Cartel Clock Case, 1715–25; Gilles-Marie Oppenord (French, 1672–1742); Pen and black and brown ink, brush and watercolor on off-white laid paper, lined; 31.6 x 13 cm (12 7/16 x 5 1/8 in.); Purchased for the Museum by the Advisory Council, 1911-28-226

0959. Drawing, Wall Elevation for an Antechamber or Salon, ca. 1785; Louis-Gustave Taraval (French, 1738–94); Pen and black ink, brush and watercolor, black chalk on laid paper; 45.5 x 63.2 cm (17 15/16 x 24 7/8 in.); Purchased for the Museum by the Advisory Council, 1911-28-281

0960. Drawing, Textile Design: Indian Heads, 1943; Angelo Testa (American, 1921–84); Brush and gouache, graphite on heavy cream paper; 60.2 x 45.5 cm (24 x 17 15/16 in.); Museum purchase through gift of Eleanor and Sarah Hewitt, 2001-11-2

0961. Sidewall, Acorn, 2000; Francesco Simeti (b. 1968, Italy); Digitally printed; 195.6 x 78.7 cm (77 x 31 in.); Gift of Francesco Simeti, 2000-62-2; © Francesco Simeti

0962. Border, France, ca. 1810; Block printed and flocked on handmade paper; 74.9 x 25.4 cm (29.5 x 10 in.); Gift of Carolle Thibaut-Pomerantz, 1998-62-10

0963. Border, France, 1820–40; Block printed on handmade paper; 92 x 28 cm (36 1/4 x 11 in.); Gift of Josephine Howell, Inc., 1959-160-33-a,b

0964. Border, France, 1810–20; Block printed on handmade paper; 66.5 x 28.5 cm (26 3/16 x 11 1/4 in.); Gift of Eleanor and Sarah Hewitt, 1928-2-68; Photo credit: Ken Pelka

0965. Dado, France, 1820–30; Block printed on handmade paper; 183 x 54.5 cm (72 1/16 x 21 7/16 in.); Gift of Josephine Howell, 1972-42-165; Photo by Scott Hyde © Smithsonian Institution

0966. Dado, France, 1820–30; Block printed on handmade paper; 4.29 m x 58 cm (14 ft. 1 in. x 22 13/16 in.); Gift of David Marshall, 2007-55-2

0967. Border corner, England, 1850–60; Block printed on machine-made paper; 26 x 17.5 cm (10 1/4 x 6 7/8 in.); Gift of Martin Battersby, 1951-117-5

0968. Border, France, ca. 1850; Machine printed on ingrain paper; 76 x 43 cm (29 15/16 x 16 15/16 in.); Gift of Josephine Howell, Inc., 1959-160-30

0969. Border, France, 1830–60; Block-printed, flocked and gilt paper; 72 x 25 cm (28 3/8 x 9 13/16 in.); Gift of Josephine Howell, Inc., 1959-160-40

0970. Border, France, ca. 1850; Block-printed and flocked paper; 65.5 x 25 cm (25 13/16 x 9 13/16 in.); Gift of Josephine Howell, Inc., 1959-160-42

0971. Border, France, 1825–45; Jean Louis Mery; Block-printed on handmade paper; a: 87.5 x 50 cm (34 7/16 x 19 11/16 in.), b: 134 x 5.5 cm (52 3/4 x 2 3/16 in.); Gift of Josephine Howell, 1972-42-54-a,b

0972. Window shade, USA, 1875–1900; Machine printed on paper; 314 x 89 cm (123 5/8 x 35 1/16 in.); Gift of Norman Hasselriis, 1980-45-6

0973. Sidewall, France, ca. 1860; Block printed, stamped foil, applied chromolithograph, paper support; 73 x 515 cm (28 3/4 x 202 3/4 in.); Gift of Eleanor and Sarah Hewitt, 1931-45-72

0974. Chasuble back, England, 15th century; Silk velvet, appliquéd with silk and embroidered with metallic yarns; 135.3 x 61 cm (53 1/4 x 24 in.); Gift of John Pierpont Morgan, 1902-1-653

0975. Window shade, USA, ca. 1860; Machine printed on paper; 89 x 152 cm (35 1/16 x 59 13/16 in.); Gift of Elinor Merrell, 1961-175-1

0976. Sidewall, The House that Jack Built, 1886; Walter Crane (British, 1845–1915); Manufactured by Jeffrey & Company (London, England, 1836–1930); Machine printed on paper; 61.8 x 56.4 cm (24 5/16 x 22 3/16 in.); Gift of Grace Lincoln Temple, 1938-62-57

0977. May Tree frieze, 1896; Walter Crane (British, 1845–1915); Made by Jeffrey & Company (London, England, 1836–1930); Block printed on paper; 137 x 57.5 cm (53 15/16 x 22 5/8 in.); Gift of Roger Warner, 1955-144-7

0978. Sidewall, Golden Relief, 2014; David Nosanchuk (American, b. 1969); Made by Flavor Paper (Brooklyn, New York, USA); Digital print; 365.8 x 137.2 cm (12 ft. x 54 in.); Gift of Flavor Paper, 7640.1.2014

0979. Kimono length, Japan, late 19th–early 20th century; Plain-woven agave fiber, warp tie-dyed before weaving (ikat); 11.51 m x 35.9 cm (37 ft. 9 in. x 14 1/8 in.); Gift of Mrs. Benjamin Ginsburg, 1956-72-1

0980. Book cover, Ornamented Grapevine Patterns, 1907; Firm of Francis Sangorski (1875–1912) and George Sutcliffe (1878–1943); From John Addington Symonds, translator, *Wine, Women, and Song; Mediaeval Latin Students' Songs* (London: Chatto & Windus); Tooled green Levant Moroccan leather with gold stipple and embedded amethysts; 17.14 x 11.43 x 2.5 cm (6 3/4 x 4 1/2 x 1 in); Gift of Mrs. Dorothy M. Rogers and Ms. Katherine Epler, 1962, Smithsonian Libraries, PA8164.S98; Photo by Ellen McDermott © Smithsonian Institution

0981. Photograph, Storefront of Printer and Bookbinder Brodard & Taupin, ca. 1924; M. Thérèse Bonney (American, 1894–1978, active France and USA, 1919–78); Photograph; 19.5 x 5.5 cm (7.75 x 6 in.); Purchase, Cooper-Hewitt Museum, 1978, A5F037A

0982. Color lithograph, Scene of De la Rue's Stationery Stand and Envelope Machine, 1851; Edwin Thomas Dolby (fl. 1849–70); From *Recollections of the Great Exhibition, 1851* (London: Lloyd Brothers & Co., and Simpkin Marshall & Co., 1851); Color lithograph on paper; Smithsonian Libraries, fT690.C1 R43 1851

0983. Sidewall, Antoinette with Black Stripe, ca. 1956; Elsbeth Kupferoth (German, b. 1920); Made by Marburger Tapetenfabrik (Kirchhain, Germany); Machine printed on paper; 108 x 56.5 cm (42 1/2 x 22 1/4 in.); Gift of Marburger Tapetenfabrik, 1957-116-9; © Marburg

0984. Casket, Coventry, England, 1654; Frances Basnet; Wooden casket covered with silk satin and embroidered with glass beads; 23 x 21 x 28.5 cm (9 1/16 x 8 1/4 x 11 1/4 in.); Gift of Mrs. Charles Suydam Cutting, 1947-70-1; Photo by Ken Pelka © Smithsonian Institution

0985. Matchsafe, St. Petersburg, Russia, 1882–96; Champlevé enameled silver, fiber; Box: 6 x 3.6 x 1.6 cm (2 3/8 x 1 7/16 x 5/8 in.); Gift of Stephen W. Brener and Carol B. Brener, 1982-23-130

0986. Mural miniature, El Sol, from the *Mural Scrolls* sample book, 1948; Joan Miró (Spanish, 1893–1983); Made by Katzenbach and Warren, Inc. (New Canaan, Connecticut, USA); Screenprinted on canvas; 30 x 44.5 cm (11 13/16 x 17 1/2 in.); Gift of Katzenbach and Warren, Inc., 1953-61-1-3, © Katzenbach & Warren

0987. Textile, 1950–59; Paul László (American, b. Hungary, 1900–93); Printed cotton; 274.3 x 123.2 cm (108 x 48 1/2 in.); Museum Purchase from Smithsonian Institution Collections Acquisition Program Fund, 1998-57-1

0988. Fragment, Spain, 11th–12th century; Silk compound twill; 51.4 x 32.7 cm (20 1/4 x 12 7/8 in.); Gift of John Pierpont Morgan, 1902-1-222

0989. Book illustration, Color chart, 1889; Michel Eugène Chevreul (French, 1786–1889), engraved by H. Legrand; From *De la loi du contraste simultané des couleurs* (*The Principles of Harmony and Contrast of Colors*) (Paris: Imprimerie nationale), plate 38; Color lithograph on paper; 33.5 x 26 cm (13 x 10 in.); Gift of Harvey Smith, 1968, Smithsonian Libraries, f ND1280. C52 1889

0990. Bioimplantable device, England, 2004; Designed by Prof. Simon Frostick and Dr. Alan McLeod; Textile designed by Peter Butcher for Ellis Developments Ltd. (Nottingham, England); Manufactured by Pearsalls Ltd. (Taunton, Somerset, England); Machine embroidered with polyester thread on dissolvable substrate; Diam: 14.3 cm (5 5/8 in.); Gift of Ellis Developments Ltd., 2004-15-1; © Nuvasive Inc. and Ellis Developments Ltd.

0991. Foldout, 1867 Paris Universal Exposition floor plan; From *Reports of the United States Commissioners to the Paris Universal Exposition, 1867* (Washington, D.C: published under direction of the Secretary of the State by authority of the Senate of the United States), vol. 1, 1870; Engraving on paper; 23.5 x 30.5 cm (9 1/4 x 12 in.); Cooper Union Library, 1971, Smithsonian Libraries, T801.E1 U5X

0992. Textile, Turkey, 18th century; Silk velvet with metallic brocade; 87 x 65.7 cm (34 1/4 x 25 7/8 in.); Gift of Eleanor M. Delanoy, 1978-169-124; Photo by Scott Hyde © Smithsonian Institution

0993. Cabaret service, 1813; Attributed to Alexandre Brongniart (French, 1770–1847); for Sèvres Porcelain Manufactory (Sèvres, France); Enameled and gilt hard-paste porcelain; Tray: 2.2 x 42.8 x 34 cm (7/8 x 16 7/8 x 13 3/8 in.), teapot: 18.5 x 19 x 10.5 cm (7 5/16 x 7 1/2 x 4 1/8 in.); Gift of Katrina H. Becker in memory of her parents, Mr. and Mrs. Charles V. Hickox, 1981-38-1/9; Photo by Ellen McDermott © Smithsonian Institution

0994. Fashion plate, Le Jugement de Paris, Travestis de Jeanne Lanvin, pour Le Bal de la parure (The Judgment of Paris, costumes by Jeanne Lanvin for the Adornment Ball), 1924; Illustrated by Georges Lepape (French, 1887–1971), costumes by Jeanne Lanvin (1867–1946); From *Gazette du bon ton: Arts, modes & frivolities* (*Gazette of Arts, Fashions & Frivolities*), (Paris : Librairie centrale des beaux-arts), vol. 7, no. 8 (1925); Pochoir print on paper; 25 x 19 cm (9 3/4 x 7 1/2 in.); Smithsonian Libraries, GT500.G384

0995. Roasting pan and lid, probably USA, ca. 1935; Press-formed aluminum; 19 x 29 x 47 cm (7 1/2 x 11 7/16 x 18 1/2 in.); Gift of Mel Byars, 1991-59-67-a,b; Photo by Ellen McDermott © Smithsonian Institution

0996. Cylinda ashtray, 1967; Arne Jacobsen (Danish, 1902–71); Manufactured by Stelton A/S (Copenhagen, Denmark); Brushed and formed stainless steel; 6.7 x 11 x 7.5 cm (2 5/8 x 4 5/16 x 2 15/16 in.); Gift of Mr. and Mrs. Richard Stein, 1978-141-1-a,b; Photo by Ellen McDermott © Smithsonian Institution

0997. ConferenceMaster Audio teleconferencing system, 1993; Walter Dorwin Teague Associates, Inc.; Manufactured by Coherent Communications System Corporation (Lansdowne, Virginia, USA); Molded plastic, metal; 6 x 33.4 cm diam. (2 3/8 x 13 1/8 in.); Gift of Walter Dorwin Teague Associates, Inc., 1994-49-1; Photo by Ellen McDermott © Smithsonian Institution; © Coherent Communications Systems Corp

0998. Colorstone tableware, 1986; Lella Vignelli (Italian, b. 1934) and Massimo Vignelli (Italian, 1931–2014) with David Law (American, b. 1937); Manufactured by Sasaki (Japan); Glazed molded stoneware; 1, salad plate: 3 x 27 cm diam. (1 3/16 x 10 5/8 in.); Gift of Lella and Massimo Vignelli, 1990-2-1/4a,b; Photo by Ellen McDermott © Smithsonian Institution; © Vignelli Designs, 1986

0999. Pedestal stool, 1957; Eero Saarinen (American, b. Finland, 1910–61); Manufactured by Knoll International (East Greenville, Pennsylvania, USA); Lacquered cast aluminum, woven wool upholstery; 42 x 38 cm diam. (16 9/16 x 14 15/16 in.); Gift of Mel Byars, 1991-59-66; Photo by Ellen McDermott © Smithsonian Institution

1000. Sidewall, Lagoon, 1929; Edward Bawden (British, 1903–89); Made by The Curwen Press (England); Lithograph from linocut; 77 x 55 cm (30 5/16 x 21 5/8 in.); Museum purchase from Smithsonian Institution Collections Acquisition Program and Pauline C. Noyes Funds, 1996-32-8

1001. Sidewall, Austria or Switzerland, 1925–30; Josef Hillerbrand (German, 1892–1981); Block printed on paper; 31 x 31.5 cm (12 3/16 x 12 3/8 in.); Gift of Frankl Galleries, 1930-11-1-k

1002. Sidewall tile, V2, 2004; Designed by MIO; Molded recycled paper; 30.5 x 30.5 x 5.7 cm (12 x 12 x 2 1/4 in.); Gift of MIO, 2005-7-1; © MIO Company LLC

1003. Bowl, ca. 1930; George Sakier (American, 1897–1988); Manufactured by Fostoria Glass Company (Moundsville, West Virginia, USA); Molded glass; 8.1 x 26.8 x 26.8 cm (3 3/16 x 10 9/16 x 10 9/16 in.); Gift of Daniel Morris and Denis Gallion, 1993-134-12; Photo by Ellen McDermott © Smithsonian Institution

1004. Jar and lid, ca. 1915–20; Moser Glass Factory (Karlovy Vary, Bohemia, Czechoslovakia); Molded and cut glass; 11 x 8.7 cm diam. (4 5/16 x 3 7/16 in.); Gift of Denis Gallion and Daniel Morris, 1994-118-17-a,b; Photo by Ellen McDermott © Smithsonian Institution

1005. Photograph, Castel d'Orgeval, Parc Beauséjour, Paris, France, 1904; Hector Guimard (French, 1867–1942); Photographic print on sensitized paper; 26.8 x 21.2 cm (10 9/16 x 8 3/8 in.); Gift of Unknown Donor, n-d-1865

1006. Il Conico kettle, 1986; Aldo Rossi (Italian, 1931–97); Manufactured by Alessi S.p.A. (Milan, Italy); Rolled, soldered, and polished sheet stainless steel; 19.5 x 22 cm diam. (7 11/16 x 8 11/16 in.); Gift of Dr. Richard Grant, 1987-95-2-a,b; Photo by Ellen McDermott © Smithsonian Institution

1007. Drawing, Designs for Bowls, Vases, Candlesticks, and Teapots, ca. 1928; Ilonka Karasz (American, b. Hungary, 1896–1981); Graphite on tracing paper; 35.4 x 42.9 cm (13 15/16 x 16 7/8 in.); Museum purchase from General Acquisitions Endowment Fund, 2006-16-1; © Ilonka Karasz

1008. Photograph, Ilonka Karasz, Dining Room, Exhibition of American Designer's Gallery Inc., 1929; Twentieth-Century Decorative Arts Collection, Ryerson and Burnham Archives, The Art Institute of Chicago; Photo by Worsinger © The Art Institute of Chicago

1009. Tea infuser, designed 1925; Marianne Brandt (German, 1893–1984); Silver and ebony; H: 7.3 cm x Diam: 10.6 cm (H: 2 7/8 x Diam: 4 3/16 in.); British Museum, 1979, 11-2, 1

1010. Candlestick, bowl, and vase, 1928; Ilonka Karasz (American, b. Hungary, 1886–1981); Manufactured by Paye & Baker Manufacturing Company (Attleboro, Massachusetts, USA); Silver-plated metal; 1, vase: 19.8 x 10.6 cm diam. (7 13/16 x 4 3/16 in.); Museum purchase from Decorative Arts Association Acquisition and General Acquisitions Endowment Funds, 1993-111-1/3

1011. Half Teacup, 1923; Kazimir Severinovich Malevich (Russian, 1878–1935) (form) and Ilia Grigorevich Chashnik (Russian, 1902–29) (decoration); Made by State Porcelain Factory (Leningrad, USSR); Enameled, glazed, and molded porcelain; 6 x 10.8 x 5.2 cm (2 3/8 x 4 1/4 x 2 1/16 in.); The Henry and Ludmilla Shapiro Collection; Partial gift and partial purchase through the Decorative Arts Association Acquisition and Smithsonian Collections Acquisition Program Funds, 1989-41-68

1012. Bambu vase from the Pasta Vitrea Series, Murano, Venice, Italy, 1998; Yoichi Ohira (Japanese, b. 1946); Hand-blown glass canes with murine, powder; ground surface; H x diam.: 17.3 x 14.3 cm (6 13/16 x 5 5/8 in.); Museum Purchase from Smithsonian Institution Collections Acquisition Program Fund and General Acquisitions Endowment, 1998-52-1; Photo by Ellen McDermott © Smithsonian Institution

1013. Dinner plate, ca. 1937; Jean Luce (French, 1895–1964); Made by Charles Ahrenfeldt (Limoges, France); Glazed, molded porcelain with enamel, gold, and platinum; 2.5 x 21.3 cm diam. (1 x 8 3/8 in.); Gift of James M. Osborn, 1969-97-14-a; Photo by Ellen McDermott © Smithsonian Institution

1014. Flaches Modell (Flat Model) dessert fork and knife, 1903; Josef Hoffmann (Czech, 1870–1956, active Germany and Austria, 1891–1955); Produced by Wiener Werkstätte (Vienna, Austria); Silver; 1,2: 17.9 x 1.6 x 0.4 cm (7 1/16 x 5/8 x 3/16 in.), 18.5 x 1.7 x 0.5 cm (7 5/16 x 11/16 x 3/16 in.); Museum purchase from Friends of Applied Arts and Industrial Design, General Acquisitions Endowment, and Morrill Acquisitions Funds, 2002-3-1/2

1015. Cruet set and stand, ca. 1987; Roberto Sambonet (Italian, 1924–95); Manufactured by Sambonet, S.p.A. (Vercelli, Italy); Press-formed stainless steel, molded glass; 9.5 x 12 x 7 cm (3 3/4 x 4 3/4 x 2 3/4 in.); Gift of Dr. Richard Grant, 1987-95-6-a/d; Photo by Ellen McDermott © Smithsonian Institution

1016. TōFU lamp, 2000; Tokujin Yoshioka (Japanese, b. 1967); Manufactured by Yamagiwa Corporation (Japan); Molded methacrylate, aluminum, halogen light source; 29.5 x 36.5 x 7.6 cm (11 5/8 x 14 3/8 x 3 in.); Gift of Yamagiwa USA Corp., 2010-36-1; Photo by Andrew Garn © Smithsonian Institution; © Tokujin Yoshioka

1017. Prototype for domestic space heater, 1973; Designed by Bill Moggridge (British, 1943–2012) for Hoover, Ltd. (England); Sheet metal, extruded aluminum, compression-molded phenolic plastic, wood; 15.2 x 38.1 x 27.9 cm (6 x 15 x 11 in.); Gift of Bill Moggridge, 2010-22-2

1018. Lytro camera, 2012; Lytro, Inc. (Mountainview, California, USA) and NewDealDesign (San Francisco, California, USA); Engineered and manufactured by Lytro, Inc. (China); Silicone rubber, ultralight anodized aluminum, glass, plastic, Li-Ion internal battery; 4.1 x 4.1 x 11.2 cm (1 5/8 x 1 5/8 x 4 3/8 in.); Gift of Lytro, Inc., 2013-13-1; Photo by Matt Flynn © Smithsonian Institution; © 2012 Lytro, Inc.

1019. Via Portico d'Ottavia vase, 1988–91; Gaetano Pesce (Italian, b. 1939); Made at Centre International du Verre et Arts Plastiques (C.I.R.V.A.) (Marseilles, France); Mold-blown pâte-de-verre glass; 39.4 x 36.8 x 34.3 cm (15 1/2 x 14 1/2 x 13 1/2 in.); Gift of Kim and Al Eiber in honor of Caroline Baumann, 2013-43-1; Photo by © Smithsonian Institution

1020. One of a pair of pier tables, Dublin, Ireland, ca. 1785; Attributed to William Moore (Irish, d. 1814); Turned, joined, and veneered satinwood inlaid with tulipwood, harewood, and other woods; 89.5 x 119 x 50.5 cm (35 1/4 x 46 7/8 x 19 7/8 in.); Gift of Neil Sellin; 1967-87-1-a,b

1021. Book illustration, Signs for the 5 Groups of Men, 1936; Otto Neurath (Austrian, 1882–1945, active Germany, Netherlands, and England, ca. 1919–45) and Gerd Arntz (German, 1900–88, active Austria and Netherlands, ca. 1928–88); From Otto Neurath. *International Picture Language* (London: K. Paul, Trench, Trubner & co., ltd), p. 47, fig. 15; Photomechanical process on paper; 15 5 x 9.5 cm (6 x 3 3/4 in.); Gift of Henry Dreyfuss, ca. 1972, Smithsonian Libraries, PM8999.N48X

1022. Book cover, *Selected Poems* by Kenneth Patchen, 1946; Alvin Lustig (American, 1915–55) for New Directions (New York, New York, USA); Offset lithograph on white coated paper; 18.4 x 17.8 cm (7 1/4 in. x 7 in.), irregular; Gift of Susan Lustig Peck, 2001-29-8; © Estate of Susan Lustig Peck

1023. Endpapers, This Is Josephine, the Average American Female, and Joe, a Typical 6-Year-Old, 1955; Henry Dreyfuss (American, 1904–72); From *Designing for People* (New York: Simon and Schuster); Offset lithograph on paper; 33.5 x 24 cm (13 1/4 x 9 1/2 in.); Gift of John H. Duddy, 1998, Smithsonian Libraries, TS171.D77

1024. Poster, International Women Workers Day, 1930; Valentina N. Kulagina (Russian, 1902–mid-1930s); Lithograph on paper; 108.3 x 71.6 cm (42 5/8 x 28 3/16 in.); Museum purchase through gift of George A. Hearn, 1992-164-1

1025. Textile, La Moisson (The Thresher), ca. 1922; Raoul Dufy (French, 1877–1953); Produced by Bianchini Ferrier, Inc. (Lyon, France); Block-printed cotton with linen weft; 134.6 x 120 7 cm (53 x 47 1/2 in.); Museum purchase from Au Panier Fleuri Fund, 1934-14-1

1026. The Reds and the Whites chess set, 1922–32; Natalya Yakovlevna Danko (1892–1942); Manufactured by Lomonosov Porcelain Factory (Leningrad, USSR); Glazed porcelain; a: 10.8 x 3.8 x 3.5 cm (4 1/4 x 1 1/2 x 1 3/8 in.), b: 10 x 4.1 x 3.9 cm (3 15/16 x 1 5/8 x 1 9/16 in.); Gift of Charlotte Y. Salisbury in loving memory of her husband, Harrison E. Salisbury, 1994-122-5-a/ff

1027. Poster, Graphic Design China 2005 (GDC 05), 2005; Bi Xue Feng (Chinese, b. 1963); Offset lithograph on aluminized plastic foil; 100.6 x 78.9 cm (39 5/8 x 31 1/16 in.); Gift of Bi Xue Feng, 2010-30-1; © Bi Xue Feng

1028. Drawing, Design for Candlestcks with Figurines, 1950–70; Tommi Parzinger (American, b. Germany, 1903–81); Brush and gouache, graphite on paper, lined; 55.7 x 71.8 cm (21 15/16 x 28 1/4 in.); Gift of Donald Cameron, 1998-19-77; © Parzinger Originals

1029. Book cover, *Three Lives* by Gertrude Stein, 1947; Alvin Lustig (American, 1915–55) for New Directions (New York, New York, USA); Lithograph on white coated wove paper; 18.5 x 16.2 cm (7 5/16 x 6 3/8 in.); Gift of Tamar Cohen and Dave Slatoff, 1993-31-165-1; © Elaine Lustig Cohen

1030. Sidewall, Nana, 1971–72; Niki de St. Phalle (1930–2002); Made by Marburg (Kirchhain, Germany); Flexograph printed on paper; 58 x 53 cm (22 13/16 x 20 7/8 in.); Museum purchase from Sarah Cooper Hewitt Fund, 1992-110-8-a,b; © Marburg

1031. Fashion plate, La Danseuse aux jets d'eau, Robe de danse de Worth (Dancer with water jets, Dance dress by Worth), 1924–25; Illustrated by George Barbier (French, 1882–1932), costume design by House of Worth (France, 1858–1956); From *Gazette du bon ton: Arts, modes & frivolities* (*Gazette of Arts, Fashions & Frivolities*), (Paris: Librairie centrale des beaux-arts, 1925), vol. 7, no. 8. plate. 61; Pochoir print on paper; 25 x 38.5 cm (9 3/4 x 15 1/4 in.); Smithsonian Libraries, GT500.G384

1032. Poster, 1999 Season, Ballet Tech, 1999; Paula Scher (American, b. 1948); Screenprint on paper; 116.8 x 152.4 cm (46 x 60 in.); Gift of Paula Scher, 2013-25-6; © Paula Scher

1033. Figurine, early 19th century; After a design by Johann Joachim Kändler (German, 1706–75); Manufactured by Spode Ceramic Works (Stoke-on-Trent, Staffordshire, England); Molded porcelain with overglaze decoration; 15.3 x 12 x 8 cm (6 x 4 3/4 x 3 1/8 in.); Gift of Irwin Untermyer, 1952-17-2; Photo by Ellen McDermott © Smithsonian Institution

1034. Allegorical Figure of America from the Four Continents, 19th century; Manufactured by Meissen Porcelain Manufactory (Meissen, Saxony, Germany); Molded hard-paste porcelain, polychrome enamel, and gilt decoration; 13 x 3.8 x 5.6 cm (5 1/8 x 1 1/2 x 2 3/16 in.); Gift of the Estate of James Hazen Hyde, 1960-1-35; Photo by Ellen McDermott © Smithsonian Institution

1035. Sidewall, Nofretari, 1951; Peter Mijer; Made by Piazza Prints, Inc. (New York, New York, USA); Screenprinted on paper; 96 x 76 cm (37 13/16 x 29 15/16 in.); Gift of Harvey Smith and Benjamin Piazza, 1952-34-4; © F. Schumacher & Co., all rights reserved

1036. Panel, Spain or Portugal, ca. 1600; Linen with withdrawn element work and needle-lace fillings; 23.6 x 70.8 cm (9 5/16 x 27 7/8 in.); Gift of Richard C. Greenleaf Esq. in memory of his mother, Adeline Emma Greenleaf, 1950-121-27-a

1037. Plaque, possibly 1909; Marc-Louis Emmanuel Solon (French, 1835–1913); Made by Mintons Ltd. (Stoke-on-Trent, Staffordshire, England); Pâte-sur-pâte glazed porcelain; 0.7 x 15.8 x 16 cm (1/4 x 6 1/4 x 6 5/16 in.); Gift of Leon V. Solon, 1920-30-1; Photo by Ellen McDermott © Smithsonian Institution

1038. Print, Woman Bathing Her Feet at a Brook, 1658; Rembrandt Harmensz. van Rijn (Dutch, 1606–69); Etching on laid paper; 15.9 x 8 cm (6 1/4 x 3 1/8 in.); Gift of Leo Wallerstein, 1950-5-10

1039. Furniture mount, France, 19th century; Gilt-cast and chased bronze, 44.8 x 24.3 x 1.3 cm (17 5/8 x 9 9/16 x 1/2 in.); Gift of Jacob H. Schiff, 1904-20-15; Photo by Ellen McDermott © Smithsonian Institution

1040. Frontispiece, *The Wood Beyond the World*, 1894; Edward Burne-Jones (British, 1833–98) and William Morris (British, 1834–96), (London: Kelmscott Press); Woodcut on paper; 20.5 x 14 cm (8 x 51/2 in.); Gift of Calvin S. Hathaway, 1962, Smithsonian Libraries, PR5079.W6 1894X

1041. Drawing, Design for Sandblasted Glass Mural: Mercury Gathering Air Waves amidst Planets and Stars, 1932; Hildreth Meière (American, 1892–1961); Brush and white gouache, black wash, graphite on tan paper; 43.3 x 46 cm (17 1/16 x 18 1/8 in.); Museum purchase from Drawings and Prints Council Fund, 2001-10-1

1042. Overdoor, France, 1800–10; Block printed on handmade paper; 99 x 64 cm (39 x 25 3/16 in.); Gift of Eleanor and Sarah Hewitt, 1931-45-76

1043. Sidewall, Paris, France, 1925–30; André Groult (French, 1884–1967); Block printed on paper; 86.5 x 51.5 cm (34 1/16 x 20 1/4 in.); Gift of Jones and Erwin, Inc., 1945-13-3-a,b

1044. Safavid velvet, Persia (present-day India or Iran), ca. 1640; Silk voided velvet with metallic facing wefts; 217.2 x 74.6 cm (85 1/2 x 29 3/8 in.), repeat H: 215.9 cm (85 in.); Gift of Anonymous Donor, 1977-119-1

1045. Print, Nemesis, 1501–02; Albrecht Dürer (German, 1471–1528); Engraving on white laid paper; 33.5 x 23.3 cm (13 3/16 x 9 3/16 in.); Gift of Leo Wallerstein, 1954-89-24

1046. Ornament, Mother and Child, from the series The Ages of Man, ca. 1850; Block printed on machine-made paper; 138.5 x 69.5 cm (54 1/2 x 27 3/8 in.); Gift of Deutsches Tapetenmuseum, 1955-51-3

1047. Print, Four Nude Women or The Four Witches, 1497; Albrecht Dürer (German, 1471–1528); Engraving on laid paper; 19.5 x 13.7 cm (7 11/16 x 5 3/8 in.); Gift of Leo Wallerstein, 1950-131-152

1048. Poster, Levi's, The Strongest Thread, 2009; Art directed by Stefan Sagmeister (Austrian, b. 1962); Design by Joe Shouldice (American) and Richard The; Photographed by Tom Schierlitz Photography (New York, New York, USA); Offset lithograph on coated wove paper; 118.9 x 84.3 cm (46 13/16 x 33 3/16 in.); Gift of Stefan Sagmeister, 2011-34-1; © Stefan Sagmeister

1049. Drawing, Design for a Candlestick, 1820–30; Joseph Anton Seethaler II (German, 1799–1868); Red crayon, pen and black ink, brush and wash on paper; 30.3 x 17.8 cm (11 15/16 x 7 in.); Purchased for the Museum by the Advisory Council, 1911-28-383

1050. Poster, Stefan Sagmeister AIGA Program, Detroit, Michigan, USA, 1999; Stefan Sagmeister (Austrian, b. 1962), Martin Woodtli (American), and Tom Schierlitz (American); Offset lithograph on paper; 99.1 x 69.9 cm (39 x 27 1/2 in.); Gift of Sagmeister, Inc., 2000-61-4; © Sagmeister Inc.

1051. Textile, Attush robe, 19th century; Ainu culture (Hokkaido, Japan); Woven elm bard (ohyo) with cotton appliqué and embroidery; 128.9 x 118.1 cm (50 3/4 x 46 1/2 in.); Gift of Alice Boney, 1962-67-1

1052. Noh robe, Japan, ca. 1800; Twill woven silk and metallic yarns with supplementary weft patterning; 174 x 147.3 cm (68 1/2 x 58 in.); Gift of Eleanor and Sarah Hewitt, from the textile collection of Mrs. Abram Stevens Hewitt, 1931-4-62

1053. Child's dress, England, early 18th century; Silk damask; 73 x 66 cm (28 3/4 x 26 in.); Gift of Mr. and Mrs. DeWitt Clinton Cohen in memory of Eleanor and Sarah Hewitt, 1940-93-68

1054. Sidewall, Modernistic, 1927; Charles Burchfield (American, 1893–1967); Made by M. H. Birge & Sons Co. (Buffalo, New York, USA); Machine printed on embossed paper; 118 x 56 cm (46 7/16 x 22 1/16 in.); Gift of Ms. Edna Lindemann, 1992-109-3; © Charles E. Burchfield Foundation

1055. Textile, Wonda ya chi, Zomo ya chi gudu (Whoever catches a hare has to run for it), mid-20th century; Manufactured by Heinrich Habig Aktiengesellschaft Stoffdruckerei (Herdecke, Ruhr, Germany) for African market; Cotton printed by engraved roller; 82.5 x 50.1 cm (32 1/2 x 19 3/4 in.); Gift of Paula Habig, 1958-73-9

1056. Child's dress, Europe of Indian fabric, late 18th century; Mordant-painted and resist-dyed cotton (chintz); 82.6 x 59.1 cm (32 1/2 x 23 1/4 in.); Gift of Mrs. Robert P. Brown, 1960-81-9

1057. Bed hanging, France, 1730–70; Silk embroidered with silk satin stitch and couched metallic yarns; 381 x 102.2 cm (150 x 40 1/4 in.); Gift of Anonymous Donor, 1952-166-46-a

1058. Waistcoat, England, 1770–80; Silk embroidered with silk in satin, stem, and chain stitches; 76.8 x 32 cm (30 1/4 x 12 5/8 in. each front); Bequest of Richard Cranch Greenleaf in memory of his mother, Adeline Emma Greenleaf, 1962-54-21; Photo by Steve Tague © Smithsonian Institution

1059. Tekke woman's mantle (chyrpy), Turkmenistan, 19th century; Cotton appliquéd with wool and embroidered with silk; 121 x 61 cm (47 5/8 x 24 in.); Gift of Samuel A. Howes, 1950-106-1

1060. Coat, France, ca. 1790; Silk embroidered with silk; 124.5 x 69.9 cm (49 x 27 1/2 in.); Gift of Mrs. Edward C. Post, 1913-33-1

1061. Petticoat, Coromandel coast, India for European market, 1700–50; Cotton, mordant and resist painted and dyed; 96.5 x 160 cm (38 x 63 in.); Museum purchase from Au Panier Fleuri Fund, 1957-188-1

1062. Print, Tailleur d'Habits, details (Suit Tailor, details), from *Encyclopédie, ou, Dictionnaire raisonné des sciences, des arts et des métiers* (*Encyclopaedia, or a Systematic Dictionary of the Sciences, Arts, and Crafts*), 1763; J.R. Lucotte (French, 1750–84) for Denis Diderot (French, 1713–84); Engraved by Robert Bénard (French); Engraving on white paper; 35.1 x 22.3 cm (13 13/16 x 8 3/4 in.), irregular; Gift of Mrs. George A. Kubler, 1949-152-191

1063. Daoist priest's robe, China, 19th century; Silk satin embroidered with silk and metallic yarns in couching, satin, stem, and knotted stitches; 128 x 184.2 cm (50 3/8 x 72 1/2 in.); Gift of Harvey Smith, 1968-135-77

1064. Robe, Turkestan region, 19th century; Cotton velveteen, roller-printed cotton lining, warp ikat facings; 130.8 x 175.3 cm (51 1/2 x 69 in.); Gift of Eleanor and Sarah Hewitt, from the textile collection of Mrs. Abram Stevens Hewitt, 1931-4-66

1065. Robe for a statue, China, late 18th century; Silk and metallic slit tapestry (*kesi*); 43.2 x 47 cm (17 x 18 1/2 in.); Museum purchase from Au Panier Fleuri Fund, 1960-32-2

1066. Book illustration, The Goblin Spider, ca. 1900; Lafcadio Hearn (American, 1850–1904); From *The Goblin Spider* (Tokyo: T. Hasegawa); Woodblock print, crepe paper; 15.25 x 10.25 cm (6 x 4 in.); Gift of Sarah Cooper Hewitt, 1931, Smithsonian Libraries, PZ49.4.G63 1900z

1067. Drawing, Costume Design: Two Pirates, for *Daphnis et Chloé*, 1913; Léon Nikolajewitsch Bakst (Russian, 1866–1924); Brush and watercolor, graphite on illustration board; 26.8 x 39.5 cm (10 9/16 x 15 9/16 in.); Gift of Mrs. G. Macculloch Miller, 1947-77-2

1068. Book illustration, Ancient ceremonial costume and musical instruments, 1903; Kōrin Furuya (Japanese, 1875–1910); From Asamaro Inokuma, *Kyūgi sōshoku jūrokushiki zufu* (*Sixteen Pictorial Charts of Ancient Ceremonial Decoration*) (Kyoto: Bijutsu Kyōkai), plate 13; Woodcut on paper; 25 x 74 cm (9 7/8 x 29 in.); Purchase, Lillian Saxe Fund, 1997, Smithsonian Libraries, fNK1484.A1 K98 1903

1069. Textile, Japan, early 20th century; Cotton, resist applied by stencil, indigo-dyed (*katazome*); 906.8 × 35 cm (29 ft. 9 in. × 13 3/4 in.); Museum purchase through gift of Jacques Seligmann, 1948-10-2

1070. Print, Great Wave at Satta Beach, Suruga, from the series The Thirty-Six Views of Fuji, 1858; Ando Hiroshige (Japanese, 1797–1858); Woodblock print on paper; 37.5 x 25.4 cm (14 3/4 x 10 in.); Gift of the Estate of Mrs. Robert H. Patterson, 1941-31-120

1071. Print, Seki, Early Departure, from the series Tokaido Gojusan Tsugi-no Uchi (The Fifty-Three Stations of the Tokaido Road), ca. 1834; Ando Hiroshige (Japanese, 1797–1858); Woodblock, brush, and watercolor on paper; 24.1 x 36 cm (9 1/2 x 14 3/16 in.); Gift of Mary Rutherford Jay, 1948-134-48

1072. Print, Hakone Lake, from the series Tokaido Gojusan Tsugi-no Uchi (The Fifty-Three Stations of the Tokaido Road), ca. 1834; Ando Hiroshige (Japanese, 1797–1858); Woodblock, brush, and watercolor on paper; 23.7 x 36.4 cm (9 5/16 x 14 5/16 in.); Gift of Mary Rutherford Jay, 1948-134-11

1073. Print, Ejiri, View over Mio-no-Matsubara, from the series Tokaido Gojusan Tsugi-no Uchi (The Fifty-Three Stations of the Tokaido Road), ca. 1834; Ando Hiroshige (Japanese, 1797–1858); Woodblock, brush, and watercolor on paper; 23.9 x 36.4 cm (9 7/16 x 14 5/16 in.); Gift of Mary Rutherford Jay, 1948-134-19

1074. Mural Miniature, Arches, from *Mezzotone Papers* sample book, 1948; Ilonka Karasz (Hungarian, active United States, 1896–1981); Made by Katzenbach and Warren, Inc. (New Canaan, Connecticut, USA); Mezzotone printing process; 28.5 x 22 cm (11 1/4 x 8 11/16 in.); Gift of Katzenbach and Warren, Inc., 1959-134-1-17; © Katzenbach & Warren

1075. Frontispiece, *Architectural Iron Works*, 1865; Daniel D. Badger (American, 1806–84), lithographs by Sarony, Major & Knapp; From *Illustrations of Iron Architecture, Made by the Architectural Iron Works of the City of New York* (New York: Baker & Godwin); Color lithograph on paper; 34.5 x 26.5 cm (13 1/2 x 10 1/2 in.); Purchase ca. 1993, Smithsonian Libraries, fNA3503.7.B32 1865X

1076. Clock, Paris, France, 1807–10; Made by Antoine-André Ravrio (French, 1759–1814); Fire-gilt bronze, blackened bronze, enameled metal (dial), blued steel (hands), glass; 56 x 49.7 x 18.5 cm (22 1/16 x 19 9/16 x 7 5/16 in.); Gift of the Estate of Carl M. Loeb, 1955-82-1; Photo by John Parnell © Smithsonian Institution

1077. Mural miniature, Arabian Nights, from *Mezzotone Papers* sample book, 1948; Designed by Ilonka Karasz (Hungarian, active United States, 1896–1981); Made by Katzenbach and Warren, Inc. (New Canaan, Connecticut, USA); Mezzotone printing process; 28.5 x 22 cm (11 1/4 x 8 11/16 in.); Gift of Katzenbach and Warren, Inc., 1959-134-1-22; © Katzenbach and Warren, Inc.

1078. Frieze, England, 1850–60; Block printed on paper; 168.5 x 50 cm (66 5/16 x 19 11/16 in.); Gift of Josephine Howell, 1955-85-15-a

1079. Scenic wallpaper, Psyche Bringing Venus a Goblet of Water from the Fountain of Youth, from Les Amours de Psyche, ca. 1820; Merry-Joseph Blondel (French, 1781–1853); Made by Joseph Dufour et Cie (Paris, 1752–1827); Block printed on handmade paper; 182.9 x 137.2 cm (6 ft x 54 in.); Gift of Elizabeth Werter and Henry Trevor, 2013-9-1

1080. Drawing, Bathroom and Boudoir Interior, 1807; Jean-Claude Rumeau (French, active 1806–23); Pen and black ink, brush and watercolor, gouache, varnish, graphite on off-white paper; 29 x 23.7 cm (11 7/16 x 9 5/16 in.); Thaw Collection, 2012-5-4

1081. Drawing, Sepulcher in Egyptian Style with Sphinxes and an Owl, 1779–84; Louis-Jean Desprez (French, active in Sweden, 1743–1804); Pen and black ink, gray and blue-gray wash, traces of graphite on off-white paper; 18 x 28.5 cm (7 1/16 x 11 1/4 in.); Museum purchase through gift of various donors and from Eleanor G. Hewitt Fund, 1938-88-3953; Photo by Ken Pelka © Smithsonian Institution

1082. Sample book, Paris, France, 1785–95; Jean-Baptiste Réveillon (French, 1725–1811); Block printed and gilded on handmade paper; 59 x 42 x 6 cm (23 1/4 x 16 9/16 x 2 3/8 in.); Museum purchase from General Acquisitions Endowment and Decorative Arts Association Acquisitions Funds and through gift of Anonymous Donor and Bequest of Mary Hayward Weir, 1986-34-1-1/314

1083. Sidewall, Sacred to Washington, ca. 1800; Ebenezer Clough (Boston, Massachusetts, USA); Block printed on handmade paper; 122 x 53 cm (48 1/16 x 20 7/8 in.); Gift of the children of the late Edith Parsons Morgan, 1960-103-1

1084. Sidewall, England, ca. 1750; Block printed and flocked on handmade paper, varnish; 139 x 58.5 cm (54 3/4 x 23 1/16 in.); Gift of Josephine Howell, 1972-42-187-a

1085. Drawing, Embroidery Design Commemorating the Marriage of Napoleon I and Marie-Louise of Austria, ca. 1810; Attributed to Jean-François Bony (French, ca. 1760–ca. 1825) for Fabrique de St. Ruf (France); Brush and white gouache on two sheets of laid paper, coated with resin, joined; 62.2 x 48.9 cm (24 1/2 x 19 1/4 in.); Gift of Eleanor and Sarah Hewitt, 1920-36-327

1086. Textile, Turkey, 19th century; Silk and metallic velvet with linen weft, 158.1 x 64.1 cm (62 1/4 x 25 1/4 in.); Gift of Harvey Smith, 1958-104-1

1087. Textile, Tulip and Rose, 1876; William Morris (British, 1834–96); Manufactured by Morris & Co. (Merton Abbey, England); Wool triple cloth; 268.9 x 80.6 cm (105 7/8 x 31 3/4 in.); Gift of Harvey Smith, 1967-20-1-a,b; Photo by Scott Hyde © Smithsonian Institution

1088. Textile, Lyon, France, ca. 1924; Herman A. Elsberg (American, 1869–1938); Silk and metallic cut and voided velvet; 101 x 103.3 cm (39 3/4 x 40 11/16 in.); Anonymous bequest in memory of Albert and Rebecca Elsberg, 1938-82-194

1089. Sidewall, Versailles, 1951; Piazza Prints, Inc. (New York, New York, USA); Flocked paper; 91.5 x 76 cm (36 x 29 15/16 in.); Gift of Harvey Smith and Benjamin Piazza, 1951-168-1-a,b; © F. Schumacher & Co., all rights reserved

1090. Leather, Vlaanderen, Netherlands, ca. 1750; Embossed, painted, and gilded leather; 76 x 63 cm (29 15/16 x 24 13/16 in.); Museum purchase through gift in memory of Josephine C. Howell and through bequest of Edith M. Henderson and from Sarah Cooper-Hewitt Fund, 1989-34-1; Photo by Ken Pelka © Smithsonian Institution

1091. Brooch, ca. 1898; Fortunato Pio Castellani & Sons (Rome, Italy); Engraved and modeled gold set with sapphires, diamonds, rubies, emeralds; 7.2 x 4.5 x 1.3 cm (2 13/16 x 1 3/4 x 1/2 in.); Museum purchase through gift of Anonymous Donor, Annie Schermerhorn Kane, and various donors, 1969-40-46

1092. Drawing, Design for Woven Fabric with Neoclassical Motifs, France, ca.1820; Brush and gouache on laid paper, prepared with brush and brown pigment and squared; 47.4 x 18.7 cm (18 11/16 x 7 3/8 in.); Gift of Eleanor and Sarah Hewitt, 1909-13-130

1093. Sidewall, Crystals, 1953; Janice Hart White (American); Made by Bassett & Vollum, Inc. (Davenport, Iowa, USA); Screen-printed on paper; 114 x 56 cm (44 7/8 x 22 1/16 in.); Gift of The Wallpaper Magazine, 1953-51-1; © Bassett & Vollum, Inc.

1094. Caduceus-form hair ornament, ca. 1875; Fortunato Pio Castellani & Sons (Rome, Italy); Cast and granulated gold, carved ivory; 17.8 x 4.2 cm (7 x 1 5/8 in.); Museum purchase through gift of Anonymous Donor, Annie Schermerhorn Kane, and various donors, 1969-40-83; Photo by Ellen McDermott © Smithsonian Institution

1095. Stick pin, France, ca. 1867; Gold pavé set with diamonds, enamel, freshwater pearl; 8.8 x 2.2 x 2.4 cm (3 7/16 x 7/8 x 15/16 in.); Gift from the Thomas W. Evans Collection from University of Pennsylvania School of Dental Medicine, 1983-69-9

1096. Cuff buttons, probably France, ca. 1860; Bright-cut engraved aluminum, gold; a: 1.5 x 2.1 cm diam. (9/16 x 13/16 in.), b: 1.5 x 2.2 cm (9/16 x 7/8 in.); Gift of Mrs. Gustav E. Kissel, 1928-5-3-a,b; Photo by John Parnell © Smithsonian Institution

1097. Buckle, Paris, France, ca. 1900; Attributed to Edward Colonna (German, 1862–1948) for Samuel Bing (German, 1838–1905), Company L'Art Nouveau (Paris, France); Sculpted gold set with opal, pearls, garnets; 8 x 6 x 2 cm (3 1/8 x 2 3/8 x 13/16 in.); Gift of Mr. and Mrs. Maxime Hermanos, 1967-88-3

1098. Sidewall, Lincrusta-Walton, 1884; Attributed to Christopher Dresser (British, 1834–1904); Painted and gilded Lincrusta; 60 x 54.5 cm (23 5/8 x 21 7/16 in.); Gift of John Davidson Rockefeller, Jr., 1937-57-3

1099. Sidewall, Aesop's Fables, 1952; After designs by Thomas Beckwith; Made by Herndon Papers (New York, New York, USA); Screenprinted on paper; 91.5 x 76 cm (36 x 29 15/16 in.); Gift of The Wallpaper Magazine, 1953-198-12

1100. Suite of micro-mosaic jewelry, Italy, 1800–25; Gold sheet and wire, glass mosaics; Necklace: 0.4 x 45.5 x 2.8 cm (3/16 x 17 15/16 x 1 1/8 in.); Gift of Frederick Saal in honor of Dr. and Mrs. Joseph Saal, 1991-160-1/8

1101. Dish, France, ca. 1920; Jean Cros (French, 1884–1932); Pâte de verre and molded glass; 4.1 x 23.8 x 15.9 cm (1 5/8 x 9 3/8 x 6 1/4 in.); Museum purchase through gift of Georgiana L. McClellan, 1969-90-1

1102. Panel for a cabinet door, France or Flanders (present-day Belgium), late 16th–early 17th century; Silk embroidered with silk, metal threads and coral beads; 33 x 28 cm (13 x 11 in.); Gift of Marian Hague, 1959-144-1

1103. Sampler, colonial Boston, Massachusetts, 1734; Embroidered by Ann Peartree (American, 1722–44), student of Susanna Condy (American, 1686–1747); Linen, embroidered with silk in cross-, herringbone, satin, stem, back-, running, chain, couching, and detached-looping stitches; 36.8 x 29.2 cm (14 1/2 x 11 1/2 in.); Bequest of Gertrude M. Oppenheimer, 1981-28-157; Photo by Ken Pelka © Smithsonian Institution

1104. Embroidered picture, England, late 17th century; Plain-woven silk embroidered with silk, metallic yarns, and sequins in knot, split, satin, surface-satin, and couching stitches and linen backing; 21 x 28 cm (8 1/4 x 11 in.); Museum purchase through gift of Eleanor and Sarah Hewitt, 1950-98-1

1105. Embroidered picture, colonial Boston, Massachusetts, 1760–70; Linen embroidered with silk; 34.5 x 35 cm (13 9/16 x 13 3/4 in.); Bequest of Emily Coe Stowell from the Coe Collection, 1970-28-2; Photo © Smithsonian Institution

1106. Sampler, USA, 1828; Embroidered by Ann E. Kelly (American, b. 1814), student at Mrs. Leah Merguier's School (Harrisburg, Pennsylvania, USA); Embroidered in silk in buttonhole, cross-, and satin stitches on a cotton foundation; 48.9 x 48.9 cm (19 1/4 x 19 1/4 in.); Bequest of Mrs. Henry E. Coe, 1941-69-119

1107. Adoration of the Magi figural group, Flanders (present-day Belgium), ca. 1525; Carved walnut; 67.5 x 20.7 x 58.5 cm (26 9/16 x 8 1/8 x 23 1/16 in.); Gift of George Arnold Hearn, 1910-12-1; Photo by Hiro Ihara © Smithsonian Institution

1108. Adoration of the Magi plaque, Limoges, France, 1500–50; Enamel-painted and fired on copper; 21 x 15.9 x 1.3 cm (8 1/4 x 6 1/4 x 1/2 in.); Gift of Mr. and Mrs. Maxime Hermanos, 1966-6-1; Photo by Ellen McDermott © Smithsonian Institution

1109. Drawing, Wallpaper Design: Reconciliation of Venus and Psyche, 1815; Merry-Joseph Blondel (French, 1781–1853) for Joseph Dufour et Cie (active Paris, France, 1802–51); Graphite, black, white chalk, brush and black ink on brown coated paper mounted to paperboard; 39.8 x 35.2 cm (15 11/16 x 13 7/8 in.); Museum purchase through gift of Mr. and Mrs. Christian H. Aall and from Smithsonian Institution Collections Acquisition Program Fund, 1996-57-2

1110. Tapestry fragment, possibly Grenada, Spain, 13th century; Silk and metallic slit tapestry; 34.9 x 17.8 cm (13 3/4 x 7 in.); Gift of John Pierpont Morgan, 1902-1-82; Photo by Scott Hyde © Smithsonian Institution

1111. Vase, 1923; Dagobert Peche (Austrian, 1887–1923); Produced by Wiener Werkstätte (Vienna, Austria); Chased, raised, cast, and applied silver; 23.9 x 21.6 cm diam. (9 7/16 x 8 1/2 in.); Gift of Ely Jacques Kahn, 1962-227-2; Photo by John White © Smithsonian Institution

1112. Print, Design for a Footed Vase, from *Vasses de la Maison Royalle de L'oo* (Vessels for the Royal House of L'oo), ca. 1700; Daniel Marot (French, 1661–1752; active Netherlands and England); Etching and engraving on white laid paper; 35 x 23.5 cm (13 3/4 x 9 1/4 in.); Museum purchase from General Acquisitions Endowment Fund, 1988-4-33

1113. Locket, St. Petersburg, Russia, 1899–1908; August Hollming workmaster for workshop of Fabergé; (b. Finland, 1854–1913), workmaster; Raised and cut yellow gold (18 kt), rolled and engine-turned white gold (18 kt), enamel, diamonds; 0.5 x 3.3 cm diam. (3/16 x 1 5/16 in.); Bequest of Lorey Katz, 2004-12-1

1114. Print, Pendant Design with the Temptation, from *Pendants with the Virtues*, 1615–23, plate 1; Daniel Mignot (French, active Augsburg, 1593–1625); Engraved by Jan Theodor de Bry (German, 1561–1623); Engraving on paper; 15.6 x 10.8 cm (6 1/8 x 4 1/4 in); Museum purchase from Drawings and Prints Council Fund, 2001-22-1-1

1115. One of a pair of candelabra, Paris, France, 1739; Claude Ballin II, the Younger (French, 1661–1754); Cast and chased silver with traces of gilding; 48.3 x 24.5 cm (19 x 9 5/8 in.); Gift of Anonymous Donor, 1949-131-2-a/c

1116. Print, Ewer with Handle, 1548; Cornelis Floris II (Flemish, ca. 1513/14–1575); Engraving on white laid paper; 22.7 x 15.6 cm (8 15/16 x 6 1/8 in.); Museum purchase through gift of Mrs. John Innes Kane, 1946-3-3, p. 789

1117. Bratina (ceremonial vessel), stand, and tcharkas (cups), Moscow, Russia, 1884; Pavel Akinov Ovchinnikov (Russian, active 1853–c. 1917); Raised, repoussé, chased, and engraved parcel-gilt silver; a, b: 23 x 33.9 cm (9 1/16 x 13 3/8 in.), c–h: 5 x 10 x 6.7 cm (1 15/16 x 3 15/16 x 2 5/8 in.); Gift from the Thomas W. Evans Collection from University of Pennsylvania School of Dental Medicine, 1983-69-16-a/h; Photo by Ellen McDermott © Smithsonian Institution

1118. Panel, France, 18th century; Linen embroidered in silk and metallic yarns in satin, stem, and counted stitches; 59 x 55.9 cm (23 1/4 x 22 in.); Gift of Anonymous Donor, 1952-166-44

1119. Drawing, Design for Two Andirons and Sconce of Gilt Bronze, 1777–90; Jean Démosthène Dugourc (French, 1749–1825) for François-Joseph Belanger (French, 1744–1818); Pen and black ink, brush and watercolor on paper, lined, framed with brown paper and pen and black ink lines; 20.5 x 29.3 cm (8 1/16 x 11 9/16 in.); Purchased for the Museum by the Advisory Council, 1921-6-61

1120. Drawing, Project for a Fireplace with Sphinx Andirons from Projets de Cheminées, 1777–90; François-Joseph Belanger (French, 1744–1818); Brush and gray wash, yellow and green watercolor, pen and black ink, black chalk on off-white laid paper; 33.5 x 49.5 cm (13 3/16 x 19 ½ in.); Bibliothèque Nationale de France, Cabinet des Estampes, Ha 58 f. p. 15

1121. Drawing, Project for Eight Lighting Fixtures and Clocks, 1777–90; Jean Démosthène Dugourc (French, 1749–1825); Black chalk, pen and brown ink on white paper; 50.8 x 34 cm (20 x 13 3/8 in.); Louvre, RF41599

1122. Drawing, Project for Andirons with Sphinxes and the Monogram of the Comte de Provence, ca. 1780; Jean Démosthène Dugourc (French, 1749–1825); Black chalk on white paper; 18.4 x 25 cm (7 1/4 x 9 7/8 in.); Musée des tissus et des arts décoratifs, Lyon inv. 3129

1123. Sidewall, Oakleaf, 2004; Marthe Armitage (British); Linoleum block printed on paper; 318 x 61 cm (10 ft. 5 3/16 in. x 24 in.); Gift of Marthe Armitage, 2005-26-2; © Hamilton Weston

1124. Sidewall, Angela, 1953; Gene McDonald (American); Screenprinted on paper; 91.5 x 77 cm (36 x 30 5/16 in.); Gift of The Wallpaper Magazine, 1953-198-3-a

1125. Textile, England, 1750–59; Silk, metallic threads; 87 x 54.9 cm (34 1/4 x 21 5/8 in.); Museum purchase through gift of Eleanor and Sarah Hewitt, 1950-49-3

1126. Scenic wallpaper, China, 1800–30; Hand-painted on joined sheets of handmade paper; 342.9 x 111.8 cm (11 ft. 3 in. x 44 in.); Museum purchase from General Acquisitions Endowment Fund, 2013-10-1

1127A. Textile, Lyon, France, ca. 1919; Herman A. Elsberg (American, 1869–1938); Silk cut and voided velvet; 28.9 x 75.6 cm (11 3/8 x 29 3/4 in.); Anonymous bequest in memory of Albert and Rebecca Elsberg, 1938-82-206-b

1127B. Textile, Lyon, France, ca. 1919; Herman A. Elsberg (American, 1869–1938); Silk cut and voided velvet; 27.9 x 75.6 cm (11 x 29 3/4 in.); Anonymous bequest in memory of Albert and Rebecca Elsberg, 1938-82-206-d

1128. Drawing, Textile Design: Tropical Flowers, 1912–13; Raoul Dufy (French, 1877–1953) for Bianchini Ferier, Inc. (Lyon, France); Brush and gouache on paper; 39.2 x 38.1 cm (15 7/16 x 15 in.); Museum purchase from General Acquisitions Endowment and Friends of Drawings and Prints Funds; 1985-50-1

1129. Tulip dish and lid, 1760–90; Probably Volkstedt (Principality of Rudolstadt, Thuringia, Germany); Enameled and glazed, molded, hard-paste porcelain; 11 x 11.6 x 19.2 cm (4 5/16 x 4 9/16 x 7 9/16 in.); Bequest of Erskine Hewitt, 1938-57-550-a,b

1130. Drawing, Textile Design: Honeysuckle and Hollyhocks, 1897–98; Alphonse Maria Mucha (Czech, 1860–1939); Brush and watercolor, graphite on dark cream wove paper; 57.4 x 40.5 cm (22 5/8 x 15 15/16 in.); Gift of Aimee B. Troyen, 2012-15-1

1131. Sidewall, France, 1925–30; André Groult (French, 1884–1967); Block printed on paper; 57 x 50 cm (22 7/16 x 19 11/16 in.); Gift of Jones and Erwin, Inc., 1945-13-2-a,b

1132. Sidewall, Geraniums, 1938–40; The DeAndrado's; Made by D. Lorraine Yerkes; Screenprinted on paper; 91 x 74 cm (35 13/16 x 29 1/8 in.); Gift of D. Lorraine Yerkes, 1940-117-28

1133. Drawing, Design for a Printed Border, France, 1810–20; Black chalk, brush and gouache, blue ink on paper; 30.6 x 45 cm (12 1/16 x 17 11/16 in.); Gift of Eleanor and Sarah Hewitt, 1909-13-136

1134. Purse, France, 1820–40; Silk moiré embroidered in silk in satin, stem, knot, and couching stitches; 21 x 21 cm (8 1/4 x 8 1/4 in.); Gift of Richard C. Greenleaf, 1951-105-12

1135. Reticule, France, late 18th century; Silk bobbin lace lined with woven silk, flowers of silk ribbon, painted paper, and silk floss; 17.1 x 19.1 cm (6 3/4 x 7 1/2 in.); Gift of Richard C. Greenleaf, 1951-105-11

1136. Textile, ca. 1928; Ruth Hildegard Geyer-Raack (German, 1894–1975); Manufactured by Deutsche Werkstätten GmbH (Hellerau, Germany); Printed linen; 461 x 129.5 cm (181 1/2 x 51 in.), repeat: 63.5 x 62.5 cm (25 x 24 5/8 in.); Gift of Bertha Schaefer, 1962-18-1; © DWH

1137. Letter case, France, 18th century; Silk embroidered with silk and metallic yarns; 17 x 17 cm (6 11/16 x 6 11/16 in.); Gift of Eleanor and Sarah Hewitt, 1925-2-65

1138. Letter case, France, 18th century; Silk satin embroidered with silk and metallic yarns; 15 x 15 cm (5 7/8 x 5 7/8 in.); Purchased for the Museum by the Advisory Council, 1925-1-50

1139. Letter case, France, late 18th century; Silk embroidered with silk and metallic yarns, paste jewels, and gilt foil spangles; 24.1 x 22.2 cm (9 1/2 x 8 3/4 in.); Gift of the Marquis Val Verde de la Sierra, 1924-27-5

1140. Letter case, England or Netherlands, 19th century; Linen embroidered with silk; 12.7 x 14 cm (5 x 5 1/2 in.); Gift of Anonymous Donor, 1926-1-4

1141. Letter case, Spain, late 18th century; Silk, mica, bast fiber; 18.1 x 14 cm (7 1/8 x 5 1/2 in.); Gift of Marquis Val Verde de la Sierra, 1923-51-14

1142. Letter case, Spain, 18th century; Silk and metallic brocade; 19.6 x 14 cm (7 11/16 x 5 1/2 in.); Gift of the Marquis Val Verde de la Sierra, 1924-27-2

1143. Hanging, Röd Crocus (Red crocus), 1945; Ann-Mari Forsberg (Swedish, 1916–92); Wool and linen tapestry; 214 x 140 cm (7 ft. 1/4 in. x 55 1/8 in.); Gift of Elizabeth Gordon, 1964-24-41

1144. Drawing, Three Studies of Poppies, before 1907; Sophia L. Crownfield (American, 1862–1929); Brush and gouache on gray paper; 55.2 x 65 cm (21 3/4 x 25 9/16 in.); Gift of Starling W. Childs and Ward Cheney, 1937-59-59

1145. Hanging, Syrian Pomegranate Tree, 1919–26; Lydia Bush-Brown (American, 1887–1984); Wax-resist dyed (batik) on silk; 209.6 x 90.2 cm (82 1/2 x 35 1/2 in.); Gift of Lydia Bush-Brown, 1974-23-3

1146. Textile, Japan, 1936; Stencil-resist printed cotton; 54 x 32.1 cm (21 1/4 x 12 5/8 in.); Gift of American Council, Institute of Pacific Relations, 1937-69-28

1147. Title page, *La Alhambra Palais* (*The Alhambra Palace*), 1842–45; Jules Goury (French, 1803–34) and Owen Jones (British, 1809–74); From *Plans, Elevations, Sections & Details of the Alhambra* (London: Owen Jones), vol. 1; Color lithograph on paper; 68 x 49 cm (26 3/4 x 19 3/8 in.); Smithsonian Libraries, f NA387. G64X

1148. Sidewall and attached border, République Française Liberté Égalité, ca. 1792; Block printed on handmade paper; 45.5 x 77.5 cm (17 15/16 x 30 1/2 in.); Gift of John Jay Ide Collection, 1986-106-1; Photo by Ken Pelka © Smithsonian Institution

1149. Border, France, 1775–99; Block printed on handmade paper; 182.9 x 47 cm (72 x 18.5 in.); Gift of Carolle Thibaut-Pomerantz, 1998-62-3

1150. Man's mantle (hinggi), Sumba, Indonesia, 19th century; Cotton warp ikat; 243.8 x 134 cm (96 x 52 3/4 in.); Gift of Alan L. Wolfe, 1962-233-13

1151. Ceremonial cloth (pewo), South Sulawesi, Indonesia, late 19th–early 20th century; Cotton slit tapestry, tie-dyed; 247 x 30.5 cm (97 1/4 x 12 in.); Museum purchase from General Acquisitions Endowment Fund, 1983-36-1

1152. Sidewall, Le Marin (The sailor), 1920–30; Jean-Émile Laboureur (French, 1877–1943); Made by André Groult (1884–1967); Block printed on paper; 43.8 x 47 cm (17 1/4 x 18 1/2 in.); Gift of Frankl Galleries, 1930-11-1-e

1153. Sidewall, Blutengarten (Blossom Garden), 1913–32; Felice Rix-Ueno (Austrian, 1893–1967); Made by Wiener Werkstätte (Vienna, Austria); Machine printed on machine-made paper; 122.5 x 75 cm (48 1/4 x 29 1/2 in.); Gift of Harrison Cultra, 1971-62-5-a/e; Photo credit: Ken Pelka; © The National Museum of Modern Art, Kyoto

1154. Sidewall, Kolibri (Hummingbird), ca. 1920; Josef Hillerbrand (German, 1892–1981); Machine printed on paper; 7.93 m x 48.5 cm (26 ft. x 19 1/8 in.); Gift of Cincinnati Art Museum, 1990-129-24

1155. Textile, England, 1774–1811; Bromley Hall (Middlesex, England); Cotton, printed by engraved plate; 95.9 x 70.5 cm (37 3/4 x 27 3/4 in.), repeat: 95.3 cm (37 1/2 in.); Gift of Mrs. William D. Frismuth, 1911-7-6

1156. Sidewall, 1934–40; Made by Imperial Wallcoverings, Inc. (Glens Falls, New York, USA); Machine printed on paper; 168 x 48.5 cm (5 ft. 6 1/8 in. x 19 1/8 in.); Gift of Mr. Robert L. and Mrs. Jean L. Thompson, 1992-157-10-a,b; © Imperial Wallcoverings, Inc.

1157. Textile, New York, New York, USA, 1930s; Made by S. Kahn, student at The Educational Alliance, a project of the Works Progress Administration; Hand screenprinted cotton; 97.8 x 86.4 cm (38 1/2 x 34 in.) repeat: 21 x 21 cm (8 1/4 x 8 1/4 in.); Gift of the Estate of Ella Ostrowsky, 1976-98-8

1158. Sidewall, Robinson Crusoe, ca. 1875; Machine printed with engraved copper rollers; 56.5 x 38 cm (22 1/4 x 14 15/16 in.); Gift of Frances Irene Clark, 1959-117-2

1159. Box, Paris, France, 1858; Made by Louis Toussaint (French, active 1856–ca. 1880); Chased, engraved, and enameled gold; 1.7 x 8.6 x 6 cm (11/16 x 3 3/8 x 2 3/8 in.); Gift from the Thomas W. Evans Collection from University of Pennsylvania School of Dental Medicine, 1983-69-15

1160. Sidewall, Japonaiserie, 1883–85; W. N. Peak (Brooklyn, New York, USA); Machine printed on continuous paper; 75 x 48.5 cm (29 1/2 x 19 1/8 in.); Gift of Grace Lincoln Temple, 1938-62-18

1161. Paper construction, *Alice's Adventures in Wonderland: A Pop-Up Book*, 1980; John Strejan (American, 1933–2003), paper engineer James Roger Diaz; From Lewis Carroll, *Alice's Adventures in Wonderland* (New York City: Delacorte Press), pp. 11–12; Offset lithograpgh, cut paper; 30 x 42.5 x 16 cm (11.81 x 16.75 x 6.3 in.); Gift of Dr. Daniel J. Mason, 1986, Smithsonian Libraries, qPZ7.C319Al 1980b

1162. Book illustration, Glove-Making, Women's gloves in preparation, ca. 1769; From *Encyclopédie, ou, Dictionnaire raisonné des sciences, des arts et des métiers* (*Encyclopaedia, or a Systematic Dictionary of the Sciences, Arts, and Crafts*) vol. 2, plate 178; Denis Diderot (French, 1713–84) and Jean le Rond d'Alembert (French 1717–83), editors (Paris: Antoine-Claude Briasson, Michel Antoine David, André Le Breton, Laurent Durand, ca. 1769); Engraving on paper; 40 x 26.5 cm (15 3/4 x 10 7/16 in.); Gift of Marion Hague, Smithsonian Libraries, fAE25.E53X 1751

1163. Book, *Making Design: Cooper Hewitt, Smithsonian Design Museum Collection*, 2014; Designed by Irma Boom (Dutch, b. 1960); Published by Cooper Hewitt, Smithsonian Design Museum (New York, New York, USA); Paper and ink, 15.24 21.59 x 7.14 cm (6 x 8 1/2 x 2 13/16 in.)

Subject Index

Index Note: Locator references in **bold** indicate image numbers instead of page numbers. Images are numbered sequentially throughout the book and in the "Long Captions" section. Unbolded locator references indicate essay page numbers.

Name Index

Index Note: Locator references in **bold** indicate image numbers instead of page numbers. Images are numbered sequentially throughout the book and in the "Long Captions" section. Unbolded locator references indicate essay page numbers.

Acknowledgments

The individuals and institutions listed below provided immense support in making this collection book. We want to express our great appreciation and sincerest thanks to:

Cabelle Ahn, Airo AIDA, Masao AIDA, Sue Ellen Appleman, Reinier Baarsen, Laurent Bastard, Allison Barr, Sam Bigio, Christianna Bonin, Kamalika Bose, Knut Astrup Bull, Steve Burges, Chelsea Butkowski, Demian Cacciolo, Ashley Callahan, Mary Christian, Perry Choe, Adriane Dalton, Virginie Desrante, Edouard L. Desrochers, Heather Douglas, Kira Eng-Wilmot, Russell Flinchum, Peter Fuhring, Keira Gruber, Goethe-Institut New York Library, Williamena Granger, Sarah Gibbons, Erin Gillis, Widar Halén, Allison Hale, Annie Hall, Joelle Herr, Kaja Hjort, Yuki IKUTA, Stephanie Keating, Alex C-M Kelly, Jackie Killian, Jay Kreider, Thierry de Lachaise, Tiffany Lambert, Stacey Leonard, Nicolas Luchsinger, Caroline O'Connell, Tamara Préaud, Cindy Prasnal, Danielle Mastrangelo, Elizabeth Mattison, Ingo Maurer, Virginia McBride, Rebecca McNamara, Melissa Okan, Andrea Osgood, Kristina Parsons, Benjamin Peery, Rebekah Pollock, Barbara Reed, Letitia Roberts, Bertrand Rondot, Sara Rubinow, Megan Schoenbaum, Arielle Schraeter, Georges and Margaret Segal, Anna Shuster, Milton Sonday, Jewel Stern, Adriana Turpin, Merle Strätling, Kevin Tierney, Isao UCHIDA, Carolina Valdes-Lora, Hampton Wayt, and Karin Zonis

1163. Making of *Making Design*
Irma Boom

From: "McCarty, Cara" <McCartyC@si.edu>
Subject: Getting together?
Date: 22 March 2011 23:47:56 CET
To: "Irma Boom (i.boom@irmaboom.nl)" <i.boom@irmaboom.nl>

Hello Irma,

If I recall you mentioned you would be in the US during March and April. If you are coming to NY at some point, please let me know as I'd like to get together. I showed your extraordinary Every Thing Design book to the curators and everyone loves it. In fact, they (we) are jealous that you didn't do it for us first. I'd love to talk with you about our upcoming collection Handbook.

Can you please email me a few days and times when you'll be in NY. Otherwise, you may be the good excuse to go to New Haven.

Best,

Cara McCarty
Curatorial Director
Smithsonian Institution
Cooper-Hewitt, National Design Museum
...

The Contract: 10th day of December, 2012:
1. SCOPE OF WORK. The Artist agrees to create a book design in accordance with the terms herein.

- Description of Commissioned Works.

The Work is a full-length illustrated book with the following tentative specifications:

- COLLECTIONS COLLECTION:

Text: a. Preface of 1,500 words;
fifty Essays by CHNDM curators of between 300-800 words each;
approximately 800 illustrations integrated throughout the Work;
and Back Matter (Acknowledgments, Photo Credits, List of Works, Copyright Page); text to be provided by CHNDM. Trim size and specifications: not-to-exceed 500 pages, hardcover only, suggested trim size of approximately 6 3/4" x 8".

The Work shall also contain links to the CHNDM website, the CHNDM collection database and be reconfigured as an eBook.

- Deliverables. The Artist shall deliver to CHNDM:
- No fewer than two distinct design directions, including trim size, for the cover and interior of the Work, to be submitted in electronic (PDF) as well as hard-copy maquette format.
- Three rounds of full hard-copy layouts of the Work, with text, captions, and edits and corrections keyed in by the Artist.
- Final print-ready InDesign files of the Work upon acceptance of the final layout by CHNDM.

c. Coordination with CHNDM staff. The Artist shall coordinate all Work performed under this Agreement with relevant members of the CHNDM staff, as identified by the Contracting Officer's Representative in Section 14, herein.
...

On 8 Jan 2013, at 18:01, Horn, Pamela wrote:
1. I haven't received anything from you on the contract and I'd really like to get that settled. Can you please let me know what the status is?
2. I have attached a new schedule for the collection handbook. We have moved the publication date from Spring 2014 to September 2014. As you can see I have you submitting your sample interior design pages by 2/15/13, final text, captions, and hi-res images to you 8/25/13, and final files to the printer 2/15/14. Please let me know if you are on track for this.
3. We are now calling the book *Making Design*. This title really gets to the essence of what this book is. Since we last met, the museum has been going through some good exercises in trying to identify and clarify what this redesign and rebranding is going to represent. Cooper Hewitt wants its collection and the institution to be recognized as a museum about design process. The organization of the collection book should be the physical representation of those ideas. Below is a memo I sent to the curators after a series of discussions about our book. I hope this will provide a good sense for you about the content. Of course, your sequenced sections of the objects don't necessarily need to be organized that way—let's talk further about your thoughts on this.

Editorial direction 1/2/13 *Making Design* will be a snapshot of our understanding of Cooper-Hewitt's collection relative to design ideas today. The collection handbook will look at objects through a process lens. The objects that are the focus of the essays will be selected for how well they best tell the design process story. These process-driven narratives will continue to be useful to the museum and its audiences. The objects themselves will remain relevant and fluid.
Think about writing for audiences C-H hopes to build—design students ages 18 to 30, individuals and families curious about basic elements of design who want to learn about techniques and processes. Put yourselves in the shoes of these visitors and readers who are asking WHY? Why are we looking at this object and what does it have to do with us today?
The following questions can help shape your essays, and further, the label, table, and web content.
What is the significance of the object to the design discipline?
Where does this object fall on the innovation scale?
What was it used for?
What did it replace?
What was it a precursor for?
Why is this object important to our collection?
What is its justification for being acquired?
Thank you--
All best, PH

From: Irma Boom <i.boom@irmaboom.nl<mailto:i.boom@irmaboom.nl>>
Date: Tue, 8 Jan 2013 12:14:35 -0500
To: "Pamela A. Horn" <hornp@si.edu<mailto:hornp@si.edu>>
Subject: Re: Making Design

Hi Pamela,
Will get back to you about the contract.
Sorry for not getting back to you about this.
I get back to you on the things you have sent.
Very hectic at the moment!
All best, Irma

From: "Horn, Pamela" <HornP@si.edu>
Subject: Contract
Date: 11 January 2013 15:58:20 CET
To: Irma Boom <i.boom@irmaboom.nl>

Here you go Irma. As I mentioned, please make three copies, sign, and send back to me for countersigning.
Thanks-
Pam

846 emails from PM to IB

Actual facts:
912 pages
6 x 81/4 in.
5 different color covers
5 different color stained edges

37,323

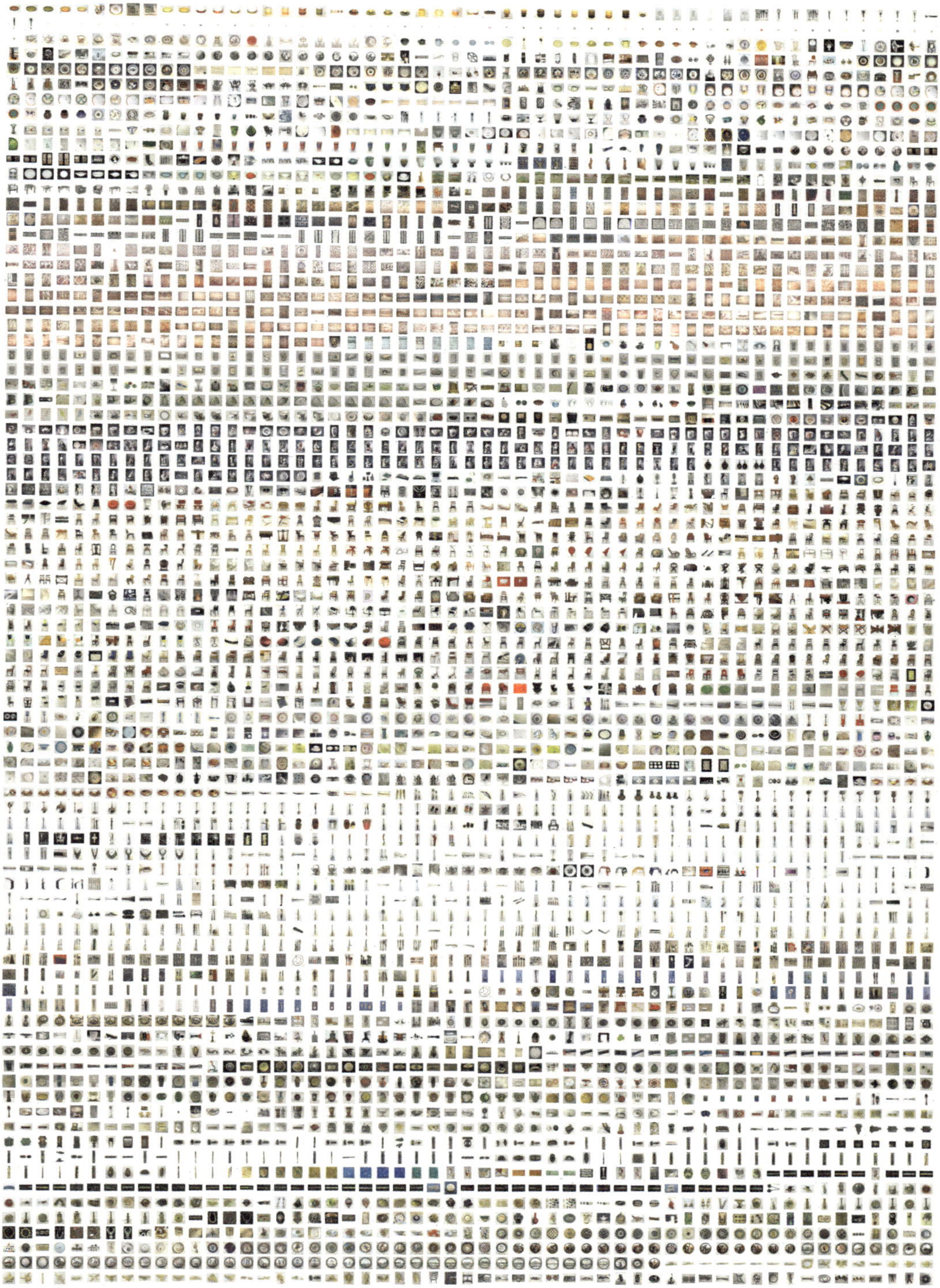

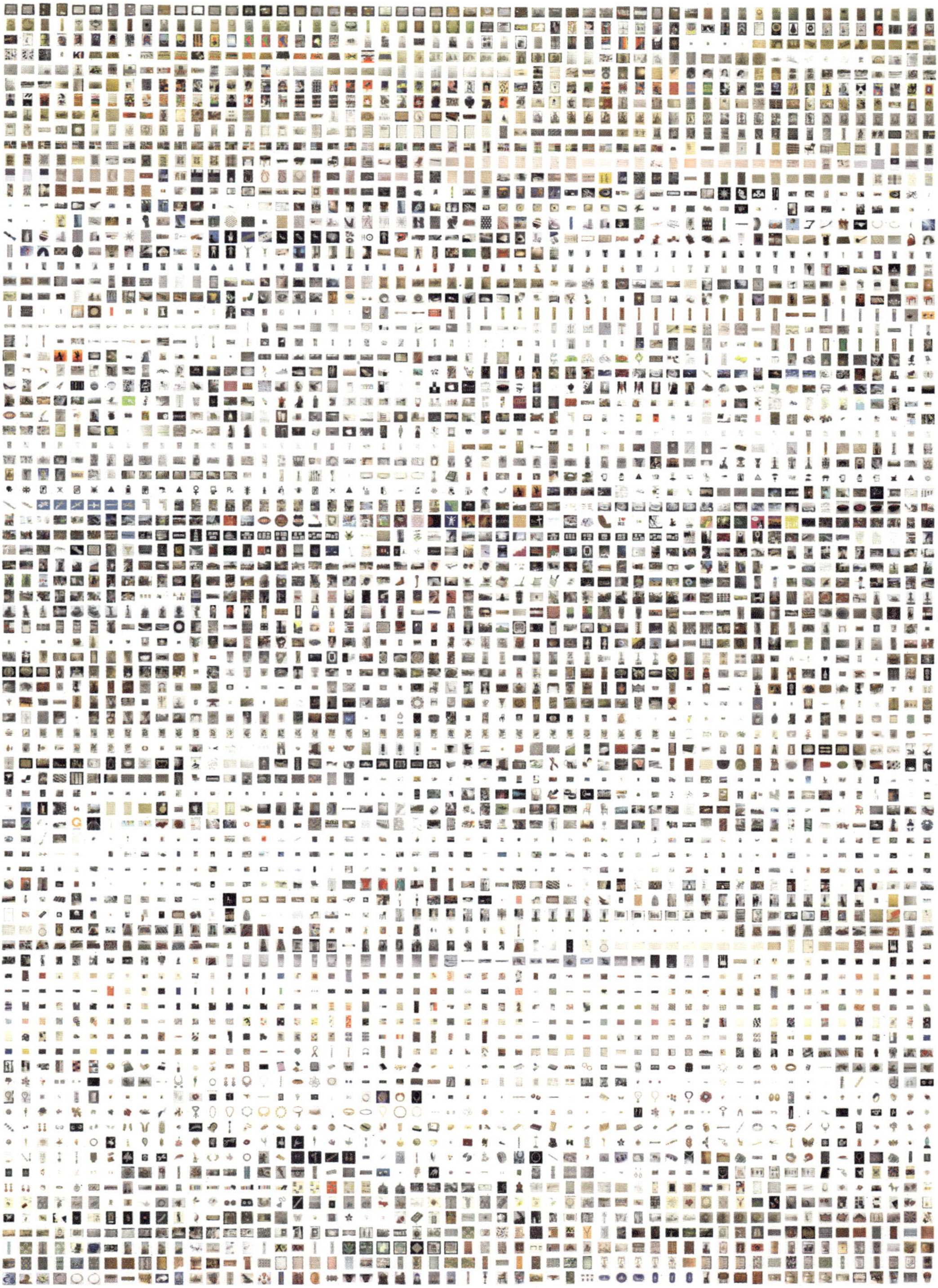

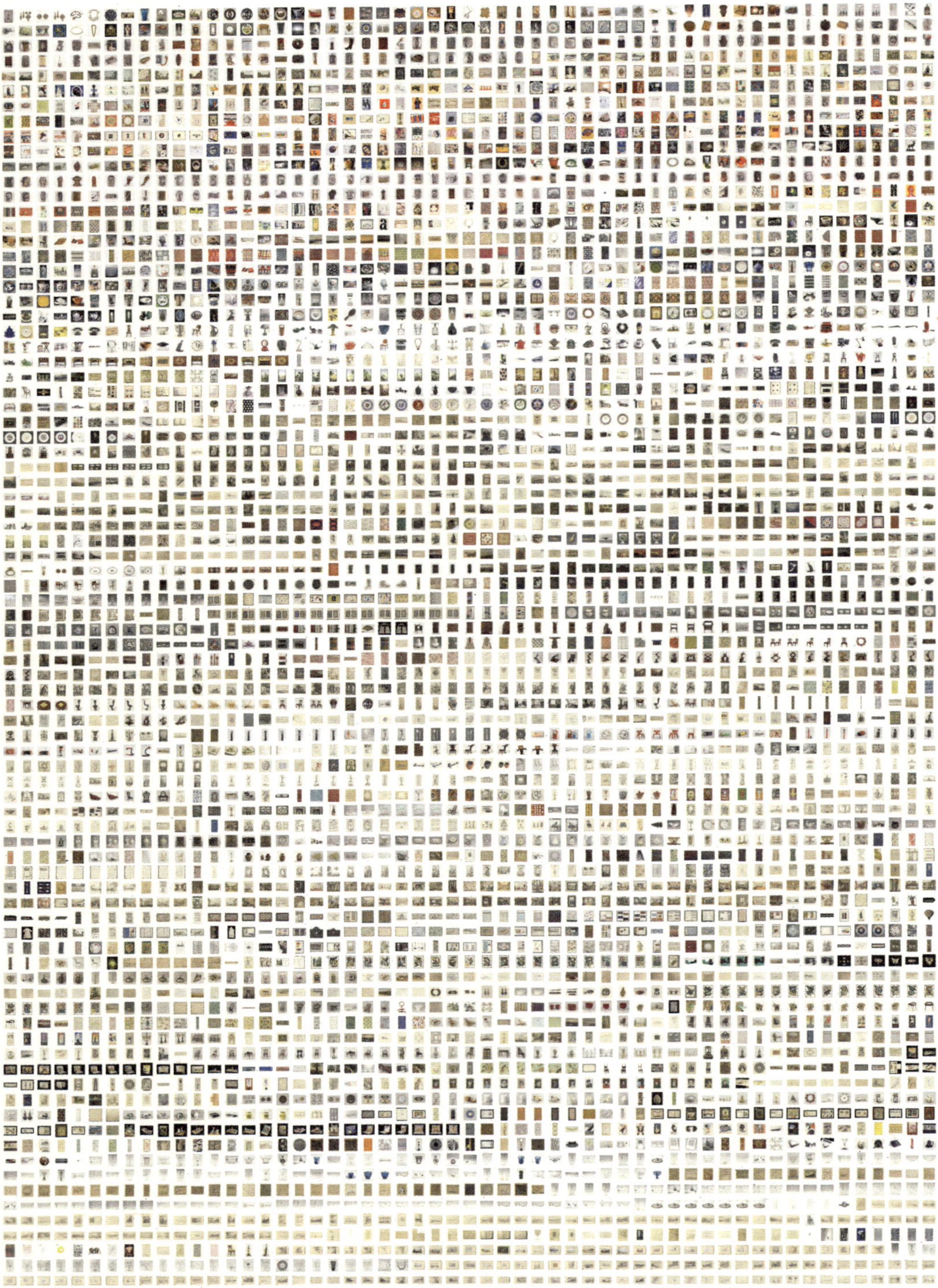

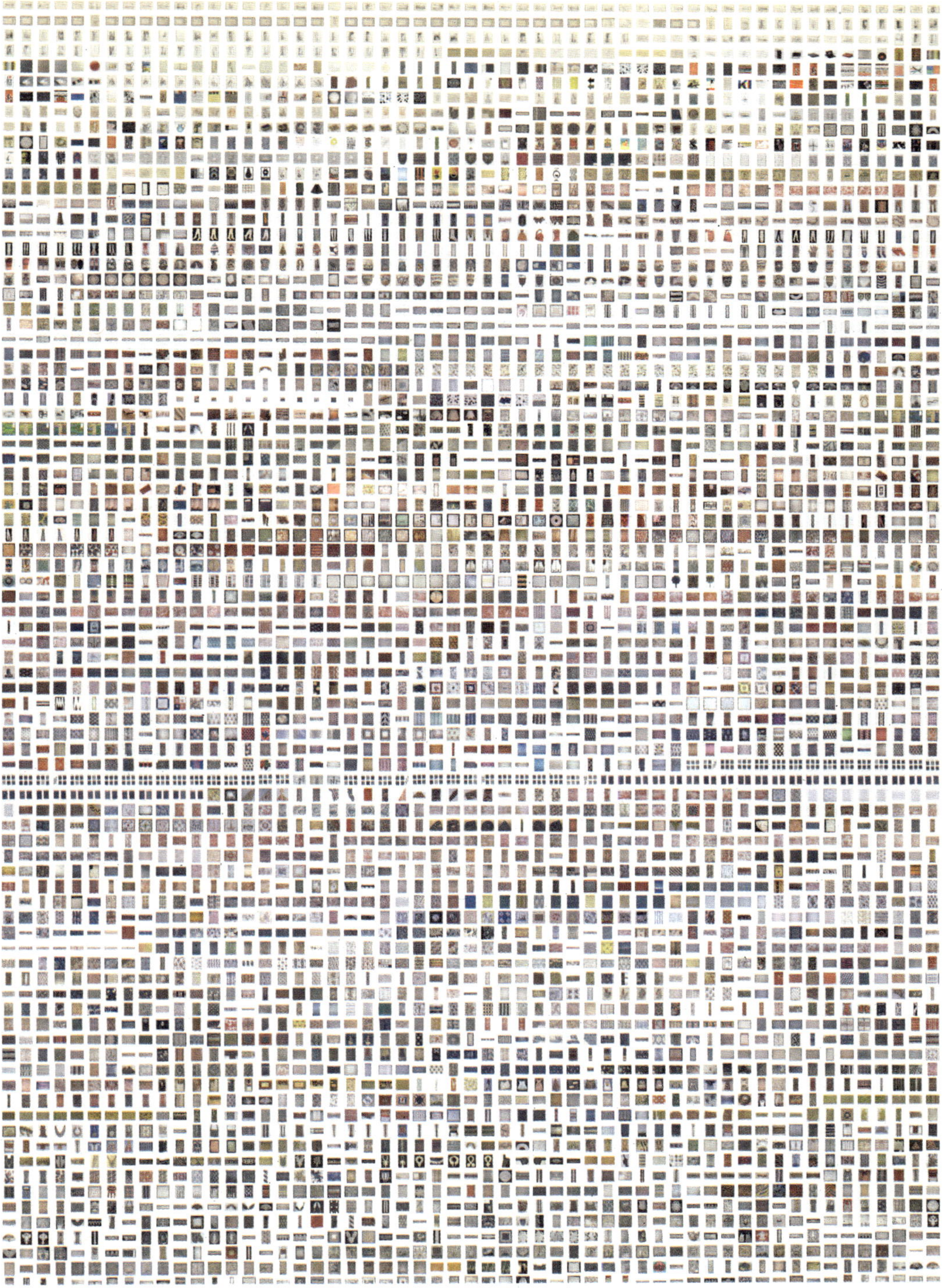

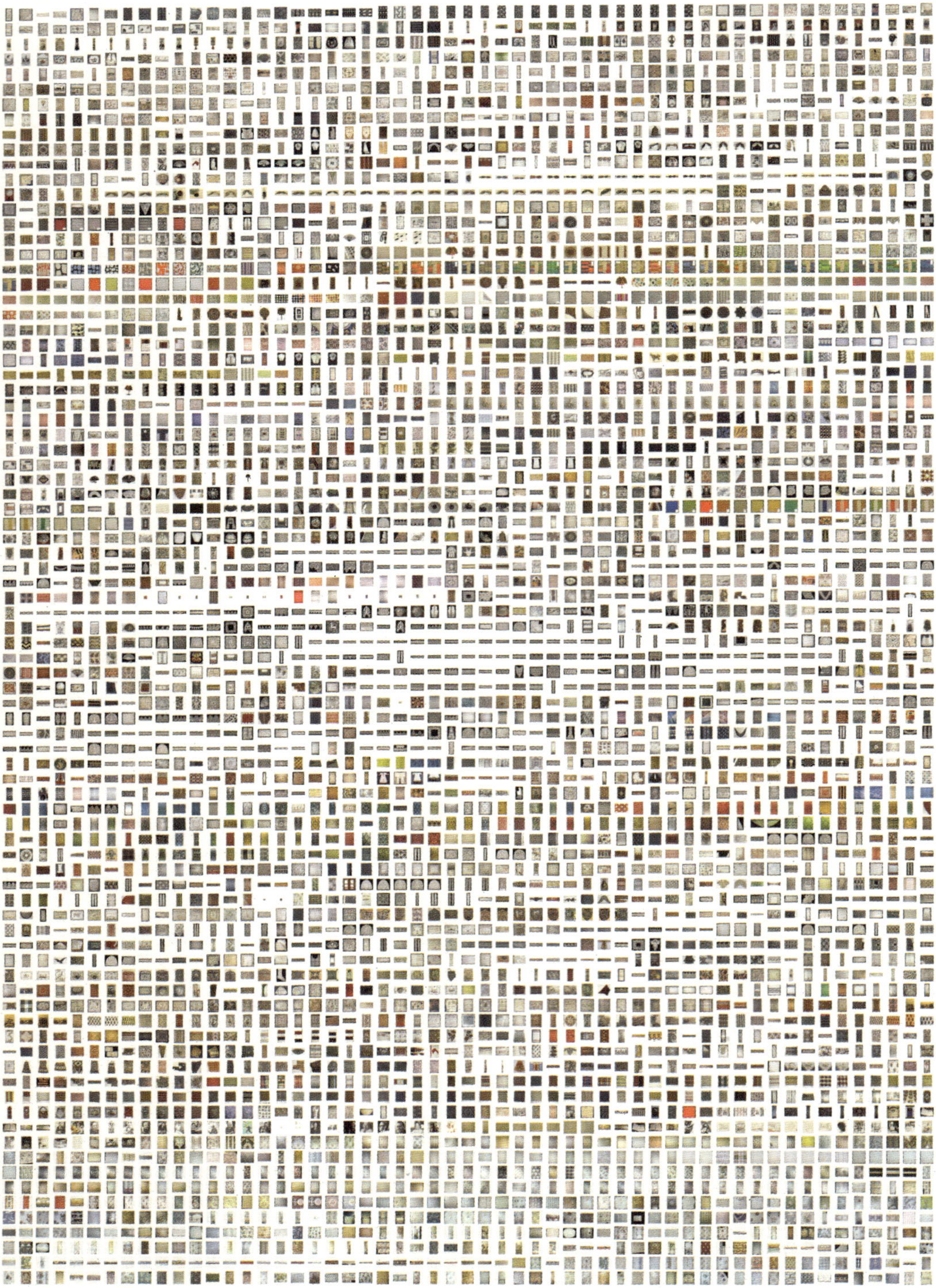